791.43 S331d   FV
SCHICKEL
D.W. GRIFFITH : AN AMERICAN
LIFE
                                    24.95

WITHDRAWN

St. Louis Community College

Library

5801 Wilson Avenue
St. Louis, Missouri 63110

D.W.

An

GRIFFITH
American Life

RICHARD SCHICKEL

SIMON AND SCHUSTER · NEW YORK

Copyright © 1984 by Gideon Productions, Inc.
All rights reserved
including the right of reproduction
in whole or in part in any form
Published by Simon and Schuster
A Division of Simon & Schuster, Inc.
Simon & Schuster Building
Rockefeller Center
1230 Avenue of the Americas
New York, New York 10020
SIMON AND SCHUSTER and colophon
are registered trademarks of Simon & Schuster, Inc.
Designed by Edith Fowler
Manufactured in the United States of America
10 9 8 7 6 5 4 3 2 1

Library of Congress Cataloging in Publication Data

Schickel, Richard
   D.W. Griffith: an American life.

   Bibliography: p.
   Includes index.
   1. Griffith, D.W. (David Wark), 1875–1948.
2. Moving-picture producers and directors—
United States—Biography. I. Title.
PN1998.A3G778   1983   791.43'0233'0924 [B]   83-20151
ISBN 0-671-22596-0

For My Daughters,
Erika and Jessica

"We possessed together the precious,
the incommunicable past."

Contents

Introduction

THIS is a very large book, as befits a long life and a career that included high achievement and deep failure. It aspires to the definitive, and yet its author knows better than anyone else that the life of D. W. Griffith probably will never—probably *can* never—be fully defined in print. For Griffith, though he gave many interviews and caused much publicity about himself to be generated, had two personal characteristics that are a biographer's despair; he was both secretive and a mythomaniac. About his family's history, about his own early life, about his work and his motives for undertaking this or that project, about his financial dealings, about his personal life—about almost every significant aspect of his activities—he maintained a profound silence, which he later covered with an excess of explanations that nearly always tended toward the grandiose and the improbably noble. When, along his way, he encountered those difficulties with the marketplace that finally doomed his career, we will see that he came to be, in his desperation, not just secretive but somewhat shady—by the standards of our times if not his own. As for his romantic life, which was as singular as his artistic and financial life, he spoke not a word (although much of it was an open secret to his coworkers).

More than in most cases, then, the Griffith biographer is forced to sift through mounds of misinformation, trusting his own common sense, critical intelligence and speculative abilities in order to arrive at a plausible and coherent historical narrative. I am well aware that much of what is to be found in this book runs counter to the received view of Griffith's life, which tends to portray him as a heroic visionary betrayed and destroyed by a crass and unfeeling industry, forgotten in his later years by a fickle public. There is some truth in this portrait—just enough to make it convenient for the hurried historian or acceptable to the casually concerned reader. But it is not the whole truth, or the most interesting truth.

11

Like the rest of us, D. W. Griffith was the principal author of his own misery, just as he was the author of his own greatness.

Much of what is true about Griffith is true of early film history as well. It is largely the product of an oral tradition, and most of the talkers were show folks, in the habit of improving upon stories, many of which were already greatly enriched by their travels along the gossip circuit before reaching the people who finally set these tales down for posterity to wonder at. Yet one cannot fully comprehend Griffith's career—the choices he made, the achievements he recorded, the disasters that befell him—without trying to understand the fast-moving historical currents in which, like everyone else in those early days of the movies, he had to try to plot at the same time he was navigating them. Again, one is offering the most plausible account of how that flow ran, not necessarily its definitive chart.

But enough for warnings, which I hope will not be mistaken for apologies. Several people before me—and while I was at work—set forth on a task similar to mine and were stopped, or stalled, as I several times was, by the daunting problems this life presents to anyone trying to penetrate beyond its superficial aspects. For that reason, I offer this volume with considerable pride, because it presents a portrait that I know comes closer to any offered heretofore of the man with whom begins the history of film as a self-conscious art, as a major financial institution, as a significant shaping force on the modern mind and the modern world. I believe as well that Griffith's life has continuing relevance, for many of the problems that confounded him—the problem of celebrity management, for instance, the business of keeping a grip on oneself, on the audience and on the filmmaking process—continue to bedevil directors for whom the blessing of vast success turns into a curse.

Beyond all that, of course, I believe that the life of D. W. Griffith has an intrinsic fascination. It may be argued that his contribution to the development of film technique—a contribution that may be summarized by saying that he had the insight to understand that a technological novelty could be converted into an instrument capable of sustaining complex narrative development, an instrument that partook of some of the qualities of several other arts, yet had its own remarkable language and imperatives—would ultimately have been provided by someone else. Indeed, we will see in this book that others quite quickly built on the foundation Griffith laid down and, in a matter of years, took the movies into realms of technique and expression where he could not follow. But no matter. The stubborn fact remains that it was he who made this contribution first, this strange and even unlikely man. He did it out of astonishing energy, long-suppressed (but vaulting) personal ambition and cultural aspiration, some profound (if ultimately inexplicable) psychic connection with the unspoken yearnings of his audience and the imperatives of his historical moment. And it was a great achievement, one that has few parallels in the history of art, one that was conditioned, in ways that are both simple and complicated to comprehend, by the fact that he was an American, the product of, and perhaps ultimately the victim of, our particular history, our particular spirit—the best of it and the worst of it.

This life has long required a careful recounting that is at once sympathetic and quizzical—and aware that Griffith lived in a world that was not completely defined by his films, his legend, his own view of himself, or the generally defensive memories of those with whom his life intertwined. It continues to amaze me that someone did not complete this task long before I began it, long before I finished it. I offer this book not only to those who care about the history of film, but to everyone who cares about the life of our century as it was refracted through the work and life of one of the figures who, as much as any politician, thinker or artist in the traditional forms, shaped the way vast numbers of us perceive its course, and perceive ourselves.

R. S.

CHAPTER ONE

Oldham County

WHEN he was at the height of his success, *The Birth of a Nation, Intolerance, Hearts of the World* and *Broken Blossoms* among literally hundreds of other movies already behind him, a new career as the generalissimo of his very own movie studio stretching, as he thought, prosperously and endlessly ahead of him, David Wark Griffith told the man preparing an authorized biographical sketch that "the sword remains the first memory I have of existence."[1] The sword belonged to his father, Jacob Wark Griffith, late Colonel (and possibly breveted Brigadier General), C.S.A., and David remembered him donning his old uniform and taking up the saber to thrust and parry with imagined enemies for the amusement of his children. And for their edification—since Jacob Griffith believed he was a descendant of Welsh warrior kings[2] and had, himself, led an extraordinarily adventurous life even before the Civil War provided him with a canvas broad and brave enough to match what he, apparently, and his son, surely, regarded as a truly heroic spirit. David—next-to-youngest of the seven Griffith children who survived childhood—learned well from his father. He believed, as his father had, that he was peculiarly suited to the leadership of men in great and daring enterprises and responded readily, as his father had, to the lure of far horizons, the thrill of gambling for very large stakes. These were, in the view of both father and son, the manly, perhaps even the kingly, virtues. And so, when it appeared to the son that by practicing them he had achieved a position more powerful than any of his father's wartime commands, and in a winning rather than a losing cause, it was not surprising that he claimed the sword as his first and therefore most influential memory.

A decade and a half later, however, he had changed his mind. By the time he attempted the autobiography he never finished, his studio had vanished and he had failed in his attempts to continue his career in a less grand manner. Now, he said, his first memory was not of a sword

15

but of a yellow dog, a sheep dog, he supposed, used on the Griffith farm to help round up cattle. "The dog too was a cavalier dog like all our family which was supposed to be of a cavalier species," Griffith said. As he told the story, the dog could not control his emotions and so fell into hopeless and forbidden love with a sheep, which in its passion it bit to death. Jacob Griffith tied the yellow dog to a tree and dispatched it with a single shot from his rifle. David ran from the scene. "But I couldn't run fast enough to get away from the report of the gun."[3]

Thus, late in life, the central image in D. W. Griffith's memory of childhood changed from one charged with romantic heroism to another of a more modest, not to say self-pitying, nature. His father, in the second instance, ceases to be the bold cavalryman and becomes simply a country-man offhandedly performing a routinely unpleasant chore which his son—identifying with the victim—could not bear to witness.

The contrasting stories represent the poles of Griffith's personality, his art, his life. For he was both weak and strong, both a romantic and a realist, and these contrasting impulses struggled—inconclusively—for dominance within him all his life.

He was born in the midmorning of January 22, 1875, on a farm near Crestwood, Kentucky, in Oldham County, just off the turnpike that joined Louisville, some 20 miles to the west, and La Grange, the county seat. It was a sizable place, 264 acres, and, before the Civil War, its main house had been considered, if not exactly a manor house, then an ex-ceedingly comfortable home by the standards of the time and place. A family tradition[4] held that the house had been destroyed during the war, possibly (and ironically, considering the family's Southern sympathies) by John Morgan's raiders on one of their periodic depredations into Ken-tucky. Actually, however, Lofty Green, as the farm was known, apparently survived the war by a few weeks, then burned to the ground in a fire of unexplained origin. No Griffiths were in residence at the time, Jacob hav-ing prudently moved his family into the nearby town of Floydsburg when he went off to war, but most of the home's furnishings, as well as family records, were destroyed. The most prominent reminder of its former pre-tensions to grandeur was a double row of poplars lining the drive from the turnpike to the place where the great house had stood. Jacob Griffith was never able to restore the farm to a semblance of its former prosperity; over the years he took out no fewer than three mortgages on Lofty Green, the paid and unpaid interest on which amounted to no less than 60 percent of their combined principal.[5]

So Griffith was born to people who had quite recently known better days, and his father, in particular, dwelled to excess on the life that had once been, not only at Lofty Green but throughout the antebellum South.

Moreover, Jacob Griffith had reason to believe—whatever the facts were about his descent from Welsh kings—that his American ancestors were at least moderately distinguished. It appears that the family was founded in the United States sometime in the early eighteenth century by an exiled Lord Barrington or Brayington who settled in Somerset County, Maryland, and took his wife's maiden name—Griffith—as his own. His son Salathiel married one Nancy Owen in 1760 and they had a daughter and five sons, one of whom was to be Jacob's father. The mother died when four of the boys were still of common school age, and Salathiel turned their upbringing over to a slave named Sarah while he pursued extensive private and public interests. In the Revolutionary War he served as deputy constable in the Wicomico Hundredth, a volunteer unit. Thereafter he was appointed sheriff of Somerset County, a position he might have also held before the war under a king's commission. His will, dated January 8, 1796, left the 100-acre estate Safeguard, on which he lived, and property called Little Belleau, to his daughter, who by this time had married. There were two other tracts—Abergildie and Snow Hill, as well as other property, which included slaves. One of the boys was bequeathed Abergildie, but his brothers were not to share in it unless he decided to sell it, in which case he was instructed to split the proceeds with them.

Daniel Wetherby Griffith, Jacob's father, was only six when Salathiel died. As one of the younger children, he was ignored not only in the will but educationally as well. Ill-prepared for either a profession or a trade, he drifted to Charles Town, in Jefferson County, Virginia, where he married, lost his first wife, and married again. During the War of 1812 he served for a month as a corporal (not a captain, as D. W. Griffith later claimed) with the Virginia Militia in its unsuccessful defense of Washington against the British invaders. Eventually, Daniel fathered five sons and at least four daughters. His son Jacob Wark Griffith was born on October 13, 1819.

Jacob was seventeen when his father left him behind in Virginia and moved to Kentucky to take up land in Shelby County, on the border of Oldham. Jacob joined his father in 1839, when he was 21 years old, and almost immediately apprenticed himself to two of the county's medical practitioners. Formal training at a medical college was not required of a doctor in those days and, in due course, Jacob, who had no more than a grammar school education, set up his own practice. In 1845 he purchased a horse to carry him on his rounds, but a year later that restlessness that was to be the one constant of his life came over him and he rode off to fight in the Mexican War. He served for a year in the First Regiment of the Kentucky Cavalry, mostly as a surgeon, and saw action at the battles of Buena Vista and Saltillo before being mustered out at New Orleans. The following year, on September 18, 1848, he married Mary Oglesby, daughter of a prominent Oldham County family. The couple moved into a five-room cottage owned by Mary's father, and Jacob hung out his shingle.

The Oglesbys, who had settled in America before the Griffiths, were a more extensive and a more prosperous clan. William Oglesby, the first of the family to leave Virginia, moved to Kentucky, where he had been granted land in return for services in the Revolutionary War. Others followed, among them Thomas Oglesby, Mary's father, who apparently acquired Lofty Green with money inherited from his first wife, Sarah Easley. Mary was the daughter of his second marriage, to Nancy Carter, whom Griffith identified, without firm proof, as a member of the prominent Carter family of Virginia. In any case, as of 1840, Thomas Oglesby held no less than 495 acres of land, six slaves, eight horses, 20 head of cattle and a mule. He was thus one of Oldham County's important citizens and his daughter an extremely eligible belle.[6]

Mary Oglesby Griffith was, in her son's words, "a silent sort of woman . . . so silent and quiet . . . that I never dreamed she loved me until she was about 70 years old when I discovered that stern, cold, hard exterior covered a tremendous emotional and an affectionate nature that was terrible in its intensity."[7] Aside from the comment of a friend, who claimed Mary "had the knack of dryly saying the funniest, funniest things,"[8] little else is known about the personality of this woman who "had been raised in the easy conditions of the rich in the South."[9]

Apparently she was too shy and retiring to hold Jacob's complete interest. Or perhaps he felt compelled to try to acquire his own wealth to match hers. Anyway, on May 2, 1850, less than 20 months after his marriage, Jacob Griffith set out for the gold fields of California with a party that included Mary's brothers, Richard and Miller Woodson Oglesby and John Grove Speer, one of the doctors to whom Griffith had once apprenticed himself. In Lexington, Missouri, they joined what D. W. Griffith claimed was the longest wagon train ever to cross the plains for the gold fields—35 to 40 mule-drawn wagons, containing at the start more than 100 men and a few women and children, with others joining as they proceeded. It was called, he said, the Lone Jack unit and, he said, his father was elected captain of it.[10] It appears that Jake was, indeed, captain of the train for a time, but it also appears that Jake's bad temper caused him to be dismissed from the post.[11]

In Utah the party split up. One group headed south to pick up the Santa Fe trail, the other, Jacob's group, proceeded, via Donner's Lake, to the junction of the American and Sacramento rivers, where Jake and Dr. Speer prospected as one team, the Oglesby brothers as another. They spent some two years in California and all were successful. Jake and his partner purchased a claim on Deer Creek in Nevada County which netted them around $16 a day. There must have been other, equally prosperous activities, for in due course Jacob was dispatched eastward carrying $16,000 of his own money and $8,000 belonging to Richard. He reached Louisville, just a few hours from home, with his sum intact; but there, in a burst of self-destruction, he gambled away the fruits of two hard and dangerous years, money in an amount he had never before seen (and would never see again) and very possibly Richard's money as well.[12] His only taxable property during the year of his homecoming was a span of mules valued at $120.

But he did salvage something from his adventure. Besides taking up medicine again and helping out on his father-in-law's farm, he acquired the beginning of his local reputation as an orator, with the Gold Rush as his topic. It may be in this period that he achieved his nicknames Thunder Jake and Roaring Jake; at any rate, his oratory naturally led into politics, though his career in public life was not long or particularly distinguished. He served one term in the state legislature in 1854–55 and returned to Frankfort for another term in the same body 23 years later.

It is possible that Jacob interrupted his political life because, as a result of his father-in-law's death in 1856, he became, at long last, a man of property. Oglesby had divided Lofty Green between his son Woodson and his daughter Mary, whose share included the main house as well as five slaves and goodly herds of cattle and horses. In prosperous times her share of the farm provided a comfortable livelihood for her, Jacob and their growing family. (Their firstborn, Thomas Jeremiah, died while Jacob was serving his first legislative term, but in the years prior to the Civil War two daughters, Mattie and Ruth, and two more sons, Will and Jacob, were born.) On the other hand, Mary's inheritance was not large and prosperous enough to withstand the hard times that came with war and its aftermath.

Nor could farming fully occupy a spirit like Jake's. If the outbreak of the Civil War struck others as a tragedy, it appeared to him a heaven-sent opportunity to escape the bonds of domesticity and agriculture. At the age of 42, Jake eagerly left the farm to fight for the Confederacy. This was, obviously, a quixotic decision, for not only was he rather mature to take up his old, brief career as a soldier, but Kentucky was not secessionist. Perhaps only one family in six held slaves, and the plantation system had never rooted itself there. Shelby and Oldham counties were both strongholds of slaveholding sentiment, however. The farmers there had long owned slaves and they had convinced themselves that their economic welfare depended upon this cheap labor. Jacob Griffith may very well have held a principled belief in the Southern cause, though there is no evidence that in later years he spent much time discussing the ideas at issue in the war. All his talk was about the fighting, the camaraderie, the gallantry and (to a degree) the danger and the hardships. For whatever else he was, Jacob Griffith was a brave man, and one gathers that he was completely happy, fully alive, only when he was testing his courage.

Jacob Griffith was to fight a long war and an active one. He fought almost from its beginning until after its official end; he was wounded at least twice, perhaps more often, and performed with valor and skill, so that he rose through the years to commands of ever-greater responsibility. But aside from its intrinsic interest, one attends to Jake Griffith's career principally because in it he found the stuff that he would weave into a personal legend in which he wrapped himself against the chill of the Reconstruction Era. That legend, in turn, would shape the life and fancies of his son, David, his strengths and weaknesses too. And it would, of course, cause him to turn to the War Between the States for the subject of the work that brought him first to fame and finally to a portion of his immortality.

When war was declared, Jacob immediately set about recruiting and organizing men from his region into a company of cavalry under his command. On October 15, 1861, they were sworn in as a unit of the First Kentucky Cavalry, a regiment that, in turn, was part of the Kentucky Brigade, organized at Bowling Green, Kentucky, on October 28 of the same year and stationed there until forced to retreat from its native state in February 1862. Units of the brigade fought at various times in Tennessee, Mississippi, Louisiana, Alabama, Georgia and the Carolinas, winning a reputation as an outstanding fighting force and a colorful appellation— the Orphan Brigade. It is sometimes said that the name was applied to them by their first commander, John C. Breckinridge, who, upon seeing the unit broken but trying to reform after an unsuccessful charge, exclaimed: "My poor orphans! My poor orphans!" More likely, however, it gained its name "by reason of identification with a cause Kentucky had not formally approved; its complete isolation from its people; its having been time and again deprived of its commander by transfer to other service or death in battle."[13]

Jacob Griffith led his company during the Army of the Tennessee's retreat toward Nashville in the late winter of 1862, after Grant's victorious capture of the Tennessee River forts to the west had turned the flank of its defensive line. Thereafter, Jake did brief duty guarding railroad bridges. He rejoined the brigade at the Battle of Shiloh in April 1862 and saw very active service in the rear guard, covering the disorderly Confederate retreat to Corinth, Mississippi. He was wounded in his shoulder in the fight at Hewey's Bridge, Alabama, on May 9, but he recovered sufficiently to take command of his company when it was detached to join Nathan Bedford Forrest's and Morgan's raiders on a sweep north toward Louisville. Thereafter Jacob Griffith's cavalry left Forrest to join General Joseph Wheeler's command. They must have seen some action at the terrible battle of Stone River, which ushered in the new year of 1863 on a tide of blood. The brigade suffered one-quarter casualties and retreated beyond Chattanooga. There was, however, plenty of fighting left to do and on March 1, 1863, Jacob Griffith was appointed lieutenant colonel, third regiment, of the Orphan Brigade. From now on, Griffith would frequently command the regiment (a full colonel's job) and would fight only under Joe Wheeler, in whom he found a truly kindred spirit— so much so that they agreed one night to name their post-war firstborn after each other, which is why one of D. W. Griffith's sisters would carry through life the awkward burden of a man's name, Wheeler.[14] The Orphan Brigade was transferred from the Tennessee front to Mississippi, where it participated in the unsuccessful attempt to relieve Vicksburg from Grant's tenacious siege. The brigade and other elements of this exhausted army returned to Tennessee just in time to participate in the Confederacy's Pyrrhic victory at Chickamauga.

Once the siege of Chattanooga began, preoccupying major elements of the Confederate army in this theater, most of Wheeler's cavalry corps, Jacob Griffith's Kentuckians among them, was sent north of the Tennessee River with orders to interdict Union supply lines. The Third Kentucky had now been combined with Jake's old outfit, the First Kentucky Cavalry and, Jake still in command, fought under the latter unit designation until the end of the war. On October 2, only two days after he set out, Wheeler encountered, in the Squehatchie Valley, a train of 32 mule-drawn wagons; he took the animals and destroyed the wagons. A little later, at Anderson's crossroads, he was met by cavalry, which turned out to be escorts for a ten-mile-long supply train of anywhere from 800 to 1,500 wagons. Unable to penetrate the defense thrown up by the two regiments of infantry defending the train's flanks, Wheeler summoned his reserves and asked Jacob Griffith if his Kentuckians could do the job. "Griffith's answer was to dismount; and in less than two minutes the First Kentucky was going up the ridge. In less than ten minutes the train, with a number of prisoners was ours. And the commander of the escort, with his surviving men, was going toward Chattanooga on short rations."[15] Again, Wheeler fired the wagons and selected mules for his own use. Then, just before dark, a large force of Northern cavalry and infantry appeared and Wheeler retired. Jacob Griffith fought with the rear guard and was mentioned, along with two other officers, as "distinguished for gallantry,"[16] in Wheeler's dispatches. Griffith was wounded, it is impossible to say how seriously, in the engagement.

This represents the only occasion Jacob Griffith was mentioned in the official records of the war, except in routine fashion. Nevertheless, if family tradition and one reference in an unofficial source are to be credited, his finest hour was yet to come. Grant, with Sherman and Sheridan leading the way for him, broke out of Chattanooga, and by mid-November, the Confederates were fleeing toward Georgia. At Charleston, Tennessee, however, the Orphan Brigade, again serving as a rear guard, was required to turn and fight. The date was December 28 and Jacob Griffith was still not sufficiently recovered from his October wound to mount a horse. Frustrated at his inability to ride with his men, Jacob commandeered a horse and buggy, was helped in and led his regiment to a temporary victory.[17]

One hopes the story is true, for there was to be little enough glory for Jacob Griffith or anyone else in Joe Wheeler's command thereafter. They spent most of 1864 attempting to impede Sherman's advance on Georgia, mainly—and vainly—trying to sever the railroad that linked the Northern army to its supply depots—Chattanooga and Nashville.

On September 1, Atlanta fell. After this, the First Kentucky was ordered to Virginia, where they joined the motley army that had been assembled under General Joseph Johnston's command to protect Lee's rear and to defend Charleston, South Carolina, regarded as the spiritual capital of the Confederacy. Sherman was now in Savannah and could strike at either Augusta or Charleston, to his left and right respectively. Johnston deployed his army in both directions—and found Sherman coming for his center at Columbia, driving Joe Wheeler before him through the swamps of South Carolina. Jacob Griffith and the First Kentucky were reunited with their leader one last time. They were employed as scouts both before and after the Battle of Bentonville, where Johnston was defeated. He surrendered as Sherman crowded him toward the sea, but Jake Griffith, possibly breveted both full colonel and even a brigadier general in these last days of the war, did not.[18] John C. Breckinridge, the last Confederate Secretary of War as well as the first commander of the Orphan Brigade, had joined the surrender negotiations between Johnston and Sherman, which, among other matters, took up the problem of Jefferson Davis and his cabinet. Sherman was aware that Lincoln, by this time martyred at Ford's Theater, had once expressed the wish that Davis "unbeknownst to me" could escape the country. He suggested to the Confederate negotiators that a ship to take Davis and his party quietly to Europe might be arranged. Davis refused; as long as there were any Southern troops still fighting and as long as they could defend him and his cabinet, then the Confederate States of America could continue to exist and, who knows, from this center of resistance it might rise again. In late April two small Confederate armies were still in the field, one under General Richard Taylor in Southern Alabama, another in the so-called "Trans-Mississippi Province" in Texas. Davis would make his way to one of them. At the very least he would avoid being under obligation to the Yankee, Sherman; at most he might perhaps manage to leave the stage of history with some dignity.

Breckinridge gave the dubious honor of escorting Jefferson Davis to one of these small remaining spots of "Confederate soil," to an element of his beloved First Kentucky, with Jacob Wark Griffith in command. They made their way across South Carolina and into Georgia and there, on the rainy dawn of May 10, 1865, elements of the Tennessee Cavalry, which had swung as far south as Selma, Alabama, and were now galloping eastward to undertake such mopping up as might be required, stumbled upon the Davis camp. It happened very quickly—no one was hurt in the engagement—and Jeff Davis's war and Jake Griffith's war came simultaneously to an end. It could at least be said of the latter that very few men fought longer for the lost cause; indeed, only the handful in Texas did, surrendering just three days later to close out, finally, the long agony.

2

When the war ended, Jacob Griffith's life effectively ended, too—though he had two decades left to him. His physical capacities were diminished in some measure by his exertions in behalf of the Confederacy. Indeed, D. W. Griffith claimed that his father had been wounded five times during the war, though only two of his injuries are anywhere set forth in the published record. He also claimed that on one occasion his father had been left for dead on the battlefield, "virtually disembowelled by a shell explosion." He was, according to Griffith, found by an army surgeon, operated upon where he lay, without anesthesia, biting through the old gray campaign hat he stuffed in his mouth to stifle his cries. In the same passage, Griffith claims, with no proof, that the Northern naval blockade had prevented good quality surgical thread from reaching the South and that the surgeon's use of an inferior material, under crude conditions, led indirectly to his father's death over two decades later.[19]

Whatever the truth of these claims, we know that with no property except his side arms and his uniform, Jacob returned home either unable or unwilling to rescue his family's fortunes in the postwar period. We know, too, that his wounded arm had not healed properly and was, to an unknown degree, crippled. He also suffered from a less glamorous ailment—hemorrhoids.[20]

Worse than any physical ailment, however, was the feeling that he had lost something more than a cause when the war was lost. He felt that he had lost, as well, the one calling that peculiarly suited his temperament, which was for military leadership of a very special kind. All his life he had possessed, and been possessed by, the innocent, arrested adolescent's courage of the cavalryman he had loved being—all hot blood pounding and damn the consequences. In peace, and in age, he would find no useful outlets for that spirit. Jake's boozy yarns about his early and wartime adventures were eventually transformed into a life-shaping legend by his son, David. The latter's taste for a wandering and deliberately unsettled life, as well as his capacity for great and heedless risk, were learned at the parental knee. There are other, even more unhappy parallels between Jake's life, when his great adventure ended, and that of his son, when his high tide had receded.

For Jacob Griffith did little with the twenty years of life left to him when the war ended, other than to produce three more children. And drink. And give orations and tell tales. And play the fiddle at home and at country dances. And gamble. One winter he even gambled away, it is said, his own and his neighbor's proceeds on crops he had taken to Louisville to sell. He does not appear to have been particularly close to his wife, despite the increase of their family in the postwar years. An indication of the extent of his contemptuous alienation from Mary is evident in a remarkable story told by a neighbor. "I'd give anything," he said to his cousin, Elizabeth White, "if Mary had a walk like you." She replied: "Well, why don't you take time to amuse her, to show her that you love her?" To which Jake snapped: "What do you think buck niggers are for?"[21] D. W. Griffith would later speak of his father's remoteness, and it appears that none of his children, with the exception of his favorite, the eldest girl, Mattie, were capable of penetrating his reserve.

Mattie was a plain, slender, black-haired girl with large protruding eyes and a remarkable ability to put people at ease. She was strongly attached to her father; and Jake loved her enough to borrow money from Henry Watterson, the famous Louisville newspaper publisher, to buy her a piano and to sell cows to pay for her tuition at Millersburg Female College, which was both a finishing school and a normal school that supplied teachers for a school system that offered no tenure and, in many cases, no guarantee that salaries would be paid in full. Mattie lived at home after she graduated, teaching at various private and public schools and, more importantly, overseeing the education of the younger Griffith children as well as teaching the family's former slaves to read and write. She also did chores around the farm. She and her sisters, Ruth and Wheeler (when the latter was old enough), habitually arose at 4 A.M. and worked until 8 A.M., the time the former slaves, who lived some distance away, arrived.

It was quite clearly a hard life economically and hints of emotional poverty are discernible despite the warm, nostalgic cast to the reminiscences of childhood in Griffith's unfinished autobiography. To his surprise at discovering, late in life, that his mother actually cared for him add this summary of his relationship with his father:

"I think the one person I really loved the most in all my life was my Father. I often wondered if he cared anything about me particularly. I am forced to doubt it. As far as I can remember he never seemed to show anybody his feelings toward them. But he must have had a deep emotional nature behind his sternness. What he did, which he only did occasionally, was to put his hand on my head and say, 'Son, how are you this day?' This simple action seemed to be an overwhelming miracle of some kind."[22]

There is some evidence that Jake Griffith cared more for young David than he showed. He termed David "one of the first in point of beauty and sense"[23] in one of his letters and in another, written to Mattie when he returned to the legislature for a term in 1878, he says, ". . . The question here is not asked is he rich but is he a man of brains. I want to prepare you for life, to be able to meet and act with life—to be able to hold the 'mirror up to nature.' Force upon your brothers and sisters the dire necessity of cultivating their minds."[24]

Mattie followed this injunction faithfully. Through teaching, she financed her brother Jacob and her sister Wheeler's advanced education at Kentucky Wesleyan after Jake died. She also indulged young David, who referred to her as "Thith Mat." He had a pronounced lisp as a young child and even when he was as old as eight acquaintances regarded his speech as singularly childish, drawling and slurring, quite at odds with the grand manner of his adulthood, when every sentence he spoke insisted on the "cultivated" quality of his voice.[25] His sisters and many female cousins made him the family pet. Even his mother, as remote emotionally from him as his father (and lacking that sense of self-dramatization that made him such a vivid figure notwithstanding), frequently reminded him that in Welsh his name meant "dearly beloved."[26]

So the first years of David's life were strangely mixed: on the one hand he was indulged, made much over, by the womenfolk; on the other, he was too often ignored and beset by doubts about his father's love. In his memoirs he speaks not at all about his brothers and sisters, contenting himself with a listing of their names. The figure who dominates the first chapter of the book is his father—remote enough and imposing enough to be a wonder and a mystery to his son, yet close enough to serve as a model for manhood.

Griffith remembered, for example, sneaking out of bed, as a small child, and creeping back into the parlor, there to take his place beneath the table and listen quietly to his father's readings from Shakespeare as well as from various romantic poets and novelists. On another occasion, David hid behind a sofa to observe a dance his family gave, an affair that went on, he says, until dawn. From this vantage point he heard one young woman say to another, "Goodness, gracious me, I would like to get another dance with Col. Griffith."

Griffith also liked to tell a story—there are at least three versions of it—about his father's relationship with the servant who had accompanied him throughout the war. His name was given variously as Uncle Easter or Uncle Zeke or Uncle Henry. In any case, he took it upon himself to give a haircut to one of David's older brothers, who had been to Louisville and there observed the new shorter hair fashion just coming into style. He prevailed on the elderly black to barber him. Roaring Jake, upon seeing the results, roared: ". . . You've ruined my best-looking son, you black ***," he cried. Whereupon he dashed into the house, fetched his saber and proceeded to chase his servant around the yard. In one version of the tale Griffith recalled being frightened at his father's violence until, as he said, he observed "the twinkle" in his father's eye and heard the laughter of the black man. In another version, he has the black returning with a glue pot and pretending to paste the trimmings back on the barbered head. On all the occasions of its retelling he adds some variation on this sentiment: "Looking backward, it seems that father enjoyed [the servant's] company more than that of any other member of his family," perhaps because, Griffith speculated, they had shared so many hardships during the war.

Griffith's reminiscences about his family impress upon an observer familiar with his later career that he organized his motion picture company—the only family he knew in his adult life—along the lines that had first been laid out to him as a child at Lofty Green. Like his father, he was capable of a certain humor in his dealings with subordinates at odd moments, and he was almost unfailingly courteous in all his dealings. But he remained, again like Jacob, extremely remote emotionally. He rarely spoke of his own troubles and made no inquiries about anyone else's. Indeed, one can find in none of the reminiscences of those who worked with him a single incident in which an exchange of confidences took place, let alone an exchange of intimate emotions. But he was always a soft touch for a loan and he was good at keeping people's spirits up in the midst of adversity. There is, in recollections of him, a tone very similar to that which marks his memories of his father—respect bordering on awe and a longing for love that is often so intense it can almost be mistaken for love. But always there is that sense of distance, a sense among his co-workers that they can only speculate about his deepest feelings.

One does not wish to press too hard on this point, but it seems that as a child Griffith received only two kinds of psychic rewards: either he was smothered in sentimental affection by the older sisters who made him a "pet," or he was asked to be a brave little man. Later, his films would be marked by a highly sentimental regard for the innocent and by a celebration of the heroic virtues. But one would find in them, or in him, little understanding of mature love, little regard for masculine responsibility exercised quietly, patiently, tenderly. His men were either callow or brutal, and when he tried to work in the middle range his heroes became stiff, even rather prissy. And entirely unpersuasive.

One of David's most vivid memories was of a journey with his father one winter's night, to a country schoolhouse, its eaves glittering with icicles reflecting the light of lanterns held by farmers gathered outside it to await the beginning of a magic lantern show. The mostly educational and religious slides were, Griffith wrote, "quite exciting to my childish mind." No less exciting to him was the opportunity for undistracted intimacy with his father—"to sit close to him and feel the warmth of his great body was as much rapture as a childish heart needed." Still, there was more than his father's presence, more than the slides to stimulate the little boy. There was a strong man who, "in the dim light from the lanterns placed around the school platform . . . bared his hairy chest," lay down across two chairs, and had his assistants cover his chest with a piece of leather, on which they then placed a huge rock. After these preparations an assistant picked up a sledgehammer and attempted to break the rock. "Crash! Again and again. You could hear the ring of steel on stone resound through the little room. The audience was spellbound. I remember to this day how the strong man's body seemed to quiver and shake. It seemed almost about to break in two as each blow of the sledge hammer fell. . . . Could that human frame endure the agony until the rock was broken? . . . We wanted someone to stop it, and yet again, we wanted the struggle to go on until the strong man won. Finally, there came a terrific climactic smash of the sledge hammer and the rock actually split, the fragments falling to the floor."

More than half a century later, Griffith commented that "to this day that drama of the strong man fighting the rock and sledge was as thrilling as any I have ever seen since. Certainly, none has ever impressed me more than this contest in the old country school house." By the time he attempted to write his autobiography perhaps he felt deep identity with a man attempting to endure, fatalistically, a series of heavy blows. Perhaps he sensed some symbolic connection between his family's condition and that of the strong man in the midst of his demonstration. In any case, that night at the school was his introduction—and an appropriately dramatic one—to the theater.

Most of his pleasures were more modest. In the country, he recalled, "entertainment consisted mostly of listening to whittling oldsters by the horse-trough before the general store fight the Civil War over again—with ever increasing victories; reading *Leslie's Weekly* by a kerosene lamp; listening to the old sentimental vocal and piano music in the parlor where gathered our sisters' beaux. Picnics, ice cream socials, camp meetings and county fairs were events."

There was also a lively and extensive relationship with numerous kinfolk in the area, particularly with John Whyte, a cousin who lived some fifteen miles away in Shelby County. Cousin John, a prosperous farmer active in politics, apparently reveled in being pompous. Griffith recalled him getting into a dispute with his eldest son over the veracity of some Latin tags the old man had introduced into a breakfast table conversation. "Cousin John banged the table with his fists, rattling the dishes and knocking several to the floor, as he stormed . . . about the general 'cussedness' of modern youth." Even more to David's taste was a political debate between Cousin John and Jacob Griffith's old commander, General Breckinridge. The latter challenged the former's expertise in the law. And Cousin John, in the great oratorical tradition, responded by building a reply that rose sonorously to a truly gorgeous climactic simile: "My knowledge of the law as compared to that of J. C. P. Breckinridge is as the refulgence of the mid-day sun to the infinitesimal light on the tail-end of a glow-worm."

Then there was Aunt Becky Oglesby, "a small yardage of alpaca completely filled with brains and energy." She sent four children to college, including Woodson R. Oglesby, sometime congressman and latter-day advisor to D. W. Griffith, partly by exercising a frugality that caused her to repair her own buggy harness with string, and partly by selling vast quantities of butter and eggs. A deeply religious woman, she "fully trusted in the Lord, but unlike most, she refrained from placing all her burdens on His shoulders." Versions of this lady in particular would appear in many of Griffith's films.[27]

Finally, "there also came a most welcome visitor—at least to the children. This was an old Jewish peddler who carried an enormous load on his back as he walked through the countryside." His name was Isadore Kahn and he often traveled with his teenaged son, also named Jacob. He usually paid for room and board by barter—some tinware or crockery in exchange for a night's stay.[28]

Griffith recalled him as an indifferent businessman, spreading out his wares and allowing the family to pick over them, but never pushing the sale of anything very hard. One late winter evening he stopped with the Griffiths and after dinner, as apples roasted, slowly turning on strings over the fireplace, Kahn took out an accordion and "began to play strange airs," apparently Jewish folk songs. Between songs he paused to tell stories of his travels, and the children loved it all—not least because they were allowed to stay up past their usual bedtimes. "The old peddler loved his music," Griffith recalled, "and there was a strangely abstract smile on his face while he played on. Then he seemed like a painting of some old patriarch in the family Bible."

In short, and despite the isolation and provincialism of D. W. Griffith's young life, there was no lack of the kind of talk, experience and characters that can enrich and stimulate the open imagination. And despite the hard work of farm life, there was no lack of time for dawdling and dreaming, and for all of this—the people, places and events of his childhood—D. W. Griffith would retain a regard that was more than merely sentimental. Some of the best, most strongly felt passages in his later movies (often, contained in films that were not great successes and are today, perhaps erroneously, regarded as minor) were evocations of country people, country life. He respected the values he learned here, mourned their passing and, indeed, suffered because he clung to them at a point in our history when the more sophisticated members of his audience were gratefully setting them aside.

He wrote: "There was a small field close behind the farmhouse, I went out to it early one spring morning, when a boy, with a little pail to gather dewberries. The berry patch was on a gently sloping hillside. Behind it was a double log cabin where lived two Negro families that had been slaves of my parents. Beside the rambling cabin flowed a small stream and on one side of the patch there was a stake-and-rider rail fence. Several larks were soaring up and down from this rail fence, singing ecstatically in the clear spring morning. In memory I always seem to see around this entire scene a luminous glow of joy. As I walked it seemed that my bare feet hardly touched the ground. Of course, I did not realize that never again would I know such pure joy, such singing, soaring ecstasy. . . .

"Often afterwards, I have thought what a grand invention it would be if someone could make a magic box in which we could store the precious moments of our lives and keep them with us, and later on, in dark hours, could open this box and receive for at least a few moments, a breath of its stored memory."[29]

There can be no doubt that for Griffith the movie camera often functioned as just this sort of magic box, that is, as a means of recapturing a lost sweetness, a lost innocence and beauty. But it functioned in other less poetic ways as well—that is, in the realm of ideas.

Jacob Griffith might have been somewhat confused as a political philosopher, but it seems his views were not entirely reactionary. His economic problems—like those of most small farmers of his time and place—were too pressing to waste much time in nostalgia for a system irrevocably canceled by the outcome of the war, a system in which, in any case, he had only an emotional stake. To be sure, he had held a few slaves, but in his wildest fantasies, he could not have regarded Lofty Green as a plantation or himself as a great landholder. No, Jake Griffith was some kind of populist. And there can be no doubt that David Wark Griffith, if he may be said to have held to a coherent body of political beliefs, was also something of a populist, at least until old age, coinciding with the arrival of the New Deal, turned him into a mild reactionary. He was, of course, tainted by the almost unconscious racism of his time and place, and, indeed, so was populism itself—and not only in the Southern and border states. But any objective examination of Griffith's work, writings or statements to the press leads one inescapably to the belief that given the social and economic conditions that largely controlled the life of the Griffith family in this period, racism was no more a dominant factor in conditioning his sensibility than the hard times he and his family endured.

To be sure, Kentucky and the other border states were spared some

of the postwar economic and social upheaval visited on the states of the
Deep South, where sharecropping proved to be as disastrous in its way
as the plantation system it replaced. But the region could not escape the
effects of the agricultural depression that, except for brief intervals, held
rural America in thrall for most of the latter portion of the nineteenth
century. Between 1880 and 1900 the percentage of tenant farmers rose
from 25 percent to 35 percent of the agricultural population and it would
rise still higher in the early years of the twentieth century. For smallish
farmers like Jake Griffith and his family there were only two escapes—to
the city or into capitalistic enterprise, for only the large landholder, working his holdings with the new heavy equipment being made available by
a technological revolution, could hope to rise out of poverty. Jake had no
taste for the former alternative, no money for the latter.

Under the impress of economic hardship, rural America fostered all
sorts of movements designed to restore what it regarded as the old virtues
to their rightful place in the nation's life. There was the WCTU and the
Anti-Saloon League, there was the Ku Klux Klan and the American Protective Association, there was, eventually, the cry for free silver, cheap
money, which lay at the heart of that diffuse movement (or spirit, really)
that we call populism.

There is no evidence that, in his on-again, off-again political life Jake
Griffith formally aligned himself with any particular faction in the Democratic party, though it is dubious that he could have achieved any success
at all without advocating cheap money and without voicing the common
rural resentments of eastern banking and railroad interests that were seen
as the farmers' oppressors. We may be sure he had little to do with the
temperance wing of populism and although around the time that *The
Birth of a Nation* was released his son would sometimes claim Jake had
ridden with the Klan, there is no reliable evidence that he did so. All that
can be certainly said is that Jake Griffith shared the general sentiments
of his time and place and that the Populist attitudes that manifested
themselves in so many of Griffith's films certainly had their beginnings
at Lofty Green.

3

In 1885, David's tenth year, as Jacob Griffith was approaching his sixty-
sixth birthday, he died—suddenly and shockingly. Or so it seemed to
David, anyway. It is not quite certain what the cause of his death was.
His son simply says that the poor surgical thread used on him during the
battlefield surgery so long ago "rotted and broke and nothing could be
done for him. . . ." However, evidence gathered by Barnet Bravermann

suggests that the immediate cause of Jake's death was much more singular. Jake Griffith liked to eat when and where he pleased (a habit that David Griffith inherited). It seems that on the night of March 30–31, 1885, he hitched his chair up to the whiskey barrel he kept on the front porch and repeatedly dipped into it with the tin cup he kept handy. He also indulged himself in no less than eight homemade pickles from another nearby barrel. The combination soon caused paroxysms and, in the early morning, Mattie Griffith sent for the doctor. The truth of Jacob's brief, final illness may be found in a combination of the Griffith and Bravermann accounts of it. Very possibly the stomach cramps caused by the odd combination of food and drink ruptured the old, badly stitched stomach wound, causing the peritonitis that carried him off.[30]

In any case, D. W. Griffith was pleased to think of this as "a blow out of the past." He adds: "I was outside standing on the rear porch when the country doctor came out and told one of the country cousins there was no hope. He was dying. It was only a question of a few hours. I went around the house and got behind the chimney in my favorite corner when I was in trouble, and of course I broke out in tears."

Sometime later he was summoned to pay a farewell visit to his father: "The four old niggers were standing in the back at the foot of the bed weeping freely. I am quite sure they really loved him. Around the bed the family was gathered. As was the custom in the old South he had a word of goodbye to say to each one of us. When it was my turn I came beside the bed. He looked at me for quite a long time with those brave eyes that now seemed so soft and tender. Finally he said, as I drew close to him, 'Be brave my son, be brave.' . . . Then after he had said goodbye to the last of the family it was only a short time until he lay still forever."[31]

The funeral was at the Mount Tabor Methodist cemetery, hard by a modest wooden church, painted white, the very graveyard in which D. W. Griffith himself chose to rest when he died. Hundreds of neighbors turned out to pay their last respects, the minister wept as he read the ceremony, and the body was borne to the grave between files of Jake's old comrades from the First Kentucky Cavalry. There was a rifle volley at the very end.

After Jake's death the family learned about the three mortgages on Lofty Green, one of which, apparently, had been made as settlement for a gambling debt. In all, $2,642 was owed on these instruments, a good deal of it representing accrued interest. In addition, the family would finally have to deliver over to Mary's brother the 89 acres for which he had paid a thousand dollars seventeen years previously.

The county court directed that Jacob's personal effects be sold at auction to settle his debts. A bay horse, a sorrel horse, a spotted cow named Sally, a red cow named Cherry, some other livestock and poultry, a few farm implements and books, worth in all $434.50, were reserved by the court for Mary Griffith and the children still remaining at home. A total of $590 was realized for the rest of their possessions, some of which were bought back by Mary and her son Will, who, the year before, had married Ann Crutchers of Southville in neighboring Shelby County and received, as a wedding gift, a 130-acre farm, complete with a five-room house, where he now lived. Specifically mentioned as one of their purchases was Mattie's piano, for which they paid $20.

A month later 18 acres of land near the turnpike were sold for $560 and, in the fall, the remainder of Lofty Green was sold for $5,447.28 in cash plus a note for $1,552.28, which was not paid in full until 1897. When all claims and debts were settled it appears that Mary Griffith and her children had about $3,500 in hand.[32]

Their situation was thus by no means hopeless. They were able to move in with Will and his bride at their farm (which Griffith remembered as poor and rocky but nicely situated on a rise in a meadow, with a stream arcing around it). Mattie went off to Louisville to teach, and young Jacob got a job as an apprentice printer on the *Spencer County Courier*, a weekly paper owned by Will's new brother-in-law. Mary Griffith applied for a pension as the widow of a veteran of the Mexican War, claiming that Jake had been disabled by "organic diseases of the heart" as a result of his service. After an 18-month delay, she received an eight-dollar monthly pension, which continued until her death in 1915.

Griffith remembered the time immediately after his father's death as harder than any he had ever before known. About the only provender available for his school lunches was apple butter, since the only thing his brother's farm had in abundance was apple trees. Each day David faced a two-and-a-half-mile walk to and from school: "In the event of rain or snow we always arrived at our destination thoroughly drenched and chilled to the bone. Then we would have to sit on our hard benches and depend upon the small stove or the mercy of the good Lord to dry up and prevent pneumonia." It seemed to him, in retrospect, that "here my first real battles with life began."[33]

Griffith records differing versions of schoolyard fights in the two drafts of his autobiography, but the themes are similar: he is set upon because he is a stranger and because, at this time, owing to the softening influence of his mother and sisters, he refused to fight back. In both versions there is the moment when he turns upon his tormentors and, singling out the worst of them, wrestles fiercely with him. The bully starts pulling Griffith's hair, Griffith retaliates, and in so doing discovers, to his stomach-turning horror, "a crop of large fat lice." He breaks off the engagement and runs.

He was, it would seem, a rather shy and easily frightened child. He was afraid of snowballs, some of which were, he says, built around rock centers; afraid to walk by the small graveyard at the corner of the farm after dark; afraid of exposing his poor spelling in the school's weekly bees (he particularly remembered being sent down for making a mistake on "deceive"). In time he learned to defend himself and as a director he was always willing to impose discipline on his sets with his fists if necessary. Indeed, he became something of a physical culture faddist. He swung Indian clubs and he paid Kid McCoy, the sometime boxing champion and latter-day movie hopeful, to spar with him.

The necessity for self-defense was not the only lesson Griffith learned in his country school. One morning on the way to school he had a vision-ary experience that stayed with him for a lifetime. It was after a sleet storm and the branches of the trees were gleaming with glaze. One group of branches was struck by the sun in such a way as to create a halo effect; Griffith thought the face of Christ appeared to him in its center, and he politely introduced himself: "My name is David and you know that means dearly beloved. I do hope you may like me a little, that I might even become your dearly beloved, because I love you and always have." Needless to say, Christ did not reply.

Though Griffith was raised a Methodist and eventually became a Mason with no strong sectarian beliefs, there can be no doubt that he harbored somewhat loftier, somewhat more romantic, somewhat vaguer religious sentiments. And, of course, at the end of several films, most notably *The Birth of a Nation* and *Intolerance*, there are visionary re-ligious allegories—Christ pacifying the nations in the former, a flight of angels bringing peace in the latter—that may have owed something to this childish (and as he admitted, quite ambiguous) vision.[34]

More important to David, was the first appearance of love, or more properly, romantic longing, in his life. The object of his shy affection was "a slim, nut-brown maid with curling chestnut tresses" and "beautiful legs." The children often played "prisoner's base," a kind of tag, and this quick, lively girl was a much sought-after team member. In one version of his memoirs Griffith said he was never able to catch and tag her; in the other she allows him to catch her once and then informs him, coquet-tishly, of her trick. In this version Griffith bursts out: "My God, how I loved her." In the other he says: "All my life I have been accused of being a devoted admirer of the opposite sex and somewhat of a connoisseur of feminine pulchritude" and adds that people are always asking him who his first star was—Mary Pickford, the Gish sisters, the Talmadges? No, he replies, this child was the first—and he no longer knows her name.[35]

In a way she was, for she surely worked powerfully on his imagina-tion, a golden, unattainable creature, perhaps the prototype of those golden, unattainable child-women who populated his films. In his last years he even attempted to write a short story about her, clumsily mingling several threads of memory—the prisoner's base games among the beech trees of his schoolyard; an imagined expedition to town in which he escorts her, trembling, past a graveyard and is rewarded by an embrace when an owl screeches nearby and frightens her; the introduction, by visiting relatives, of views of women less noble than his own. They gossip to him about an incest relationship between another girl and her father living on a nearby farm; there is, in the story, even a hint at masturbatory fantasies about the girl.[36]

It is a strange little fiction, but more revealing, perhaps, of his sexual confusions than anything in the more formal autobiographical attempts. Its title was "It Never Happened," so one is tempted to note that one of the things that never happened in Griffith's life was a resolution of the conflict between the differing versions of this girl as his memory presented her—the virgin whom one somehow could not tag and the wanton who both titillated and appalled. In memoir and story he finally retreated physically before both. In life he would retreat emotionally before both—thinking himself perhaps not worthy of the former and regarding the latter as unworthy of him, though he certainly did not lack sexual relations with women of all types. But his inability to see that a single woman might be both a sexual and a spiritual creature cannot be fully explained by the simple notation that he was the product of a rural, Victorian society. Indeed, he noted himself in the 1930s: "Today the movies are accused of corrupting the morals of youth and contributing to the 'degeneracy of modern adolescence.' This is all so much bologna. The sex morals of some of these country youths of my day were lower than a snake's belly. They had never read obscene books, certainly had never seen a motion picture, yet their conversations and actions were unprintable."[37]

One thinks again of Jake Griffith and the powerful yet contradictory image of masculinity he presented to David. If the discontinuity between the heroic soldier-adventurer of self-perpetuated legend and the disheartened farmer coping ineffectually with post-war reality was a confusing legacy, so too was the attitude toward women which David absorbed from him, for if he presented himself most attractively, attentively to them on social occasions, his remoteness from his wife afforded his son no model of a mature, loving, balanced way with women. They would remain for David distant, almost ethereal creatures, to be worshiped from afar. Or they were pals, sisters, "little disturbers" (to borrow one of Griffith's phrases for Dorothy Gish). Or they were wicked, fallen things to be used and pitied almost simultaneously. Never would he be able to sustain for any length of time a relationship with a woman in which the physical, the intellectual, the spiritual, the companionable elements were in balance. In any event, with no father to consult, his older brothers either away or otherwise occupied, with little capacity to make friends with the boys at school, he was very much on his own. At a very early age, he confesses, he was preoccupied with matters of dress and grooming and so he remained for the rest of his life, selecting clothes with an admirably theatrical flair. He was never, it seems, very confident about his looks, feeling they needed all the enhancement good tailoring could provide, though he was, to most observers, never less than a striking figure. Moreover, he admits that as a youth he spent hours studying himself in the mirror, pondering the irony that though "I would feel perfectly beautiful inside . . . the mirror would not agree with me."[38] One thinks that perhaps this self-scrutiny is subject to a less obvious interpretation—that he was studying the only material at hand in a search for clues as to who he was, what he was supposed to be and become.

And now, four years after his father's death, his first great and confusing transition was at hand. He was about to put the country, and boyhood, behind him, and become a city youth. In 1889, at the urging of Mattie and Ruth (who had now joined her there), the family left the Shelby County farm and moved to Louisville. Just what, specifically, impelled Mary Griffith to pack her three youngest children into a farm wagon in midwinter and head for town we do not know. But young David was glad, for the moment at least, to go: "No more back breaking toil in the tobacco patch; no more yanking a plow around row ends; no more struggles with obstinate cows—of all females, the most ornery. . . ."[39]

For all his excitement over the possibilities the city would surely offer him, the rural environment of his boyhood had exerted an influence on Griffith as profound as that of his father's tales of heroic chivalry and high adventure. Some of the most spontaneous and most deeply felt passages in his films would be evocations of the simple pleasures of farm life, the simple goodness he felt resided in the people who lived that life. The turnpike that ran past Lofty Green would be recreated as accurately as memory would allow in A Romance of Happy Valley; the idea of selling cows to finance a college education would be the point on which the plot turned in True Heart Susie; the use of the gentle barnyard animals as symbols of innocence would recur throughout his work. And although he would occasionally, as in Way Down East, show the narrow outlook and repressive morality of country people, he would in that film, and others as well, posit them as symbols of basic human goodness. Interestingly, too, one of his favorite stories was of the young man—very often a writer—who goes off to the city, finds his fortune but loses at least part of his soul, regaining it only when he returns to his native ground. Griffith always allowed this figure what he apparently regarded as the greatest pleasure—that of coming home in triumph, admired and envied by his neighbors—but insisted that he pay for this by some kind of admission that he had strayed from the sustaining rural values. He was simply not allowed to savor success fully until he acknowledged his roots and paid his psychological debts to the friends and relatives who had sustained and shaped him in childhood. As we shall see, Griffith himself would seek such approval—and the inner peace that he thought might come with it—in later life.

For the moment, however, the Griffith family must be seen as a small unconscious unit in one of the most significant mass movements of the time, the steady drift of large numbers of people from the country to the city. Both the South and the West were held in a "colonial economic position in relationship to the Northeast," as one economic historian puts it. They lacked the manufacturing on which the prosperity of the ruling region was based and yet their basic "extractive" industries (agriculture, forestry, mining) were exploited, particularly through railroad rate making, in such a way that it was almost impossible for the extractors to achieve steady prosperity.[40] On the other hand, the cities were late and slow in making humane provision for the work force they were drawing and so offered all immigrants, whether from the native countryside or abroad, less than they dreamed they might find. In short, though driven from the land, the Griffiths could not reasonably expect to greatly improve their fortunes in the city.

Nor was their entrance into it propitious. "Right into the city of Louisville we trundled with our furniture piled onto an old two-horse wagon. I was piled on top of the furniture. From all sides, as we creaked and rattled towards our new home, came jeering cries from street urchins.
" 'Country jakes! Country jakes!' "[41]

Still, they were there. And of all the cities of the South none was in fact more prosperous, progressive and interesting than Louisville. There, at least, one could catch a glimpse of the great, changing world. There David Wark Griffith would gratefully open himself to that world.

CHAPTER TWO

The Curve of the River

IN the 1890s the population of Louisville edged its way up to, and finally over, the 200,000 mark; comfortable growth for a comfortable city that masked its drive for economic progress under easy, graceful manners. Situated on a sweeping curve of the Ohio River, some 20 miles long, the city offered eight miles of waterfront to serve the boats and barges that moved endlessly up and down the great stream. In addition to the thriving river trade the city generated prosperity from local manufacturers, notably its distilleries and tobacco factories, and by the time the Griffiths arrived "Marse" Henry Watterson was urging, in his *Courier-Journal*, still further expansion of Louisville's commerce and industry, as well as thundering against such reactionary forces as the Ku Klux Klan and the racism endemic in populist political thought. He was a civilized and sophisticated editor, well suited to his time and place, for Louisville, perhaps because of its location on the river, possessed a lively, cosmopolitan spirit that few southern or western cities of its size could match. The memory of being awakened in the middle of the night by the cry of a steamboat whistle announcing the arrival of some floating palace figures prominently in the memoirs of people who were D. W. Griffith's contemporaries in Louisville. So does the pleasure of repairing to the levee to watch *The Big Sandy* or *The Fleetwood* or *The City of Cincinnati* nose out into the current. And if one of these glamorous boats was not to be seen, there were stern-wheel freighters chugging along on the broad river, or tugs pulling strings of barges, forty or fifty of them at a time.[1]

Like most port cities, Louisville enjoyed a reputation for raffishness that was entirely justified. Among the many part-time jobs Griffith was to hold during his decade in Louisville was covering what was politely known as "the District," as a stringer for the *Courier-Journal*.[2] Several blocks on Green Street and on Tenth Street were given over to the better class of brothels and on the side streets there were others, less fashionable,

37

which Griffith later described with obvious familiarity. He recalled that the scions of the best families patronized the more famous houses on a regular basis, that the better-known madams regularly rode up and down the main thoroughfare—Fourth Street—in open carriages, in effect advertising themselves. During the racing season at Churchill Downs—the first Kentucky Derby was run in the year of Griffith's birth—visiting madams would place discreet advertisements in the papers, announcing that they were "receiving friends" and giving their addresses. The District also housed the dance halls that, all his life, Griffith enjoyed visiting, and the more wide-open saloons where black piano players offered "chop-beat," a form of ragtime, at this period just beginning to make its way north from New Orleans.

Of course, a prosperous gentility existed side by side with this more colorful world. There was, for example, the Pendennis Club, named for Thackeray's character, who "did not claim to be a hero but only a man, a brother." The manly brotherhood of the club revolved around poker at the beginning and evolved into an exclusive eating and drinking establishment, locally famed for its cuisine. Its members were of that class who took particular pride in the cleanliness of their sidewalks, sending retainers out on Saturday morning to wash and sweep and to finish the job, if the walkways were brick, by dusting them with a fine layer of red dust; if they were cement, by whitewashing them. The ladies devoted several afternoons a week to making calls. Each carried a card that listed the hours of the afternoon they would be "at home," and these were left at each house visited. It was a highly stylized exercise—the ladies on one street arranging their receiving hours so that ladies from another street might easily make a sequence of several calls during an afternoon's outing, with fifteen minutes considered the proper length for a visit. Children were expected to be seen but not heard, tea or punch was offered at each stop and, outside, the coachman waited orders to take his party down the block to their next stopping place. On Wednesday afternoons there was dancing instruction for young ladies and gentlemen at Miss Mamie Wastell's classes at the Woman's Club and, when they grew older, debutante cotillions were held there or at the country club. For less formal entertainment there were picnics at Fontaine Ferry, the amusement park, which could be reached by coach or streetcar after an hour's ride. For special occasions one could rent a handsomely decorated open car, the "Allegro," from the street railway company, go to the end of the line and, on the return trip, stop off for homemade ice cream in someone's parlor. There was also a Bicycle Club in Iroquois Park, and at twilight on a summer's evening young men and women would pedal slowly out to it along Third Street, receiving greetings from older and younger friends and relatives taking the air on the verandas of the great houses that lined the avenue.[3]

The Griffiths, in their genteel poverty, were part of neither the lei-surely and comfortable upper-class life of the city nor its more exotic underworld. In the nineties they lived at no less than seven different ad-dresses in the downtown area; at all of them they took in boarders and from all of them David sallied forth in search first of odd jobs at which he could work after school, then of permanent employment, although he was too ashamed of the family's reduced status to apply for assistance to his father's prominent friends like Breckinridge and Watterson. A young friend from that period, Edmund Rucker, recalled that David did not fit in at all with his contemporaries in the public school he at-tended at the corner of Second and Gray streets. "The kids in our neigh-borhood used to 'gang-up' at First and Gray," he wrote. "When Griffith first appeared among us we regarded him as a hick—as indeed he was. Tall for his age, loose-jointed and beak-nosed, he wore jeans that barely reached his ankles, red suspenders and rawhide shoes. He badly needed a haircut."[4] Other fragmentary testimony about Griffith's first days in Louisville mentions the dirt ever present beneath his nails, the frayed sleeves of his coats and shirts, even that his face was often unwashed. About the only outstanding trait he revealed to his schoolmates was a good memory for quotations.

There were circumstantial explanations for his lack of popularity. To begin with, he immediately acquired an after-school job selling news-papers and, in his first summer, he took a full-time job selling vinegar on commission to grocers. Now there was no time to join the other boys on their adventures—nickel ferry rides across the river, or renting rowboats for a quarter or climbing the rocks at the falls, which drought sometimes exposed to be as big as houses. Worse, in that first summer Mattie Grif-fith died of tuberculosis, denying the family not only the stability of her presence but the knowledge of city ways that might have eased the tran-sition to their new life.

Still, in time, he adjusted. "In the loneliness of . . . this new en-vironment young Henry Watterson, who had lots of his father's generous spirit, being older than I and also very well to do, became quite friendly and I could walk peacefully, if I was with him, down Chestnut Street without being much jibed at. . . ." Moreover, Griffith was naturally in-telligent and, after taking his exams, he was allowed to skip two grades. In high school, a new teacher, "name of Wasabeer," the influence of his remaining sister, and the discovery of the *Tales of Homer* helped him "begin to see the light."[5]

But high school was a luxury the Griffiths could not afford for very long and sometime in 1890 David was forced to seek full-time employ-ment. He found a job in the J. C. Lewis Dry Goods Store, where for a time he worked as a cash boy, taking money from the sales counters to the cashier, hurrying back with the change. After a short time he was promoted to running the elevator. It was not easy work; the machine was stopped and started by tugging hard on the wire ropes on which it was suspended. They "gently tore off the skin on my hands to such an extent that they were swollen and bleeding for weeks. My chief trouble was keeping the blood from showing to the customers as I couldn't afford to buy real heavy elevator gloves and had my hands wrapped in cloth. . . . They were afraid that I'd lose a hand and my mother went to the boss to get me fired. But when the boss approached me, I told him I was doing great and finally the hands got used to it."[6]

Griffith was to stay at this job for more than two years and his feelings about it, once his hands healed, were ambivalent. From his mother he gathered the distinct impression that "gentlemanly farming, ministry and the law" were the only honorable careers he might embark upon, though possibly a genteel literary life could also be considered. But "to go into business was frowned upon. It took me many years to discover just how silly this idea was. Many good American dollars slipped through my fingers . . . and all on account of that poisonous belief."[7] On the other hand, this was the age of Horatio Alger, a period when the popular press was full of stories about lads who had worked their way up to positions of power and affluence from beginnings at least as humble as Griffith's. Even the populist press, antibusiness on many specific issues, was full of ads, as Richard Hofstadter, the movement's distinguished modern historian, pointed out, for courses in business skills and other forms of self-improvement that might help readers, whose sense of social indignation was often based on resentment over their failure to share the wealth of this age of expansion, rise into the owning and managerial classes. Indeed, the very idea of a department store like Lewis's was a new one: the first three such emporia had been created almost simultaneously in the 1880s by A. T. Stewart in New York, John Wanamaker in Philadelphia, and Marshall Field in Chicago, so it was very much in the vanguard of the revolution in merchandising that characterized the age no less than did the rise of the great luxury restaurants and hotels and the invention of such humble aids to efficient commerce as the cash register, the time clock, the fountain pen and the adding machine. In this newly urgent atmosphere Griffith, it is no wonder, occasionally felt his mother's attitude toward "trade" to be as old-fashioned as it was, in their situation, impractical.

In any case, he was not immune to the general spirit of self-improvement, though he bent his efforts toward cultural rather than business education. He read constantly in the elevator, and began taking advantage of Louisville's rich theatrical life, saving a few cents each week for a cheap seat at one of the city's many playhouses. There was melodrama at the Avenue, burlesque at the Buckingham, variety at the Bijou, "ten-twent-thirt" (inexpensive melodrama named after the price scale of tickets) at the Grand and the Harris, a stock company and, best of all, there were the Auditorium and Macauley's, where the touring companies from the East usually stopped to play split weeks. Mary Anderson, a Louisville native, had given the American premiere of *Hedda Gabler* here before Griffith arrived, but in his decade in Louisville he might have seen, among many other attractions, *Henry VIII*, with Modjeska and Otis Skinner, *The Scarlet Letter* with Richard Mansfield, *A Society Fool* with Tyrone Power, *The Masked Ball* with John Drew and Maude Adams. Then, too, there was E. H. Sothern in *Sheridan* or *The Maid of Bath*, Joe Jefferson in his famous *Rip Van Winkle* role, Lily Langtry in repertory, Eddie Foy in *Little Robinson Crusoe*, Ada Rehan as *The Shrew*. There were also companies featuring such celebrities as Lillian Russell in *The Grand Duchess of Gerolstein* and *La Périchole*, Gentleman Jim Corbett in *Gentleman Jack* and DeWolfe Hopper doing his Dr. Syntax routine.[8]

Griffith's first theatrical memory was Pete Baher's recitation of "America's National Game," and the first dramatic star to make an indelible impression on him was Julia Marlowe in *Romeo and Juliet*. He claims, indeed, that "the die was cast" as far as his future career was concerned when he saw that famous lady in her most famous role.

In fact, however, it would be at least five years before he seriously attempted acting. For the moment he chiefly harbored literary and musical ambitions; in these years both exerted a stronger influence on his imagination than the theater did. The first was somewhat hampered by his penmanship, which never progressed much beyond a scrawl and by a certain insecurity about grammar, punctuation and spelling which remained a constant of his life. Nevertheless, he spent a great deal of his spare time at the Polytechnic Library and it was there that his friendship with Edmund Rucker deepened considerably. Rucker recalled Griffith reading Browning, possibly Tolstoy and even Hardy, as well as Civil War history. Doubtless his lifelong addiction to Dickens, perhaps begun earlier, ripened in this time. One day Rucker invited Griffith to accompany him to a lecture by Mrs. George Pickett, widow of the general who led the famous charge at Gettysburg. On another occasion he and Rucker took a long walk out to the southern outskirts of town to a place known as "the fort," actually the remnants of the breastworks General Braxton Bragg had thrown up in his unsuccessful defense of the city during the late unpleasantness. Rucker also recalled Griffith's interest in the legend that the Duke of Orleans, later Louis Philippe, the dauphin deposed by the French Revolution, had once passed some of his exile near Louisville. Griffith apparently felt that the tale had the makings of a great romantic novel and outlined a plot for Rucker in which the Dauphin falls in love with a Kentucky belle but gives her up in order to make a convenient marriage to the daughter of the King of Sicily. Together, they explored the banks of the Ohio searching for the remains of the cabin in which Louis Philippe had, according to local legend, stayed.

For a time, according to Rucker, Griffith "was stiff, and there was little talk between us. But gradually he thawed a bit. . . . Awkward and moody, yes, but actually precocious." He had, his boyhood friend recalled, a propensity for long words, and as soon as he had a bit of money in his pocket he improved considerably on his style of dress—flowing bow ties were particularly well remembered. His emergence from the protective shell in which he had insulated himself during his first years in the city was now nearly complete. Rucker remembered a part-time job David took directing a crew of girls, decked out in funny, colored paper hats distributing merchandise samples door-to-door, work that apparently satisfied, in some small way, his growing need for theatrical self-display.[9]

Then there was his interest in singing which was apparently stimulated by his brother Jacob, who was a choir member at the Portland Avenue Methodist Church and once told a friend that "if I should ever lose my voice and be unable to sing, I would want to die." For Jacob his voice was apparently a compensation for a withered leg, the result of an attack of malarial fever in childhood. For David, who seems to have discovered the power of his own bass voice by singing hymns at the Cavenaugh Camp Ground near Beard's station when he returned one summer to visit his brother Will's farm, it may have been a compensation for a not very happy existence in the mercantile world. In any case, he apparently experimented with it in the basement of the Lewis store during breaks. An unnamed Negro, overhearing him one day, told him that with a voice of such quality he should not be working in a department store. Frank Coyle, a friend who worked with him, agreed. And this chance remark had two immediate results. Griffith, Coyle and Albert, youngest of the Griffith siblings, and the one with whom David would remain closest, joined Jacob in taking lessons—as a quartet—with Mrs. Annie H. Boustead, a voice coach of some local repute. She applauded the range and volume of David's voice but deplored the theatrical yearnings he was more and more openly expressing.[10]

He never abandoned his fond belief that he had a talent for music. Indeed, one of the most frequently expressed memories of those who worked on Griffith's movie sets in later years was of him singing, and not softly either. On the set, though, some said that he experienced considerable difficulty staying on pitch. Whether it was this problem, or simply the fact that the theater was more appealing to him, that caused him to turn away from music, we do not know. But sometime during his employment at the Lewis store, he went on the stage for the first time. The occasion was an amateur production of *The District School*, staged by Thomas Coffin Cook at the Broadway Baptist Church. Griffith played the dunce, sitting on the traditional high stool and wearing the traditional pointed cap. He had only one line: "The breeze from the lake blows chilly tonight." In one version of the tale of his debut Griffith said he reversed the word order so that, in his nervousness, the line came out, "The lake from the breeze blows chilly tonight."[11] But his friend Coyle found Griffith's acting quite natural and remembered that in his first test, his voice carried well. He urged him to go on with dramatics.[12]

Griffith followed the advice. He made himself known to local managers, announcing his availability as usher, stagehand and super. And in his bedroom, with its photograph of his father, a copy of the Griffith coat of arms and a Confederate war map for wall decorations, he took to reading aloud from the family's small library of books. Passersby could see him pacing up and down and gesticulating as he worked to cultivate his voice, an effort in which he succeeded admirably. He turned it into a well-placed instrument with no more than a soft, attractive trace of a regional accent, though he was perhaps more "actorish" in manner than was desirable, since among the more advanced professionals a more naturalistic style was beginning to replace the affected manner that had been popular earlier in the century.

Although Mary Griffith did not approve of the theater any more than she did of smoking and drinking (habits Griffith took up much later in life), she did nothing to discourage her son's theatrical ambitions at this point. Perhaps she thought they were no more than a youthful whim in which she could afford to indulge her otherwise dutiful son. Perhaps Griffith at first thought they were no more than that too, though there is some ambiguity on this point.

If, sometimes, he liked to claim that he was stricken with the acting virus almost from the first time he was exposed to it, he also liked to claim, when the mood was upon him, that he never intended to make a life's work of performing. On these occasions he would say that he had gone on the stage only because show people had advised him that acting was the best way to gain the practical knowledge of stagecraft he would require to fulfill his real ambition, which was to be a dramatist. There is probably some truth in this conceit; he is known to have written copiously during his many years as a touring actor. But it is also true that when he finally gained fame as a director he liked to pretend that he was made of finer, more richly creative, stuff than the typical player, that "authorship" of a kind yet more formal than the movies finally gave him the chance to practice, had been his goal from the start. This claim, of course, lent legitimacy to his ambitions for himself and his work in a suspect new medium.

Yet the need to give film a certain cultural cachet—which he brought to the medium at a timely moment—had more to it than late-blooming opportunism. The fact that he continued to use a stage name throughout his acting career, even when he was many miles and many years away from home, indicates that his mother's sense that an actor's life was somehow *déclassé* had obviously made a powerful impression on him. In contrast, a number of forces combined to impress upon him the virtue of the literary endeavor, the literary life as a higher calling.

Among these factors were his father's impressively dramatic readings when David was a boy, the consolation books provided him in the first lonely days in Louisville and, perhaps most important, the glimpse of a genteel and delightful life they afforded him when he took a job selling them in 1893. When a cousin, Albert Shipp Oglesby, decided to leave his job at Flexner's Book Store, he introduced Griffith to Benjamin Flexner, the manager, who hired him to succeed Oglesby as a clerk in what was then Louisville's leading book shop as well as one of the city's centers of intellectual life. "You'll rue the day you ever left this store," said the nephew of the owner of Lewis's when Griffith announced he was leaving. "And I will rue the day I ever came here if I don't," Griffith replied.[13]

The Flexners were leaders in the intellectual and artistic life of the community. One brother, Simon, was the physician who as director of research for the Rockefeller Foundation wrote its famous report on medical education which, among other things, helped put an end to the apprenticeship system that, so long ago, had allowed Jacob Griffith to practice medicine; more importantly, of course, it established standards for medical education, driving diploma mills out of existence. Another brother, Jacob, was also a physician, while a brother named Washington was a successful businessman and another named Lincoln was a school principal. Their sister, Mary, was a playwright who achieved several Broadway productions. The store, founded by their father, Abraham, specialized in fiction, poetry, drama and history, particularly ancient history. Its being a meeting place for celebrities, both local and visiting, was perhaps its great attraction to Griffith. "The Flexners were gentle, cultured people," he wrote, "and the intelligentsia of Louisville and the countryside usually gathered in the back room of the store after closing hours to talk of mighty subjects." They were often joined there by actors from the touring companies as well as other famous people who were passing through—especially when the Kentucky Derby drew them to the city. Griffith commented: "It was one of the few jobs I suppose where a boy would find various excuses [to stay] at his workshop instead of going home. I think I did my best work then. I would dust industriously and find something to do in order to stick around and listen to people talk who had something to say."

There were other fringe benefits as well. Theatrical managers and press agents used the store as an agency to handle free passes when they were papering houses. Then, too, there was the store's stock of books temptingly available and the only word of criticism for his performance on the job came when "Mr. Ben" told Griffith: "David, I don't blame you for wanting to read the books, but don't you think you should give a little time to dusting them, too—at least during working hours?"[14] Finally, a cousin of the Flexners, Edward Klauber, kept a photographic store in the adjoining building and his son, Adolph, six years older than Griffith, was "one of the handsomest men I had ever seen." For a time David modeled himself on this young man, later to be a drama critic for the *New York Times* and husband of the actress Jane Cowl. Griffith was impressed by his wardrobe, his dashing manner and the beginning he had made in his literary career, for he was writing articles on the arts for such regional publications as *Fetter's Southern Magazine.*

There can be no doubt that the atmosphere around the Flexner shop refined Griffith's literary tastes, though in ways difficult to specify. It also undoubtedly encouraged his ambition for a career in art. Surely, too, it gave him a new definition for the word "culture," though, so far as we can tell, it was fairly narrow. The habitués of Flexner's took little interest in contemporary affairs or in the burgeoning social sciences. On Main Street there was a public forum in a hall where every Sunday afternoon the whole panorama of leftist, reformist thought was displayed—trade unionists, Populists, Socialists, single-taxers. The Flexner crowd did not, as a rule, attend these meetings, and Griffith's attitude toward them has been described as one of "amused detachment."[15] Later, he would indeed become passionately antireformist, despising the meddlesomeness of the breed, but he remained essentially apolitical, except about the historical inequities of Reconstruction, about freedom of speech and later, about the income tax—all matters that had touched and would again touch his life directly.

Griffith continued to live with his family at their various downtown addresses. Not much is known about his emotional life during this period, but it is obvious that he was a frequent visitor to the District. He was clearly fascinated by the women he referred to as "geishas" and "houris." Prostitutes have always been the refuge of sexually shy men, and Griffith was a very shy young man at this time. When he fell in love with a blond young lady who lived some forty blocks from him he took her on long walks, "miles and miles," along the boat canal, but he was unable to bring his ambulatory courtship even to the mild climax of a kiss, although he and the girl did hold hands while he "talked her to death," sometimes passing off quotations from Homer as his own. The young lady's father disapproved of his daughter's walking out with a mere bookshop clerk and doused Griffith with the garden hose (more than once, he claimed) when he brought the girl home, effectively cooling his ardor.[16]

2

In 1896, Sarah Bernhardt appeared in Louisville. Griffith was engaged as a super in *Gismonda* and *The Lady of the Camellias*. "Standing in the wings, I would forget all about the old wolf [poverty] as the golden voice of Bernhardt chanted those poetical lines," he recalled. Everyone backstage had to wear rubber-soled shoes so that no heavy tread would upset the star's concentration on her art. He remembered her ferocious display of temper when someone in the flies, leaning forward to see and hear her better, dislodged some heavy object which crashed to the stage floor, causing her to go up in her lines. Somehow she got through the rest of the performance, bestowing the most gracious bows and smiles on the audience. Afterward, however, she cornered her stage manager, a French-man, against a wall and, according to Griffith, lectured him for close to two hours about the incident. "Madame's hands flayed the air; her whole body quivered; each hair on her head trembled as she eloquently excori-ated the lout. He would try sneaking along the wall, but she always headed him off. He would flee back to the corner and essay the other side. No dice. Madame was too quick. Next, he would face about like a cor-nered rat and try to alibi—but before he could open his mouth, the grande dame was on him with another burst of invective. . . . What a woman!"

When Bernhardt reported for rehearsal the next day she came on stage bowing to left and right, "like a gracious queen to her subjects. To her favorites she extended her hands to be kissed." The offending stage manager stopped the rehearsal, bowed low and as the star advanced on him she rewarded him first with a box of jewelry, including several gold pieces, then by embraces and kisses. "Now she consumed as much time and energy to apologize as she had in berating him. Tears . . . raptures . . . forgiveness . . . joy."[17]

No wonder the stage—especially the melodramatic stage of that time—appealed so powerfully to Griffith's imagination. It could be to him what war had been to his father, a place that could comfortably en-compass grand emotions, sweeping gestures. Moreover, it was a place for wanderers; and Griffith, no less than his father, would need to be free of confining domesticity and imprisoning roots.

By this time, the Flexners had sold out. Griffith had stayed on under the new owner, Charles T. Dearing, but their relationship was not a happy one, and when Dearing asked him to leave—possibly for reading on the job—he was ready to go. By this time he could no longer deny his passion for the theater, and his desire to make a serious attempt at a theatrical career.

When Griffith told his mother that he had signed on with a touring company, she reminded him of those Welsh kings from whom he was allegedly descended and noted that after the English conquest of Wales history had heard little from the Griffiths "doubtless because they have in the interim committed various assorted villainies." Nevertheless, she concluded, according to her son, in all that time "none is on record as having fallen so low as to have become an actor."

Griffith undoubtedly exaggerated his mother's response to his new career, and it was, perhaps, irrelevant, since he had now attained his majority. In any event, the first record of Griffith the actor appears in a few lines of small type in the *New York Dramatic Mirror* for May 23, 1896. It says simply that an actor named Robert Haight produced and starred in a production of *Damon and Pythias* for a "small but well-pleased audience" at the Opera House in New Albany, Indiana, adding that Carroll Hyde as Lucullus and Lawrence Griffith as Dionysius "were excellent."

The following fall Griffith joined Ada Gray in what was billed as her farewell tour. Her repertory included *East Lynne, Ring of Iron* and *Camille*, and although he was only twenty-one, while Miss Gray was now seventy years old, he had a good part in the first-named "great moral sensational play," as it was sometimes billed. He was the villain, Sir Francis Levinson, and playing under the name "Alfred Lawrence" "cleverly depicted" the role, according to one notice.[18] *East Lynne* did not become famous by accident. It was regarded as a sure-fire attraction, especially in the hinterlands, and it would continue to be so regarded for another twenty years. The other Gray presentations were also not without appeal; but as the tour proceeded, the reviews grew more and more unfavorable, and business dropped, according to the trade press, from "good," to "moderate," to "poor" to "extremely poor" as they trouped through the small towns of Indiana in the winter months. Griffith was to claim that the tour ended when the stage manager absconded with the box office receipts one night, stranding the company, but he tended to dramatically exaggerate his reminiscences of his touring days. It seems more likely the company simply expired for lack of business and future prospects. It is also possible that Griffith left it for a lesser job in a more stable company.

In March 1897, he is reported working with a small company headed by a John Griffith in Urbana, Ohio, playing an unknown role in *Richard III* and singing with an off-stage quartet in *Faust*. The engagement represented two months of work, playing small towns in Ohio, Michigan, Minnesota and North Dakota. Early in the tour he wrote his mother a letter, the only one from him in this period which has survived. He had changed his name again, this time to Lawrence Brayington, to avoid conflict with John Griffith's name, and he wrote quite uncomplainingly of the rigors of life on tour. Griffith had not yet been paid, but since touring companies traditionally bore the cost of their actors' room and board, he was not suffering. Indeed, he was quite impressed with what seemed to him lavish accommodations. In Grand Rapids he had "a beautiful room and steam heat for $1.25," which seemed to him "fine enough."[19]

In May of 1897, Griffith left the John Griffith company for unexplained reasons and returned to Louisville, where he got his first brief engagement with the Meffert Stock Company, a group that would be very important to him over the next two years as a source of steady employment, over many later years as an influence that significantly shaped his theatrical sensibility. Colonel William Meffert was not himself an actor or director. Rather, he managed the Temple Theater, which operated in a one-time Masonic lodge, located above a drugstore in downtown Louisville. One climbed to the theater via an outside staircase, but once inside "the prettiest playhouse in the city" as it advertised itself, one found a good-sized house seating some 700 in the orchestra, another 300 in the balcony. The stage was large (65 feet wide, 30 feet deep) and, by the standards of the day, well equipped with electrical lighting equipment. It had been some time since Louisville had a stock company in residence, but in the winter of 1897 Meffert engaged two brothers, Ralph and Robert Cummings, to organize one and they offered Griffith a small role in Belasco's *Men and Women*. Though Griffith claims that the stage manager dismissed him before he ever got a chance to play the role, he more than likely played out the run and found himself not needed for subsequent Meffert productions.

His luck continued to run strong, however, for at this time an Irish comedian named Ned Risley (Griffith refers to him, incorrectly, in his memoirs as Ridgely) and a character actor named Willard Blackmore were organizing a company they called the Twilight Revellers to make a summer tour of the small towns of Indiana and Kentucky. They were backed by a stagestruck blacksmith named Jim White, who, in exchange for the promise of acting experience, put up seventy-five dollars to get the group started. Griffith joined the company, which counted among its other members, he says, a carpenter, a harness maker, a waiter and a banjo-playing barber. Their repertory was to include *Pygmalion and Galatea* and *The Arabian Nights*. Their rehearsal hall was the back room of White's shop, "our wild histrionic shoutings . . . punctuated rhythmically by the assistant blacksmith hammering out iron in the adjoining room."

The Twilight Revellers made their debut in New Albany, Indiana. Griffith was singled out for playing Leucippi in *Pygmalion* "in a thoroughly competent manner." From this and the next three stops on their tour, Griffith laconically comments, the troupe "escaped alive." At the fourth, however, management informed them that there was no money for their board bills, but that if they could escape without paying they would find the next stop in their itinerary "a great show town." That night, as Griffith had it, doubtless improving on the facts, "the entire company attempted to forsake the boarding house via a rear second floor window and a bed clothes rope." Their landlord was on to them, however, and he materialized out of the darkness to grab each actor as he reached the ground. Risley, the last one down the rope, was adept at dealing with this kind of crisis. He promptly put his smooth tongue to work on the landlord, suggesting that he accompany the Revellers to their next engagement, where he could take what was owed him off the top of their receipts and, in addition, enjoy with them the pleasures of backstage life. The man was easily persuaded and, according to Griffith, the little company was swelled by the presence of no less than five similarly stagestruck hosts as it proceeded on its way. One of them, he claims, was even talked into pawning his gold watch, "a biscuit-like family heirloom" in order to keep them all going. The end came when several of the landlords' wives appeared in a body and put an end to their foolishness. Says Griffith, "I . . . was forced to beat my way back to Louisville and home."[20]

As the years passed, Griffith managed to turn reminiscence into a very tall tale. One of his last projects was a screenplay based on this and other touring experiences. Yet one feels that he was basically true to the spirit of the adventure in all his recollections. Whatever its financial and artistic defects, life in the Twilight Revellers company was apparently fun. There is a gaiety in his account of this tour that is missing from most of his other theatrical reminiscences.

What he did next is unclear, but most likely he visited Chicago for the first time, though there is no record of his finding theatrical work there. It is also possible that on his return to Kentucky he took a summer job peddling the *Baptist Recorder*, a weekly paper, as well as an encyclopedia, from farm to farm outside Louisville. He recalls taking some steaks along with him in an attempt to woo a notoriously difficult customer. A storm broke out and he was forced to take shelter in a forest, where he was stalked by a mountain lion. He abandoned the steaks to the beast and took dripping shelter with his own prey, who even without the gift of the steaks took pity on him and agreed to buy a set of the encyclopedias.[21] Again, the anecdote strikes one as more than a little fanciful, but the job did tide Griffith over.

The new theatrical season brought new management to the stock company at the Temple in Louisville. Colonel Meffert had found the Cummings brothers excessively rude and arrogant with patrons so he decided to replace them with Oscar Eagle and his wife, Esther Lyon, who in addition to managing and directing were to play leading roles. The season began on September 6, 1897, with a dramatization of Ouida's novel, *Moths*, but Griffith did not immediately get an acting job with the company.

Two men claimed to have been most influential in getting Griffith work with the company. They were Adolphe Lestina, who played heavies (and, later, character parts in many Griffith films), and Tony Sivori, the company's propman. Lestina praised Griffith's voice; the latter recalled that "with that thick mop of brown hair and his high winged collar, that fellow certainly looked the part of the 'legit.' And how he loved to act."[22] Sivori's claim that he gave Griffith twenty-five cents a performance to do scene shifting and act as call boy and that Griffith soon graduated to supering and bit roles seems improbable. By this time Griffith surely regarded himself as a thoroughly professional actor and was unlikely to accept the indignity of backstage work and small parts, unless he was in desperate straits, which also seems unlikely, since his family could provide him with bed and board. Sivori also recalled suggesting Griffith for the role of a butler in *Little Lord Fauntleroy*. This he might have done, but that part was by no means Griffith's first at the Temple that season.

The earliest mention of Lawrence Griffith in a playbill occurs during the week of October 4, when he played Thomas Bagot in an adaptation of George du Maurier's *Trilby*. Griffith had a role in *The Wife*, a naturalistic study of marriage written some ten years before by Belasco and Henry DeMille in an imitation of the "cup and saucer" realism that Thomas Robertson had introduced in England as early as the 1860s. He played a servant in Wilde's *Lady Windermere's Fan*, a relatively up-to-date and sophisticated work for a company of this kind, and a considerable novelty for Louisville. So was the next production, *The Silver King*, which had premiered in London only three years earlier and won praise from no less a critic than Matthew Arnold. In it, Griffith played the role of a landlord.

In all, it would seem that the Eagle regime at the Temple was more serious, more *au courant* and more wide-ranging in its choice of material than other stock companies in similar cities at this time. Indeed, Griffith was fortunate in attaching himself, at this early point in his career, to this group. Eagle himself went on to a solid career directing musicals (and some films) in New York and several members of his Louisville company became well known to the theatrical public. Among them were Kate Toncray, who would also work on and off for Griffith in his early films; Henry Hull, a native of Louisville who played occasional child roles at the Temple and would also later work for Griffith; and Edmund Day, whose play *The Round Up* became a sort of winter substitute for the Wild West shows in the period 1907–17, since it called for spectacular staging, including real horses in its great climactic Indian fight. In short, the Eagle company was a good training school, ambitious, literate and very professional.

There was no work for Griffith at the Temple for several weeks after *The Silver King* completed its run and he might have returned to the John Griffith company during this hiatus. He was back at the Temple by January 10, 1898, however, and Eagle asked him to double in two small parts in one of the most beloved and oft-performed melodramas of the nineteenth century, Adolphe d'Ennery's A Celebrated Cause, which was written the year Griffith was born. Its plot, involving a good man wrongly accused of murdering his wife, and forcibly separated from his beloved child when he is sentenced to a prison galley, is too complicated to summarize in detail. Griffith's roles as a corporal of the guard and as a sergeant were of no great significance in it, but this was his first professional association with the work of the prolific French playwright, who specialized in a plot that he was to find irresistible—that of the lost child. Much later, Griffith would risk much with a film adaptation of another d'Ennery work which revolved around the same theme. That, of course, was The Two Orphans, which, as Orphans of the Storm, Griffith expanded into a spectacular—and costly—drama of the French Revolution.

Griffith's roles continued mainly to be small during the rest of this season. He doubled again in The Lights o' London, another famous success of the time, particularly noted for its realistic portrayal of slum life in the city—another subject that Griffith would later master in his own medium. He also played a servant in The Wages of Sin and a nobleman in Jim the Penman and it was in this period that he did the butler's role in Little Lord Fauntleroy. Possibly as a reward for his patience, or as evidence of his growing skill, he got a larger part in Eagle's last Meffert show of the season. He played Christopher Dabney, the "Broken-down music teacher" in William Gillette's All the Comforts of Home.

Eagle thought well enough of Griffith to invite him to join him at the Alhambra Theater in Chicago, where Eagle was to direct a season of summer stock for the James Neill Company. The repertory there included plays new to Griffith, The Lost Paradise and Ferncliffe and, most important, The Ensign. In it Griffith played Abraham Lincoln and scored "a remarkable success," so remarkable, apparently, that he received a pay raise—from fifteen to eighteen dollars a week. The portrayal gained such a measure of local fame that on June 9 and 10 he was invited to don his makeup and appear as Lincoln in an Elks club minstrel show. "Lawrence Griffith of the Neill Stock Co. made his famous Lincoln pose in the tableau finale and received deserved praise," a trade paper noted.[23]

It was probably during this summer that Griffith saw a movie for the first time. In interviews he sometimes tried to place the date of this rather consequential meeting of man and medium much later, as if to imply that he was so grand a stage actor that he had not noticed the beginnings of this very humble competitor (though if he had been paying attention he might have noted that some of the Louisville vaudeville houses were already using films as "chasers" to empty the theater at the conclusion of performances). He did not enjoy his first film. "It was a weary, dull affair, exactly what I have forgotten. But my friend [he does not name the man who insisted on taking him] liked it greatly. I found it silly, tiresome and inexcusably tedious. It was in no way worthwhile and I considered the time wasted." He conceded only that the line at the box office was impressive.[24] Griffith's Chicago season ended on the Fourth of July and it is impossible to say how he spent the remainder of the summer.

By September 1898, however, he was in Clinton, Iowa, working in a touring company led by an actor-manager named Walker Whiteside. Griffith played a general in *The Red Cockade*, a cape-and-sword melodrama set in the French Revolution, and a country squire in *Eugene Aram*, an adaptation of Bulwer-Lytton's popular novel. All he had to say about this experience was that "it probably accounts for my lack of sympathy with Iowa ideas,"[25] whatever that may mean. The tour extended beyond Iowa to small towns in Minnesota, Indiana, Ohio and Michigan, where, in Dowagiac, it finally ended on March 28, 1899.

Griffith returned to Louisville in time to work briefly for the Meffert Company, again under Oscar Eagle. He opened in *Aristocracy* by Bronson Howard, one of the first playwrights to work firmly in the American popular tradition; in *A Gilded Fool* by Nat Goodwin, the beloved comedian; and, most important for Griffith, in an adaptation of *The Three Musketeers*, in which he played Athos. This production closed the season on a small note of triumph for Griffith. By this time he was convinced, by the growing importance of his roles and by the steadiness with which he had worked in the past couple of years, that he was now ready for a full-scale assault on New York. In any case, he probably knew that Eagle and his wife had decided not to return to Louisville for the next season, so the mainstay of his provincial career was about to disappear. An ambitious and courageous man, he could not help but realize that he had arrived at a propitious time to try his luck on larger stages.

He stayed around Louisville for a month or two, and it was at this time he probably free-lanced items for the *Courier-Journal*'s "Stage of the River" column, a compendium of information for shippers and navigators on the Ohio and handling assignments as a stringer covering the District. Living at home, he saved what he could, sold the bicycle he had used to get around the city and finally bought a ticket for the East. When he set off he was twenty-four years old and had just nineteen dollars in his pocket. But he knew, if no one else did, that his apprenticeship was behind him, that now, for better or for worse, he was a committed man of the theater.

CHAPTER THREE

On the Road

GRIFFITH had bought a round-trip ticket to Atlantic City, possibly to disguise from his family his intention of making a full-scale assault on the New York theater. When he reached his destination he cashed in the unused portion of his ticket, used part of the proceeds for a one-way fare to New York, then spent the day strolling the boardwalk, taking in what were undoubtedly, to him, the exotic sights, sounds and smells. They were nothing, however, compared to what he would encounter in New York.

He quickly discovered that with his limited resources he could not afford even a modest hotel room. He stayed for a few days in a flophouse—fifty cents a night—in Brooklyn, under the shadow of the great bridge. Then he moved to another, even less attractive place, on Houston Street, not far from the Bowery. It was a dormitory, accommodating perhaps fifty inmates, who paid just fifteen cents for their cots. The beds were very close together and Griffith was fearful of thieves and homosexuals. In these cramped quarters it was easy for the former to lift what money one had or for the latter simply to crawl into bed uninvited. The floor was covered with dust, and the bedspreads stained by reddish brown spots that marked the places where cockroaches had been dispatched.

In these dismal rows of beds "men made out of the image of their God [sic] reposed as best they could through hopeless nights. The wailing voices—shut the sounds out of your ears for God's sake . . . shut the memories out of your mind . . . stop your thoughts, all of them, from whirling around and around. You must get some sleep. . . . Do you hear the clock striking the hours now—then daylight . . . and Big Jim will pull the cord and your lousy cot, along with the rest, will flop to the floor and drop you into the filthy dust."[1]

The atmosphere and the human wreckage were appalling, but Griffith was a very strong young man, buoyed by faith in his talent and toughened by the years of near poverty he had already experienced. For all his

53

innocence about the city's ways, for all his inbred romanticism, he was not greatly fearful either of menacing surroundings or of undertaking hard physical labor to survive. Though the next nine years would be hard, they were quite possibly a necessary tempering of his spirit, grounding him in the harsh reality of contemporary urban existence. From this experience would come that vigorous sympathy with the poor, the suffering and the lost that caused his early films to speak so directly and unpatronizingly to the nickelodeon audiences. It must be remembered that the man who adapted Poe and Tennyson and Browning for the screen also adapted Jack London and Frank Norris and invented dozens of other short tales about modern hardships. If the romantic side of his nature had fattened on his reading and his provincial dreaming, the second, less-often-remarked side, the realistic side, was now beginning to develop as he pounded the pavements of New York, looking for work.

Considering the meanness of his life in New York, and the hardly exhilarating economic rewards when he actually found work in the theater, Griffith's memoirs of this period are remarkably cheery. "Actors were then engaged either late in the summer or early in the fall. That is generally a perfectly gorgeous time in New York. Many crisp autumn days and that enticing street of dreams—the Rialto; youth; lifting your feet scornfully from the sidewalk in the crisp, clear air. Actors hurrying from agent to agent, or talking magnificently in little groups about past contracts; fascinating women . . . dancing girls, singing girls, dramatic hopefuls . . . the perfume of their carefully gotten up enticing rigs filled the offices. Bright eyes attempting to lure susceptible managers. Oh Boy! It was the life."[2]

At first, even the streets of the Lower East Side were exciting to Griffith. "The Ghetto, Mulberry Bend, the Bowery and Chinatown were all well-known to me, but Rivington Street was the lively one, eternally jammed with push-cart peddlers hawking their wares. . . . Rivington Street never appeared as a melting pot to me, but more as a *boiling pot* [italics Griffith's]. Here were Italians, Greeks, Poles, Jews, Arabs, Egyptians, all hustling for a living. Emotional, tempestuous, harrowing Rivington Street was perpetually a steaming, bubbling pot of varied human flesh. . . ."[3]

In vividness it compared, in memory, only with the Bowery at night: ". . . pianos banging, violins screeching, braying instruments of brass, and every popular song of the day. Gaudy women swung in and out of the doors of the various bagnios and bistros. Sometimes the street was alive with sailors ashore from the seven seas and avidly searching for life, women, drink, excitement. Maybe I passed the store where Irving Berlin hammered away on his inspired old piano. . . ."[4]

But it was not the music, primarily, that excited him. In this chapter

of his memoirs, as in his section on Louisville, Griffith devotes a disproportionate amount of space to a rather lyrical description of the prostitutes and their environment. "The skin of the Bowery women was of
every known hue. After the age-old manner of the siren, they chanted in
many languages and accents the one hymn to lust . . . the same against
which Ulysses roped himself to the mast." He adds, slyly, "That was one
man who had the right idea."

For the sake of propriety Griffith notes that there were no "respectable" clubs where a young man might meet a young woman. Instead, he
recalls, "I polished my shoes until they shone; brushed my suit and it also
shone; set my hat at a rakish angle and walked mile upon mile" hoping
to pick up some girl. He was notably unsuccessful, and he claimed, interestingly, that the only women available to men in his situation were prostitutes. Maybe so—but perhaps he was not looking far beyond these girls.
His best memory was of the time he had enough money to go to a dance
hall in the Tenderloin on Sixth Avenue and Twenty-seventh Street. He
could not afford the main floor, but he could buy some beers for a girl he
encountered working the mezzanine. He pretended that he was an English lord (and, later in the evening, a royal duke) out for a bit of slumming. "She took this without a shudder, having been lied to by professionals." No consummation ensued, and Griffith vividly contrasted this
one exciting night with the world of derelicts he encountered on the way
home: "How often was I assured in my soul that I would never get out of
these grimy streets! I could even picture the kind of rags I would wear
when I held out a cup to indifferent passersby . . . or the coming day
when I would not have even the price of admittance to that nadir of
existence, the five or ten-cent flophouse."[5]

Such gloomy forebodings were by no means unjustified. Before long,
however, he got a job, a good one, as the lead, "Happy Jack" Ferrers, in
London Life, a popular melodrama of the day. The pay was $25 a week,
out of which Griffith sent a "chunky slice" home regularly. The tour
opened in Albany, wended its way through New York State, darted over
the border into Ontario, and then on into Ohio, Michigan, Indiana, Illinois, Tennessee, Georgia, Alabama, Mississippi, Arkansas, Wisconsin
and Minnesota, with Griffith achieving generally good notices. In Buffalo, for example, he was called "a capable actor, who at times betrays
considerable dramatic ability." The Saint Paul critic for a trade paper
noted that he "carried the role with spirit" and the man in Minneapolis
said he "caught the house as Happy Jack."[6]

Something odd happened in Minneapolis, however. Griffith claims
that the show closed abruptly, leaving him once again broke and stranded
far from home. But the trade papers indicate that the London Life company continued west to San Francisco, probably without him. Why did

he leave—or get fired—if his notices were good and there were no other jobs in the offing (the record does not disclose him to be working again until the following October)?

We cannot say for certain, but in his memoirs Griffith makes a curious confession. There was a girl in the company whom he identifies only as "the Snow Angel," and of whom he writes: "In my memory she stands out as one of the two most beautiful feminine creatures I have ever seen. She was long of limb, slender, but very full-busted. She had real blonde hair, exquisite white skin, great blue eyes, shaded with silky lashes." As had happened before and would happen again, he found himself unable to confess his feelings to a respectable young woman. However, he reports, approvingly, an incident in which another actor in the company, a short man who resembled Edgar Allan Poe and was generally "razzed" for his habit of reciting highly romantic verses to the women he constantly pursued, brought the Snow Angel to his couch with these lines:

> To hold you 'till one stilled you
> To feed you 'till one filled you
> To kiss you 'till one killed you
> Sweet lips—if love could kill

The girl lay half the night on the actor's bed; all the fellow could do "was to sit and gaze upon her." The sentiment commended itself to Griffith as did the man's words when he reported his feelings: "I knew I would never see anything as beautiful as she again, and I wanted to keep that unspoiled lily in my memory forever."[7]

It is an odd anecdote to record in an autobiography that is so reticent about so many other more central matters. It is indeed one of the few pages Griffith wrote that does not directly involve him in the action, and needless to say its tone was radically revised for the book's second draft. There is almost no question that Griffith himself was, in fact, the watcher in the shadows and that he chose to disguise his identity since the male figure acts with strange—even unmanly—reticence. Griffith's strong literary identification with Poe, his habit, in those days, of writing verse to women he admired support this view. But one feels that even if he was not actually a participant in this scene, it is here because it so perfectly expressed one of Griffith's basic attitudes. Parker Tyler has observed that Griffith was one of the inventors of the "Morality of the Single Instance," that basic convention of the American film in which the relationship between a man and a woman is continuously conditioned by the circumstances of the first time they indulged their carnal passion. In the moral system that derives from this convention, marriage, for example, becomes "not a complex spiritual and physical union to be revitalized by all manner of devices, and sustained by culture and imagination. It is, rather, a series of repetitions of an originally legalized sin; it is a compulsory, mono-lithic act of nature one has received legal permission to repeat indefi-nitely." As Tyler points out, this amounts to "an overemphasis placed on the First Time—a sort of shock, a persistent subflowering of shame and guilt."[8]

A persistent sub-flowering of shame and guilt. The phrase summa-rizes the most important aspect of Griffith's feelings when they were aroused by "good" (and always very young and very innocent) women almost as perfectly as the incident involving "the Snow Angel" prefigures emotions he would obsessively explore in his films. As Tyler says, he had a very "forthright" conception of the premarital "single instance": "rape or the marriage proposal."[9] Quite obviously he (or his surrogate) could bring himself to no such definitive action in this incident and so retreated to a romanticized passivity, a passivity that would be duplicated by his camera as it mooned over such Griffith favorites as Lillian Gish and Carol Dempster in later years.

His guilty sexuality, however, would have more significant conse-quences than that. It severely limited his range when he was dealing with romantic love. He could be free, even humorous with women who did not arouse strong emotions in him. Dorothy Gish, for example, was easily turned into a hoydenish comedienne by him, and other actresses, ranging from Mae Marsh (once his infatuation with her ended) to Lupe Velez, were allowed an expressive range that his special favorites were denied (Gish, of course, often conquered his limits; Miss Dempster was incapa-ble of so doing). These limits—frequently ascribed to, and no doubt in-fluenced by, the Victorian sentimentality that was so much a part of Griffith's sensibility—played a role in his fall from favor with audiences in the 1920s, when his endless preoccupation with fates worse than death came to seem to many rather laughably anachronistic. There were other consequences as well, the most important of which was his inability to create genuinely virile roles for the male leads in his pictures. Whatever their abilities as actors—and many of them proved to be talented indeed—Henry Walthall, Richard Barthelmess, Ivor Novello, Neil Hamilton, Al-fred Lunt, William Boyd, shared, as physical specimens, a preternatural handsomeness that made them seem rather abstract and bloodless—sym-bols of the masculine principle rather than realistic representations of the male animal. Moreover, Griffith's direction of them tended to be stiff and tentative, overidealizing them, as if he preferred not to think of them as harboring any of those lustful qualities that he apparently feared in him-self. This capacity—this need, really—to despoil childish innocence, inno-cence of the unguarded, sleeping kind that he wrote about so vividly in his memoirs, he embodied, instead, in the bestial villains, most notably, Lynch and Gus, the mulatto and the black who threaten, respectively, Lillian Gish and Mae Marsh in *The Birth of a Nation*, but also in characterizations like those by Donald Crisp in *Broken Blossoms* and by Lionel Barrymore in *America*. Without wishing to seem too schematic about it, one can say that Griffith was never able to integrate the conflicting demands of the light and dark sides of his sexual nature, either in life or in his films.

One runs the risk of overinterpreting this moment in Minneapolis only because it is one of the clearest revelations Griffith made of his attitude toward sex. As such, it offers insights into the attitude he brought to sexual relationships as he dealt with them in his art, but also in understanding his own busy, if confusing, romantic life.

If Griffith was, in fact, the male figure in the anecdote, was he asked to leave the company as, later in life, he was asked to leave certain bars, for annoying a young woman? Did he, perhaps, make advances to more than one of the young women in the troupe? It has been noted, for example—on possibly dubious authority—that at roughly this time Griffith, worried about a sudden inability to perform sexually, visited a Dr. Oglesby, a cousin, who advised him to abstain from his energetic sexual activity.[10] Was he, conceivably, suffering from venereal disease, which prevented him from consummating the sex act with "Snow Angel," and did his shame over this drive him from the company? Or was he merely so smitten with unrequited passion that he could no longer bear to be near her?

The questions are endless, and all we know for certain is that it was midwinter in the Upper Midwest, no place for a penniless actor to be stranded, voluntarily or involuntarily. So, in subzero weather he "grabbed the blinds" of a Chicago-bound passenger train and managed to get a considerable distance before he was discovered by a brakeman and forced off. Thereafter he had to ride the rods of a freight train into Chicago, arriving there, he says, "a well-frozen ham." He thawed out at the free-lunch counter of a tavern near the American Theater, which was well known to actors, grabbed the blinds of a Louisville-bound passenger train and, some eighty-five miles out of Chicago, was discovered and derailed by a brakeman inspecting the train at a water stop. By this time Griffith was, he says, so "done up" that he "was ready to call the whole thing off and stay there" (and possibly freeze to death). However, he summoned some hidden reserve of strength and hiked into the nearest town, his shoes tied to his feet with rags. In the early morning hours he found a baker at work in his kitchen and the man let Griffith warm himself by toasting his feet in one of the ovens. Unheeded while the baker went about his work, Griffith crawled all the way into the oven, so bone-cold was he. "Ach, Gott," said the man, who was German, when he discovered what Griffith had done. The baker presented Griffith with twenty stale doughnuts, nineteen of which he claims to have eaten on the spot, "making Louisville on the twentieth."[11] The incident, comically heightened, with W. C. Fields actually falling asleep in the oven and almost burning to death when its door was inadvertently locked, became one of the best bits, a quarter century later, in Griffith's comedy *Sally of the Sawdust*.

Eventually Griffith made his way back to New York, where he again slept in flophouses, although this time he was apparently able at least to afford a small cubicle, partitioned off from the other lodgers. Even so, he says, he was kept awake nights by a neighbor whose battles with delirium tremens could be plainly overheard through the thin walls of his room.

It is impossible to say what, if anything, Griffith did theatrically between January 1, 1900, and October 29, 1900. It is one of three extensive "lost" periods in his theatrical record. In his autobiographical writings, as well as in interviews, he spoke of going out with a "ten-twent-thirt" melodrama that stranded in Tonawanda, New York, and this might have occurred in this first blank period. All information about the company and its activities is lost, but Griffith spoke in such detail of his experiences after the show closed that one must record his adventures in cheap melodrama as true, despite the absence of documentation. Perhaps the place of this company's death, deep in the sticks, gives us an adequate clue to the quality of its life. In any event, Griffith got a job in Tonawanda shoveling iron ore in the holds of the steamers that carried it across the great lakes. "To do real muscle-stretching work, and to mingle with the men who did such work, was my ambition," he later claimed, giving the impression that he had done this work by choice. However, the description of the work that he gave his interviewer belies the glamour with which he tried to invest it: "Men would shovel down in that grimy, stuffy hold until they dropped where they stood from utter exhaustion; then they would be chucked into one of the steel buckets, hoisted to the deck and flung to one side, to come, or to go to, as the strength of their hearts decided." He claimed he could work twenty hours at a stretch, and though he saw that for the older workers the toil was "weakening," it was for him "healthful and body-building," adding: "I feel the benefit of it every day I live; it gave me physical resiliency, fortitude, determination to go all the way through to a given ambition. And it gave me some little muscle which has been of particular value to me on many occasions."[12] Still the most immediate benefit of the shoveling was the wherewithal to "ride the cushions" back to New York, with a little bit left over to support him while he searched for a new job.

This was not the only hard physical labor Griffith undertook to keep himself going while he looked for work as an actor. He speaks, for example, of being a day laborer, scraping rust from the iron supports of a new subway. He claims he got the job by affecting an Irish brogue to work on the sympathies of the Irishman who was foreman of his crew. He was living in a theatrical boardinghouse at this time and to prevent his fellow actors from discovering what he was up to he says he changed into his work clothes in the alley, having jauntily set forth in his best garb, ostensibly to make his rounds of the theatrical agencies.

It would appear, too, that he occupied some of his free time in literary endeavors, none of which were profitable with the exception, he claims, of a piece he wrote on southern cooking for the *New York World*. He got five dollars for this effort and says it was illustrated by a photograph of a brick, covered with grass stolen from Battery Park to make it look like some exotic dish or other.[13] As is so often the case with Griffith's autobiographical musings, it is impossible to date these adventures or even to guarantee their truthfulness.

Griffith's next known work in the theater was in *Richelieu's Stratagem*, a vaudeville sketch that played at the Fifth Avenue and Proctor theaters in New York before going on a month's tour to Boston, Providence, Rochester and, following a break for the Christmas holidays, Toronto, Cleveland and Washington as well. Griffith implied that the piece was drawn from the hoary historical drama by Edward Bulwer-Lytton, the title role of which had, since 1839, provided actors like William Macready and Henry Irving with a wonderful leading role. He also implied that he played the most important supporting role, that of De Maupret. In fact, he was praised by the *New York Dramatic Mirror* as "dignified and effective as Henri (de Talleyrand)," and we have no way of knowing what, in fact, the sketch really was, though it starred a fairly well-known actor, J. E. Dodson.[14] We do know that it provided him with employment through February 2, 1901, when it finished its run in a Brooklyn vaudeville house.

The following month Griffith was again on the road, this time (and for the first time) working on the Pacific Coast in what he referred to as the Memphis Stock Company, though it appears to have been known as the Harry Glazier Company as well. He says he played the role of "The Italian" in *The Three Musketeers*, though he was not listed by name in reviews.[15] While he was out with this company, however, he had his first small success as a writer. A vaudeville playlet he devised and entitled *In Washington's Time* opened in Washington, played by Mary Scott and Company, and apparently went on to Boston, Philadelphia, Chicago and New York as well, possibly playing the Keith Circuit.[16] It appears to have been about a rebel spy who insinuates himself into the home of a Tory during the American Revolution in search of some unnamed document of military significance.[17] This was a period, and a theme, he would return to later in both his theatrical and motion-picture careers.

What Griffith might have realized financially from this little work is unknown, but his subsequent silence about it indicates that it offered him little pride of authorship. He had, it would seem, the legitimate actor's contempt for vaudeville money, vaudeville success. Nor do we know what, exactly, he did from the time *The Three Musketeers* ended its West Coast tour in Vancouver until we pick him up again, nearly a year later, touring with another show. It may be that he was forced to stay for a while on the West Coast to look for employment. Though he dates the occasion somewhat later in his life, this was probably the time when, with seventy-five dollars saved, enough to pay his fare back to New York, he attempted to increase his slim stake at the gambling table and ended up by losing it all, playing craps.

The only theatrical center within convenient reach was San Francisco, and so he signed on as a deckhand on a coastwise lumber schooner and worked his way to what he called "the castle of the coast defenders." There he was offered a week's work in a stock company in Portland, but the fee was so small he determined to work his way back up the coast on another lumber schooner. Sometime soon thereafter, he managed to beat his way back to New York and there, "stepped into my happiest days as an actor." He found a theatrical boardinghouse on Thirty-seventh Street, where he discovered "one or two pals" and "wasn't so lonely this time." From its rooms, he recalled, "accordions groaned, guitars tinkled, voices trilled the scales, as one and all rehearsed over and over the popular tune[s] of the day. Day and night you could hear the tapping of hoofers' routines and the mighty voices of Shakespearean actors rehearsing their lines." The camaraderie in this boardinghouse was, apparently, unlike any Griffith had previously known. There was a common kitchen where after meals the young players would declaim from their favorite roles, and the dancers and singers among them would demonstrate their specialties. "Despite our troubles, I imagine there was as much jesting and horseplay among we [sic] clowns as there was anywhere in the great city of New York."

Here, too, there was a girl. Her name was Cathy, and Griffith declines to give her surname because, he says, she later became famous. "She was slim and pale, possessing lustrous large brown eyes. . . . She would busy herself fixing her own poor meal and then get in a corner alone and eat with her face turned to the wall. . . . I wrote her sonnets and songs, words and music, and even slipped some of my alleged poetry under her door. In my imagination I walked mile after mile with her, dreaming countless dreams of purple adventures of love in which she was always the heroine." Again, however, he could not find it in himself to declare his feelings for her.

"We were hustling every day, trying to land a job," he says, but "one was virtually always too tall or too short, too lean or too fat." He recalls, on one occasion, hearing about a part for a tall man, having 2-inch lifts put into his heels (increasing his height from 5 feet 11 inches to 6 feet 1 inch), only to hear from the agent that he was now too tall. "But Mr. Brown, I thought you wanted a tall man." "Yes, that's so—but you're too tall for your width." "What could one do?" Griffith asks rhetorically. ". . . That was the life."[18]

We do not know how many odd jobs Griffith took at this point to tide him over another gap in his career, but his old friend Oscar Eagle came to his rescue and from February 5 through April 16, 1902, and possibly longer, Griffith toured with him in a play called *The Gypsy Cross*, opening in Troy, New York, and proceeding at least as far as Indianapolis. After that, there is a summer of silence and we encounter him next on a New England tour of *Miss Petticoats*, a dramatization of a novel by Dwight Tilton about a rather obnoxiously good girl and her efforts to clear her name of a slander—and to have her revenge on those who committed the slander. The star was Kathryn Osterman, and her company played split weeks and one-night stands in Massachusetts, Maine, New Hampshire and Connecticut for a little more than a month, until the star suffered an injury in Hartford and the rest of the tour was canceled. Thereafter, there is no record that Griffith obtained any theatrical employment until January 1904 (a period of almost fifteen months) when he received praise in a trade paper for his performance in a supporting role in Edward McWade's *Winchester*, which also toured briefly in New England, and finally ended its run in Philadelphia in March. It was at this point, apparently, that Griffith decided to move his home base to San Francisco, working out of there instead of New York.

2

The decision to look for work in California was among the more shrewd— and consequential—moves of Griffith's acting career. Ever since Gold Rush days San Francisco had been a theatrical capital second only to New York. From the start it had been a haven for "players of recognized merit who, in the East, had attained only secondary rank or even less. . . . It offered the prospect of far greater earnings; even more beguilingly, it held the promise of a new, more illustrious career." The important thing about the city was its attitude, a kind of proud provincialism that "refused to take an actor's prior celebrity in the East as proof of excellence, and often bestowed prodigal favor on actors and actresses who previously had enjoyed no such good fortune."[19]

No great fame came to D. W. Griffith, still playing under the name of Lawrence Griffith, in San Francisco. But he did achieve there, and elsewhere on the West Coast, two seasons of nearly steady work as an actor. Of course, the great national touring companies stopped in the Bay City, offering opportunities to catch on and work one's way back East again as, indeed, Griffith finally did in 1906. But there were also West

Coast touring companies passing through and even setting forth from San Francisco and they, too, often needed players. Best of all, there were two resident stock companies in the city, more across the bay in Oakland.

Both of the San Francisco stock companies were managed by Fred Belasco, brother of David Belasco, the famous specialist in the spectacular, who had begun his own career here. The Alcazar presented serious drama; the Central was a "bucket of blood" house presenting melodrama. It was at the latter that Griffith found work. He had an unspecified role in William Gillette's *All the Comforts of Home*, a work that he had first appeared in with the Meffert's company. When it closed, Griffith crossed the bay to work with the Harry W. Bishop Players at Ye Liberty Playhouse in Oakland, which boasted a revolving stage. There, as Rupert of Hentzau, in a dramatization of Anthony Hope's splendid novel of adventure, *The Prisoner of Zenda*, he obtained one of his best parts since leaving Louisville. He was, apparently, a success, for one of his acquaintances later told an interviewer that Griffith was "immense" in the part.[20]

It is difficult to gain a clear picture of Griffith's talent because he was a very unimportant actor. Fred J. Butler, the father of David Butler, who also became a movie director, remembered that Griffith was quite good when he had a decent role.[21] On the other hand, George Stevens, a more famous film director, whose father had also acted in San Francisco at this time, remembers his father telling him that "Larry" Griffith was a bad actor—"too busy," always doing distracting bits of business with his props and costumes.[22]

The two judgments can, perhaps, be compromised. Griffith was very likely the sort of actor who could rise to the occasion when he was given a meaty role that suited his romantic temperament; chafing in a small role, one he judged beneath his gifts, he might very well have been a fussy performer. As we know from his films, he had something like a genius for inventing business that could reveal the inner dynamics of a character or a situation and he may have occupied his alert intelligence by experimenting with such detail work on stage. Moreover, the "busy" actor is often an actor trying to call attention to himself, and there can be no doubt that Griffith liked to call attention to himself, no matter what he was doing.

In any event, his stratagems worked. He went almost immediately from *The Prisoner of Zenda* into six weeks of repertory with Melbourne MacDowell, an actor-manager who had taken over the proud old Opera House on Mission Street, the very house at which Caruso was engaged when the earthquake and fire struck San Francisco in 1906. The Opera House "languished in lonely glory" on a street that now housed saloons, cheap restaurants, secondhand and pawn shops,[23] and by this time MacDowell and his female star, Fanny Davenport, were in a position roughly analogous to that street. That is to say, they were in decline, trading largely on Miss Davenport's reputation as an agreeable comedienne, established some thirty years earlier. Still, they were offering an ambitious season of works by Victorien Sardou, including *Fedora, Cleopatra, La Tosca* (which of course provided the libretto for Puccini's opera), *Gismonda, The Captain of Navarre* and *Theodora*. Sardou's reputation was also in decline by this time. Shaw had coined the word "Sardoodledom" to describe not only Sardou's works but the whole tradition he represented. Henry James called him "that supremely clever contriver" in order to dismiss him. The successor to Scribe, he was a prolific and brilliant craftsman, especially of historical plays offering magnificent roles for leading actresses, most notably Sarah Bernhardt. Being a facile writer with an eye to the main chance, however, he also wrote melodramas and even dramas of social conscience during his long career. As Griffith, DeMille and others were to do later in the movies, he insisted on great accuracy of historical detail in settings and decor, possibly to compensate for the liberties he took with more significant historical material and with the more subtle nuances of psychological motivation. But in a theater dominated by actors, writers like Sardou, in fact, performed a useful function. The stars liked to test themselves in long roles that provided a free range for their emotions and though Shakespeare provided the basic material they required, they also needed modern vehicles. The audience for serious theater was a knowledgeable one, despite the hesitations it felt about the new stage literature, and they enjoyed the sport of comparing and contrasting the efforts of leading actors in these parts. Undoubtedly, MacDowell hoped that by proving herself in the famous Sardou roles, Miss Davenport could rescue her career by making the transition from comedy to tragedy, or what passed for tragedy at this time. She was not totally without success. The MacDowell company played out its full six weeks in San Francisco and then obtained a five-week booking in the late summer and early fall at the Baker Theater in Portland, Oregon.

Still, Griffith's career with MacDowell and Davenport had a significance deeper than the fact that it provided him with eleven weeks of work in good roles with a better-than-average company, for it was during his stay at the Grand Opera House that he met a young local actress named Linda Arvidson Johnson. Three or four years younger than Griffith, she was the daughter of a ship's captain, whose mother had died when she was a child. She had gained her first professional experience in the theater by taking small parts at the Alcazar and at Ye Liberty, by doing nonspeaking roles with the traveling companies, and by making a two-week tour with a college play. She had even organized an evening of dramatic and musical entertainment at San Francisco's Carnegie Hall, designed to showcase her talent and that of her friend, Harriet Quimby, later to gain some fame as both an aviatrix and a drama critic (surely the first time in human history those occupations were combined). The venture had not proved profitable and they were unable to repay the $20 they had borrowed from James H. Phelan, then the mayor of San Francisco, later to be senator from California, to hire the hall.

Now Miss Arvidson got a job with the MacDowell company, among her tiny roles being that of a boy servant in *Fedora*. She had one line, a reply to a question posed by a magistrate about the time at which her master had left the house on the night a crime was committed. The actor playing the role had "a deep stern voice that seemed to rise from some dark depths" and the young actress "shivered and shook and finally stammered out the answer and was mighty glad when the scene was over."[24]

The actor's name was "Lawrence" Griffith, which Miss Arvidson did not like. She was glad to learn, she recalled, that his real name was David Wark Griffith, which pleased her ear better. He told her, however, that "he was going to keep that name dark until he was a big success in the world, and famous." Interestingly, he appeared to her "very lackadaisical" about whether he would make his mark as an actor, stage director, grand opera star, poet, playwright or novelist. This unconcern impressed the girl, as did his casually knowledgeable conversation about the important stars and producers in New York, with whom he affected an intimacy not entirely warranted by his personal history. Finally, it would appear that he had, by this time, developed certain graceful ways with which to please a woman. He told Linda, for example, that she had "wonderful eyes for the stage," whose expressive qualities would surely win her a job if she ever went to New York.

What other qualities he found in Miss Arvidson—to call her by her professional name—is hard to say. She was a rather plain-faced woman, handsome rather than pretty, and she was, in spirit, not at all the sort of helpless fluttery woman he liked to focus on in his films. Nor was she a "houri." Instead, she appears to have been an intelligent and extremely strong-minded young woman and, as it would turn out, far more practical in spirit than Griffith, and through the years more in touch with the fresh intellectual currents of their time. One can imagine why she invited him to take some meals with her family—he was older, literate, so much more experienced in the larger theatrical world she longed to join. For his part, Griffith must have relished a taste of home life after so many years in boardinghouses and cheap hotels, and he might have sensed in her the calm and practicality he had not known in a woman since his sister Mattie had died. Perhaps more importantly, she encouraged his literary ambitions. She was a willing audience for the poems, plays and stories he read to her when they strolled in Golden Gate Park or along Ocean Beach. She even took his dictation of new pieces. Still, they were not a particularly well-matched couple and one surmises that their marriage was more the result of her persistence than his ardor.

After six weeks at the Opera House the MacDowell company had a layoff of another six weeks before beginning its run in Portland. The romance between Griffith and Miss Arvidson apparently took firm root during these idle days. It is likely that it was around this time, too, that he conceived an admiration for Lewis Stone. The man who was to become best known to the world as Andy Hardy's father was then a young and well-regarded leading man in San Francisco's theaters. Griffith says he used to drop in to watch Stone's acting, and "try to figure out what was wrong with my own." He also frequented the Chutes, a ten-cent variety hall that featured eccentric dancers and freaks of a more exotic nature, and visited a similarly priced production of the musical *Princess Tan-Tan*. He claimed, too, that he fell in with the circle around Jack London, "that mighty word juggler," as Griffith described him.

The year before, London had published what proved to be one of the great best-sellers of the era, *The Call of the Wild*, a paean to the primitive life that captured the imagination of a nation then beginning to feel an acute sense of loss over the wilderness it had just spent so much time and vigor taming. Now, amidst outward confidence, there was inner uneasiness, a growing sense among intellectuals in particular that the culture had seen its greatest moments, that the nation might be beginning the decline that many believed inevitably followed a great flowering. London's story, about a dog that reverted to its primitive heritage and became the leader of an Alaskan wolf pack, thus symbolically fulfilled a dream that many citizens were entertaining at the moment.

In a very few years Griffith would be turning out many little films that dealt with similar themes—the nobility of the savage world, the necessity for individuals to rediscover their roots in simpler lives. It is impossible to determine whether it was direct contact with London or merely his works that encouraged Griffith along these lines. He speaks ironically of conversations in which London blithely "kicked the old world out the window and hauled a new one in the door." He recalled, as well, a nonstop party that "rolled on for three days and three nights," but one suspects his connection with the writer—if not his circle—was brief, since the record shows London was otherwise and elsewhere occupied during much of this period. Still he gathered a piece of advice from one of this author's friends that, he said, served him well: ". . . if one suffered heavy reverses [one should] throw what little remains into the breach and luck would be sure to return." Griffith claims he followed this advice assiduously, throwing parties for friends when a show closed or he was fired.[25]

Indeed, he might have had occasion to resort to it in Portland, where, he says, he was fired by MacDowell. More likely, however, the company simply disbanded when it was unable to get more bookings after the run at the Baker ended on October 1, 1904. In any event, Griffith made his way back to San Francisco; finding no work in the theater, he decided to join the migrant laborers harvesting hops, which he thought might be "a healthful, colorful and more remunerative experience than picking up theatrical odd jobs." Linda, who had found work as "a leading ingenue" with a stock company headed by Florence Roberts, reported that "in California in those days, quite nice people picked hops," adding that whole families participated, since the weather in the dry fall season was so pleasant that they could live out of doors and "pick hops by day and at night dance and sing."[26]

It was, perhaps, not all *that* idyllic, but we also have Griffith's word that it was not so bad. He sent Linda a box of sweet-smelling hops and he also began consciously or unconsciously to gather material for the one full-length play he ever managed to get produced. In it, the life of the agricultural workers is made to seem very attractive and interesting—a notion that surely suited the belief that heeding "the call of the wild" was restorative to sensibilities jaded by city life. His play rings with folk music and dance. The people his leading character—suspiciously like Griffith in background and attitudes—encounters are, for the most part, warmly and colorfully drawn and such poverty as they suffer is of a very decent sort. Quite clearly, he enjoyed his month or so in the fields.

But again, there is no record that he immediately obtained theatrical work when he returned to San Francisco. It may be that he began his directorial career at this point, handling some high school productions in the Bay area. Here, as at many other stops in his life, one must pause to wonder at the principles of selectivity Griffith exercised when he attempted his memoirs. Surely there is no shame in beginnings that, if humble, were honorable. Anyway, there is only the word of two fellow actors, Lloyd Ingraham and Bobby Lawlor, recovered by a third party, that he did well in these assignments and that he talked seriously of embarking on a career as a director.[27] There is no clue as to what plays he did.

He did not, apparently, find any professional work until January 1905, when he journeyed to Los Angeles to undertake a role in an adaptation of Helen Hunt Jackson's famous romantic novel *Ramona*. The story of a Spanish mission girl who, persecuted for daring to bear the child of an Indian, Alesandro (the part Griffith played), the book would subsequently be filmed by Griffith as well as by three other directors. This stage version, written by and featuring an actress named Virginia Calhoun, was no more than a mild success. It played briefly in Los Angeles and then toured through Oakland, Fresno and Woodland before ending its run in San Francisco, where it was greeted by dismal reviews: "No one in the company knows how to act," said the *San Francisco Argonaut*, "and Miss Calhoun does not know how to write a play. . . ."[28]

Griffith's part at least brought him back to San Francisco and to a role in a farce by Henry Cottrell called *The Financier*. He played Warburton, a cigar-smoking detective who, over the course of four acts, finds it necessary to adopt various comic disguises—as a grizzly bear, a drunkard and a society matron—in order to pursue his profession and the crooks. The star of this enterprise was Barney Bernard, until then a vaudevillian, later to gain more lasting celebrity as Potash in Montague Glass's well-known *Potash and Perlmutter* farce. Griffith, possibly hired as a last-minute replacement, received $35 a week. He probably got about six weeks of work out of the play in San Francisco, Oakland, Los Angeles and a return engagement in San Francisco, with possible split-week stops along the way.

It might be that he was reunited with Miss Arvidson in Los Angeles, where she may have been playing ingenues in stock at this time (her dates are shaky on this point). One of the actors in this company was Marshall ("Mickey") Neilan, later to be one of Griffith's assistants, Blanche Sweet's first husband, a meteorically successful director in the teens and early 20s, a hard-drinking failure in the 30s and, through it all, one of Hollywood's most famously convivial souls. "That Griffith is the goddamdest ham actor," he remembered thinking at the time, adding modestly, "you can imagine how we both stunk." Perhaps his most significant memory of this time with Griffith was of being dragged to nickel-odeons by him at every opportunity. "I see a great future in them," he recalled Griffith saying—a remarkable change in attitude if Griffith's description of his first contact with film in Chicago is to be credited.[29]

Griffith might have had to return to the hop fields the following fall. In any case, there is no record of theatrical employment until late November 1905, when he managed to book *In Washington's Time*, his vaudeville sketch, into Martin Beck's Orpheum Theater in San Francisco. Linda Arvidson, Bobby Lawler and a man named Olaf Hanson appeared with him in it and there was talk of their being booked on the entire West Coast Orpheum Circuit, but Beck "could not offer enough consecutive bookings to make a road tour pay, so that was that."[30]

This bit of bad luck turned into good luck quite quickly. Nance O'Neil—a great theatrical name at the time—had just returned from a triumphant tour of Australia and was hiring actors in San Francisco for the smaller roles in her repertory. Griffith was able to catch on with her for the longest sustained employment, in the best company doing the best group of plays that he had ever encountered. There was a long run in San Francisco, followed by a cross-country tour of nearly four months. O'Neil had an established reputation for her Lady Macbeth, and she would do that role during the year. The rest of her plays included Paolo Giacometti's *Queen Elizabeth*; *Camille*; two plays by Ibsen, *Rosmers-holm* and *Hedda Gabler*; two by Ibsen's German admirer Hermann Sudermann, *The Fires of St. John* and *Magda*; and, in San Francisco but not on tour, *Judith of Bethulia*. The last is significant because Griffith would choose it as the vehicle for his transition from short to longer films a few years later, though he did not appear in O'Neil's production of it.

O'Neil was a striking figure on stage—tall, vital, warm, intelligent— and her repertory is more than usually interesting, acknowledging as it does the fact that the American theater was entering a transitional phase. *Macbeth, Queen Elizabeth* and *Camille,* of course, were traditional favorites with audiences of the day, Ibsen and Sudermann were considered virtually avant-gardists in America, while *Judith* represented a bow by O'Neil to the flourishing conventions of the spectacle stage, conventions that would profoundly inform Griffith's approach to the cinema.

The play is in four acts and seven scenes and was based by Thomas Bailey Aldrich on a tale from the Biblical Apocrypha. First produced in New York in 1904, it is about a courtesan who saves the city of the title from the Assyrians who are besieging it by giving herself to their leader, Holofernes. She must, finally, kill him, a task made difficult by the fact that she has fallen in love with her people's enemy. It had not been warmly received by the New York critics when it premiered there, and the San Francisco critics were equally unkind to the O'Neil production. It is clear that the sophisticated theatrical centers were by this time becoming if not perfect Ibsenites, then imperfect ones. It is also clear that *Judith,* along with several similar works, represented a kind of culmination for a theatrical manner—"photographic realism"—that had been developed over the course of several decades and taken to perhaps its most artful extreme by the actor-manager Henry Irving, who as theatrical historian A. Nicholas Vardac said, "moved to the very threshold of cinema" but could not, of course, step across it no matter how brilliant his mechanical and electrical effects. Still, he had approximated such cinematic devices as the fade-in and fade-out, the iris shot, quick crosscutting from one line of action to another, the smooth flow of one scene into another.

All these techniques were on view in the O'Neil production of *Judith,* so much so that when he came to write his definitive and invaluable study of the transition *From Stage to Screen,* Vardac, perhaps influenced by the presence of the screen's first master in O'Neil's company, used it to prove his point that "the cramping of . . . spectacular, cinematic conceptions [was] appalling" and to observe that by trying thus to exceed its physical and technological limits (while ignoring its strengths as a medium for writers and performance) "the stage had played thoroughly into the hands of the screen."[31]

It is impossible to know if, at the time, Griffith sensed this developing restlessness with the conventions of the spectacular stage, or saw in the very humble films of the moment the potential for redeeming those conventions in a medium more suited to them. We know only that when his moment came he turned to the literature and techniques of this theater frequently and gratefully. For the moment, perhaps, he merely reveled in being with a first-class company, doing (mostly) first-class plays receiving generally good notices and doing fine business. Moreover, Linda Arvidson, his wife-to-be, is not exaggerating; he was, personally, a success. When Miss O'Neil's manager, director and leading man McKee Rankin fell ill and had to be replaced as the minister, Hefterdinck, in *Magda*, Griffith got the call. Miss O'Neil liked his work. Besides an increase from $40 to $75 a week, he was given the part to play permanently along with the good roles of Sir Francis Drake in *Queen Elizabeth* and Ulric Brendel in *Rosmersholm.*

The tour covered ten states and three Canadian provinces and though Griffith had apparently been reluctant to leave Linda in San Francisco, he had also promised to return for her, adding, according to her, that "when he came back things would be different,"[32] though whether he meant he intended to marry her or merely to walk out with her in a more prosperous style is unknown. In any case, Linda was out of work and 'rested' until eighteen minutes to five on the morning of April 18, when "something happened."

That something, of course, was the great earthquake and fire of 1906. Linda does not mention any serious injury to herself, her family or their property, but she did, apparently, hint strongly, in a telegram to Griffith in Minneapolis, that it would be very nice to get out of the devastated city. Either the wire was delayed in delivery or Griffith delayed answering it as he thought over the implications of Linda's desire to join him in the East. Indeed, one of his later intimates would claim that she cast herself in an uncharacteristically pitiful light in order to play upon Griffith's gentlemanly feelings and, in effect, force him to rescue her from destitution through marriage.[33] Whatever the case, he finally wrote her from Milwaukee, where the O'Neil company staged a benefit for the survivors of the San Francisco disaster, asking her to join him in Boston, where his season would end on May 26. On May 9, she boarded a refugee train, carrying a box lunch and wearing, she says, clothes provided by the Red Cross. She arrived in Boston a little less than a week later. Griffith met her at the station. "Everything a bustle! People and people and people! Laughing, happy, chattering people who didn't seem to know and didn't seem to care what had happened to us out there by the bleak Pacific. I was annoyed at them; their life was still normal. Though I know they had helped bounteously, I was annoyed.

"But here HE comes! . . ."[34] They got a cab, discovered that neither of them had thought of getting a ring, which necessitated a delay before proceeding to the Old North Church, where they were married. The date was May 14, 1906; she gave her age as twenty-seven, he as thirty (a year less than the truth). Significantly, he gave his occupation as "writing."[35]

CHAPTER FOUR

To the Biograph

THEY arrived in New York in a thunderstorm. Linda claimed she had never seen a storm like it. "The wind blew a gale, driving papers and dust in thick, swirling clouds. Of all miserable introductions to the city of my dreams and ambitions, New York City could hardly have offered me a more miserable one."[1]

After a few days at the Hotel Navarro, they found a sublet—"a ducky little place," according to Linda—on West Fifty-sixth Street, where they lived for the rest of the summer. Their apartment overlooked a YMCA's outdoor athletic field and Linda enjoyed looking down on the fat men, swaddled in sweaters, jogging around it, trying to get into shape. It would be some time before she and Griffith could sensibly begin to make the rounds looking for work for the fall season. He decided to use the time—and his savings from the long engagement with Nance O'Neil—to complete the final draft of a play he had begun in San Francisco. We have his wife's word that his concentration was intense. Apparently the writing went well, for his wife remembers these as "happy days. The burdens were shared equally. My husband was a splendid cook; modestly said, so was I." For the moment, at least, Griffith seemed to enjoy his domesticity—the first he had known since he had left home and a condition that would remain a rarity in his life. Griffith sang "Negro songs" while he cooked and was earnest and cheerful whether doing domestic chores or writing. The only small cloud scudding across the horizon that summer was Linda's old friend, Harriet Quimby, now writing a regular column in *Leslie's* and enjoying a free summer at a fashionable beach hotel in return for publicizing the place. She called on the Griffiths one day beautifully dressed and conveyed in an expensive car belonging to wealthy friends. Linda recalls Griffith watching them draw out of sight at the end of the visit and musing in a sad voice: "She's a success."[2]

The fact that he had been working professionally in the theater for

71

nearly a decade with such a singular lack of what Miss Quimby—and others—had achieved with apparent ease weighed heavily on him. One can detect no direction in his career to this point, no movement that would have imparted to him a sense of progress toward a well-defined goal. Indeed, he seems to have had none, beyond a generalized desire for economic well-being derived from a career in one art or another. He had a feeling he was destined for great things, but no specific idea of where or how he would realize the promise that was more apparent to him than to others. This yearning for greatness, for fame, was too long denied and was to have consequences later in his career. One needs training in success if one is to handle it intelligently—the economics of it, the psychology of it. Griffith never did comprehend that and when, at last, he found his rewards he literally did not know how to capitalize on it. The reckless, heedless grandiose side of his nature—Jake's side—would come forth to revenge itself on the cautious side, which had necessarily dominated during the long years of poverty and struggle.

Without Griffith's knowing it, the elements of the success that would soon be his were now beginning to coalesce. The most important of them, a sudden spurt in the popularity of film, based on recent technical and commercial innovation, he seems not to have noticed, so preoccupied was he by his own writing. But the lasting significance of the play he completed late this summer, and which he called A Fool and a Girl, was that it would, in a short time, ease his passage into the studios as a scenarist, since it provided him with literary credentials superior to those possessed by most of the people doing this humbly paid and regarded work. Of course, that was an unintended consequence. Griffith had much higher hopes for the work, and naturally that sense of anxious satisfaction which always attends completion of a complex piece of writing. And whatever the crudities of the work, viewed objectively, his feelings of accomplishment were not entirely misplaced. For A Fool and a Girl does manage to summarize much of his experience to this point and some of what he had gained from it emotionally and intellectually.

In the play we find a hero named Albert (after, no doubt, Griffith's younger brother) who is a bit of a poet and a dreamer, rather like his creator, and rather like him, too, in that he had suffered considerable hardship in the course of a wandering life. The contrast between creator and character was that the latter, before the curtain rises, has suddenly come into a large sum of money. The plot revolves around attempts by a group of bunco artists to do him out of it. Their number, interestingly, includes two sisters, representing the twin organizing principles of femininity as Griffith understood them, one being quite clearly a prostitute, the other a virgin of surpassing sweetness. It is with the latter, of course, that Albert falls in love and it is a misunderstanding about her intentions—he gains the false impression that she has knowingly participated in the plot to gain his wealth—that precipitates the play's crisis. Renunciation followed by lengthy expiation of guilt are the girl's lot until, with her hair turning gray, she and Albert are at last reunited. In all, it is a clumsy play, but besides expressing many of the ideas, attitudes and preoccupations of his young manhood, he also made use of some of the more interesting settings he had encountered during his West Coast stay—the hop fields where he had worked, and the Poodle Dog café, a well-known San Francisco bistro where upper-class slumming expeditions could encounter both the bohemians and the lower classes of the city. (Griffith called it the Bull Pup in the play.) He also did his best—none too good, alas—to render realistically the slang of the streets in his dialogue, the results being awkward and flat in themselves and unconsciously humorous in close juxtaposition with the poetic flights Griffith also permitted himself.

The vernacular is represented by such expletives as "Kazoozles!" and "Cheese it!" and "Oh, splash!" A few dollars is "a few plunks," and people constantly refer to one another as "kiddo" and "youse." Set against this we find passages in which Albert awkwardly attempts to mingle romantic feeling and religious sentiments. For example, as the lovers watch a sunset, there is this exchange:

EFFIE: What makes it do you suppose—all this?
ALBERT: Why *God* created it, little one.
EFFIE: Who for? Not just for everybody, not just for common
  everyday people.
ALBERT: Yes, for everyone—everyone who has eyes to see.
EFFIE: And you believe this sort of thing, don't you?
ALBERT: Why, why shouldn't I *believe* it? It's the truth.

His declaration of love for the girl comes not long thereafter as they listen to Mexican migrants singing a folk song about "something beautiful they have found." After telling Effie that in the moonlight she seems "too beautiful to be anything born of this earth," he continues:

Yes, something they [the Mexicans] have found. But they couldn't dream what I found here when I just saw you,—everything—everything. I have been as blind as death all my life.

. . .

Yes, blind. I never saw anything until I came to see all things with you. You took away the blindness from my eyes and everything was sweet. You! You! YOU! I knew of course there was a God. They made me kneel down to him when I was that high and pray to him—but I never really knew him—but tonight when I was with you, I felt that you were on one side and on the other there was some mysterious, undreamed of god's arm around me, and that he was leading us on, over the hills—over the hills.[3]

The style clearly prefigures that of the subtitles he encouraged—and often wrote—for his films, a style that, incidentally, alienates modern audiences from his work on occasion. The play, in fact, represents a first attempt to blend the elements of romance and realism that he would more success- fully conjoin in his movies, and one gains from it a sense of a fully formed—but not particularly subtle—sensibility attempting to express it- self at length for the first time. As such, the play does not seem any more laughable than hundreds of similar efforts by young authors. If the over- all design is absurdly melodramatic, individual scenes are well constructed; if the characters have more about them of the cartoon than they do of life, they are nevertheless determinedly colorful and occasionally sur- prising; if the tone of the writing is more often pretentious or the product of an ear badly in need of tuning, there are nevertheless passages of some crude power and feeling in the piece.

One's interest in A Fool and a Girl does not depend entirely upon knowledge of the work and the career to come. The play is a failure, but a respectable one, especially at a moment when the theater was in transi- tion and playwrights in general were groping toward forms that would preserve the dramatic values of the melodramatic stage yet also attempt to deal more realistically with ordinary experience. Griffith's attempt to reproduce the language of the lower classes was not much less successful than Eugene O'Neill's strained efforts in the same direction a little more than a decade later. Then, too, Griffith was attempting to express feelings that had grown naturally out of his own experiences. Albert's sudden ac- cession to wealth was a projection of his own dreams of sudden success; Albert's naïve delight in the discovery of "real life," that is, of a poverty culture quite different from that of the genteel poor in which Griffith had grown up, represents, one imagines, Griffith's own delight in discovering that he could survive in such an arena. Who knows, he might have be- lieved that his adventures as a wandering player were the equivalent of his father's youthful adventures. Whether Albert's elaborately expressed feelings for Effie derive from Griffith's feelings for Linda at this time seems more problematical.

The exact nature of their relationship is one of the mysteries of his life—she is guarded about it in her book, he never mentions her in his autobiographical manuscripts, and their friends and co-workers from this time recall little about their public life as a young married couple, noth- ing at all, even in the nature of gossip, about their private affairs. All that is certain is that, for a few years at least, Linda's strength and sense served both of them well. At the very least, she believed in him and his future when few did. But a grand passion, grandly expressed, as in the play? No, that seems unlikely. The air around them is much cooler.

2

Still, their first summer together ended well. Not only did Griffith complete his play, but he and his wife managed to get jobs together in the same company, work that completes our sense that, without their knowing it, their future was beginning to take shape. For the play in which they were cast was *The One Woman* and its author was Thomas Dixon, Jr., who was, of course, also the author of the two novels *The Clansman* and *The Leopard's Spots*, on which, some eight years later, Griffith was to found not only his greatest movie success but also the beginning of the modern feature film and, in a sense, the reconstituted industry necessary to produce such films.

When Griffith met Dixon, the latter was at the height of his fame and prosperity as a popular novelist and playwright. He was a tall, spare man in his early forties with iron-gray hair, heavy black eyebrows and small, shining black eyes. His face was long and narrow; and he had a straight, delicate nose and firm, thin lips. Someone correctly said of him at the time: "The man will have till long past middle age the energy of youth."[4]

This energy might well have been the shaping force in Dixon's scattered life, for it seemed there was no single profession that could fully absorb it. He was graduated from Wake Forest College at the age of nineteen and had spent a year in graduate study at Johns Hopkins, where he had been influenced, to an unknown degree, by that school's circle of Anglo-Saxon historians who sought to trace the origins of American democracy back to the primitive democracy of the Germanic tribes. Thereafter, he had been briefly an actor (unlike Griffith he had quit the stage for good upon being stranded for the first time in a small town), a lawyer, a legislator in his native North Carolina and, finally, from 1887 through 1899, one of the nation's most famous preachers and platform personalities. As such, he had aligned himself firmly with the Social Gospel Movement, even going so far as to desert his Baptist faith for four years to form a nondenominational "Peoples' Church" in downtown New York. From his pulpit and on the lecture circuit he spoke out endlessly for women's rights, for justice for the immigrant, the slum dweller, the weak and the helpless of every social level. Above all, he believed, in the years of his ministry, that religion and science together were working to create the conditions in which democracy would soon flourish in every corner of the world.

And yet, sometime during the latter portion of the period when he gained his first national fame as a dramatically brilliant orator, he became a racist of the most virulent sort. It was, despite his southern heritage, a late conversion. True, as a child he had been frightened by the sight of Ku Klux Klan night riders sweeping past his home and had been consoled by his mother's statement that "they're our people—they're guarding us from harm."[5] But as late as 1896 he was capable of thanking God "that there is not to-day the clang of a single slave's chain on this continent," since "democracy is the destiny of the race, because all men are bound together in the bonds of fraternal equality with one common love."[6] What happened to change his mind in the next few years is unclear, though the historian Maxwell Bloomfield speculates that for Dixon, as for many other Populists and reformers, the problems posed by the success of the American imperialist adventure against Spain caused a reexamination of racial relations at home. It seemed to them that the Pacific and Caribbean populations for which the United States had acquired responsibility were incapable of democratic self-government. They would have to be governed, it was thought, without their consent until such time as they set aside their semibarbarous ways, until, with the white man's beneficent aid, they achieved the judgment and self-control to manage their own affairs.

It required no great leap to move from this position to one in which the same arguments were applied against American blacks. Indeed, Dixon's earlier fears of a riotous immigrant mob tearing down democratic institutions were now refocused on the black population. All he added to the old nightmare were fantasies of rape and mongrelization of the races—together with an increasingly strident argument in favor of states' rights and opposition to the growth of federal power. He retained a few small notes of civility. He despised, for example, the cavalier pretenses of many southerners, arguing that the clansmen of his books were, instead, representatives of the great Jeffersonian tradition—small freeholders careful to protect the rights of all minorities other than the black one. Later on, he would decry the terror and brutality of the reorganized Ku Klux Klan of the 1920s.

But in the context of his major argument these were minor gestures. For he believed that the tragedy of the black was not the comparatively brief historical moment when he endured slavery in America, but rather the thousands of years he had been sunk in savagery on the African continent while the Anglo-Saxon races were building a great civilization in Europe. He insisted that this was all the evidence any reasonable man required to believe that there was an unbridgeable evolutionary gap between the races.

Why, it might be wondered, did it seem so pressingly important to Dixon to raise these issues at the time he did? The condition of black Americans in the period between 1895 and 1915 was, as the historian C. Vann Woodward has recently pointed out, the worst it had been since Emancipation. Most of them were still trapped in the rural South as sharecroppers, with many of this group in a state of virtual peonage. Beyond that, most of the rights extended to them during the Civil War and Reconstruction had been withdrawn, with many freedmen disenfranchised, segregation legally and generally established, lynching and race riots cruel facts of life. In short, the danger the blacks presented to the whites was not, as Dixon and others in the vast racist chorus of which he was a member, implied. They were not a race trembling on the brink of rebellion but rather a race on the verge of becoming a permanently victimized underclass. Given these facts, one cannot help but think Dixon's vision of a racial apocalypse was at least partially created out of his nearly insatiable need for self-dramatization. He was self-cast in the role of the lonely defender of the Anglo-Saxon race and its institutions against a black horde that he alone—as he thought—could discern marching toward the citadel. And he loved the role, devoting all his demonic energy to playing it. He seized upon the pitifully small and quite isolated advances the blacks had made since emancipation and claimed that "the beginning of Negro equality is the beginning of the end of this nation's life."[7]

It seems likely that Thomas Dixon, now a nearly forgotten figure in American cultural history, except as the man who provided the tainted literary source for its first film masterpiece, was among the individuals who must share the heaviest responsibility for the radical deepening and broadening of race hatred that occurred during the first decades of the twentieth century in the United States. For no sooner had he formulated his ideas than he set about casting them in an easily apprehensible form. First came *The Leopard's Spots*, his novel about the agonies of Reconstruction in his native North Carolina. He began it during a lecture tour in the summer of 1901, finishing it in sixty days, scribbling away at it in hotel rooms and lobbies, even after a train wreck while waiting for crews to finish clearing the tracks. And though he never made any claims for his fiction as art, he did have the capacity to create a compelling story. Indeed, when he submitted it to an old friend, Walter Hines Page, who had moved from newspaper editing in North Carolina to book publishing in New York, that august gentleman, latterly the American Ambassador to Great Britain during World War One, after whom a distinguished graduate school in diplomacy would be named, literally stayed up all night reading the manuscript. With it still unfinished he set forth the next morning in search of breakfast, and reading as he walked, he was struck down by a streetcar, the blood from his cuts actually staining the manuscript.

As with Page, so it was with less sophisticated readers. The book sold more than 100,000 copies in its first three months of publication and was one of the foundations on which the relatively new house of Doubleday, Page and Company built its prosperity. On one level it was a conscious attempt to answer Harriet Beecher Stowe's *Uncle Tom's Cabin*, and it even carries on the history of Simon Legree, who has ceased here to exploit blacks physically as a slave trader in order to exploit them politically as a scalawag. Another character is George Harris, the very child Eliza Harris escaped from slavery with, carrying him across the frozen Ohio River with bloodhounds nipping at her heels. In Dixon's novel he has become a graduate of Harvard, a poet and scholar who overreaches himself by asking to marry the daughter of a great white defender of the Negro cause—prefiguring a similar incident Dixon used to strengthen the drama and give vent to his obsession with miscegenation in the sequel, *The Clansman*. For the rest, the novel was a lengthy recital of the evils of Reconstruction and its aftermath in the South, with plenty of attention paid to what Dixon was sure were the prophetic implications of that experience—namely, that the only hope for racial peace lay in separatism, possibly even the establishment in Africa of a new national home for freed American slaves and their descendants.

Few responsible journalists praised Dixon's work either as ideology or as literature. Indeed, the attacks on him were quite ferocious. On the other hand, the view of Reconstruction which Dixon popularized was by no means a purely personal or even regional one. The standard view of "The Tragic Era" (to borrow the title of the book in which as late as 1929 Claude Bowers summarized the accepted scholarly interpretation of Reconstruction) was that the idealism that motivated both sides during the Civil War was betrayed almost instantly upon the signing of the truce. In this view Lincoln's mild and benign policies, briefly instituted by Andrew Johnson, were savaged by the Radical Republicans of Congress, bent upon imposing a harshly punitive peace on the South and misled by their belief that the Negro, once freed from slavery, would quickly achieve equality with the white. In this opinion, the military occupation of the Confederate states was sadistically harsh and, indeed, the instrument by which corrupt officials of both races were given license to plunder the conquered states. Little wonder, then, that organizations like the Klan grew up to defend, as best they could, by whatever means they could muster, the old values.

It cannot be too strongly stressed that this view was almost laughably simplistic. In fact, as Kenneth M. Stampp, a modern revisionist, has argued, the alleged brutalities suffered by the white southerners are difficult to find in any records; compared to the lot of almost any defeated nation in history, their "punishment" was unprecedentedly mild, consisting of: "First, the freeing of their slaves; second, the brief incarceration of a few Confederate leaders; third, a political disability imposed for a few years on most Confederate leaders; fourth, a relatively weak military occupation terminated in 1877; and, last, an attempt to extend the rights and privileges of citizenship to southern Negroes."[8] Except for the loss of his slaves, the typical southern citizen lost no property, suffered no untoward humiliations or brutality, was allowed to resume the customary patterns of his daily life as soon as he could recover from whatever devastations the war itself had wreaked upon him. About the only hope thwarted—and then only briefly—was that he might substitute a rigid caste system for outright slavery and even that was not, in the end, denied him, as, late in the nineteenth century, the Jim Crow system was permitted to grow unhindered. Obviously, there were individual tragedies in this period, not to mention mistakes in governance, but it does not, by any stretch of the imagination, qualify as a truly "tragic" era.

How it acquired that reputation is a nice question. Stampp argues persuasively that sympathy for the South and its "Negro Problem" grew as the great waves of immigration from abroad struck northern shores and an analogy between these newcomers and the Blacks became fashionable; both groups were seemingly unassimilable, both were threats to Anglo-Saxon hegemony, both were victims of Social Darwinism, that first, but not last, perversion of scientific method by the social sciences, which argued that government intervention on behalf of underprivileged groups was unnatural, preventing the most fit from rising naturally to deserved eminence. In short, the popularity of Dixon's first attempt at fiction is explicable if not very inspiring.

No sooner was *The Leopard's Spots* safely launched than Dixon began planning *The Clansman,* the while drafting a three-volume attack on socialism, *The One Woman.* The latter was published in 1903, the former in 1905, and both outsold his first book, although *The Clansman* was in many respects but a reworking and expansion of the first section of *The Leopard's Spots,* now with a heavier stress on the heroism of the KKK and with a quite obvious attack on Dixon's great *bête noire,* Thaddeus Stevens, the leader of the Radical Republicans, who is given, in the fiction, a mulatto mistress and a venality of character the historical record does not support. Dixon also indulged himself in borrowings from Walt Whitman's writings which come perilously close to plagiarism, but none of this stayed the popularity of the work.

The One Woman, the novel on which he was to base the play in which he asked D. W. Griffith and Linda Arvidson to take parts, at least had some autobiographical overtones, which may have given it a slight edge in quality of feeling. It is about a minister who, like Dixon himself, attempts to found a nonsectarian people's church, is wooed away from his family by a wealthy young woman who is a heavy contributor to this enterprise. He is shown to be what Dixon apparently thought himself to have been as a younger man—a naïve and impractical dreamer who has staked too much on his belief that the common man is fundamentally good and needs only gentle guidance to realize fully his innate moral potential. He learns a terrible lesson when a more cynical friend wins his first wife's love. The minister kills him and is twice sentenced to death before winning a last-minute reprieve. To Dixon, this melodrama somehow demonstrated the folly of any philosophy of "sharing." What was true in the sexual realm, he implied, was also true in the social realm. Any scheme or ideology that encouraged breakdowns in the concept of private property could lead only to devastation.

It was, of course, the propagandist—as well as the money-conscious popularizer—who, in 1905, produced a dramatic version of *The Leopard's Spots* and *The Clansman*, under the latter title. It toured successfully for four months, in the South and Middle West before opening in New York, where the critics despised it. "It is difficult to do justice to so bad a play as *The Clansman*," the *New York Dramatic Mirror* said, while another critic would only grudgingly concede that it might just "appeal rather forcibly to the lovers of crude melodrama." The best anyone could do was praise as spectacle the concluding scene, a torch-lit night meeting of the Klan.[9] Nevertheless, the thing was a considerable commercial success, especially on the road, where two companies toured for some five years and where it found, particularly in the South, critics who would term the unfavorable New York reviews "sheerest nonsense."[10]

The play added greatly to Dixon's fortune, which, on the sole basis of his literary efforts, reached a point where he had close to $400,000 to risk (and to lose in the panic of 1907) in the stock and commodity markets. He would win most of it back again (and lose it again, this time in real estate), but *The Clansman* convinced him that he could add yet another vocation to the others he had already mastered—that of playwright. So, while pressing on with the final volume in his Klan trilogy and on the last two volumes in his trilogy criticizing socialism, he worked on plays as well. "A hell of restlessness/I have drained, drained," he once wrote in a poem and no truer words did he ever speak.

The dramatization of *The One Woman* was the first fruit of this new ambition. And, as usual, his flair for the sensational was to serve him well. As a novel, *The One Woman* had already outraged many Victorian sensibilities with its frank portrayal of a minister seduced away from his wife by a wealthy woman. Moreover, the idea of a man of the cloth becoming a murderer—however he justified the crime—had appalled many moralists. The outcry was revived and even, perhaps, intensified when these actions were rendered more vividly immediate on the popular stage.

Griffith, however, was spared from much of the controversy surrounding *The One Woman*. He had the leading role when Dixon, seeking to repeat the pattern that had proved successful with *The Clansman*, opened his new play's tryout tour in friendly Norfolk, Virginia. And he held on to it for two months as the company trouped through the South, playing short stands in the smaller cities. His salary was $75 a week, Linda's $35. But for reasons that remain unclear he was fired before the play came into New York. Very possibly, as Mrs. Griffith reports, Dixon simply found a less expensive actor to replace him. In any event, it would appear that there were no hard feelings between Griffith and Dixon, since it was on the former's initiative, in 1914, that the latter was finally able to turn *The Clansman* into a film. And although there is no record, either at this point or in their later dealings, that the two southerners ever became truly intimate friends, they maintained cordial relations— they were often separated by distance—and there can be little doubt that Griffith's ideas were strongly influenced by Dixon's. It should be noted, for example, that one of the major themes of *The One Woman* was that reformers were "meddlers," intervening without warrant in the lives of people who did not ask for their assistance and who would have been better off without it. This, of course, would become one of the major themes of Griffith's *Intolerance,* as well as of several earlier, shorter films. Then, too, there was a remarkable coincidence between the endings of *The One Woman* and *Intolerance,* both of which involve desperate heroines racing with reprieves to save a condemned man from the gallows.

Indeed, it is tempting to stress the similarities between the two men; both were inordinately proud of their Anglo-Saxon blood, both were strongly shaped by and increasingly nostalgic for the values of the rural South of their boyhoods, both were inordinately energetic, ambitious and in love with public performance, and both seem to have come naturally and without much self-questioning to the racist views they shared. In time both would endure shocking reverses of their economic fortune as well as psychologically devastating reversals in the public's esteem. There was, however, one important respect in which they were different. Dixon never rose above the level of the publicist, and his ventures into the arts were always, it would seem, either in search of fortune or in aid of some idea that was important to him. Griffith, to be sure, wanted wealth and in his last years was bitter about the fact that it had eluded him. But only in desperation did he do anything solely for money, while ideas always remained of secondary importance to him. His spirit, in short, was classically that of the artist—self-absorbed, and only dimly aware of the larger political issues of the day, perhaps excessively so. He might have been a naïve, and even primitive, artist, but an artist he surely was. And that is the one thing Dixon, so like him in other ways, was not.

3

Still, as of autumn 1906, Griffith had yet to prove himself as anything but a competent journeyman actor possibly more imbued with the art spirit and a sense of some larger destiny awaiting him than some of his theatrical colleagues. And now, once again, he was out of work. The Griffiths moved into a furnished railroad flat on West 100th Street in New York and he went back to his rounds of the agents' and producers' offices, this time offering not only his services as an actor but his playscript, A *Fool and a Girl*, as well. Only one very small job turned up. Edward Ellsner was producing, for one performance only, the first American staging of Oscar Wilde's *Salome* and it seems that Griffith was broke enough to take the small role of the "Young Syrian" under the pseudonym George Lawrence. The brief engagement turned out, however, to be very lucky for him. James K. Hackett, whose career as the romantic hero of swashbuckling dramas had been dimmed by the vogue for realism, had turned producer. Now, Ellsner happened to know, he was looking for a vehicle for Pauline Frederick, then a promising ingenue, but, like Griffith, soon to find a larger fame in film. Ellsner suggested Griffith send his play to Hackett, which he promptly did.

A lengthy silence ensued. Even on Christmas Eve, according to his wife, Griffith was out looking for work while she stayed at home preparing a meal more humble than festive—hamburgers with gravy, baked potatoes, a bottle of beer for the master and a five-cent pie for dessert. He entered. There was a strange look on his face. Linda was distressed to discover that she had placed her plate on the table wrong side up. Or had she? Perhaps her husband had overturned it. Irritated, she picked up the piece of china. There was a piece of paper under it. "I wished people wouldn't be so silly. I supposed this was a verse about Christmas. But why the mystery?"[11] But it was not a poem. It was a check. For $700. An advance against royalties from Hackett. He had bought A *Fool and a Girl*.

It was the first time in his life that Griffith had been in possession of so large a sum of money, and though he and Linda knew it could not last until the play went into production, the immediate financial pressure on them was greatly lightened. "Now came wonderful days," Linda writes. For the moment Griffith decided he would take no work that forced him to tour. And with this first acceptance in hand, he felt justified in pursuing literature in a more single-minded fashion than he ever before had. He wrote "yards of poetry and several short stories," according to Linda.

He was further encouraged by the appearance in *Leslie's Weekly* of a poem for which he was paid six dollars. It was in the issue of January 10, 1907, and it was called "The Wild Duck":

> Look—how beautiful he is!
> Swift his flight as a bullet
> As he comes in from the sea in the morning.
> For the wind is from the sea in the morning.
> See! He is bound for the hilltops,
> The gold hilltops, the gold hilltops.

There he will rest 'neath the flowers,
The red flowers—the white and the red,
The poppy—the flower of dreams,
The crimson flower of dreams.
There must be rest in the morning.
Happy wild duck! Happy wild duck!
For the wind is from the sea in the morning.

So will he rest 'neath the roses,
The red roses, the love roses,
And their petals will fall around him,
Sweet and warm around him,
Warmer and warmer around him,
Till even in the daytime the stars shall be shining.
Happy wild duck! Happy wild duck!
For the wind is from the sea in the morning.

There by the roses bloom the lilies, the flowers of peace,
The white flowers of peace,
Red and white together, red and white and red,
Waving and blowing together,
On the gold hilltops in the morning,
For the wind is from the sea in the morning.

Ah me! but the wind soon changes in these parts.
Ah me! Ah me!
It was not so in the old days.
Look, look, ah, look, see, even now it is changing out,
  out to the sea!
Look, look, above the hilltops,
With eyes turned back to the mainland,
And tired wings wearily beating, but vainly,
For the wind blows out to the sea in the evening.
Poor little wild duck! Poor little wild duck!
In the evening,
For the wind is out to the sea in the evening.

Look! He is falling, falling out to the sea.
Ah, there is mist on the sea!
There is always mist on the sea in the evening.
Perhaps his nest is beyond, I know not;
Only with tired wings wearily beating,
And eyes turned back to the mainland,
To the red and white and red,
Waving and blowing together,
Blooming and blowing together.

He is falling out, out to the sea.

Poor little wild duck! Poor little wild duck!
In the evening when the wind blows out to the sea!
Ah me! Ah me! Ah me!
In the evening when the wind blows out to the sea.

Ah me, indeed! Yet despite its flatness of tone, the lack of inner tension in its lines and its conventionalized sentiments, one senses a shadow of the gift that he would soon be exploiting in a medium more congenial to him. For the poem is obviously an exploration of an image, an attempt to find the meaning (perhaps more properly *a* meaning) in a glimpse of the natural world. If the poem is analogous to anything it is to a symbolic shot in a movie, the kind of shot that Griffith would be the first to use to establish a mood, suggest an overtone or undertone in a sequence. No director, before or since, has been, in fact, more drawn to the animal world as a source for such material and no one has used it more unabashedly—or more successfully—than he did.

But if "The Wild Duck" suggests the direction in which he was heading, it suggested nothing to Griffith except that perhaps he might, after all, have some small future as a writer. If anything, he seems to have been more excited by seeing it in print than he was by the acceptance of his play. He later recalled buying the copy of *Leslie's* containing the poem at a newsstand and getting on a subway to carry it home. "I read the verses carelessly . . . trying to register indifference. Then I folded the magazine with a gesture of nonchalance and endeavored to appear absorbed in the virtues of Doan's kidney pills, Sloan's liniment and Sapolio. But my eyes wouldn't behave and I had to direct them from the advertisements to my fellow passengers, only to discover that everyone was looking at me and trying to discover the cause of my flushed face and the Cheshire grin. . . .

"I scanned the table of contents . . . but the only thing I could see was 'The Wild Duck.' There it was, as big as an elephant and utterly dwarfing everything else in the list of contents. And there, in type, flaming at me in letters of fire, was my name. My very own name—DAVID WARK GRIFFITH."[12]

But despite apparently prodigious labors during the rest of the winter and the spring of 1907, Griffith was unable to sell anything else, and the following summer he was back in Norfolk again, this time to appear in an historical pageant, *Pocahontas*. It appears to have run for about two months, and again we gain a sense of the forces of his future gathering around him, for in the company were two actors who would soon be working with him at Biograph—Spottiswoode Aitken and Herbert Pryor.

To save money, Linda was left behind in New York—their first separation—where she particularly remembered that she "sewed like mad" to make a dress of some green silk material she had bought at Macy's. She hastened because the rent on her sewing machine—$1.50 a week—unnaturally strained her tight budget, for as usual, Griffith was having trouble collecting all of his agreed-upon salary and he was able to send only small amounts home to help out. Once he sent three dollars in cash because he didn't want to put his wife to the shame of cashing so small a check. Speaking of her in the third person, which apparently was a form of endearment between them, he ended the accompanying letter: "I bet you I get some good things out of this world for her yet, just watch me and see. . . ."[13]

While Griffith was working in Norfolk, James K. Hackett, that curious man, was proceeding with plans for A *Fool and a Girl*. His father, James H. Hackett, had been the first "gentleman" actor in America, that is, the first man of wealth and social position to become a player for hire, and he had been particularly successful in a series of New England rural comedies, which made him one of the beloved figures of the stage in the middle of the nineteenth century. His son, despite his early success as a matinee idol, always felt himself somewhat in his father's shade—the son was a legendary drinker—and at this moment, with his acting career in decline, he was perhaps not as strong and as sure a producer as an inexperienced playwright might want. Moreover, his backing was provided by Klaw and Erlanger, and this syndicate, then the most powerful economic force in the theater, producing and packaging plays for the dozens of houses it controlled, required confident fending off—especially when it was involved in a marginal and troubled project like Griffith's. This was beyond Hackett's skill and will, although his later productions of *Othello* and *Macbeth*, financed by a surprise inheritance, and with himself in the leads, would be hailed in England (where Mrs. Patrick Campbell was his costar) and on the Continent as capstones of his career, restoring a sweep and grandeur to Shakespeare that had been missing since the realistic fashion had taken hold.

These, however, were precisely the qualities Griffith had neglected to include in his play and for which Hackett's skimpy production could not compensate. Pauline Frederick dropped out of Hackett's plans quickly and when A *Fool and a Girl* opened in Washington the lead was played by Fannie Ward, with an actor named Jack Deane, whom she later married, opposite her. Alison Skipworth, later to score a notable success in George Kelly's *The Torch-Bearers*, in which she played a harassed drama coach, had the chief supporting role. All were better known as comic than as dramatic actors. Miss Ward in particular seemed miscast to both Griffith and Hackett. Constant rewrites were apparently made by the cast as they rehearsed—especially the star—and Griffith recalled that "frequently I was ejected into the alley behind the theater for objecting to changes in the script." He also recalls Hackett commiserating: "Well,

Griffith, they have certainly done a lot of spoiling of the play I bought—but it's too late now to do anything about it."[14]

It cannot have been a happy situation for Griffith, who might have been able to take direction as an actor but who had, as he amply proved later, an imperious will about his larger conceptions. Writing about it later, Griffith passed the whole incident off as a youthful folly, making jokes about himself and his play. At the time, however, it was anything but a joke. He received one or two good notices. The Toledo *Blade*—of all strange places—reported that A *Fool and a Girl* was "a play with a purpose, and presents realistic pictures of vital human interest." Its anonymous correspondent praised Griffith for his strong characterizations and for his depiction of "a love that is noble and victory that comes to those who 'fight the good fight.' " The *Dramatic News* was, if anything, more enthusiastic: ". . . a strong story that the author has handled admirably," it reported, accurately predicting that Griffith was "a craftsman of whom more will be heard."[15]

Alas, however, the play was by no means the "instant success" the *Dramatic News* claimed it was. The local critics, writing out of the genteel tradition, were far less kind than these out-of-towners were. F. B. Morse in the *Washington Post*, for example, wrote: "If I entertained any fear that A *Fool and a Girl*, the play that tried out . . . at the Columbia Theater would last through the season, I would yield some space to its disgusting vulgarity" and indeed yielded only a few more lines excoriating it.[16] Morse at least waited until the weekend, when his review could no longer harm the play. The response that deeply hurt came from Hector Fuller of the *Washington Herald*, whose notice, the day after the opening, was particularly savage: "It may be said that the dramatist wanted to show where his hero's feet strayed; and where he found the girl he was afterwards to make his wife, but if one wants to tell the old, old and beautiful story of redemption of either man or woman through love it is not necessary to portray the gutters from which they are redeemed." There was much more in this vein, with Fuller finally crying, "If this be art, it is the art of Zola, and Washington wants none of it."[17]

The review stung and Griffith had his first—but by no means last—opportunity to respond to a misunderstanding critic. Two days after Fuller's piece appeared, he dispatched a letter to the editor of the *Herald*, as lengthy as it was aggrieved. "In the name of justice," he began, "I ask you the courtesy of printing this letter," and it was no small favor he required, for his missive ran on for some 1,200 agonized words, defending in detail both the veracity of what he had placed on the stage and his high moral intent. In both realms he was on solid ground. His troubles lay elsewhere—in the realm of art. His concluding passage gives a fair sense of his tone and his position:

I am exceedingly sorry that I should have had to waste so much time on such a foolish and childish string of words that have fallen from Mr. Fuller's erudite pen, but I suppose we should bear this as one of the unavoidable tribulations of life. That the play is candid I admit, but that it is in the least immoral I do most emphatically deny, instead it preaches unmistakably and strongly the old, old sermon of redemption through love, which even Mr. Fuller must admit is one of the most beautiful to our possible imagination and also despite the gentleman's morbid impeachment without in any way hurting the intelligent sensibilities of any man or woman. As for your compliment, Mr. Fuller, in saying that my play was as inarticulate as a novel of the great Zola, who according to the most eminent literary critics has been esteemed as one of the greatest literary geniuses of the time, I can only say whatever else Zola may have been, it would be childish to call him inartistic. . . .[18]

Griffith's protest—so similar in tone to those he would direct to critics of *The Birth of a Nation* in its sensitivity to hypocrisy, in its outrage that anyone could possibly suspect his motives and its quite feverish tone of address—was to no avail. The play, according to his memoirs, did very poor business in Washington, although it played, on its final night, to a full house, a considerable improvement over an opening night that grossed only nineteen dollars. At the end of the week it moved on to Baltimore and after another week there, during which Klaw and Erlanger refused Hackett's request to make cast changes, it quietly folded. Griffith returned to New York, and neither he nor Linda found any theatrical work that winter. Checks from his brother Jake and a few hundred dollars sent to her from a San Francisco bank, belatedly settling accounts after the earthquake, supported them.

Undaunted—even cheerful (he used to recite Keats's "Ode to a Nightingale" to revive his wife's flagging spirits)—Griffith devoted himself to a new play about the American Revolution, which he called *War*. Weeks were spent in research at the Astor Place library, where he and Linda read histories and copied soldiers' diaries and letters. The piece was long (four acts) and very grand in conception (requiring, for some scenes, a goodly portion of an army), but it marked only a very small advance in Griffith's skills as a playwright. In his handling of his main character, an indentured servant named Jack White, who is by turns brave, cowardly and finally brave again, he created a figure of greater depth and interest than any in *A Fool and a Girl*. On the other hand, the play, though longer, is thinner than its predecessor. The plot, which involved White's falling in love with Jennie Randolph Graves, daughter of a great

Virginia family, and his sacrifice of her honor in order to complete a mission as a spy for George Washington, is not strong enough to sustain our interest over the inordinate length of the play. Nor is there any compensation for the work's lack of psychological depth in the panoramic view of the Revolution which Griffith offers. The action moves from Massachusetts to Valley Forge to Trenton (on the night of Washington's celebrated Christmas Eve attack on the Hessians) to Philadelphia, but the minor characters are feebly drawn and nothing very affecting happens in any of these settings.

The play's overall design, many of its specific incidents, and some of its characters prefigure Griffith's Revolutionary War drama of 1924, *America*, which was also a failure. Equally interesting, however, are a few speeches in which Griffith articulated his opinions on at least one matter that would arise again in his career. That was slavery. In the very first act he has this dialogue between Samuel Snow, Jack White's owner, and one Farmer Brown. Says Snow: "Well, of all the lazy, loafing culls—that was a fine bargain when I bought you. Wish I'd bought a nigger instead." To which Brown adds: "I told you, Sammy. I told you he wasn't no good. You ought to bought a nigger. Niggers is best cause you can knock *their* heads with a club, an' if you beat these white polecats, they get the law on ye." Given his reputation as a racist, one should note that this exchange was not between characters Griffith in any way showed in a favorable light and it did not express attitudes of which he approved. Indeed, throughout this opening scene he is at some pains to stress the unconscious cruelty of the times. One character, reading a newspaper, looks up from it and idly says, ". . . they're going to whip Moll Mitchell Friday morning, fifty lashes for being a wench—by Gilly, I'll have to see that. . . ." There are similar speeches, by similarly dislikable characters, one of whom insists, "There must be a master everywhere. If we don't obey the king, how can we expect our servants to obey us. . . ." Indeed, the first description of White, Griffith's hero, tells us that through all this he "shows no spirit of life, the dead ugly sullenness of bondage he typifies." It should be observed, however, that Jack White is not a typical indentured servant; it is made quite clear quite quickly that he is of finer stuff, perhaps the illegitimate son of a good family, though he appears not to know this for certain.

The play also prefigures the near-obsessive concern with two characters that would haunt Griffith's films; the virgin imperilled by a bestial male tormentor. In the third act of *War* Jack White has entered the Hessian camp at Trenton to spy out their intentions. He is disguised as a Quaker pieman and he comes to a tavern where the enemy officers meet, so he is privy to their sensual revels. Considering the taste of the time the scene carries quite a heavy charge of perverse sexuality. He has, for example, two soldiers gambling for the possession of a girl. At another point four women are forced to impersonate horses and are driven on stage with a whip flicking at their heels. We are reminded of Fellini and Genet, not of Griffith's playwriting contemporaries as we read this passage. One can only be thankful that Hector Fuller was never exposed to this scene, or to the archvillain of the piece, Captain Robert Cunningham, he of the "powerful frame" and "massive head"—"dark, brutal, animal, contemptuous, sensual." He is a man, according to Griffith's stage directions, born a thousand years too late, since he should have been "hairy and naked, a son of Thor." He is, in short, the precursor of Griffith's most memorable monsters—Silas and Gus in *The Birth of a Nation*, Von Strohm in *Hearts of the World*, Battling Burrows in *Broken Blossoms*, Captain Walter Butler in *America*, to name only a few of his lustful sadists.

He behaves in a manner that would be entirely familiar to any viewer of the films that were to come. Two of his men bring in a captured girl, shrouded in a cloak. When it is stripped off she is revealed to be Jennie, the high-spirited Virginian of the first act for whom Jack White, the bondsman, has long nursed a secret passion. Cunningham orders her tied to a pillar to await ravishing at his convenience. Jennie, of course, cries that she will commit suicide if he dares touch her, to which he replies: "Now, don't, don't—that is book talk, not real life." A brother officer, who is also Cunningham's cousin, protests, but is quickly disarmed.

The girl is hidden behind a curtain when White, disguised, enters on his mission of espionage. Suspicious of him, Cunningham and his band force whiskey down him, certain that it will loosen the tongue of a man whose religion forbids drink and that he will then reveal his true intentions. He survives this ordeal, however, only to be put to a sterner test. For he discovers the presence of his beloved. And he must choose between rescuing her (which would reveal to the enemy that a spy had been in their midst) or reporting to General Washington with news of the British-Hessian plans. Jones, his companion on the mission, urges stern duty on him: "It's not your life . . . but the thousands waiting on the other side of the river for you." "God! God! God!" cries White in the beginning of an agony of indecision which will reach considerable heights before the scene ends. Jennie, true to the stage heroine's creed, understands where White's larger obligations lie but begs him to kill her. He is prevented from doing so and in the ensuing melee escapes, fulfills his military obligation and, when the Americans move on Trenton, returns to the tavern, where he finds Jennie ravished. He then kills Cunningham in a duel.

In the play's final act White, now freed of his indenture and rewarded for his heroic services with a land grant in Virginia (or Kentucky as it would eventually turn out to be), encounters his "Lily Lady" (as he calls her) in a military hospital where both have come to visit Jones, and the one-time bondsman proposes. She replies: "You of all men know that

I MUST GO THE PATH ALONE UNTIL THE END. You know
why, bondsman." The capitals are Griffith's, and the sentiment expressed
is pure, pure Griffith.[19]

War represents Griffith's first attempt to create a spectacle. He was
aware enough of the stage's limits not to call for huge battle scenes, as
other writers for the spectacular stage did, but there is hardly a scene that
does not throng with people and, of course, he did not stint when it came
to fights and duels and all the other bloody conventions of the spectacle
tradition. Nevertheless, as he would show in the best of his later movies,
the thing that interested him most was the private moment that a couple
of people might share amidst the hurly-burly of the crowd and its passions. His language in some of these scenes might be either stilted or
flowery, but there was often a kernel of truth in them. One especially remembers an antiheroic moment at Valley Forge where the bondsman,
showing himself as discouraged as the rest of Washington's army, has to
be talked into the hard labor of struggling out of camp to rescue a supply
train mired on the road. In brief, he has some dimensions beyond those
of the standard hero. Even his early sullenness, conquered by love and
by the adventure that war offers, contributes to a somewhat deeper understanding of his character than we might ordinarily expect in this kind of
enterprise.

According to Linda, Henry Miller was briefly interested in doing the
play but finally rejected it as too expensive to produce, and no one else
stepped forward. Meanwhile the Griffiths kept up the pretense of leading
a literary life. She says he had sold a short story to Perriton Maxwell, editor of *Cosmopolitan*, for $75 (though if this is true, Maxwell never ran
it), and they invited the editor to a rather sad little dinner. Linda had to
pawn a gold bracelet to pay for the food and she recalled placing signs on
various pieces of their rickety furniture—"Do not sit here; the springs are
weak"; "Don't lean; the legs are loose"—in an attempt to forestall embarrassing accidents. Maxwell reciprocated with a more elegant affair, including at it the editor of *Good Housekeeping*, but nothing came of it.
There is no record of any further literary success for Griffith at this time.

4

Still, it was as a writer of scenarios, not as an actor, that D. W. Griffith
approached the movie studios of New York, looking for work to tide him
over a difficult winter. The precise circumstances of his first visits to them
are in dispute, but there is general agreement that it was an old acting
friend from Louisville, Max Davidson—late of the Twilight Revellers—
who suggested that he turn to films. One day, in the Automat on Forty-

second Street, a favorite oasis for actors making the rounds, Griffith ran into Davidson, whom he had not seen since leaving Kentucky, and another actor, Harry Salter. They told him that the going rate for movie performers was five dollars a day, that much of the work was outdoors, which was pleasant, and that, since these were silent films, there were no lines to learn, which was even more pleasant. As Griffith remembered it, he replied: "But I'll lose standing as an actor with theater people if they see me in a movie." To which Salter responded: "None of them has seen us yet and it hasn't hurt us. The money is worth going after." Davidson added that if Griffith didn't want to appear in films he could, given his writing ability, sell scenarios to the movies,[20] the rate for which ranged from five to 30 dollars per script.

It was the anonymity of that work that appealed most powerfully to Griffith—especially since a scenario could be cobbled up in an evening. The studio at which Davidson and Salter had found the most work, and which they commended to Griffith's attention was—according to his wife—the Biograph. (Early movie people nearly always prefixed the article to the studio's name, as if in compensation for the fact that no one could possibly use the organization's full title—the American Mutoscope and Biograph Company—in a conversational sentence.) Griffith himself remembered that Biograph's name came up at a slightly later time and from a different source[21] and it would appear that in this instance his memory is the more trustworthy, for the first movie work by D. W. Griffith for which there is documentary evidence took place earlier in 1908 than his wife places it and at a different location, the Edison Studio in the Bronx, where Edwin S. Porter, creator of the first American story films, was in charge of production.

Griffith journeyed to the Bronx with a scenario in hand, apparently a reworking of *La Tosca*.[22] The script, probably no more than a couple of pages in length, was of no interest to the studio—not probably, because it was plagiarized, but because it contained more scenes than the budget could stand. "So far as I know . . . it is still there; I've never heard anything from it since," Griffith said in 1920.[23] He did, however, get an acting job.

Edwin Porter is generally credited as the man who engaged Griffith for this assignment, but by this time, four years after the success of *The Great Train Robbery*, Porter was not casting, directing or taking an active part in finding stories for *all* Edison productions. Given the rapid expansion of the business and its new emphasis on fictional material (both direct results of the success of Porter's little western film), this is not surprising. For one thing, his studio was turning out at least two one-reel films a week, more than he could attend to single-handedly; for another, Porter a one-time sailor, then a newsreel cameraman, and always an inveterate inventor of mechanical gadgets, had no training in dramatic or literary construction and probably realized that, despite his lucky accident with *The Great Train Robbery*, he needed strong assistance in choosing and mounting his little fictional screenplays on a regularly scheduled basis.

So, in 1907 he had hired J. Searle Dawley, a playwright and actor, to aid him and, until 1913, when he left to join another company, Dawley staged some 300 films for the Edison company. In the beginning, Dawley often directed the actors while Porter, a rather self-effacing sort, handled the camera (later he even abandoned that activity). Dawley had considerable freedom in choosing subjects and players, routinely presenting his ideas to Porter, who just as routinely approved them—so long as they could be made within the rather stringent budgets imposed on him by Thomas A. Edison and his managers, who were entirely uninterested in the esthetics of moviemaking and who, indeed, saw very little future in theatrical motion pictures at this point.

It appears, then, that it was Dawley who hired Griffith to play the leading role in *Rescued from the Eagle's Nest*, which was shot, on a four-day schedule, in late January or early February 1908. Griffith, anyway, gave Dawley informal credit for giving him his first movie job, for some years later he encountered Dawley in an elevator in New York and called out to him: "Say, Dawley, you got me into this picture business, why not get me out of it?"[24]

The picture was fairly typical of its time: a baby is snatched from its cradle by an eagle, there is much consternation on the part of family, friends and neighbors, whereupon a brave mountaineer, played by Griffith, climbs to the bird's aerie, fights off the predator and restores the child to its home. There are a few exteriors shot on location in New Jersey, but most of the scenes were done in the studio, as painted canvas flats attest. The bird itself was obviously stuffed and manipulated by wires in its climactic struggle with Griffith, who makes a stalwart but not particularly animated hero.

At the end of shooting, Dawley, who kept track of production costs in a notebook, went to Porter and, as he did in the case of all actors, told the studio manager how many days work the thespian had put in, Porter handed over the cash, and Griffith's initiation was ended as casually as it had begun. He probably went to see the movie when it was released—Dawley's wife so recalled—but there is no record of his response, except that in his rounds he began to call in at some of the other studios looking for work.

It was Frank Marion, manager and co-owner of Kalem, in Manhattan, who sent him to Biograph, perhaps with a letter of introduction. Griffith recalled that Marion owned stock in the rival concern, but there is no reliable record of when or in what circumstances Griffith entered the studio, located in a five-story brownstone, once a fashionable residence, then the office-showroom of a piano company, before Biograph leased it as a studio. More than likely he hoped both to write and act for the company—though he liked to claim that he was engaged forthwith and full time as a writer of screenplays.

In fact, no one except executives, cameramen, stagehands and technicians worked full-time at Biograph and there was only one full-time director, George McCutcheon, although he was occasionally assisted by his son, Wallace, a musical comedy star who would later become the husband of Pearl White, the "Perils of Pauline" girl. It was undoubtedly "Old Man McCutcheon" (as he was called) who first hired Griffith and it was as an actor that he was engaged, not as a writer. There is no evidence in anyone's reminiscences that the thirty-three-year-old actor had any sense that the forces of destiny were playing about him as he stepped over the threshold of 11 East Fourteenth Street and entered the grimy little world of Biograph. He was, then, just another actor—one of many—looking for some work to tide him over until the summer stock season began.

CHAPTER FIVE

"Painter
of the Passing Moment"

GRIFFITH was entering the movies in general, the Biograph in particular, at a propitious moment, the former having entered upon a period of incredible expansion, the latter—belatedly—about to join in the general prosperity. Only twelve years had passed since the first exhibition of movies in the United States had taken place at Koster and Bial's Music Hall in Herald Square, on the spot where Macy's now stands. Much of the industrial history of the movies for that period was written in legal briefs, as claims and counterclaims for a swarm of inventors were put forward in the courts (with Thomas A. Edison being the most persistent plaintiff, defending his firm's rights in a chain of invention he personally had little to do with and in which he had originally had so little faith that he had been careless in protecting it with adequate patents). But it is also true that since the turn of the century real progress, both esthetic and commercial, had been made.

Prior to 1900 the only fictive form films took was anecdotal: usually a bit of slapstick, though J. Stuart Blackton, a sometime newspaper cartoonist and cofounder of the Vitagraph Studio, had had a great wartime success with something called *Tearing Down the Spanish Flag*, which consisted of just that—a hand pulling the Spanish standard off its staff and running up Old Glory. Mostly, however, the early producers, releasing mainly through the vaudeville houses, offered the public little more than the novelty of pictures that moved. There were excerpts from well-known variety turns, glimpses of newsworthy events, a huge number of scenic views. Often enough, they simply set their cameras up on a New York street corner and shot the passing parade—imitating the Lumière brothers in Paris in taking advantage of the enormous provincial curiosity about life in the metropolis.

The novelty, however, wore off and aside from a brief renaissance during a strike of variety performers in 1900, their drawing power steadily declined. They might have disappeared from the theaters altogether had not Georges Méliès achieved, also in 1900, a considerable breakthrough. The French magician had already produced a catalog of some 200 "magical, mystical and trick films," each no more than a minute or two long, but utilizing a full range of wondrous effects—double exposures, matte shots, stop-motion, fast and slow motion, reversed film, animation, fades and dissolves. These little films were the most popular (and the most frequently pirated) pictures of their day, but now he surpassed himself by creating what most historians consider to be the first full-scale story film, a version of *Cinderella* in twenty "motion tableaux," or scenes. He followed it with more filmed fairy tales, as well as with fantastic adventures of his own devising, the pictures growing longer and longer in order to encompass the inventions of a mind that remains, to this day, one of the most charming, unpretentious and uninhibited ever to turn to the movies.

It was, indeed, Méliès's demonstration of the power of arranged scenes that inspired Edwin Porter to attempt something similar, though in a more realistic vein, *The Life of an American Fireman* (1902). Despite a dull initial reception, this film has enormous significance in the history of screen technique. Porter worked mostly with stock footage, arranging it so it told the simple tale of a mother and child rescued from a burning building, but he did make use of a close-up (of a fire alarm box and of a hand reaching in to set off the signal) and, perhaps more important, he employed, for the first time, more than one camera setup in a single scene (at the film's climax he showed fire apparatus arriving at the blaze, a shot of the imperiled woman and child and, finally, a shot of them being carried down a ladder to safety).

Edison's managers, sensing Porter was on to something, encouraged his enthusiasm for arranged scenes and—among other projects—set him to work on a version of *Uncle Tom's Cabin*, which was rather perfunctorily managed by Porter, who was already nursing the idea for *The Great Train Robbery*, which he was finally allowed to put into production in 1903. In a sense this movie, too, was retrograde, for like *Uncle Tom*, each of its fourteen scenes was shot from a single camera position—there were no changes of angle within the scenes. Yet there was simple crosscutting from the point of view of the bandits to that of the honest citizenry pursuing them. More important, however, the film was realistic (it had been inspired by accounts of holdups then taking place in the West) and melodramatic, both values highly prized by the popular audience of the time and heretofore entirely absent from the movies. Yet even this does not fully account for the astonishing success of this little film. At least as important as its creator's insights into the editing principle was the establishment, while he was preoccupied in the studio, of new and more efficient methods of distributing and exhibiting films.

In the beginning, movies had been sold outright by producers to exhibitors—a slow and costly process in which the producers encountered heavy sales resistance, since the effective commercial life of most movies in any given location was no more than a few days. What was needed, obviously, was some sort of rental system, increasing the velocity at which films could be circulated and lower the unit cost of them for exhibitors. And that is what Harry and Herbert Miles, sometime cameramen and exhibitors, established when they set up the first film exchange in San Francisco in 1902. Their idea was simplicity itself: they stood ready to buy almost anything the producers turned out, assuring them of a steady market for their wares. The middlemen, in turn, offered these films to exhibitors at first-run rentals that amounted to no more than a quarter the cost of outright purchase. The exchange men, of course, were free to peddle any given picture at many locations and, obviously, they began to make a profit once they had rented a film more than four times—a simple matter to accomplish on a regional basis. It was a neat solution to a vexing problem and by the time Griffith entered the movies there were more than 100 exchanges in some 35 key cities.

The exchange system helped extend a parallel—and more far-reaching change—in the manner of exhibiting films. It also began in 1902, and it began, appropriately, given its later centrality in movie history, in Los Angeles. There Thomas Tally, proprietor of a penny arcade where he offered projected films among many other attractions, observed that they were bringing larger returns than any of his other novelties and decided to devote his establishment exclusively to movies. It was the first such theater in America and he advertised it as "The Electric Theater. For Up-to-Date High Class Motion Picture Entertainment Especially for Ladies and Children."[1] Among his other innovations were matinees to which the admission charge was only a nickel.

It was an idea whose time had come. By 1905, when John P. Harris and his brother-in-law, Harry Davis, coined in Pittsburgh the pretty name by which these little theaters quickly came to be generically known, there were hundreds of "nickelodeons" in the United States. By the time Griffith found his way to Biograph, the estimate is, there were 10,000 of them. The movies had thus begun to find, in the space of about a decade, and, as it were, just in time for their first great master, the great commercial destiny that their early promoters—Edison notably excepted—had so eagerly predicted and toward which they had been energetically groping.

In this period of rapid, if quite unpredictable, expansion, Biograph had failed to maintain its original position as Edison's prime competitor. The company did not notably lack technological know-how or managerial skill and it had rather more sound financial resources than most of its competitors. Yet, as of winter 1908, it was an invalid—mostly because it

had found no one with Porter's vision of the screen's storytelling potential. Or Griffith's.

The company had been founded in 1895 by four disparate individuals: Henry N. Marvin, a college teacher; Herman Casler, a skilled ma-
chinist; Elias B. Koopman, a wholesaler of toys and novelties; and, most
silent but most important of the partners, William Kennedy Laurie Dickson. Born in Scotland, he had been raised in Virginia. It was he who had
supervised, while in Edison's employ, the development of the Kinetoscope, a device that had made possible the showing, as early as 1891, of
movies on a peepshow basis. Though not a terribly popular novelty, it was
clear to Dickson that the Kinetoscope, using flexible celluloid film developed by George Eastman and requiring a motion picture camera to
record images upon it, represented half the system necessary to achieve
practical projected movies, and that the development of the projector itself would be a comparatively simple matter. Important refinements,
later incorporated in the Edison equipment, were made by other inventors in the period 1891–95, resulting in a steadier image and a capacity
to handle longer films, but by 1894—two years before Edison was ready
to unveil his perfected system—Dickson had decided to strike out on his
own and was making overtures to Marvin. He had come up with a good,
even elegant, idea for an alternative to the unsatisfactorily delicate Kinetoscope—which tended to break film—and did not want to share this
new notion with his old employer. It became the basis for the first prosperity of the four-way partnership that located its shop in the small town
of Canosta, New York.

What Dickson had in mind was placing each frame of film shot by
the motion picture camera on a card, placing the cards on a drum and
having the viewer, peering into a tiny magnifying window, crank the
drum past a simple metal bar which would riffle them just as the thumb
does when the edge of a deck of cards is pressed glancingly against it. The
advantage of the drum, of course, was that it could hold many thousands
more cards than a hand could—enough to tell a little visual anecdote, for
example.

The Mutuoscope, as his gadget was shortly named, was sturdy, simple, portable and inexpensive and it is this device (along with some variants on it) that persisted in splendidly functioning condition, almost to
the present day in amusement arcades, and is still to be found in the recreation rooms of people with a taste for antique novelties. It was an instant
success, driving the Kinetoscope out of the market and providing the new
partnership with a solid base of steady profits on which to operate in the
highly competitive and speculative business of marketing the moving
image. Indeed, because of their patent on the Mutuoscope they were able
to obtain capitalization amounting to $200,000 from the New York Se-

curity and Trust Company—the only early movie firm able to attract solid support from the financial community.

Yet even before the Mutuoscope went on the market Dickson had begun work on the camera-projector system that was eventually to be known as the Biograph. It differed from the Edison system in two important respects. It used film approximately twice the size of the one-inch strip its competitor required and the film went into the camera without sprocket holes. As each frame was fixed in place behind the lens, so an image could be recorded, it was neatly punctured, left and right, by two small pins. The first of these differences gave the Biograph a competitive advantage over Edison's Vitagraph, for the larger film resulted in a distinctly larger and infinitely clearer projected image. On the other hand, the puncturing device was cumbersome and often broke down. In fact, the Biograph camera weighed some 300 pounds and resembled, according to a contemporary account, "more than anything else a cedar clothes-chest some five feet long and two feet wide, the only photographic evidence being a suggestive lens poking out of one end."[2]

But perhaps more important than the question of which motion picture system was superior, was the timing of the work on the Biograph. It was going forward at precisely the time Edison's technicians were putting the finishing touches on his Vitagraph and though it was the latter that was exhibited to the public first, the Biograph people had virtually completed their work by that time, too. The race was close enough to support their later contention, in the courts, that they had not infringed on Edison's patents but had simultaneously solved, by methods sufficiently different from Edison's, a well-known technological puzzle. The argument was plausible enough to keep the case dragging through the courts for many years, thus allowing Biograph to establish itself firmly in the movie business, a process it began almost immediately after the Vitagraph debut.

The partners spent the summer of 1896 getting material together for a debut of their own. Even before the Edison screenings they had erected a stage on the roof of their New York headquarters at 841 Broadway—a facility very like Edison's famous first movie stage, the Black Maria—and were taking pictures that could be utilized by both the Mutuoscope and the Biograph. In the spring and summer Dickson, now aided by Billy Bitzer, later to gain lasting fame as Griffith's cameraman, shot a wide variety of subjects. To begin with, there was a dancer named Annabelle doing genteel gyrations on the roof stage. Later there was Sandow the Strongman, a scene from the stage hit *Trilby* and a group of three little films featuring black performers—"Hard Wash," "Watermellon [sic] Feast," "Dancing Darkies." The pioneers also took views of Union Square (on which their office building was situated) and of Bicycle and Carriage parades on Broadway north of Columbus Circle. In July they journeyed to Atlantic City and Philadelphia and shot what amounted to moving postcards in both cities as well as en route. In August they traveled to Buzzard's Bay on Cape Cod to record, at his summer home, Joseph Jefferson doing several scenes from *Rip Van Winkle*, the play in which he almost endlessly toured during this period. Immediately thereafter the Biograph promoters essayed their first newsreel subjects—shots of the Chinese diplomat Li Hung Chang, who visited both President Cleveland and Grant's Tomb as he passed through New York on his way home from the Coronation of Nicholas II of Russia. After that it was on to West Point to obtain views of the cadets on parade and to Niagara Falls for more scenic shots.

By this time they had a sufficient variety of subjects to risk a theatrical debut on a bill with Sandow at the Alvin Theater in Pittsburgh during the week of September 12. The notices were enthusiastic, one newspaper noting that the Biograph image was twice the size of other motion picture projectors and praising it as "clear-cut and distinct." Another flatly called it "the best . . . [in the] new process of photography" observing that "Mr. Jefferson's lips moved so naturally that one could almost imagine he heard the words that he seemed to utter."[3] The Pittsburgh papers thus enunciated a theme that was to be repeated throughout this era, namely that the Biograph system was technically superior to all its competitors.

Shortly thereafter, the Biograph achieved its first great reportorial coup. Eighteen ninety-six was an election year and the Republican candidate, William McKinley, following the advice of his campaign manager, Mark Hanna, was running largely by sitting—on his front porch in Canton, Ohio—while William Jennings Bryan thundered up and down the land rallying farmers and labor to the cause of free silver. During the Pittsburgh engagement a Biograph crew headed by Dickson and including Bitzer joined the more conventional journalists on the pilgrimage to Canton, where the candidate was photographed strolling on his lawn. In this little sequence an aide was shown rushing up to him with a telegram which, after taking his spectacles from his pocket, the soon-to-be president read with evident happiness, after which he walked on, appearing to discuss the good news contained in the wire with his associates. As Bitzer later said, "Not much, was it? But it was what the public wanted. A picture which could go down for posterity. . . . The first time a President had been photographed in action. There is a thrill in that!"[4]

The *New York Herald*, when it got around to discussing the film some months later, took an ironic tone about this little scrap of footage: ". . . the President elect toes out like a ballet girl when walking. His clod crushers are quite respectable in size, too, if anybody should ask you. In the machine one can readily see that he is not a reckless pedestrian. He is slow and methodical and is careful where he puts his feet."[5]

Modest though it was, the McKinley sequence, along with a shot of the crack Empire Express train rounding a curve at 60 mph on its New York–Buffalo run was the hit of the Biograph New York debut at Hammerstein's Olympic on Monday, October 12, 1896. To be sure, the house was full of Republican faithful—supplied by the party organization—and they gave their candidate a standing ovation when he appeared on screen. But there was again much favorable comment on the quality, size and sharpness of the Biograph image and the show moved over to Koster and Bial's, where it attained an unprecedented run—almost three months. Other triumphs followed, notably an election-night projection on a screen that stretched across the front of the *World* building and then, after the close of the run at Koster and Bial's, the beginning of an eight-and-a-half-year period when Biograph was the sole purveyor of film to Keith's Union Square Theater.

Obviously, whatever the merits of Edison's case against Biograph for patent infringement, Biograph had begun life as an aggressive, confident and imaginative competitor. In the days before the story film its managers, indeed, continued to demonstrate the same venturesome spirit they had evidenced in scoring their coup with McKinley. By the turn of the century their catalog contained an impressive list of name performers from both the legitimate and vaudeville stages miming their most memorable routines for the camera. In addition, Biograph was among the leaders in providing newsreel coverage of events ranging from the Spanish-American War to McKinley's funeral. Its managers were also more willing than many to enliven their scenic views with technical experiments—like mounting their cameras on moving vehicles or by trying time-lapse photography. Perhaps its most enterprising early project was an attempt, in November 1899, to photograph in its entirety a prizefight between Jim Jeffries and Tom Sharkey. No one had ever successfully made movies of anything using artificial light as the only source of illumination, but the movie people—Bitzer again among them—rigged no less than forty huge hot arc lights over the ring, their heat combining with that generated by the crowd of over 11,000 to exhaust the fighters in the early rounds. It also warmed the electrical connections to a point where short circuits threatened and Biograph crew members applied ice—hastily obtained from a nearby saloon—to these connections, the melted water dripping into the ring below to make the going for the fighters slippery as well as hot. Alas, technical daring was not to be rewarded on this occasion. The rival Edison and Vitagraph companies, brought together by an unnamed promoter, slipped into the arena and, protected by bodyguards, made a film of their own, using Biograph's expensive lights without permission. Attempts to eject them were foiled by the crowd, already irritated by the effects of movie pioneering on the quality of the boxing. Hot pursuit, led by Jeffries himself, once he had won the fight, failed to separate the pirates from their film. The Vitagraph highlight film reached the theaters and skimmed the market before the Biograph product, running to 5,575 feet and taking a long time to process, reached it.

This rather comic setback did not prevent Henry Marvin from attempting, a few months later, a bold stratagem to settle the patent fight with Edison. Biograph was only one of many firms that had for two years been skirmishing with Edison's lawyers in the courts, but it was the biggest, most solidly established of them, and Marvin, seeing that the struggle was going to be virtually endless (and endlessly costly), conceived the notion of bringing it up short by the simple expedient of buying Edison out. The idea appealed to Edison, who still had not come to enjoy the movie business, and he agreed, in principle, to a purchase price of a half million dollars. Had not the bank from which Marvin intended to borrow this amount failed just at the intended moment of consummation, it seems likely that Biograph might have achieved a dominant, perhaps unassailable position in the new industry. As it was, however, this near miss represented the high watermark of Biograph's early economic history. Edison returned to the courts with renewed vigor, and more and more of Biograph's corporate energy was devoted to fending off his lawyers. Worse, Biograph management was temperamentally unsuited to the new phase their industry was entering.

As long as the machines themselves were the attractions that lured the people into theaters, so long as film content needed only to adequately demonstrate the qualities of this equipment, the Biograph managers were on safe ground. Their models were the industrialists who had dominated America's great age of economic growth in the last decades of the nineteenth century and they supposed, quite erroneously, that movies would turn out to be a sober, rational industry in which the big profits would derive from the manufacture, sale and lease of hardware. So it had been for the inventors and promoters of other communications equipment, ranging from the telephone to the typewriter, from the rotary press to the mimeograph machine. Very close to their own field they had the example of George Eastman and the multiplying fortune he was deriving from the sale of cameras and raw film stock. What was characteristic of all this equipment was that the people who manufactured it didn't have to spare a moment's thought for what their consumers might do with it—that was entirely their business—and rather beneath a capitalist's dignity to contemplate.

So the owners of the Biograph, and their competitors, patterned themselves on models inappropriate to their business. They simply never understood that the power and wealth of the movies was not in hardware but, to borrow a more recent term, in software. Not one of the people who engaged in the desperate struggle for control of the patents they imagined were key to their industry, actually obtained significant, long-term power in the movies. That went, instead, to men who, in the early years of the new century, were learning, as exhibitors and distributors, what the public wanted and, perhaps more importantly, how to make the public want what it was within their power to give.

"Old Man" McCutcheon actually gave Biograph some successful story films in the pre-Griffith days. Terry Ramsaye, an early historian of the cinema, cites *Personal* and *The Moonshiners* as films that developed the potential of the comic chase and the big climactic fight in the 1904–5 period. The former, in particular, appears to have been an amusing piece in which a Frenchman places an ad in the *New York Herald*'s personal column, stating that he would like to meet a handsome American girl with a view toward matrimony. "The rendezvous is at Grant's Tomb," says a contemporary catalog. "When the hour for the appointment approaches and he sees the great crowd of girls waiting for him, he flees in dismay across the country, over bridges, through wheat fields, down embankments, over fences, the girls following close behind. He is finally captured at the point of a revolver and carried triumphantly to the nearest clergyman. This is in many respects the funniest chase film that has ever been made."[6]

Yet these successes were isolated and by 1907, according to Ramsaye, "Biographs were openly called 'rotten' on the market."[7] Whether they were much more "rotten" than the average of the competition is an open question, but the fact remains that by early 1906 the Empire Trust Company, which had extended a sizable loan to the studio, was sufficiently concerned about its future to dispatch one Jeremiah J. Kennedy, a consulting engineer, northward to East Fourteenth Street, in order to survey the studio's faltering operations. His instructions were either to liquidate the company or to revitalize it—whichever seemed most profitable (or perhaps least costly).

Kennedy was a hard man who had worked his way up through railroad construction and mining camps, where he had gained a reputation as an organizer (and reorganizer)—"blunt, pungent, swift and positive."[8] Withal, his portraits reveal, besides a strong jaw and a bold mustache, a hint of the ironist in his glance, a man perhaps amused to find himself engaged in so erratic an enterprise as the movies, which surely presented the challenge of a lifetime to a man with a rage for order.

In any event, installed as president, retaining H. N. Marvin, last of the four original Biograph partners to maintain an active interest in the firm, as vice president and general manager, Kennedy determined that the company was strong enough to undertake a more energetic fight for survival, a decision no doubt buttressed by the knowledge that pressure for industrial peace was growing throughout the motion picture business. In Chicago, in the fall of 1907, a federal judge had handed down a decision holding that, indeed, cameras used by the Selig company, another independent, infringed on Edison's patents, and a group of the companies most likely to be adversely affected by that decision, should it be upheld on appeal, combined to sue Edison for peace. Under terms arranged by George Kleine, a Chicago Exchange man, seven major firms agreed to pay royalties to Edison in return for licenses to manufacture movies using his patented equipment. Marvin, however, refused an offer to join what came to be known as the Motion Picture Patents Company, or more familiarly, "the trust." Considerations of strategy rather than of principle motivated him. For in the winter of 1907–8 he scurried about acquiring a new patent right of his own, specifically to the Latham Loop, key to the projection of long films without breakage. He also acquired an option to purchase shares in a company formed by Thomas Armat, inventor of the stop-motion device that was the key to Edison's camera-projection system. Thus Biograph was poised to take control of a small but vital part of the very machinery on which Edison's power was based.

All this was largely bluff, since the company had small likelihood of raising the $3 million required to exercise its Armat stock options. By creating an impression of strength, Kennedy and Marvin were simply trying to force Edison and his new allies to treat Biograph as an entity in a class by itself, threatening to go back into manufacturing equipment themselves—a line Biograph had abandoned when it conformed its film size to the industry's standard at the turn of the century.

Meantime, and of more direct concern to Griffith, efforts were being made to strengthen the quality of the stories the studio was filming. Lee "Doc" Dougherty, a onetime newspaperman, was engaged as head of the story department and he, in turn, employed as his chief scenarist Stanner E. V. Taylor, also a sometime journalist, latterly an unsuccessful playwright, who would, in time, become a Griffith familiar. He wore thin white gloves even when he typed and carried a bar of soap with him at all times, for he was a compulsive hand-washer, but he was quick, could plagiarize a plot as readily as anyone, and the money, which could reach $50 a week if both efforts were used, was far better than daily press space rates. It is dubious that Taylor had any discernible immediate influence on Biograph productions, but he was a reasonably literate man and, in a very short time, he along with another journeyman of similar gifts, Frank Woods (later to be both Biograph's and the Griffith company's story editor), would be providing Griffith with the largest portion of his scripts, scripts that reflected some of his aspirations for the medium he was now reluctantly embracing.

2

And, surely, the embrace was reluctant. There is no precise record of what Griffith's first role for Biograph was. Mrs. Griffith recalls simply that it was a western, requiring two days of work under Old Man McCutcheon's direction, the second day of which was on location in New Jersey. When it was all over Griffith reported to his wife: "It's not so bad, you know, five dollars for simply riding a horse in the wilds of Fort Lee on a cool spring day." He added: "I think it wouldn't be a bad idea for you to go down and see what you can do. Don't tell them who you are, I mean, don't tell them you're my wife. I think it's better business not to."[9]

And so she also fell into the movies, briefly and in the long run less happily than he did, since she was neither attractive enough nor gifted enough to establish a strong demand for her services outside of the films her husband directed—and even in those she was soon relegated to character roles as younger, more dewy-eyed creatures came under his tutelage. It was not a pleasant fate for a strong-willed and intelligent woman and, in time, Griffith would have to pay heavily for her frustrations.

For the moment, however, they were both content to have discovered a line of work that was steady and not without its charms. Griffith sold a scenario, *Old Isaacs, the Pawnbroker*, in which he acted and in which he enunciated for the first time one of the themes to which he would obsessively return—criticism of organized philanthropy, which was invidiously compared to the kind heart and highly personal touch of the ghetto moneylender of the film's title. There were other roles, some of them in scenarios he also provided throughout the spring—*The Music Master*, *Ostler Joe* and *The Stage Rustler*, uncredited adaptations of well-known theatrical melodramas, for which—the copyright laws not having been extended to film as yet—no royalties were paid the original authors or producers.

Of them all perhaps the most interesting were *At the Crossroads of Life* and *When Knights Were Bold*. The former was based on a Griffith scenario in which he played a worldly fellow attempting to seduce a chorus girl whose father rejected her because she had gone upon the wicked, wicked stage. One thinks immediately of Griffith's tale, in his autobiography, of the idealized actress he had been so strangely drawn to in his trouping days. One is reminded again of his ambivalence about the morality of theatrical life. And, of course, of his ambivalence about the women with whom he had shared that life. It was not much of a film. There were but nine shots in it, all taken from the same camera position, well away from the action and only when McCutcheon does an exterior (of the girl mailing a letter) does the screen come to life, with glimpses of passersby and horse-drawn vehicles in the background. Still, it was probably intrinsically better than the medieval romance *When Knights Were Bold*, which is notable mainly because it is the one film in which David and Linda Griffith appeared together.

Some of these films were photographed by Bitzer and he has left a description of Griffith, the actor, which may be somewhat colored by his later bitterness over Griffith's less than generous acknowledgment of the cameraman's contributions to the developing syntax of the screen. Nevertheless, he does not contradict the prevailing opinion of Griffith's thespic gifts. He noticed him for the first time lurking near the edge of a scene, his arms in such constant motion that to Bitzer he looked as if he had three or four of them. "He acted as jerky as a mechanical doll because— I later learned—he had never seen pictures where the actor seemed to do other than jerk and he supposed it was what was expected."[10] The next time he appeared before Bitzer's camera, the photographer told him to stop mugging. Griffith replied that he had been told that this manner was expected of movie players but he ceased to overplay. He might have been dissembling, for the description squares neatly with the frequent criticisms of Larry Griffith as an excessively busy stage actor. What is most interesting, though, is that it was Griffith who introduced the principle of stillness in movie acting, thereby indicating that his natural sense of the new medium's demands quite transcended his own ingrained habits of style.

Whatever his skills as an actor, Griffith and his wife found themselves being drawn into the informal and unpretentious ambiance of the Biograph company. "It was a conglomerate mess of people that hung around the studio," Linda later wrote and it was only occasionally, she said, that "among the flotsam and jetsam appeared . . . a few real actors and actresses."[11] Their habit, of course, was to depart as quickly as a legitimate role presented itself, and there was some ambiguity regarding them. On the one hand, the studio's tiny executive corps was annoyed at the inconvenience of being unable to create a reliable repertory company of talented players. On the other, the people who actually shot the movies were impressed by individuals who gave evidence, if only by their absences, that they were in demand on the stage. Old Man McCutcheon, anyway, was very understanding and would arrange to work around an actor who announced that he had an appointment, during the workday, with an agent or manager uptown.

So a comfortable routine began, for the first time, to assert itself in the Griffith home, and Griffith began to speak occasionally of his desire to direct. Bitzer recalled warning him off, on the ground that if he failed he would probably not thereafter find acting jobs at Biograph. Mrs. Griffith recounts a rumor that Sigmund "Pop" Lubin, one of the jollier film pirates, was looking for a director in this period, claiming her husband wrote a letter of application and even journeyed to Lubin's Philadelphia headquarters for an interview, of which nothing came. Again, we have an early example of Griffith's instinct for the nature of the medium, for at this time the director's role was not as significant as that of the cameraman, especially if he was as strong-willed as Bitzer. It was the latter who chose the setups and since these were rarely changed in the course of a scene, there was not much for the director to do after he had chosen his players except make sure that, in carrying out such bits of business and action as he might devise with them, they did not step outside the guide-lines, marked on the floor, which indicated the limits of what the lens could record. Nor did he have any serious postproduction responsibili-ties, since there was rarely more than one take of any scene and thus not much to edit—if anyone thought seriously about film editing, which no one did. Obviously, then, it required considerable creative imagination just to visualize how significant the director could become in the creative process of filming.

Nevertheless, Griffith came close to missing his opportunity. For in the late spring he received the offer of a job in summer stock at Peake's Island, Maine—at "forty per." This is the way his wife recalled their dis-cussion of the opportunity: "If I turn this job down, and appear to be so busy, they soon won't send for me at all. Of course, if this movie thing is going to amount to anything . . . we could afford to take chances. In one way it is very nice. You can stay in New York, and *if* I can find time to write too—fine. But you know you can't go on forever and not tell your friends and relatives how you are earning your living."

To which Linda replied: "How long is Peake's Island going to last? What's sure about summer stock? What does Peake's Island mean to David Belasco or Charles Frohman? We've got this little flat here . . . and the rent's so low—twenty. You don't know what's going to happen down at the Biograph, you might get to direct some day. Let's stick the summer out anyhow, and when fall comes and productions open up again, we'll see, huh?"[12]

And so they stayed. And were rewarded for their small gamble more quickly than they might have anticipated. For Old Man McCutcheon shortly thereafter fell ill—Bitzer claims it was drink that laid him low—and Henry Marvin began looking for someone to fill in, at least tempo-rarily. As usual, Wally McCutcheon was willing to help out briefly; Mar-vin himself occasionally laid aside his managerial duties, mounted the stairs to the ballroom on the third floor which served as the main interior stage, and handled an occasional picture; even Stanner Taylor was pressed into service for one film—in which Linda, coincidentally, played the lead. But these were all stopgaps and by this time Marvin had convinced him-self that quality might be served, even should the elder McCutcheon re-turn to full strength, if he had two directors permanently on staff. After all, the company was committed to grinding out two one-reel films a week and the minimum shooting schedule for each was two days.

So Marvin continued to make inquiries among his employees and the other Biograph faithful, discovering that no one really wanted so am-biguous a job, until he talked to his brother, Arthur. He was the studio's other cameraman, and apparently quite a competent one, but, as Bitzer said, "seldom affected with the exuberance of ambition" and self-described as "the captain of the good ship Take-It-Easy with nine decks and no bottom, which sails on forever and forever sails on."[13] Good-naturedly, he answered his brother's question by recommending Griffith as a fellow who "seems to have a lot of sense and some good ideas."[14]

So Griffith was called in, offered the job and responded with a decent hesitation. "I am working regularly for McCutcheon now. If I try directing he will not like it and if I fall down he won't give me any more parts." Marvin, however, reassured him, and Griffith left the office carrying one of Taylor's scenarios, *The Adventures of Dollie*.[15] "Gossip around the studio had it that the story was a 'lemon,'" according to Linda, but Griffith appears to have been unworried by the plot itself, which involved a child stolen off the lawn of her home by Gypsies, nailed up in a barrel and floated down a river and over a falls before she is rescued by some boys fishing in a quiet part of the stream. What he needed were strong actors to play the roles of the anguished parents and so he repaired to the studio's projection room to study what he had apparently not bothered to study before—the on-screen presences of the Biograph players. There he discovered, of all people, his own wife, whose work in one of Taylor's melodramas—which ended in her suicide—he liked. "You're good," he said, "quite surprised me."[16] He did not, however, like any of the studio's regular leading men, and so set forth to discover one, by the simple process of strolling Broadway in the area where actors made their rounds. There he saw, according to his own account, a man "something over six feet tall, dark, slightly waving hair" who "had the air of a gentleman." He approached the stranger and asked if he was an actor. "Well, some say 'yes,' but most say 'no,'" was the reply. Griffith then confessed that he was a Biograph director, quickly adding "that the pictures [they] were making were different." "Judging by the pictures I have seen, it would be a pretty good idea to make them different," the actor noted coolly, and Griffith, who was looking for a quality something like this, engaged the man on the spot.[17]

His name was Arthur Johnson, he was a minister's son (with that type's proverbial penchant for wild behavior) and he would be Griffith's leading man for the next two years, before decamping for Lubin and then falling victim, as so many of the first generation of stars did, to drunkenness. He died in 1916, but Linda Griffith, his first leading lady, would write, "To my mind no personality has since flickered upon the screen with quite the charm, lovableness, and magnetic humor that were his," and she adds that he remained throughout his brief time as lacking in affectation as he was when Griffith first encountered him.[18] In fact, he was one of the few movie actors ever to turn down a raise. And for a good reason—namely, that he was making plenty to take care of his modest needs and feared the effects of more. Indeed, it can be said that just as

Dollie initially stated another theme to which Griffith would again and again return—that of innocence imperiled—so Arthur Johnson was the model for a Griffith leading man—classically handsome, good-natured and easy to handle on the set. The male star of a Griffith film was Griffith himself, and he had no intention of contending with another strong masculine ego during production.

Still, Johnson, like Linda, was more than adequate to his immediate purpose, and with the addition of Charles Inslee, an actor he had known on the West Coast, to play the leader of the Gypsy band, the major parts in Griffith's debut film were cast—again characteristically, with fresh faces. He was also wise enough to consult the veteran Bitzer about locations—and, perhaps, about the protocol of working with a cameraman, though Bitzer's notes on this point do not entirely jibe with more formal records. In any event, Bitzer recommended the nearby Bronx River to Griffith as a stream wild enough to give the barrel supposed to contain the captured child a suitably thrilling ride. Griffith, however, chose to go elsewhere—Bitzer says to Hackensack in New Jersey, Mrs. Griffith to Sound Beach, Connecticut, where, indeed, according to studio records, exteriors were shot. It seems likely that both are right—that Griffith went with a small crew—and no actors—to do the barrel sequence in New Jersey, then matched this footage to that taken on the Connecticut location. The barrel was kept on course (that is, in focus) by piano wires attached to it and manipulated by technicians on shore and it appears that the day's work went well, except for Arthur Marvin, who was forced to wade into the stream repeatedly in order to get the shots the director wanted. It may be that the easygoing Marvin objected to these immersions, for, according to Bitzer, Griffith appeared at his rooming house around this time, saying, "So there you are! I have been looking for you. I need your help, Billy."

"What's the use telling you anything? . . . You'll end up taking someone else's advice anyway," Bitzer replied, still miffed that Griffith had gone to the wrong river. But Griffith prevailed, and Bitzer conducted him to his room, where they discussed *The Adventures of Dollie*. According to Bitzer, he took a piece of shirt cardboard and schematized the story in this way:

Heart Interest   Drama   Danger   Comedy   Rescue

Underneath each heading he entered the appropriate elements of the scenario. Just how this little diagram helped Griffith visualize his work in progress is unclear, but Bitzer did have some sound advice on how to induce Marvin to greater activity. Bribe him with beer, he suggested. And so it came about that when Griffith requested changes in camera setups Marvin would ask: "How far in, Mr. Griffith? Three feet? That will cost you just three bottles of beer—now, if you had said one that would have only cost you one bottle."[19]

Griffith seemed to feel confident about the little one-reeler and later claimed that "on the night *The Adventures of Dollie* went into the can, I went up on the roof of my cheap hotel to watch Haily's [sic] comet flash through the sky. Down in the street Gypsy fortune tellers were predicting a new era."[20] Never mind that Griffith was not then living in a hotel, never mind that the return of Halley's comet was two years off. For as his wife put it, "this movie business had gotten under his skin. David Griffith had tasted blood—cinema blood."[21]

More important, he might have sensed that he was the right man at the right time and in the right place for once in his life. He was older than most of the people he was to direct (he would continue to see to that), but he was not so old that he rejected new ideas. He had also just put in several years working on problems of dramatic construction and, as a result of his playwriting, was keenly attuned to the new medium's need to improve its storytelling methods.

Then, too, he was hungry. He may well have sensed that, after his failures as actor and writer, he had stumbled on one more chance—perhaps a last chance—to assert himself as the artist he hungered to be. Certainly we get a sense that he worked in a state of feverish creative excitement in the Biograph years which he had not attained before. This excitement cannot be entirely explained by the thrill of discovery, though that certainly entered into it; one gains the distinct impression that he was impelled from behind, from memory of all the dreary and bitter years that had gone before, as well as pulled on by the brightly beckoning future that he, almost alone, imagined for himself and this medium that other artists and would-be artists of that moment—in contrast to the businessmen and the technologists—so lightly dismissed. Finally, Griffith must have realized that Biograph, seemingly so near death, was the perfect place for innovation. It had nothing to lose—and if a man could possibly turn it around, his reputation would be made. Halley's comet should have burned the sky that night, for a new era was beginning for the thirty-three-year-old failure.

3
———

Even so, he had to endure a slight delay in whatever practical plans he might have designed up on his roof as the studio chiefs waited to see what their directorial candidate had achieved. There is some dispute as to how that time was filled and what the response to the 713-foot film was when it was finally projected. Bitzer claims that Griffith (and Linda) were set to work on "blue" movies, one of which he recalls featuring Linda sitting in a chair that was overturned, in the process of her fall exposing petticoats and ankles.[22] There is a certain persuasiveness in this. The studio was still cranking out material for the Mutuoscopes and it offered a line of slightly racy stuff to the penny arcades. We know, too, that Linda occasionally worked before the Mutuoscope cameras, appearing, for instance, in a re-creation of Harry Thaw's murder of Stanford White.

As for *Dollie* itself, Linda recalls that at the end of its first screening in the little projection room on the top floor of the studio, a moment's thoughtful silence broken at last by Henry Marvin: "That's it—that's something like it—at least."[23] Bitzer, however, says there was resistance to the film from exhibitors and that it was not until the public had spoken, by creating a demand for the film, that Griffith's future was assured.[24] There may be some truth to that, because Griffith did not receive a formal contract as a director until August 17, by which point *The Adventures of Dollie* had surpassed the house sales record. Prior to it, the most prints of a single film Biograph had been able to sell had been 15. They moved 25 prints of *Dollie*.

And for understandable reasons, since by the standards of the day the picture had quality. Its simple little story was told efficiently, in swift, strong action sequences, and despite its essentially preposterous central situation, Griffith obtained a true sense of audience identification with the anguished parents of the stolen child. Despite the stylized panto-mimic gestures employed by Linda and Arthur Johnson in these roles, some small transcendence of types and situation was achieved.

Whatever the exhibitors might or might not have said about the film when they previewed it, Griffith was given his next assignment two weeks later—and two weeks *before Dollie* went into release. Indeed, he had completed the first day's shooting on his sixth film, *The Greaser's Gaunt-let,* by the time *Dollie* opened its run at Keith and Proctor's in Union Square, within hailing distance of the Biograph headquarters on East Fourteenth Street.

Linda Arvidson describes that opening night: "What a day it was at the studio! However did we work, thinking of what the night held? But as the longest day ends, so did this one. No time to get home and pretty up for the party. With what meager facilities the porcelain basin and makeup shelf in the dressing room offered, we managed; rubbed off the grease paint and slapped on some powder; gave the hair a pat and a twist; at Silsbee's on Sixth Avenue and Fourteenth Street, we picked up nourishment; and then we beat it to Union Square.

"A world's premiere indeed—a tremendously important night to so many people who didn't know it. No taxis—not one private car drew up at the curb. The house filled up from passersby—frequenters of Union

Square—lured by a ten-cent entertainment. These were the people to be pleased—they who had paid out their little nickels and dimes. So when they sat through *Dollie's* seven hundred feet, interested, and not a snore was to be heard, we concluded that we'd had a successful night."[25]

Biograph's satisfaction with Griffith's work is manifested in its first contract with him. It called for a base salary of $50 a week, plus a royalty of one-twentieth of a cent on each foot sold to the exchanges. Biograph soon dispensed with all other directors and in the last six months of 1908 Griffith churned out 60 movies, an average of slightly better than two a week. So far as one can tell, he had virtual carte blanche in matters of story, casting and shooting. This does not mean that Griffith was entirely happy. Despite his newfound prosperity and the pleasure of command, his wife reports that "times came, agonizing days, when he would have given his life to be able to chuck the job. Mornings when on arising he would gaze long, long moments out the window, apparently seeing nothing. . . ." Then he would threaten to call in sick before setting forth, finally, on "heavy, leaden feet."[26]

The problem was a nagging sense that he was betraying his true calling, the theater, and it was compounded by the contempt of his old theatrical colleagues for his new career. But, unwittingly, they provided him with a new impetus. "It was *his job* and he would dignify it," Mrs. Griffith understates. And as soon as that resolution was made, "The leaden mornings came to be quite the exception to the rule. Many days were greeted with bright and merry song."[27] Here, in fact, we find the first—and perhaps more important—of the singular qualities Griffith brought to the movies. Many had held high aspirations for film, but for the most part they had been economic aspirations, tinged occasionally by vague notions that somehow they might make some ill-defined contribution to the general progress of humanity, probably as a useful adjunct to history, journalism or perhaps even science. Griffith was the first to conceive of movies as—potentially—an art form, and the first to hold consistently to that belief long enough to make a series of practical experiments aimed at realizing that potential. Simply stated, his belief, not yet articulated and, indeed, never directly stated, was that if the traditional art forms would not find room for him, then he would make an art form of his own.

4

Griffith was not immediately able to set about realizing this huge ambition. The pressure of turning out two films a week to meet the unyielding studio release schedule was enormous. In the Griffith canon, these first six months merely make the promises he was later to fulfill. But having said that, one must concede that the accomplishments of this period were enormously significant.

Griffith himself, his latter-day publicists and not a few film historians have emphasized the technical achievements of the Biograph years—the invention (or rediscovery) of the various devices (close-ups, fades, cross-cutting, etc.) that he brought together for the first time to create a coherent, basic screen grammar. And, indeed, almost from the beginning Griffith experimented, in the course of his sixteen-hour working days, with his cameras and with the resources of the laboratory—showing a particularly keen eye for the possibility of making conscious use of effects that, heretofore, had been thrown out as technical mistakes.

But he also had, right from the start, a natural ease with the camera. In his ninth film, *The Fatal Hour*, the heroine—a detective trying to break up a white slave ring—is tied to a chair, a gun is aimed at her and set to be triggered when the hands of a clock reach a certain point. While she struggles to free herself, a carriageful of rescuers races to save her, and Griffith, besides showing the gun and the ticking clock in occasional close-ups, also crosscut between helpless maiden and would-be saviors, thus greatly enhancing the suspense. It was, of course, merely an adaptation of the techniques of stage melodrama, which often put parallel actions on stage simultaneously, but Griffith was the first to discern and stress the not-obscure analogy between this stage form and the screen—probably because he was the first film director with a solid background in melodrama.

There was, apparently, no objection from studio, exhibitors or audience to such a novel structure. But in September and October, when he shot the first of his three versions of Tennyson's *Enoch Arden*, under the title *After Many Years*, incidentally giving first expression to a theme that would haunt him throughout his career, that of the wanderer's longing for the home he once left too blithely, he ran into objections. The film lacked a chase, in itself a considerable novelty, and indeed it contained very little action of any sort. Moreover, he risked a pair of parallel shots: Annie Lee at the seaside, visualizing her shipwrecked husband on his desert isle (how she knew he was on an island at all was never explained); Enoch on that barren strand, visualizing the long-gone comforts of home. When he proposed this scene, an unnamed executive asked: "How can you tell a story jumping about like that? The people won't know what it's about." To which Griffith replied, "Well, doesn't Dickens write that way?" "Yes, but that's Dickens; that's novel writing; that's different." "Oh, not so much, these are picture stories; not so different."[28] And he went ahead, to the confusion of no one, it would seem. In an interview he gave in 1922, to a reporter from the *Times* of London, Griffith claims he went home, "re-read one of Dickens' novels, and came back next day to tell them they could either make use of my idea or dismiss me."[29]

Whether, in fact, he found it necessary to take such a stern line, or whether it was even possible for him to do so this early in his career, is debatable and as one considers the incident, one imagines that it was less the switchback that was being protested than the novel use of the camera to plunge, however momentarily, into the stream of his characters' consciousness. In any event, Dickens, the most popular storyteller of his time, had influenced (and had been influenced by) the melodrama, and both, no doubt, were drawn upon by Griffith as he attempted to broaden the scope of screen storytelling. Indeed, one rather imagines that Griffith's reference to Dickens was a rationalization and that the novelist's influence, as Sergei Eisenstein was the first to point out, was both more profound and less conscious than this incident might lead one to believe.

The point is worth pausing over. Both men were the sons of fathers who were, at best, rather cold in their relationships with their sons (though both, it appears, made some attempts to have it otherwise). Both knew relatively comfortable circumstances as youngsters, then suffered shocking plunges into near-poverty while they were still children (though Griffith suffered no experience as devastating as Dickens's six months in the blacking factory). Both, thereafter, lived lives poised dangerously between destitution and the lower rungs of middle-class respectability, looking down in fear, looking up in envy. Their most characteristic works, as a result, often feature figures who endure great rises and falls in status, and often pursue parallel plot lines—one showing lives of great wealth, the other showing the lives of the poor, nearby and unacknowledged.

Nor is this the end of the comparisons between the great writer and the filmmaker who so frequently acknowledged him as his master. Both were men of prodigious energy, turning out vast bodies of work almost without pause. Both were men with a taste for theatrical self-display (though ironically, it was the writer, not the professional actor, who enjoyed the greatest triumphs on stage, Griffith never knowing, as a performer, anything like the acclaim Dickens achieved with his readings). Both, finally, were men with an obsessive interest in adolescent girls, each finally irreparably damaging their lives by their infatuations with young actresses.[30]

Of course, these uncanny (and mainly unconscious) connections between master and distant student would not become clear for many years. And meantime, Griffith was pursuing some purely filmic innovations that owed little to either literary or theatrical precedent. Even before he began his relatively sophisticated experiments in parallelism, Griffith had begun the steady process of moving his camera closer and closer to the action. In a film he shot almost simultaneously with *The Fatal Hour*, an adaptation of a Jack London short story, which the studio called *For Love of Gold*, he even dared to change angles in the middle of a scene (though his second shot was not yet a medium shot, let alone a close-up). By eliminating the foreground in the new angle he hoped to suggest to audiences that his players were thinking. Interestingly, both of these films were shot by Marvin, not Bitzer, indicating that Griffith was beginning to free the camera from its distant, immobile, conventionalized position well before entering into his creative partnership with the latter. He seems instinctively to have sensed that the camera had an unrealized potential as a more active participant in the creation of the mood, the manipulation of audience response, and as a kind of psychologist.

This liberating process, of course, accelerated when Griffith went to Henry Marvin, sometime in the early fall, and asked to replace Arthur Marvin with Bitzer. The very fact that he could without apparent difficulty get the boss's brother replaced indicates how quickly he had gathered prestige within the confines of the studio. He simply said that though he liked Arthur Marvin, he thought he could achieve better teamwork with Bitzer, and it was done—though Marvin occasionally worked for him thereafter.

In these first six months Bitzer and Griffith made their first primitive fade-outs, a major contribution to film grammar. It was the necessity for stopping the lens down outdoors that suggested the technique. If Bitzer went to a slower setting while the camera was turning, a perceptible dimming of the image resulted. At this time it was a movie convention that all comedies and romances must end with a kiss, which was all right with Griffith, except that when the embrace was held too long, audiences began to giggle. What was needed, he thought, was some film equivalent to the theatrical slow curtain. He had seen out-takes of the fade effect—which seemed only to be ruined film to everyone else—and now he simply ordered Bitzer to deliberately create the effect when they were working on a kiss sequence. It had the desired suppressive effect on audience risibility.[31]

There were many more such innovations—all rather casually introduced as practical solutions to practical problems rather than as historically momentous experiments—but at the outset, it is well to bear in mind the wise remark of Edward Wagenknecht that "none of this is very important. What matters is the use Griffith made of all these devices," simply because *"This was the right way to tell a story on film"* (Wagenknecht's italics). He adds significantly that upon going back to look at Biograph films in the 1960s he was "surprised" at how sparingly Griffith used them, since "If one were to judge by what many film critics have written, one would conclude that all Biograph films were a tightly woven tissue of tricky, brilliant technical devices, a never-ending show of virtuosity for its own sake." Actually, as he says, the opposite is true.[32]

Wagenknecht places equal stress on the fact that Griffith used charming people, and he used them, for the most part, "while the dew of morning was fresh upon them." There is high truth in this observation and there is an important corollary to it, especially worth noting at this point, that when Griffith was reaching out beyond the "flotsam and jetsam" of the Biograph hangers-on, he was looking not just for fresh, youthful faces but, as importantly, for people willing to take movies with the same seriousness that he did. One has no doubt that the grammar of film would have developed without Griffith's work, but one is not so certain that the tense, unending dialectic between art and commerce would have been established without Griffith to show the way. It might have been all commerce; there might have been, in the United States anyway, no tradition of rebellion against the conventional commercial wisdom to which others could repair. Indeed, already the voice of the censor was heard in the land, objecting to a film version of *The Great Thaw Trial*, to a thing called *Murphy's Wake*, in which the mourners at an Irish funeral were observed tippling at the side of the bier, to a dozen other racily titled and no doubt valueless movies which a Chicago judge was moved to declare "cause, indirectly or directly, more juvenile crime coming into my court than all other causes combined."[33]

The movies, therefore, had need of Griffith and the people who gathered around him, people who would, under his influence, come to see what the courts did not formally recognize until 1948 (in *The Miracle* case): that they were not inevitably "a common show," that at the very least, movies could be an uncommon show, and very possibly an art—thus entitling them to the protection of the First Amendment. It was Griffith, and at first only Griffith, who insisted, mostly because his starved and aching ego demanded it, that they be treated by others as seriously as he treated them. Without his example—and without his films—there is little doubt that censorship would have been imposed on the movies even more heavily, and with even more stultifying effect, than it was. Beyond that the magnetism of his presence and the force of his early idealism attracted to the movies a class of craftsmen and actors that they desperately needed in order to grow.

In the beginning the statuesque and worldly seeming Marion Leonard, whose experience had also been chiefly in melodramas, alternated with Linda Arvidson playing dramatic leads and, within a year, she would be among the first to make what seemed to the producers an unconscionable salary demand—$100 a week, which was compromised to $75. But even before Griffith had signed his own Biograph contract, he had heard, probably from the actor Harry Salter (who appeared in the second Griffith film, *The Redman and the Child*), about a young actress, then working for Vitagraph, who had a youthful, exuberant quality that his other women lacked. Her name was Florence Lawrence and she would achieve lasting fame as the first "Biograph Girl" and, indeed, as the first actress to receive publicity in her own name and thus to be the first movie "star" in something like the modern sense, when Carl Laemmle lured her away from Griffith to work under his IMP (Independent Motion Picture Company) trademark. Griffith saw her first, in company with his wife, at a nickelodeon on Amsterdam Avenue and 169th Street. The film was *The Dispatch Bearer*, a western of sorts, and she was "a vivid, gallant little person"[34] whose appeal was not unlike that of Dorothy Gish. She had begun her career as "Baby Flo, the child wonder-whistler," had worked for several other movie companies before going to Vitagraph, where, for $15 a week, she not only acted but sewed canvas scenery and costumes, too. Griffith gave her $25 and told her she could leave her needle at home. She proved to be his kind of worker. "The movies were the breath of life to her. When she wasn't working in a picture, she was in some movie theater seeing a picture. After the hardest day, she was never too tired to see the new release and if work ran into the night hours, between scenes she'd wipe off the make-up and slip out to a movie show."[35]

Eventually she married the similarly ambitious Salter and they were fired for daring to discuss, with Lubin, the possibility of a better contract (Griffith was always rather hurt and sullen when his people left and generally refused to bargain with them over money). Her career as a star was cut short when, in 1915, she turned back into a burning studio to help rescue coworkers and was temporarily paralyzed as a result of the injuries she sustained. Salter died a few years later, other marriages failed, she tried a comeback, settled into bit roles under an M-G-M contract and then, in 1938, committed suicide. For the moment, however, she was a potent factor in Griffith's burgeoning success and, teamed with Arthur Johnson, she formed part of a highly appealing romantic team.

Not so immediately important, but still a man whose enthusiasm for the movies commended him to Griffith, was one Michael Sinnott, who would become better known as Mack Sennett. He had been a boxing trainer, a small-parts performer in musical comedy, a drifter like so many other early movie people; not well educated, he was held in a certain contempt by Mrs. Griffith and the other ladies of the gathering Biograph stock company because he lacked polish and an aspiration for the higher things. With his "burly bear-like figure; long gorilla arms . . . a wide, good-natured grin on his face" he struck Griffith as an interesting and photographically useful human type and so he gave Sennett small roles on an irregular basis, allowed him to hang around and enjoyed the close friendship this odd-looking fellow struck up with Johnson, who was in every way his opposite—"tall, nonchalant, with the easy air of an aristocrat." He reports that on their frequent pub crawls Sennett would mime the role of Johnson's idiot brother while Johnson arrogantly refused him food and drink and told vicious stories about him to the other drinkers.

"They took great delight in making sillies of themselves," Griffith mildly commented.[36]

He also discovered he shared a couple of convictions with Sennett. One was that there was some sort of future to be had in the movies; the other was that walking was healthful and mentally stimulating exercise. "When Griffith walked, I walked," Sennett later declared. "I fell in, matched strides, and asked questions. . . . We used to stroll about, gaze at the river, wander the streets." In the process, Griffith advised him that being a director seemed to him to hold more potential rewards than acting; he also confided some of his aspirations for the medium. " 'I want to put together full-length stories,' he would say. 'Not merely little scenes such as we photograph now. And I don't see any sense in always showing so much. For instance, we have a scene in Room A. We finish with it and the characters go to Room B. Why do we have to photograph the people walking from Room A to Room B? Just cut to Room B. Writers do it. It's done on the stage. Why not in movies? And in pictures we can do so many things we can't do at all on stage. Why not move a camera up close and show an actor's full face? That would reveal his emotions, give him a chance to show what he is thinking. . . .' "[37] There was more, much more, according to Sennett in the perambulating seminars—talk of mood lighting, for example, talk of showing in full the great spectacular scenes the melodramatic stage had been able only to suggest. It may be that, recalling all this many years later, Sennett imputed to Griffith conscious prefigurations of what were still only unconscious stirrings. But if Griffith was able to point out to his bosses that Dickens, too, had used cross-cutting, isn't it equally possible that he saw in Dickens's marvelous narrative drive, in which he gathered together seemingly disparate plot elements and allowed their relationships to become clear in their own good time, and almost incidentally, as the story moved along, the beginnings of what came to be called montage? So it seemed to Sergei Eisenstein, in what remains the best single essay on Griffith's art, and so Sennett's memoirs would seem to prove.

At all events, the crude but highly intelligent Sennett, who called Griffith—in a lovely and oft-quoted tribute—"my day school, my adult education program, my university,"[38] became a member of the team, a well-regarded inventor of, and actor in, comic scenes—a gift not highly valued or generously distributed in the Biograph stock company. He never did sell Griffith on his greatest comic insight—that cops were funny—but by the fall he had worked up a passable imitation of Max Linder's comic boulevardier (widely seen in America as a result of his Pathé films) and got his first leading role in a scenario—the only one—dreamed up by Billy Bitzer and called *The Curtain Pole*. In it, gorgeously spifflicated, he had to maneuver the ungainly title object through the streets of Fort Lee, New Jersey, by various modes of transportation and at considerable peril to himself and to innocent passersby. It remains one of Griffith's few ventures into pure farce and for an essentially humorless man, it is a rather surprisingly successful one, very possibly because Griffith allowed Sennett a full, free rein.

So the Biograph nucleus began to form. Hard-drinking Owen Moore, later to become Mary Pickford's first husband, signed on in these first months—another leading man not too dissimilar from Arthur Johnson, though lacking his off-screen charm. And, already there, waiting to be discovered, as it were, when Griffith came on the scene, were two recent graduates of Saint Joseph's parochial school in the neighborhood, both of whom had been introduced to the studio by the parish priest. One was Jimmie Smith, who started out in the shipping room but who became Griffith's film editor, a job for which there were few precedents and which was to become an extraordinarily taxing one, given Griffith's habit of working without scripts, as he moved on to feature films. The other was Robert Harron. A prop boy when Griffith arrived, he was quickly promoted to bit parts as an adolescent before becoming Griffith's leading juvenile and one of the best male actors he ever had. "If he loved anyone, he loved Bobby," a Biograph worker of the time has recalled.[39]

There is no question that, from the first, Griffith's will completely dominated them all. Given a position of command, he discovered a talent to command that he had never before exercised. Nearly everyone who came under his sway at Biograph had been an orphan, usually fatherless, very often on the theatrical road since early childhood. Many of them—especially the women—needed a patriarchal figure in their lives and that is what, by accident and design, Griffith gave them. People remembered the reverential hush that fell over the assembled cast when Griffith strode onto the set, they remembered the distance he maintained at the breaks—Sennett's walks and talks were definitely the exception to the rule—they remembered that even his own wife was addressed, in public, as "Miss Arvidson." Indeed, it was not for close on a year that it became generally known that they were married. At first, Bitzer recalled, "we none of us suspected they knew each other outside the studio walls, for they were never seen together, neither entering nor leaving the studio."[40]

One cannot help but feel that in these first months, as Griffith formed his professional manner, he was creating the elements of future failure as well as future success. His secretiveness would grow, and his inability to develop, among his coworkers, critics whom he could freely trust would result in a dangerous isolation and, in time, it would seem to even so sympathetic a friend as Lillian Gish that there was no one near him "who loved him enough to be able to say 'no' to him."[41]

Or perhaps one might more accurately say that he let no such person penetrate his reserve.

5

For the moment, though, that was no problem. The Biograph sales curve began its steady upward trend in 1908 and if that first half year did not result in any short masterpieces of the sort he would very soon start delivering to the exhibitors, it did demonstrate the remarkable range of material he could handle. His cultural aspirations were served not only in his 1908 adaptation of *Enoch Arden* but also in a tabloid *Taming of the Shrew* ("Too much praise cannot be bestowed on this picture," a trade journal said[42]), as well as in his Jack London adaptations. "Literary" productions of this sort would come to represent a larger share of Griffith's Biograph output and they would have their effect in increasing the studio's prestige as well as that of the movies in general. But there were also crime melodramas and stories about the sea and many that were set in various vanishing American wildernesses and reflected the prevalent nostalgia—the first but not the last we would suffer—about the loss of these unspoiled lands to civilization. Some of these films were notable for their extremely sympathetic treatment of the Indian as a natural nobleman, and that, too, represented a recognition of shifting popular attitudes, a first, guilty observation that the Red Man had been ill used in the century just past.

Virtually no setting was a stranger to Griffith in these first months. He ranged back in history as far as the Middle Ages and he ranged geographically as far afield as Japan. But even so, the bulk of his films were contemporary in time and local in setting. He took his cameras to Hudson Street and to the Curb stock exchange to capture some of the vitality of city life, to Cos Cob, Connecticut, and, of course, to Fort Lee, that first American motion picture capital, in search of the middle class, in the process beginning, according to some authorities, the genre we now know as the situation comedy in a series of split reels about the Jones family, a typical American family encountering typically American *contretemps* in the course of attending a fashionable ball, throwing a card party, staging amateur theatricals and so on. It can fairly be said that of all the screen forms he would undertake in his career, only one—the spectacle—was entirely absent from his 1908 work.

But one should not be deluded by Griffith's apparent range. Taking these films—and most of the later Biographs—as a group, one is perhaps more impressed by their unity than by their diversity. Again, it is Eisenstein who gives us the clue. "In order to understand Griffith, one must visualize an America made up of more than visions of speeding automobiles, streamlined trains, racing ticker tape, inexorable conveyor-belts.

One is obliged to comprehend [a] second side of America as well—America, the traditional, the patriarchal, the provincial."[43] It was the Soviet director's contention that as Dickens's narrative manner gave Griffith the clue as to the techniques he might employ to capture, on film, the greatness and speed and, yes, the terror, of urban, commercial America, so the writer's obsessive concern with the intimate details of humble private lives may have inspired Griffith to a similarly obsessive concern with similar material.

There is more to it than that, of course. The life of the farm and the life of the urban poor were the subjects Griffith knew best, knew by this time instinctively. What could have been more natural for him than to turn this most realistic medium to the task of recording the very texture of these life-styles. Moreover, though ambition urged him on to grander, more "poetic" subjects, to material he did not know as well and never handled as surely as he did this, he remained throughout his career attached to "the traditional, the patriarchal, the provincial." In the worst and most pretentious failures of his later years, whenever he turned to poverty, to street life, to the dusty rural roads of remembered childhood, the films would suddenly ring with truth. And, indeed, the two unquestionable masterpieces of the 1920s, *Way Down East* and *Isn't Life Wonderful*, attain that status mostly because of the director's sympathy for the problems and values of the poor, the simple, the modest.

After giving due credit to Griffith the technical innovator, Griffith the romantic poet *manqué*, Griffith the product of the melodramatic and spectacle stage, the important thing to note is that in these first months at Biograph he had found his best and truest line and that his later "development" away from it represented an acquiescence to commercial pressure for grandeur, as well as an acquiescence to the less attractive elements of his own ambition. Many years later, when Eisenstein met Griffith and praised him for his "intimate" films, the old man reported, rather sadly, that "they were made for myself and were invariably rejected by the exhibitors."[44]

The second half of the statement was untrue, a product of the self-pitying mood of Griffith's later years, when he liked to pose as the unappreciated artist. For the mix of subjects produced at Biograph during the Griffith years remained essentially as it was in these first months, meaning that his intimate pictures achieved sufficient commercial acceptance to permit him to go on making them even as he pressed on with more ambitious projects. Still, there emerges a very strong impression that the conditions under which Griffith worked at Biograph—the necessity to average close to two films a week—suited his natural—and essential—gift better than any others he would encounter and one retreats to Baudelaire's essay on "The Painter of Modern Life" to suggest the nature of his first greatness: "For the sketch of manners, the depiction of bourgeois life and the pageant of fashion, the technical means that is the most expeditious and the least costly will obviously be the best. The more beauty that the artist can put into it, the more valuable will be his work; but in trivial life, in the daily metamorphosis of external things, there is a rapidity of movement which calls for an equal speed of execution from the artist." In this connection, Baudelaire spoke of the uses of lithography, of the art of Daumier and Gavarni, but one rather imagines he would have appreciated very well what the movie camera could do to render into art the materials and feelings of everyday existence. In any event, he described Griffith when he described the type of artist suited to this recording work: "Observer, philosopher, flâneur—call him what you will; but whatever words you use in trying to define this kind of artist, you will certainly be led to bestow upon him some adjective which you could not apply to the painter of the eternal, or at least more lasting things. . . . Sometimes he is a poet; more often he comes closer to the novelist or the moralist; he is the painter of the passing moment and of all the suggestions of eternity that it contains."[45]

Novelist and moralist Griffith certainly was, and one cannot escape the observation that it was often when he attempted the poetic that he succumbed to afflatus, that it is when he tried to intellectualize about the things which caught his eye that he became the most pompously literary and rhetorical. There were times, of course, when the sheer majesty of his pictorial gift carried all before him, swept away all objections as niggling. But the fact remains that Griffith was at his most approachable, his most exciting and his most charming—in short, close to the height of his powers—as he pressed against the formal limits imposed upon him in the Biograph years. In time he would produce several flawed, large-scale masterpieces, but as 1908 ended so did his apprenticeship, and he was now ready to produce literally dozens of smaller but more nearly perfect masterpieces—complete in a single reel. Nowhere is his art less debatable than it is in these films. "Every country, to its pleasure and glory, has possessed a few men of this stamp," Baudelaire concluded his discussion of the painter of manners, and there can be no doubt that in this century, regardless of the medium in which they worked, Griffith belonged to that select few.

CHAPTER SIX

Mastery

IN the summer of 1908, just after Griffith began directing, J. J. Kennedy met with Edison's managers in an attempt to compromise their differences about Biograph's joining the Motion Picture Patents Company. He offered to guarantee Edison $150,000 in profits if it would finally accept Biograph's patent claims as genuine and in effect let his company join the alliance on its own terms. The people who remembered and resented William K. L. Dickson's departure had by this time left Edison, and the inventor himself had disposed of his interests in Biograph. So the moment seemed ripe for compromise and to further soften Edison's resistance Kennedy invited its representatives to come to the studio, inspect the Biograph camera, watch it in operation and even take its film back to the Edison laboratory for development. It was a bold and unprecedented breach of industrial security and, sometime that summer, Edison's people came to see D. W. Griffith and company at work.

There were no immediate results, perhaps because Biograph's precarious financial position commended to the Edison management a policy of watchful waiting for bankruptcy. It was not until mid-December that an Edison lawyer called Kennedy to discuss terms and then Kennedy adamantly refused to bargain, insisting that he would put his cameras on the market, licensing all nontrust companies to use them and thus deepen the state of anarchy that the trust firms so devoutly wished to end. Within a day Edison capitulated and when all the agreements were signed it was J. J. Kennedy who emerged as the new president of the Motion Picture Patents Company.

The acceptance of Griffith's films by exhibitors and public was probably a factor in Edison's coming to terms, since it was now obvious that the studio's product was, for the first time, able to compete on equal terms—more than equal terms, as it turned out—with that of the major trust firms. Griffith directly benefited from the prosperity his work brought to Biograph: for one thing, there was now enough money for larger casts, more expansive stories and more location work than ever before. Indeed, only a handful of films were shot entirely in the studio and the company ranged all over Connecticut, New Jersey and New York State in search of novel locales. Perhaps more important was the general sense of security the studio's new prosperity brought. Other directors, working for the independents, might have to carry revolvers on location to protect their camera from the trust's saboteurs or be prepared to quickly hide their patented equipment from spies (hence the term "blanket outfits" for independents) or simply to use inferior machines, but there were no such distractions for Griffith. And if Biograph never entirely abandoned its pinch-penny habits, he was still able to get most of what he wanted—an extra day's shooting when he needed it, the right to make "special arrangements" with a particularly desirable performer, above all, the right to be left alone to make his little pictures as he felt they ought to be made. The risks, after all, were tiny—the negative cost of a one-reel film was never more than a few hundred dollars—and the returns were increasingly gratifying. Indeed, George Pratt has argued that 1909 "was the first of Griffith's two miraculous years, matched later on, in 1914, when he finished the shooting of *The Birth of a Nation* and began *Intolerance*."[1]

Outwardly, the studio did not change. Early in the morning a little knot of actors looking for day work would congregate on the steps of the unimposing brownstone building, or, if the day were cold or damp, in its front hall. Those who were beckoned farther in would be directed past the front offices on the first floor, where Doc Dougherty studied scripts and wrote the weekly bulletin describing new releases, and Henry Marvin and a changing cast of bookkeepers (including one who was fired for allowing extra girls to keep the stockings the studio had bought for them to wear in a picture) kept track of expenses, and on up the stairs to the ballroom-studio where Griffith's small oak rolltop desk stood in a corner. There, amidst a permanent confusion of folded flats and rolled-up carpets, under the banks of arc lights and Cooper-Hewitt lamps, he would look them over and assign them roles. Whereupon they would be sent to the basement to select and change into costumes in an area that was permanently permeated by the smell of chemicals from the laboratory. Most of the space here was given over to prop storage and it was among them that costumers carelessly deposited trunks of rented finery. It was among them, in a sometimes mad scramble to find items that fit their roles and themselves, that the actors selected the day's wardrobe. It was here also that the crap game, attended by male actors awaiting their calls, endlessly flourished. The trunks also doubled as dining tables at the lunch break, which was often delayed until midafternoon if the director lost track of time. When that happened there was a good chance that the evening meal would be taken here as well and that the workday would stretch to midnight or beyond.

The regimen was no less arduous when location shooting was in order. If, for example, they were working in New Jersey, the actors would dash from homes to subway, get off at the 125th Street stop of the West Side IRT and dash for a saloon called Murphy's, where they would congregate to eat a longshoreman's breakfast before catching the eight forty-five ferry for Fort Lee. A couple of hotel rooms would be rented to serve as dressing rooms and when the players were suitably costumed, "Old Man Brown" and his son, each driving a two-seater buggy, would appear to take them to whatever location had been chosen for them by Miss Gene Gauntier, who, besides scouting scenery, also did a bit of story editing for Doc Dougherty. In due course an express wagon, bearing props, cameras and wardrobe changes, brought out from the studio on a run that often began as early as 4 A.M., would arrive and the day's work would begin—not to end until the light failed.

Sometimes location filming was decided upon on the spur of the moment, as when, early in 1909, a lovely snowstorm blanketed the city and Griffith improvised *The Politician's Love Story*—in which Mack Sennett played the first of his few straight leads—in order to take advantage of the snowscapes in Central Park. The film looked so handsome, despite a rather trivial story, that the Biograph Bulletin was able without much hyperbole to sell it as "a photographic work of art, comprising the most beautiful winter scenes ever obtained."[2] Here Griffith was the beneficiary of a lucky accident, for Arthur Marvin was forced to shoot into the sun and he obtained some strikingly beautiful backlight effects. Or was it luck? Griffith was pushing his people hard—insisting on more outdoor work, for example, than his competitors—and the cameramen in particular were frequently forced by his demands to go against the customs of their craft, discovering in the process that they could be bent and even broken to happy effect.

There must have been people who resented Griffith's demands, others who, if they worked willingly enough, did not take the movie medium as seriously as he and his favorites did. At least one Biograph worker has told later interviewers that if he had known that those little films were going to be shown in museums and discussed in books and articles he would have practiced his craft with more care. But, for the most part, the reminiscences are colored in warm hues. The problems the Biograph people were called upon to solve were novel and therefore stimulating, the comradeship was fun and, at least at first, there was little serious rivalry or jealousy.

What there was of these emotions was generally stirred deliberately by Griffith. In the morning rehearsals, he might ask two or three people to try each leading role, about which they generally knew only what he cared to tell, comparing what they delivered with his imagined ideal and making his choices in his own rather mysterious way. He was always a secretive man, but in the early years, at least, he had "a happy way of working. He invited confidence and asked and took suggestions from anyone sufficiently interested to make them. His enthusiasm became quite infectious," his wife wrote.[3]

The model for the organization he was beginning to build was the theatrical stock company. By forcing his people to play a lead one day, an extra role the next, he kept them in a state of malleable anxiety and he also prevented most of them from getting exaggerated notions of their importance in the Biograph scheme of things. Moreover, this policy prevented other centers of creative or artistic power from developing within the studio. As Blanche Sweet was later to say, "Griffith was the whole show." She added: "I think he liked the idea that he could take anyone and make her into an actress," though she thought it "just a fluke" that so many of his casually recruited players turned out so well and rather resented his belief that he was almost solely responsible for the development of their skills.[4]

Perhaps as Sweet suggests, Griffith overestimated his contribution to the many careers that began under his guidance. In later years, certainly, he rather meanly regretted that he had no share in the financial rewards that were paid these careers—contrasting his position with that of the studios that, through their long-term contracts, did share the benefits derived from their taking risks on untried talent, patiently building up their contract players. Be that as it may, Griffith indeed clung to the repertory system to his disadvantage in later years, and shied away from star casting when it would likely have been to his advantage to embrace it. Still, looking back over the star system's history, who can say that Griffith was wrong in opposing it? Can anyone honestly say that better work or happier lives resulted from the custom of paying huge wages to players? Can anyone honestly say that the atmosphere of the industry was improved by the unreality and hysteria that million-dollar star contracts created? Didn't these have the effect of enormously increasing the risks, and hence the pressures on creative people?

It's impossible to say, of course. And one has to bear in mind that in this period the movie business began to grow at an annual rate of some $25 million. Actors would have been less than human if they had not shown a desire to participate more fully in these huge, sudden profits; producers would have been less than human if they had not offered such participation to performers with a proved ability to attract the largest share of the growing audience.

In the early Biograph years, there is evidence of only one case of open rebellion over Griffith's primacy. The evidence indicates that it was Griffith's old pal Charles Inslee, who had worked quite steadily for Griffith since *The Adventures of Dollie,* who made the challenge. The setting was an island in Long Island Sound, and Inslee, as he often was, was engaged to play an Indian brave. At lunchtime he indicated that he wanted to be waited on, but none of the crew would serve him. Finally, sulkily, he approached the table, only to discover that the beer was all gone. "Where's my beer?" he cried, pounding his bare chest. A girl laughed, then everyone did. "Heap big Indian Charlie's lost his beer," someone shouted. Angered, and no doubt feeling something of a fool, Charlie retired, took off his costume and makeup, donned his street garb, appropriated a rowboat and struck out for the mainland. Griffith spotted him, ran down the beach yelling to Inslee to stop. "Go to hell," was the reply. Griffith waded into the water, grabbed the actor by his collar and hauled him back to shore, telling him to "stop being an ass."

"I'm the one that makes the hits in all the pictures you make," shouted the aggrieved thespian. "If it wasn't for me, you wouldn't be so God almighty. I didn't get my beer, so I'm walking out on you right now."

"Charlie, I'll give you just three minutes to take off that coat and get back into your make-up."

"I'll take off my coat . . . but I won't get into my make-up," came the threatening reply.

Whereupon Griffith threw a punch at the actor and knocked him down. Inslee grabbed for a beer bottle and came up swinging it. He missed, and Griffith knocked him out with another punch, then turned quickly away.

"Leave him alone," he said. "Everyone back to work." There was a pause while the amazed group struggled to digest what they had just witnessed. "Children! Come! Come!" said Griffith. "We can't be here all day, the sun will be leaving all too soon. We're losing time."

They were back before the camera when Inslee appeared, sheepish but made up. "Sorry to have kept you waiting, boss," he mumbled.

"Oh, that's all right, Charlie . . . I knew you wouldn't fail me. Sorry about the beer."

It was the first, but by no means the last, time that Griffith maintained discipline on one of his sets with his fists—which came in particularly handy when he had to recruit platoons of extras for his spectacles from the lower reaches of the social order. But, despite his forgiving tone, he and Inslee apparently came to blows a second time—when Griffith was demonstrating a fight sequence—and the actor disappeared from the Biograph records early in 1909, never to appear there again.

Said Bitzer: "Griffith recognized temperament in a woman, but never in a man. He reasoned a woman was delicately molded, her nerves easily fagged and upset, and when she showed signs of extreme fatigue it would be better to send her home to rest . . . for she would be sure to show up the next day refreshed . . . and the danger of temperament entirely gone. But in a man it was impudence, cussedness, or he was just a damn fool, and should be treated as such."[5]

It should not be imagined that Griffith's early achievements were simply the result of charm reinforced, when necessary, by strong discipline. There is no doubt that his dawn-to-dusk, seven-day-a-week work habits impressed his people. He was on the set before them and he stayed after they left (their last contact with him came when he made out vouchers for them to take to the paymaster in order to collect their day's wages). They knew that he spent his free evenings and his Sundays editing his own work, studying that of the competition, reading scenarios. They were aware, too, of his rather impressive reserve. Even on location, he rarely unbent or mixed with the crowd; he tended to take his meals with Bitzer and perhaps one or two special favorites among the stock company. When they lunched off the costume trunks in the studio basement, they knew he was down the street at Luchow's, savoring an extra beer or two—he drank nothing stronger in those days—with key staff members, planning the afternoon's work.

But they also knew that in order to get the effects he wanted he would go to any length, play any sort of psychological game he thought might be helpful. Sometimes the techniques were simple. On location one very hot day, there was a certain understandable reluctance to clear a path through some high grass to the door of an old house being used as a background. Griffith grabbed a shovel, worked for a while, paused to remark that one certainly felt a lot cooler after he'd worked up a bit of a sweat—Tom Sawyer's ploy. On another occasion, a large group of actors, engaged to portray society leaders having a high old time at a bachelor dinner, simply could not be worked into the requisite mood of gay abandon, mostly because the rented costumes fitted particularly badly this time. After trying everything he could think of, Griffith simply announced that he was going out for a walk and that if, in his absence, they could work the scene out he would see that they all got a bonus of five dollars for the day's work. One of the actors proposed that they invent a college yell to be shouted as they raised Owen Moore, playing the bridegroom, on their shoulders and carried him around the room. The cheer went:

> Biograph!
> Hah! Hah! Hah!
> Ten Dollars,
> Ten Dollars,
> Rah! Rah! Rah!

And it gave the scene exactly the exuberance it needed.

So it went. He would have a gun fired off, without warning, near an actress who was having trouble registering surprise and fear. Or he would insult Mary Pickford's lover—and eventual first husband, Owen Moore—

getting her angry enough to fly at him, and then turning the camera on her before all her passion was spent.[6]

Not, perhaps, master strokes of psychology, but good enough, and successful, stimulating variants on his basic techniques. To hear some of the women tell it, Griffith spent most of his rehearsal time talking things over with his players, gently encouraging them to try various bits of business he suggested, asking them to counter with ideas of their own. Doubtless, there was a fair amount of this kind of give-and-take, and no witness disputes Griffith's willingness to accept ideas from any source. But the fact is, as one man recalled, "He loved to act himself and he would practically act out entire scenes, playing all the roles, on some occasions. On others he would minutely correct an actor's gesture or expression."[7] In short, he dominated his sets and only occasionally, despite his unfailing correctness, were those sets governed by anything like the democratic spirit.

The departure of old friends and the arrival of new faces served to keep the company in a state of stimulating, more or less constant flux, as did Griffith's habit—lifelong as it turned out—of encouraging jealousies to enhance competition. In this first full year of Griffith's regime the new arrivals included among the women Kate Bruce, who would play mothers and grandmothers for Griffith at every stage of his career and Blanche Sweet, who made one film and then departed for a stage contract, delaying her full-scale membership in the stock company for over a year.

Among the men, none was more curious than Henry "Pathé" Lehrman. Legend has it that he was conductor of a streetcar that plied Fourteenth Street and whose curiosity was aroused by the colorful comings and goings at Biograph. The facts are scarcely less curious. He was an usher at the Unique Theater whither Mack Sennett repaired one day to watch some movies. Lehrman approached him, flattered him and insisted that he was recently back from Paris where he had learned all the tricks of the art at the highly regarded Pathé studios. It is doubtful that Sennett believed his tale, but he was never one to resist a bold and slightly improbable importuning, and so he introduced him to the studio where Griffith employed him as a technical advisor and extra on a French swashbuckler he was then directing. Lehrman endeared himself by eagerly taking a fall off a set two stories high in rehearsal, then, slightly woozy, repeating it with the cameras running. The reasoning behind hiring him thereafter was that anyone who wanted to be in the movies that badly *ought* to be in the movies. Lehrman became an assistant to Sennett on the Biograph comedies and, later, a staff director and resident decadent at Sennett's own studios. It was Lehrman who introduced Fatty Arbuckle to Virginia Rappe, the extra girl (and prostitute) who died in mysterious circumstances after the infamous party that cost Arbuckle his career.

More immediately significant among the men was James Kirkwood, a leading man whose stage reputation was somewhat stronger than that of most of those who took parts in the movies at this time. He did not stay long with the company, but it is probably the easygoing Kirkwood who introduced the similarly relaxed but wonderfully romantic-looking Henry Walthall to the Biograph. They had worked together in a play and were friends from the Lambs Club, most of whose members were still carefully avoiding the movies. Walthall, of course, would stay with Griffith throughout his Biograph career and achieve his small, but secure, immortality as the Little Colonel in *The Birth of a Nation*. It was in this year, too, that Bobby Harron first ventured out of the prop room to try a few roles.

But certainly the most significant arrival was that of Mary Pickford, in a startlingly short time to become the most powerful feminine star in the history of American film. Born plain Gladys Smith in Toronto in 1893, she had gone on the stage at the age of five when her mother was suddenly widowed and found herself with three children and her own aging mother to support and no special skills to capitalize upon. Charlotte Smith's first response to this turn of fortune was the traditional one—she rented out her spare room to a man and his wife. That anonymous gentleman boarder turned out to be the stage manager of the Cummings Stock Company in Toronto and it was he who made the historic suggestion that little Gladys and her sister Lottie could bring in extra money by appearing in the schoolroom scene of *The Silver King*. Their mother, setting aside the customary moral objections middle-class ladies harbored against the stage, saw that it might be the answer to her economic plight and in the next decade the Smith family, sometimes together, occasionally separated, played out the familiar actor's odyssey of the time—stock company, touring companies, an occasional Broadway show. The experiences of Gladys Milbourne Smith—she used her impressive full name at first— were not dissimilar to those of D. W. Griffith earlier, except that she was a good deal more successful, achieving finally, in 1907, a kind of pinnacle—an engagement in the New York run of a David Belasco production—*The Warrens of Virginia*, written by witty William DeMille, who was Cecil's brother and the father of Agnes, the choreographer. It was Belasco, in fact, who gave Gladys, now 15 years old, the stage name that was to become, along with Chaplin's, one of the first great screen names. Pickford was the middle name of her maternal grandfather and one of a series of family names that tumbled forth when Belasco requested a list from which to pick something more glamorous than Gladys Smith for his posters and playbills.

The play provided her with about a year and a half's work, counting the tour, but when she returned to New York in the spring of 1909 little Gladys Smith had managed to save only $200, a bit more than her mother and Lottie had to show for a year's touring with Chauncy Olcott in another show. There was a little splurge of dress buying and then, rather more quickly than they would have thought, the rest of the money began to dwindle away. It was at this point that Charlotte Smith thought of the movies, principally, her daughter was to recall, because it seemed a way for the family to avoid the long separations theatrical touring entailed.

Her daughter objected: "Oh, no, not that, Mama!" But her mother persisted and promised Gladys that she might have her first high heels and silk stockings if she would try. It is perhaps an indication of the stature that Biograph films had attained in less than a year under Griffith's direction, that it was to his studio that shrewd Charlotte Smith sent her daughter first.

Gladys Smith's mood, as she set forth from their apartment, was no more than dutiful. She intended merely to pay the briefest possible call at Biograph and then head uptown to make the rounds of the theatrical agencies. "I would be able to say to Mother, honestly and truthfully, 'I did what you asked me to.' In my secret heart I was disappointed in Mother: permitting a Belasco actress, and her own daughter at that, to go into one of those despised, cheap, loathsome motion-picture studios. . . . Belligerently I marched up the steps of Biograph."[8]

A prop boy, probably Bobby Harron, announced her to Griffith. "He paused and then commented that she was certainly a good looker." And so she seemed to Griffith when he went downstairs to meet her: "She was small—cute figure—much golden curls—creamy complexion—sparkling Irish eyes, but eyes that also had languorous capabilities."[9]

He did not, apparently, allow Miss Pickford to know his first impression was so favorable. She recalled him looking her over "in a manner that was too jaunty and familiar for my taste," and speaking rather rudely to her as he inquired about her credentials. "I thought him a pompous and insufferable creature," Miss Pickford wrote, "and I wanted more than ever to escape." Instead, he conducted her to the basement, where he told her to wait. A few minutes later he reappeared, announced that he would give her a test. A costume was rounded up, Griffith himself applied a makeup that she thought entirely wrong for Pippa of *Pippa Passes*, the Browning poem he was toying with the idea of making, and she was shocked to overhear the other players addressing one another by their first names, a familiarity not common in theater. She was also interested to hear that the director was invariably referred to as "Mr. Griffith" (although a few of his old friends from trouping days continued to call him "Larry," the only familiarity he permitted).

In time she was conducted to the top floor studio, handed a guitar and told to mime playing it. That was awkward for her, but she was stopped cold by the improvised entrance lines of the actor assigned to play opposite her. "Who's the dame?" asked Owen Moore.

A dame to Pickford was a loose woman and she broke character to upbraid Moore. Now it was Griffith's turn to be outraged. ". . . Never, do you hear, never stop in the middle of a scene. Do you know how much film costs per foot? You've ruined it! Start from the beginning!"

As if this gaffe were not bad enough, Miss Pickford thought her performance was terrible and she was convinced that she would not be invited back. But when it was over and she emerged from the dressing room in her street attire, Griffith was waiting for her, with an invitation to dinner. She turned him down, on the ground she'd never had dinner with a boy her own age, let alone a grown man. Still, he asked her to return the next day, offering her the standard five dollars a day. She said she would require $10 and he gave in, after swearing her to secrecy. (After a few weeks the terms were changed to a $25 weekly guarantee for three days' work, overtime to be paid at the rate of $10 for extra days.) Griffith escorted her to the subway through a rainstorm, sheltering her with his umbrella, but she was soaked anyway by the time she reached the theater in Brooklyn where her mother and sister were working with Olcott. And despite the five-dollar bill she clutched, along with the promise of more to come, she still did not regard her triumph as anything but ambiguous.

Next day, however, she began her movie career in earnest by working in one of the veins that would continually distinguish it—playing a child much younger than she was. Linda Arvidson, no less, was recruited to accompany Mary to Fifth Avenue and supervise the purchase of a costume for her debut, a split-reel comedy called *Her First Biscuits*. It was not important—Griffith would soon turn over the direction of these little comedies to Sennett—and in the nature of a second trial. But she did well enough, and Griffith asked her if she felt up to playing the lead in a longer film the next day. She agreed and he inquired: "Do you know anything about love-making?"

She assured him she did, but he did not entirely believe her. A carpenter was passing by at the moment, carrying a papier-mâché pillar. The director ordered him to set it down and told the young actress to demonstrate her technique on it. She demurred on the not unreasonable ground that it would be difficult to mime emotion with only a prop to help her. Owen Moore materialized and was pressed into service. The young woman refused to kiss him, saying she would not be a party to so vulgar a public display, but as he embraced her, she did manage a look of loving adoration. She would later record her opinion that her efforts were "pathetic," but they more than pleased Griffith, who regarded her demure behavior as suitable for one of her years.[10] It is too much to say that he already had an image in mind for her, but he did not have in his company a young woman quite so versatile as she was. For in two days "Little Mary" (as she would soon be generally known) had already demonstrated that she could play under her true age with a certain sweetness and charm and she had also demonstrated that she was spunky, even willful. In short, she miraculously combined the two seemingly contradictory qualities of adolescent femininity that fascinated Griffith—a certain virginal unworldliness and a certain humorous practicality. He would, as it developed, never find another girl who so comfortably provided these elements so successfully. It required, for example, two Gish sisters to give him what "Pickford," as he called her in these years, could give him. And none of the other gifted young women who worked for him ever had quite her range.

Posterity has not treated her kindly, probably because of the tenacity with which she clung to ingenuous roles long after she had passed the age when they were really suitable for her, possibly because her well-known drive and shrewdness as a businesswoman unconsciously imparts to her screen image, as now we imperfectly glimpse it, a slightly grotesque air. But if she had chosen to be an actress in the traditional sense, rather than a movie star, she would have been a great one, for there was something magically paradoxical about this girl, something at once knowing and innocent, that the camera caught.

In any event, her impromptu performance with Moore secured for her the lead in *The Violin Maker of Cremona*, opposite him, but both essentially in support of Herbert Miles, playing the title role of the crippled craftsman. A week later she was in *The Lonely Villa*, as one of Marion Leonard's children, threatened by thieves (who have lured the father out of the house, leaving its women undefended). It was not a very subtle thing, and it required very little of Pickford, but the scenario, attributed to Mack Sennett by at least one authority, called for a chase to rescue the women and Griffith did it in bravura style, with splendid crosscutting. It is probably the best early example of the technique that was his trademark and of which he was the master.

It would be some time before the public began identifying her with the sobriquet they had first bestowed on Florence Lawrence, "The Biograph Girl" (Miss Lawrence departed in mid-July). Nevertheless, she quickly became a considerable presence in the studio, an ambitious, intelligent girl who took the trouble to learn the smallest details of her new craft—makeup, for instance; ". . . none of the others gave it much more than a passing thought," Bitzer remembered, "but Mary would use first one make-up, then when she would see it on the screen she would re-blend it and come to me saying: 'Do you think this is better, Billy?' We would then study it out together, much as though she were a canvas and we the artists. 'Do you think I should put a little more yellow—pink—?' "[11] In so doing, of course, she was pioneering one of the wiles on which female stars have ever since depended—enlisting the sympathy of her cameraman. And it worked. In his autobiographical notes Bitzer has more praise for her than for anyone who passed through the Biograph: "Mary is the sort of person that gets ahead in any business, no matter where you find her."[12]

Pickford's relationship with Griffith was a much more complex one. He was obviously smitten by her at first. Everything from his request for a dinner date their first meeting to his ready acquiescence to her salary demands indicates this. Right along she received special attention—though some of it was admittedly harsh—and she and her mother were among the very few women permitted to join Griffith at his lunch or dinner table when they were on location, sister Lottie was engaged as a stand-in (very possibly the first in film history), and brother Jack began working regularly with the company within a year. More important, Griffith was her chief defender against company executives who resented her demands, insisting that she wasn't attractive enough to be worth them.

Yet there was a tension between them. In part it was based on esthetic differences. "I refused to exaggerate in my performances, and my brother Jack wouldn't either," she told Kevin Brownlow, the oral historian. "Nobody ever directed me, not even Mr. Griffith. I respected him yes. I even had an affection for him, but when he told me to do things I didn't believe in, I wouldn't do them. I would *not* run around like a goose with its head cut off, crying 'Oooooh . . . the little birds! Ooooooh . . . look! A little bunny!' That's what he taught his ingenues, and they all did the same thing."[13]

According to Miss Pickford, she informed the director that she was 16 years old, after all, and unwilling to play the perpetual child (though, in fact, she spent most of her adult career doing precisely that). She claims that she would threaten to quit when these crises in interpretation arose and Griffith would tell her to go ahead and do it. And she did quit him—twice—both times because more money was offered her elsewhere, but also because she craved to be more nearly her own boss.

Of course she had some words of praise of her first film director. One incident she remembered in particular, and which illustrates a point raised repeatedly in memoirs of him, concerns his attention to realistic psychological detail. In some film or other Miss Pickford was playing a poor child and, entering a scene, she carelessly tossed her hat on the bed and dropped her coat over it. Griffith stopped the camera, spoiling the take. "Pickford, you'll never do that again," Griffith lectured sternly, instructing her to place the hat down carefully and to shake the coat before placing it neatly next to the hat. "You must take care of your clothes. No heroine is untidy."

So it went—and would continue to go—between Griffith and Pickford. There *was* mutual respect at times and certainly shrewd little Mary absorbed everything she could from the Master, the tragedy perhaps being that he refused to learn anything from a young woman whose intelligence about the medium, and especially about how to behave in front of a camera, was equal to his. "I think in his way he loved me," she told Brownlow, "and I loved him."[14]

But the remark has an obligatory air about it; it seems to represent an old woman's sensible desire not to stir up ancient, nearly forgotten, quarrels. The fact is that there is no real warmth toward Griffith in this interview or in her autobiography. The only hint of nostalgia for what must sometimes have been between them appears in a little tribute she wrote as an introduction to Homer Croy's hopeless, fictionalized biography, *Star Maker*: "I see D. W. now, standing beside the camera, a lean, hawk-like individual with an old straw hat, the top unravelled (he believed the sun would stop him from losing his hair). He wore a large, black, Chinese prayer ring, which he constantly twirled while directing us, and at the same time he jingled silver coins in his trouser pocket. Eccentric? Yes. But certainly no poseur. D. W.'s presence was magnetic. Nothing before or since has given me the warm satisfaction of a performance that pleased Mr. Griffith."[15]

Griffith has little to say about her acting in his autobiographical notes. There is mention of her appealing looks, a story or two about her romance with Owen Moore (which began in that first Biograph summer), and a memory that at some point in their salary discussions she told him that "he could say what he pleased, but one day she'd be making $100 a day." Four years later, as he notes, she was making $10,000 a week."

Of course, by the time they came to write about one another much had happened. The Biograph years were associated in her mind with her dreadfully unhappy marriage to Moore and were filled with people who had known her before she became a remote and glamorous world figure. Then, too, Griffith and her second husband, Douglas Fairbanks, Sr., often rubbed one another the wrong way, and in his later years Griffith could not help contrasting his diminished financial circumstances with the wealth and social position maintained by Little Mary.

2

All of this, of course, was far in the future. For the moment the important thing was that Biograph was a going concern and that it was generally recognized as the new leader in the industry. The reviewers for the entertainment trade journals—the general press had yet to regularly employ anyone in this capacity—quickly perceived Griffith's work as superior to all competitors'. The journalists were particularly impressed by the studio's willingness to tackle material of a sort previously untouched by moviemakers—an adaptation of *Rigoletto*, under the title *A Fool's Revenge*, was called by the *New York Dramatic Mirror*, "the first American film that we have felt justified in pronouncing the equal in smoothness of construction and power of dramatic action of any of the Pathé 'films d'art,'" adding that Biograph "is entitled to the warmest praise for its undoubted success in producing a work of moving picture art that must rank with the very best." A little more than two months later *The Moving Picture World* declared that "Step by step the Biograph Company is making for itself a unique position among American film manufacturers." The occasion for this outburst was the release of *Resurrection*, an adaptation of the Tolstoy novel. The anonymous critic noted that within recent months the studio's reputation with exhibitors and the public had increased "by leaps and bounds." It was not just good photography that sold them, he said, it was "dramatic quality." "The Biograph picture today tells a story and tells that story well. Moreover the Biograph film is one in which one is almost sure to see good acting. A very ordinary person indeed can act before a crowded house of interested men and women, but it takes a genius to do so with real feeling on a moving picture stage. For there is no eager, sympathetic audience of thousands before you there, but only the staff of the company or the very matter-of-fact person who turns the handle and exposes so many feet of sensitized celluloid per minute. . . ."[16] This last was a particularly telling point and if it naïvely underestimates Griffith's ability to stand in for the missing audience, it at least evidences an understanding of the medium and an awareness of the nature of the problems of film performance.

This year, like all the others at Biograph, was punctuated at regular intervals by the production of films based on well-known, if not always great, literature. All contributed to Biograph's growing image of respectability, but, quite obviously, they do not represent anything like a majority of the 151 films Griffith made in 1909, and it is impossible to generalize about them all, for he touched on subjects ranging from the evils of drink and of card playing to medieval romance. But among this miscellany a few stand out, either because of their special qualities or because they represent early statements of themes that were of peculiar interest to Griffith. Among the first of them was *Edgar Allan Poe*, with Herbert Yost, a reputable Broadway actor, as the poet and Linda Arvidson as his dying wife. It is about Poe as he tried to write "The Raven" while nursing his wife in her final illness. Of special interest, perhaps, are the points of identification between Poe and Griffith—both southerners of a highly romantic persuasion; both particularly attracted to very young women and peculiarly moved by thoughts of their premature death; both poetic spirits who labored much of their time in popular media; both, finally, alcoholics.

Slightly later in 1909, *In Old Kentucky* offered Griffith an early opportunity to deal with the Civil War and, more importantly, a story in which brothers fight on opposite sides, as the good friends do in *The Birth of a Nation*. It also contains a homecoming scene that clearly prefigures that of the Little Colonel in *Birth*, not least because the scene features the star of the later film, Henry Walthall. Indeed, one is struck by the persistence of Griffith's preoccupation with stories dealing with wandering and absence and the dream of returning home either in triumph or with the return's dramatic impact enhanced by the wanderer's having been given up for dead. How often he must have dreamed this dream during his own years of wandering! How frequently it animated his films. Another variant on it appeared in this same year, *Lines of White on a Sullen Sea*. The title is from a poem by William Carleton and, like the first version of *Enoch Arden* in 1908, it featured Linda Arvidson, who obviously symbolized for him, in these years, conventional stability as the woman who waits for a lost love's return.

Another of his favorite subjects was the American Revolution and in the summer of 1909 he made *1776, or, The Hessian Renegades*, which clearly looked back to his play *War* as well as forward to *America*, his 1923 feature about the American Revolution. Then, too, there were the potent contemporary melodramas like *The Lonely Villa* and *Through the Breakers*. In the latter the high living of parental social butterflies is starkly contrasted, through expert crosscutting, with the illness of their little daughter who finally dies. It is a moralizing and sentimental work but effective in its spareness. Also interesting, not to say curious, is a little item entitled *The Voice of the Violin*, in which a youthful musician is lured, without entirely understanding what's happening to him, into an anarchist bomb plot which, he discovers, is aimed against the father of one of his students—whom he loves, naturally. In the end, he betrays the plot to save the girl, and the film could conceivably lend credibility to the opinion of some modern observers—Jean-Luc Godard, for example— that Griffith was some sort of unthinking reactionary. In fact, however, the film seems commercially rather than politically motivated, capitalizing on the widespread fear of the bomb-throwing anarchist legions that the popular press regularly conjured up at this time.

Several of the year's films, as well as a remarkable group that dealt with extraordinary sympathy with the American Indian, were doubtless dictated by the fact that in the summer J. J. Kennedy suggested a new location site to Griffith. It was Cuddebackville, in the Orange Mountains of New York, not far from the New Jersey state line and the Delaware Water Gap. Kennedy had once stayed at a small hostelry, the Caudebac Inn (it took its name from the original Indian word for the area), and thought that it would be a convenient and economical place for a film company to spend a few days shooting.

In that first summer Griffith and assorted groups of players came at least twice to the inn. The actors regarded these outings as something like vacations with pay, and, after his first stay, the director, in a letter to his wife, who was apparently visiting his relatives in Kentucky, declared that "it's very fine up there," despite the fact that on the first stay he lost six pounds—"hard work if you please"—and was now faced with the boring necessity of making out expense accounts for the eight days of shooting.[17] On the next trip she joined him, was charmed by the ride from the railroad station to the inn in what she called the Red Devil, a brightly painted Thomas car owned by the Predmore family, proprietors of the hostelry, which was "no towering edifice—just a comfy place three stories high, with one bathroom, a tiny parlor, rag-rugged, and a generously sized dining-room whose cheerful windows looked upon apple orchards. It was neat and spotlessly clean."[18]

Griffith and Bitzer rose with the sun to prepare for the day's work, but for everyone else, the living was easy. There was time for swimming and canoeing. There was a poker game in one of the outbuildings and a more genteel card game in the parlor of an evening. Often they gathered around the piano for songfests, in which Griffith occasionally joined. "Griffith had a voice he thought was pretty good," said the late William Beaudine, Sr., later to become a director himself (he was best known to modern audiences as one of the regular directors of the Lassie television series) but then the newest member of the Biograph crew—a prop boy. It does not seem that Griffith joined in the vacation spirit very often, however. Beaudine remembered that "I never saw him put his arm around anybody. He was a god, and without seeming to try, he mesmerized those people."[19] His strongest memory was of Griffith emerging from his room late one night to break up a seance that had grown particularly noisy in its attempt to rouse some spirit or other from the dead.

On the last stay in Cuddebackville this summer, he might well have been preoccupied by other matters. He mentions fearing calls from the studio, thinking that each might be to give him the message that he was fired, despite the fact that such calls invariably dealt with practical matters of developing and printing the films he was sending back. The reason for his concern—which Griffith does not mention—was that he was in the process of negotiating a new contract with Kennedy, one in which he sought a raise in his percentage on film sales. The president of the firm was proving to be a hard bargainer, while Griffith, after only a year, was probably not as secure about his value to the company as he would be later.

Other crosscurrents were swirling about him as well. Owen Moore and Mary Pickford had definitely discovered one another at Cuddebackville, and often appropriated one of the canoes—which Griffith used for an imaginative chase in Leather Stockings—for courting purposes, a development that could not have pleased Mrs. Pickford and of which Grif-

fith, too, might have disapproved. Then, too, there is some evidence that
a certain distance was creeping into his own marriage. Linda, that strong-
minded woman, gave Beaudine the impression, this summer, of being "a
completely dominated wife." She was, he thought, "wonderful, sweet,
nice, very well liked" by the rest of the company, but he could not fail
to observe that Griffith still called her Miss Arvidson when they were
together in public.[20] It may be that it was around this time that Griffith,
aware of his growing success, began, in Mack Sennett's phrase, to make
"pronouncements as if he were handing the Ten Commandments to
Moses," to adopt a style that the comedy producer likened to that of "an
emperor who gives away continents." Sennett, despite being permitted
to draw closer than most to the director, was often condescended to by
him as well as by many of the actors whose earlier theatrical experiences
were more elevated than his own. He also concedes that there were sufficient practical reasons for Griffith's growing imperiousness. Stage actors
would more willingly work for a director they regarded as a genius than
for one who seemed just a humble craftsman. The front office would
more willingly accede to the demands of such a grand figure. And, as
Sennett says, "Griffith was the first person to realize he *was* a genius."
Since "there was no one else to announce it,"[21] Sennett concluded that
he was forced into this posture. But a young and intelligent wife, who
had known him before the great self-discovery, was bound to seem something of a handicap, no matter how assiduously she demonstrated her
agreement with this new evaluation of his abilities.

But the work—the demanding, satisfying, successful work—went on.
Earlier in the year Bitzer, possibly with Griffith's encouragement, began
experimenting with a new lighting technique. One day when Pickford
and Moore separated themselves from the rest of the company during a
lunch break, Bitzer noticed that gravel from a walk at their feet was reflecting a soft and attractive light into their faces. As a result, and even
though the sun was at their backs, there were no harsh shadows. He got
out his camera and peering into the ground glass, he saw that besides a
slight rainbow effect, he could get a much more beautiful close-up than
had heretofore been possible.

Griffith's memory of the incident was slightly different. He recalled
that Bitzer commandeered a white tablecloth to act as a reflector for his
test shots. No matter. Griffith recognized the merit of the new technique
and recalled defending it against some in the front office, who found the
results soft in comparison with work shot in direct light. To them these
pictures looked out of focus. It was J. J. Kennedy himself, according to
Griffith, who finally settled the dispute. "Why, they look like steel en-
gravings," he said. "Stick to that idea."[22]

Out of this line of work there also came the technique that was to
become the hallmark of Griffith's early work—the iris-in, or vignette, in

which most of the frame was black, leaving only a tiny, circular portion of the action visible to the audience. Griffith, apparently, was more bothered than he need have been by the change in perspective when camera positions were changed in midscene. He found it annoying visually and imagined audiences would agree. He asked Bitzer if there weren't some way to simply throw the background out of focus briefly in order to highlight a single player or bit of action without changing setups. Bitzer experimented with a gauze filter with a hole cut in the center of it. But it blurred the background without eliminating it, and Bitzer found the effect distracting. Worse, it looked to the uninitiated as if the cameraman had been careless and that was intolerable to a man who prided himself on the sharpness of his images. But the new technique of backlighting combined with reflected light required a lens shade. Bitzer at first had used his cap, but it had a way of flopping into the shot. So he improvised a shade out of a Le Page's glue bottle, the bottom of which he had tapped out, the remainder of which he had fastened around the excellent two-inch, f. 3.5 Zeiss Tessar lens (undoubtedly the best then in use in the movies) with which the Biograph camera was equipped. The shade worked admirably indoors, but outdoors, when the lens was stopped down to compensate for the increased light, its depth of field was increased and the edge of the glue pot was thrown into focus, blacking out a large portion of the screen. It was precisely the effect Griffith wanted and, in time, the glue pot gave way to a specially made masking device, which could provide the director with a vignette of any shape he desired.[23] Griffith recalled that it was a blacksmith at Cuddebackville who made this gadget for them.

In Griffith's development as an artist, however, the most important work he did at Cuddebackville was a remarkable series of Indian films—*The Mended Lute, The Indian Runner's Romance*, the Cooper adaptation and, most important of all, *The Redman's View*. No doubt he was influenced toward these subjects by the romanticizing of the savage and of the natural environment which coincided, in this period, with the nation's first awareness that the frontier had finally closed, that it had just lost something it had always taken for granted—untamed, untouched lands to the west. But he approached this material with great sobriety, even going to the lengths of hiring as technical advisor one Young Deer who, with his wife, accompanied the acting company to Cuddebackville, largely to teach them authentic dances. Though most of the films were rather romantic and melodramatic in style, the last, *The Redman's View*, was clearly seen by contemporaries for what it was: ". . . symbolical of the fate of the helpless Indian race as it has been forced to recede before the advancing white, and as such it is full of poetic sentiment and artistic beauty, and it is at the same time an important step out of the beaten path." Thus spake the *New York Dramatic Mirror*.[24] A week later, writing in the same journal, Frank Woods was moved to write in his "Spectator Comments" column that "the injustice that the red race has suffered at the hands of the white, is held up to our eyes in convincing picture language, and the conclusion is conveyed that they are now receiving as wards of the nation only scant and belated attention."[25]

Curious! Griffith could sympathize with, and romanticize, a race he did not know, yet was full of unconscious racism toward blacks, whom he knew better. Similarly, his critic. For it was Woods who, having moved on from trade journalism and reviewing, would, as Griffith's story editor, bring *The Birth of a Nation* to him and draft its first scenario. Woods is, indeed, a most problematical figure in Griffith's career. He was a sensible and perceptive critic, perhaps the first more-or-less responsible journalist to comment more-or-less responsibly (and regularly) on the developing art of film. As such, his widely read column was largely responsible for spreading the reputation of Biograph films, building up Griffith in the process—a crucial element in the creation of a "genius," with immediate benefits and long-term hazards for his subject. Yet Woods might already have been selling scenarios to Griffith, and definitely would be within the year. In short, he had an undeclared interest in puffing Griffith.

But, perhaps, no matter. He certainly was not wrong in his critical judgment. It may be, indeed, that the little series of films about the Indian which Woods praised was more significant than the achievement of this year which is more often remarked—the production of *Pippa Passes*, which was shot in August, back in the studio. The film had its merits. For example, Griffith used in it for the first time a linking device between sequences. It was a single shot of an actress named Gertrude Robinson singing a song. It recurred at the beginning of each of the film's four sections (Morn, Noon, Evening, Night), each lit in a mood suitable to the hour. It, of course, prefigures the use of Lillian Gish in a similar shot in *Intolerance*.

Bitzer had thrown up his hands when Griffith's difficult idea posed a difficult lighting problem, but Arthur Marvin was intrigued by it—he really was a more venturesome cameraman than he has received credit for being—and Bitzer has described how Marvin solved it. "He figured on cutting a little rectangular place in the back wall of Pippa's room, about three feet by one, and arranging a sliding board to fit the aperture much like the cover of a box sliding in and out of grooves. The board was to be gradually lowered and beams of light from a powerful klieg shining through would thus appear as the first rays of the rising sun striking the wall of the room. Other lights stationed outside Pippa's window would give the effect of soft morning light. The lights full up, the mercury tubes a-sizzling, the room fully lighted, the back wall would have become a regular back wall again, with no little hole in it."[26]

There was considerable dubiousness around the studio about the project, but when the film was screened the comments, according to Mrs. Griffith, were "awed and hushed" and it appears that the general enthusiasm within the studio for what Griffith had wrought was in part responsible for the settlement of his new contract on terms favorable to him. For shortly after the film was completed that long-debated document was signed and it provided a raise in Griffith's royalties from one-twentieth of a cent per foot of film sold to one-tenth.

This internal judgment of his work was confirmed by the *New York Times* of October 10, 1909, which, a week after its release, accorded *Pippa Passes* the first review any movie ever received in its pages. Heretofore the newspaper had covered movies as technology but never as art. Nor could it be said that its small, anonymously written article was very knowledgeable. It attributed the new cultural pretensions of the movies—Browning, indeed!—more to the pressure emanating from censorship boards than to the ambitions of filmmakers. Moreover, in its slighting comments on "cheap melodrama" and its approving, if ironic, prediction of still more intellectually rarified adaptations to come, it set the tone of much of the middle-class film reviewing to come, a criticism that would for the most part turn a blind eye to films that defined and advanced the "movieness" of movies and lavish praise on those who aped the norms established by the other arts.

Still, this little item, tucked away in an obscure corner of the paper, is perhaps more historically significant than the film it discusses. It is an annunciation of respectability if you will, and the allusion it contains to the "Secessionist Photographers," grouped around Alfred Stieglitz's famous gallery at 291 Fifth Avenue, is an important—if ironic—cross-reference. It is perfectly true that the effects obtained in many Griffith films were very like those achieved by Stieglitz and his cohorts. Irony enters when one remembers that Stieglitz in particular was in revolt against the school of photography that found its ideals of lighting in the Barbizon school of painters and in Rembrandt, while the movie people, Griffith among them, would shortly begin publicizing their "Rembrandt" lighting, trying to put behind them the flat, contrasty style that resulted from the early reliance on orthochromatic film.

In any event, the *Times's* historic notice is worth reprinting, headlines and all:

BROWNING NOW GIVEN IN MOVING PICTURES

"Pippa Passes" the Latest Play
Without Words to be Seen
In the Nickelodeons

THE CLASSICS DRAWN UPON

*Even Biblical Stories Portrayed For
Critical Audiences—Improvement
Due to Board of Censors*

"Pippa Passes" is being given in the nickelodeons and
Browning is being presented to the average motion picture audiences, who have received it with applause and are asking for
more.

This achievement is the present nearest-Boston record of
the reformed motion picture play producing, but from all accounts there seems to be no reason why one may not expect to
see soon the intellectual aristocracy of the nickelodeon demanding Kant's Prolegomena to Metaphysics with the "Kritik of Pure
Reason" for a curtain raiser.

Since popular opinion has been expressing itself through
the Board of Censors of the People's Institute, such material as
"The Odyssey," the Old Testament, Tolstoy, George Eliot, De
Maupassant, and Hugo has been drawn upon to furnish the
films, in place of the sensational blood-and-thunder variety
which brought down public indignation upon the manufacturers
six months ago. Browning, however, seems to be the most rar-
efied dramatic stuff up to date.

As for Pippa without words, the first films show the sunlight waking Pippa for her holiday with light and shade effects
like those obtained by the Secessionist Photographers.

Then Pippa goes on her way dancing and singing. The
quarreling family hears her, and forgets its discussion. The tap-
room brawlers cease their carouse, and so on, with the pictures
alternately showing Pippa on her way, and then the effect of her
"passing" on the various groups in the Browning poem. The
contrast between the tired business man at a roof garden and
the sweatshop worker applauding Pippa is certainly striking.
That this demand for the classics is genuine is indicated by the
fact that the adventurous producers who inaugurated these expensive departures from cheap melodrama are being overwhelmed by offers from renting agents. Not only the nickelodeons of New York but those of many less pretentious cities
and towns are demanding Browning and the other "high-brow"
effects.

3

There was truth in the report that exchanges and customers were "demanding" more films like *Pippa Passes*. "Even we children sensed that

Biograph pictures were 'different,'" Edward Wagenknecht has written, "though we could not, for the life of us, have told you wherein their difference might consist, and sometimes I think we felt more at home with the less adventurous and disturbing Vitagraphs."[27] In any event, by this time theaters were advertising "Biograph days" and if the names of those responsible for the company's movies were still unknown, the general feeling that they were by and large extraordinary achievements was quite widespread.

And not a moment too soon, for the controversy over the morality of movies continued unabated. There were a few liberal reformers like Jane Addams of Hull House in Chicago who understood that they represented, potentially at least, a source of mass education, that they were a sort of people's theater more accessible to the mass public, both physically and financially, than any previous form of entertainment. But Miss Addams was distinctly in the minority among opinion makers of the time. The clergy and the judiciary railed at nickelodeons as if they were saloons—even though temperance dramas were a staple genre (and one not ignored by Griffith, either). Thus the Biographs based on literary material performed an incalculably valuable public relations job for the entire industry.

Moreover, Griffith's last major release of the year must have satisfied nearly everyone with a serious interest in the potential of film—the liberal reformers, who surely applauded its political message, the middle-class literary intellectuals, who must surely have applauded its source, the general public, which could certainly appreciate, by this time, a tautly made melodramatic masterpiece. The film was called *A Corner in Wheat* and its unknown scenarist had in essence lifted his material from a Frank Norris short story called "A Deal in Wheat" and published after the writer's death. A review in the *New York Dramatic Mirror* summarized both the film's plot and its impact:

> This picture is not a picture drama, although it is presented with dramatic force. It is an argument, an editorial, an essay on a vital subject of deep interest to all. The theme is the rising cost of living, the inability of the masses to meet the increase and the part played by the speculator in bringing about this unfortunate condition. No orator, no editorial writer, no essayist could so strongly and effectively present the thoughts conveyed in this picture. It is another demonstration of the force and power of motion pictures as a means of conveying ideas. It was a daring step for the Biograph producers to take, to thus step out of the domain of the picture drama as they have done in this film and in the one last week, *The Redman's View*, but having taken the step and done so successfully, they are entitled to all the praise

they will undoubtedly receive for having opened up a new vein for motion picture subjects. The film opens with an artistic farm scene after the style of Millet, showing sowers of wheat, hopeless and worn down by hard work. From these depressing scenes we turn to the affairs of the speculator where the great wheat corner is being arranged. The master mind issues his orders and the brokers appear in the wheat pit, where we see them struggling like ravenous wolves to control the wealth they did nothing to create. The corner wins and the defeated gamblers are brushed aside like the chaff of the grain for which they had fought. Another change and we see the city poor paying the increased price for bread or going hungry for want of enough money to buy. We get a glimpse of the dreadful breadline contrasted with the scenes of high life where the successful speculators are lavishing the money they have won. A sensation turn is given to the film when we see the speculator showing his friends through one of his elevators. He is handed a message telling him that he has cornered the world's supply and in the midst of his exultation he makes a misstep and falls to a terrible death in one of his own bins of wheat. We see him struggle and disappear from view in the dusty grain and we see again the breadline and the weary farmers. The film closes in the darkening night on the farm. The effectiveness of the subject is enhanced by the superb acting of the company. Every part is powerfully presented with telling truthfulness, except in one instance only, when we see the farmers sowing the wheat. No wheat would ever come up from the sort of sowing they do, but this slip is lost sight of in the artistic atmosphere of the scene and in the compelling pictures that follow.[28]

A little later the same journal would report that the film received special billing in its New York debut as the closing presentation of the vaudeville bill at Keith and Proctor's—unprecedented prestige for a movie in this context.

But even now one can scarcely speak too highly of the film. It is a model of compression and at the same time a bold and slashing attack on economic injustice. The final sequence of the wheat baron (played by Frank Powell, who also served as one of Griffith's assistant directors) being smothered by wheat cascading in from the top of his grain elevator remains one of the most powerful and affecting film images ever created and one cannot help but reflect that Griffith's poetic impulse was never more effectively used than when it was grounded in social realism, which checked his tendency toward the too pretty, the too flowery.

Equally important, if accidentally, this film related more directly to the advanced intellectual currents of the time than any Griffith had previously done. As we have seen, his best instinct was for a kind of realism, but it was an essentially untutored instinct. It had nothing to do with the conscious rebellion of his literary contemporaries against the genteel and romantic tradition which had for so long ruled American letters. If he knew about this rebellion at all, it was only through hearsay, for as we know, Griffith's tastes ran to writers of quite a different sort, very often, indeed, to the established writers of the moment. Norris, however, was representative of a group who, coming to maturity in the 1890s, were denied recognition not only in that decade, but in the first decade of this century as well. As Larzer Ziff has persuasively argued in his fine literary history *The American 1890s*, this was the generation that was truly lost. Norris himself, Stephen Crane, and Harold Frederic all died prematurely; John Jay Chapman suffered a shattering mental breakdown; Kate Chopin ceased to write when her last book was ill received; Dreiser managed to get *Sister Carrie* published in 1903, but was unable to get his next published until 1912, when fashion shifted. In short, there was an opportunity here for Griffith to attach himself, and his emerging medium, to the literary and intellectual forefront, rather than to the rear guard. It would have suited the strongest aspect of his sensibility, and at least some portion of his audience, with its taste influenced by a decade of muckraking journalism, might have responded well to more works of realistic social concern. Griffith, however, did not move firmly in this direction. This was regrettable not only for him, but for the movies in general and perhaps for the larger public as well. He, especially, needed to attach himself to a stronger artistic tradition than he ever found. Its lack, in his career, was a factor in the withering of the realistic elements in his talent (they never entirely died) and the decline in regard for his work in the 1920s. Still, it is difficult to imagine a work more appropriate—if more falsely promising—than *A Corner in Wheat* on which a director might end one decade and begin another.

CHAPTER SEVEN

Great Expectations

As *A Corner in Wheat* went into the theaters, Griffith, who was not to be denied any reasonable request in these days, received the front office's permission to spend the winter months in California. It was a decision of some moment. His would be the first group representing a Patents Company firm to shoot in California—a significant step in the transformation of Los Angeles into a film capital. Perhaps more immediately important, the trip required him to confess his marriage to Linda Arvidson to his superiors at the studio so that they could travel together in a drawing room on the train west and live together as man and wife while on the Coast.

Until this time only a few of their Biograph co-workers knew of their marriage. Two of them had known the Griffiths before they had come into the movies and one of them, Harry Salter, had been told of their arrangement when he discussed with Griffith the possibility of a secret marriage to Florence Lawrence. There was some surprise, but no consternation, and Doc Dougherty's comment was interesting: "Well, that is bringing coals to Newcastle."[1] Whether this meant that Griffith had already acquired a reputation as a lady's man or whether Dougherty had merely noticed a certain warmth between the two is unclear. What is astonishing is the implication that they had been able to keep their liaison secret during the previous summer's stays at Cuddebackville.

In any event, theirs was not the first movie company to make the trek westward in search of winter sunlight and virgin locations. For the last few years movie people had sought warm weather in order to continue making outdoor dramas when the snows came to the Northeast, ranging as far afield as Florida and even Cuba in their quest. The honor of pioneering Los Angeles probably belongs to a company sent forth from Chicago by Colonel William Selig in the fall of 1907. The producer thought that Los Angeles might be far enough away to give his companies surcease from harassment by Patent Company agents and so a director named Francis Boggs, a cameraman named Thomas Parsons and several assistants entrained for the West. They left behind a half-finished version of *The Count of Monte Cristo* and since they took no actors with them, the rest of the film was finished on the West Coast with an entirely different cast—and mostly in extreme long shot, one imagines. After that came, if not a deluge, then a steady trickle of independent producers, including perhaps most notably New York Motion Picture Company owned by Baumann and Kessel, who would later back Sennett's Keystone operation. They fled when shooting on one of their films, which involved a crowd scene of some twenty actors, was interrupted by a like number of toughs recruited by the trust's agents. Whether, in fact, these companies chose Los Angeles over San Francisco because of its closer proximity to the Mexican border and its sanctuary from process servers, as legend would have it, is unprovable. But the steadiness of the sunshine in the more southerly location, along with its generally warmer and drier airs, doubtless was a factor in the favor of Los Angeles. It is also possible the less formal, less stratified social climate of Los Angeles appealed to the raffish movie people, as did the ready availability of cheap studio accommodations. At all events, the public liked the pictures that emanated from the West Coast. And soon the phrase "A California Picture" or some similar designation in the advertising had something like the same cachet that the Biograph trademark had.

The departure of Griffith's company of some thirty actors and technicians did not go entirely smoothly. Griffith, his wife and an officer of the company were to travel in isolated splendor on the Twentieth Century Limited while the rest of the group proceeded by the Lehigh Valley line's less grand Black Diamond express to Chicago and thence to the coast. Frank Powell was in charge of the larger party, but Griffith went down to the ferry to see them off (the Lehigh had no tracks into the city and its terminal was in Jersey City). There he found the Smith-Pickfords in full cry. To begin with, Little Mary was saying tearful farewells to Owen Moore, who had asked for, and been refused, a ten-dollar raise for undertaking the westward trek. Meanwhile, Mary's mother had waited until the last minute to threaten to keep Mary at home unless *she* got an extra ten a week. Griffith smoothly countered with the information that Gertrude Robinson was standing by, ready to depart at the standard salary, and that rather slowed Mrs. Smith down. Happily for her, Jack Pickford chose the occasion to throw a tantrum over his sister's departure and so, at the last moment, a guarantee was pried out of Griffith for him and he was allowed to accompany the little troupe—one less mouth for Mrs. Smith to feed.

Moore never worked for Biograph again and was probably instrumental in luring Mary Pickford away a year later; on the whole, however, it was a happy company en route and a happy company once it settled down in Los Angeles. They travelled in coaches especially reserved for them, in trains marked "Biograph Special" and they each had three dollars a day to spend in the dining car. The cards slapped down and the dice rolled and when they paused in San Bernardino before making the final dash into Los Angeles, all the ladies received tiny bouquets of welcome.

Their rented studio space was at the corner of Grand Avenue and Washington Street. It was an empty lot, surrounded by a board fence, a baseball field to one side, a lumberyard to the other. The carpenters erected a wooden stage, open to the sun (which was softened by diffusers made of linen or cotton), on which flats, probably made of composition board, could be erected. There were two small dressing rooms for men against one fence, similar facilities for ladies across the lot. When large numbers of extras were required they were provided with a tent for dressing. And that was all. A loft nearby was rented for laboratory space and on rainy days the actors used it for rehearsals. Costumes were also stored there.[2]

The company found housing nearby. The Griffiths and some of the leading players stayed at the Alexandria Hotel, beginning its history as the first in the long chain of favorite movie industry hotels in Los Angeles. Most of the company stayed in rooming houses and a survivor recalled that they could save money out of the two dollars per diem the studio provided for expenses—some of them stole such necessities as potatoes, vegetables and coffee and some bunked with two or three other Biograph people in a single room.[3]

The city of Los Angeles was not quite the sleepy little village that has been described in some film histories. By 1910 the regional population stood at around 800,000, and the first large population to overlie the original pueblo—mostly middle-western farmers, who contributed the community's basic values ("Los Angeles is the Middle West raised to flash-point," architectural historian Reyner Banham once wrote)—had itself been overlaid. This new group, slightly rougher in manner, was composed of those who had come to search for—and find—oil in the period 1890–1910. The place was, in short, a boom town. It easily absorbed the seekers after the new El Dorado and they, in their turn, found the no-questions-asked atmosphere congenial. Only on those occasions where they sought to use some enclave of wealth such as Pasadena for backgrounds did they encounter any difficulties—and there was compensation in that they could sometimes simply take a streetcar to find mountain, desert and seaside locations. Actually they weren't streetcars, but "the big red cars" of the Pacific Electric Railroad, an interurban line that had pushed out in almost all directions from the central city at this time, forming the skeleton of the metropolis that was to be. Along its right-of-way, urban and suburban backgrounds of many types were also readily available, and if these occasionally appeared strange to the eyes of eastern viewers, they also had the charm of the exotic.

Almost everyone found the routine agreeable. Griffith began each day by having his bathtub filled with ice cubes because he was convinced a cold plunge was therapeutic. Less strenuous souls tended to stay up late over cards, often with little Jack Pickford as a kibitzer, and to eschew Griffith's nearly recreation-less routine, which included, as a rule, full Sundays of motoring in search of locations. If anyone was unhappy it was probably Mary Pickford, mooning over the absent Owen Moore, but she didn't let her moods interfere with her work—she was too much the professional (and far too ambitious) for that.

The films made during this first visit of a little less than three months were not, by and large, terribly distinguished. From them, as from the rest of the 1910 work, one gains the impression that Griffith was consolidating the techniques and skills he had uncovered the previous year. In the California films one gets the sense that he was often simply entranced by the great vistas suddenly opening up before his camera and that, freed from the daily supervision of studio executives, Griffith allowed some of the creative tension to uncoil for the first time in almost two years. Whatever the reasons, the most striking quality about these first California efforts is their scenic beauty.

There is, in almost all of them, a sense that the director is experimenting with the possibilities of backing away from his human subjects, the better to reveal the environment that shapes their actions, if not their characters. It is, in effect, the reverse of what he had done the year before—moving in closer and closer to his people, the better to read their thoughts. He was, then, joining expansiveness to intimacy, increasing the range of choice available to him and demonstrating again his essential abhorrence of the middle distance, the commonplace view.

Quite naturally, his subject matter on this trip tended to emphasize western history. There were stories of miners, of oppressed Indians and, most often, of life in Spanish and Mexican California, for Griffith had the true romantic's feeling for the monuments and ruins of the past. The first film he shot in California was *The Thread of Destiny*, a romance of an orphan girl brought up as a ward of a mission. The one at San Gabriel was used as a location and at it Bitzer achieved an exquisite camera effect. Shooting with available light inside the mission, he caught a sunbeam illuminating the pulpit where actor Christie Miller, playing an aged *padre*, was standing to bless his congregation. Bitzer didn't really expect the scene to work, but it came out considerably better than the similar effect Marvin had worked so hard to achieve by artificial means in *Pippa Passes*. It was something of an omen of loveliness to come.

The next film, *In Old California*, was billed as a melodrama of Spanish California and it had no particular distinction, except that it was probably the first movie ever entirely shot within the boundaries of Hollywood, predating by three years DeMille's *The Squaw Man* and the famous barn at the corner of Sunset and Gower. Griffith was attracted to the suburb only because he wanted to shoot in the Hollywood hills and there was a conveniently located inn in which to hire dressing rooms. He would return to Hollywood toward the end of the stay in order to use a flower garden he had spotted for a film called *Love Among the Roses*. On that occasion he lost the opportunity for a modest real estate killing. He offered the owner of the garden $50 for location rights and the man countered with an offer of free shooting rights if Griffith would purchase a nearby lot he happened to own for $300. It was on Hollywood Boulevard, but with that lack of financial acumen so characteristic of him, Griffith insisted on the rental arrangement.

For all his stress on history, Griffith did not entirely ignore contemporary subjects. Indeed, Frank Powell's comedy unit continued grinding out split-reels, all of which were modern in setting, and Jack Pickford graduated from bits to a leading role with the group during this sojourn. Characteristic of Griffith's best work was a simple little story of a widower, attempting to raise his child unaided while condemned by circumstances to a menial job. The picture was called *As It Is in Life* and what transformed it was Griffith's choice of setting. He had his leading character employed at a pigeon ranch and the constant swoopings and soarings of the birds, astonishingly beautiful in themselves—it was worth inventing a story to make use of them—formed a memorable and ironic counterpoint to a story that might otherwise have been rather banal.

A similar feeling for beauty of place informed *The Unchanging Sea*. Inspired by the verses of the Victorian cleric-poet Charles Kingsley, it was essentially another remake of *Enoch Arden* (with Linda Arvidson again in the role of the woman who must suffer and wait). This time the setting was the then entirely unimproved Santa Monica beach, a wilder and more exciting seascape than any conveniently available to Griffith in the East. The movie was distinguished by the director's efforts to capture the broad sweep of sea, beach and horizon, emphasizing the smallness of his players against this background and stressing, as well, a certain naturalness of movement and a certain slowness of pace, which was duly noted by reviewers in the trade press. Indeed, as Griffith's California films began to go into release in June, Frank Woods devoted one of his columns in the *Dramatic Mirror* to praise of Biograph for pioneering a movie style "distinguished by deliberation and repose," adding that the studio's "first experiments along this line were undertaken with no little hesitation and fearsome doubt. . . . So deeply rooted was the notion that speed was the thing, that the experimenters were fearful that their attempts to introduce acting into the films would be met with derisive laughter."[4]

There was still, even in Griffith's films, plenty of posturing, exaggeration, excessive movement (a couple of years later another reviewer would speak irritably of one of his "bounding" heroines), but in fact he was managing to tone this down and sometimes, as in *The Unchanging Sea*, to almost totally eliminate it. Again, one gets the sense that, as with camera placement, so with rhythm, Griffith was deliberately working in a direction opposite the one he had pursued the previous year, attempting to extend his poetic range.

Alas, practical matters often interfere with the poetic muse and not long after the stately and picturesque Santa Monica production was completed, Griffith found himself some 70 miles south of Los Angeles in Mission City, prowling a hotel lobby, pestering Billy Bitzer with questions about when the weather would clear so they might begin filming *The Two Brothers* in and around the mission of San Juan Capistrano. The morale of the rest of the company was not much better than their leader's. He might have been oppressed by the thought of what their accommodations were costing, but they were depressed by what they were getting for Biograph's money—cramped, damp rooms, with Mack Sennett loudly roaming the halls late at night crying out: "Hey, how many in this bed? . . . Got three in my bed. Can't sleep three in a bed." Periodically another of the players would shout in panic to his bed partner, "Don't crush me." Only Dell Henderson, an assistant and sometimes actor-scenarist, was content. Sizing up the situation instantly, he had chosen tiny Jack Pickford—who took up far less than half a double bed—as his bunkmate.[5]

The company's troubles did not end when the weather cleared. On the day prior to shooting there had been a funeral procession involving most of the mission's Mexican-American parishioners and the first order of business for the Biograph people was staging a wedding fiesta that involved a similar procession. According to Bitzer, the trouble began when they borrowed from the obliging priest-in-charge the same cross that had been used in the funeral the day before. According to Mrs. Griffith, the problem was the date—Good Friday—and a sacristan who regarded a mock wedding feast on so holy a day as sacrilege. She says that he threw a straw effigy of Judas out of his bell tower into the middle of one of Griffith's takes. The tradition was for such effigies to be attached to the horns of a lively bull and bucked through the town on Good Friday, but in this instance the flinging of the straw man was the cue for the large crowd of onlookers to turn ugly. Rocks were thrown, according to Bitzer, and the company retreated to the hotel, where a bartender suggested that the way to placate the crowd was to have the cowboys engaged for this picture (and whose gun-blasting arrival the previous night had disturbed everyone's restless sleep) put on an impromptu rodeo for the crowd. In particular he suggested that the star rider, one Bill Carroll, attempt to ride the neighborhood's most famously unridable horse. It was arranged,

Carroll managed to stay on the nag and he and his cohorts climaxed the event with a display of trick riding that won everyone over. Ironically, the wedding scene had to be reshot elsewhere—Bitzer's film stock turned out to be streaked, not by light, but by static in the camera—a common, endlessly irritating phenomenon in those days.

Undoubtedly, however, the climax of this first California expedition—though it was, in fact, the second-to-last movie shot there—was a production of *Ramona*, the first of three film versions of Helen Hunt Jackson's enormously popular novel, in the stage version of which, of course, Griffith had appeared in his trouping days. Mary Pickford, whom Griffith liked to use as an Indian maiden because of her high cheekbones, played the lead in yet another reworking of a favored theme—the white man's injustice to the Indian. In his later publicity Griffith sometimes claimed that it was in this picture—shot in Ventura County—that he first used the extreme long shot, and it does seem that in some of his camera placements he had backed away from his actors farther than ever—but it is a matter of degree, when compared to other works of the same period. The real departure from established practice lay in the fact that the story was not simply filched from Mrs. Jackson. Biograph actually paid her publishers $100 for the motion picture rights—and it is possible that this was the first such sale in movie history.

Anyway, it was a strong picture, in Griffith's best romantic vein, and, given its setting, an appropriate note on which to close out this first venture to the West Coast. He would make, all told, well over a hundred films out here, including his two most famous films; he would know both the high point of his career and the low point of his life in these landscapes; he would, within two years, see Los Angeles surpass New York as a production center, in no small measure because of the prestige he brought to it with his yearly trips; but it would never truly be his home.

2

When he returned to the New York studio, it was obvious that Griffith was restless within its confines. Almost every film he made in New York in the spring of 1910 contained at least some location filming, and, often as not, it would be shot entirely outside the studio. If nothing else, the California trip appears to have convinced Griffith that whatever advantages the studio conferred in controlling the conditions of work, they were more than offset by the inability of stagecraft to duplicate reality, of Cooper-Hewitts to match the quality of light that could be obtained outdoors.

The large general issue attracting his attention at this point was the beginning of the star system, now raising its first serious challenge to the status quo. The defection of Florence Lawrence had been a major victory not only for the independent producers, fighting the trust with all the weapons they could imagine, but for the freedom of the actor. And throughout this year, the practice of granting actors billing in movies continued to grow; indeed, within two years it would be standard practice. For the moment, however, Biograph held out and Frank Woods observed that in the case of Biograph, "We have seen the personnel of its stock company changed from time to time until now scarcely one of the original faces is ever seen in its films [this is something of an exaggeration] and yet the Biograph standard continues steadily to advance. Players with little or no reputation and others with big reputations have appeared in Biograph pictures, some of them becoming favorites, but none of them individually essential to the advancement of Biograph's reputation."[6] One imagines Griffith's position on this question to be ambivalent. On the one hand, some companies were now giving directors credit and surely he would have liked his name to become known in households outside the industry. On the other, he must have understood that the star system threatened his own power to command his players. Very likely at this point he set aside his desire for personal publicity and consoled himself with the fact that for the first time ever he had money in the bank— $5,207.40 by the end of the year and a new contract that called for a $75 base salary and a $200 weekly guarantee against his share of film sales, which was raised again—to one-eighth of a cent per foot sold.[7] This time, for the first time, the contract was not signed "Lawrence Griffith" but with his real name. Obviously a form of commitment had been made. Equally obviously, for his new prosperity was unprecedented in his personal history, that salary was a powerful incentive in his temporary support of the status quo.

Indeed, after the California expedition, Griffith seems to have marked time for the rest of the year. In general, the quality of his work remained high; consistency at this time being one of his great virtues. But for the most part he was not reaching out, stretching his talent and the medium's range as he previously had. His best film of the spring, for example, was *The Usurer*, but it was essentially a remake of *A Corner in Wheat*. This time, as the title implies, the central figure was a money-lender and not a grain dealer, but there was the same crosscutting between his machinations and their effect on plain people, and he came to much the same end as the earlier villain—instead of being suffocated in a grain elevator, he was suffocated in a safe in which he was accidentally locked. (Griffith must have been something of a claustrophobe, for from *The Sealed Room* in 1909 to Lillian Gish's celebrated entrapment in a closet in *Broken Blossoms*, suffocation, as a suitably terrible end for villains and as an awful peril for heroes and heroines, recurs. He was also fond of trapping large numbers of people in cabins or shacks that were too close for comfort, there to be menaced by a populous, ever-narrowing circle of enemies, often racial, until somebody rode to the rescue.)

He went back over previously explored ground in other ways. There were three more trips to Cuddebackville, and, again, Indian romances figure prominently in the shooting schedule there. And whether working out of New York or Cuddebackville, he continued to turn out, at regular intervals, historical romances, set in times and places that ranged from eighteenth-century Ireland and France to the Puritans' America to the Middle Ages. It may well be that these projects, with their rather elaborate costumes and their increasingly literary subtitles were, more than anything, responsible for separating Griffith's work from that of his competition at this time. They were all making, as he had been, plenty of films that revolved around contemporary social issues and the daily life of ordinary people. But it was Griffith who most consistently ranged farther afield historically than the Wild West, only he who would be termed, before the year was out, "the Belasco of motion pictures," in tribute to the ambitiousness (as well as the realism) of his designs.

If a slight trend in his development can be discerned in the latter part of this year it is away from adaptations (there was only one after *Ramona*, *The Golden Supper*, based on Tennyson's awful poem about a young woman revived from the tomb by her lover and restored to her husband at the banquet of the title) and toward a quickening interest in the Civil War. There were four films on this subject—*In the Border States*, *The House with Closed Shutters* (they hid the disgrace of a coward), *The Fugitive* and, by far the most important film of the year's latter half, a two-reeler, released serially (against Griffith's wishes) as *His Trust* and *His Trust Fulfilled*, which he made in November in Fort Lee.

In it, Griffith's old friend Wilfred Lucas, in blackface, plays an old family retainer whose master departs for the Civil War begging the servant to protect his wife, child and home while he is fighting for the South. Naturally the soldier dies. Naturally his home catches fire and, naturally, the servant upholds his trust by braving the flames to rescue first the child and then his master's sword, which has been hung in the place of honor over the mantel. He takes them to his own humble cabin and there the child grows up. In the second reel we see her attending seminary, her education financed by the old servant's small savings. When they run out, he is tempted to steal and cannot, so fine a spirit is he. His faithfulness, however, has been observed by one of the girl's cousins, who takes over the financial burden of her support and, finally, meets and marries the girl. The film's last shot shows Lucas fondling his late master's sword, tearfully happy that he has been able to fulfill "His Trust."

This film represents Griffith's first direct confrontation with a family's reduction of circumstances as a result of the war, a subject about which, of course, he had the strongest personal feelings, and so it, like *In Old Kentucky* of the previous year, can be regarded as a preliminary sketch for *The Birth of a Nation*, particularly in its patronizing, if affectionate, regard for the "good Negro," its tragic vision of war's effect on innocent victims, and perhaps even in the expansiveness that contemplation of the Civil War typically engendered in him.

His Trust prefigured *Birth* in another way as well. As most people know, Griffith was moved, a little later, to attempt the feature-length spectacle because he was stung by the popular success—and the prestigious play dates, in legitimate theaters—of such lengthy foreign spectacles as *Quo Vadis?*, *The Last Days of Pompeii*, *Les Misérables*, *Cabiria*. Something similar was happening now. No doubt the artist in him urged him to tell stories of greater length and complexity, but the fact was that his competitive spirit had been aroused almost a year earlier when J. Stuart Blackton had made a *Life of Moses* some five reels in length. His Vitagraph studio, second only to Biograph in reputation, followed with a four-reel *Les Miserables* and a three-reel *Uncle Tom's Cabin*. In addition, there was a three-reel life of Buffalo Bill—quite profitable—and Pathé had sent over from Paris a two-reel version of Zola's *L'Assommoir*, a title that would have its resonances far later in Griffith's career.

Exhibitors and exchangemen, underestimating their public, had complained about longer films (although the Zola film in particular had been successful where it could get bookings) and the trust leaders were firmly set against them, for no good reason that anyone has adduced, though probably they feared the higher unit cost per picture and the higher risk these pictures represented. Then, too, their innate desire not to disturb a system that was finally running smoothly must be counted. They insisted, therefore, on distributing these films serially, one reel at a time, as Biograph did *His Trust*. The important thing to Griffith, however, was that talk of longer films was in the air and that meant that his reputation as an innovator was at risk. He simply had to try something of greater length—and the reviews indicated to him, to anyone of any commercial or artistic sensibility that the future belonged to longer films, though the highest praise was reserved for *His Trust*'s battle scenes—"managed with a skill that baffles criticism," as Woods put it.[8]

For the moment, however, his major problem was not lack of personal publicity or the dispute over how to release *His Trust*. The fact was that as 1910 drew to a close, nearly all the important actors and actresses he had developed in his first years at Biograph were leaving—lured away by the independents' offers of bigger salaries and, more important, star billing. Marion Leonard had married Stanner Taylor, the scenarist, and they went as a team to Reliance. Walthall, Kirkwood and Arthur Johnson also received better offers, and this left Griffith with an acute shortage of leading men. Indeed, a decade and a half later Mrs.

Griffith, who had a shrewd eye in these matters (and a financial interest in them as well), commented that her husband "never found anyone to take [Johnson's] place exactly."

But the most serious defection was Mary Pickford's. The previous spring she had quietly informed Mrs. Griffith that "some day I am going to be a great actress and have my name in electric lights over a theater." "I turned pale and felt weak," the director's wife recalled, and others who had overheard the remark had been, she said, "shocked." They all assumed she was planning a return to the stage; none imagined—as Pickford apparently did—that screen stardom could possibly grow into the institution it was about to become, entailing for its leaders a quantum change—in prestige and in problems—compared to starring on the stage.

But then, few of them had as clear an insight into the management of careers and money as Little Mary possessed (and was possessed by). Even on the short West Coast trip she and her brother had managed to save an astonishing sum—$1,200 between them. She had made $40 a week and $14 expense money. Jack got five dollars a day. But he supplemented it by doubling falls from horses, windows and other heights for the young women of the company—feats for which Griffith rewarded extras at the rate of a dollar a fall. On top of that, Mary took to writing scenarios—palming off a reworking of *Thais* for a split reel that Griffith needed in a hurry, an original that was called *May and December* and a couple of things he rejected but which she sold to a rival company. When they returned East they changed their earnings into 24 crisp new $50 bills, tucked them into a handsome purse and presented it to their mother as a kind of first return on her investment in their careers. She thought they were playing a joke on her; never having seen bills of this large denomination before, she thought it was stage money.

There might have been more than simple gratitude at work in this gesture. Absence from Owen Moore had simply made Mary Pickford's heart grow fonder of him and that imposed upon her the necessity of winning Mother over to this romance—no easy matter given Moore's reputation as drinker and all-around wastrel. For a time Mrs. Smith made the best of it, welcoming him to her home, but then someone informed her that Mary's feeling for Moore, now playing leads for Carl Laemmle's Independent Motion Picture Company (IMP), was deeper than she was allowing her mother to see. At this point Mrs. Smith "made one of the few big mistakes of her life," as Mary was to put it; she forbade her to see Moore. The girl was far too willful to abide an ultimatum and began seeing Moore secretly. Finally, one night in the fall of 1910, she borrowed a "grown-up" dress with a long train from Biograph's wardrobe mistress and ran off to New Jersey with Moore for a secret wedding. She spent her wedding night in the double bed she shared with sister Lottie. There followed months of feeling guilty of "a monstrous betrayal" of her family, which soon extended to a betrayal of sorts of Griffith and of Biograph.[9]

She signed with IMP, too, at a salary of $175 a week. But money, one imagines, was not the major question, since Griffith and Biograph were paying Wilfred Lucas, a useful nonentity, $150 a week at this time. Surely Laemmle's promise of billing influenced her. And then, too, there was her feeling that Griffith did not use her much or as well as he should have, possibly because she was the most strong-spirited of his girls. Later she would say: "I got what no one else wanted, and I took anything that came my way because I decided that if I could get into as many pictures as possible I'd become known and there would be a demand for my work."[10] She was, in short, too intelligent and too sure of her own value to accept for very long Griffith's rather patronizing attitude toward her. But her autobiography leaves little doubt that Moore played a leading role in her change of allegiance, that she hoped, by working with him, to further his career as well as her own. Perhaps success would make him more palatable to her family.

Because goons from the trust were harassing IMP productions whenever they moved outside the studio, Laemmle decided to send the company to Cuba. At this point, Moore insisted, not without justification, that the Smith family be informed of the marriage. Mrs. Smith cried for three days and three nights and the children apparently did not speak to Mary or her husband on the voyage out. To make matters worse, Moore took an instant dislike to their director, Thomas Ince, soon to gain a major reputation as an efficient and gifted manager of action dramas as well as one of the prime inventors of the assembly-line system of producing films in quantity. Quite soon, Mary and Moore would leave for Majestic Pictures, a new firm, formed specifically to make Mary Pickford movies (it was the creation of Harry Aitken, soon to be a major factor in Griffith's career), where Moore was to be the principal director. As it developed, he could not handle his star-wife—ego problems—and by the beginning of 1912 she would leave him—and IMP—and return to Biograph.

3

Still for the moment Griffith was shorthanded. The most notable male newcomer was Donald Crisp, experienced both as an actor and a stage manager, but Griffith at first used him sparingly and, in any event, he was not a very romantic figure. When the Biograph company left for the West Coast at the turn of the year, Griffith's best leading man was the forgettable Lucas and his most promising leading lady was the inexperienced Blanche Sweet. Griffith had wanted to take her West the previous year, but she had opted for the theater. Now, however, her stage work had evaporated, her grandmother, who was her surrogate mother, remembered Griffith's interest and she appeared, job hunting, at the Biograph studios at the perfect moment. Griffith signed her, though by Miss Sweet's own admission, she had, in her fourteenth year, "grown in all directions" and was, physically, something more (and therefore less) than Griffith's ideal of youthful beauty. She has also said that she did not match his ideal temperamentally either. "I was always a rather independent child. I was rebellious. I wanted to do what I wanted to do and he was a very dominating man."

She thinks Griffith was disappointed by her manner as well as her appearance. But she did not particularly care. "I was without vanity and I was not particularly impressed with Griffith that first season." This, she says, set her apart from the rest of the company, "not one member of which was not completely enthralled by him; without a doubt the men just as much as the women."[11]

Thus Griffith lacked an ingenue of the type he particularly favored, for the other leading women who accompanied him to California—and there were literally a dozen of them—tended as a group to be darker and older (or, at any rate, less girlish) than his ideal. And this, it would seem, dictated a new emphasis in choice of subject matter. There were far fewer of the Spanish-Mexican-Indian romances that had preoccupied him in the previous year and, especially later in the stay, he turned toward straight action-adventure subjects, much less intimate than his best previous work.

In other respects, too, the tone of the trip differed from that of the previous year. For one thing, there was a new studio, this time at Georgia Street and Pico Boulevard, with a larger stage and generally better facilities for the actors and technicians. For another, Griffith's pace was slower. He averaged only about one film a week, handing over melodramas to Frank Powell, giving Sennett a chance at comedies and at some of the players in whom he was less interested—among them Mabel Normand and Ford Sterling. It is perhaps a measure of the growth in his prestige that this time he brought with him his sparring partner, a boxer named Spike Robinson, with whom it was his habit to go a few physically improving rounds almost every day. There was also, as Miss Sweet recalls, a growing estrangement between Linda Arvidson and the rest of the company. "She was very quiet, and she made no attempt to join in the studio's life, which was more important than home life or any other kind of life. I knew her only well enough to say 'good morning' when she did turn up."[12]

Maybe Linda felt that a certain reserve was a requisite for the wife of so important a figure. More likely, estrangement was growing between them. In 1910, Griffith was interested enough in a young Biograph actress named Dorothy West for Bitzer to comment on it. "There was hell to pay," he wrote.[13] In any event, Linda had worked for him only twice in 1910 and would work for him only twice again this year—at the seaside, of course, in dramas about women who must stand and wait for their far-darting husbands. By these castings Griffith was obviously trying to tell her something.

The first of these tales, *Fisher Folks*, was also the first film completed on this trip and in it, perhaps significantly, Linda played a crippled girl married by Wilfred Lucas, not out of love but as a form of revenge against the village flirt. He is lost at sea for a year, during which time his wife bears his child. When he returns he reforms, resists the blandishments of the local siren and settles down to hearth and home in a satisfyingly sentimental way, no doubt something of a dream projection of Griffith's.

But though Griffith would return to his same beach at Santa Monica for what would come to be regarded as the most important film of the 1911 trip, as well as for other sea-faring tales, the picture is less interesting than the third California film—*The Lonedale Operator*. The story could not be simpler or more melodramatic, with Blanche Sweet playing the young girl who relieves her father, a telegraph operator, at his post in the station so aptly named in the movie's title, a payroll shipment being due in on the same train that carries a pair of hoboes who imagine an easy theft from the girl. They of course reckon without her marvelously spunky nature (the role was perfect for Miss Sweet) and her frantic efforts to summon help by telegraphing down the line while the bandits batter at the station's locked door (the claustrophobic image again) are splendidly exciting. There are good, inventive little twists in the story's development. The nearest operator is literally asleep at his switch when she sends out her S.O.S.—with a train that could be used to rescue her idling outside under the command of her sweetheart (Bobby Harron). Griffith works this irony for all its worth in his crosscutting and once Sweet gets through to another telegrapher the director handles the locomotive's dash to the rescue brilliantly—alternating close shots of Harron, shots taken from the front of the engine of the country sweeping by, ground-level pictures of the train steaming down the tracks, and footage of the bandits breaking in on the girl and her holding them at bay with what appears to be a revolver but which turns out, in the end, to be a small monkey wrench she had disguised with a kerchief.

Griffith had never totally abandoned the melodramatic chase form with which he had won his first success, but surely *The Lonedale Operator* represents a return to it with renewed energy, possibly in delayed recognition that the open spaces available to him on the West Coast presented him with an opportunity for sweeping cinematic gestures that were denied him in the more cramped spaces of the East. Anyway, in this film, as in the westerns he would make on this trip, he set aside his deliberate efforts to slow down the pace of his productions as well as his interest in developing an historically romantic *mise en scene* to present his audiences with thrill-a-minute movies that seem to race through the projector even today.

He was still preoccupied, however, by the desire to make two-reel films. Perhaps to gain more respectful attention for it than he had received from *His Trust*, which was an original scenario, he reverted again to a generally recognized "classic"—that obsessive favorite of his, *Enoch Arden*. This time, however, he would release it under Tennyson's title. This time, too, he would devote a full week to shooting. There can be no doubt that he regarded it as the major effort of the winter schedule, for he dispatched an assistant all the way to San Francisco to rent costumes of a quality then unavailable in Los Angeles, rented a boat suitable to the story's period in San Pedro and had it towed to the Santa Monica location. In remaking the picture this one last time he carefully introduced each character with a vignette close-up and the subtitles here were more self-consciously literary than they had for the most part been in the past. The picture, indeed, opened with a spectacularly beautiful backlit shot of Enoch and the other sailors departing on their fatal voyage. That shot announced the film's intention—Art!—in no uncertain terms.

And as art it was received. Biograph tried to release it serially, then found theaters running the two parts not a week apart but a day apart in an attempt to satisfy, at least partially, the public's demand to experience the thing in something like its totality. The studio finally capitulated and allowed the two parts to be played on the same program—which was a victory not only for Griffith but for everyone who believed in the necessity for longer films. For Griffith was not just any director—he was now increasingly seen as an artist who seemed to be answering the call of his conscience—and Biograph was not just an independent studio trying to cash in on a sensation but the leading member of the trust and the most artistically reputable of all American studios. In short, *Enoch Arden* represented a famous victory. And it also became one of the first movies to have an extensive afterlife in the schools, where, being such a faithful rendering of the famous poem's story line, it became a much-booked audio-visual aid—long before that graceless term had been invented.

Successful though the film was, it was not necessarily the most venturesome effort of the trip. Frank Woods, in his column, singled out *A Knight of the Road* as possibly most qualified for that distinction. It is a melodrama about a tramp who rescues a family from robbery by other tramps, is rewarded by an invitation to settle down with the family but then succumbs to the lure of the open road. The picture is marked by Griffith's sympathy for a fraternity he had occasionally joined in his younger days (and which was greatly feared in these days, in part for political reasons, since itinerant workers were often supporters of the revolutionary IWW), and by a fragmentation of scenes into individual shots that one trade reviewer, at least, felt was unprecedented. The average movie might have twenty-five or thirty "changes of scene"; but this one had "at least fifty and maybe a hundred—the reviewer couldn't count them." He was disconcerted by all this, as critics continued to be for some time, as more and more directors made more and more setups per scene. Still, he manfully concluded: "As an experiment, just to show what Biograph can do, the film is a success, but unless one watches sharp, not to miss a scene or a half dozen scenes, it may be hard for some to follow."[14]

Griffith's steadily growing technical sureness was evidenced in other ways as well. For example, in his increasing adroitness in cutting on action (in *The White Rose of the Wilds*, for instance) and in handling large-scale action as in the last two films made on this trip, *Fighting Blood* and *The Last Drop of Water*, which is a brief, classic statement on that staple western situation, the wagon train fighting for its life against encircling savages. Perhaps its most striking detail showed members of the train who were killed by the Indians being covered over by the desert's shifting sands and it caused a moment's rebellion in the usually redoubtable Dell Henderson, who, upon finally being dug out of his picturesque but highly uncomfortable grave, quit the company. He was back in 24 hours, but the sense that Griffith asked a great deal from those who participated with him in the discovery of the art—and didn't always give a great deal in return (beyond the experience itself)—was not singular with Henderson. Mack Sennett was apparently growing increasingly restive, even though he was beginning to direct. On one occasion Griffith had quietly ordered steaks for himself, his wife, and his leading actors while crew and extras received the traditional sandwiches from the nearest restaurant. Sennett, however, noticed that culinary status-line being drawn and announced the lunch break in succinct fashion: ". . . steaks that way . . . and sandwiches this way."[15] He knew, as did everyone else, that they were lucky to be getting lunch before they were famished, for Griffith preoccupied with his work had a habit of forgetting the meal entirely. On one occasion, when he was supposed to lead an infantry charge with a rebel yell on his lips, actor Charles Mailes cried instead, "For godsake Bobby, bring the lunches."[16]

Griffith's drive for success was, of course, entirely forgivable and these small inconveniences were laughable. But the Pickford defection, Sennett's increasingly strong desire to go out on his own (which, legend has it, occasionally took the comic form of dressing up in a tux and hanging around fashionable restaurants and hotel lobbies, waiting to be discovered), the complaints about Griffith's high-handed method of assigning a leading role to an actor one day and making him an extra the next, and his habit of creating needless rivalries, took their toll. Actors have easily bruised egos and it required a special strength to stay the course with him, especially as it became clear that they had to be the pliable instruments of his will or they would be nothing—unless, of course, they were one of his handful of special (usually female) favorites.

Worse, in terms of Griffith's long-range development, his choice of subject matter was changing. The emphasis was more and more on historical material which spoke powerfully to his romantic nature, but which left less and less room for the things he did superbly—urban poverty, the simple verities of rural life, contemporary problem dramas. One can't escape feeling that in discovering California he was also helping to discover what others found there later—a debilitating distance from the reality of their times.

Yet, it could be argued that he was doing what circumstances seemed to dictate. By 1911, there were no less than three permanent movie studios in Edendale (Selig, Pathé and Bison); Kalem was in Glendale. And these represented only the major competitive installations in Los Angeles. Others came and went. It was, quite simply, easier to work here and the talent pool and the supporting services necessary for large-scale production were growing apace. Besides the nearly unfailing sunshine, the ease with which a company could move from studio to countryside to urban locations had to be considered. Biograph veterans would recall that if a few hours were required to change sets at the studio it was a simple matter to hop into one of the three waiting cars and grab a few exteriors in almost any atmosphere they needed.

Moreover, as Griffith's purely technical innovations were incorporated into the everyday vernacular of the screen, the best way to maintain his competitive edge, and his individuality, was to make more and more spectacular productions. Unlike the other directors of the time, he nearly always found a way to particularize and humanize these films with intimate moments and gestures, and it was this ability which kept even the largest of his efforts (including *Birth* and *Intolerance*) in some sort of human scale. Even so, there is something just a little bit hollow about movies like *The Last Drop of Water*. With its eleven prairie schooners, its cast of hundreds, its huge horse herd, logistics get in the way of sensitivity. There is a feeling of a mob lost in these vast western expanses in a way they would not have been in the more intimate landscapes around New York. Still, it must be admitted, the action sequences in *The Battle*, filmed only a little later that same year, are much better. Compelled to these large efforts by ambition, Griffith was also compelled to learn fast. He had to maintain his position as film's leading innovator, whatever the cost in the relationship with his cast and crew, whatever the strain it placed upon his basic sensibility. Perhaps he didn't notice any of this, for although he was at heart a kindly man, he was also, as Raoul Walsh, one of his assistants, would say, "a lonely man, a dreamer."[17] And these were characteristics already deepening as his reputation and his power grew.

4

The loner, the dreamer, the poet was, moreover, a sensual man. In his new eminence attractive young women were ever available to him. And he took advantage of their availability and of their feeling that he could advance their careers. When it started is impossible to say. About why it started one can only speculate. Perhaps his need to exercise the power so long denied him as a struggling actor just naturally had to be extended beyond the purely professional and into the personal realm. And perhaps, too, Griffith, this creature of hotels and boardinghouses and quick-lunch restaurants, could not make himself settle permanently into the domesticity his wife had tried to provide. Perhaps her restrained manner and the fact that she knew too much about him as he had been, before he asserted his claim to greatness, and had that claim validated by his industry's growing acclaim, was a factor in his desire to be free of her. In any case at some point on the 1911 trip to California she apparently found a love letter addressed to him by one of his actresses, possibly West. She taxed him with it, they agreed to separate and then he wrote to Linda admitting far too much. Declaring that all he was about to say was "the solemn truth," he begged her to "abide by it and don't try to find any other way out of it, as you value your soul. For there is none . . . turn your face to your own future." The truth was, he said, that, "after your discovery of that letter written by a certain other woman I have not been able to see how we could possibly live together any longer." More damagingly, he added: "There were others before her, and there are sure to be others just as objectionable in every way after her. . . . Let me lead my own life and you yours," he concluded. ". . . I am better off morally, and all ways, outside of marriage and so will you be. . . . Don't think there is some other woman in the case. It is not one, but many."[18]

A deeply felt letter, perhaps the most deeply felt piece of writing Griffith ever did. And the most costly, since Mrs. Griffith held it over him in order to obtain a very satisfactory separation agreement (a guarantee against a share of his income that would, through the years, amount to over a million dollars), not granting him a divorce until 1936, when, in effect, he stole one from her.

But the document, which comes to us in fragmented form, in a newspaper account of a suit Linda brought against Griffith in 1937 for $50,000 in alimony she alleged was owed her, deserves further analysis. To begin with, it is obviously a response to an overture from her about reconciliation and as such it is terribly blunt, even brutal. It might have been honest, but it was also vain and heedless of her feelings. Moreover, it was self-destructive, for even Griffith could not have been unaware that a wounded lady would use it against him, that it would ensure that no quarter would be given when the legal battles began.

But if their bitter breach was financially costly to him, it was emotionally ruinous to her. Much of her life was devoted to revenge; far too much of her strong intelligence and will were focused on it. Yet, ironically, she seems never to have fully accepted the fact that their alienation was irreparable. Her reminiscences of these years, published fourteen years later, is bylined "Mrs. D. W. Griffith," which was legally factual but hardly reflected the truth of their relationship. And the book never, in any way, suggests that anything had altered in their lives after this year—simply trailing off into digressions, evasions and, finally, silence. Worse, from her point of view, she did not follow his advice to turn her face to her own future. Instead, because of her economic interest in him, she remained tied to him, a kind of remittance woman who—excepting her rather charming memoirs—never did harness herself to any project more worthwhile than seeing to it that her check arrived on time and that it reflected her rightful (15 percent) share of his income.

As to Griffith, it is impossible to say what caused him to write the fatal note. We do know, from an interview with a former Biograph employee, that at some point in this period he was wearing a ring presented to him by Harriet Quimby, the aviatrix-journalist whom he had met through his wife—and that five of his 1911 productions were based on scripts by her.[19] We also know that he betrayed no outward sign of strain when his marriage broke up. He was as polite and distant as ever to most of his associates. He went on making a picture almost once a week. He attended all his supervisory functions with due diligence. He picked up a couple of valuable new players for his stock company. Perhaps only his films betray him. As a group, those of the last six months of 1911 are the weakest he turned out during the Biograph years.

The most important new face Griffith encountered on his return to New York was the cheerful countenance of Lionel Barrymore, who had been a leading man with his Uncle John Drew's company and had quit to paint and was now broke. He ran into Griffith at lunch one day and, in search of some easy money, made the journey to 11 East Fourteenth Street and braced the director for a job. "He looked me up and down, peering over that fine, cantilevered nose of his, and he said: 'I'm not employing stage stars.' 'I am not even remotely any such creature,' I said. 'I will do anything. I mean absolutely anything. Believe me, I'm hungry. I want a job.' "[20]

The onetime strolling player having forced so humbling an admission out of a member of the nation's leading theatrical family, Griffith relented. He told Barrymore to report the next day and to bring a dress suit. He used him as an extra throughout the spring and early summer and Barrymore, having proved that he could handle the rude suspicions and rough kidding of the men's dressing room, fitted in gracefully enough. One of those early extra jobs was in *Swords and Hearts* and he recounts a comic anecdote about its shooting. Along with nine others, he was assigned to die in battle on Griffith's signal. "The charge came, finally, with the 'Southern' troops roaring, lurching, and falling off their horses. It was a terrifying maneuver. Griffith called my number and I died like a dragon, clutching my throat and gasping horribly. I staggered under the eaves of the cabin, near a corner, kicked convulsively, and expired. It was a performance that would have pleased Fred Remington. My object, though, was to fall in a corner where the horses wouldn't step on me. The other Union gentlemen caught on and did the same thing. We fell in a heap and died en masse, a pile of corpses under the eaves as the horses thundered around us. Griffith made more noise than the cavalry. He worked us over in his excellent and blistering rhetoric, but he had to call us back for another day's work. We had to do it right the second time, and a horse's hoof missed my face by a twentieth of an inch as I perished miserably out in the open."[21]

Griffith used Barrymore a little more prominently in his next Civil War movie, *The Battle*, which is one of the best-made of the year's big-scale productions, and took a liking to the literate, intelligent actor, who represented for Griffith a level of the theatrical hierarchy he was anxious to attract to the movies. Barrymore was, in addition, an unpretentious man, a good companion at the lunch table and a performer whose skill and taste the director could trust. "Hard-bitten players like me he largely left alone, but . . . his younger people . . . he directed . . . minutely in every gesture they made, from the lifting of an eyelid to the correct way to scream."[22]

Barrymore played gently on Griffith's respect for the tradition he represented. He, too, sold occasional scenarios and later, having not made the company's 1912 trip to California, he employed a nice ruse to make sure he was included on the 1913 trip—the last, as it happened, for Griffith under Biograph aegis. While the director was mulling the composition of the group, Barrymore received a feeler from Minnie Maddern Fiske, who remembered him as a juvenile, and now sought him as such for her company. Barrymore knew he had outgrown such roles, but he decided to use her interest to pique Griffith's, and so arranged for her to call him at a restaurant where he was dining with Griffith and further arranged that Griffith could overhear his end of the conversation: "Why, yes, indeed I would. Work with you? Delighted. I'm sure I'd like the play. Why, yes, Mrs. Fiske. Yes, I could start at once. Shall we meet and talk it over?" When he returned to the table, Griffith's hesitation disappeared, "just before a forkful of spaghetti touched his mouth. 'How would you like to go to California, Barrymore?' "[23]

It was precisely the right strategy to employ and Barrymore sensed that, plagued by defections and what he took to be personal disloyalty, Griffith increasingly required proof of an actor's devotion to the medium and to the master. Throughout the period 1911–1913, Griffith was searching not just for talent and physical attractiveness but for loyalty as well. He wanted no more defections, and it is not too much to say that the search for this kind of personal devotion would be a constant of his career from this point onward.

In fact, the most obvious thing about his work throughout 1911 would be his refusal to commit fully to performers unless they demonstrated a prior commitment—and a properly serious air—toward him and what he was trying to do. Two instances of the growth of this attitude are particularly vivid at this time. The first involved Dorothy Bernard, daughter of one of the stock company managers he had worked for in Portland. He had encountered her on the street late in 1910 and he had given her a couple of small parts, picked her up again in the spring and used her sparingly through this period. She was, according to Miss Sweet, "better than any of us,"[24] an experienced, intelligent actress, but, perhaps, too high spirited and, by her own admission, not as serious about movies as she might have been. "Making movies was all a joke to me," she told an interviewer much later. "It was all haphazard. We didn't take the pictures seriously. . . . It was all fun. Actors didn't cut each other's throats. Nobody had this awful conceit. It was just a way of making a little extra money." This attitude did not, of course, commend her to Griffith, who liked her cheerfulness and, later, would indulge her to the extent of letting her bring her newborn baby on the set and call breaks for the actress to nurse her, crying: "Time for the baby to eat."[25] He gave her good roles, but he made no attempt to draw her more tightly into his circle, possibly because she had clearly decided to place husband and child above career.

Another excellent actress whose virtues somehow escaped him was Mabel Normand, a blythe and lovely spirit soon to reach star status under Sennett's guidance only to have her career destroyed in the twenties by the scandal surrounding the unsolved murder of director William Desmond Taylor, with whom she, along with another actress, Mary Miles Minter, was mysteriously involved. In the absence of Pickford, Griffith gave Normand a chance at better roles than she had been used to and, in Cuddebackville, in the summer of 1911, she was the subject of what might have been the first movie scene to be covered by three cameras. It was a fight on a cliff between Dorothy West and Miss Normand, playing Indian maidens in love with the same brave in *The Squaw's Love*. The climax would see Miss Normand being pushed over the edge and executing a back dive into the river below. Griffith did not want her to risk the stunt more than once, and thus arranged this elaborate setup, getting his take the first time. Despite Miss Normand's convincing demonstration of devotion to his art, Griffith failed to recognize her natural gifts. Sennett comments: ". . . he never saw that Mabel was a born actress. She was no intellectual . . . Mabel was pure emotion. All you had to do was say act out this or that emotion, feel this way, or look like you feel this way, and Mabel could instantly do it, throwing herself into the part so thoroughly that she believed it. But on account of the pranks that went on all the time, and on account of her being with me so much, Griffith never took her seriously."[26]

These represented the first signs of a weakness—a blindness, really— that were to have serious consequences for his career. Because of the long years of insecurity, he could never quite quell the inevitable doubts about himself and what he was doing and so had a ceaseless need for disciples— and no jokes allowed. His apparent strength was in fact a weakness, fed by his womanizing, by the presence of those who worshiped him, and would never say no to him. He was, underneath his courtly manner, an emotional cannibal and if this year only his wife felt the full destructive force of his appetites, their power was obvious to many who made a few films with him and drifted on, those who, looking up after a year or two, saw the danger they were in and fought free of him.

Now, as later, his work left almost no time for introspection—and that, too, was one of his curses. His 1911 Biograph contract raised his royalty to one and three-fourths mills per foot of film and it has been estimated that his income now was $3,000 a month—a huge amount by the standards of the time. But to earn it he still had to average more than a film a week and even though others were handling the comedy reels and even some of the melodramas, he took his supervisory duties seriously. No story was bought without his approval, no crank turned until he approved a film's cast and, nights, he could join Jimmie Smith in the editing room to check out the footage provided by Sennett, Dell Henderson, Frank Powell and others who took occasional turns directing the lesser units. In addition, he continued to check out the competition, prowl the streets for new locations and new faces, still stimulated by the excitement of his work and, perhaps, driven by an ambition for which he saw no need to conceive bounds, an energy that was, almost to the end of his career, equally boundless.

What matter that he had never known precisely who he was? Why stop now to puzzle on that question? He would be defined by his work and by his success. He would be a genius and that would be sufficient. And there would be no one to deny him. All are agreed on that point. Around him were gathering the yes men, forerunners to a breed that would find its happiest hunting ground in Hollywood. And soon enough they would drive out the truly independent spirits, the ones who might have tested Griffith and his ideas more severely and helpfully.

Perhaps the pictures he made between June and December of 1911 suffer from the twin hazards of being too busy and too isolated as much as they do from his emotions over his wife's departure. If *The Battle* was his most successful military spectacle to date, that was mostly because it demonstrated greater sureness in the way it was shot and edited, not because story or characterizations were much improved over similar efforts in the past. In fact, one trade critic muttered disapprovingly of the dance sequence in the picture—"too much hoydenish action and undignified jumping around," he wrote[27]—alluding to a problem that had already been noted by other critics and would plague Griffith in the future. He never really did understand simple joy. He tended to encourage mugging and excessive movement to indicate it. He never found a way to express it serenely, confidently.

For the rest, what is there? *Through Darkened Veils*, a rather treacly story about a blind man; an adaptation of Browning's *A Blot on the 'Scutcheon*, more pretentious than satisfying; a resurgence of melodramas about life in the slums, but with the emphasis distinctly on the melodrama rather than on life as it really was. In all, with his company in the weakest condition it had been since he formed it, with Griffith unable to find ways of transcending his recent achievements, he was coasting on his reputation, secure in the knowledge that almost anything he turned out was going to be commercially successful, and that, so far as the studio's executives were concerned, the less ambitious he was, the safer they felt.

5

Still, only about to turn 37, Griffith's creative energy was hardly used up and was bound to reassert itself. And he departed for the West Coast, at the beginning of 1912, with a renewed company. Mary Pickford had returned, not notably chastened by her experiences outside the fold, but noticing "some resentment . . . among the girls who had stepped up during my absence."[28] These include, most notably, Blanche Sweet and Dorothy Bernard in the New York contingent, and a young woman who would join them almost as soon as they arrived on the West Coast—Marguerite Loveridge, who would shortly introduce one of Griffith's most important players to the company. Among the men were the redoubtable Wilfred Lucas, and another veteran of no greater stature, Charles West. Bobby Harron, long since graduated from prop boy to light juvenile roles, was along and he was about to get his first steady succession of stronger (though still youthful) roles. Also present was a new assistant and some-time actor, Christy Cabanne, one of many such who would move on to directorial careers of their own.

Cabanne was quite close to Griffith during 1912 and 1913 and he remembered his mood as expansive. He recalled that Griffith particularly hated the nickelodeons, feeling that their ambiance was not sufficiently impressive and that they were holding back recognition of films as a proper art form. One day Griffith sketched for Cabanne—he was quite gifted with a pencil—a plan for a 7,000-seat motion picture theater, demonstrating a prescience about the commercial and technical direction of movies that he would shortly show in more public forums. He also had a word of advice for the younger man: "Keep away from Doctors of Divinity, Doctors of Law and Doctors of Medicine and you'll do all right."[29] Another assistant in this period, George Beranger, was struck by Griffith's relationship with his ingenues. He continued to toy with them profession-ally, encouraging rivalry by passing the better roles around among them on a seemingly whimsical basis, but, in Beranger's words, he "was quite obsessed by these little creatures." He speculated that this might have been a manifestation of his hidden feelings of inferiority, noting that, in general, he "fought shy of bigger people" and that his friends in the com-pany, like Cabanne, tended to be "simple" in taste and outlook.[30]

Free as he was of the constraints—and possibly the memories—of New York, a new vigor manifested itself in Griffith's work this winter. One of his strongest films was a remake of *The Lonedale Operator*, this time called *The Girl and Her Trust* and this time starring Dorothy Bernard instead of Blanche Sweet. The little film offers a convenient measure of how much Griffith's technical mastery had grown in just a year's time. For the first time he used a camera mounted on a car and driven parallel to the train which is pursuing the thieving tramps, who this time have a handcar at their disposal for their attempted escape (and, incidentally, have the heroine on it along with the stolen strong box). Griffith does violate a basic law of editing—the eyeline rule, which holds that a mov-ing object must always seem to move in the same direction in each cut to it—but it doesn't really matter, so compelling is the film's rhythm. It was a harbinger of the most sophisticated of all Griffith's Biograph chases, which he shot toward the end of this California trip for *A Beast at Bay*. In it he handled three elements—a train, a touring car and a rac-ing car—with similar brilliance (and, of course, foreshadowed the won-derful car-train chase at the conclusion of the modern section of *Intolerance*).

Between these two technically complex, if emotionally simple, films, Griffith, in addition to the customary number of genre efforts, attempted some nobler experiments. Of these, the one that strikes a modern viewer as the most interesting and the most successful, was a savage little creation called *The Female of the Species*. In it three women (Mary Pickford, Dorothy Bernard and Claire McDowell) leave a played-out mining camp with a man who is married to one of them and is the brother of another. They must trek across a bleak desert to civilization and in the course of the journey the man dies, as it happens in the arms of the one woman who is not related to him. The wife and the sister wrongly suspect her of doing him in (and, implicitly, of having been his mistress). "Half mad with lonely brooding" as a sub-title puts it, they turn on her and it appears likely that they will kill her for her imagined transgressions. What saves her is their discovery of an Indian mother, dead of thirst, and her infant who is still alive. The child awakens their maternal instincts and these blot out their jealousies and suspicions. There is a single-word sub-title, "Womankind," and a final shot of the three resuming their journey across the wasteland harmoniously sharing their new burden.

Despite this ending, which suggests a rather limited view of "womankind's" psychology, this is as strange a film as any in the Griffith canon. It is shot with a chilling, unblinking objectivity and it gives vent to a misogyny found nowhere else in his work. It is impossible not to see it as a symbolic representation of Griffith's own life—the wandering male, surrounded by women bickering over their claims to him and achieving peace only in death. There is also, in the lack of sentiment with which he views these three young women, a departure from his customary attitudes that is strikingly radical. One feels that in this film, alone among his works, his truest feeling for "the little creatures" that obsessed him is allowed to show—the womanizer's essential fear of the opposite sex, expressed in Griffith's case through his inability to sustain relationships with his young discoveries when they matured, the contempt implicit in the film's subtext, which was that only through assuming their proper roles as mothers they might achieve full human stature. From it one gains a measure of the duplicity involved in his usual public attitude toward women.

Ironically, he was within a few months of experiencing his most serious difficulties thus far with the girls of his company. Marguerite Loveridge's sister, then seventeen, had envied her sister's employment in movies, persuaded her to take her along to the studio one day and put in a good word with Griffith. He couldn't use her and sent her on to Sennett, who gave her work as an extra in a comedy he was shooting at Redondo Beach. At the end of the day, since Sennett had nothing else immediately available for her, he took her back to Griffith and he, too, interceded on her behalf. Griffith was shooting one of his Mexican romances (which Miss Marsh misremembered as *Ramona*) with Mary Pickford and told the would-be actress to report at seven the next morning on location. Bobby Harron gave her an old costume of Miss Pickford's, showed her how to make up and for the next months she worked something like three days a week as an extra. Her mother, who had been twice widowed, told her it was all right to quit school so long as she earned money. Griffith told her it was all right to earn money as long as she continued her education—which meant private tutoring. Thus Mae Marsh (she used her true patronymic but changed her first name from Mary to Mae to avoid confusion with Mary Pickford) joined Griffith.

The more he saw of her, the more attracted Griffith was to her—yet another fatherless girl for whom he could act the patriarch. Pauline Kael has aptly contrasted Marsh to Lillian Gish, who was—to Griffith, and thus to his audiences—"idealized femininity, and her purity can seem rather neurotic and frightening." Mae Marsh, as Miss Kael says, "is less ethereal, somehow less actressy, more solid and 'normal,' and yet, in her own way, as exquisite and intuitive. She is our dream not of heavenly beauty, like Gish, but of earthly beauty, and sunlight makes her youth more entrancing. She looks as if she could be a happy, sensual, ordinary woman. The tragedies that befall her are accidents that could happen to any of us, for she has never wanted more than common pleasures."[31]

There is no doubt that Griffith was smitten by these qualities—by the girl's lively intelligence and sweetness of spirit, by her becoming modesty and lack of driving ambition, which was, of course, her chief contrast with Pickford. And at some point in the next year or so, he would form a romantic attachment with her that would elevate her to special status in the stock company. "Your talking and giggling make me forget my worries for a time," he once said to her.[32]

Of all his players, Marsh was perhaps the most interested in the theory of screen acting and in 1921 she brought out a little book on the subject. Her memories of Griffith at work are among the most detailed available. When he gave Marsh her first featured role, in *The Lesser Evil*, he observed: "They always say you don't have any lines to remember. But you do have lines to remember in your head. You don't speak them, but they are in your mind. Think of your lines first and have them register the same way as they do when you're speaking." On another occasion he cautioned her: "We don't want actresses. We want people to think what they're doing. If you think what you're doing, the expression on your face will be right."[33]

What Griffith was thinking about at this time was a very wide range of films. He did a strongly felt movie called *The Old Actor*, which not only effectively portrayed the trials implicit in the chancy theatrical world but also demonstrated a strong feeling for the anomie of the aged. He indulged a scenarist named Mary Pickford in a sort of fairy tale romance called *Lena and the Geese*, which coincidentally contained a fine role for the actress of the same name; he did a moralistic melodrama about *Man's*

Lust for Gold that again utilized the nearby desert landscapes with great force and these subjects give some indication that he was again reaching out for novelty.

Never more so than in a project he had been nourishing for some time under the working title "Primitive Man." It was to be set in prehistoric times and it would be a parable about reason and unreason, the pacifistic impulse opposed to the aggressive instinct. Many were dubious about it, Lee Dougherty in particular warning him that cave men dressed in animal skins and brandishing clubs could be used only for comic purposes.

In a sense, history proved Dougherty right. It is impossible to see it today as anything but a pioneering example of the camp spirit. Nevertheless, at the time *Man's Genesis*, as it was finally titled for release, was considered a formidable "art" film, a major experiment. And Griffith had no trouble recruiting Bobby Harron to play "Weakhands," who uses his intelligence (he invents the stone axe right before our eyes) to overcome Wilfred Lucas, who plays "Bruteforce." His problem was to find someone to don a grass skirt and essay the role of "Lilywhite," the object of their contention. Pickford, Sweet and Dorothy Bernard rejected the role on the ground that the costume required a public display of their nether limbs. Cheerful Mae Marsh had no such compunctions. She happily wrapped the skirt around her—in truth it was quite modest—and went to work.

She left an extremely detailed description of the director at work on this film: "On the first day, he explained, 'I want you to sit on that rock wall over there. This boy you're sitting next to, you're very, very much in love with him. But don't do anything but look at him like you're in love with him. Have you ever been in love?' And I said oh yes, which I hadn't. He said, 'Just think that you're terribly in love and look up at him shy-like.' So I did, and then he said, 'Look up at him again and then put your head down,' which I did. Then he said, 'Now get up and run away.' So I got up and ran away. That was my first acting part. I loved it. I said to Mr. Griffith, 'When am I going to do it again?' He said, 'You've done it once. You can't do it again. That was fine. Maybe you can do something else tomorrow.' "[34]

In fact, he had already decided what tomorrow would bring—for when he had announced to the rest of the company that Marsh had agreed to do the lead in *Man's Genesis* he had added, as Pickford remembered it, "for the benefit of those who may be interested that as a reward for her graciousness Miss Marsh will also receive the role of the heroine in *The Sands of Dee*."

This was to be Griffith's major "literary" film of the winter, another adaptation of a Charles Kingsley poem, this time about a simple country lass, beloved by a simple country lad, who falls in love with a painter when that rascally fellow works her into a seascape she has been watching him do. She refuses to bring the artist to meet her father, who falsely accuses her of wrongdoing and whom she leaves to bitter loneliness. "The creeping tide came up along the sand and never home came she," as the poet put it.

On the face of it, the leading role in this film does not seem much of a prize, but for all those young women with absent fathers a film in which one of them would get to walk out on *him* must have seemed very appealing and the more experienced actresses who had turned down *Man's Genesis* were appalled by Griffith's assertion of authority in so peremptory a manner. A stage mother, Mrs. Smith (ruler of the Pickford clan), and a stage grandmother, Blanche Sweet's guardian, briefly set aside their tight-lipped rivalry to make common cause against Griffith. He, however, stood firm and Marsh, as Pickford put it, "gave a beautiful performance. Indeed, we were all so stirred, we swallowed our pride and gave her our sincerest congratulations."

Still, even four decades later, the incident continued to rankle—Pickford, at least. "The whole episode set me thinking: if a little girl fresh from a department store could give a performance as good or better than any of us who had spent years mastering our technique, then pictures were not for me. I would return to the theater, where the years of study and effort were a safeguard against the encroachment of amateurs."

She naturally chose to tax Griffith with this decision. She recalls an incident in the dining car on the train bearing the Biograph company eastward that spring in which she dared criticize Billie Burke and Griffith replying: "You—criticizing Billie Burke! You can't hold a candle to her!"

"Well . . . I can have my likes and dislikes—"

"No. . . . You're not privileged."

To which she responded: "And you're not privileged to criticize me."

It was on this occasion that she flung out a boast that within a year her name would be in lights on Broadway. And it was on this occasion that Griffith informed her that she was, theatrically speaking, damaged goods. One version of his remarks: "Do you suppose for one moment that any self-respecting theatrical producer will take you now after spending three years in motion pictures? My advice to you, young lady, is to stay where you are."[35]

Griffith never did quite get over the feeling that film was a second-class citizen in the world of art—even when he was widely regarded as one of the few genuine artists to be functioning within the benighted medium, and in later years, when he was not so regarded, he liked to tell people that he had always been primarily a man of theater who had unfortunately been led astray by film. He undoubtedly understood that Mary Pickford had, in her youth, already achieved more in the theater than he had in more than a decade of trying, could very well go back to it anytime she wanted to. Surely that knowledge galled him. And surely she knew that it did. The unspoken tension between them never really abated, despite the veneer of gentility with which they were always careful to cover it.

Still, she would have to wait until the fall before returning to Belasco and the lead in *The Good Little Devil,* which, ironically, would advance her movie career more than did all the work with Griffith. Meantime, Griffith continued to use her as an Indian maiden and one of her consolation prizes this spring was the lead in what he thought might be his definitive Indian romance, *A Pueblo Legend.* It was a two-reeler and for it he took cast and crew to Isleta, New Mexico, in order to obtain an authentic setting. Indeed, he and Bitzer were so struck by it that dramatic tension is sacrificed to static views of the pueblo where Pickford, Bobby Harron and Wilfred Lucas play out their drama. Yet even this failure reflects the resurgence of Griffith's ambition in this season of shooting.

6

There were reasons, besides those of artistic conscience, for Griffith to continue to extend himself when he returned to New York. For one thing, Biograph had by this time begun construction of a new studio, one which, incidentally, still stands and is still sometimes used for television production, on 174th Street in the Bronx. It was spacious, well lit both by skylights and banks of artificial light, comfortably appointed for the actors—perhaps the most elaborate studio facility in the country at the time. It was visible evidence of Biograph's new prosperity, a prosperity that could be traced solely to Griffith's efforts and in which, now, he wished to be more directly included. He was becoming a man of property, having joined his cousin, Woodson Oglesby, a prominent New York attorney and sometime congressman, in purchasing controlling interest in the Cascadian Spring Water Company (a venture which would not, in the end, prove very profitable), and also having begun a series of California land purchases that would, in the short term, represent a drain on his finances, but would, in the long run, prove to be reasonable investments. As befitted a man of his station he bought a new Packard touring car in 1912 for $1,250.[36] What he appears to have wanted from Biograph now was either stock in the company or a solid percentage of the profits. These, at any rate, were the subject of discussion a year later, when he made his break with Biograph. For the moment, it seems, he continued to work under the terms of his 1911 contract, though at a slower pace.

His company was strengthened, when he returned to New York in

June, by the return of Henry Walthall and by the recruitment, the following month, of the Gish sisters. With their mother they had, at one time,
shared an apartment with Mary Pickford and her family. Their backgrounds were similar—the Gishes' father had deserted them in childhood
and, along with their mother, they had taken to the theatrical road, with
approximately the same success as the Smiths prior to their daughter's
rechristening as Mary Pickford. Now, having seen their old friend in *Lena
and the Geese*, all three Gishes appeared one day at Biograph, between
engagements, interested in the movies as a stopgap and, no doubt, hoping
their old friend could help them out. There was a momentary confusion
when they asked the doorkeeper (Biograph and its people were now
famous enough to need protection from the idly curious) for Gladys
Smith, but it was soon straightened out and Little Mary appeared from
the depths of the studio to greet them with hugs, squeals and kisses. And
with the news that she had done so well in the movies that the family
now owned a car and that it had not set back her theatrical career either—
that it looked as if she would be working for Belasco the next season. She
offered to introduce the Gishes to her director. "Just then a tall slender
man came down the stairs, singing in a fine baritone, '*La ci darem la
mano, la mi dirai di sì.*' "[37] Mary called D. W. Griffith over.

Griffith's own memory of the details of this first meeting was slightly
different (as were Miss Pickford's), but he did have a most vivid impression: ". . . suddenly all the gloom seemed to disappear. This change of
atmosphere was caused by the presence of two young girls sitting side by
side on a hall bench. They were blondish and were sitting affectionately
close together. I am certain that I have never seen a prettier picture."

He went on in his autobiographical jottings, to quote a review by
Alexander Woollcott of Lillian Gish's appearance, in 1932, in a stage
production of *Camille*. In it the reviewer noted that in her death scene
there was around her "a strange mystic light not made by any electrician."
Griffith added: "When I first saw her in this dingy old hall I remember
well there seemed to be a luminous glow around her that did not come
from the skylight." Dorothy he remembered as "pert—saucy—the old mis-
chief just seemed to pop out of her, and yet with it all she had a tender
sweet charm." He remembered her teasing her sister, calling her "Old
Lil."[38]

He, in his turn, teased Mary Pickford: "Aren't you afraid to bring
such pretty girls into the studio?" he asked. She replied either that she was
afraid of no little girls, especially friends (Miss Gish's version), or that if
they could take her job away from her, then, obviously, she didn't deserve
it (Miss Pickford's version).

In any event, Griffith soon inquired of Mrs. Gish whether her daughters could act and Dorothy interrupted with comic pretension: "Sir, we

are of the *legitimate* theater." "I don't mean just reading lines. We don't deal in words here," Griffith replied, following up quickly with an offer to demonstrate what he meant.

He conducted them upstairs to the studio and recruited Lionel Barrymore, Bobby Harron, Henry Walthall and Elmer Booth, an actor new to the Biograph, to help out with their screen test. He told the puzzled sisters to remove their black hair bows and gave a blue one to Dorothy, a red one to Lillian, so he could shout instructions to them by color rather than by unfamiliar names.

Quickly, he sketched in the story. They were children alone in a house under assault by burglars; the men were instructed to pry open windows, knock down doors, shove a revolver through a hole left by a stovepipe they had broken off. It was all so strange to the girls, Griffith's commands were so startling, the activities of the other actors so realistic that they had no trouble looking scared when he told them to.

Still it was not enough for him. He yelled at them to hold each other and cower in the corner. Whereupon he hauled another revolver out of his pocket and began firing blanks, ceilingward, quite genuinely frightening the girls, who were only 14 and 16 years old (Lillian was the elder). Suddenly he stopped, put away the gun and smiled. "That will make a wonderful scene. You have expressive bodies. I can use you. Do you want to work for me? Would you like to make the picture we just rehearsed?"[39]

They offered some mild demurrers. They would have to ask their mother. They really wanted work in the legitimate theater. He told them he couldn't use them every day, which would leave plenty of time to make their rounds. And he won Mrs. Gish over by offering all three of them jobs that very afternoon as extras at five dollars apiece, sitting in a theater audience. Next day the sisters reported for their first starring roles in *An Unseen Enemy*, which was *The Lonely Villa* all over again, but in final form slightly different from what they rehearsed.

The Gishes did not get, in that first summer, a great deal of work. Dorothy, in fact, made only two more films in which she had long roles, and Lillian totaled only eleven films during all of 1912. Indeed, there was some doubt in those early days as to their gift. From afar, Mrs. Griffith was to write that she thought Dorothy was the more talented of the two—natural enough, considering Lillian's subsequent close relationship with D. W.—and Bitzer, when he came to attempt his own embittered memoirs, was scathing about Lillian. (She introduced Griffith to the cameraman who would replace Bitzer.) "It seemed too much trouble to light Lillian, and to make matters worse, she couldn't act, and when we finally did use her she just wanted to be beautiful." In particular, Bitzer had trouble softening her strong jaw so that it met his standards of beauty. He also thought her movements were too mechanical, doll-like. But even he had to admit she was a girl of extraordinary composure: "She would stand for so long a time without moving—waiting for the signal that at last . . . we had the lights just right on her face" and that quality finally won Bitzer's grudging admiration. "As I never could get a subject to be so patient, it was that about her that impressed me most, and I commenced to get some very beautiful effects with her." Even so, he claims that Griffith at one point nearly gave up on both sisters, saying, "They'll never amount to anything in pictures."[40]

If true, the condemnation must have been the result of a moment's irritation. It is true that Dorothy Gish was a spirit too independent, too satiric for him to be entirely comfortable with, but Lillian was to prove to be the perfect embodiment of the highest feminine principle as he understood it and eventually he would fall in love with her. No doubt at first he saw only her intelligence and independence and missed what was to be a crucial factor in their relationship, which was that she was a girl for whom the perfection of art for its own sake was not enough; she needed art to be placed in the service of some higher ideal and she came upon Griffith at roughly the moment he had begun to articulate such an ideal.

She has recalled that in her first summer at Biograph she heard Griffith raise his voice only once—when he heard one of the girls in the company refer disparagingly to the "flickers." "Never let me hear that word again in this studio," he said. "Just remember, you're no longer working in some second-rate theatrical company. What we do here will be seen tomorrow by people all over America—people all over the world. Just remember that the next time you go before the camera."

Overhearing, Lionel Barrymore said to Miss Gish: "Don't let it upset you, Lillian. It wasn't so long ago that D. W. himself used to talk scathingly of 'flickers' and 'galloping tintypes.' But now he has a vision. He really believes we're pioneering in a new art—a medium that can cross barriers of language and culture." Barrymore, according to Miss Gish, came to believe that this desire to advance the medium as well as his own career was the chief reason that Griffith drove himself so single-mindedly and unceasingly. And he added that he had himself come to think Griffith was right about the movies' potential for mass enlightenment.[41] Nor were he and Miss Gish the only ones to note this element in his ambition. Cabanne, for example, remembered Griffith holding forth at some length that the movies were the ideal medium "to bring out the truth about unjust social and economic conditions."[42]

Surely there was an element of rationalization in this, a way of making an unrespectable field seem more respectable. Surely the ideal was often lost sight of in the crowded and sometimes desperate years to come. But so far as one can tell, Griffith was the first important figure in the field to consistently enunciate this position, to define the movies in terms of highest aspirations rather than common commercial practice. And the effect this argument had on those whose emotions were touched by it is significant. One need only compare the strength of Miss Gish's reputation over the years to that of the equally gifted but more materialistic Miss Pickford. The former is, by common consent, an artist—and a lady who has, to the present moment, continued to function actively as one. The latter interests most people only as the phenomenon of another age's peculiar fashions, remote and enigmatic. For Miss Gish, Griffith's definition of the enterprise in which they were jointly engaged became a significant element in forging an identity strong enough to weather the many buffetings of a public life that has now stretched over seven decades. And one cannot help but believe that if Griffith could have retained this clarity of purpose after he achieved great fame and the potential for great wealth a few years later it might have had a beneficial effect, not only on the industry but on Griffith's future career.

Still, it was only in retrospect that Miss Gish began to see Griffith's idealistic side with some clarity. In that first summer, she remembered, Griffith used her to pique Miss Pickford's jealousy, telling her Miss Gish's costume and general appearance were more attractive than Mary's, suggesting that perhaps, in the circumstances, she should replace Mary in the leading role of some forgotten little film going into production. Both actresses saw it for the stratagem it was and refused to be drawn into the rivalry he thought would create better performances. According to Miss Pickford, she went to the director after work and informed him it was too bad "you can't get a good performance without trying to come between two friends."

"I'll have none of your lip," he is said to have replied. "I'll run my company as I see fit without the insolent criticism of a baby."

"I won't be treated like a baby."

"Well, that's all you are, and you know it."

This turned Miss Pickford into a self-confessed "hellcat." "Mr. Griffith, I don't care for the way you direct. I never have. If you were a real director you wouldn't have to try to turn me against Lillian to get a good scene. Why don't you think of a more honest way of directing me?"

"I'll have no more back talk from you, you half-pint."

Whereupon, according to Miss Pickford, he gave her a "rude shove," she tripped and fell to the floor, from which position she informed him that he was no southern gentleman and was, indeed, a disgrace to North as well as South. She threatened to leave their location and return to New York and she claims Griffith recruited the Gishes, her own brother and sister and Bobby Harron to serenade her ("So long, Mary, we hate to see you go!") through her locked hotel room door, melting her anger and leading to a reconciling glass of sarsaparilla.[43] The incident, one guesses, has gained something in the retelling after the passage of many years, for the mock serenade is the only recorded incident of Griffith-organized fun-

and-games on location. And yet, the notion that the years of unspoken tension between director and leading lady might be discharged in some sort of physical violence, however mild, rings true, particularly since this was a difficult season for both of them.

Since Pickford already had strong hints from her "darling" Mr. Belasco that he had something for her in the fall, she was marking time at the Biograph this summer. As for Griffith, he was in contention with J. J. Kennedy over his new contract and there is reason to believe that he knew Kennedy, adamantly opposing him on the matter of longer films, had helped a new firm, which included Edwin S. Porter and Adolph Zukor, obtain a trust license to show Sarah Bernhardt's four-reel *Queen Elizabeth* in the United States. The thing actually had a promotional showing in a legitimate theater, something Griffith had never had. Worse, the production was nowhere near as sophisticated cinematically as Griffith's. For all its length, it contained fewer shots than Griffith might use in the first quarter of a one-reeler, and the staging within the shots was static. In short, promoters with nothing more in hand than a great, if fading, theatrical name could blithely enter his field and obtain favors and the prestige that eluded him. Nor was that the end of his catalog of envies. For in this summer Mack Sennett—crude, eager, artless Mack Sennett, his oft-patronized assistant—found financing for his own studio and departed for the West Coast to set up shop in Edendale. And so, perhaps, Griffith can be excused for not immediately apprehending Gish's obviously distinctive qualities. And for sulking.

For sulk he eventually did. July was a normal Griffith month. He personally directed six films, among them *Friends*, a western in which he employed extreme close-ups of Miss Pickford, which she did not entirely appreciate; a rather good romance called *So Near, Yet So Far*; *A Feud in the Kentucky Hills*, which was another exploration of the brother-against-brother theme and which included another of his claustrophobic climaxes in a beleaguered cabin. Then, abruptly, he slowed his pace, doing only two movies in August, two in September. Only one of them—*The Musketeers of Pig Alley*—was distinguished. But despite its inelegant title, it was very distinguished indeed—one of the masterpieces of the Biograph period.

In the year it was made, New York City was reaching the climax of what had been, to borrow a more modern word, a highly permissive period. Under Mayor Richard Gaynor, something of a civil libertarian, gambling and other vices had been allowed to proceed more unchecked than ever in the city, as long as they did not become an obviously visible public nuisance; the gangster mobs from the Lower East Side, now run by Jews and Italians, more ambitious than the Irish, who had previously controlled the underworld, were extending their reach "above the line" (Fourteenth Street); the city's WASP and German-Jewish establishment was in a swivet about them and about police corruption, always a favorite subject among these uplifters. As the best historian of the seamy side of the city's life in this period, Andy Logan, has noted, the reform movement in part diverted attention from other serious matters, notably the ease with which the rich got richer, often on the profits from sweat shops and tenements.

At any rate, the reform agitation reached a climax when a petty gambler named Herman Rosenthal was gunned down by rival gangsters and a corrupt policeman named Charles Becker "took the splash" for the crime, as Miss Logan says, quite against the evidence and, for that matter, against all reason. The papers this year were full of that crime and full of colorful details about gang life. No doubt, this piqued Griffith's interest in a timely topic; no doubt he drew upon his own Bowery days for detail; no doubt the studio was once again delighted to have an easily promotable film dealing with a subject of such intensive journalistic scrutiny. Perhaps, since this particular crusade against crime had more than the usual overtones of religious prejudice, it can be seen as an early example of Griffith's unthinking distrust—"hatred" would be, and would remain, too strong a word for his attitude—of minorities. Be that as it may, Griffith had once again—and once again successfully—grounded his filmmaking not on his cultural aspirations but on one of the common concerns of the common viewer. It cannot be emphasized too strongly—it was this unthinking but constant touching of the roots of his experience that, in the long run, makes Griffith's Biograph films so rewarding.

Specifically, *Musketeers* starred Miss Gish as a young wife who becomes the object of a gangster's attentions and it concludes with a ferocious gunfight. As usual, Griffith displayed remarkable sympathy for the family attempting to maintain its decency in sordid surroundings and against heavy economic odds (Miss Gish's husband is a struggling musician). But perhaps the most exciting thing about it is the use of authentic locations in New York's slums. Advertised by the studio as an exposé of the gangster menace and often erroneously referred to by film historians as the first such work (Griffith himself had dealt with the subject earlier), its lasting interest is as a documentary; it is like a series of Jacob Riis photographs come to life. And it is also, of course, a sketch for certain aspects of the modern sequence in *Intolerance*.

In fact, as Griffith recovered momentum in the fall, there were among the many films that covered familiar territory at least three that gave hints of things to come. The first of these is *Brutality*, with its scenes of drunkenness and wife beating that prefigure—especially in the dark animalism of the male figure played by Walter Miller—*Broken Blossoms*. For it, as well as for several subsequent productions of the late fall, Griffith had sent for Mae Marsh, indicating that he had had more forewarning of Mary Pickford's departure than the three days she mentions in her autobiography. Indeed, according to Gish, he made an offer of $300 a week to Pickford in an attempt to retain her, this proving to be $200 a week less than her mother deemed suitable. He was, however, a graceful loser. "Well, Pickford, bless you," he replied when she broke into a rehearsal to announce her leaving. "Be good. Be a good actress."[44]

Miss Gish was also offered a part in the Belasco production, at $25 a week, which Griffith offered to double, although he told her she would be foolish to accept: "The name Belasco is worth ten times my offer," he said, again indicating his awe of a great theatrical name.[45] This is one of the few recorded incidents in which Griffith tried to bid against other producers to keep his protégés with him, but obviously he did not extend himself greatly.

He did, however, extend himself on Miss Pickford's last film for him, *The New York Hat*. And though it ended his association with her, it was the beginning of his association with a teenage scenarist who called herself A. Loos. Griffith, Doc Dougherty, and Frank Woods, who had now joined the story department after a brief but significant stopover at Kinemacolor, assumed their distant contributor was male—and considerably older than she was. Living in San Diego, where her father ran a not very successful stock company (and showed movies between the acts), Loos, thanks to her intimate acquaintance with theatrical literature and with show people, had developed a sophistication beyond her years. Like nearly everyone else she had observed that the Biograph one-reelers her father ran were much superior to their competitors, and when she got an idea for a scenario she just naturally sent it to that company, obtaining its address from one of the film cans in her father's theater.

Her story was exceedingly well constructed—even by Griffith's standards. Miss Loos demonstrated a sharp observational and satirical sense. It is about the daughter of a miser whose mother, on her death bed, pressed on the attendant minister (Lionel Barrymore) a small legacy, intended to buy the girl—anonymously—an occasional luxury the mother knows the father will deny her. Naturally small town gossips and do-gooders (the setting is Vermont), observing the minister buying the New York hat out of a shop window and then seeing Mary Pickford wearing it, jump to the conclusion that an affair is in progress and the minister must, finally, produce a letter, in which the mother explains the trust she levied on the man of the cloth. The story's appeal to Griffith is obvious; it gave him another opportunity to exercise his contempt for busybodies. But what is so appealing about the film is its essential good humor, its fine feeling for the pleasures (as well as the prejudices) of small-town life and the cleverly twisted plot in which just deserts are parceled around very sensibly. As much as any picture of the Biograph period, *The New York Hat*—on which Griffith spent three days of shooting—demonstrates the truth of James Agee's observation that Griffith "was remarkably good, as a rule, in the whole middle range of feeling" and if the movie does not represent him at the very top of his form ("just short of his excesses," as Agee so aptly put it), it again demonstrates that "he was capable of realism that has never been beaten" and that "he might, if he had been able to appreciate his powers as a realist, have found therein his growth and salvation."[46]

But no. Mere realism was never enough for him; it was not poetic enough and not spectacular enough. He distrusted it—it was so like what everyone else seemed to be doing—and undervalued it, not seeming to understand that he somehow invested his street pictures and his rural romances with an intensity, a frame-filling liveliness, that no one else was able to realize. But then, what artist—especially what primitive artist—really understands where his greatest strengths lie?

Most of the pictures he made in the last two months of 1912 were rather dull. Perhaps he was distracted. He attended Mary Pickford's farewell party and he journeyed, with other Biograph workers, first to Philadelphia, then to Baltimore, to see how she and Miss Gish were faring in the play *The Good Little Devil*, then began making plans for the annual California trip, succumbing to Lionel Barrymore's aforementioned ploy and including him in the company, along with another promising new leading man, Harry Carey. Henry Walthall came too, along with Walter Miller and Elmer Booth, a reliable heavy. Together they represented the strongest contingent of male actors Griffith took to the Coast in his entire Biograph career. Mae Marsh and Blanche Sweet were along to play female leads and he agreed to take Dorothy Gish with the company, at a weekly guarantee of $15, though he still did not quite know what to do with her. One suspects he was merely being obliging, since her sister had her engagement with Belasco and her mother had decided to return to Ohio, where they had all started from, leaving Dorothy somewhat at loose ends.

He completed one last temperance drama in the studio—it was the thirteenth filmed sermon on drink that he did at Biograph, evidence that the abstemious beliefs of his Methodist boyhood were still in force and representative of an ironically large preoccupation with the evils of drink for a man later to have serious problems with alcohol. He then began a romantic comedy, *Love in an Apartment Hotel*, was unable to complete it before it was time to leave for Los Angeles and, planning to finish it there, walked out of the old Brownstone on East Fourteenth Street for the last time. When he returned, the new studio in the Bronx would be completed and his relationship with Biograph would be near its end. He probably did not realize it, but when he closed that door he was closing the door, not merely on a chapter in his life, but on a chapter of film history as well. Movies would never again be made as casually as they were in that brownstone. In large part because of his own efforts, they were now beginning to require the kind of technical facilities—and the huge casts—that only a studio specifically designed for large-scale production could possibly house. A future that he would for a time master, then grow increasingly unable to live in as man and artist, was beginning to open up for him.

He never publicly expressed any regrets about the passing of the dim little world he had so comfortably dominated, but only briefly, rarely in the future would he be able to exercise the kind of easy and uncomplicated control over his art and his life that he had in these years when he first gained mastery over the new medium. One imagines that he did not even have any silent regrets. He was an essentially rootless man, "at home only in hotel lobbies and movie stages," as Lillian Gish was to express it,[47] and there were many stages—far bigger stages—for him yet to pass through. They would blot out whatever sentiment he might have had about the place where he invented not only his art but, to a very large degree, the self the world came to know so well.

CHAPTER EIGHT

"The $100,000 Idea"

"GRIFFITH's bold juggling with and breakneck pacing of film editing in 1912 and 1913—his use of motion continually intercepted, and continually resumed—exactly coincided with the American public's growing awareness in those years of the restless 'crisis which threatens all the arts,' " George Pratt writes.[1] In Paris, Schönberg's *Pierrot Lunaire* had been greeted with "hysterical yelling," as reports had it. In New York, Alfred Stieglitz had published samples of Gertrude Stein's prose in his little magazine *Camera Work*, writing that she later revealed had been influenced, at least in its structures, by the example of the cinema. And while Griffith was working in Los Angeles in the spring of 1913, three of the watershed events in the history of modernism took place. The first was the Armory Show in New York, which gave Americans their first extensive view of postimpressionist art and, of course, scandalized both polite society and the academicians of art, who probably wrote more prose they lived to regret on this occasion than on any other. Then there was the premiere, in Paris, of Debussy's *Jeux*, with its allegedly incomprehensible and "cinematic" choreography by Nijinsky. Which was shortly followed by the riotous debut of Stravinsky's *Le Sacre du Printemps*, with the same choreographer again directing the Diaghilev ballet, and making even the composer somewhat unhappy with his extremely fragmentary patterns of movement—"arcs of motion continually intercepted, continually resumed."

There were many, of course, who believed that such nonsense could not happen here, not in sensible, self-satisfied America. Though, of course, the Republicans had finally been thrown out of office in 1912 and Woodrow Wilson and the Democrats were beginning to translate into law a good many of the reforms for so long advocated by populists and progressives. And, too, there was the disturbing realism of the ash-can school of painters, not to mention the strange career of Isadora Duncan,

184

to contemplate. Still, it was easier to imagine the political activity of the moment as a minor readjustment, the artistic activity as a temporary aberration, than it was to see either as an end. Or a beginning.

So it was with Griffith certainly. He had no politics, except on those occasions when some manifestation of the *zeitgeist* reached out and touched him directly. (For instance, the enactment of the income tax law, in this year, drove him into a frenzy of resentment and in later years he would write articles denouncing it as an intolerable intrusion on individual freedom. Similarly, he would not become a civil libertarian until censorship threatened *The Birth of a Nation,* and World War I would interest him more as a subject for sentimental and chivalric films than as a world tragedy.) Nor did he recognize film as part of a revolution in sensibility. There is no evidence that he ever took the slightest interest in new developments in literature, painting, music. Quite the opposite; throughout his career he continued to resort to the literature of the nineteenth century—and often at its less exalted reaches—for material, and later turned a blind eye even toward such developments in his own art as German expressionism and the epic cinema of Russia. Nor did he seem aware that film was itself an example to the other arts. That a sometime theater manager named James Joyce had probably learned something from Griffith and his colleagues would be of no consequence to him. His was to be a career singularly insulated from the great intellectual and artistic movements of his time—an irony considering how much, unknown to him, his work contributed to these movements, technically and structurally, if not in terms of plot, characterization, attitudes.

In time, of course, he would pay heavily for this lack of self- and cultural awareness. But in the spring of 1913 it could be excused. For Griffith went West for the last time as a Biograph employee in a state of considerable self-absorption and, probably, irritation. He had been unable to negotiate a new contract with J. J. Kennedy and was still working under the terms of his 1911 agreement, which, though generous, did not give him 10 percent of the studio profits, which is what he originally asked for. Worse, he could observe that many people who had begun in the industry under his direction were beginning to move on to greater rewards.

Some small attempts had been made to placate Griffith. Management had at last agreed to permit personal publicity about him and his leading actors—though they were still denied billing on the films themselves. And Griffith had been told that he might at least make a few two-reel films while he was in California—if he cleared these projects with New York before undertaking them.

None of this satisfied Griffith. With remuneration still pegged to the amount of footage sold, he felt he had no alternative except to go on grinding out as many feet of film as humanly possible. And though his name was obviously well known within the industry he was still denied recognition as author of his films in credits and paid advertising. Finally, he had argued with Kennedy that it was not possible to clear, in advance, those titles he felt deserved expansion beyond one-reel length; such decisions, he said, must be dictated by the demands of the material and he couldn't tell about that until he actually began shooting. Besides, communication with New York had previously proved to be very poor and there was no reason to imagine it would improve.

Griffith's heart was not really in the one-reelers he turned out in California during his longer-than-usual stay in 1913. Of the shorter works none continues to exercise a very powerful hold on the viewer. There were no experiments with new kinds of story material, nor were there any striking technical advances or, for that matter, performances. The director's creative energy was poured into the longer films, of which there were, during this trip, eight, or slightly more than one-quarter of the company's production.

The trend toward what would shortly be called "feature" films was continuing to gather momentum, most notably with the successful imports from Italy, which in 1911–12 sent over such subjects as *The Fall of Troy* (2 reels), *The Crusaders* (4 reels), and *Homer's Odyssey*, which had somehow been crammed into three reels. They were precursors of a much greater challenge soon to come from that country; namely, a series of longer spectacles climaxing with *Cabiria* in 1914. The sensation of that year, however, had not been an Italian import but the Sarah Bernhardt *Queen Elizabeth*, hugely successful at the box office. Technically, neither the early Italian literary-historical spectacles nor the Bernhardt film represented a great threat to Griffith. The latter, as Robert Henderson has observed, contained but twelve different camera setups while Griffith, to take a typical example, had used 68 in the single reel *Sands of Dee*.[2] On the other hand, it rankled that America's leading director had not been the first to make a grand film. And Griffith, like most of the people who had any prescience at all about the future of film, could see that it belonged to features, that the brief day of the nickelodeon was fast ending.

Griffith himself was partly responsible for this. He had pressed as hard as he could against the constraints of the single reel, developing it to a point where it was obvious that nothing more in the way of drama and feeling could be jammed into it. It seems likely that the public, though perhaps unable to articulate the feeling, also sensed that a limit had been reached and was ready for new excitements.

Griffith began the process of stretching his vision modestly enough. He made nine one-reel movies in January and February before essaying something longer—*The Little Tease*, with Mae Marsh in the title role, the setting that favorite of his, the Kentucky Hills. The film was not quite two reels in length, short enough for Biograph to handle as an ordinary part of its program and thus unlikely to raise an outcry from New York.

Nor was his first full two-reel production, *The Yaqui Cur*. It was another Indian drama—picturesque, romantic, sufficiently action-filled. Attractively exotic, not very challenging intellectually, it too seems to have been handled by the studio without demur. And within the month (April) Griffith had found another project that seemed to him worth more than a reel. Shot under the title "Mother Love" but released as *The Mothering Heart*, it was to provide the first really strong vehicle for Lillian Gish. There is some dispute as to the circumstances of her arrival in California. Her role in *The Good Little Devil* had required her to do a bit of flying (by means of wires and a harness) and in Baltimore the wires had come undone and she fell rather than flew off a five-foot wall. When the play reached New York, Gish settled into a rented room and, determined to save at least $10 a week to send to her mother and sister, she subsisted on an unbalanced diet and grew more than usually ethereal in appearance. Belasco began to fear for her health—or so the story goes— and also to fear that her apparent illness might be traced to the onstage fall and subject him to a lawsuit. He proposed a vacation in warmer climes and, finally, she decided to visit the rest of her family in California.

This account may be true enough as far as it goes, but it would be a mistake not to enter Miss Gish's shrewdness and ambition into the equation of this decision. Her friend Pickford had the lead in this production and she faced a lonely winter's run in a part that afforded her few opportunities. In the meantime, on the Coast, Griffith was operating without his greatest star, Mary Pickford, with Dorothy Gish, Mae Marsh and Blanche Sweet not quite able to fill certain sorts of romantic roles. In short, convenience and opportunity coincided.

And *The Mothering Heart* proved to be, as Gish says, "a milestone in my career, primarily because, with two reels to work with, Mr. Griffith could concentrate more on the effects that he wanted and exercise more subtlety in his direction." Initially Griffith thought her too youthful for the role and rejected her at the first rehearsal. Miss Gish, however, was determined to try to "play old" and she showed up at a second rehearsal wearing falsies to give her a more matronly figure and won the part, that of a wife rejected during pregnancy by her husband, who favors a cabaret dancer. She bears her child alone, it dies, and in a famous bit of business, she wanders into a garden, picks up a stick and, in her grief, beats all the blossoms off a rose bush—the kind of pantomime only Griffith was capable of creating at this time.

Miss Gish, alone of the Biograph players, took an intense interest in those aspects of filmmaking which did not involve acting. It was her habit to look at the rushes every day, even to go into Jimmie Smith's cutting room to see, from his point of view, what worked and what did not in a performance. In the course of this activity during *The Mothering Heart* she concluded that she was overacting and asked Griffith about it.

"The camera opens and shuts, opens and shuts with equal time," he said. "So half of everything you do isn't seen. Then take away the sound, and you lose another quarter. What's left on the screen is a quarter of what you felt or did—therefore, your expression must be four times as deep and true as it would be normally to come over with full effect to your audience."

Griffith's explanation of camera technology was inaccurately mechanistic, and as everyone has noted, it led to some unfortunately broad bits of pantomime. Nonetheless, his concern with emotional truth in acting at a time when most movie acting was itself rather mechanical, also set his films apart. "The first thing an actor needs is soul," he told Miss Gish. "The actor with soul feels his part; he is living his role, and the result is a good picture."[3] *That*, of course, was the key—the stern insistence that screen acting was not just make-work, that the camera could reveal, as the stage could not, an actor's deepest emotions, even his unconscious motives. Perhaps Griffith sensed already that it had the potential to steal his soul, just as primitive people have always believed, and as, indeed, happened to some players in the next few years as the star system developed.

Griffith was never at a loss to theorize about screen acting, but just now it was not his greatest preoccupation. Feature films were—the ones others were making, the ones he was not being allowed to make. His sense of urgency about this matter was heightened by word reaching him from the East of the continued—and, it would seem, improving—flow of long films from abroad. Most notable among them, this spring, was *Quo Vadis?*, presented in three acts and running over two hours at the Astor, a legitimate house on Broadway. Griffith did not see this picture until his return to the city in the summer, but he perhaps saw or heard about the *New York Times* review, which was typical of the comment that greeted it. Calling it "the most ambitious photo drama that has yet been seen here," the paper's anonymous critic noted that it was "plain that a wealth of effort has been spent on details and nothing occurs to spoil the illusion"—adding that in particular "the arena scenes are almost painful, so faithfully do they paint a picture of ruthless cruelty."

The review concluded: "In none of the pictures is there the slightest suggestion of canvas and paint, all of them being taken with a natural background. It is said that a huge arena was specially built for the production and the film gives visible proof of the statement. The films are fine examples of motion-picture photography, all of them being perfectly lighted and free from blemish. The acting of the principals was calculated to help the illusion at all times, and the handling of the small army of supernumeraries admirable. If a feature moving-picture production can fill a Broadway theater, 'Quo Vadis?' ought to be able to do it."[4]

It did. *Quo Vadis?* ran for 22 weeks. And there is every reason to believe its reception filled Griffith with envy. Realistically speaking, there was little direct competition he could offer, given the straitened circumstances Biograph forced on him and his company. Nonetheless, *Quo Vadis?* further strengthened his belief that the future lay with features, as well as his determination to fly his flag in this field.

Around the time *Quo Vadis?* went into release, Griffith managed to slough off still more of his routine production responsibilities, turning over all the films destined for Monday release on Biograph's implacable schedule to an assistant named Tony O'Sullivan (with Dell Henderson becoming the new director of the comedy split-reels). From April 1 to the end of July, Griffith would personally direct only nine films while supervising the rest of the studio's production in only the most superficial manner.

Of these nine films four would be greater than one reel in length and two of them, *The Battle of Elderbush Gulch* and *Judith of Bethulia*, represented unprecedented commitments of his time and the company's money. For, in this period, he ordered his carpenters to sites in the San Fernando Valley, there to begin construction of a three-dimensional western town for *Elderbush Gulch*, a walled, Biblical city for *Judith*. Eventually, the latter, built in a defile in the hills near Chatsworth, and surrounded by the encampment of the besieging Assyrian enemy, would become the largest set Griffith had yet shot upon. Realistically, this Bethulia would have been indefensible against a troop of Boy Scouts, who could have assaulted it from the hills that formed two of its walls, but that Bitzer's camera did not reveal. It was also indefensible to Biograph's management back in New York. Members of the company have recalled Griffith arguing at long distance with the New York office about the costs of these constructions. Adding to them, there were huge expenses for costumes, extras and props. Why, the thing might eventually cost $30,000, $50,000—they didn't know. All management was sure of was that Griffith's extravagances would ruin them—especially since *Judith* was a tragic love story. Undaunted, Griffith fell into the habit of visiting, almost daily, the sites on which the physical manifestations of his dreams were rising. He was full of confidence that spring. Blanche Sweet remembers that when he sang on his sets his voice was louder than ever.

The shorter films he made in April, May and June were not particularly memorable. Nor was the first of the climactic four long pictures much of an improvement over his previous work. Titled *The Reformers: Or The Lost Art of Minding One's Business*, it can be seen as another preparatory sketch—again in a comic vein—for the attack on social uplifters which he was to make at greater length, and with far greater dramatic intensity, in *Intolerance*. His next film, however, was perhaps the best of the longer Biograph releases and must, indeed, rank among the

best work he did for the studio. *The Battle of Elderbush Gulch*, two reels
in length, is a simple little thing. Indians attack a settlement, a baby
escapes the shelter of her cabin and must, at great peril, be rescued—before the settlers themselves are rescued by a posse from another town. The
plot is primitive, but the shooting and editing is markedly superior to that
of Griffith's last big western, *The Massacre*, shot earlier in this California
visit. The rhythm as the film approaches its climax grows smoothly and
steadily more compelling, the detailing is more careful, and there is a
genuine sense of terror as the circle of marauders draws more tightly
about the settlement. The masses of riders, both Indian and white, are
also handled with deftness; there is no sense, as there was in previous
Griffith films, that they have been left to mill about on their own. On the
whole, Griffith's westerns are less good than his action dramas in other
settings, but this one, perhaps because it is set in a little hillside town
rather than on a vast, boundaryless plain, is an exception. Put it another
way: Griffith often worked most strongly within tightly defined physical
limits.

The next film seems something of a regression, rather more casually
handled than *Elderbush Gulch*. A sort of sequel to *Man's Genesis*, it was
made as "Wars of the Primal Tribes," referred to as "In Prehistoric Days"
during the long gap between completion and release under a final harder-
selling title, *Brute Force*. In it, Bobby Harron, the "Weakhands" of the
earlier film, portrays the leader of a community struggling upward toward
civilization and defending it against assault from neighbors still lost in
darkness. The moral is obvious—and the theme has a peculiar appropriateness to a man engaged in "civilizing" the primitive movie medium and
presently, indeed, fighting against the reactionary forces in his own front
office. It should also be observed, of course, that Griffith's interest in the
prehistoric surely represented an extension backward in time of the mys-
tique of the Noble Savage, which so intrigued American middle-class
culture at this time. At any rate, the film was neither worse nor better
than its thematic predecessor and, given the success of *Man's Genesis*, it
probably appealed to both Griffith and his employers as a solid box office
prospect.

By the time it was finished, the *Judith of Bethulia* location was ready.
And Griffith began working on what he might have sensed would be
his last Biograph film—certainly a test case of his relationship with the
studio—in a mood that can only be described as soaring. As he would at
every turning point or crisis in his career, he went to the melodramatic
and/or spectacular stage for his raw material.

Its attractions were obvious. To begin with, the play was well known,
which meant that a film based on it would find what has come to be
known as a "pre-sold" audience. Of at least as much importance in Griffith's commercial calculations was the fact that the material's source lay

in the Biblical Apocrypha, which meant that he could compete directly with the religious films coming out of Europe. Moreover, the author of the play on which it was based (though, in order to avoid copyright troubles, Griffith had commissioned a scenario by one Grace A. Pierce of Santa Monica) was Thomas Bailey Aldrich, a leading figure in the genteel tradition of American letters—editor of *The Atlantic*, clever light versifier and novelist, author of that perennial favorite among nostalgic books about childhood, *The Story of a Bad Boy*. His literary reputation was, no doubt, as eminent as that of, for example, Henryk Sienkiewicz, author of *Quo Vadis?*, making him a writer with whom Griffith was pleased to associate himself and the movies in his drive for respectability.

Most important of all, however, was the story Aldrich told, or, more properly, retold with suitably romantic embellishments. For his Judith is a respectable young widow, anxious to contribute something to the defense of her surrounded and starving city, willing—after decent hesitation—to undertake the mission her elders impose upon her—namely, offering herself to Holofernes, the Assyrian commander, in order to obtain the opportunity to kill him and thus disorganize his army so it can be defeated by the desperate Bethulians. Given Griffith's lifelong preoccupation with the question of what constituted sexual respectability in a woman and what put her beyond the pale, this story of a good-bad woman had obvious attractions for him. This was especially so given the major twist Aldrich had imparted to his basic material, having Judith fall genuinely in love with the man she was required to kill. Indeed, the strongest scenes in the finished film are those in which Blanche Sweet acts out this dreadful inner conflict.

Still, it must be said that once Griffith went into production he rather lost sight of such intimate dramatic detail. He had never attempted a film on this scale before and it is obvious that, as he proceeded, both the thrill of working on so large a canvas and the problems this entailed, distracted him. But his intentions remain obvious and Vachel Lindsay described them well in *The Art of the Motion Picture*: "There are four sorts of scenes alternated: (1) the particular history of Judith; (2) the gentle courtship of Nathan and Naomi, types of the inhabitants of Bethulia; (3) pictures of the streets, with the population flowing like a sluggish river; (4) scenes of raid, camp, and battle, interpolated between these, tying the whole together." He added, quite correctly, "The real plot is the balanced alternation of all these elements. So many minutes of one, so many minutes of another."

But despite the poet's belief that it was "one of the two most significant photoplays I have ever encountered" (he was writing in 1915 and his other favorite was the pageant-like *The Battle Hymn of the Republic*); despite his prescient hope that Griffith would go on to make "American patriotic crowd-prophecies";[5] despite Blanche Sweet's persuasive portrayal of the title role (she was good both in widow's weeds and vamp's attire, and even better at conveying guilt both over her love for Holofernes and over killing him); despite gentle Henry Walthall's surprising success at portraying a leading man of a sexual vitality rare in Griffith's work; despite the winsomeness of Bobby Harron and Mae Marsh as the young lovers; despite Lillian Gish's beautiful portrayal of a young mother increasingly desperate in her efforts to find food for her baby as the siege wears on for forty days; despite all this, the film is, on the whole, unsuccessful.

Edward Wagenknecht praises *Judith* as "certainly the greatest achievement of the early American film" particularly noting its "rich, brooding splendor" so suitable to its "semioriental subject."[6] No doubt that is the quality for which Griffith was striving; no doubt in occasional scenes he achieved it. But more often than not, he achieved merely the *idea* of this quality—a hint, a suggestion of what, given a larger budget and more experience, he might have achieved and would achieve in the Babylonian sequences of *Intolerance*. What one applauds here is a noble ambition, not a fully realized one. This is particularly noticeable in the action sequences. It is hard to believe that the man who had just finished *Elderbush Gulch* and was within a year of making *The Birth of a Nation* could handle these scenes so distantly and with such slackness. There is very little detailing in them—few smaller combats, for example, within the larger ones. The attempts to build suspense when the Assyrians assault the city are sketchy. In all, one has the impression of mobs milling about, waving swords, making a fuss, but not believably locked in mortal combat. Similarly, the exotic costumes and decor in the love scenes between Holofernes and Judith seem to bring out in Henry Walthall and Blanche Sweet exotic behavior that interferes with belief. Compared with the spectacles from abroad, *Judith* was perhaps superior. But compared with the standards Griffith had set in his shorter films and would shortly establish in his longer works, it cannot be judged as more than a most interesting transitional film.

It was, however, a thrilling production to work on. The Biograph people had never before attempted anything of this grandeur and their memoirs give a picture of an exuberant, youthful group uncomplainingly, even joyously, overcoming hardships, minor disasters, exhaustion simply because they were so excited to be part of what was obviously a great and unprecedented enterprise.

Everyone worked. And worked. And worked some more. The men who had just been appointed directors reverted temporarily to the status of assistants, in which capacity they were joined by others. Many actors played more than one role; Lionel Barrymore claimed to have done no fewer than six different extra and walk-on parts in *Judith*. Family members, too, were pressed into service and Lillian Gish's mother acquired a painful sunburn wandering the wilderness in a flimsy extra's costume. Indeed, everyone had trouble with costumes and makeup. Some of the extras' beards were made of crepe paper, which curled and sagged and demanded constant refurbishment in the heat. Miss Sweet's costume, in a scene that required her to ride a horse, was also made of crepe paper, giving her skin no protection at all against the unyielding leather saddle.

Confusion was everywhere. The whole company had to be bussed to and from the location. The extras were responsible for their own costumes—the wardrobe department was simply not big enough to oversee such enormous numbers of them. This ensured a frantic, endless scramble every day, one that was intensified by the knowledge that loss of costume was ground for dismissal. According to Lillian Gish, however, the most memorable hardship of the film was lunch. It was delivered in boxes and cost each actor a quarter. The contents were unvarying—a dry sandwich, usually cheese on thick white bread, a hard-boiled egg if you were lucky, a piece of fruit, a container of milk. Standard Biograph location fare, but somehow less appetizing than usual in the broiling desert. "I lived for so many years on those box lunches," Miss Gish writes, "that to this day I cannot eat a sandwich."[7]

Griffith's high spirits, however, seem to have carried everyone along. He was always, of course, a confident, even serene, director on the set, but while preparing and shooting *Judith of Bethulia* he appears to have been extraordinarily forthcoming. He had been taking dancing lessons from an instructor named Gertrude Bambrick and he hired her to choreograph dances in the Denishawn manner for *Judith*. Between takes he would turn to her and say, "Well, Miss Bambrick, how about a few steps?" and off they would whirl. Early in his instruction, "He didn't know his right foot from his left," she later recalled. "But within six months he was a beautiful dancer. He never gave up on anything. He'd stick to it until he succeeded."[8] Dancing would remain, for the rest of his life, his favorite recreation, and Miss Bambrick would work for him, as rehearsal pianist and occasional choreographer, for some years.

His first encounter with a young woman who was to play an important role in his developing career is a good indication of his bustling good cheer at the time. Anita Loos, the teenage scenarist, came up from her home in San Diego at this time to meet Doc Dougherty, the story editor who was amazed to discover that "A. Loos," author of sophisticated screen material, was barely twenty, and a woman at that. Griffith, in effect, did a long double take on being introduced to her (and her mother, who had chaperoned her on her visit to the dangerously glamorous movie studio). Mrs. Loos and her (for once) tongue-tied daughter had actually left the lot and were proceeding in the direction of a streetcar stop when they heard a hail behind them.

It was Griffith, standing in the studio gate, beckoning them to return. He mispronounced her name ("Miss Looze") as he would continue to do throughout their long association, and that day he had chosen from his extensive collection of eccentric hats a huge, battered Mexican number, but "even under that ridiculous sombrero he looked so compelling and fateful that mother's hackles must have risen; she must have known that this might be good-bye forever to her little girl." Nevertheless, "like an invisible magnet, Griffith pulled her back, with me in tow."

He took them to the studio's outdoor stage, lavishly dressed and populated, at this point, largely by semi-nude dancing girls, "their faces dead white, with black smudged eyes and violent red lipstick." Griffith gave Miss Loos the place of honor next to his camp chair and while her mother "tried to look at the shocking spectacle without actually seeing it," he went to work on a love scene between Henry Walthall and Blanche Sweet. Describing it, Miss Loos gives us a Griffith more obviously stimulated, excited by this project than by any other project in the later Biograph years. Indeed, no other description of him at work stresses, as Miss Loos does, the notion that he actually found pleasure in doing it: "He stepped onto the set from time to time to demonstrate some tactics of seduction which he did with a sense of fun that prevented any harm to his male dignity. Sometimes he put his arms about the semi-nude Miss Sweet and whispered in her ear, obviously to save the young actress the embarrassment of his criticism's being overheard." To Miss Loos's mother these embraces looked like "sheer license," evidence that "we were in an anteroom of hell."

The relationship between Griffith and a mother who had divined his sexual nature quite accurately was not improved when Griffith took them to lunch at the corner drugstore, and Griffith—not without his own ability to read character—drew from Miss Loos the confession that she had ambitions as an actress and that it was a constricting home life that had led her first to the library, then to writing. They had a lively literary discussion, Miss Loos enthusing about Plato, Montaigne, Spinoza, Voltaire—the last of whom Griffith thought rather too cynical, at least as Miss Loos described his work. She, on the other hand, found his ranking of Whitman in his personal literary pantheon rather too high. Too hysterical, she thought.

By the end of lunch Griffith was saying, "I think we'll have to get you out of San Diego." And not just to Hollywood. "I think you belong in New York, Miss Looze." This, of course, was too much for Mrs. Looze and she forthwith whisked her daughter back home, from which the young writer escaped only through a brief and comically disastrous marriage that apparently convinced her mother that a creative career in the movies, if it did not involve immodest public displays as an actress, would absorb her willful daughter's bounding energy.[9]

Griffith's expansive mood extended in all directions. Blanche Sweet, for example, remembers a discussion about the casting of her leading man in *Judith*. There was a body of opinion in the studio that favored Alfred Paget. Griffith, however, leaned to Walthall from the beginning. Too short, he was advised. "Well, Wally will play him tall," the director said with a smile. And that settled the matter,[10] though it must be added that under Griffith's direction the gentle Walthall did, indeed, play him tall and, more significantly, with a fierceness not often seen in his acting.

There is, however, no better evidence of Griffith's confidence than the fact that he invited his old employer and leading lady, Nance O'Neil, to visit his set. He had previously shown no inclination to introduce the more respectable of his old theatrical colleagues to the movie world. It is doubtless a measure of his medium's growing prestige that Miss O'Neil asked for such an introduction (though she did not work in the movies until the arrival of sound, when she did character roles in minor films). It is doubtless a measure of his own growing pride that he permitted the visit. After all, he was in command of a cast larger than any stage could hold, in charge of a production as costly as any stage spectacular.

Among the scenes Miss O'Neil witnessed was one in which Miss Sweet, dressed in sackcloth and ashes, mimed her grief at widowhood. Before beginning it, Griffith approached the young actress and said, "show her," show the great lady from the stage, that is, what a movie actress, one of the director's most apt pupils, could do. Whether Miss O'Neil was suitably impressed we do not know. There is, however, evidence that Griffith was certain he had found his metier in *Judith of Bethulia*. During the production, according to Miss Sweet, he was full of plans for production of another exotic, romantic adaptation of a work about a woman who was also a courtesan, though from choice rather than necessity—Flaubert's *Salammbô*.[11]

Given his circumstances, it was not a very realistic idea. Biograph executives had sent out from New York a small, mustached, bespectacled accountant named Johannes Charlemagne Epping, whose function was to prevent Griffith's romantic excesses from being translated into financial ones. His worried, fussing presence was felt on location and on the studio's stages nearly every day, insisting on conferences, being put off until the master finished whatever scene was in progress. One can only imagine Epping's response when he heard about the incident at the well.

The well was a fake, a thing of canvas and wood set up at the Chatsworth location as the place where the juvenile and the ingenue (Bobby Harron and Mae Marsh) would meet and fall in love. Griffith insisted that the well be practical, that his players could be observed drawing real water from it. Alas, repeated rehearsals and takes drained it dry one day and Griffith required a new tank of water, special delivery, at a cost of $80. He would not, could not, wait for the regularly scheduled delivery.

And so it would continue to go—until *Judith of Bethulia* had cost Biograph an estimated $36,000, about twice the figure at which Griffith had budgeted it. And yet, in the course of what must have been very tense conferences, Griffith won a convert—none other than the man many around Griffith regarded as a management spy, J. C. Epping. Whatever Griffith's excesses, the little man apparently grasped that the director was on to something important, that his future was brighter than Biograph's and that he would need someone like . . . well, like Johannes Charlemagne Epping . . . to assert the reality principle, to keep the vaulting ambition within financial reason. He would become Griffith's business manager and he would serve him loyally almost to the end of his career, quietly, efficiently patching and bailing the endlessly leaking ships that were Griffith's various production companies.

2

Marvin and Kennedy, back in New York, were not so easily converted. In fact, they were not converted at all. When Griffith reported to the new studio in the Bronx—the studio many believed had been built for him and all knew had been built *by* him, by the profits he had created for Biograph—his reception was vague and distant.

His position was not as strong as it might have been. *Judith of Bethulia* was not quite finished—a few interiors and the titling (which was undertaken by Frank Woods) remained to be completed. And there was the matter of cutting it from six to four reels. It appears that Kennedy and Marvin focused on these defects, as well as on a plan to release the film serially in their discussions with Griffith. They were trying to assert control over their errant director; there is no other explanation for their peculiar behavior.

For it would seem they were no longer in principle opposed to longer films. During Griffith's absence, they had actually concluded an agreement with Klaw and Erlanger, the theatrical syndicate, to make five-reel films out of their most successful plays. These, apparently, were not to be drawn from the realm of the spectacular stage but from the repertory of smaller-scale drama. The material would have suited Griffith, but it would pointedly not be offered to him.

Curious, this need to discipline—if not humiliate—the man who had, in all probability, rescued their corporation—and whose departure would send it to quick ruin. Perhaps they resented the near-absolute authority over stories and casting he had, through the years, arrogated to himself. Perhaps they resented his growing reputation in the industry and his increasingly imperious ways with them. Perhaps they felt that, forced, he could continue to achieve good results while still paying decent attention to cost control. Certainly they understood *Judith of Bethulia* for what it partially was, a challenge to their authority and to their style of doing business, a rebellion they were compelled to put down.

So they put him to work "supervising" other Biograph pictures. And when he again raised the issue of a new contract, Kennedy belatedly informed Griffith of the recently concluded arrangement with Klaw and Erlanger, catching the director off balance. Other directors would be hired to make the K and E films, Kennedy said, but he would like Griffith to oversee them. He would, of course, have to relinquish control over casts and stories and make a more serious effort to stay within budgetary limits. In short, he was being asked to cease direction and become a member of middle management. The only consolation was that he would be allowed to complete work on *Judith of Bethulia.*

Of course, all this may have been, at bottom, no more than a negotiating ploy, a duplicitous attempt to demonstrate to Griffith his dispensability before negotiating his long-delayed contract. Surely Kennedy understood that Griffith was, by common consent, the industry's leading director. Surely he also understood that many of the studio's most popular players and gifted technicians owed their primary loyalty to Griffith, not to the corporation, and would probably follow him elsewhere. But Griffith either could not or would not understand Kennedy's offer as an invitation to bargain. He was not by nature a bargainer. Compromise was alien to him. The only thing he wanted now, or later, was autonomy. All other considerations were secondary, details to be worked out, if necessary, by associates.

This was the true Griffith, commander of all he surveyed on his sets, Jake's boy and finally enjoying it. But it was also a Griffith that Kennedy had probably not seen in his previous negotiations, the Griffith whose self-esteem had been crushed by his many luckless years and who had been glad to enjoy steady work at ever-improving pay in the years between 1908 and 1912. Now the world had at last come around to his own view of his gifts and now he would find a way to exercise them to the fullest, without the nagging interference of smaller spirits.

There was a second conversation with Kennedy, no more satisfying than the first. This time there was no talk of supervisory work. But as for directing . . . , "The time has come for the production of big fifty thousand dollar pictures," Kennedy is reported as telling him. "You are the man to make them. But Biograph is not ready to go into that line of production. If you stay with Biograph it will be to make the same kind of short pictures that you have in the past. You will not do that. You've got the hundred thousand dollar idea in the back of your head."[12]

When Griffith refused this grudging second offer, one suspects that among J. J. Kennedy's emotions relief loomed large. After Griffith's performance in California this past summer there was no reason to suppose that even if he promised to stay within a budget he would actually do so.

Kennedy thus became the first—but by no means the last—film executive
to understand that, carried away by grand conceptions that always grew
grander in the execution, Griffith would literally lie, cheat and steal in
order to realize them on film. And defend himself by raising the cry of
"Art." He was, in short, a man politely but persistently possessed. Which
meant that he required now, as he would later, backers with more sporting spirit than Jeremiah J. Kennedy, who still thought the movies could
be, ought to be, as rational as any other form of enterprise. Griffith would
also need entrepreneurs who could entertain the possibility that movies
might be art and thus have available to themselves high-minded conso-
lations when his gambles failed.

He was never to find anyone, or any group, with both these attributes. But in the fall of 1913 there were, at least, plenty of high rollers
interested in plunging on so reputable a director. The Motion Picture Patents Company had never succeeded in squelching its independent competitors and in 1912 the Edison Company had lost one of the many suits
brought against it under the Sherman Anti-Trust Act. This had em-
boldened the independents. But perhaps more significant was their steady
drift away from the business style set by patents company members. They
did not insist that their exhibitors limit a successful film's engagement to
a single day; instead they were encouraged to let them play as long as the
public would support them. Independents were also the ones who were
pioneering the star system and who were most interested in long films.
In the end, the courts would repeatedly find in their favor in their litigation with the patents company, but these decisions would be largely irrelevant. The important thing was that beginning in 1912–1913 the public
began to find in their favor, responding eagerly to their innovations,
knowing little and caring less about the legal technicalities of the matter.

Griffith could not, of course, turn to the other members of the trust
for employment. Kennedy was president of the combine and, in any
event, most of its members agreed with him about the proper course to
follow; the rest were unwilling to risk an open break with their leadership. Obviously, the independents were the ones Griffith would have to
approach. They were already far fewer in number than they had been
when he started out in movies, but those who had survived this first era
of consolidation were proving to be, just as the lately fashionable social
Darwinists had said they would be, tougher and smarter than those they
had defeated. They were also rich enough; not as rich as they shortly
would be, most of them, but well enough off to contemplate financing
Griffith in the style he thought suited him.

They spent, alas, as much time squabbling among themselves (perhaps too mild a term for their cutthroat competition) as they did fighting
the trust, but that was perhaps an inevitable, even a necessary, defect.
They were the founding fathers—the founding pirates, really—of the mo-

tion picture industry as it would soon be constituted in its economic maturity. Indeed, most of the institutions they created continue to exist, albeit in revised forms, in the present day.

Typical of this breed was William Fox, a New York theater owner who was one of the trust's most vociferous opponents. He had gone into production in order to ensure a steady supply of films for his ever-expanding chain and is generally credited as the first man to combine in one corporation production, distribution and exhibition, a feat he accomplished, not through acquiring pre-existing firms, but by creating his own organization. To the public at large, however, he was shortly to become known as a shrewd discoverer of talent and an even shrewder publicist. In the next few years he would mount the famous campaign that turned Theodosia Goodman, a tailor's daughter born in Cincinnati, Ohio, into Theda Bara, alleged to have been born in the Sahara, love child of a French artist and his Arab paramour, and, according to the publicity, a seer who constantly surrounded herself with the symbols of death— mummy cases, ravens, skulls. Her name was supposed to be an anagram for the phrase "Arab death," but for a brief time she was a potent life force at the box office and Fox seemed to enjoy hugely the game he created for her to play. Besides having his gift for publicity, he was a nimble production executive—never above rushing a quickie into production in order to beat a competitor with a similar idea to market (as he did with a *Carmen* designed to steal the thunder from Cecil B. DeMille's much-publicized 1915 version of the Mérimée story), never too inflexible to imitate another man's success or to instantly revamp his plans when circumstances dictated (once blithely changing a picture already sold to exhibitors as a Spanish romance into a Russian one when snow fell on his New Jersey set). In all, he was a raffish figure, but not, like some of his contemporaries, one to carelessly neglect the basics. While winning (and losing) spectacularly on his major films he would, after 1917, quietly keep Tom Mix under contract. From the literally dozens of westerns in which he starred Fox created the on-going prosperity of his studio.

Diminutive, soft-spoken Adolph Zukor—sometimes known to his later employees as "Creepy"—lacked Fox's personal magnetism and he conducted his affairs differently. A one-time furrier, he drifted into what he called "the penny business" in 1903 as an investor in an arcade on Fourteenth Street in New York. A little later he took over as manager, expanded into a small chain, then partnered with Marcus Loew, an old friend, and, in time, turned the Fourteenth Street place into what has been described as "a (for the time) semi-palatial cinema." It was from this vantage point that he first observed Griffith in his comings and goings at the old Biograph studio. He was apparently impressed by his bearing, his personal style. At any rate, he followed Griffith's career with interest and once or twice tried to lure him away from Biograph. Now, in

1913, having left Loew and having made a sizable profit on the Bernhardt *Queen Elizabeth*, he was in the process of organizing his Famous Players ("in Famous Plays," to complete the slogan), an idea that was the logical outcome of that first success. His partner was Daniel Frohman, the theatrical producer, and he was within a few months of concluding a distribution deal with a new firm, Paramount Pictures (which he would ultimately absorb), and he already had in hand contracts with a large group of "famous players," including a young woman not yet truly famous by Broadway standards but destined to outdistance them all— Mary Pickford.

In comparing Fox and Zukor, one is tempted—in part by the accidental congruence of a single key word—to apply quite literally the phrase Isaiah Berlin has made famous in our own time: ". . . the fox knows many things, but the hedgehog knows one big thing." The fox (or Fox) was willing, at this moment, to try anything that might sell a picture. The hedgehog (Zukor) knew one big thing—that whatever else might help sell a film (subject matter of current journalistic interest, a great title from literature, a striking promotional campaign), one factor could be made into a stabilizing constant. That, of course, was the star. Properly built up, he or she simply by appearing in a film could bring the public in, regardless of the quality of the surrounding work. As of the fall of 1913, Zukor was prepared to extend this concept to include one director— Griffith.

There were others, at this point no less powerful than Zukor, who were, perhaps, less in thrall to the star concept, but similarly preoccupied with the creation, through combination, of large-scale corporations that would operate at every level of the business. This was a quarrelsome process, with partners endlessly trying to gain the upper hand in these arrangements and falling out with one another in the process. The leaders in what might be termed the agglomerating style were Carl Laemmle and Harry Aitken. Laemmle had taken his IMP company into Universal Pictures, a production and distribution outfit organized by Pat Powers, who was essentially a distributor and essentially a small-timer. (He was later to be the first distributor of Mickey Mouse cartoons.) Laemmle and his partner, Robert Cochrane (who was the author of a spirited series of trade paper ads that helped rally opposition to the trust), quickly fell to squabbling with Powers and his allies.

This escalated to warfare in the literal sense, with the Laemmle forces occupying the New York offices and physically resisting the efforts of the Powers people to enter. Process servers and strong-arm men were both rebuffed. At one point a jewelry salesman named Lewis J. Selznick—later to be a prominent producer himself, and the father of David O. and Myron, producer and agent *extraordinaire*, respectively—penetrated the fortress and in the confusion managed to appoint himself general manager of the company by the simple expedient of printing up some stationery bearing that title beneath his name.

At another point the Powers group managed to halt an annual meeting by the similarly simple expedient of tossing the firm's books and its corporate seal out the window when it appeared that the stockholders would not support the insurgents' charges of mismanagement. Indeed, a probably exaggerated legend has long held that one of Universal's first big box office successes, a study of white slavery called *Traffic in Souls*, was made by a group of employees working without Laemmle's knowledge and without his approval after he screened the first time. It was only on the second showing that he grudgingly gave his consent to release—and to a box office bonanza. In short, until Laemmle finally bought out Powers a few years later, the operation was a shambles—if a profitable one.

The other great agglomerator, Harry Aitken, was one of the most remarkable figures in this phase of movie development and, because he turned out to be one of its remarkable losers as well, one of the least-known of the group later to be known, on ceremonial occasions, as "pioneers of the industry." With his brother, Roy, Aitken had been in the movie business since 1905, mostly as an operator of film exchanges in the Middle West, where the Aitkens, like so many others, had gone from cooperation with to opposition to the trust. In search of product, they had acquired a half-dozen small but well-known independent production companies and also began acquiring foreign product through Western Import (which was Roy's special concern), were producing at two major studios, Reliance in New York and Majestic in Los Angeles, and were releasing mainly under the famous Mutual trademark—a winged clock with the hands spinning around the dial, accompanied by the legend, "Mutual Movies Make Time Fly."

Harry Aitken's chief asset—in addition to 35 exchanges scattered around the country—was a quick mind and a ready tongue. His chief defect, like that of a later generation of even more spectacular grand acquisitors, was impatience. He loved new beginnings but was bored by the day-to-day business of managing his creations, consolidating what could have grown into an empire on the order of Paramount or M-G-M. A medium-sized, balding man with a disarmingly open face, Aitken had already made contact with a group that had not, so far, had much to do with movies—the private investment bankers of Wall Street—and though he was never able to get huge commitments from the likes of Crawford Livingston, Felix Kahn, and W. B. Joyce, prominent names in this field, their modest flyers increased Aitken's prestige in the industry and enabled him, as well, to acquire backing from more innocent investors impressed by the smart money's apparent interest.

These men—Fox, Laemmle, Zukor, Aitken—were the leading independents and the logical ones for Griffith to turn to at this point. Fox was, perhaps, too much the promoter to interest, or be interested by, the sober Griffith. Laemmle was essentially creating a factory, tooled to produce large numbers of program pictures with only an occasional major film on the schedule (Von Stroheim would get his first chance to direct at Universal and Lon Chaney would be Universal's most important star in the 1920s). But Zukor and Aitken both responded to Griffith's overtures.

It was probably Griffith's assistant Tony O'Sullivan who told Zukor that Griffith and Biograph were unable to reach an agreement, and when the two met, Zukor could assure Griffith of a prestigious salary—$50,000 a year—and prestigious associates. James O'Neill had agreed to recreate on screen his famous interpretation of *The Count of Monte Cristo*. And James K. Hackett, Griffith's old theatrical producer, his career as an actor-manager now in the ascendant, had signed to do *The Prisoner of Zenda*. Pauline Frederick? Mary Garden? They, too, were "Famous Players." Griffith, the actor who had yearned to work with the elite of legit, must have been tempted.

Many years later Zukor would remember their discussions warmly. "He approved what I was trying to do, he approved it 100 percent." He also liked Griffith's style. "He wasn't a conversationalist. He wasn't a glib talker. He asked straight questions and demanded straight answers."[13] Which, as it turned out, didn't satisfy the director. Zukor could not offer him the free choice of subjects, control over casting and budgets, that he felt he deserved and needed at this moment in his career. They parted amicably, their careers destined to cross significantly at two later points.

Griffith's meetings with Harry Aitken were more productive. As far as anyone could tell, he was as well established as Zukor and just as far along the way toward creating an empire. He had stars and adequate financing (or so he said) and though his salary offer—$300 a week—couldn't match Zukor's, he could give Griffith stock in what appeared to be a growing concern, plus a percentage participation in some of the films he made for Majestic and the right to make two independent productions a year.

With these boons came greater freedom as to material, casts, budgets, as befits a coventurer. "Does Griffith know we have very little available capital and an oversupply of nerve?" Roy Aitken recalled asking his brother when they discussed this arrangement for the first time. "I think he likes our nerve," Harry replied, adding that Griffith saw their enterprise as a growing force in a growth industry and welcomed the chance to get in on the ground floor.[14] It made sense after his frustrations with the established and stodgy Biograph organization.

So it was done. And on September 29, 1939, the famous full-page ad appeared in the *New York Dramatic Mirror*, for the first time publicly declaring Griffith "Producer of all great Biograph successes," which, it went on to say, had had the effect of "revolutionizing motion picture drama and founding the modern technique of the art." The bulk of the ad was taken up with a listing of what had come to be regarded as the most famous of his Biograph films—151 of them—but before that the copy stressed his claims to invention of the close-up, the long shot, crosscutting and "restraint in expression."

The ad was significant in two respects. It represents the first public statement of a theme that would echo and reecho through Griffith's publicity and through the standard histories as well, namely, the notion that Griffith had actually been the first to devise certain techniques that were to become—indeed, already had become—standard practice in screen storytelling. In fact, others could lay prior claim to these inventions; Griffith's real contributions had been those of widening the range of the screen as a storytelling medium and of writing the basic book of screen grammar, setting the rules of composition which, of course, others would bend and break, but only with a sense of experiment, of risk. In a way, the claims of the ad were simultaneously too broad and too modest.

Another interesting point about the ad was that it was signed by Albert H. T. Banzhaf, who styled himself "counsellor at law and personal representative." Where and how Griffith met Banzhaf, who was to prove undistinguished in both roles he assigned himself in the ad, is unknown. But he was to be an extremely important figure in Griffith's life, his key advisor on all business transactions, holder of various offices in Griffith's production companies, his man on the board of United Artists when that bold venture was formed, and, unfortunately, a man consistently overmatched in his dealings with the shrewd and tough "counsellors" and "personal representatives" of Griffith's peers. A trusting and kindly man, his inability to defend Griffith's best interests against outsiders was matched by his inability to defend them against an increasingly imperious Griffith himself.

But perhaps the most intriguing thing about the ad was the timing of its appearance. Griffith was clearly not seeking work when it appeared. A couple of days later the trade press would carry news of his deal with Aitken. What he—and Aitken, too—wanted were bookings for their first Mutual releases and that required building up the Griffith name, so that the most backward backwoods exhibitor could not mistake it. In that sense, the ad was extremely valuable, the beginning of a fame unprecedented for a director, but a fame that would soon be *the* precedent for all who would claim to be truly creative artists in the newest art.

3

About three months passed between the appearance of this ad and the start of Griffith's first production for Mutual release. Some old friends were available to him through the Aitken interests—Stanner E. V. Taylor, Marion Leonard, James Kirkwood, Arthur Johnson—though Griffith would make little use of any but Taylor, perhaps because he was unforgiving of their earlier defections, more likely because his newer recruits were generally more gifted. He spent most of this period persuading members of his last Biograph company to follow him into the Aitken organization. Only one important actor, Lionel Barrymore, anxious to try the stage again, refused him. All the rest—the Gish sisters, Blanche Sweet, Henry Walthall, Donald Crisp, Mae Marsh, Spottiswoode Aitken, Bobby Harron, Jack Pickford, to name just a few—came along. So did the man who would set in motion the next phase of Griffith's life, Frank Woods, the story editor. Christy Cabanne, one of his principal directorial assistants, also joined him, though Dell Henderson, the comedy specialist, stayed on for a time at Biograph.

This loyalty was not without its cost, for it meant going without salaries until Griffith was ready to go into production. Lillian Gish says she and her sister were offered Biograph contracts, but "never even considered the offers. Nor did others of his company. . . ."[15] Indeed, of its key members only Billy Bitzer—who had just directed his first film, a Bert Williams comedy at Biograph—proved hesitant, despite a proffered trebling of his salary. "We will bury ourselves in hard work out at the coast for five years, and make the greatest pictures ever made, make a million dollars and retire, and then you can have all the time you want to fool around with your camera gadgets . . . and I will settle down to write," Griffith told the cameraman, who was at first dubious. "Now I thought how can he be so sure of that when even now in the pictures we had . . . we never did know whether we had a best seller until it went out."[16]

So Bitzer debated with himself. Meantime, he helped Griffith, who was worried that, using other equipment, he could not achieve a quality of camera work comparable to that which he had been getting with the patented Biograph instrument. Bitzer assured him it was possible and borrowed a Pathé camera and shot some reassuring tests. Biograph then offered him a paid vacation in Florida to get him away from Griffith and his importunings. Aitken countered by putting a car more or less at Bitzer's disposal—a car that somehow always ended up at Aitken's office. One day, when he had some errands downtown, he accepted a ride in it, but only on condition he not be taken again to Aitken's place for more persuasion. The chauffeur, however, called in to report Bitzer's adamancy and came back with the word that Aitken would fire him if he did not deliver his passenger. To protect the man's job, as Bitzer later told the story, he agreed to speak to Griffith and Aitken again and this time they finally extracted his agreement to work for them with a salary of $200 a week and a 10 percent participation in the profits of Griffith's independent productions.[17]

Bitzer's doubts about Griffith's "sure thing" were to prove prophetic; as it turned out, no one—and most especially not D. W. Griffith—was ever able to count upon making (and, more difficult, keeping) a million dollars in the movie business. Especially in the creative end of it. But even though drink would destroy Bitzer's career and he would end his life as virtually a charity case, subsidized by the Museum of Modern Art to write his autobiography and to hang about as a sort of consultant, he got a good, wild ride out of the years he would spend with Griffith—in the process, of course, securing his claim on immortality.

Still, when he and the other Biograph regulars reported for work in December they couldn't help but contrast their situation with the luxury of the new Biograph facility they had abandoned. Aitken had acquired the Clara Morris estate in Riverdale to use for outdoor locations in the East and had a small studio on Twenty-first Street for interiors. Unfortunately, the former was of no use to Griffith in midwinter and the latter had been rented out to a lithographer. As a result, until Griffith could move the company to Los Angeles, they were forced to work in two stories of a loft building at Sixteenth Street near Broadway—a former rug factory—Bitzer had found for them. Worse, Aitken was short of cash and needed inexpensive product in a hurry. So, although he wanted Griffith to make four- and five-reel films, he insisted on budgets not to exceed $5,000 apiece and on hasty shooting. The first project was *The Escape*, starring Blanche Sweet, who remembers having to work the full day before Christmas Eve and then on into the night. She also remembers breaking out in a mysterious rash, signaling the onset of scarlet fever and four weeks of illness and recuperation, during which the half-finished production was suspended. "They had invested in the rights to the stage play it was based on and that money was all tied up. Everyone hated me, no one sympathized. It was a catastrophe."[18]

Griffith quickly turned to another work, a novel, *The Single Standard*, which was retitled *The Battle of the Sexes* and went before the cameras starring Lillian Gish, Owen Moore, Mary Alden, Fay Tincher, Donald Crisp and Bobby Harron. "This is a potboiler," Griffith told his cast at their first rehearsal and he shot it as such in five hectic days and nights, the long hours finally taking their toll on Miss Gish; Bitzer found he could not bring his camera in for close-ups because her eyes were bloodshot from lack of sleep. A few hours' rest cured that condition and the film turned out to be commercially quite successful when it was released the following April, so successful, indeed, that in 1928, his career in decline, searching for something that looked like a sure box-office bet, Griffith returned—unfortunately—to this story of a philandering middle-aged, middle-class husband and the effect his transgressions have on his family with Jean Hersholt in the lead.

This, however, was the only movie Griffith was personally able to complete in New York. Since his name was already worth something, especially in light of the publicity campaign about him that Aitken was beginning to orchestrate, he agreed to act as "supervisor" on productions actually directed by such contract workers—and Griffith disciples—as Christy Cabanne, Marshall Neilen and James Kirkwood, among others. He also directed a manikin whom Aitken had dubbed "The Mutual Girl" in a series of newsreellike short subjects designed primarily to familiarize the theatergoing public with the corporate name. Griffith also attended to the further building of his reputation by granting two important and fairly lengthy interviews to the leading trade papers, the *Moving Picture World* and the *New York Dramatic Mirror*. Most important of all, he began to think about, and then promote actively, the project that would transform both him and his medium—a film version of that sometime best-selling novel and provincially popular theatrical melodrama, Thomas Dixon's *The Clansman*, which would become Griffith's *The Birth of a Nation*. It was Frank Woods who brought *The Clansman* to his attention. He had worked briefly at Kinemacolor, a firm experimenting with an early color process, and had drafted a scenario when it had acquired control of the rights to the novel. Griffith was overwhelmed by the melodrama's possibilities—so much so that one can't help but think his lack of more routine production—especially when his new employer so desperately needed it—represented a quiet slowdown, a warning of what might happen if he did not get his way in this matter.

For Griffith's mood, as revealed by the trade paper interviews, was serenely confident. It was not overbearing, as it often was later. One simply senses, beneath a commendably poised and modest surface, a man who was, for the first time, fully assured as to his worth and the worth of his talent, a man with a sense that his great moment was finally at hand. Anyway, Griffith impressed the man from the *Moving Picture World* by his willingness to praise films other than his own, and perhaps by revising his opinion about theatrical players in pictures; he now held they could succeed in the new medium, though he stressed the special need, in film, to cast actors and actresses in roles that more or less matched their own ages, and held forth with some passion about how the public was only aware of the sudden successes of movie performers but had no knowledge " 'of the hundreds who are tried and fail to show the possession of that indefinite quality, that something in here'—as he tapped his temple— 'which gives them the power to impart to others a clear realization of a given situation.' "[19]

In the second interview he made a true observation, one that often got lost in the later publicity about him as a discoverer and molder of stars. "There is no secret," he said. "I did not 'teach' the players with whom my name has been linked. We developed together; we found ourselves in a new art and as we discovered the possibilities of that art we learned together." As he told it, all were in search of greater realism and moved toward the close-up as a means of eliminating unrealistic panto-mime to indicate emotion. Similarly, the switchback, though here Grif-fith used the occasion to comment rather sourly on others who had taken up the technique, "The switch-back I use with fear. . . . It must give a very good sound reason for its existence before I will attempt to use it."[20]

Of course, he revealed nothing about *The Clansman* to the press. But it is obvious why this strange, tainted work appealed so deeply to him, why it occupied so much of his thoughts at this moment. It had, of course, that strongly melodramatic flavor for which he had such a power-ful, and ultimately destructive, affinity. More importantly, Griffith found in it dozens of points in common with his family's mythology. Most im-portant of all, he sensed in *The Clansman* the raw material of a great *American* epic, story and characters with which both he and his audience could identify as they could not with material taken from Biblical and European history. Moreover, American epics seemed to be coming into vogue. Thomas Ince, the leading producer of westerns, and Griffith's lead-ing domestic rival, had a great success in 1913 with a five-reel *Battle of Gettysburg*, confirming Griffith's sense that the Civil War was the place to look for a subject of wide general appeal.

Even in the talking stage, Griffith was sublimely confident about the picture—and quite innocent about Harry Aitken's true financial position. The latter told his brother, Roy, that he had agreed to be Griffith's part-ner in two long "special" films per year, not because he had any great faith in such pictures, but because only by so doing could he get Griffith to sign with him. Griffith had claimed that he could work on these films in odd moments while overseeing—and occasionally directing—a regular Majestic-Reliance schedule that called for the completion of two four-reelers every week.

At his first meeting with both Aitken brothers and Thomas Dixon, Griffith contented himself with the mild observation that "this *Clans-man* picture will be worth a hundred of the other movies." This did not soften the shock of his estimate that it would run ten to twelve reels and cost at least $40,000. Nor were the Aitkens reassured by the price Dixon placed on screen rights to his book—$25,000.

This did not daunt Griffith. Harry Aitken, as an aid to his promo-tions, maintained a lavish 10-room apartment on Fifty-seventh Street, staffed by an English cook and butler. His brother, just back from Lon-don, boasted a yellow Leon Bollee automobile (with green leather seats) and a sizable wardrobe of bespoke tailoring. Griffith took down the name of Roy's tailor and was further convinced that he was dealing with men of solid substance. "I look to you," Griffith said to the Aitkens, "to get the money together for this production. Surely you can get it from Majestic, Reliance or Mutual or from Wall Street," he said blithely.

What he did not know was that Aitken, who was by this time also financing both Ince and Mack Sennett, was dispensing cash at a rate somewhere between $60,000 and $100,000 a week and was not, as yet, seeing anything like that amount returning from the exhibitors. He told Griffith and Dixon as much, but Griffith, who had suffered the presence of the Wall Streeters Kahn and Livingston on his *Battle of the Sexes* set, shrewdly observed that those gentlemen were "not so hard-headed but what the glamour of the movies appeals to them." Their interest in the extra girls had been, he said, quite obvious to him.

Anyway, at this first conference it was agreed that Harry Aitken would approach his board of directors at Mutual for financing and the next morning Roy Aitken took Griffith for a cruise of the New York streets in his smart car. A day later they were all to meet again for lunch to hear Harry's report from the directors' meeting.

It was not a happy one. The risk seemed too great to these gentlemen and they rejected the proposal. In a gloomy atmosphere the Aitkens agreed to try to form a syndicate of individual investors, hoping at least to obtain enough money to permit Griffith to begin production. Actually, however, it appears that Harry Aitken was putting on a show of activity in order to temporarily placate Griffith so that he would keep working happily on his program features. Aitken appears to have honestly believed—or anyway hoped—that in a few months Majestic and his other firms would establish a cash flow sufficient to finance Griffith's vaulting dream. In any event, he had no immediate luck forming a syndicate, whether because this project was so without precedent or because knowledge that he was overextended was now general it is impossible to say. But things were so tight, according to Bitzer, that the producers were forced to mortgage the negative of a Cabanne film Griffith had supervised—*The Great Leap* (rather an appropriate title)—in order to obtain the cash needed to send Griffith and company to California for the winter shooting season. The importunate director entrained, convinced the project was in hand, though it would seem Aitken had not yet closed with Dixon and had no more than verbal commitments from a few financiers, some of whom indicated that though they did not want shares in *The Clansman* syndicate, they would lend him money on his personal notes, one of whom, Felix Kahn, told him that he would lend him some more if he would put up his stock in Majestic as security.[21]

And a good thing, too. For Griffith was now belatedly ensconced in the old Kinemacolor studio at 4500 Sunset Boulevard, that venture having failed despite the presence of Linda Griffith on its roster of players. The studio, renamed the Fine Arts, would remain Griffith's headquarters until 1920, and now it was frantically busy. For full of enthusiasm for *The Clansman*, and wanting to keep the pressure on Aitken, he began researching the picture, renting land on which to shoot the battle scenes, the while making commitments for costumes, horses, and so on. He perhaps even began formal rehearsals at this time. Meanwhile, he supervised the regular Mutual release schedule and contributed two productions to it that, in any year but *The Birth of a Nation*'s year, would not have been regarded as considerable achievements.

There is some dispute as to whether Miss Sweet's suspended vehicle, *The Escape*, was finished in New York or "at the coast," as the phrase then went (Miss Sweet says the latter). If he did finish *The Escape* at the Sunset Boulevard studio, Griffith didn't dally over it, and almost immediately plunged into one of the most interesting of his transitional productions, *Home, Sweet Home*, a highly colored version of the life of John Howard Payne (Henry Walthall), author of the song from which the title of the movie was borrowed. It presented a series of vignettes in which the song itself was shown to have a profound effect on the fates of a diverse group of characters, as Miss Gish, who played Payne's patient, abandoned sweetheart says, "inspiring loves and saving marriages." The film is quite handsome pictorially, but its chief interest lies in Griffith's treatment of Payne, whom he saw as another of his unappreciated artist-wanderers. As the story had it, Payne struck bottom far from his home sweet home, in an unnamed Arabic country, maddened by drugs. So sorry an ending for a protagonist Griffith admired was not to be countenanced, of course, and so there was an epilogue in which the songwriter was reunited with his long lost, but faithful, sweetheart.

The setting, necessarily, was Heaven, or more properly, somewhere en route to it. Payne, for his sins, had been condemned to the place beneath—"hell being rocks and smoke pots in Chatsworth Park," according to Gish. She, of course, had directly ascended and now, as a most favored angel, was vouchsafed the power to raise Walthall up. As a practical matter this involved flying actor and actress past the camera by means of wires. But, as the shot was set up "the most prominent things are Wally's feet," as Griffith noted, and he called a cut and extensive discussions were held while Miss Gish and Walthall hung in their harnesses in midair. "Wally, a true southern gentleman, didn't raise his voice, didn't complain; he simply fainted and hung there limply." This was observed, they were lowered, and a complicated shot, in which the camera was trucked back while Miss Gish and Walthall were flown backward, was arranged. And so, at last, perfect love was perfectly rewarded.[22]

Griffith's next picture was both more psychologically acute and more poetically realized. Entitled *The Avenging Conscience*, it is essentially a version of Poe's *The Tell-Tale Heart*, with an artful reference to the theme of "Annabel Lee." Four reels in length, the movie is a compact and quite chilling rendition of the famous tale in which a young man, without motive, kills his benefactor and then betrays his crime because he believes he and the investigators hear the dead man's heart continuing to beat under the floorboards where he had been buried. Once again, Griffith was able to evoke terror by emphasizing the claustrophobic dimensions of the room in which the crime took place and Gilbert Seldes, writing as late as 1924, was disposed to consider this little film not only Griffith's masterpiece but the greatest American film to its date. "A sure instinct led him to disengage the vast emotion of longing and lost love through an *action* [Seldes's italics] of mystery and terror. . . . The picture was projected in a palpable atmosphere; it was *felt*. After ten years I recall dark masses and ghostly rays of light." Neither before or after, in Seldes's opinion, did Griffith achieve so perfectly proportioned a picture. Acting, the critic felt, began to replace "playing" in the later works, while the public and the industry's demand for spectacle corrupted him as well as other directors and he lost his ability to give us the "delicate or fine," with "beautiful effects" replacing a simpler and rarer kind of beauty in his work.[23]

Seldes was perhaps overstating the case against Griffith the better to make his less-disputable case against the industry's later pursuit of self-conscious importance. Yet there is also truth in what Seldes wrote. Without knowing it, Griffith's ambition, his drive to work on a vast scale, was continuing to push him away from the most singular aspect of his gift. Still, it may be unfair to contrast *The Avenging Conscience* with the longer, more complex films that followed it—as unfair as it is to contrast a short story and a novel. If nothing else, the ambition and the influence of Griffith's next films set them definitively apart, not only from his previous work, but from the work of all other directors in this period. If he lost something as an artist, he gained something, too—scope and scale and grandeur—and not just for himself. The tragedy is that, as his career worked out, he could only occasionally go back to the style and themes of films like *The Avenging Conscience*, his success with spectacle making all his attempts to return to shorter, simpler works about ordinary life seem to the critics, the public, the industry, and himself, regressive. And this pressure of opinion, combining with his own megalomania, forced him yet further away from the basic core of his talent.

Of course, this was not at all apparent to him in the spring of 1914. True to a verbal agreement with Griffith, Aitken opened *The Battle of the Sexes* in a legitimate theater (the Cort) in New York and this marketing strategy helped to proclaim Griffith's importance to the world—and to build grosses for Aitken. Indeed, Banzhaf was able to tell Griffith, at the end of the latter's first month in Los Angeles, that Aitken expected his companies to be turning a profit within ten days. A couple of weeks later, just after the opening of *The Battle of the Sexes*, Aitken wired Griffith that there was "A GREAT DEMAND FOR HOME, SWEET HOME, SO WILL CHANGE POLICY TO HIGHER PRICE AND FEWER PRINTS." He also proposed a remake of Griffith's *Elderbush Gulch*—which Biograph had just brought out and which was doing well—because, he said, the more routine productions, handled by Griffith's assistants, were not big enough for a market that was opening up to lengthier, more expensive films in a way that apparently surprised even the congenitally optimistic Aitken.[24] In a letter written the same day, Aitken expanded:

"I am having a great time showing your film [probably *The Escape*] in my apartment to Mr. Irving Cobb, Otto Kahn, May Wilson Preston, Daniel Frohman, editors and society people. This method of presenting them is getting a kind of recognition, which I am sure will be a great boost to you."

He added that Frohman, the theatrical producer, was "very enthusiastic" about Griffith's work and predicted that *Home, Sweet Home* "should make a lot of money for us if it is what I think." Aitken was, however, still cautious about the superproduction: "I think your next feature should be an Elderbrush [sic] Gulch film, and then we will get after 'The Clansman,' "[25] an indication that Aitken either (a) didn't have all the front money he needed in hand or (b) that he was still not sure the world was ready for a film as mighty as the one Griffith was proposing. This was sensible. The policy was not as conservative, surely, as Biograph's, and perhaps not as headlong as Griffith would have liked, but, rather, a sound middle course.

At this moment, however, common sense, the middle ground, meant nothing to Griffith. In the spring and early summer Aitken continued to successfully release Griffith's films as he had promised, either in legitimate theaters or at the Strand, entrepreneur Mark Strand's daring new concept—an elegant Broadway theater devoted exclusively to showing movies. There were to be, however, no more personal productions from D. W. Griffith for Mutual to release in the ordinary way. The master's assistants, when not forced to work directly under him on his great new enterprise, would continue to turn out program features for Mutual. But Griffith was now completely in thrall to the obsession called *The Clansman*. He could not, would not, bring himself to work on anything but that.

CHAPTER NINE

Re "Birth"

The Clansman was in almost every respect a miraculous production: miraculous in its length, in its combination of spectacle and intimacy, in its complexity of structure, in its cost. In time, all these miracles would be equaled and surpassed by other films. Three miracles, however, would retain even to this day their capacity to astonish: the amount of money it grossed, which can only be estimated, but which has been exceeded with any consistency only in very recent times, when admission prices are much higher; the fact that a film could attain such tremendous popularity—however great its artistic and technical novelty—despite a morality actively offensive to perhaps half its worldwide audience and profoundly disquieting to everyone not a rabid racist; the fact that a movie as long and as difficult as this one was made without a detailed shooting script.

We shall return to the first two matters later. But since all movies are supposed to begin with a script, any discussion of this film must begin with the fact that it had none. Griffith had never used anything more elaborate than a modest scenario, generally little more than an outline of the plot, for his shorter films and saw no reason to change his ways now. Indeed, in his autobiography Griffith claims that when Woods brought *The Clansman* to him he "skipped quickly through the book until I got to the part about the Klansmen, who, according to no less than Woodrow Wilson, ran to the rescue of the downtrodden South after the Civil War. I could just see these Klansmen in a movie with their white robes flying." The implication is that he started agitating for purchase of the property almost sight unseen (though he must surely have known the theatrical version). That may represent an *ex post facto* attempt to expand his creative claim to it at the expense of the original author, and of Woods, who either prepared some sort of treatment for him or brought one along from Kinemacolor; it may also represent an implicit plea of innocence regarding the book's more noisome moral qualities. But the fact remains that

212

film directors often interest themselves in projects simply because of the imagistic possibilities a first reading suggests. And Griffith did see this one, from the start, in the simplest imaginable terms. "We had had all sorts of runs-of-the-rescue in pictures and horse operas. The old United States Cavalry would gallop to the rescue—East, one week; West, the next. It was always a hit. . . . Now I could see a chance to do this ride-to-the-rescue on a grand scale. Instead of saving one poor little Nell of the Plains, this ride would be to save a nation."[1] The stress, in short, was to be on melodrama, on sentiment. And though, during the spring, Griffith and his associates consulted a fair number of standard histories and personal reminiscences of the Era of Reconstruction—consultations that led to quite accurate reproductions of high historic moments in tableaulike scenes—there is no evidence that any thought was devoted to the racist implications of Dixon's story—except by Dixon himself, passionate and half-baked ideologue that he was.

In defense of Griffith and his cohorts, it should be noted that the weight of the time's scholarship was on their side. The historians generally agreed that, as one of them put it, the Republican scheme for reconstruction was "repressive" and "uncivilized," that it "pandered to the ignorant negroes, the knavish white natives and the adventurers who flock from the North," that it might have been, indeed, "the most soul-sickening spectacle that Americans had ever been called upon to behold."[2] It is only in our own time that this view has been extensively revised, that the crimes committed against white southerners after the Civil War seem not to be part of a studied pattern of repression but a series of more or less isolated incidents in a brief and relatively painless period of postwar adjustment.

Be that as it may, Griffith and his colleagues should have been far more aware than they were of a shift toward greater militancy about their lot and their image (as we would now say) among American blacks. It is possible, of course, that Griffith intended his film as an answer to the black agitation for equality. Certainly Dixon, now as before, continued to believe blacks not yet sufficiently civilized to practice political or any other form of self-determination. But Griffith naïvely supposed that his film was uncontroversial and incontrovertible, an exercise in historical truth-telling—and not merely *a* truth, but *the* truth. He might have been the first but he was not the last movie director to be so convinced, filmmakers inhabiting as they do an extremely narrow and parochial world in which the play of ideas, as a political or literary intellectual understands it, is virtually nonexistent. In short (and on balance), as he prepared his great project, D. W. Griffith's motives appear to have been quite pure.

Despite the fact that Frank Woods shared the first copyright of the film with Griffith, he never received any creative credit from the director. "We wrote no script. I never did for any of my pictures." (This is untrue;

scripts of his later films exist in his files.) "We would get the idea of the story, carry it around with us; eat over it; walk over it; drink over it; dream over it until every action and scene was catalogued in our minds. Then we would start rehearsing."[3] In any event, the Woods scenario is lost. All that remains are a few pages of notes in Griffith's handwriting, a cutting continuity he presented his editor, Jimmie Smith, at some point during the time the film was being shot and Smith was making his first assemblages. It is scribbled on the back of some research about the activities of the Union League clubs during Reconstruction.

Griffith seems to have worked more from Dixon's play than from the novel and he expanded greatly on the basic story, especially in the first half of the film, with its spectacular battle sequences. These are made with enormous sympathy for the suffering endured by soldiers of both sides and are colored by a pacifist sentiment that may have been a response to the beginning of World War I in Europe, which occurred while the movie was shooting. These sequences, of course, give the film a scale not to be found in Dixon's novel and they also provide a general humane and high-minded context that somewhat—and somewhat duplicitously—disarms objections to the second half of the film with its heavy-handed racism and its glorification of the night-riding defenders of "Aryan" purity (the word actually appears in a subtitle). Indeed, the film was, and is, a great deal more pleasurable to view than any mere plot outline can suggest. The action sequences impart to it a sweep, even a grandeur, that, at least while we are watching it, tend to dull criticisms of its message. Then, too, the humanizing vignettes of life in the genteel Cameron family of Piedmont, South Carolina—idealized archetypes of the southern gentry, who treat their slaves gently (and in turn are the subjects of adoring loyalty)—have the effect of further disarming us. They are depicted as owners not of a huge, exploitative plantation but of something like a prosperous farm and they are, all of them, civilized and charming people.

It could, of course, be argued that all this was shrewd calculation on Griffith's part, a supremely clever attempt to make audiences lower their guard so he could get across his repellent beliefs. But that gives him too much credit for intellectualization. Griffith was a man—in his work, anyway—who followed and trusted his feelings more than he did reason; and besides, all the available evidence suggests that he did not for a minute believe he was making a "controversial" film. Very simply, he thought everyone thought as he did about the matters he was taking up. The surprise he repeatedly expressed as the storm broke around him after the film's release was genuine. Why, he loved Negroes! And believed (as have many southerners before and since) that he had a special understanding of their natures not vouchsafed northerners, honestly felt that these good, childlike people had been grievously misled by outsiders and agitators.

To be sure, by modern standards—and even by the standards of the liberal and humanistic circles of Griffith's day—this is a poor and thought-less performance. But if our century has taught us anything it is that high artistic vision does not necessarily correlate with a similarly elevated so-cial vision.

So Griffith retained the core of Thomas Dixon's novel, in which the Camerons are friends of a northern family, the Stonemans, the patriarch of which, Austin Stoneman, is a radical Republican who keeps a mulatto mistress and has as a henchman another mulatto, a lustful politician named Silas Lynch. The latter aspires not only to political leadership in South Carolina but also, in time, to marriage with Stoneman's blond and virginal daughter as well. The families, of course, are separated by the war (though there is a very touching scene of lads from the two families find-ing each other and dying together on the battlefield at Petersburg, during the campaign that concluded the war); become enemies during the days of Reconstruction; are reconciled—those who survive these events, any-way—when the "Little Colonel" (the eldest Cameron son) in the end marries Elsie Stoneman, while her brother marries the Camerons' sur-viving daughter.

It is, to put it mildly, a highly coincidental plot and in sketching it, one gets some idea of the difficulties Griffith and the Aitkens must have had in selling it to backers without a script to indicate, in detail, what the director's treatment would be, without the magnificent images he cre-ated—images that did not simply bring the story to life but are, in fact, the life of the film, the source of its energy and its continuing fascination.

The conception, existing in the spring and summer of 1914 only in Griffith's mind, enormously enlivened him. We have Bitzer's testimony that it "changed D. W. Griffith's personality entirely. Where heretofore he was wont to refer in starting on a new picture to 'grinding out another sausage' and go at it lightly, his attitude on beginning this one was all eagerness. He acted like here we have something worthwhile." Bitzer did not share his leader's vision. "I had read the book and figured out that a negro chasing a white girl was just another sausage after all and how would you show it in the South?"[4] It is probably fair to add that his atti-tude was typical of the majority of Griffith's employees when they heard the story for the first time and even as they worked on the picture later.

This had little effect on Griffith, who simply set to work. Lillian Gish has recalled that Griffith drew her aside one afternoon during a break in shooting one of his program pictures, requesting that she stay on after work. It was not an unusual request; Griffith often held after-hour re-hearsals for a forthcoming project while another work was in progress, and a sizable percentage of those who would eventually have featured roles in the finished film assembled with Miss Gish to hear him announce his plans for *The Clansman*. She remembers only two unusual facts about this small beginning to a mighty project. The first was that she had observed for some days that Griffith's pockets were overflowing with notes as well as scraps of printed material. She therefore correctly assumed that he was brooding about a work of unusual scale, since he carried no *aide-mémoire* when working on films of routine length. The other was that on that first night he swore his actors to secrecy about his intentions. He might control rights to Thomas Dixon's novel, but he owned no patent either on the Civil War or Reconstruction, and it would have been a simple matter for a competitor to cobble something together and beat him to market with a picture taking up the themes he regarded as his by birthright.

According to Miss Gish, Griffith did not make his final casting decisions until rehearsals were well along and he had seen more than one player essay most of the larger roles. The center of this nocturnal activity was the extras' makeup room on the Griffith lot, "a make-shift building of cheap, rough pine," where everyone sat on hard kitchen chairs, because Griffith felt that if anything more easeful were provided, "You were apt to get too comfortable and lean back, instead of keeping busy."[5]

The rehearsals went well. And despite the director's determination to keep his options open, there seems to have been no doubt as to who would play the central role in this drama, that of Ben Cameron, the "Little Colonel." From the start it appears that Henry Walthall had the part, despite the fact that he was somewhere between 36 and 38 years old (the year of his birth is in dispute) and thus a trifle old for the part, and more than a little intemperate in his drinking habits. His age could be de-emphasized, Griffith thought, by having him wear wide-brimmed hats whenever possible, thus softening the light on his face. Since "Wally" was a well-liked member of the company, there would be no dearth of volunteers to see to it that he arrived on time, and in a reasonably sober state, for each day's shooting. Slight of build, with long, curly hair and sometimes a romantic mustache, he carried something of the air of a poet about him, this actor who could, as his friend director Raoul Walsh said, "speak volumes with his eyes."[6] His seeming fragility and his natural gentleness of spirit would render his heroics on the battlefield and as the Klan leader more exciting and, of course, they would also enhance his many tender moments in the film. Indeed, so right was he for the part that after the actor's death in 1936, Griffith told a reporter that his demise should effectively quell all talk of a remake. "I can never imagine any actor taking his place,"[7] the director said.

According to Lillian Gish, it appeared for some time before production began that Blanche Sweet would play opposite Walthall as Elsie Stoneman, daughter of the abolitionist senator, eventually to become the loved-from-afar sweetheart of the Little Colonel. She, however, was absent at one rehearsal at which Griffith decided to run through what was to become one of the film's most famous scenes, in which Silas Lynch forcibly tries to persuade Elsie Stoneman to marry him. "Come on, Miss Damnyankee, let's see what you can do with Elsie," said Griffith, and soon enough Gish found herself being chased round and round the rehearsal room by George Siegmann—who besides functioning as Griffith's chief directorial assistant was to daub himself with burnt cork and play Lynch in the film (all the major black roles were played by white actors, though some blacks were used as extras). In the course of evading his miscegenational clutches, Gish lost some hairpins, causing her long blond hair to flow freely over her shoulders as, finally, she fell into a swoon over the horror of it all. It was one of those images of imperiled innocence that was bound to fire Griffith's imagination, and besides, Gish's slender form suggested to him a vulnerability that a woman of fuller figure (such as Miss Sweet) might not be able to give him.[8] Beyond that, of course, there was Gish's considerable talent to recommend her. She was, as everyone knows, a master of those fluttery, childlike gestures that Griffith required of his heroines when he wanted them to suggest—as he often did— a virginal condition. She was, as Parker Tyler wickedly put it, "a permanent lyric of jumpiness."[9] Yet there was also about Gish spunk, humor and practicality, and, setting aside her confrontation scene with Lynch, these qualities were more significant to the success of her performance than her ability to suggest sexual inexperience.

Finally, in assessing his choice of Gish for this role, it should be borne in mind that Griffith was beginning to be romantically taken with her. In her autobiography, and in her many other recollections of Griffith, Gish has never suggested that their relationship was other than platonic in character. Yet it is clear that sometime prior to the start of *Birth* she had begun to supplant Mae Marsh as the most favored of his actresses. He did not switch allegiance suddenly. As he would in the future, with other actresses, he encouraged, reveled in, their rivalry—both personal and professional. Miriam Cooper, another member of the company, recalled that Marsh, whose dressing room was on a second floor of one of the studio buildings, would peer through the cracks in a balcony's floorboards to spy on Gish at the end of the working day. If she emerged from her first-floor room dressed for a date, Marsh would know that Griffith was squiring her that night and she would make other plans. If Gish exited in street clothes Marsh would then put on her finery in hopes that Griffith would favor her.[10]

Anita Loos has said that favorite replaced favorite on the Griffith lot, "like the wives of Henry VIII," and that Marsh was "very bitchy" about Lillian Gish's rise to favor. Close to both the Gish girls, she remembered speculating with Dorothy Gish, a much more mischievous spirit than her sister, as to what, exactly, her sister and Griffith did when they walked out together. One night the two youngsters followed them in hopes of finding out. But the director and his leading lady were models of propriety; they dined in a restaurant and Griffith escorted Gish home at a seemly hour, not lingering in the house where the Gishes' highly protective mother awaited.[11]

Not that Griffith was anything less than courtly—as far as anyone knows—in his cooling relationship with Marsh—"an Irish leprechaun . . . very strange," according to Loos. She was to winningly (if overactively) play Gish's younger sister, she who, rather than submit to the rapacious embraces of Gus, a low-caste black man (Walter Long) whose libidinal energies have been freed by Reconstruction, flings herself through "the opal gates of death." Marsh would later recall that, in effect, she was type-cast by the director. "You remind me so very much of my little sister. You are a little sister,"[12] he said to her, and though in the later sections of the film she played her age (nineteen), she obviously had to play Flora as a much younger adolescent in the antebellum section. Most of the time her pantomime suggests a child of perhaps twelve or thirteen, and she (and Griffith) made rather heavy weather of it. Still, no matter what the fate of his romantic feelings toward her, Griffith (as was not always the case with him) remained very loyal to Marsh. She would have the best female role (and perhaps the most memorable of her career) in his next film, the monumental *Intolerance*, and though she would leave him after Gish had completely supplanted her for a Goldwyn contract and for roles abroad, he summoned her back for another excellent role, in *The White Rose*, as late as 1923.

It would seem that in the cases of both Gish and Marsh, Griffith made his familiar equation between blondness and purity, behaving with them in public in the most respectful, indeed fatherly, fashion, whatever other feelings he might harbor for them. This was not completely the case with *Birth*'s third leading lady, the dark and very handsome Miriam Cooper, cast as Marsh's older sister, Margaret. As a schoolgirl Cooper had modeled for Charles Dana Gibson, among other New York illustrators, and as early as 1909 had done a day's work as an extra in a Griffith one-reeler (*The Duke's Plan*), had gone on to work for Kalem, a rival concern, was dismissed and returned to her studies at the Cooper Union, hoping to become an artist. But in need of money, she found herself drifting back to film. In her autobiography she states a belief that Griffith had her in mind for her role in *Birth* even before his company left for California. This seems dubious, since she recalls heading West with no formal contract in hand, just the promise of employment and ten dollars in her purse. That, somehow, rings true, very much in the business style of the day. Doubtless Griffith had seen in her a striking young woman for whom, surely, he would find something useful to do.

At any rate, she remembered, years later, that Marsh told her she sometimes called Griffith "Mr. Heinz" (behind his back, we may presume) because he liked to have "57 Varieties" of girls on hand on his stages, and there came a moment when he attempted to add Cooper to his more personal string. One day after location shooting, whether before or during *Birth* is unclear, he offered her a lift home in the large auto that was ever at his command. Exhausted, she leaned back against the cushions, closed her eyes, prepared to enjoy the cool evening breeze as they glided through the hills. Suddenly, she felt an arm snaking across the seat behind her head, and opened her eyes "just as Mr. Griffith leaned over and kissed me on the mouth. He smelled of butter: we'd had corn on the cob for lunch. I was so startled I pushed him away and he landed on the floor. He looked so silly that I'd have laughed if I hadn't been scared. He was amazed that anyone would do this to him. I was amazed that he would make a pass at me with the chauffeur sitting in the front seat."

Startled, Griffith inquired: "Don't you want me to kiss you?" Cooper "damn well didn't," but she also thought, probably erroneously, that lack of compliance might cost her job. So, good Catholic that she was, she said she would be delighted if she didn't have to tell about it in confession. Surely, Griffith said, the church did not consider kissing a sin. No, said Cooper, but the sisters had taught her not to put herself in the way of temptation, and that, precisely, was what Griffith was doing with his advance. It was a smooth answer, turning him away with flattery, and she heard no more from him on this subject.[13]

However much his actresses excited the director's sexual interest, though, his feelings for them were not allowed, at this point in his career, to interfere with his professional activities. Discretion was then, and for most of the time that he was in the public eye, his watchword. Added to this was a natural reticence about sex, perhaps a certain guilt about the nature of his needs in that area and, as his fame grew, a certain concern for the dignity of both his own image and that of his industry, which the public tended to perceive—even before the scandals of The Twenties— in rather raffish terms. In short, he did not number among his problems on *The Birth of a Nation* any insoluble ones between himself and his leading ladies: those who did not worship him as father-elder brother or actual or potential lover were sufficiently in awe of him to respond with absolute alacrity to his directorial commands. As for the men, few figured large in Griffith's life. For example, there were three heavies in *Birth*, all equally nasty in image, therefore memorable to the public, but only one of them appears to have had any special closeness to Griffith. Ralph Lewis, a character man who would have a long career in villainy, played Austin Stoneman, the Radical Republican Senator, much influenced by his mulatto housekeeper-mistress to stir southern blacks to vengeful rebelliousness during Reconstruction. His character was, in fact, a caricature, based on Thaddeus Stevens, the distinguished Abolitionist leader, and as such the focus of much of the controversy surrounding the film after its release, especially in the Northeast, where Stevens's historical reputation approached the heroic. Walter Long, who played the renegade Gus, who pursued Miss Marsh to her doom, went on to have a steady career as a character actor and passed unremarked through more prominent lives. George Siegmann, however, is another matter. He had a rather round, bland face, almost innocent in appearance, and it contrasted effectively, memorably with his villainy as the overreaching Silas Lynch. Moreover, as Griffith's chief assistant, the man who passed the director's orders to the vast cast, oversaw all the logistical details of the production, he was an inescapable and invaluable figure during shooting. He has been described by Karl Brown, Bitzer's youthful assistant, as a "gentle-hearted, soft-spoken human elephant, sensitive to Griffith's every whim, yet powerful enough to bend everyone else to his will."[14]

None of those featured in the more benign supporting roles achieved great prominence. Spottiswoode Aitken, who played Dr. Cameron, *pater familias* of the much put-upon clan, was a veteran Griffith character man, a specialist in playing kindly older men. His wife was Josephine Crowell, one of those women born to play mothers. She did so for Griffith for years, and then achieved an immortal screen moment playing the apotheosis of the awful, interfering mother-*in-law* in a Harold Lloyd comedy, *Hot Water*—a glorious comic performance. Playing their other sons were George Beranger (also known as "André" and also a directorial assistant and, latterly, a character actor of no great fame) and Maxfield Stanley, of whom little else was ever heard. Playing the Stoneman sons were Bobby Harron and Elmer Clifton, another assistant director, who would direct a number of important features in the 1920s and continue making pictures, mostly of the low-budget variety, until his death in 1949.

Clifton, indeed, was representative of the most interesting class of people employed on *Birth*—the small-parts players and assistant directors—nearly all of whom achieved greater fame and longer-lasting careers than the players—always excepting Miss Gish—who were billed above them. Among the former were Wallace Reid, cast as a strapping village blacksmith who, toward the end of the picture, takes on a barroom full of lawless blacks (he's searching for Gus in the aftermath of his assault on Marsh) and wipes them all out in a brawl. He was, of course, shortly to become a highly publicized romantic lead and to gain a tragic immortality as the first major Hollywood personality to die as a result of drug addiction. Then there was Elmo Lincoln, soon to become one of the screen's most enduring footnotes as the first movie Tarzan. He is most prominently visible as "White Arm Joe," Reid's chief opponent in the aforementioned fight, but he has been identified in at least eight other small parts in the picture. Eugene Pallette, far more slender then than he was in his later incarnation as a chubby, gravel-voiced and constantly working character man, played a tiny role—listed in the credits merely as "Union Soldier."

More prominently on view in the vignettes, which Griffith based on true historical incidents, were Joseph Henabery, who played Lincoln, Raoul Walsh, who played John Wilkes Booth, and Donald Crisp, who impersonated Ulysses S. Grant. Henabery was a movie-struck youth, adept at makeup and much interested in historical research—both qualities that aided him, a young extra, in obtaining his role in *Birth* and in making it memorable through careful detailing. He would go on to become a very prolific silent picture director. Walsh had, oddly enough, made his theatrical debut in a touring company of *The Clansman*, replacing an injured horseman, galloping his steed across a treadmill in the piece's climactic ride to the rescue. An expert rider, he had drifted into the Biograph orbit a little late as a rider and bit player, moving up to assistant director. A darkly handsome young man—he would woo and win Miriam Cooper, to their subsequent sorrow, on the Griffith lot—Walsh got the role of John Wilkes Booth because Griffith happened to glance up one day to see Walsh, as usual, surrounded by admiring girl extras. Obviously, he had the magnetism to impersonate a man who, if he was not a matinee idol, surely aspired to be. Walsh, who would, of course, go on to become one of Hollywood's finest directors of action films, was one of the several performers invalided by his work on the film. When it came time for his big scene, Lincoln's assassination, hundreds of extras were assembled in the L-shaped set, which included the full stage and the entire side of the auditorium in which the presidential box was situated, but was open to the sky above and on the left side of the house, which there was no reason for Griffith to shoot. Everything went well, until Walsh, having shot Lincoln, was required to leap from box to stage. Unlike the historic Booth, he did not catch a spur in the bunting that draped the box, breaking his leg, but a hard landing on stage jarred a bad knee Walsh had acquired during his roustabout youth, and sprained an ankle. So when he limped off stage, it was a very convincing imitation of Booth's exit after his dreadful act. Finally, there was Crisp, who also worked as an assistant on the picture, and who would establish himself in a later Griffith film, *Broken Blossoms*, as a character man of distinctive force. He would himself become a director and would also be a familiar figure to a later generation of moviegoers as a kindly, fatherly type in films like *How Green Was My Valley* and *Lassie, Come Home*, among many others.

The large corps of assistants also included, besides those who doubled as actors, Monte Blue, another man who would achieve modest fame as a leading actor in the years to come; Herbert Sutch, an Englishman, who would be with Griffith on all his large productions thereafter, and who here functioned as the munitions expert; Fred Hamer, another Englishman who had served in the "other ranks" in sundry colonial wars, was in charge of extra casting and achieved a certain local fame for his knowledge of the kind of barracks room ballads Kipling could not print.

Christy Cabanne also took a hand when needed; so did Erich von Stroheim, whose introduction to the movies this was. His arrogance, if not his genius, was already apparent. And useful in the big scenes. He quickly rose from extra work to stunting to the ranks of the A.D.s.

Thus, as spring turned into summer 1914, the pieces began to fall into place. For Griffith. Back in New York, however, the Aitken brothers were still unable to raise enough money to start production, let alone see it through to a conclusion. Griffith, however, forced their hand. The picture already sketched out in his mind, his players rehearsing scenes for it, and money for sets, costumes and props already being spent, he blithely called the producer in New York and asked for the money to cover expenses. Within hours of receiving that call, the elder Aitken received another call—this time from Dixon, who now scaled down his original demand for a $25,000 advance against the picture's eventual royalties. He would settle now for $2,000 cash in front (retaining the 25 percent of the producers' grosses he had unwaveringly insisted upon and from which, eventually, he would net a million dollars). He needed the $2,000 immediately, however, to cover some pressing obligations. Happily for Aitken these calls (which it is hard to believe were coincidental) arrived on a Friday, after the banks were closed. The hard-pressed Aitken would write the author a check for $2,000 and have the weekend to scurry around, writing personal notes, to obtain the cash to back the check first thing Monday morning, before Dixon presented it for cashing. So, at last, Harry Aitken put his money where his mouth had for so long been—behind Griffith's dream.

The $2,000 represented, in effect, the ante. Aitken was finally, definitely, in Griffith's game. And sport that he was, he would support this small investment with a still larger investment. The details of it are murky, but it seems that the deal Felix Kahn imposed on them became a model for other backers as well, with Harry and his brother Roy pledging percentages of their salaries plus such stock in their various enterprises as was not yet being employed as collateral on other loans, to various high rollers acting for themselves, not their Wall Street firms. By this method they raised $25,000, according to the younger Aitken, turning it over to Majestic to pass on to Griffith, the Aitkens taking unsold Majestic stock in return for this cash. It appears, however, that his memory might have been faulty. In time, the Aitkens and Griffith formed a corporation, Epoch Productions, for the sole purpose of releasing *Birth*, and its first auditor's report, issued March 19, 1915, shows Majestic holding a very modest amount of Epoch stock—2,400 of the 107,910 shares outstanding, with the brothers Aitken holding either in their own name or in that of Mutual, the corporation they totally controlled, shares roughly equivalent in value to the total amount of cash they advanced the production.[15] The logical explanation is that they returned most of the stock they acquired in Majestic as a result of this dealing, allowing them to take a controlling interest in Epoch after they saw that they were in on a good thing.

Better late than never, perhaps. Though one may imagine other Majestic stockholders, lacking the Aitkens' privilege of seeing the picture take exciting shape, eventually being more than a little disappointed to be dealt out of what turned out to be the greatest game in movie history to date. On the other hand, the Aitkens had certainly given everyone they knew every opportunity to take a hand and all had refused the risk.

No sooner had Griffith received the $25,000 that the Aitkens had scrambled so hard to amass than he was wiring to remind them that, in their earlier talks, they had promised to provide him with $15,000 more. Since this sum represented the last amount due on the total budget that Griffith had outlined to his backers, and the picture was still entirely unshot, Griffith knew at this point that more—much more—was going to be required. He must have been beginning to see, even then, that he was going to require something near three times his original cost estimate to complete the picture. So he was either deluding himself or he was cleverly escalating the level of financial pain slowly, trying to keep it within a range he calculated would be tolerable to the Aitkens. Be that as it may, they eventually made another contribution to the film that was almost as important as their cash. That was silence. For the fact was that the direct costs of the film, which was eventually released independently, under the Epoch name, would have been much higher had Griffith not had the resources of "the Majestic" behind him. It is impossible to calculate how many of *Birth*'s expenses (Griffith's salary among them) were simply charged off to that firm, as part of its general overhead, but it is certain that all the principal players were simply assigned to *The Clansman* and paid for their work on it as if it were an ordinary Majestic film. So far as one can tell, no compensation was ever offered the corporation for these salaries or the production services it provided, probably unknowingly, for the film.

The Aitkens certainly never said a word about all this to their investors. They hid their considerable anxiety over *The Clansman* from their New York financial sources, and mostly maintained a calm and businesslike manner in dealing with their profligate producer out West. If they had small confidence in the box office potential of his project, they were loath to anger him, for they continued confident in his ability to make profitable pictures on a smaller scale once he had worked this madness out of his system. Indeed, as his vast new production ground along, the smaller films he had made for them in the early months of his Majestic contract moved, one by one, into profit. The strategy, obviously, was to hold him in check as much as possible, hope that their losses would not be devastating, and pray for a quick return to normalcy.

2

After Griffith finally "took" his first scenes for the picture, all such hopes were feckless, of course. For once the cameras turned, Griffith had the money men where he wanted them, where independent producers ever since have wanted to have their backers, with an expensive picture no longer being talked about or developing—stages at which it is comparatively easy to walk away from a project—but actually rolling. For once there is exposed negative in the can, the money people are faced with an exquisite dilemma. If they stop the flow of capital, they must accept a dead loss on the footage already shot. If, on the other hand, they press on with the production, the only hope of recouping whatever they have already spent, they are at the mercy of their possibly mad genius. To shut him down at a later date is, obviously, to face a still larger loss. To keep going means that they will have to continue pouring money into the production at whatever rate he deems necessary to realize his vision. He may be reassuring as can be, but for every *Birth* there are many more expensive deaths.

Griffith chose to begin work on a film that he must have sensed would change his life, and the life of his medium, on July 4, 1914, Independence Day. Symbolically, he was announcing his own independence not only from the niggling concerns of the Aitkens back East, but of all the conventions that had ruled American films in their infancy. Indeed, he was proclaiming their independence from childhood, and declaring (as he would make clear in his later statements to the press) that this new art must now be permitted to take its place with the older arts as a medium of ideas and of highly personal expression.

No one seems able to recall reliably what scene he made that first day, but it appears that he worked either within the confines of his "Fine Arts" studio or perhaps on the vacant lot across the street, which had been rented as the site for the set representing the main street of Piedmont, the small town where the Cameron family lived. That street was the largest standing set created for the picture, and it was built in forced perspective, the buildings farthest away from the main camera position being smaller than normal size, so the thoroughfare would appear longer and more impressive to the lens. The street on which the Cameron house stood was built on the studio street that led back into the lot from its main gate, and the interior of that house, like the other interiors, was constructed on the studio's open stages, where they were lit by sunlight and reflectors.

Most of this construction was completed by the July 4 start date, the handiwork of taciturn, tobacco-chewing Frank ("Huck") Wortman, a stage carpenter with no formal training as a designer but a naturally gifted architect who remained with Griffith through the mid-twenties. Wortman's crew consisted mainly of carpenters recruited from the stage. Karl Brown, then a young assistant cameraman, latterly a distinguished cinematographer and director and author of the best record of this production, said that all of them, at one time or another, must have built sets for *Uncle Tom's Cabin*, that staple of American melodrama for over 60 years, and that, ironically, the design traditions that had grown up around that classic piece of Abolitionist propaganda influenced the look of this soon-to-be classic—if belated—piece of anti-Abolitionist propaganda. He also notes that these craftsmen were so used to hinging scenery (so that it could be folded flat and shipped from tour stop to tour stop) that they went right on doing so for their movie sets, which would be destroyed once the picture was completed.

Griffith hoped to do most of his large-scale scenes—the Battle of Petersburg, the Klan's ride to the rescue of the beleaguered citizens of Piedmont in general, the Cameron family in particular—first, so that he would have time to reshoot if he did not like the dailies. But he had all the sets ready for the smaller scenes so that he could work on the stages if delays in recruiting extras or securing matériel occurred. Or if he simply lacked the cash to meet the large payrolls for the big scenes.

These scenes were made, with one exception, at various locations within fairly comfortable distances from the studio. According to Seymour Stern, a Griffith scholar who went over the ground with Elmer Clifton in 1946, the battle scenes were shot in the San Fernando Valley, in the area between the present day locations of the Burbank Studios and what is now MCA's Universal City Studios, which has grown, on the same site, from Carl Laemmle's old company. Universal at that time either owned or rented some thirty or forty acres of gently rolling countryside—now at least partially occupied by the famous Forest Lawn Cemetery—which it found useful for the many outdoor dramas it produced, and Griffith apparently sublet the land from his rival. This acreage was surrounded by hills, which afforded Griffith excellent camera placements for panoramic views of both his battle scenes and of Sherman's march to the sea, which he also reproduced. The sequence showing the Little Colonel's "inspiration" for the Klan (little black children being frightened by "ghosts"—white children draped in bedsheets for a game they were playing) was shot in the surrounding hills, possibly intercut with some material shot elsewhere. The famous Klan ride was shot mostly, according to Clifton, in the southern part of Los Angeles County, spilling over the line into Orange County, near Whittier. Some additional shooting was done north of the city, in the Ojai Valley in Ventura County, when it was discovered that it was cheaper to take actors to the horses at a stable there than it was to bring the horses to the actors. The other major location, and the most impressively beautiful one in the film, was in the pine forest surrounding Big Bear Lake. It was there that Walter Long pursued Mae Marsh to her doom while himself being pursued by Walthall, who arrived too late to rescue his little sister.

Griffith and his associates encountered few technical delays, no insoluble problems on these locations or in the studio—surprising considering the unprecedented nature of their enterprise. Good planning and careful rehearsal were well rewarded. Griffith's struggle, through the summer and fall of 1914, was not with his art, but with his finances. Most days on the set Griffith was his usual cheerful self, singing arias, shadowboxing, sweeping Miss Gish up for an impromptu waltz when there was a break in the action.

Which is not to imply that the work was without physical rigor and occasional danger. To begin with, there was the communications problem to solve. For Petersburg, Griffith sometimes has his "armies" spread over distances that have been estimated up to four miles. They were often well out of reach of his megaphone, so he had to resort to flags and mirror semaphores to start their advances and retreats. Occasionally, Griffith would signal starts and stops by having the troops nearest him fire a volley of blanks, though ammunition was expensive and he preferred to save it for use when the camera was turning.

The communications problem was sharpened by the nature of the people with whom the director was trying to communicate. Publicity would later claim that as many as 18,000 were employed in the cast. In fact, there were no more than three to five hundred extras on hand for the largest of Griffith's battle scenes. It is, of course, a tribute to Griffith's directorial powers that he could make so few seem like so many. Most of these men, however, had never worked in pictures; they were day laborers and drifters for whom two dollars a day and a box lunch represented a windfall. It was hard to keep them from degenerating into a mob. On one occasion one of them discharged his musket after the director had called a halt in the action and, then after being reprimanded, did so again after the next shot was completed. Griffith deserted his station by the camera and moved into the trenches where he ordered the man off the location, enforcing his authority with his fists. "You go, now you go," he said, spitting the monosyllables through clenched teeth. On another occasion, Howard Gaye, doubling as a Confederate officer of lower rank than Robert E. Lee (his credited role in the picture), came running up to the parallel on which Griffith, Bitzer, Brown and the camera were perched to cry, "These men are utterly crazy! Why I—I actually had to *defend* myself!"[16]

Raoul Walsh found he had a somewhat similar problem. He had been in charge of loading his "unit" onto trucks for transportation to the location and he had, without difficulty, got them into uniform, showed them which end of the rifle the bullet emerged from and even put them through a half hour of close order drill to get them in the proper frame of mind—all this before nine in the morning, a typical start to a typical day's work in the life of an assistant on this picture.

And the day's first shots went well. As he did throughout the picture, Griffith had the men playing Confederate soldiers moving from left to right across the screen, the Yankees doing the opposite, so the audience always knew which was which. The length of the field over which they struggled ran north and south, with the camera generally placed at its southern extremity, so that he was shooting in fairly even cross light throughout the day, thereby gaining well-matched exposures as well as good modeling on their figures.

The trouble came when Walsh was told to have his charges change uniforms, doffing their Confederate gray for Union blue (in effect, many of the extras fought themselves). One of them snapped: "My daddy rode with Jeb Stuart. I ain't no goddamned Yankee." So saying, he threw down his rifle and stalked off, never to return, not even to pick up his pay. A few others followed his lead.

Walsh wisely decided to let them go, having enough troops left to fill the corner of the scene assigned to him. He counted his men off so that those assigned to fall down as if shot would do so when he shouted their number, and recalled that even the day laborers got so deeply into their scenes that they died most photogenically. When the sequence was finished, Griffith pumped his hand and even offered a rare grin. "Mr. Walsh, if you had been a Confederate general, the South would never have lost the war."[17]

Griffith was throughout a thoughtful leader, concerned about the safety of his command. Munitions were a particular hazard on this film, many of the techniques later used to simulate warfare on screen not yet having been fully developed. Incredible as it may seem, live cannon rounds were actually employed in order that shots could be seen to land and explode fairly near the soldiery—the technique of planting charges to imitate explosions not having been invented. Elaborate warnings were signaled when these rounds were used—fired from cannons lent by the U.S. Army but repainted, with their carriages remodeled to conform to those represented in the book that was the company's Bible when it came to military matters, *Leaders and Battles of the Civil War*, recently republished by a New York newspaper in a cheap edition to mark the war's fiftieth anniversary.

These caused a few anxious moments, but they were as nothing compared with the difficulties of obtaining the effect of men fighting under, indeed, through, artillery barrages. There is public mention of a man named Walter "Slim" Hoffman as the explosives expert on *Birth*, but Karl Brown's vivid memory is of a man named "Fireworks" Wilson being in charge of this effort. He was missing one arm, and although he claimed never to have been injured by his wares, Brown was boyishly convinced that a professional miscalculation had cost Wilson, who was also pock-marked by powder burns, that extremity. He was a small man, with a Mephistophelean beard, who moved mostly in a rapid scuttle, an assortment of "thunderflashes" tucked between stump and body, a lighted fuse sputtering in his clenched teeth, his good arm free to seize and toss these fireworks as required. He had originally planned to create the effect of "bombs bursting in air" by using mortars. They, however, sent their missiles arching too high, out of range of cameras recording infantry attacks at ground level. His solution was to equip twenty or thirty men with firework "bombs" and have them stand just out of camera range, lobbing the things among the advancing troops. "Only you got to time it just right," he advised during a test. "Too soon and you get a lot of wiggly white trails from the fuse. Too late and you might get scorched a little."

"Suppose the boom is thrown too soon and it lands down among the soldiers?" Griffith inquired—by boom he meant "bomb," just as he meant girl when he said "gell," these being among his several verbal idiosyncrasies. "No problem," said Fireworks. "They just kick it out of the way." "Suppose someone kicks it right into the path of someone else?" came the logical next question.

"Look, Mr. Griffith. You're staging a battle, right? You want realism, don't you? Suppose someone *does* get hurt a little. Not much. A foot blown off or something. What you want to do is hustle right on down to where he is and get a good big picture of it, and I tell you, sir, it'll *make* your picture. Yes-sir-*ee*-sir, it'll make your picture!"[18]

Griffith might have been making the supreme effort of his life, but that degree of realism was more than even he required. Even so, injuries of a minor sort were common. Tom Wilson, a sometime sparring partner of Jim Jeffries, worked all through the picture in a variety of odd jobs and, since he had a good throwing arm, was stationed near the camera to toss grenades during the battle. He held on to one a shade too long and nearly had his hand blown off. One of the two or three doctors Griffith had present on the location ran to him with bandages and vaseline, but Wilson eluded him and ran to the camera platform, waving his powder-blackened hand, dripping with blood. He called up: "I ain't dogging out on you, Mr. Griffith. See my hand?" Griffith ordered him to stand still for immediate first-aid, but Wilson took off and was caught and forced to accept the doctor's ministrations only with difficulty.[19]

The unprecedented production was calling forth unprecedented devotion, unlikely exertions. Partly, no doubt, this was attributable to the obviously heroic scale of the enterprise. Partly it was due to Griffith's exemplary, steadfast behavior. He was a man of enormous reserve, not in the least given to warm camaraderie on the set. He was, indeed, in Anita

Loos's description, "secretive"—a trait she attributed to his Welsh heritage—"very peculiar people," in her view.[20] But not a single reminiscence of the picture reveals even a moment when he panicked or showed the slightest gracelessness under pressure. On the contrary, he did his best to minimize the physical risks the production imposed on his coworkers and was ever ready to demonstrate his own great physical courage when necessary while keeping his emotions under tight control.

He never quibbled about money—dismissing talk of the cost of something he wanted with a brief, vague wave of the hand. He kept his instructions succinct, his criticisms even briefer. Bitzer would later recall that the only certain sign of Griffith's displeasure with a scene as it proceeded was a slight wiggle of his foot as he sat next to the camera, legs crossed, watching the action. If he received a telegram from New York, complaining about costs or the quality of one of his products, he might start singing: "Save your money, for the winter time is coming soon," was a lyric he favored on these occasions. Brown, however, remembers that the notes he sounded most frequently to let off steam and, of course, to keep people at a distance while he thought things out during the action sequences were not from *Tosca* or *I Pagliacci*—two former favorites—but a pair of notes doubled and extended in almost infinite variety: "Ha-ha-Yah! Ha-haaa-Yah! Hi-yah! H-yah! Hi-Yah! Hi-haaaaa . . . *Yah!*" He was especially generous with these sounds during the filming of the Klan's ride, and Brown was at once bewildered and fascinated by this unconscious obsession. They must, of course, have been variations on the rebel yell.[21]

Beyond fulfilling the demands of his artistic conscience, even (perverse as it now seems to us) his moral vision, beyond being a suitable response to the dictates of his ambition, *The Birth of a Nation* answered a far deeper need on Griffith's part, the need to cast himself in the heroic mold of his father. That he handled himself without Roaring Jake's bluster, with a decisiveness and a reserve that won him not just respect but enthusiasm from his company, was a mark of his own mature character. *Birth* was Griffith's high tide, that moment in life when his creative powers, his hard-won skills as a craftsman, his self-confidence and his confidence in the suitability of his work for the particular historical moment in which he was pursuing it all flowed together, energizing him and all who were around him.

This was never more apparent than during the week in which he shot the famous ride of the Clansmen, the climax of the picture and perhaps the most powerful action sequence yet placed on film. To be sure, it was yet another "ride to the rescue," but here it was accomplished on a scale, and with an intensity of movement and suspense, that no one had attained before.

Years later, Elmer Clifton would recall that as preparation for the sequence was undertaken Griffith "went hogwild over horses." He wanted literally to fill the screen with mounts and riders and was "beside himself" because he couldn't bear the thought of empty or blank spots in the distant background of his shots. The problem was that with war about to break out in Europe, a war everyone imagined would require cavalry just as the wars of the nineteenth century had, there was a growing shortage of horseflesh in the U.S. Griffith's people did what they could. During the period The Ride was being shot, western production all over Los Angeles was shut down, Griffith's wranglers having rounded up all the horses and riders that worked regularly in the movies, even adding some steeplechasers from a nearby track. But that did not satisfy his needs and, at the last moment, according to Clifton, horses were shipped in, at considerable expense, from the ranches of western Arizona to help realize the director's vision.[22]

But if the temporary shortage of horses was overcome, there was little that Griffith, or anyone, could do about the permanent shortage of expert riders to mount them. Most movie riding was done then—and later—by a handful of men, mostly former cowboys, who had drifted into the movies from the open range, mostly when they brought herds in to sell in Los Angeles. They were sufficient in number to provide all the riding necessary in the ordinary western or war drama and this small band made a reasonably good living moving from picture to picture. There were not enough of them, however, to fill all the saddles when a director required a mass charge, and on *Birth* it was necessary to fill out the ranks with inexperienced men, men desperate enough to hide their ignorance and fear of horses in order to get a few days' work. Right from the start they were a peril to themselves, to more experienced riders and to the cameramen forced to move close to the flying hooves in order to get insert shots. In the battle sequences Bitzer, lying prone in a ditch—and collecting powder burns from bombs that burst too close to him—had obtained a spectacular shot of a horse-drawn wagon thundering right over the camera, blotting out the lens with its bulk. Now, working on the Klan's ride, Griffith wondered if the cameraman could get a similar effect. He wanted the horses to leap Bitzer as he lay prone on the ground with his camera pointing skyward. Bitzer thought it could be managed and Wally Walthall, in the van, was an expert horseman, making his leap effortlessly. Those immediately behind him, the steeplechase jockeys, also negotiated it easily.

Now, however, the less-experienced riders came on, hindered not only by their lack of expertise but by the fact that both they and their horses were swathed in sheets, which had a way of twisting about as they rode, temporarily blinding horse or rider, or both. Bitzer was sure he could roll out of the way if any of the horsemen lost control, but one man, blinded by his sheet, decided discretion was the better part of valor and reined in and dismounted in order to get himself straightened out. There were horses behind him, however, and they, still coming full tilt, panicked the halted horse, which bolted, pulling free of his rider's grasp. The runaway was heading directly toward Bitzer, out of control, when Griffith rushed forward, seized its trailing reins and deflected his course before managing to pull it to a halt—a courageous act in that melee.[23] Bitzer, it appears, thereafter decided to stay safe on the parallel, doing the master shots while spry Karl Brown worked the ground level camera.

This was not the end of the near disasters attending the Klan's ride. America almost lost one of its great directors, before his career behind the camera began, down there in Orange County. John Ford was one of the extras who rode with the Klan, and his bedsheet too twisted and blinded him as he pounded along. He failed to see an overhanging tree branch, which swept him from the saddle and plunged him, unconscious, to the ground. He came to with no less than Griffith kneeling over him, offering a brandy flask. The director insisted that he retire from the field for the day, and Ford would remember stretching out comfortably under a tree to watch the rest of the day's shooting on a sequence that he would have cause to duplicate (and surpass) during his great career.[24]

After these exertions, young Brown was glad enough to be chosen to make a little outing to Big Bear Lake, high in the mountains north of San Bernardino. The sequence to be made there was simple enough—Walter Long's pursuit of Mae Marsh, climaxing with her entrapment high on a canyon wall, where she had to choose between dishonor and death. They set forth in three cars and the trip should have been a pleasant enough break in the rigorous production schedule. Already Big Bear was a well-known vacation spot for those seeking refuge from the summer heat of the Los Angeles basin, and the little company, which besides the actors included the director, Bitzer, Brown, Siegmann, Clifton, and a couple of driver-assistants, had booked rooms at one of the lodges there. Unfortunately, however, Griffith's driver did not know about a new road across the desert of the San Gabriel valley, and they bumped dustily along rutted roads that were not much more than dry washes for the first day, exhausting themselves. They stopped the night in San Bernardino, and found the occupants of the other cars, rested and refreshed after a quickly made, entirely pleasant journey along the new, nicely paved roadway that parallelled the Santa Fe tracks across the valley. As usual, Griffith's comments about this mix-up were mild, ironical, and next day they set forth in good spirits for what they knew would be the really rugged portion of the journey—through the mountains to the lake above. It was a nightmare for those in Griffith's car. The road was in almost total disrepair and had been thoughtlessly built to begin with. Again, Griffith's group arrived frazzled and frightened (they had been negotiating hairpin turns at the edge of sheer cliffs all day) to find the rest of the party awaiting them calm and refreshed. It seems Griffith's driver had been deliberately misled by a local garageman having his little joke on the greenhorns in their impressive Packard, while the others, having phoned ahead, received directions for a longer, but less hazardous and therefore quicker, route.[25]

At last they reached their destination unharmed—and it must be said that the results are worth the trouble. The tall pines of the location are distinctly Californian, there is nothing quite so grand in the pine forest of the South, but no matter. These great trees very successfully suggest the majesty and indifference of nature to the meanness of man. They dwarf the small figures acting out their primitive, indeed distasteful, drama in their shade.

The action of the scene is straightforward enough. Mae Marsh has come to the woods to draw water from a well, but childish and innocent, she is distracted by the beauty of her surroundings—cutaways to small, equally innocent, woodland creatures which seem to be observing her, underline that message—and she gambols deeper and deeper into the forest, all the while stalked by Long, whose burnt-cork makeup is ludicrous, as are the skipping and fluttering that attends Marsh's progress. Griffith was not playing the scene for subtlety. Indeed, during the shooting, Brown found Griffith's instructions to both players preposterous. Long, for example, was forced to run doubled-over, transforming his movements into an animalistic scuttle. Moreover, frequent resort was made to the prop box, wherein several bottles of hydrogen peroxide were habitually kept, since Griffith was convinced that lustfulness was best suggested by having those caught in its grips literally foaming at the mouth, and a swig of peroxide, held behind the teeth, was a sure way of getting that effect.

Yet somehow the scene works. The physical contrast between the two principals, strong enough naturally, is hugely heightened by the powerfully contrasting manner of movement the director insisted upon. And the breathtaking beauty of the stage on which their fatal drama is acted out creates yet another contrast, ironic in nature, that further tightens the scene's grip upon us. Finally, Griffith's editing technique was most artfully applied to his material, crosscut shots of the players coming in more and more rapid alternation as Long draws closer and closer to Marsh. When they must finally be contained mostly in the same shot, another, more hopeful kind of suspense is created by cutting to the searching Walthall, who is, of course, too late to effect a rescue on this occasion.

Curiously, in shooting the scene Griffith suffered one of his rare technical lapses, perhaps a sign of how profoundly it caught his emotions. When he got back to the studio from the Big Bear Lake location, he discovered that he could not cut around Mae Marsh's leap to her death, that audiences would have to see her actually falling through the air if the sequence was to have its full emotional impact. So Bitzer and Brown were sent back, carrying a well-weighted dummy dressed in the actress's costume. This Brown tugged and hauled up the heights, while Bitzer set up his camera below. After much signaling back and forth, Brown launched the dummy and very nearly launched himself along with it, having somehow got tangled up in a ribbon or a belt dangling from the 100-pound figure. He managed to save himself, and stay out of shot, but it was a near thing.[26]

In the end, one is struck by how much Griffith managed to overcome in this sequence—the antique melodramatic conventions with which he started, the deliberate overplaying of the principals and, finally, its implicit racism. One does not wish to rationalize the indefensible, yet the fact that Griffith chose a white man to play the black, Gus, the fact that his makeup cannot and does not fully transform him into a Negro, and his weird less-than-human movements, all conspire to somewhat mitigate the sequence's racism. One is reminded of how often, before and after *Birth*, Griffith arranged confrontations between the beautiful and the bestial, how obsessive was his belief that innocence must, almost inevitably, be brutally despoiled. One cannot help but think that this theme, not the racist one, was paramount in his mind as he staged this sequence. Indeed, it is the major theme of his work, while the racial question was one that he returned to less often, and then more in patronizing rather than inflammatory terms.

It is curious, certainly, that he did not employ a black actor to play Gus. One is aware, of course, of the minstrel tradition, still pertaining in show business in those days, which insisted that even black performers darken their skin with burnt cork in order that there be no ambiguity about their negritude when they were on stage. Yet if anyone knew the revelatory power of the camera, it was Griffith. He must have been aware that if a white man was playing a black man there was no way to disguise that fact, no way to prevent the audience from being aware of this duplicity every moment he was on screen. Why, then, did not Griffith go all the way and hire a black to play a black? He would say later that there were few Negro actors available in Los Angeles and that in any case he wanted to draw on his own repertory company for important roles. It may also be, as Andrew Sarris has speculated, that Griffith was suggesting "that blackness itself [is] a state of being so inferior that blacks themselves are incapable of interpreting and communicating its inescapable baseness."[27]

But if it was rape more than race that motivated the sequence as Griffith visualized it, he was ambiguous in stating even that point—peroxide bottle and scuttling movement notwithstanding. Gus keeps insisting that he merely wants to talk to Flora. That he may be harboring larger hopes of sinister passions is certainly implied. But it is really the girl's reading of his intentions, nothing that he himself overtly indicates, that leads, finally, to the scene's tragic denouement.

About none of this can we ever be certain. Griffith never discussed his intentions about the scene. And dispassionate analysis of its character, however detailed and specific, can never overtake the passionate rhetoric that has been lavished on it from all sides. Best perhaps merely to return to the most obvious point about it—the lengths to which Griffith went to separate this scene texturally from the rest of his film. The long, and as it turned out hazardous car journey he undertook to make it proves that. He could just as well have staged it in the handy Hollywood Hills, losing something pictorially perhaps, but gaining, of course, a more seamless join with the rest of the film. Again, one cannot help but think that unconsciously he wished to set this one blatantly sexual assault apart, to indicate that, despite his generally horrified view of Reconstruction, this action was, even in his own eyes, atypical.

It may be objected that Lynch's rather vigorous proposal of marriage to Gish, later in the film, is of the same character as the woodland scene. But, in fact, its implications are quite different. For one thing, Lynch is a mulatto, therefore a living ambiguity. If "blood" is driving him, is it his white heritage or his black heritage that is doing so—or a desperate need to resolve this ambivalence in violence? Beyond that, it should be noted that Lynch's patron, Stoneman, has, throughout the film, insisted on Lynch's equality in all matters. Lynch's problem is that he has finally come to believe that Stoneman and his sin, indeed his tragedy, are as much social as they are racial; he is at least as much the overreacher as he is the Black Stud of America's oldest and most common racial nightmare. Even when he binds and gags Gish after she faints at the very notion of marriage to him one does not believe, after repeated viewings of the film, that his intention is to carry her off and work his will upon her at leisure. What seems to be moving him is shame, fear that she will tell others of his proposal and thus bring him to ridicule—and possibly to more dire punishment. One imagines, indeed, that his true intention may be to kill her rather than allow her to expose his terrible secret, which is not that he lusts after her but that he truly loves her.

Be that as it may, it must be observed that at the end of the scene between Long and Marsh, Gus, too, is afflicted by conscience. When he sees the mortal panic into which he has thrown the girl, comprehends that she will indeed fling herself into the abyss rather than submit to his embraces, he drops his menacing manner. His final moves toward her, just before she makes her fatal decision, are intended to be reassuring, to demonstrate that, whatever his original intentions, he surely does not want her to die. The panicked girl does not believe him—though there is no hint in Long's playing that this is a ruse to lure her back to him—and she goes over the cliff with Long clutching at her, trying to save her.

Looking at this scene, and the scene between Gish and Siegmann, one is tempted to argue that Griffith was more sexist than racist. That is to say, the most melodramatic consequences occur in this film because of his conviction that the only possible response his girl-women can make to danger is a loss of control over their emotions—and their reason—followed perhaps by a swoon. Couple this with his conviction that at least half the male sex, no matter what their age, color or station in life, are always poised on the edge of rape or some other violence toward women and one has the basic crisis toward which many—if not most—of his longer films are aimed.

This does not, of course, excuse Griffith from the charge of racism. He shared with southerners of his age and background, indeed with most of his audience, an unconscious—but not especially passionate or vicious—racism of a familiar kind. We need but refer to the scene of the Little Colonel's inspiration for the Klan, in which black children are seen to be frightened by "ghosts." This belief that blacks are peculiarly fearful of supernatural apparitions was a common bit of folk wisdom until very recently. It forms, for instance, the basis for a great deal of film comedy throughout the silent period and on through the first decade of sound pictures. It is now offensive, and surely was then to the minority who were sensitive to racial stereotyping, but the white majority unthinkingly accepted this as a reasonable theatrical convention, though just what observed reality it was based upon is hard to determine.

Even when he showed "good" Negroes, Griffith was condescending. The Camerons' house servants, for example, are seen to be impervious to the rabble-rousing of the carpetbaggers, and willing actively to oppose their police-state tactics. Yet they are referred to in subtitles by the patronizing phrase "Faithful Souls," and the male is an Uncle Tom type, while his wife is a Mammy. In the prewar scenes residents of the slave quarters are seen as happy children, dancing and singing for masters who are perceived as benign guardians of a people incapable of ruling their own lives. After the war we are given to understand that the blacks are in the largest sense guiltless of whatever crimes are committed in the name of Reconstruction. It is merely that their new leaders, scalawags and carpetbaggers, do not understand that such juvenile natures dare not be indulged. Unchecked by the kindly sternness of the Camerons and their ilk, the blacks are seen to lapse easily into drunkenness, for example, or stirred with equal ease to casual discourtesy (bumping whites off sidewalks, for instance) when they are in small groups, to riotous excesses when they are massed. But they are not *blamed* for these affronts, any more than we blame small children for pre-moral lapses in conduct. As Griffith tells his story, that blame is consistently laid at the feet of the northern interlopers, who, lacking the southerner's intimate and, indeed, affectionate understanding of the blacks, woefully overestimate their capacity for self-rule, even their capacity for civilized personal conduct.

This view of the blacks, which did not preclude (at least in theory) their coming after the passage of time to a true state of equality with whites, was and remained until very recent times the conventional wisdom of "enlightened" southerners. One might have expected more of someone like Griffith, who had lived long in the North and had some pretensions to culture and cosmopolitanism, but he was not alone in his blindness. It was, as we shall see, shared by, among others, the President of the United States, who was a scholar and a man of great formal cultivation.

It must also be stressed that as Griffith improvised scenes he had not written out in advance, and which fitted into a structure that was only lightly sketched out, he was quite incapable of stepping back and objectively observing all the implications of what he was doing. Add to this the burdens he was carrying when he was not on location or stage—problems of logistics and finance—and one can at least partially rationalize the moral insensitivity of his work.

Finally, he was, as we have seen, one of the pioneers of his industry's move to California and, in this instance, he became one of the first victims of its isolation from the main currents of contemporary thought and newly developing social consensuses. It is hard to believe that, if he had been working out of New York, he would have been unaware of the founding of the NAACP and the Urban League, for instance. Or of the fact that in the Negro press voices were beginning to be raised at the thoughtless continuation and intensification on stage and screen of outworn black stereotypes, mostly taken over from nineteenth-century southern writers specializing in rural regionalism. Or of the fact that strong voices drawn from the white liberal intellectual community were now being raised in protest against segregationist practices and the racial stereotyping that supported, falsely justified, those practices.

Beyond all that, he was also a victim of the independence he had fought so hard for and was the first director to gain. There was no one in his organization with the power or the prestige to act as a sounding board, to look at the footage he was assembling and dispute the point of view that informed it. He might not have listened, and there would have been no way to prevail on him to abandon his vast project, but there might have been ways to get him to temporize, to present a more balanced view of the era he was determined to recreate on the screen. Had there been someone to say him nay—at least in his more outrageous conceits— the fate of his film might have been quite different, since we know that once it was released, and he became aware of the (to him) surprising objections to it, Griffith busied himself with the shears, trying to modify those sequences that had raised the greatest outcry. At which point, of course, it was too late, since much of the work would have had to be reshot and restructured in order to still the controversy.

As it was, his film was far less vicious in tone than Dixon's shrill novel, far less obsessive in its anxiety about racial "mongrelization." There are several reasons for this. The most important, of course, is that Griffith does not get down to the heart of Dixon's book until the second half of his picture. The first part, with its idyllic portrayal of antebellum life in the South and its powerful realization of the terrors of war, is almost pure Griffith. The effect of this material is to provide, first of all, a human context for the Klan material that is to follow. The Camerons are established as a decent, kindly, loving family, and their prewar way of life, modest, pleasant and law-abiding, provides a kind of benchmark against which to measure the impositions of war and Reconstruction. The contrast between the way things were and the way they become is what motivates the Little Colonel to form the Klan—even before the death of his young sister. Inescapably, we care for these people, and that caring is intensified by the battle sequences, in which the Little Colonel is seen to be both brave and compassionate (as are his enemies)—no small feat given the huge scale of these scenes. To be gallant and humane in a frightening and inhumane terrain is not an inconsequential matter, and the unassuming manner with which Walthall plays the role establishes a reassuring air about the Little Colonel that carries over into the film's second half. We cannot believe he is motivated by anything as mean-spirited as bigotry.

It is also true that however much Griffith enjoyed playing the role of a general when directing the battle scenes, he was careful to surround them with pacifistic sentiments. "War's Peace" says the ironic subtitle preceding wide shots of the dead and dying on the bloody ground at Petersburg. This, too, serves as an earnest of the filmmaker's high intentions. This, too, was a theme he would revert to in later spectacles. In *Birth* it serves to disarm us partially, for at the end of the film, after the Klan has restored peace through its warlike exertions, there are symbolic shots of Christ banishing Mars from the scene, a painfully obvious statement by the director that he deplored the fact that events had reached such a pass that they could be resolved only by bloodshed. Clearly, the attempt here is to dissociate Griffith from the uglier aspects of his material, to establish a feeling that he was as pained by its violent implications as anyone else, and that he hoped, by exposing to public view an unpleasant historical chapter, he could contribute his mite to seeing that it would have no sequels.

The guise of the objective historian was one Griffith liked. By being as authentic as possible in details of decor and costume, by stressing to the point of exaggeration in his publicity the amount of historical research that underlay the film, by inserting throughout the picture recreations of well-known historical incidents (the signing of the Emancipation Proclamation, Lee's surrender, Lincoln's death, and so on) he was attempting to wrap his inventions in a cloak of fact, to insist in yet another way that he was functioning here as an objective historical observer, bringing painful material into the healing light.

Viewing the film from the perspective of almost 70 years, it is harder to dismiss the simple humanity with which Griffith realized his many moments of the quotidian realities. Returns and farewells, the love scenes and the scenes of domestic life—these he managed with unaffected charm, with rue and romance and even occasional humor, just as he always had, right from the start of his directorial career. As Andrew Sarris has wisely written, "there is more of eternity in one anguished expression of Mae Marsh or Lillian Gish than in all of Griffith's flowery rhetoric on Peace, Brotherhood and Understanding."[28]

What is on view in these moments is the best side of Griffith's gift and nature. And that, too, disarms, contributing to the ambiguity surrounding the picture, that ambiguity which made it possible for millions of people to see it, if not in total moral comfort, then as concerned citizens eager to witness, first of all, this great advance in the art of the screen, second of all, to make up their own minds regarding the intense, highly publicized "controversy" that swirled about it.

We may, far after the fact, and with much testimony to hand regarding the fundamental decency of his spirit, his essentially untutored and rather innocently romantic view of complex historical matters, make excuses for Griffith, enter at least a plea of invincible political and social ignorance for him. But there was no reason for those who rose up against him and his work to know any of this or to accept any excuses on his behalf. They had to deal with the film they saw and with the terrible fact that the art that had been lavished on it made it a peculiarly potent demagogic weapon. They had a right to expect more of Griffith, of anyone who called himself an artist and therefore laid claim to special awareness of such tragic human conditions as blacks had found themselves in on this continent. To put the matter simply, Griffith should have known better. And if he had he would not have had to pass the rest of his life in the knowledge that his first masterpiece, the screen's first masterpiece, was a profoundly tainted one.

3

Thus it was that in the summer of 1914 he labored exhaustively, exhaustingly on the many troubles afflicting his film, without ever addressing its central trouble, a trouble whose existence he seems never to have consciously acknowledged. And this, of course, becomes one more excuse for him. Many a director since, caught up in the logistics of managing an enterprise of epic proportions, oppressed by a million and one details, has failed to see those large issues of story, character, theme, underlying philosophy which will fatally flaw the critical reception of his work, no matter how brilliantly he has solved those practical problems of technique and management the day's work presents to him.

Back East, Griffith's backers continued to wonder where their money was going. They therefore journeyed westward sometime after shooting commenced and were present when Griffith did the lovely ballroom sequence, in which a dance is interrupted with the news that Fort Sumter has been fired upon, and the Little Colonel and the other officers of his regiment depart in order to march to war the next morning. He also apparently took them along on location for part of the Clansmen's Ride. But Roy Aitken remembers that the atmosphere was distinctly chilly, with Griffith pressing for more money, Harry Aitken refusing. His last words to Griffith, who came to the station to see the brothers off on their return trip, were: "Make the picture with the $40,000 you already have. . . . This isn't the only picture we are financing."[29]

While the younger Aitken was in London, where he spent most of his time overseeing distribution of the product rolling out of the several studios his brother controlled, he heard from Harry that Griffith had finally persuaded him to put another $19,000 into the picture, but that Harry had sworn that would be the last money the director would get from him. And it was. He also reported to his brother rumors that Griffith had shot 150,000 feet of negative—a ratio of almost twelve feet of film for every foot that was incorporated in the movie's final print, which ran—before postrelease cutting—13,058 feet. It is a generous ratio, far more than the standard of the time, but it is not exorbitant by the standards that came to pertain on epic productions of this sort.

Harry Aitken made a second visit to Los Angeles, in the early fall, and there he and Griffith found themselves in disagreement even more intense than it had been on the earlier trip. Roy Aitken would claim that it was only sometime later that his brother heard that Griffith was selling stock in *The Clansman* to any and all comers, and that he was concerned at this dilution of the picture's ownership. But it appears that Griffith must have started doing so sometime in the summer, for there is scarcely a memoir of this filming that does not speak of Griffith cadging money out of sundry bystanders. Adela Rogers St. John, then a young reporter on Hearst's *Los Angeles Herald*, remembers Griffith appearing in the paper's city room and, with the drama editor's sponsorship, passing the hat to accumulate $250 to meet a payroll.[30]

Billy Bitzer came in for a far larger investment than that. He claimed later that it all started one morning when he picked Griffith up at the Alexandria Hotel, his usual home in Los Angeles. The director showed him a telegram from Aitken informing Griffith in no uncertain terms that no more money would be forthcoming from him and that the director must "FINISH PICTURE IMMEDIATELY." Bitzer, upon reading it, advised the director to do as he was told. "I will like hell," Griffith snapped. Then, in more reasonable terms, he asked Bitzer if he had any money tucked away. He said that he needed four hundred dollars to pay the extras.

Bitzer, as it turned out, had a thousand dollars in a savings account. And after a quick handshake from Griffith, they took off for the bank, and then to the studio. As Bitzer recollected, only $385 was required to meet the extra payroll, and the principals, that day, received nothing. That, however, was not the end of Bitzer's financial contributions to the film. Over the weeks ahead, the cameraman invested some $7,000 all told, withdrawn in smallish amounts from a savings account he held jointly with his wife. Oddly, his name does not appear in the first list of Epoch stockholders. It seems likely that to settle accounts Griffith and Harry Aitken simply handed over to him some of their stock at some later date, for after the picture opened, Bitzer recalls receiving weekly checks for his share of the profits.[31]

One sees from all this what a near thing the birth of *The Birth* was, and though we have the names of those who invested in the picture after the Aitkens' front money ran out, their identities—as anything other than names on a list—are for the most part lost. We do know that Griffith's attorney, Albert Banzhaf, invested $100 and prevailed on his brother to come in for $5,000. We also know that "O. Wimpenny" ran the little restaurant near the studio. But just who was Mae B. Rogers, holder of 5,000 shares in the company that was eventually founded to market the picture and protect the interest of those who lent money to the producers, it is impossible to say. The same goes for R. J. Huntington, and L. Hampton—to name just two of the larger shareholders. Where and how Griffith or Aitken recruited them to the ranks is hard to say.

Tales do hang on the inclusion of two other names on the list. One was W. H. Clune, owner and manager of Clune's Auditorium, latterly the Philharmonic, one of the larger Los Angeles theaters and obviously a desirable location for the picture's first run. Griffith arranged for Clune to come out to the lot when he shot the big, impressive scene in which Walthall led his troops down the main street of Piedmont, heading for the war. For the occasion, he hired a small brass band to put soldiers and the townspeople who lined the street in a properly martial mood.

Clune watched—and listened. And looked pained.

"That's not much of a band," he complained.

"No, it's not," Griffith agreed. "But think of how that tune would sound if your orchestra played it."

"I've got the best orchestra west of the Mississippi," said Clune.

"Think of how 'Dixie' would sound in *your* auditorium, with *your* orchestra!" the director pressed on. "Why, you'd charm the audience right out of their seats! All we need is $15,000 more. . . ."

Whereupon Griffith guided the theater man off the set, in the direction of the director's office, from which they shortly reappeared, wreathed in smiles.

As soon as Clune had left the lot, Griffith held a staff meeting. "Let's start shooting right away. Clune might change his mind. And for heaven's sake, send that band away."[32]

Obviously, Griffith's persuasive powers could be magnetic. Faced with a bill for costumes he could not pay, he somehow persuaded Robert Goldstein, president of the firm supplying them, to take shares in the production amounting to $6,200 in his company's name and got another thousand out of him as a personal investment. Deferrals of this sort have since become common enough in the film industry, especially among independent producers, but they certainly were not common in those early days, when the number of fly-by-night producers was huge and the continuing tradition of doing business on a cash basis grew up among the smaller suppliers of motion picture equipment and services—a tradition still very much in force today. Once again, Griffith can be said to have been a pioneer, this time in the realms of low (but vital) finance.

As far as one can tell, Griffith never lost a day's shooting for lack of money, though Miss Gish recalls him saying things like, "Come on, let's shoot this scene. If we don't get it today, there's no money to make it tomorrow." She also remembers him walking around with a highly visible hole in the sole of his shoe, declaring he wouldn't even buy new shoes "until we start getting money back at the box office." Only once did activity come to a standstill at the studio and that was the only occasion his people became vividly convinced that he had finally, irrevocably run out of money. And, indeed, when he appeared on the lot after lunch he looked weary and there was something grim about him as he said, "All right, let's get to work." Obviously, he had been out trying to round up money. And obviously he had failed, for on the next payday J. C. Epping had to tell everyone that there was nothing to put in their pay envelopes. He, however, convinced them that if they were patient they would be rewarded and no one left the company or failed to report if not to *Birth*, then to one of the several other pictures that were produced simultaneously with it, as the studio kept up with Harry Aitken's implacable demands for product. One suspects that since everyone was working on the Majestic payroll, the problem here was not of Griffith's making but was the result of cash flow troubles back in New York. But those few hours on that single morning represented the only time Griffith lost as result of underfinancing. And in a matter of weeks, the shortage was made up, the payroll regularized.

Griffith's only known refusal of financial aid occurred around this time, when Lillian and Dorothy Gish's mother came forward offering to invest all their savings in the production. "How much money do you have saved, Mrs. Gish," the director inquired. "Three hundred dollars," was the reply. "Mrs. Gish, I can't let you do it. You'd be taking too great a risk."[33] It was a shame, in a way. She would have made thousands on the investment.

Finally, sometime in early November 1914, the last scene was shot (though no one seems to remember what, precisely, it was). There was no celebration, no wrap party, nothing to mark what should have been a memorable day. It was just that from this time forward, for a period of two months, no one saw much of Griffith. Even while he was still shooting, it had been his habit to retire to the projection room in the evening to work into the small hours of the night with his cutters, Jimmie Smith and his wife, Rose, to make preliminary selections of his material. Now, however, he was fine-cutting the enormous work, and it was a brutal task. For the Moviola had not yet been invented. What he had to do was run the picture back and forth through the projector, a buzzer at hand to signal the projectionist whenever he wanted him to slip a piece of paper into his machine's uptake reel, a signal to the editor either to begin or end a cut. He in turn, would stand by, taking notes and, in time, literally attack the film with shears, hoping to approximate the director's necessarily approximate instructions. With 150,000 feet of film piled up around him, Griffith had three projectionists working night and day with him in the screening rooms and the work, in these circumstances, must have been maddening and exhausting.

Nor was editing his only task. There were the titles to be done. Here Frank Woods—known to Griffith as "Mr. Woooods"—came into his own. Woods was not quite a gray eminence; he was intellectually too lightweight for such a role. But when Griffith had problems on the set it was noted that he would head for Woods's office to talk them over, get the views of a sensible, highly practical, reasonably literate man who was not caught up in the day-to-day confusions of production. Somewhat older than Griffith, he was noted for habitually sporting a tam-o-shanter, made of rough tweed and surmounted by a large, flat button, the shape of a tea biscuit. He was also noted for appearing unshaven on the lot during daylight hours, betaking himself to the barber only at the end of the working day. After that it was his habit to repair to his favorite table at the center of the Hoffman House Café, where, it would seem, his real life began. For he was a journalist of a familiar type, the sort of man who prided himself on knowing, at least slightly, everyone who was anyone and who was at his best as the focus of a group of convivial males, drinking and swapping yarns, and in the process—during this period—making sure that his journalistic cronies heard all the most impressive gossip emanating from the production of *The Clansman*.

It was surely in the admiring talk of Frank Woods, at the Hoffman House, that the legend of D. W. Griffith, the profligate genius, began to take shape. Certainly it was from that center that word of mouth regarding Griffith's monumental undertaking began to spread, generating the excitement that would begin to crest at Clune's Auditorium in the early spring of the following year, sweeping eastward in what would prove to be an irresistible tide.

Now, however, there was something more (or less, or anyway different) than a legend to create. There was a movie to be polished and Woods contributed enormously to this process. There can be no doubt that Griffith took a large hand in the process of writing and rewriting the subtitles (which Karl Brown was shooting and reshooting by a new method of his own devising which made them much clearer). But it is also clear that the process began with Woods, who would make first drafts of them in batches, have them inserted into the film for Griffith to see, then take down the master's revisions, perhaps cut and polish them a bit, then resubmit them. After which, more often than not, Griffith would order up more revisions. And more. Titles were cheap to change; they were, indeed, the only footage in the film that the director could now have reshot to his heart's content. So his heart was never content.

While all this was going on, Griffith was also conferring with a musician named Joseph Carl Breil, a popular composer in the sentimental vein ("The Song of the Soul" was one of his hits) about a score for the film. As early as 1909 Griffith had employed him to compile cue sheets for some of his Biograph releases. These were nothing more than listings of the film's major scenes, with suggestions for appropriate music, drawn from the most familiar sources, for the theater orchestra or pianist to play as accompaniment. They were thought to be an improvement on the practice of letting musicians freely improvise as they followed the action on screen. For such later Griffith releases as *Home, Sweet Home* and *The Avenging Conscience*, Breil devised scores for small orchestras (no more than a dozen players), again drawing upon familiar sources, and these were sent out with the release prints to the theaters.

The Clansman presented the arranger with a challenge far larger than any he had faced before. There were no fewer than 214 cues in the score that was eventually sent out. It called for an orchestra of 40 pieces, plus offstage chorus and sound effects, and it drew on a huge range of material. Schubert, Dvořák, Schumann, Mozart, Tchaikovsky, Grieg, even the contemporary Mahler, and, of course, Wagner, contributed to it. Beyond that, nearly every Civil War song of note was represented by at least a few bars of quotation. Then, too, Griffith, who had fond memories of parlor music of his younger days, insisted on plenty of quotations from that, too. Stephen Foster was generously represented, as might be expected, but you could also hear "Turkey in the Straw" and "Home Sweet Home" and "Beautiful Ohio" and "After the Ball." Finally, Breil composed some original material—a tom-tom rhythm for a historical sequence showing black slaves arriving in America (the picture's first shots), an orchestration for brasses of Griffith's rebel yells, which many contemporary sources noted as a particularly effective bit of underscoring. It, naturally, occurred and recurred during the climactic ride of the Clansmen. Finally, Breil managed to compose the first hit song ever to be taken from a film score. It was a love theme he created for the tender moments between the Little Colonel and Elsie Stoneman. It was later published as "The Perfect Song" and by one of those weird ironies of popular culture it lived on well past its moment—as the signature music for yet another widely popular bit of racism, the *Amos 'n Andy* radio show.[34]

None of this was easily accomplished. The procedure, according to Lillian Gish, was for Breil, having looked at this or that portion of the film, to play selections he regarded as appropriate to it for Griffith. Whereupon they would wrangle. "If I ever kill anyone," Griffith once said in exasperation, "it won't be an actor, but a musician." She recalls that their big quarrel was over what came to be known as the "Clan Call," the orchestration of those two notes that had been on Griffith's mind since he shot the sequence. They were apparently very close to some of the brass sounds in "The Ride of the Valkyries"—close enough for Breil to accuse Griffith of tampering with Wagner, or to express fear that he, Breil, might be charged with that offense. But Griffith persisted. It was mood he was after, not the approval of musicologists, and in this instance he was proved right by the singular effect those notes had on audiences.[35]

4

Finally, sometime before the turn of the year, it was done—and for all the struggles over its cost, at a remarkably reasonable price. Before charges for prints and advertising were added, the picture cost just a little more than $100,000. Griffith, according to Gish, arranged a screening for his principals, without orchestra, of course, in the small projection room where he had now spent so many nights. When the last frame had flapped through the projector, there was a stunned silence, followed by a great crowding around of the director, a babble of amazement, congratulation and gratitude for inclusion in so monumental a work. Then, on January 1 and 2, 1915, Griffith took his work to Riverside, California, for sneak previews, another innovation of his, to see how it played before a large audience of strangers. There is no way of knowing how the film fared at this first public viewing. None of the memoirists accompanied the director to these suburban showings, but obviously nothing occurred to discourage him. We may imagine that the five weeks between these screenings and the official premiere at Clune's Auditorium, on February 8, were occupied by more refinements on film and score.

And by a certain amount of wheeling and dealing. Griffith was not yet rich, as he would be after the film went into general release, but he was prospering as never before, and had become, in a small way, a man of affairs. He had acquired a small ranch in the San Fernando Valley, and he now received a report that this land, which he had others farm for him, and to which he occasionally repaired for picnics, but which he never developed as a residence, might contain enough oil to be worthy of exploitation. He discovered, as well, that he could trade in some common stock in the mineral water firm he had purchased back East for some more desirable preferred shares. And finally, he was presented, late in January, with a Majestic Pictures balance sheet showing that the company, in which he owned stock, had closed business the previous year with a working surplus in excess of $300,000. Though Griffith's own corporation owed it something over $10,000 it had obviously borrowed to help finance *Birth*, this must have pleased the director, proving that he had been correct in his surmise that the public was responding well to the longer titles his studio had been shipping forth all year. All in all, things looked to be going well as he put the final touches on a film he had no reason to suppose would do at all badly in the marketplace.[36]

Indeed, he was now clearly concerned that his rights in the film be fully protected and, unbeknownst to his partners in the East, or to the West Coast investors he had persuaded to back him, he calmly had the film copyrighted in the name of the D. W. Griffith Corporation, despite the fact that his rights in the film were cloudy. To be sure, he was in every sense its author. On the other hand, very little of his own money had gone into it and he had made it while he was a full-time employee of Majestic.

Surely pique entered into this decision, for he had not forgiven the Aitkens for failing to finance him fully, putting him to the trouble and embarrassment of finding money for the picture when he should have had nothing on his mind but creative work on it. They had, in his view, reneged on a promise, and mixed with his anger there was a mistrustfulness that would pollute his relationship with Harry Aitken from that time onward. By copyrighting the film in his corporate name, Griffith was assuring himself of a voice in planning its promotion and distribution, assuring himself that it would not simply be taken away from him and handled as his often fainthearted principal backers saw fit.

And he was right to do so, whatever the ambivalence of his legal position. For the elder Aitken remained woefully overextended. He had never consolidated and rationalized his many movie holdings so that they could be sensibly managed, and he had never acquired a staff of professional managers to help him keep things under control. Worse, he continued chronically short of cash, despite the solid front he maintained in New York, and Griffith must have realized that if *Birth* was simply taken over by one of Aitken's concerns its profits—of which Griffith was so much more confident than the money man was—would surely have been used to cover other losses and finance new ventures Aitken could not resist.

There can be no doubt, in short, that Griffith's copyright of the film was a key factor in forcing the foundation of Epoch Productions, which was formed exclusively for the purpose of distributing the film and from which, for many years, profits flowed to Griffith, Dixon and the other backers of the picture, unvexed by the troubles in which Aitken soon found himself. That company was the subject of discussions between Griffith and the Aitkens when the latter came to Los Angeles for the premiere at Clune's on February 8, but its official creation would have to wait until the following month, since everyone was preoccupied with the details of launching the film properly.

By the time of the world premiere the title under which it would eventually achieve immortality was creeping into newspaper advertising as a subtitle—*The Birth of a Nation.* Just how or under whose auspices that stirring phrase was first attached to the picture is unknown, but for the moment Griffith was sticking with *The Clansman*. After all, Dixon's book under that title had been a best seller and its theatrical adaptation had increased its fame. For the moment Griffith saw no reason to abandon it here, especially since Thomas Dixon's status in Los Angeles was that of a famous and popular writer, not a racial propagandist as he was increasingly identified in the East.

Still, there was one group of people who knew all too well what Dixon was about, what the implications of his work were. This was the small local chapter of the NAACP, and they were determined to stop *The Clansman* before it galloped into anyone's heart. They went to court to obtain an injunction against the film on the ground that other branches of the NAACP would later employ, namely that exhibiting it presented a threat to public safety. That is to say, they argued that the picture might so heighten racial tensions as to lead to riots. There was perhaps an implicit threat in this maneuver, but it was the only legal tactic available to them, since the film presented no censorable sexual material, no threat to morality as the law understood that term. To argue that its portrayal of Negroes amounted to racial slander, an offense against a larger morality, would have been feckless. There were no laws on the books applicable to such a charge and, anyway, the film's proprietors could argue that to stop exhibition of the picture because its view of historical events offended a minority would constitute an infringement of their basic rights of free expression.

The NAACP's Los Angeles injunction was a narrow one. It merely forbade the matinee showing of the film on January 8 and said nothing about the evening showing on that date or about any subsequent performance. Therefore the evening presentation proceeded on schedule. There was a vast throng milling around outside the 2,500-seat house, doubtless swollen by people denied entrance to the canceled showing and hoping to obtain tickets for the evening gala. There were none to be had, most of them having gone to people connected with the production, their friends and families, all of whom were in a state of high excitement. They had, most of them, lived with this enterprise far longer than they had with any other movie, and though they had a general idea of what to expect, they had no idea of how well, or how badly, Griffith might have done his work. They knew only that they were about to witness the longest and most expensive film ever made, knew therefore that a great deal was at risk here. Inside, they were confronted with usherettes, wearing gowns cut after the fashion of Civil War days. They were passing around petitions addressed to the Los Angeles City Council, urging that body to take no action to prevent exhibition of the film. Most signed, according to newspaper reports—not surprising considering the loyalty most of them felt they owed *The Clansman.*

Then, at a little past eight, conductor Carli D. Elinor took his place in the pit, the house lights dimmed and the first frames of the film—the main title—were to be observed blurrily on the still-lowered curtain. Then it rose, the title clarified itself as it fell upon the screen behind, and Elinor swept into the downbeat for the opening fanfare. Thereafter, said Brown, whose memories of the film's unfolding are the most detailed, the orchestra "sort of murmured to itself" until the final titles disappeared and the action of the film began, "gliding along through its opening sequences on a flow of music that seemed to speak for the screen and interpret every mood."[37]

This sense of being swept along on a flood of imagery and melody is the common note that one finds not only in memories of this occasion, but in the memories of everyone exposed to the film during its first run— when, literally, there was nothing to compare it with. It is a note, too, that recurs time and again in reviews of the film as, over the next months, it opened all across the United States. The power of the picture was simply stunning; there is no other word for it. There are even, on record, statements by members of the NAACP in which they concede that, at least while watching the film, they were swept up and away by it along with everyone else in the audience. Indeed, it is remarkable that so few critics, in their initial responses to the film, even alluded to its portrayals of blacks, its view of the historical incidents it purported to portray accurately—despite the fact that the NAACP was hauling it into court whenever it opened in major cities, while, of course, making its opinion of the film known everywhere. To a viewer under the spell of the picture, none of this made any difference; the objections seemed almost niggling.

In Karl Brown's shrewd recollections of that first First Night we gain a sense of how the picture worked on an audience. It built gracefully, quietly, with a gathering sense of foreboding, as it established characters, set out plot lines, engaged one emotionally in the fate of its characters. Then came a quickening pace as war was declared, poignant farewells said. Thereafter the sudden opening up of the picture, its vast change in scale from domestic drama to one of epic proportions, though logically enough prepared for, was breathtaking. Yes, obviously, there must be battle scenes, but no one really expected to see panoramas as vast as Griffith gave them, with action as vivid as this. There was, as Brown says, an ebb and flow to these scenes, a lack of choppiness about them, which was simply unprecedented on stage or screen.

Of course, one of the most famous moments in the battle sequence is its climax. The Southern forces have, obviously, been broken, their defeat is imminent, when Walthall snatches up a fallen flag and with it in one hand, his sword in the other, he charges the Union trenches, to cram the flag down the mouth of a cannon, in a really magnificent gesture of defiance and despair. Watching the scene when it was shot, Brown had thought it pretty silly stuff. "Hank delivers the mail," he had written sarcastically in the camera notes it was his duty to keep. But now, in the theater it was another matter. It was the low angle shot that Griffith chose for the business with the cannon—Walthall outlined against the sky—that did the trick: "I think every man in that packed audience was on his feet cheering, not the picture, not the orchestra, not Griffith, but voicing his exultation at this one man's courage—defiant in defeat and all alone with only the heavens for his witness."[38]

In the lull after this storm, there were two other privileged moments of great power. One occurred in the Northern hospital, where the Little Colonel, captured after his exploits in the field, is recovering from his wounds. It is there that he meets Stoneman's daughter for the first time—though he had fallen in love with a picture of her and carried it through the war in the back of his watch. Her comings and goings are observed by a sentry, draped sleepily over his grounded rifle. He has a remarkable face, it seems to contain the sadness of the world, and his eyes follow Gish's every movement, as if he were in love with her from afar. Or perhaps he recognizes in her ethereal beauty a spiritual quality that briefly lifts the gloom from these surroundings. No one can say quite what Griffith was after in this sequence, but it has a very powerful effect, and people began asking after the uncredited extra who played the sentry. But his name was unrecorded, and it was not until Gish, riding in a float at the opening day of the 1939 World's Fair in New York, spotted him in the crowd that he was revealed to be one William Freeman, a man with no interest in acting, who had taken a day's work in the movies one idle day in far-off California.

The other great scene in the movie's first half was Lincoln's assassination. And it remains one of the most beautifully orchestrated sequences in the film. Again, it was a surprise to Brown. When it was being shot Bitzer had ordered a large mirror brought on the set, the idea being to arrange it so it reflected the sun—remember they were working on an open stage—in such a manner as to follow Booth as a spotlight might, while he draws closer and closer to his prey. Again, Brown had thought this a silly business, but on screen that dancing, flickering light was hugely effective as it "picked out a symbol of death itself, a figure all in black with a ghost-white face and a short, villainous little mustache; you never knew or cared where that light came from, so compelling was this poetic vision of Nemesis." Indeed, here as elsewhere, Brown, the eager and intelligent young cameraman, found himself entirely unaware of Griffith's changes from shot to shot, so compelling was the editing, drawing one in from the master shots of the theater to the alternating shots of the passive Lincoln and the stalking murderer, drawing closer, ever closer to him.

By intermission, Brown was entirely lost in the film, but he pulled himself together and headed for the lobby to try to overhear comments. It was a knowledgeable crowd of professionals, and they were all wondering how Griffith could top himself. The predictions were that he could not.

But he could. Again, a famous scene, much discussed by critics ever since: it is Walthall's homecoming to the economically devastated South. His walk up to the family homestead was so slow that, while it was being shot, Brown had been desperately anxious that the camera would run out of film before the actor attained his objective. Now, however, the thoughtfulness of his return, the suggestion in Walthall's movements of a flood of memories overwhelming him, is enormously touching. So are shots of Mae Marsh decorating her dress with "Southern Ermine" (cotton) to add a festive touch to the occasion, an indication of the poverty to which he was returning and of the gallantry with which it was accepted. It was a wonderfully revealing, and moving, bit of business. And when a pair of feminine arms—we never know whose they are—reach out through the door to draw the Little Colonel into his home, one is struck by the austere beauty of Griffith's imagery, the understated rightness of his choice of action and framing in this moment.

After that, of course, there were the powerful scenes that have already preoccupied so much space in this account—the threatened rape and the death of Marsh, the riotous anarchy in the streets of Piedmont, which drives the remainder of the Cameron family out of their home and into the sanctuary of a cabin outside town where they are encircled by blacks and from which they are rescued, in the nick of time, by the hard-riding Klan. The pacing of this final crisis was cinematically irresistible.

Some recall a moment of silence when the last, peaceful frames of the film—Walthall and Gish seated on a bluff overlooking the sea, sharing pacifistic visions of Christ—had passed through the projector. Some do not. But all recall the audience leaping up, cheering and applauding and stamping their feet, not to be stilled until Griffith made an appearance, not in a triumphal mood, but an ostentatiously humble one. Or maybe there was nothing ostentatious about it. Maybe he was genuinely overawed by this response. For surely this ovation was of a character he had dreamed about in all those dismal years as an unsuccessful touring actor. At any rate: "He stepped out a few feet from stage left, a small, almost frail figure lost in the enormousness of that great proscenium arch. He did not bow or raise his hands or do anything but just stood there and let wave after wave of cheers and applause wash over him like great waves breaking over a rock."[39]

A phase of his life, his career, was ending in that moment when an audience at long last fully recognized his mastery, perhaps sensed as well that he had somehow found a way of fusing, in this film, the stuff of his childhood memories and aspirations with the craftsman's knowledge hard-won in adulthood. He could not know, in this moment, how huge his success would be, but he must have sensed that it was going to be of a magnitude as unprecedented for him as his achievement was unprecedented in his young art. Nor could he know how much pain would accompany it in the months ahead, how much anguish would attend his trip back down from the heights on which he stood this night in the years that would follow on from there. What he had to savor here was a moment that might have justified, in its triumphant lack of ambiguity, the long years of struggle and disappointment, may even have sustained him in the long years of struggle and bitterness that were to come. We must imagine him happy beyond any power of ours to quantify or express it.

David Wark Griffith, circa 1908. This is one of a group of formal portraits for which the actor-playwright sat around the time he was making his first reluctant forays into filmmaking.

"Miss Petticoats"

An actor's life: *Opposite top*, Kathryn Osterman shows "Lawrence" Griffith the door during their brief tour in *Miss Petticoats*, 1902. *Opposite bottom*, his first film appearance, in the
Edison production *Rescued from an Eagle's Nest*, 1908.
Above, Linda Arvidson Johnson, the young actress Griffith
met in San Francisco in 1904, married in Boston in 1906.

At the Biograph: *Above*, Griffith and Billy Bitzer
study a strip of the cameraman's work by the
blinding light of the studio's Cooper-Hewitts.
Below, the harrowing climax of *A Corner in
Wheat*, 1912: Frank Powell is buried alive under
a cascade of the grain the financier sought so
desperately, and without conscience, to control.

Fathers of *The Birth: At right*, Thomas Dixon, "the ranting, wandering divine," author of the novel on which the film was based. *Below*, Griffith confers on the set with Frank ("Daddy") Woods, his story editor, who wrote the first adaptation of *The Clansman*. Bitzer looks on.

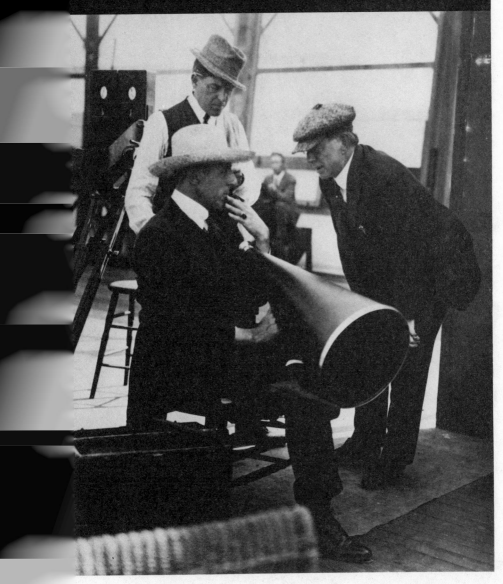

Images, innocent and infamous, from *The Birth of a N̲[...]*
Above, the Little Colonel (Henry Walthall) is we[...]
home from the war. *Below*, the Klan captures G[...]
would-be rapist who forced "the Dear One" through "t[...]
gates of death." Gus was played by Walter Long, in bla[...]

LINCOLN'S ASSASSINATION.
THE FATAL BLOW THAT ROBBED
THE SOUTH OF ITS BEST FRIEND

D. W. GRIFFITH'S
MIGHTY SPECTACLE

THE BIRTH OF A NATION

FOUNDED ON THOMAS DIXON'S

'THE CLANSMAN'

One of *Birth*'s less offensive posters showed Raoul Walsh as John Wilkes Booth escaping the presidential box after assassinating Lincoln. Most of the film's promotional art featured the Ku Klux Klan's night riders in full, menacing regalia.

Intolerance: Griffith and Bitzer mounted a camera on a racing car to film the greatest of their many rides to the rescue. Tod Browning, later famous as a director of horror films (*Dracula, Freaks*), played the driver in this climax to the film's modern story. Mae Marsh, beside him, was the wife trying to obtain a governor's pardon before her husband's execution for a murder he did not commit. The other passengers are Miriam Cooper, "the Friendless One," and the real miscreant, and Edward Dillon, the cop who broke the case.

High points: Mae Marsh, in the modern story's court-room sequence, pleading for custody of her child, achieved the apotheosis of her art. *Below*, the director prepares to lay aloft to survey construction of the Walls of Babylon. The banner in the background advertises the film's working title, *The Mother and the Law*.

"A Sun Play of the Ages": Griffith's grandiose subtitle for *Intolerance* never seemed more apt than in the moment his great vision of Belshazzar's feast in the forecourt unfolded before the startled eyes of its

1916 audience. It remains one of film's immortal images. And unlike most such expensive and highly conscious efforts to overawe the public, its power to impress seems to grow, not to diminish, as time passes.

Low society: Griffith, the sometime touring actor, remained
ever, a creature of hotel rooms and lunch counters. Here, a
newspaper interests him more than the companionship o
Bobby Harron, former prop boy turned expert juvenile lead

High society: The welcome accorded him by the English elite when he filmed there in 1917, at the height of World War One, remained one of Griffith's proudest memories. Here he directs Lily Elsie and Lady Diana Manners (with whom he said he fell in love) in a scene for *The Great Love*.

At the front: Griffith's visits to the war zone were carefully staged for maximum propaganda value and minimum risk to the world's pre-eminent director. *Above*, he poses, camera at the ready, with British flyers. His garb, *below*, suggests the trench from which he was supposed to be observing a battle was not alarmingly far forward.

At the movies: Not unnaturally, Griffith saw the war within the conventions of a Griffith movie. But *Hearts of the World* had moments of great power, notably Lillian Gish's harrowing mad scene as she wandered the battlefield convinced her lover had died on their wedding night. *Below*, a peacetime pose with co-star sister, Dorothy.

Broken Blossoms (1919) gave Lillian Gish her greatest tragic role, and was for Griffith one of his most memorable successes.

CHAPTER TEN

"History with Lightning"

So *The Clansman* was a hit. Or so it seemed. Its first-run engagement at Clune's would extend for an unprecedented seven months. But Los Angeles is not the world. Then, as now, it remained for New York, and its allegedly more sophisticated critics and audiences, to confirm or deny the producers' hopes for a film. This was, if anything, more true in 1915, when Los Angeles was genuinely a provincial city, New York genuinely the capital of the nation's culture, than it now is.

Thus it was that less than two weeks after its Los Angeles opening *The Clansman* arrived in New York. On February 13 Aitken announced that a legitimate theater, the Liberty (where nine years earlier *The Clansman* had had its brief New York run as a play), had been leased from the Klaw and Erlanger chain for the first run, which would be on a two-a-day schedule, all seats reserved, for a top admission price of $2.00, an unprecedented figure for a movie ticket and in itself a matter that greatly occupied publicists of the time. At about the same time prints of the film arrived in the East, and so did Griffith himself, who was to claim that the idea for advanced admission prices was his, and that he had to work hard to persuade his colleagues to try them. A series of screenings was arranged prior to the official opening, each of which had a significant effect on the film's fortunes.

A very early running was for a small group that included Thomas Dixon, who had yet to see what Griffith had made of his original work. As he was to recall the occasion in his unpublished autobiography, there were no more than 75 people scattered through the theater that morning and, fearing the worst, he decided to watch the film alone in the balcony from which he could perhaps escape unnoticed if the picture turned out to be a disaster. In Dixon's account, after "the last light dimmed, a weird cry came from the abyss below—the first note of the orchestra, a low cry of the anguished South being put to torture." Or so it seemed to this darkly passionate man. Like so many of the first witnesses to the film, it was the musical score—"the throb through the darkness . . . raising the emotional power to undreamed heights"—that would remain most powerfully in his memory. "Uncanny," he called it.

Still, he thought, it might be that, for obvious reasons, the movie was working more strongly on him than on the rest of its early auditors, and when the film was over he hesitated to join the rest of the audience in the lobby. "I descended slowly, cautiously, only to be greeted by the loudest uproar I had ever heard from seventy-five people."[1] It may or may not be on this occasion—there is conflict on the matter, and considerable possibility that the incident is apocryphal—that Dixon told Griffith *The Clansman* was too tame a title for so mighty a work, that he ought to call it *The Birth of a Nation*. If he did encourage this retitling, it must be remembered that the recommended phrase had already appeared as a secondary title in early advertising, so the author was at most proposing what amounted to a revised ad campaign.

More important, perhaps, the enthralled Dixon quickly conceived a grand scheme to blunt the growing agitation against the film. He would invoke the assistance in this matter of an old acquaintance, a friend from his college days at Johns Hopkins, who had attained a certain influence in the world. His name was Woodrow Wilson and, at the moment, he was President of the United States.

Dixon wrote the White House requesting a half hour appointment, and the President granted it. In mid-February the two men met, and after an exchange of college reminiscences, Dixon told Wilson he had a favor to ask of him "not as chief magistrate of the Republic but as a former scholar and student of history and sociology." Flattered by the reference to his former scholarly preoccupations (and perhaps relieved, Dixon thought, that he was not seeking a government appointment), the President listened as the author urged him to attend a showing of Griffith's film, "not because it was the greatest ever produced or because his classmate had written the story . . . but because this picture made clear for the first time that a new universal language had been invented."

The approach was very high-minded. Not a word, apparently, was spoken about the film's disturbing theme, nor about the possibility that a public official might find himself embroiled in an exceedingly unpleasant controversy should he appear to endorse such a movie. Dixon, in his recollection of this conversation, quite tellingly adds that in making his plea for Wilson's attention he described movies as "a new process of reasoning by which will could be overwhelmed with conviction."[2] In other words, the ideologue had perceived in *The Birth of a Nation* not merely the previously unsuspected artistic power of movies but their equally unsuspected propagandistic power. That, surely, was the general point that most interested Dixon about Griffith's film, and he was right to suppose that it was the characteristic that would most intrigue Wilson, the some-time political scientist and historian.

A few months later, Dixon came close to admitting what his purpose had been with Wilson. In a letter to Joseph P. Tumulty, the President's secretary and confidant, he wrote: *"I didn't dare allow the president to know the real big purpose back of my film—which was to revolutionize Northern sentiments by a presentation of history that would transform every man in the audience into a good Democrat!* And make no mistake about it . . . we are doing just that thing. . . . Every man who comes out of one of our theaters is a Southern partisan for life. . . ."* (Dixon's italics.)[3] Even this letter, however, which was written in response to Tumulty's attempt to deny and suppress a careless Presidential endorsement of the film, was not entirely forthcoming, for Dixon dared not fully own up to the President's man the sexual hysteria that underlay his feelings about blacks. Nor did he mention his "final solution" to the racial problem, which was, very simply, to send all American blacks back to Africa—although as controversy over *Birth* grew he would become more open on both these subjects.

But all of that was, in mid-February, still in the future. For the moment the president was intrigued, but there was a problem. Wilson was still officially in mourning for the death of his first wife and it would be impossible for him to appear in public at a theater. However, if Dixon could bring projectors and screen to the White House . . . ? Of course, it would be no problem.

So it was arranged that Woodrow Wilson, along with members of his staff and cabinet, would see *The Birth of a Nation* on February 18, 1915—as far as one can tell, the first movie ever to be shown at the White House. As Dixon rose to take his leave, Wilson reminded him—although surely he had no need to do so—that the author had once been instrumental in arranging for Wilson to receive an honorary degree from Wake Forest College, in Dixon's home state of North Carolina, and an institution the latter had briefly attended. Apparently the honor had come to Wilson at a moment in his life when he had been discouraged by the progress of his career and it had a cheering effect on him, as he remembered now: "I want you to know, Tom, that I am pleased to be able to do this little thing for you," Dixon later recalled the President saying, "because a long time ago you took a day out of your busy life to do something for me."[4]

The habits of politics are apparently immutable. Then as now, then as earlier, favors are returned for favors done. What seems curious to the modern student of this incident is the simplicity with which Dixon achieved his ends. He did not have to fight his way through layer upon layer of staff to make the appointment with his sometime friend and, more important, there was no one, apparently, to warn the President off

Birth, no one to pick up the first rumbles of black and liberal protest over the film—sounds that, however muted they were that February, modern presidential staffers would quickly discern and report to their boss.

There is no detailed or reliable account of that first-ever White House screening of a film, though it is said that officials brought their families to it. We do not know to whom Wilson addressed his famous two-sentence evaluation of the movie, but it passed quickly into general circulation, despite later attempts to disown it: "It is like writing history with Lightning. And my only regret is that it is all so terribly true."[5]

This endorsement, from a chief executive who had, among his other former scholarly attainments, some reputation as a student of Reconstruction, was, of course, far more enthusiastic—and colorfully quotable—than Dixon could have hoped for, but even then he was not finished with his lobbying activities in Washington. He cadged an interview with Josephus Daniels, the Secretary of the Navy and also a native of North Carolina, prevailing upon him to intercede with Edward D. White, the Chief Justice of the Supreme Court, to grant Dixon an appointment. White, too, was a southerner, a Louisianian, but he was also a forbidding figure—even to so bold a promoter as Dixon. Still, the writer had the President's endorsement to retail, and the old jurist who claimed he had never seen a film and had no curiosity to do so, was intrigued when Dixon told him who the collective hero of the picture was.

"You tell the true story of the Klan?" he inquired.

"Yes—for the first time."

Then, as Dixon perhaps hyperbolically put it in his autobiography, "He leaned toward me and said in low tones: 'I was a member of the Klan, sir. Through many a dark night I walked a sentinel's beat through the ugliest streets of New Orleans with a rifle on my shoulder. You've told the true story of that uprising of outraged manhood?' "

"In a way I'm sure you'll approve."

"I'll be there," came the firm reply, and he was as good as his word, bringing some of his judicial colleagues with him. What their decision on the film was is lost to history, but the mere fact that members of this august body had seen the picture made for excellent word of mouth advertising.[6]

In all of this, Griffith's presence is not noted, though it appears he did preside over a screening for a group of congressmen in a hotel ballroom, and in his unfinished autobiography he mentions meetings with Wilson during the latter's presidency, but most of these were in connection with his wartime film, *Hearts of the World.* Whether he was or was not present for the White House screening, however, the film's reception in the nation's capital must have buoyed everyone's spirits, and this recognition by the political world of film's powerful potential, a recognition that would have significant consequences for Griffith, was surely gratifying to him, given his lofty ambitions for his medium. Immediately, of course, the thought that leaders of political opinion had not criticized the movie's racist stance must have been encouraging, indeed.

For word about that matter had, if anything, preceded Griffith and his prints to the East. The West Coast branches of the NAACP had, naturally, warned their brothers and sisters in the East about the film, and the black newspapers of the West Coast were full of outrage and of premature reports of successful protests against the film, suggesting that total banning of it was imminent, when, in fact, black protesters succeeded only in getting a few trims made in the prints showing in Los Angeles and (latterly) San Francisco. In New York, May Childs Nerney, the NAACP's secretary, was already sending out thousands of pamphlets, alerting her organization's local chapters and sympathizers to the film, compiling lists of pending state and municipal censorship bills that might be shaped so that *Birth* could be legally banned in some localities. She reminded members and friends that *The Clansman*, as a play, had caused a riot in Philadelphia when it played there in 1906.

It must have seemed obvious to the NAACP that it was entering upon an unequal struggle, since the producers, though they were still hard pressed financially, were already beginning to mount a publicity campaign as unprecedented in its way as the product being publicized was in its way. To one of those early screenings, perhaps the very one at which Thomas Dixon saw the film for the first time, a Schubert publicity man, Theodore Mitchell, said to have been responsible for making Lillian Russell a household name, and known to be one of the founders of an off-Broadway theater group that would grow into the Theater Guild, was invited. He had the theater devotee's contempt for film and braved a cold February morning mostly out of curiosity. By the end of the film, however, he was offering his services and those of an associate, J. R. McCarthy, and before long they had orchestrated an astonishing campaign in aid of the film. They used the night riders, clad in full white-sheet Klan regalia, as a central motif of their ads and posters, which they did not confine to Manhattan Island, or even the city's five boroughs. They spread them throughout the suburbs; appealing to an audience that did not habitually attend movies—and certainly did not think of them as cultural events comparable to a Broadway play. Perhaps the most startling of the publicity agents' ploys, however, was to hire horsemen, garb them in Klan robes and set them to galloping the streets in order to call attention to the picture. There is, perhaps, no better measure of popular attitudes regarding race than the fact that this occasioned no more than amusement among those who witnessed the spectacle.

As the March 3 New York opening of *The Birth of a Nation* approached, however, the NAACP was preoccupied not with night riding in aid of publicity but with legal and quasilegal maneuverings to prevent the showing of the film or at least to force the producers to make some cuts in the release print. At the moment their attention was focused on the National Board of Censorship (latterly the National Board of Review), which was composed of prominent citizens and had been created and at least partly funded by the motion picture industry itself, to act as a censorship board in hopes of forestalling federal censorship of movies and blunting the effect of the proliferating state and municipal censorship bodies. Up to now, the board had worked well—no federal law had been passed, and many of the local boards, sometimes informally, sometimes quite formally under the language of the legislation that had created them, looked to the National Board for guidance. If it refused to grant its seal of approval to a film, that film would face hearings, and in many cases outright bans, in 80 percent of the motion picture markets, according to one trade source of the time.

The board itself was cumbersome—it had 125 members—and there were many little movies to deal with in those days, so it did most of its work through committees. It was just such a small group that, sometime in February, also attended a pre-release screening. The National Board's chairman, Frederic C. Howe, a distinguished urban progressive and at that time Commissioner of Immigration of the Port of New York, sat on this committee, and word leaked to the NAACP that Howe, at least, had been severely disquieted by it. Inquiry, however, brought the unwelcome news that the committee as a whole had voted to approve the picture, and a request for the names of the committee and for the addresses of the full board—the NAACP wished to put its case before the entire body—was brushed off.

Whether as a result of Howe's uneasiness over *Birth*, NAACP agitation or the growing sense that it was, with *Birth*, dealing with a far more consequential picture, and a much more complex moral question, than it had ever faced before, someone decided that approval should be withheld until all 125 board members could see the movie. The NAACP asked the board to give it 12 tickets to its advance screening, which was set for March 1 in the afternoon. The board agreed to that number, then cut it to two while insisting that only white NAACP members be permitted to use them. Furious, NAACP leaders attempted to squeeze light-skinned Negroes into the theater, with what results we do not know. What is known is that the producers decided to pack the house that afternoon, filling it with what a modern press agent would call "opinion-makers"—journalists, prominent citizens—who they had reason to believe were friendly to the picture. Obviously, they hoped their enthusiasm would sway the censors—and it did. Chairman Howe and a few others still held out for cuts (Howe was said to want the whole second half of the film banned), and the entire board decided to withhold final approval until they could see a re-edited version the producers promised to prepare.

On the whole, though, the screening must have been extremely discouraging to the NAACP, for the majority of those present were quite simply enthralled by what they saw. The Aitkens had overbooked the house and they were forced to violate the fire ordinances and place folding chairs in the aisles to accommodate the overflow. The crush added to the excitement of the occasion, of course, but the audience needed no artificial stimulation. As the curtain came down at intermission, there was a hush, followed by cheers and prolonged applause. According to Roy Aitken, "Many persons were so excited they did not know whether to sit down, stand up, go take a stroll into the lobby or go to get a strong drink."[7] At the end, the applause came in deafening waves and Harry Aitken and Griffith were surrounded by well-wishers of every sort—society matrons, promoters offering schemes by which they could attach themselves to a hit, investors hoping they could still get in on Epoch's stock offering.

But it was too late for the former doubters. It was clear now that the Los Angeles reception for *Birth* was no accident, that if it had conquered this relatively sophisticated audience it would conquer ordinary folks still more easily. In the lobby Harry Aitken invited a select group of theatergoers to join Griffith and Dixon at the Fifty-seventh Street apartment he shared with his brother for a reception. Felix Kahn and Crawford Livingston from the banking community were there, and so were Richard Harding Davis, Irvin Cobb and others from journalistic and literary circles, many of whom had or were hoping to sell stories to the movies. And, of course, there was a heavy representation of show people, especially theater owners and managers. But the party, the day, the week, belonged to David Wark Griffith, who had finally arrived where he had so long wanted to be—on Broadway, with a hit. "This was his moment of glory and he loved it," Aitken would write. "I began to notice from this time on, however, how much Griffith craved admiration and the public spotlight, and how much he missed it later in his life."[8]

After the well-wishers had left, the partners (Dixon included) lingered over coffee, loath to let the evening end, and wisely so, for the phone rang as they talked. It was long distance from Boston, and the caller was none other than Louis B. Mayer. He was not yet the mightiest mogul Hollywood had ever seen; he was, in fact, just a few years away from the junk business; but he was prospering as the owner of theaters in Haverhill, Massachusetts, had begun distributing pictures around the New England area, and just this year had joined with several other small distributors to found Metro pictures—ultimately, of course, to be the first M in M-G-M. He was also well connected in the New York theatrical world and it seems likely that someone had called him after the afternoon preview to tell him to bid early—and high—for the distribution rights to *Birth* in his area. At any rate, here he was on the phone, and according to

Roy Aitken's reminiscences offering $50,000, $25,000 as an advance, a guarantee of $25,000 once the picture began playing and a 50–50 split once he had recouped his costs.

Harry Aitken did not close with Mayer that night; indeed, contracts were not signed until August, at which time Mayer was forbidden to play the picture in Boston until September 11, since Epoch had held that city out of the states' rights deal they made with Mayer until their road show engagement had, as they believed, skimmed the cream off the market. This policy of reserving the first run for their own road show in many of the "key" cities was applied all over the United States by Epoch, and though the company prospered greatly by it, distributors like Mayer did not do badly, either. He and his brethren were required to turn over 10 percent of their net profits to Epoch, although their selling costs were not small. Nonetheless, Mayer boasted that he had made $500,000 personally out of this deal, and it's reasonable to estimate that the company he threw together to raise the advance Aitken asked netted a million dollars—and that was, remember, just the New England territory.

In later years Aitken would complain that Mayer had cheated Epoch, and Bosley Crowther, attempting to reconcile Mayer's boasts with Epoch's books, concluded that Aitken was right—he had been had.[9] There is no question that the huge profits Mayer made on *Birth* were crucial to his rise in the motion picture industry. From them he derived the capital he needed to buy his way further and further into production. Ironically, he would conduct his rule of M-G-M from the lot in Culver City that Harry and Roy Aitken would, in a couple of years, build for producer Thomas Ince, and which they would sell, in distress, in 1918, to Samuel Goldwyn. It—and the Goldwyn name, of course—would be that producer's chief contributions to Mayer's M-G-M, which has waxed and waned on the Aitkens' former property these many years.

Mayer's call that evening gave Griffith, Dixon and the Aitkens the first solid evidence of just how much their film might be worth. If a man were willing to advance them what amounted to half the negative cost of the movie just for the right to distribute it in one territory, and that not necessarily the most profitable of them, and if he was willing to allow them to keep the first-run rights in the region's only great city, what more could they expect? The answer, obviously, was incalculable, and it is probably as well for the beleaguered NAACP that its leaders did not know about Mayer's call, did not as yet have any idea of the extraordinary popular appeal of the movie they were opposing. If they had, their discouragement might have been profound, for the mood was changing in the moviemakers' camp. Where previously the focus of their concern had simply been on recouping what seemed to them an enormous investment, it was now shifting to the unprecedented profit potential being hinted at. Those profits would give them the will—and the cash flow—to fight off anyone trying to interfere with their suddenly glowing economic destiny.

The next day, March 2, 1915, they devoted to reorganizing Epoch Producing Corporation, corporate owner of *The Birth of a Nation*. The company had been organized in Eddyville, New York, on the day the picture was premiering in Los Angeles, when none of the principals could be present for this legal formality. Now, however, the temporary officers stepped aside, and Harry Aitken became president, Griffith vice president of the firm, with Roy Aitken serving as secretary and Albert H. T. Banzhaf, Griffith's attorney, as treasurer. On paper, control of the corporation, and its single asset, was equally divided between Griffith and the Aitkens, but in practice the director would be far away in California as important decisions about the film's release were made in the months to come, while his man Banzhaf would have the preoccupations of his law practice to distract him as the senior Aitken managed the film, and its receipts. Ultimately, the lack of communication between the corporation's officers and the mutual suspicion that would develop out of it, would increase the strains they already felt. These would finally destroy the Aitkens and, perhaps, to a certain degree damage Griffith as well.[10]

The next morning, just hours before the picture was scheduled to begin its run, the NAACP charged the producers and the management of the Liberty Theater with maintaining a public nuisance and endangering the public peace, and all repaired to police court, where the chief magistrate ruled that he was powerless to prevent showing of the film until and unless a performance of the film actually led to a breach of the peace. Nothing of the sort occurred that evening. Indeed, the premiere was conducted in the genteel fashion of a Broadway opening night—with some elements of what would become standard movie premiere hoopla added. There were souvenir programs, male ushers were dressed in confederate and union uniforms, their female colleagues in gowns of the Civil War period, and the orchestra was augmented with a chorus that sang the more familiar songs as they were quoted in the score. A trade paper report on the evening noted that the audience included "many listed in the Who's Who of filmdom and a large number of men and women prominent in literary and society circles." It added: "No picture presented in New York has been viewed by more exacting spectators and few, if any, have elicited such spontaneous and frequent applause."

At the intermission, in response to calls from the audience, Thomas Dixon came on stage to declare the film superior to both his original novel and the stage adaptation he had made from it, which, he noted, had played this very theater some eight years previously. In bringing Griffith on, he said that he would have let no one but the son of a soldier and a southerner direct a movie based on this work and called Griffith the greatest director in the world. Griffith, as was to be his custom on these occasions, took a modest stage position, "just far enough beyond the wings to be visible from all parts of the house," and spoke but briefly, though "clearly and with dignity." He said it was his aim "to place pictures on a par with the spoken word as a medium for artistic expression appealing to thinking people."

Hundreds of people had been turned away from the box office prior to the showing and the standees were three deep in the aisle behind the loge seats. Applause began with, of all things, the showing of nothing more than street scenes in prewar Piedmont, and was "nearly incessant for a full half-hour" when the battle scenes unfolded. Apparently the sheer number of people involved in these sequences was enough of a novelty to impress this audience initially, and once it saw how masterfully Griffith had orchestrated his spectacle it was simply swept away. There was, according to report, no hesitation in its enthusiasm for the film's second half as it "felt the grip of the story and sympathized with the work of the Ku Klux Klan battling against Negro domination."[11]

Nor was there much comment on this matter in the reviews the next day. The *Times* did not play its review prominently and it was quite a short notice. The lead accurately described *The Birth* as "a film version of some of the melodramatic and inflammatory material contained in 'The Clansman' by Thomas Dixon," with "the addition of much preliminary historical matter." Thereafter the *Times*'s anonymous writer, on balance more reporter than reviewer, contented himself with the notation that "a great deal might be said concerning the spirit revealed in Mr. Dixon's review of the unhappy chapter of Reconstruction and concerning the sorry service rendered by its plucking of old wounds." Obviously, however, the newsman did not think he was the person to undertake this task, and as others were to do, he tried to separate praise for Griffith's craft from doubts about the morality of the movie's message. He wrote: ". . . of the film as film, it may be reported simply that it is an impressive new illustration of the scope of the motion picture camera," and he went on to mention the "extraordinarily large number of people" in the "historical pageant," and the achievement of "a striking degree of success" in the Civil War battle scenes. He had to admit, too, that "in terms of purely pictorial value the best work is done in those stretches that follow the night riding of the Ku Klux Klan, who look like a company of avenging spectral crusaders sweeping along the moonlit roads."[12]

It is surprising that neither the *Times* reporter nor any of the other early reviewers saw fit to mention the controversy already beginning to bubble around the movie. They must have been aware of it, but obviously did not consider it their province when discussing the film itself, a rather pleasantly purist view of the critical function by modern standards.

Indeed, most of the critics were far less reserved than the man from the *Times*, and much less careful to qualify their praise for Griffith's technique with reference to the moral implications of the work as a whole. "The mind falters and the typewriter balks before an attempt to either measure or describe D. W. Griffith's crowning achievement in screen drama," the respected Burns Mantle wrote in the *Evening Mail*, obviously still caught up in an excitement "that last night swept a sophisticated audience like a prairie fire." The man from the *Sun* averred that "never before has such a whirlwind combination of story, spectacle, and tense drama been unrolled before New Yorkers," while the *News* insisted that "never before, on canvas, by photography, or by literature has the great grapple of the Civil War been so graphically visualized." Perhaps the most interesting comment, in light of later events, came from Louis Sherwin of the *Evening Globe*, whose paper was to become, with the *New York Post*, the picture's leading editorial opponent; he called it "beyond question the most extraordinary picture that has been made—or seen—in America so far."

But perhaps the review that comes closest to giving a sense of the swept-away excitement experienced by early viewers of the film was written by C. F. Zittel, of Hearst's *Evening Journal*. "First of all," he declared, "children must be sent to see this masterpiece. Any parent who neglects this advice is committing an educational offense, for no film has ever produced more educational points than Griffith's latest achievement." The reviewer, apparently, had not the slightest doubts as to the historical accuracy of the film, as indeed most did not, so neatly were they taken in by the director's earnest insistence that all his reconstructions of past events were as accurate as research and caring art could make them. If Griffith had been painstaking about these matters, surely he was about his portrayal of general conditions during Reconstruction. Having given this earnest advice, Zittel let himself go completely: " 'The Birth of a Nation' will thrill you, startle you, make you hold on to your seats. It will make you laugh. It will make you cry. It will make you angry. It will make you glad. It will make you hate. It will make you love. It is not only worth riding miles to see, but it is worth walking miles to see."[13]

With this outpouring from the daily press, the success of *The Birth of a Nation* was assured. The next day there were lines at the box office and they would continue to form there for weeks, as the initial critical excitement over the film was supported by audience enthusiasm for it. And, of course, the continuing, indeed growing, controversy over its social implications, soon spilling into the courts and municipal legislative chambers in New York and elsewhere, served to sustain interest in the film as it continued its New York run—for an astonishing 48 weeks at the Liberty before it moved on to subruns—and opened around the country.

Nor were the critics and the other publicists done with the film the day after its opening. On March 5, for example, a clergyman, very likely suggested to the paper by the producers, was calling the film "by all odds the greatest thing that has ever come to New York." The preacher's name was Thomas B. Gregory, self-described as a Universalist minister, but apparently a regular contributor to the Hearst press as well. In his piece he claimed he had personally witnessed, during Reconstruction days, horrors of exactly the sort Griffith depicted. "That the story as told by the pictures is true I am ready to swear on the Bible," he wrote. "I am prepared to say that not one of the more than five thousand pictures that go to make up the wonderful drama is in any essential way an exaggeration. They are one and all faithful to historic fact, so that looking upon them, you may feel that you are beholding that which actually happened." This "truthfulness," he wrote, was where the chief educational value of the movie was to be found.[14]

This piece by Gregory, as well as comments the producers solicited from prominent writers and politicians, would be used by them in defending their work both in courts of law and the court of public opinion, this insistence on the historical veracity of the picture being a theme they resorted to over and over again. So was the second theme Gregory strummed hard in his article. This was the film's reverence for Lincoln, which reflected his stature as a mythic, even saintly, figure, never more so than this year, as the nation continued its observance of the fiftieth anniversary of the Civil War. The general understanding, North and South, was that had Lincoln lived the anguish of Reconstruction might have been avoided, good racial relations promoted in some vague, distant and kindly way, not involving anything as intimate as brotherhood, and, naturally, skirting the unspeakable matter that Thomas Dixon insisted on speaking about, which was the possibility of those relations becoming sexual. This was at best speculation, at worst nonsense, but the film's evocation of a kind of nostalgia for the great lost leader, its hints of an imagined world that might have emerged had he lived, its use of him as a symbolic figure to resolve those baser emotional currents *The Birth of a Nation* would stir anew was something a publicist like Gregory could borrow to rationalize the picture, blazing a trail others would follow. Indeed, this piece would, in the months to come, be employed time and again to answer the outrage of liberal clergymen as they rallied to the film's opponents.

On the same day that Gregory's piece appeared in William Randolph Hearst's *American*, Dorothy Dix, giver of advice to the lovelorn in the same publisher's *Journal*, briefly deserted her usual post to praise Griffith's film without stint. "I am a film fan," she forthrightly declared, "but I never had the slightest conception of what could be done with the moving picture as an art until I saw 'The Birth of a Nation.' . . . I had considered the moving picture interesting, instructive, amusing, diverting, beautiful, spectacular, but I had believed that the silent drama never could touch the emotions very deeply. I had thought that to grip an audience, to melt it to tears with pathos, to thrill it with high heroic sentiment, required the spoken word and the magic of the human voice."

Birth, she said, "disproves all of this theory," and she went on to describe an audience worked up to "a perfect frenzy," a film that was "the apotheosis of the moving picture." To be sure, she spoke with moral and historical equanimity of scenes showing how "the black heel was set upon the white neck of a conquered people,"[15] but, unlike Gregory's, hers was not primarily an ideological piece and the gush and rush of her enthusiasm for the way the movie worked emotionally, on the subrational level, is something to be borne in mind in considering the popular success of the film. It seems fair to say that literally millions of people first experienced the full, and really quite magical, transporting powers of motion pictures at this movie, that many had a conversion experience similar to that which "film fan" Dix described in her opening paragraphs. Indeed, in the end one suspects that the film owed far more of its uncanny power at the box office to Griffith's demonstration of his—and the medium's—gift for making powerful emotional connections with audiences than it did to Thomas Dixon's perverse message. That many accepted the truth of that message unquestioningly, as Miss Dix did, says a great deal about the state of racial consciousness in this country at this time, but that acceptance also says something about the state of the nation's movie consciousness at the time, too, the fundamental lack of knowledge about the medium's power.

There is one more early review to consider in this connection. That appeared in the trade paper *Variety* on March 12 and was the work of one Mark Vance. He was more than blithe about the material that was causing so much anguish at the NAACP. "Griffith struck it right when he adapted the Dixon story for the film," Vance wrote blandly. "He knew the South and he knew just what kind of a picture would please all white classes" was the soundly amoral judgment of this trade paper reporter, whose business it was to evaluate the commercial prospects of the work at hand—and never mind nice questions about the social impact of the picture. "Some places the censors are going to find fault," the writer allowed. "That's a persistent way censors have." In this connection he mentions a scene in which a slave is flogged and the scenes of black state assemblymen in drunken, riotous conclave. But there is no discussion of the two scenes of threatened rape, either because they did not offend Vance or because he judged them good box office. In any case, he advised his exhibitor-readers that "no matter what the censors censor there will be plenty of film action and interest left to make it the biggest-demanded film production of the present century," a picture "worth seeing anywhere," and one that many will see "twice, yes thrice and still obtain much satisfaction and interest."

Passing on from these matters, Vance commented shrewdly on the cost differential between a film playing twice a day at a two-dollar top and a legitimate play, which could be performed only eight times a week at roughly the same price scale. He noted that the payroll for actors, backstage help and such might be as much as four or five thousand a week, while a motion picture like *Birth* had to pay only an orchestra and projectionists while grossing as much if not more because of its extra performances. This seemed like good economic news to him, worth passing on to his readers, some of whom, of course, were managing legitimate theaters and thus perhaps unlikely to share Vance's enthusiasm for this competitive development.

Be that as it may, this astonishing notice concluded on a note of untroubled enthusiasm. "A *Birth of a Nation* [*sic*] is a great epoch [*sic* again] in picturemaking; it's great for pictures and it's great for the name and fame of David Wark Griffith. When a man like Griffith in a new field can do what he has done, he may as well be hailed while he is living."[16] The other trade papers generally agreed with *Variety*'s viewpoint, though in somewhat more intelligent terms, paying more concerned and serious attention to the more dubious aspects of the production. These trade notices were, perhaps, the most significant reviews *Birth* obtained, reassuring exhibitors across the country that its success in its two premiere engagements was not likely to remain local, that the profitability of the New York and Los Angeles runs could be duplicated everywhere.

So *The Birth of a Nation* was safely launched. After the success of the New York opening one detects no anxiety in the attitude of its principals as they devoted themselves to fighting the censorious efforts of blacks and liberals. Quite the contrary, Griffith, Harry Aitken and, most notably, Thomas Dixon would, in the controversies to come, conduct themselves with a confidence bordering on arrogance, secure in the knowledge that, although they might be pressured into making a minor trim here, a small cut there, nothing could stop the mighty flood they had unleashed from running its remarkable course.

2

It has been estimated that, counting the eleven-month Liberty run, and subsequent subruns, *Birth* played to 825,000 people in the New York area alone.[17] How many ultimately saw the picture across the nation and around the world is literally incalculable, and no one is absolutely certain what the box office grosses, or even the producer's grosses, were. Indeed, the film is still making money in distribution to film societies and, perhaps, to less-savory organizations, more interested in its message than its art. The reason for this lack of reliable information is that, from the start, exhibitors and distributors handling the movie on a states' rights basis, skimmed profits from Epoch by underreporting grosses. Bosley Crowther estimates that Louis B. Mayer alone might have failed to report as much as $335,000 in gross revenue.[18]

The result of these defalcations, which have become something of a tradition in the motion picture industry (yet another precedent established by *Birth*), is a myth of untold wealth generated by the film. For years, for example, *Variety* carried, in its annual listing of the all-time box office champions (a ranking by producer's gross, not box office figures), a notation that *Birth* might have returned as much as $50 million to Epoch from U.S. and Canadian sales, but never placed it on the list proper because of defective financial reporting. In 1977, however, after an examination of Epoch records, it finally revised the figure downward to a much more realistic $5 million.

By the end of 1917, when to all intents and purposes *Birth* had "played off" in the United States, Epoch reported to shareholders cumulative receipts since the picture's opening of $4,839,748.41 (close to the recently revised *Variety* estimate) and a net profit of $1,860,082.59. In this period Griffith had collected, or was owed, $683,130.85 as his share of *Birth*'s profits, which were, of course, over and above fees he was collecting from other film enterprises in which he was involved in this period. Other Epoch stockholders were doing as well, proportionately, and all, it seems, were taking their shares off the top, that is, out of the producer's gross, not out of the net profits—though it must be said that the Aitkens were not always as prompt in forwarding payments as they were in forwarding statements.[19] Since Epoch's returns from states' rights distributors usually amounted to about 10 percent of the box office take, this would seem to indicate roughly a $50 million gross in the theaters, but it must be recalled that Epoch was handling its own road show engagements, and taking in more than 10 percent in those key cities, and remembered, too, that receipts were being underreported by theater men and distributors. This means *Birth* certainly generated more than $60 million in box-office business in its first run—and perhaps more.

In the long term, money of this magnitude would have its deleterious effects on Griffith and Harry Aitken, indeed on the entire motion picture business, turning the two men into high-stakes players, the industry into a high-stakes game, and in the case of *Birth*'s principals, bringing them sooner or later to disaster as they attempted to duplicate this first success. In the short term, however, the film generated all the money they needed to fight the many efforts to censor and ban it, and, naturally, a hard economic motive for so doing.

That fight was to grow very quickly in intensity as both sides began to sense that more was at stake here, financially and politically, than they originally imagined. In the week after the New York opening the

NAACP continued to press the National Board of Censorship to come out against the picture, addressing a letter to the motion picture trade press asserting that Epoch had presented the film despite the National Board's condemnation. Which statement of course exaggerated the truth, since the board (beholden, after all, to the movie industry) was still busy backing and filling on the most important matter to which it had so far been asked to attend.

In this period the most significant progress the NAACP made was finally to get a number of its more prominent members in to see the film. On March 10, Jane Addams, accompanied by Jacob Schiff, Lillian Wald, and Dr. Jacques Loeb, all prominent in philanthropic work in New York, attended one of the film's regularly scheduled performances. According to the NAACP, a group of prominent white southerners joined them and all agreed in condemning the picture. Two days after that a revised version of the movie, from which, reportedly, Griffith dropped a love scene between Senator Stoneman and his mulatto mistress and a scene in which a black and a white engaged in a fight, while adding a new prefatory title, was shown to the National Board. The new title, pure Griffith in style and substance, read:

A PLEA FOR THE ART OF THE MOTION PICTURE

We do not fear censorship, for we have no wish to offend with improprieties or obscenities, but we do demand, as a right, the liberty to show the dark side of wrong, that we may illuminate the bright side of virtue—the same liberty that is conceded to the art of the written word—that art to which we owe the Bible and the works of Shakespeare.

As we shall see, this insert contains the essence of Griffith's strategy in dealing with his critics, which was to insist on the sincerity of his art, to associate his cause with the cause of free speech and a free press. Viewers opposed to the film emerged from the screening unmollified either by the cuts or by Griffith's high-mindedness. But the Board had gone as far as it was willing to go. Three days later, the group officially approved the film. Unofficially, the NAACP heard that when Aitken appeared before the board to testify on the film's behalf he was actually cheered by its members.[20]

These skirmishes with the Board predicted what was to come as the NAACP and its allies sought to have *Birth* proscribed elsewhere. Universally, these efforts failed. In the courts of public opinion, on the other hand, the NAACP at least made its case effectively. It is doubtful if even a handful of citizens were dissuaded from seeing *Birth* by the adverse publicity the organization generated, but at least moviegoers were placed on guard against the poisons the movie carried in its system and were perhaps even inoculated against serious infection by them.

Among the most effective weapons the NAACP commanded in this war of words was an interview the greatly respected Jane Addams gave the New York *Post* soon after seeing *Birth*, and which the NAACP sent out to newspapers across the country.

Miss Addams bluntly termed the film a "pernicious caricature of the Negro race . . . unjust and untrue." Curiously, she did not seem to notice that the principal black roles were played by white actors, for one of her major charges was that Griffith "followed the principle of gathering the most vicious and grotesque individuals he could find among colored people and showing them as representative of the truth about the entire race," a practice, she said, that "could be followed to smirch the reputation of any race."

She was on firmer ground, however, in objecting to the producers' line that the film was solidly based on historical evidence. "You can use history to demonstrate anything when you take certain of its facts and emphasize them to the exclusion of others," she said, shrewdly noting that the film was, in at least one respect, as unfair to northern whites as it was to blacks, representing them, in the second half of the film, exclusively as carpetbaggers of a viciously exploitative nature. This was, she said, as unjust as claiming that all white southerners were set upon oppressing blacks or, to get on to her main point, showing blacks to be "worse than childish and brutal and vicious—actually grotesque and primitive and despicable."

In this long and detailed interview the social worker touched on all the important defects of the film—its implications about the rapaciousness of blacks, for example, and the absurd glorification of the Ku Klux Klan, its appeal to modern racial prejudice through a cruelly selective view of historical events.[21] Good polemicist that she was, she conceded that there had been excesses on all sides during Reconstruction days, that in depicting them the movie was not entirely incorrect historically. But that, she insisted, only made it the more dangerous; "the most subtle of untruths—a half truth."

It was a strong piece—its passion effectively tempered by the speaker's manifest desire to demonstrate fair-mindedness. And within a week the NAACP had another powerful—and yet more original—assault on the film to reprint and mail out to its branches and to the press around the country. This was a review in *The New Republic*, the liberal journal founded just weeks before *Birth* opened in New York. The piece was by Francis Hackett, latterly well-known as novelist and playwright. He repeated much of the criticism the other enemies of the film had directed at it, but at the heart of the piece, which does not even mention Griffith by name, is a brilliantly acerbic analysis of the character of Thomas Dixon.

Hackett began by saying that were Dixon possessed by the paternalistic view of the black man typical of southerners of his generation it would be futile to discuss those views, since even if reactionary, southerners of this stripe were usually "genial and humane and protective" in motive and statement. But, Hackett says, there is more to Dixon's case than that. At which point he springs an arresting metaphor. "Sometimes in the clinical laboratory the doctors are reputed to perform an operation on a dog so that he loses his power to restrain certain motor activities. If he is started running in a cage, the legend goes, he keeps on running incessantly, and nothing can stop him but to hit him on the head with a club. There is a quality about everything Mr. Dixon has done that reminds me of this abnormal dog."

Hackett imagined that at some "remote period of his existence" Dixon might have had some "rudimentary" power of self-analysis, but that, he said, was "stunted," and he was now "crystallized in his prejudices." "Since that time, whenever he has been stimulated by any of the ordinary emotions, by religion or by patriotism or by sex, he has responded with a frantic intensity. Energetic by nature, the forces that impel him are doubly violent because of this lack of inhibition. Aware as a clergyman that such violence is excessive, he has learned in all his melodramas to give them a highly moral twang. If one of his heroes is about to do something peculiarly loathsome, Mr. Dixon thrusts a crucifix in his hand and has him roll his eyes to heaven. In this way the very basest impulses are given the sanction of godliness, and Mr. Dixon preserves his own respect and the respect of such people as go by the label and not by the rot-gut they consume."

This was close to the last word on the character and attainments of the Reverend Thomas Dixon, but in closing his piece, Hackett fired one last brutal volley at him. "We know what a yellow journalist is. He is not yellow because he reports crimes of violence. He is yellow because he distorts them. In the region of history . . . Dixon corresponds to the yellow journalist . . . he is a yellow clergyman. He is yellow because he recklessly distorts Negro crimes, gives them a disproportionate place in life and colors them dishonestly to inflame the ignorant and credulous. And he is especially yellow, and quite disgustingly and contemptibly yellow, because his perversions are cunningly calculated to flatter the white man and provoke hatred and contempt for the Negro." *Birth*, he added, is "spiritual assassination. It degrades the censors that passed it and the white race that endures it."[22]

The Addams interview and the Hackett review are culminations in contemporary criticism of *Birth*. Nothing essential was added to the case against the film thereafter, although, of course, it continued to be reviewed as it opened across the country and continued to break away from the amusement pages and onto the front pages as the NAACP continued to try to stop its showings.

The last act of the New York drama came at the end of March, when newspapers reported that the National Board of Censorship had been far from unanimous in passing *Birth*. John Purroy Mitchell, the "boy mayor," as he was known, a reformer who would lose his life in World War I, then announced that he would hear a delegation from the NAACP and other interested groups in the matter of *The Birth of a Nation*, though the black organization's application for a license to form a protest procession to City Hall was denied on the ground that it might lead to a breach of the peace. On March 30, representatives of most of the leading social reform groups of the city gathered in the City Council's chambers, overflowing that hall, and heard a distinguished roster of speakers vividly denounce the film. Among those protesting were Dr. W. E. B. Du Bois, perhaps the most militant black voice in the nation at that time, and the editor of the NAACP journal, *The Crisis*; Rabbi Stephen Wise, the nation's leading reform Rabbi; Howe, representing the National Board of Censorship's minority, and Oswald Garrison Villard, the New York *Post* editor, as well as clergy from other denominations and a roster of civic club chairmen and presidents.

Passions ran high. Howe, for example, declared that ten million citizens (that is the nation's entire black population) were "degraded" by the production and its portrayal of Negroes as "lustful" and "depraved." Lillian Wald seemed to imply a threat of revolution when she said, "It is impossible to measure the potential dangers that threaten us if the production is allowed to go on," though Fred R. Moore, editor of the New York *Age*, a black newspaper, went out of his way to observe: "We have never been beggars. We have never asked charity. All we have asked is a fair chance. We don't stoop to anarchy." His point, as he would soon make clear, was that historically the American black population, contrary to the view presented in the film, had been a model of social responsibility in advancing its own cause, had never advocated or employed violence to achieve its ends, though perhaps it might have had greater justification than other oppressed groups for resorting to such tactics. "We never had a man among us who fired on the President of the United States. We never had a man among us who attempted to assassinate the mayor of his city," Moore concluded. Fiery Stephen Wise, at the time certainly the Jewish community's most prominent and respected ambassador to the *goyim*, was equally outspoken. "If it is true that the Mayor has no power to stop this inexcusably foul and loathsome libel on a race of human beings, then it is true that government has broken down." Calling the National Board of Censorship, of which he was a member, "stupid or worse" and the film's producers "contemptible cowards," Wise remarked that "the Negroes in this city have been patient. They have not yet arisen, like the Irish who attacked *The Playboy of the Western World* when they recognized it as caricature not as a characterization."[23]

Mayor Mitchell listened politely to all this and reported that, having seen the film, he agreed with all that had been said about it this day and had already warned the Liberty theater management and the producers that it might incite breaches of the peace, asking them to cut out the two scenes that he felt were particularly likely to lead to disturbances (these were the attempted rape scene and the scene in which the attempt to force Lillian Gish into marriage with a mulatto is shown). The Mayor told the protestors that the film would be shown with these new, and apparently deeper, cuts that very evening, and added that he had achieved them through force of persuasion, not force of law. He did not know, he frankly said, how powerful his statutory powers of censorship might be, but he promised that he would resort to them if this matter came before him again.

It is said that the relative mildness of the Mayor's stand against the film was conditioned by the influence brought to bear by the circle around Booker T. Washington, accommodationists whose long-standing and powerful influence on the white community was one of the things the more militant NAACP had been founded to counteract.[24] Even the fact that Dixon had been attacking Washington for many years (he was convinced that the endlessly compromising educator was, in his secret heart, yet another miscegenationist) could not bring him to militancy regarding the film—not immediately, anyway. Still, one can scarcely blame the mayor for listening to representatives of the nation's most prominent and respectable Negro. He was, after all, a politician, and a politician treading strange new waters, at that, meaning he was eager to find a compromise that would satisfy to some degree the conflicting points of view that had so suddenly and noisily surfaced here.

Two days after the NAACP and its friends had retired from city hall, more or less happy with the concerned reception they had received there, Griffith and his cohorts turned up to press their case. They came armed with a remarkable statement from the Reverend Dr. Charles H. Parkhurst, a leading Presbyterian clergyman of the city, which was backed by other ministers and Christian laymen, and which made the assertion that the film showed the Negro "not as he now is at all, but as he was in the days when he had just had the chains broken from him and he was rioting in the deliciousness of a liberty so new and untried that he had not yet learned to understand it and was as ignorant as a baby of the way to use it." This representation of the way things were in Reconstruction days was, Parkhurst said, "exactly true to history," and it was his bland opinion that "if it reflects upon the negro as he was then it is a complement to the black man of today."[25] In the quarrel of the clergymen, it must be said that those opposing *Birth* certainly made the better arguments.

But endorsement by the producer's recruited ministers was not the main issue before the house that April 1. For the opponents of the film had, by now, seen the revised version of the film and found the cuts made by Griffith to be nowhere nearly as deep as Mayor Mitchell had apparently been led to think they were when he addressed the NAACP protestors just two days earlier. Still, Griffith, through his attorney, Martin W. Littleton, argued strongly for making no further excisions. Littleton claimed that enough had already been done to the film, and that in any case, the Mayor and his license commission (whom he had charged with the task of negotiating with Griffith and his backers) were responding not to objections from a broad base of the citizenry, but to "propaganda" from a group he identified as "The Association for the Intermarriage of the Races," a misnomer (sometimes slightly varied) that Dixon liked to use in identifying the NAACP in his various screeds in defense of the film. The reference was to the NAACP's protest—very frequently effective, as it was, for example, in the New York, Wisconsin and Ohio legislatures—against laws designed to make marriages between races illegal. Indeed, Littleton, who bluntly called the film a "protest against the mongrel mixture of a black and white," quoted from an NAACP statement in which it said that passage of such laws "would be publicly to acknowledge that black blood is a physical taint, something that no self-respecting colored man or woman can be asked to admit." Of course, by working against these laws the NAACP was bound to earn the enmity of Dixon, for, as we have seen, it was precisely on the question of sexual relations between the races that he most resembled the laboratory dog of Francis Hackett's image. It was, quite simply, a subject that drove him crazy. Indeed, at this very hearing Dixon offered Oswald Garrison Villard $5,000 if he could point out a single historical inaccuracy in the film—a reckless offer considering its melodramatic nature. But miscegenation was, in those days (and for many days and years to follow), a subject that greatly vexed many white Americans, and judicious John Purroy Mitchell was not about to stir that hornet's nest. In responding to Littleton he would say that if the film were, "as you suggest, merely an argument against the marriage of blacks and whites, it might be a different question, but there are two scenes that appeal to race prejudice, and I feel that they ought to be modified." He would add, referring the question of further cuts back to his licensing commission, that "the Negro citizens have certain rights that must be observed."[26]

All this maneuvering delayed the resolution of the court action the NAACP had brought against the film, the organization asking adjournments apparently in the hope that a display of reasonableness might help in the effort to have the most offensive scenes cut—the best, obviously, it could now hope for in New York, perhaps everywhere—although there were a number of strong state censorship bills pending (including one in the New York legislature). These gave rise to the hope that, given the controversy over *Birth*, clauses might be written into them prohibiting exhibition of films that stirred racial animosity as had been done well before *Birth*'s appearance in one or two localities. So despite promises to continue pressing the case in court, the NAACP did not do so, and although there were indeed more meetings with the licensing commission, there is no record of any more-substantial cuts being made in *Birth* during its New York run.

The fight against the film was shifting to new venues, and that required a shifting of energies by what was still a small and overextended organization. The blacks had vividly established their case against the film in the nation's cultural and media capital, and they had also established their right to take before officialdom, and gain some sort of response from it, cases of libel against their race—something that had not happened before in this country. If they did not win a famous victory, they did make a famous beginning in a struggle for freedom from calumny that would occupy them (with increasing success) for the rest of the century. They could be forgiven now for allowing their fight for still more cuts in the film simply to peter out; the minuscule gains they might achieve would not be worth the further effort, and would compare quite unfavorably to what they had already accomplished.

As if to prove this point, an editorial quite remarkable in the context of the discussion so far appeared on April 6 in the influential *New York Globe* under the heading "Capitalizing Race Hatred." It was an attack on *Birth*, repeating many of the arguments we have already rehearsed, but containing this ringing paragraph:

"White men in this country have never been just to black men. We tore them from Africa and brought them over as slaves. For generations they toiled without recompense that their white owners might have unearned wealth and ape the ways of aristocracy. The nation finally freed them, but has but slightly protected them in the enjoyment of the legitimate fruits of their freedom. We nominally gave them the vote, but looked on inactive when the right was invaded. We did not, in any state of the Union, grant to the Negro economic and political economy. No white man of proper feeling can be proud of the record. The wonder is that the Negro is as good as he is. Then to the injury is added slander. To make a few dirty dollars men are willing to pander to depraved tastes and to foment a race antipathy that is the most sinister and dangerous feature of American life."[27] There it was at last, and not from a black publication or a general publication that had closely identified itself with the black cause, but rather from a middle-class, middle-of-the-road journal. At last all the essentially niggling arguments about whether or not the film was faithful to historical fact were swept aside and there was issued, if the phrase may be permitted, a clarion call to guilt, which by this time we might have had enough of, but which at the time there was by no means enough of. This, the paper said, was too much, this piling of slander atop centuries of inequity. By so saying, it got to the central issue raised by *Birth*, the issue, as it were, that dared not speak its name. For after one has duly considered the enormous advance in motion picture art which it represented, after one has paused over the fact that it contained some historical truth—if rarely in sequences directly involving blacks—after one has made allowance for the primitive condition of the white American consciousness on the racial issue and for the fact that the First Amendment bids us permit even views as reprehensible as Thomas Dixon's to be publicly aired, after all this has been taken into account, the fact still remains that Dixon, with Griffith's naïvely prejudiced cooperation, a cooperation that vivified his message in a way that only this first artist of a new medium could, had used a most dubious historicism to malign a minority that had already been asked to accept far more than its share not merely of economic and political abuse, but of existential pain as well.

The editorial is, however, gratifying only to the student of this time looking for an expression of something like a modern understanding of the issues raised by this film. It had no discernible effect on the course of the film's exhibition, caused no sudden surge of censorious passion at the Mayor's office or the licensing commission or any renewal of passion for the New York fight at the NAACP. It did, of course, stir a response from Dixon, but his letter, published by the *Globe* on April 10, only briefly addressed itself to the issue of racial slander. Dixon simply denied so doing, while devoting most of his space to insisting that Thaddeus Stevens, the model for Stoneman, did indeed have a mulatto mistress, whose evil influence was responsible, in the writer's curious view, for the Senator's abolitionism and his implacable desire to punish the South in the postwar era, or "reign of terror," as Dixon preferred to call it. There were also pious invocations of Lincoln's "mighty spirit." In all, it was, for Dixon, rather a dispirited performance. Not so Griffith, whose letter to the editor appeared the same day and belatedly expressed his views about the racial conflict now enveloping his film. His name has been largely absent from this chronicle of public dispute, in part because he was heavily preoccupied by the details of the premiere engagement, in part because he seems genuinely to have been shocked by the outrage his film stirred, in part because he was enjoying himself on the esthetic high road. His line, in talking to the New York press, even before the controversy over the film began in earnest, was that of the idealistic artist who was concerned to establish the credentials of the motion picture as a medium for the sober expression of serious visions. In particular he was concerned to establish its validity in relationship to the theater and literature whose adherents were, as they would for many years remain, contemptuous of the cinema.

For example, the Sunday after *Birth* opened he was to be found asserting that "those of us who are working toward the ideal motion picture have standards of which we are not ashamed." He quite favorably compared his ride of the clansmen to the race in Browning's poem about bringing the good news from Gent to Aix. Repeating the basic theme of his film's new prefatory title, he went on: "We show the horrors of war and . . . the hates and fears of the 'times that try men's souls,' but over against these we set the glory of self-sacrifice, the stern code of honor, the loyalty of friendship, the millennium of the brotherhood of love rising from afar before the dream vision of racked and tortured humanity. Does the old-school stage do more? To speak plainly, does it achieve as much?"

Needless to say, he answered his own questions in the most self-serving terms. "For one, I firmly believe that the screen drama is hampered by far fewer limitations and by reason of range and method of treatment its emotional, fictive and historical values are superior. As I said before, we exhibit both the thought and the action, while we can boast the whole world as our stage."[28]

Less than a week later an interviewer from another paper asked Griffith what makes a man great, and received a modest enough initial response: "I dunno, how should I know?" Under encouragement, however, he added: "Beauty's the answer. Beauty is my fetish. I don't care what anyone says to the contrary. Beauty is what every human being is searching for. . . . Beauty is the one road to righteousness. . . . War is hideous, but it can be made the background for beauty, beauty of idea."[29] Again, one is conscious of his blindness. It appears he felt his last-reel call for peace and brotherhood "rising from afar," that self-consciously gorgeous vision he tacked on the end of *Birth*, was the work's central symbol, compensation for all that had gone before.

A week later in the *Christian Science Monitor*, the talk was almost entirely of cinema and the large potential Griffith saw in it, perhaps more clearly than any other man of his moment. "Cinematography," he began, "has become an integral part of our social life. We are just beginning to discover its possibilities, and the time will come when the importance of the motion picture will not be expressed in terms of amusement but in units of constructive educational welfare accomplished by its means."

He went on to muse about the problems of expressing the kind of ideas more conveniently put in a novel or play than in a silent film, saying that creation for the movies was "a sort of hybrid thought process that is founded on the spoken drama and warped into the unknown mazes of picture drama," with a result "often chaotic and unsatisfactory." He then discussed, very likely for the first time, the conflict one has since come to sense as inevitable, probably inherent, in the process of making a movie, namely the one between writer and director: "I may take another man's basic idea, but I must be permitted to develop it according to my own conceptions. This is my art . . . whatever poetry is in me must be worked out in actual practice; I must write it to my own standards."

There should, of course, have been quotation marks around the word "write," for what Griffith was saying in this first crude formulation of what would become the *auteur* theory, is that the director "writes" on the set, with a camera; that what he does there constitutes true authorship in the cinema. Griffith tried to explain himself still further by saying that "words, after all, are a clumsy method of conveying thought. They clog expression in so many ways. . . ." Somewhat overstating his case, he insisted that we do not think in words and that the form in which ideas mostly come to us is in pictures. Therefore, movies are a more direct form of expressing our basic concepts and emotions than are the more literary forms.

Griffith was groping for words in this interview, principally because he was also grasping at new concepts, concepts which, indeed, would be fully articulated only by critics, scholars and theoreticians of the media in our time, but it should also be clear that, instinctively, he was on to something about the singular nature and power of the movies, that people more oriented toward the written word were slow to see.

The interview also offers a hint of how Griffith's mind worked creatively and also a suggestion, perhaps, of why he for so long remained blind to moral criticism of his film. Griffith comes close to admitting he did not care what Dixon's subtext was. He would, as he said, "take another man's basic idea" and "develop it according to my own conceptions." And his conceptions, as the interviews make clear, had little enough to do with racist propaganda, everything to do with the statement of lofty general ideas on the one hand, the wordless but concrete characterological revelations which the new medium afforded him the opportunity to place before an audience on the other. Since he operated with great purity of purpose in these areas, his continued, indeed lifelong, failure to acknowledge the film's moral flaws, or the justice of the criticism leveled at it, become explicable.[30]

But even Griffith could be stung. And the *Globe* editorial did so. It was the paper's charge that the film had been made "for sordid reasons" (i.e., commercial gain), that Griffith had pandered to "depraved tastes" merely to make "a few dirty dollars" which caused Griffith at last openly to confront the charges of racism. Yet even here he stoutly insisted that his film was "brought forth to reveal the beautiful possibilities of the art of motion pictures" in telling a story he also insisted was "based upon truth in every vital detail." Outraged, he demanded the authority on which the charge of "sordid" motives was based, and a retraction if such authority could not be cited. Quite unlike Dixon, he refused to get into a quarrel over the history of Reconstruction, noting merely that he disagreed with the paper's interpretation of that epoch before reverting to his main theme by coming to the defense of "nearly 100,000 of the best people in New York City, who have viewed this picture from artistic interests and not through any depraved tastes. . . . Appreciative clergymen and critics" (including the *Globe*'s own man) were gratefully mentioned, before Griffith finally passed over, almost at the end of his letter, to a charge that "the attack of the organized opponents to this picture is centered upon that feature of it which they deem might become an influence against the intermarriage of blacks and whites." On this point, Griffith was imputing motives to the NAACP, for the record shows that it never specifically raised this issue, and for that matter never had to, since Dixon was the one who had insisted on riding that beast out of the dark side of his mind.

But that was still not the main issue to this artist who could never be entirely secure in his identity as artist, given his many early failures as one, and his present work in a field where artistry was only grudgingly conceded to people like him. Quoting again from the passage that charged him and his coworkers with pandering to depraved tastes, he wrote thus in his peroration:

"That statement is obviously a generality, but I wish to say that if the man who wrote it meant one iota of the sentence just quoted to apply to our picture he is a liar and a coward.

"Whether this was the intent . . . it could not fail to create an impression in the minds of your readers, damaging my reputation as a producer. Therefore, as a matter of justice, I ask that you publish my statement of the facts."[31]

One can somewhat sympathize with Griffith at this point. He simply could not fully comprehend the storm he had loosed. Knowing his motives had been of the best, knowing that he had created the largest and most powerful work in the history of film—a fact even the film's bitterest opponents conceded—how could he answer the charge of venality—especially when the movie was so visibly cleaning up at the box office, a fact that, superficially, seemed to prove the anonymous editorialist's point?

Of course, he could not. He could only maintain his dignity, his civility—and pursue the defense of his film wherever it was threatened, which was virtually everywhere it opened outside the old Confederacy. For the moment, however, it was safe enough in New York, although on April 14, the anniversary of Lincoln's assassination, a white man named Howard Schaffle threw two eggs in the general direction of the screen (they actually landed in the orchestra pit) at the evening performance. When the police arrested him, they found three more of the missiles in his pockets. As he was hustled out of the theater a black man, Cleveland

J. Allen, who was identified as the head of a Negro news agency, told the audience that it was "inappropriate" to show this film on this date. "I think President Lincoln wouldn't have liked this play," he said mildly. At the police station to which he was accompanied by the blacks from the audience, Schaffle declared he had done what he had done because he couldn't sit quietly by and see Negroes maligned as they were in the film, though, of course, the large supply of weapons found on his person indicated that his response to the movie was not exactly spontaneous.[32]

3

In almost every major northern center the film's proprietors and exhibitors were forced to endure what became an almost ritual process of protest and quasi-judicial proceedings, generally resulting in small cuts and large publicity. Only in two locales, Boston and Philadelphia, were those rites radically varied. In Boston the leader of the protest against *Birth* was an extraordinary, half-forgotten figure in the history of black militancy, William Monroe Trotter, the Harvard-educated editor-publisher of a strong-minded black paper, *The Guardian*. Trotter had begun his career in advocacy as the ally of W. E. B. Du Bois in the fight against what they called "The Tuskegee gang," those compromisers whose allegiance was to the ever-ameliorative Booker T. Washington. By 1915, Trotter was even more uncompromising than Du Bois, so much so that succeeding years would see him lose most of his influence within the newer circles of black leadership.

But not yet. Though he continually sniped at the NAACP in the pages of his paper, though he had, in two recent meetings with President Wilson, so irritated the man whom he had once endorsed that Wilson had snapped at him, "Your manner offends me," Trotter was still a force to be reckoned with—particularly on his home ground in Boston.

As it happened he was out of town, lecturing on the Wilson incident (his cheekiness had made him something of a hero to some blacks), when hearings aimed at banning the film were demanded by the local NAACP chapter. Trotter hurried back to Boston for the April 10 proceedings before the legendary James Michael Curley, the "last hurrah" mayor, who had been careful to include blacks in the coalition of the underprivileged and immigrant on which his long reign in city hall, now in its early stages, was based. There was the usual exchange of statements from the clergy and other leaders of social thought, but the session grew quite heated with the NAACP spokesmen and their supporters in the audience not appearing to their best advantage. In Thomas Cripps's account the former are described as "shaky" and "buried in their notes." Indeed, the

NAACP's national president, Moorfield Storey, was trapped into admitting that he had not actually seen the film. The floor strength was "prone to interrupt the proceeding," thus considerably trying His Honor's patience. By contrast, Griffith took a high and attractive position, arguing merely that he had a Constitutional right to present his views of a historical period—especially when, as he insisted, he had so carefully footnoted in the film the bases for his argument. Griffith was, in fact, bold enough to offer $10,000 to Storey if he could point to any incident in the film that was untrue. There is, alas, no record of Griffith's response to Storey's question as to just when a mulatto lieutenant-governor of any southern state had tied up, gagged and locked in a room a young white woman in an attempt to force her marriage to him. (After the meeting, Griffith, always the gentleman, and perhaps still unaware of just how deep the passions *Birth* had aroused, approached Storey, told him he was pleased to meet him and proffered his hand, which the black leader refused with a curt, "No sir.") Trotter listened to all this and when his turn came to testify reminded Curley that Negroes had supported him in the past, but that their future support would depend on his handling of this case. Thus, at least, he got the matter down to the political nitty-gritty. Curley, however, found it convenient to take a line not unlike that of his mayoral colleague in New York. He was powerless, legally, to do anything about banning the picture, but he would use his influence to see if cuts might not be made in the more offensive passages. And so, inconclusively, the meeting broke up.[33]

Some cuts were made under pressure from Curley, but they did not satisfy Trotter, or for that matter less radical protestors. On Saturday, April 17, precisely a week after the movie's local premiere, and after the blacks had acquired the support of the liberal *Boston Post*, whose reporters found that Curley's predecessors had actually banned Dixon's *Clansman* play in Boston on the ground that it might incite a breach of the peace, Trotter and his supporters took their fight against the movie into the streets—more precisely, the streets around the Tremont Theater, where it was playing. Some 200 blacks marched on the theater, demanding admission to the theater *en masse*. Rumors had circulated earlier that the blacks intended to storm the theater and seize and destroy its print of *Birth*, so the dozen or so plainclothes Pinkertons the management had placed on duty at the start of the run were reinforced by uniformed Boston police who were visible in the lobby as well as in the streets outside.

Trotter and a detachment of his irregulars entered the lobby intending to buy tickets, but the box office windows were shut in their faces. "Sold out," the management declared. Not so, said Trotter, pointing to a white man who had just bought three tickets. Again he demanded admittance, and again he was refused, the management now ordering Trotter and his band to leave the lobby. He shouted a charge of discrimination and the police moved in. They had billy clubs and in the melee a white plainsclothesman struck Trotter. The lobby was cleared, and in addition to Trotter, ten other blacks were arrested and taken to a nearby police station. Some blacks and their sympathizers had, however, gained entrance to the performance, which was interrupted by jeers, by egg throwing—more accurate than that a few days earlier in New York, since one struck the screen squarely during the rape sequence—and by stink bombs. After the performance fights between blacks and whites broke out in the streets, leading to more arrests. Trotter's biographer, Stephen R. Fox, judged the evening to be the most ominous racial incident in Boston's history since the Civil War, and Trotter, bailed out, told reporters as he left the police station, "It is a rebel play . . . an incentive to great racial hatred here in Boston. It will make white women afraid of Negroes and will have white men all stirred up on their account. If there is any lynching here in Boston, Mayor Curley will be responsible."[34]

Using a technique that would become excruciatingly familiar a half century later, Trotter had created a confrontation that implied the possibility of more, and more serious, confrontations to come, and he now used it as his successors would, to put further pressure on the politicians. The next day there was a mass meeting in Faneuil Hall, under the auspices of the Wendell Phillips Memorial Association, named after the abolitionist leader of old. White spokesmen were well received by the overflow crowd, but its loudest enthusiasm was for Trotter, the action-oriented agitator, whose aim was never to debate the abstract issues raised by *Birth*, to decry the injustice of it all, but was simply to get the thing shut down as quickly as possible.

Again, he verbally assaulted the Mayor, with implied threats of punishment by his former black friends at the polls. "Where," he inquired, "is the valiant Jim Curley of old—the friend of the people—lovable Jim Curley, whom we colored people supported for the mayoralty against the advice of some of our white friends?" He still insisted that if Curley had the will, there were ways to stop this movie. "Mayor Curley has stopped other plays. If this was an attack on the Irish race he would find a way pretty quick to stop it." For Trotter, this meeting was but a prelude to a much larger action scheduled for the next day, a march by a mass of predominantly black citizens on the Massachusetts state house, for a confrontation with Governor David Walsh.

Up Beacon Street they came, the next morning, two thousand strong, singing "Nearer My God to Thee," to gather, grim but orderly, before the capitol building, overflowing its steps and spreading backward into the street and the Common beyond. They were Trotter's people, responsive only to his orders, and he was inside with 60 of his closest supporters, awaiting an audience with Governor Walsh. Some of the moderate leaders had got to him first, and by the time Trotter and his group gained access to Walsh, a compromise had been worked out. The attorney general of the Commonwealth would prosecute the Tremont management under a 1910 blue law that prohibited any performance judged to be "lewd, obscene, indecent, immoral or impure" or even suggestive of any of those qualities. In a way, prosecution of the film on those grounds would have been more hurtful to Griffith, more degrading to his cherished belief in himself as idealist and artist, than anything else, and when Trotter announced this decision, which was backed by a gubernatorial pledge to seek a new state censorship law aimed at the film, the crowd broke up in orderly fashion and there were no more demonstrations at the theater until after the judicial proceedings were finished.

Alas for Trotter, the judge found nothing "lewd" in the film save Gus's threatened rape of Mae Marsh, which was odd, since the much more erotic forced marriage sequence was left intact. This was less than satisfactory to Trotter and his faction, and they pressed now for passage of the so-called Sullivan Law, which aimed at establishing a censorship board in Boston consisting of the mayor, the police commissioner and the chief justice of the municipal court, who would have powers so broad as to be undefined to revoke a theater's license for any reason "satisfactory to them." Griffith and Dixon returned to the city to testify against the law, the former very sensibly observing that any group dissatisfied by its portrayal in a film or play could use the law to get the offending drama banned. He imagined that even the Oberammergau Passion Play might be judged wanting under it, and he was probably right, given its anti-Semitic overtones. The *Boston Evening Transcript* observed that under the law all that would be required to shut down a theater would be for the opponents of its offering to stage a fake fistfight in the lobby, lending credence to the notion that the work threatened public safety.

Nonetheless, Trotter and other black organizations (including the NAACP) kept pressure on the legislature and by May 21 Walsh signed the Sullivan measure into law. Trotter immediately demanded the new board take action against *Birth* and on June 2, after a hearing and a week's deliberation, it did so. Despite a petition bearing 6,000 signatures demanding an end to the run, Curley and his cohorts refused to stop the film. Their reasoning is lost to history. The picture would play Boston until late October, for a six-and-a-half month, 360-performance run, despite a few more Trotter-engineered protests, one of which, in June, resulted in a few more arrests in front of the theater, where by this time the producers had added a bland short subject, showing the good works of the Hampton Institute, a Negro college, in an attempt to disarm critics.[35]

The Boston struggle against *Birth* was the high-water mark of the nationwide campaign against the film, and it has been judged by Thomas Cripps, the sensitive historian of the black cinema, to be a high-water mark in the early history of organized protest against racism as well. In the immediate future, that drama would be duplicated in only one other place, Philadelphia, on September 20, 1915, when some 500 blacks assembled outside the Forest Theater in Broad Street, where *Birth* was playing, to make, as one of the handbills summoning them put it, "a dignified protest against the photoplay known as 'The Birth of a Nation.'" The occasion's dignity was shattered when a brick shattered the glass door of the theater. A hundred policemen had been assigned to keep the crowd peaceable and in the immemorial manner of their trade charged into the protesting mass the minute they heard the glass breaking, their revolvers drawn, their billy clubs raised on high. They were joined by private security agents, armed with clubs and sticks, who charged out from the theater, where the management had quietly sequestered them. According to press reports the confrontation was over in a matter of two minutes, and there was no mention either of injuries or arrests, suggesting that the blacks had not intended to provoke violence and withdrew in haste when it was foisted upon them.[36] There was no repetition of the incident here or anywhere else in the United States.

What there was, instead, were endless hearings before mayors, state and city censorship boards, city councils, whatever official or body of officials were charged with keeping the screen free of disturbing material in places as large as Pittsburgh, Chicago, St. Louis, as modest in size as Atlantic City, Tacoma, Galveston, Lancaster, Pennsylvania—everywhere, in short, where the NAACP had an active local secretary. As a rule they recruited clergymen as the spokesmen for the blacks, and employed the line of argument taken over from them followed in New York and Boston. As a rule the local press, although sympathetic to the charges of race libel, tended also to deplore attempts to get the film banned or to use its showings as an occasion to pass stringent censorship laws. And for the most part the proposed laws were beaten back—if only because prohibitions on "lewd" presentations were already on the books in most places and required little toughening.

This is not to suggest that *Birth* did not face some very sobering challenges in its progress across the country. For example, its showing in the state of Ohio was long-delayed by a prohibition laid on it by a powerful board of censorship there. In Chicago, another legendary machine politician, Mayor William ("Big Bill") Thompson delayed its showing until the Illinois legislature passed by a huge margin (111–2) a bill generally prohibiting racially inflammatory material on stage and screen, but aimed quite specifically at Griffith's film. It took time and money to pursue appeals of these matters through the courts, though eventually the movie prevailed, if often in truncated form, just about everywhere.

Meanwhile, distinguished Americans from many professions were rallying against the film, attempting to counteract the generally favorable early reviews, and the unquenchable popular curiosity about the film.

Charles Eliot, president emeritus of Harvard and popularly famous for his "Five Foot Shelf" of classics, had been enlisted in the cause during the Boston fight and as the spring wore on all sorts of prominent people, ranging from Upton Sinclair, the radical novelist, to Albert Bushnell Hart, the well-known historian, to George Foster Peabody, the Georgia-born philanthropist, were heard to decry the film. Even Booker T. Washington finally came out unequivocally against it. In a widely quoted letter, originally addressed to the editor of the Chicago *Defender*, a Negro newspaper, he urged "our people everywhere to take time by the forelock and adopt in advance such measures as will prevent the production of the photoplay 'The Birth of a Nation' in any community North or South," adding: "No matter how many other artistic and historic features the play may have, its ultimate result will be to intensify race prejudice and thereby do great, lasting harm to both races."[37] Washington had, by this time, rejected feelers from the Aitkens about appearing in a short tribute to his Tuskegee Institute which they thought of doing as an earnest of their kindly interest in black progress. He began to talk about reviving an old scheme of his to produce such a film on his own, and just before his death later in 1915 he was thinking that his famous autobiography might make a good movie and serve to counter *Birth*.

As the furor over the film mounted, Joseph P. Tumulty, Wilson's confidant and chief public relations adviser, urged him to deny his widely circulated endorsement of the film. "I would like to do this," the President is quoted as saying, "if there were some way in which I could do it without seeming to be trying to meet the agitation . . . stirred up by that unspeakable fellow Tucker." (He meant Trotter.)[38]

This was a wish Tumulty was capable of fulfilling. In late April when W. H. Lewis, one of the first Negroes ever to attain subcabinet rank in the federal government (he was an assistant attorney general), and a Bishop Walters of the African Methodist Episcopalian church called on him to obtain a clarification of the President's views, the press reported that Tumulty repudiated Wilson's endorsement of *Birth*. Two weeks later Tumulty put the matter even more bluntly to Congressman Thomas C. Thatcher of Massachusetts:

> My Dear Mr. Thatcher—Replying to your recent letter and enclosures, I beg to say that it is true that 'The Birth of a Nation' was produced before the President and his family at the White House, but the President was entirely unaware of the character of the play before it was presented, and has at no time expressed his approbation of it. Its exhibition at the White House was a courtesy extended to an old acquaintance.
>
> Sincerely yours,
> J. P. Tumulty[39]

So the story of *Birth*'s first months of exhibition ends in effect, where it began, at the White House, but it ends in embarrassed murmurs, not in triumph. And it ends not with the result Thomas Dixon expected—with northern sentiments "revolutionized" and every man in the audience "transformed" into a "good Democrat." On the contrary, not a few sensible people had, in a matter of months, come around to at least a tacit agreement with William Monroe Trotter's estimation of Dixon as "Slippery Tom," "the ranting, wandering divine," the "unasylumed maniac."[40] More important, since he was one of those fervent souls who are able to brush off personal attacks so long as he seems to be getting his point across, it must be categorically stated that Dixon didn't get his point across. Doubtless *Birth* fitted comfortably with the unacknowledged, virtually unconscious racism of its white audiences, and was in no way morally disquieting to the majority of its viewers. But there appears to have been no visible upsurge of *conscious* racism in the film's wake, not even any intensification of legal efforts to solve the "problem" that so exorcised Dixon, that of intermarriage. Quite the opposite. It presented an opportunity to the minority that long deplored the racist habit of mind to place before thinking people a virulent example of that mind publicly at work, thus exposing its working to a criticism that had long been wanting.

Then, too, it brought to wide public attention the fact that there was a new, nonaccommodationist black organization in the field, an organization with the potential strength, and the manifest courage, to take on the Dixons of this world. Moreover, it gave that organization, the NAACP, a rallying point, an issue on which this first truly national Negro organization could prove the need for its existence to its own people. The mere fact that a film of this kind could so easily enter the mainstream of the popular culture, and prove to be so wildly popular, vividly indicated the need for a new and more militantly vigilant stance against the conscious racism of people like Dixon, the semiconscious racism of people like Griffith, the unconscious racism of audiences responding viscerally (and quite amorally) to the melodramatic thrills of the film.

Thus it may be a mistake to measure, as Cripps does, the effectiveness of the NAACP's fight against the film purely in terms of wins and losses on the legal front. It may also be true that, in time, there came to be an obsessional quality in its concern for the picture—its latter-day protesting and picketing of screenings of it before, for example, film study groups whose interest in the film was quite legitimately historical and esthetic. As Cripps says, some of the energy expended on these activities might better have been spent in developing a more positive approach to the image of blacks being presented in newer films—perhaps by more actively encouraging well-financed and well-made movies by and for blacks. Yet this much is certain, *The Birth of a Nation* presented the NAACP with an issue just when it needed one, an occasion to get its name in the papers on a subject that commanded mass interest far more readily than, let us say, voting rights in the Deep South. As such, the movie was something close to a godsend for the new organization. As such, it actually did Dixon's benighted cause incalculable harm.

Thanks to his dignified and high-minded conduct in this controversy, no great harm was done to Griffith's reputation. On the contrary, it helped make him a truly national figure, a name known at last outside the confines of the movie business. And the financial success of the film gave him the ability to command, for the next decade, his own fate—to make the pictures he wanted to make, in any manner he chose to employ, at whatever cost. It is no exaggeration to say that movie directors have ever since wished to regain freedom of that kind and that few have actually enjoyed it in such great measure for so long a period of time.

For the moment, however, Griffith was enjoying another sort of freedom, the freedom to act, not just as a spokesman for his film, but as a spokesman for the industry of which there could no longer be any doubt that he was the acknowledged artistic leader. He honorably defended that which he saw to be the honorable in *Birth* (as we have seen), but for the most part he remained uninvolved in the kind of controversies that embroiled Dixon. He preferred the stance of the statesman—and the visionary.

For example, he wrote—or caused to have written for his signature—a piece entitled "The Motion Picture and Witch Burners" which appeared as a guest column in a quaintly named syndicated feature "Flickerings From Filmland by Kitty Kelly." In it, he adverted to the controversy around *Birth* but preferred to press on to a general defense of the new art, which he couched in genteel but somehow affecting terms:

"It [the motion picture] is softening the hard life of the plain citizen with beauty and sweetness; it keeps men away from saloons and drink, because it gives them a place of recreation in pleasant surrounding; it brings to the poor who are unable to travel away from their own dingy surroundings the beauty and poetry of moving foreign scenes, of flowers, waving grasses, the beauty of uplifted mountain crests, and the wonders of nature.

"The motion picture will help as no other art has done in this work, if it is given a chance. We understand that all new things must go through an inquisitorial gate. Why not make the passage of the moving picture less brutal than has been that of all the other arts?"[41]

Why not, indeed? But Griffith had other visions, too, in which he foresaw interesting new psychological and technological possibilities in the movies. For example, in another newspaper piece he predicted that the next generation "will be wedded to the movies. You will not be able to satisfy them with anything else." Which was as accurate a prediction as he ever made. Moreover, he saw—as no one else did—that the moving

image would profoundly affect formal education. With film, he said—
rather too grandly—children could be taught everything they needed to
know except the three Rs, "the arts and possibly the mental sciences"
through what we now call "audio-visual" methods. He asked his readers
to "imagine a public library of the near future, for instance. There will be
a long row of boxes or pillars, properly classified and indexed, of course.
At each box a push button, and before each box a seat. Suppose you wish
to 'read up' on a certain episode in Napoleon's life. Instead of consulting
all the authorities, wading through a host of books, and ending bewildered . . . confused at every point by conflicting opinions about what did
happen, you will merely seat yourself at a properly adjusted window . . .
press the button and actually see what happened."[42]

Griffith imagined boards of experts assuring the "objectivity" of these
filmed reports—clinging still to the naïve view he took of historical research and writing which had brought him to grief in Birth but which of
course was fashionable even in academic circles in these days. And, of
course, he vastly underestimated the cost of producing this sort of thing.
But bearing in mind how the problem of "information retrieval" is
handled in our time, our video cassettes and the computers' visual displays, one begins to see that he was on to something none of his contemporaries had imagined even in crude form.

Or take another piece he put out around this time, "The Future of
the Two-Dollar Movie." In it he pursued two points. The first was comparison between stage and screen, and after the preliminary sniping about
the limits of the former—the three walls, the painted backdrops, that sort
of thing—he went on to talk about how each creates memories. On stage,
he said, the pictures that lingered were all created by the actors through
voice and gesture—"the art of interpretation glorified." On screen, however, "The poetic stimulation, the tour de force, which arrests attention
and makes memories that are to live, is a silent power. The brain behind
this power is never revealed. It lends itself to that concealment which is
one of the rarest attributes of true art," and, he added, it works subjec-
tively on the viewer, almost without his knowing that it's happening. He
was groping for a theory of the cinema, of the effect of symbolism and
montage (the latter a word not yet employed in this context) which he
lacked the language to express. But yet he was groping, trying to explain
what he had instinctively come to understand about the difference between the art in which he had been raised and the art in which he had
newly triumphed, and given the fact that few others were attempting such
definitions one is struck by his earnestness as well as by the prefiguration,
however crude, of theories yet to come.

His second major point was more clearly expressed. "The motion
picture is no longer an infant art. . . . I firmly believe the day will come
when great poetic pictures will not only compare with the best of the

legitimate stage, but will be upon a parity with the greatest productions of grand opera and at corresponding prices. Remember, a few years ago it was the limit of extravagance to spend $500 on a moving picture production. At that time we played only to five-cent audiences. Now we spend $500,000 on a picture, and we crowd the theaters everywhere at two dollars a seat. By this rationale what is to hinder the superproducer from spending three times that amount and getting five dollars a seat for it."[43]

The answer, clearly, was nothing, and having just successfully made the quantum leap he described, he was now prepared to make the one he was predicting. That leap would be the greatest extravagance of them all, an example of overweening ambition, of sheer movie madness, that, because of its very lack of precedent, remains the most remarkable act of daring in the entire history of an art that has never lacked for that quality. As he had said, "I am not a dreamer in a sense that I see fantastic things unlikely of realization. I haven't dreamed an impossible thing in seven years. That is the beauty of this work."[44]

CHAPTER ELEVEN

The Impossible Thing

IT is difficult to say at what point in 1915 David Wark Griffith began to turn an entirely possible dream, a little picture called *The Mother and the Law*, a version of which he had begun before *Birth*'s release, into the next of his several "impossible things"—that ungainly near masterpiece the world came to know as *Intolerance*. But one can say, with considerable certainty, that it owed its existence in its final form to *Birth*—or, more properly, to the overwhelming success of that film. For it surely occurred to Griffith, at some point in spring or early summer, that there was no going back to the kind of short features that had previously occupied him. The public now associated him with spectacle, and more spectacles would be expected. Indeed, the demands of his own ego, which had compelled him toward the grander form in the first place, were by no means assuaged by the success of *Birth*. On the contrary, he now saw his past hopes vindicated and must surely have felt still more fame and wealth lay ahead if he continued to turn out more large-scale films that would command similar attention from press and public. Beyond that, it is evident that much of what he was trying to say in *Intolerance* owed much to the response *Birth* had stirred in progressive circles.

The film was in no sense an apologia for the ideas expressed in *Birth*. The "tolerance" advocated in *Intolerance* was not racial in nature—not even in disguised or symbolic form. Griffith never once—not even in old age—saw any reason to recant anything he had said in *Birth*; he seems never to have allowed space in his mind for the thought that his critics might have had a justifiable point or two. No, far from being an apology, *Intolerance*—especially in what came to be known as the "modern" story—is a direct and bold assault on his critics and their "intolerance" of his right to say what he wanted to say. Or so, at length, it evolved. We have seen that in his Biograph days Griffith had more than once attacked the reform movement, largely because that branch of it which concerned itself with the individual victims of social conditions—the unwed mother, let us say, or the abusive father, or with a poverty-stricken family—unconscionably "meddled" in the lives of its clients. It outraged Griffith that a social worker, supported perhaps by some private agency that, in turn, derived its support from the untutored wealthy, could intervene in private lives, and obtain support from the law for his or her actions. Griffith was not yet a rightist. He appears to have felt that government had some obligation to regulate the pursuit of profit when it was at the expense of social justice. But he was obviously a man who would fight desperately to achieve and maintain his own freedom, and so—not entirely rationally—he saw the busybody mentality as a personal as well as a social threat.

What gave renewed urgency to these feelings was Griffith's powerful sense that he, and his masterpiece, *Birth*, had been as victimized by the "meddling" and "busybody" mentality as any slum dweller ever had been. During the time he was at work on *Intolerance* he was also kept busy not so much defending his previous film against attempts to censor it (though these continued), but defending the entire motion picture industry against attempts to impose censorship of more than a local kind upon it. In 1916, for example, there were no fewer than five motion picture censorship bills under consideration by the House of Representatives' Education Committee (including one drafted by an alliance of film producers in hopes of ameliorating more stringent measures introduced by committee members and by outside pressure groups). Around the same time the Crestman-Wheeler Bill, establishing a state commission to be appointed by the Board of Regents (supervisors of higher education), to censor movies, actually passed both houses of the New York legislature and in the spring awaited a decision either to sign or to veto by Governor Charles S. Whitman, who ultimately decided against it, perhaps responding to strong editorial opposition to the bill from the leading metropolitan newspapers and heavy lobbying by the film industry, in which Griffith took a very active part, ultimately, in fact, causing to have published under his name a pamphlet entitled "The Rise and Fall of Free Speech in America." In it, he directly linked the fight against the film censorship with the title of his new movie by using the word "Intolerance" repeatedly in headlines atop the cartoon-illustrated pages on which examples of the censorious impulse throughout history were set forth in bold type. These pages were interleaved—functioning rather like close-ups in a film—with Griffith's essay on the subject as well as other anticensorship documents and editorial opinions.

In his piece, incidentally, Griffith made a quite sound and interesting historical point, namely that after the expiration of the Alien and Sedition Acts of 1798, "the integrity of free speech and publication was *not again attacked* seriously in this country until the arrival of the *motion picture* [his italics], when this new art was seized by the power of intolerance as an excuse for an assault on our liberties."[1]

It is impossible to say what the story of *The Mother and the Law* was, in detail, when Griffith first went to work on it, for after he conceived the notion of integrating it into *Intolerance*, he did a great deal of reshooting. But in final form it tells the story of the Boy (Robert Harron) and the Dear One (Mae Marsh) who meet and marry in the slum they are forced to live in after his father has been killed and her father has lost his job, as the result of a strike at the nearby Jenkins mill. Prior to his marriage the Boy has engaged in a life of petty crime as the lieutenant of a gang leader known as the Musketeer of the Slums (Walter Long), who in turn is jealously loved by a mysterious young woman known as the Friendless One (Miriam Cooper). Married, the youth attempts to go straight, but the Musketeer, angry at his desertion, plants stolen goods on him and he is sent to jail.

At this point, social workers employed by a foundation established by Jenkins, the mill owner—a nice irony there—take the young couple's child away. The ground is that the wife of a convict must, *per se*, be an unfit mother. Despite an extraordinarily moving courtroom scene, in which the Dear One pleads to retain her child, the deed is done. With her husband in prison the Musketeer begins to insinuate himself with the Dear One, promising that he can help her regain her child. His intentions are anything but honorable, and the jealous Cooper character, seeing him enter the Dear One's apartment, informs the Boy, now released from prison. He arrives in time to join in the defense of his wife's honor, but the Friendless One has, in the meantime, stolen the Boy's gun and in the struggle fires through a window, killing the Musketeer. She then throws the revolver into the room and this evidence is enough to convict the Boy of murder. He is on his way to the gallows when his wife, aided by a sympathetic policeman, confronts the Friendless One and wrings a confession from her. There is then a wild—and enthrallingly shot—chase as the Dear One and the police officer commandeer a high-speed car and pursue a train on which the Governor is riding, in order to place this new evidence before him and secure a stay of execution. Then it is on to the prison to deliver the stay before the Boy is executed. He is on the scaffold, the black cloth already covering his face, when his rescuers arrive.

In the finished film this story is not the most spectacular visually, but of the four stories Griffith wove together in what he was to subtitle, "A Sun Play of the Ages," it remains the most affecting emotionally—and the most suspenseful. The climactic chase is a summary of all the rides to the rescue Griffith had shot for Biograph and Mutual, a brilliant example of superbly executed, basic moviemaking. The realism of his strike sequences and the slum background, the sensitive performance of Mae

Marsh and the scarcely less fine work of Bobby Harron—all of these represent Griffith at the top of his form, working with material to which he
brought firsthand knowledge both of milieu and of emotion. Pauline Kael
has correctly remembered, for example, a sequence in which Marsh, deprived of her child, becomes a kind of voyeur of other people's familial
happiness, spying on other mothers at loving play with their children.
Edward Wagenknecht has cited Marsh's unbearably poignant courtroom
scene—which Griffith shot four times at widely separate intervals as he
kept reconsidering it—and the scene where she and her husband are reunited after the last-minute rescue from the gallows as among the most
privileged moments in film history, and it is a sound judgment.

How much of the quality of *The Mother and the Law* was visible
in the early version of it, which was ready for release sometime in spring
or early summer of 1915, is problematical. Lillian Gish recalls a screening
of it for studio employees and notes "we all agreed with him that the film
was too small in theme and execution to follow *The Birth*."[2] Karl Brown
recalls that studio gossip at the time held that the picture was unreleas-
able and therefore likely to be shelved, though, of course, that possibility
was remote, given the precarious condition, at the time, of its producer
of record, The Majestic Film Corporation. About his plans for the picture, Griffith kept his own counsel and, indeed, for a time, in the months
to come, studio workers at Brown's level were under the impression that
the stories that were eventually melded with it in *Intolerance* were separate projects; indeed, they were given separate production numbers (*The
Mother* was F-1, the F standing for feature, and the others were, naturally,
F-2, F-3 and F-4).

In short, Griffith literally did not know what to do next. Thus *Intolerance* was a mighty improvisation, an attempt to salvage what would
have been, pre-*Birth*, a more-than-acceptable little picture, turning it
eventually into the sort of spectacle he—and the public—expected of
America's premier director. Yet there were distractions beyond those involved with the release of, and the continuing controversy over, *Birth*
with which to contend. He could not fully turn his attention to the business of recasting *The Mother and the Law* in grander form until the fall
of 1915.

Chief among his digressions was Harry Aitken's latest big idea, which
was nothing less than combining what he insisted on thinking of as the
greatest producing talents in the industry—Thomas Ince, Mack Sennett
and Griffith—in one distributing company, to be called Triangle. The
indefatigable promoter's new scheme was forced upon him. There was a
revolt in his Mutual distribution company's boardroom, led by J. R.
Freuler, a Milwaukee real estate man, and an old friend of the Aitkens,
who had followed them into the exchange business. He had at first resented the Griffith-Aitken concentration on *Birth* and then, after it was

a success, resented the fact that they had taken the picture away from Mutual, financing its completion and release independently. At the June 1915 Mutual board meeting, he urged the ouster of Harry Aitken as the firm's president, charging that Majestic, Aitken's principal production company, had failed to supply enough films for Mutual to fulfill its contracts with the theaters, forcing it to turn to other producers.

Before the board met, Aitken knew what action it was planning to take, and a couple of days before the meeting he announced the formation of Triangle, which, he said, would aim at delivering a full weekly program, complete with short subjects, to a chain of selected theaters that would charge two dollars admission. This announcement could have been merely a maneuver on Aitken's part, indicating to other board members that should he be removed he was in a position to make off with Mutual's major assets—Griffith and Sennett, whose Keystone company was also releasing through Mutual. At this point, he did not have their formal agreement to release through Triangle. That did not take place until July 20, when his big names, attended by their legal functionaries, met with Aitken in La Junta, Colorado.

On the basis of *Birth*'s success, Aitken had no trouble attracting what was said to be $4 million in capital from highly respectable Wall Street sources for this enterprise, but he was getting both more and less than he had bargained for—more trouble and less production of the cost-conscious yet highly promotable kind that could assure the success of a weekly program at substantial admission prices. A large part of his problem was that Aitken kept thinking of his three principals as, primarily, *producers*, when, in fact, only Ince was truly such, that is to say, a man whose approach to the making of films included a primary concern for cost efficiency and shrewd speculation about marketplace profitability. Ince, indeed, was responsible for developing what quickly became the basic studio system of production—with careful preproduction planning, careful control of the budget during shooting, specialists in all aspects of production working steadily toward the fulfillment of the weekly release schedule, with few high-risk or visionary productions to distract from steady profitability. Yet even Ince, struck by the huge commercial success of *Birth*, was this year preparing *Civilization*, a pacifist epic, on a far grander scale than any film had previously attempted, and thus a much larger risk to his backers.

Sennett, of course, was Sennett. If he did not dream grand dreams of spectacle, even he was interested occasionally in making longer and more costly features, like *Tillie's Punctured Romance*, which had been a great success in 1914. And if he did have Ince-like impulses toward organization, they frequently foundered because he was, in his way, as imperious as Griffith; nothing left the studio without his approval and gaining that could involve much fussing and, often, reshooting, which added to costs. His deepest problem, one that was to plague him through-out his career, was that short comedies, which his studio was geared to produce, simply could not command large revenues in the age of the feature. Theater owners and audiences liked them, but they were not essential to the prosperity of the former, the delight of the latter. In 1915 he lost the greatest star he ever had at his command, Charles Chaplin, in part because the Sennett lot was not large enough to contain two such powerful egos, in part because Sennett felt he could not match the offer Chaplin had from Essanay (western star Broncho Billy Anderson's outfit).

So despite the fact that Aitken was indeed obtaining the services of the three most prominent behind-the-camera talents in the industry, he was also taking them on at a transitional moment in motion picture his-tory and at a transitional moment in their own careers. Worse, each was going to be allowed to continue at his own studio, making his own de-cisions about what to produce and when and for how much. Aitken, pinned in New York, attending to problems of finance and distribution, could never get their efforts orchestrated in a way that did not cause sickening eddies in his company's cash flow in those periods when money was spilling out to his producers to cover production costs and was trickling in less quickly from the theaters.

Many years later, his brother Roy, asked why he thought Triangle had lived such a short and unhappy corporate life, replied shortly, "All of the directors—Ince, Sennett, Griffith—became conceited."[3] There was more to the story than that, of course, but there was an element of truth in the younger Aitken's statement. Fame and money had descended on all three in a short span of time, and they had little patience with the Aitkens' problems (or excuses), and little loyalty. There were always others eager to finance their work.

But this was only the beginning of the problems Harry Aitken now faced. He was as aware as anyone that stars were rapidly becoming the most significant element in assuring the success not only of individual pictures but of a studio's staying power. And now he went out and bought some stars, thus greatly increasing his overhead, but not, unfortunately, his grosses. For he ignored (or could not obtain) the services of people who had begun to build their reputations in film, and turned, instead, to the New York stage for names. Among those he signed, even before Tri-angle's incorporation was formalized, were De Wolf Hopper, Raymond Hitchcock, Eddie Foy, Sr., Sir Herbert Beerbohm Tree, Billie Burke, Weber and Fields and a rising light romantic lead named Douglas Fair-banks. Of them all, obviously, only one was to become a great name in film, though, curiously, Fairbanks and Griffith, to whose studio he was assigned, never quite hit it off, the director entirely missing (as he so often did with leading men) the charm of the man, while the actor felt rather left out of a studio where in the summer of 1915, when he arrived from New York, the emphasis was all on the film that would be called *Intolerance*.

Throughout the Triangle year Griffith contributed stories and some directorial moments to the program pictures (a credit reading "Adapted from Granville Warwick's novel" signaled a Griffith story idea, though of course no novels ever existed) and distractedly tried to fulfill his supervisory obligation to Aitken. His reluctance to involve himself more deeply in the Triangle program features was thus only a small factor in that company's failure. Still, there were tension and trouble and increasingly bad feelings between him and his backer.

2

It would be fascinating to know whether the idea of combining three other stories with that of *The Mother and the Law* occurred to Griffith in a sudden flash, or whether the notion simply grew, through a process of association, as the year wore on. There is no need to inquire about his inclusion of the Life of Christ in his "film fugue," as it is sometimes called. "Surefire. Absolutely" Karl Brown remembers thinking when it became production number F-4, reflecting the well-tested show business belief that a producer in trouble could nearly always extricate himself with a Passion Play or, at any rate, hauling the Christ figure on to stage or screen to provide a morally edifying climax for whatever nonsense was going on.[4] But what drew him to the St. Bartholomew's Day Massacre of the Huguenots in sixteenth-century France? Or to the Fall of Babylon (538 B.C.)? About those matters, nothing is directly known. Always remote and deliberately vague about his intentions, Griffith was more than usually mysterious about this picture. Anita Loos, who would eventually do much of the titling on the finished product, has written that perhaps only Lillian Gish and Frank Woods had any idea of what he was up to, but, as she says, "his secrets were perfectly safe with those intense loyalists."[5]

The best speculation is that as reports of the success of Giovanni Pastrone's *Cabiria* had been one of the goads that drove Griffith during the filming of *Birth*, then exposure to the film sometime in 1914 or 15 doubtless had a direct influence on the shaping of *Intolerance*. Having succeeded in creating an *American* spectacle, it seems that he now wished to challenge the Italians on their own ground, with a more obviously grandiose work, something that would have a universal Christian appeal. (Griffith could not know, at this point, that *Birth* would quite transcend its parochial subject matter and receive acclaim wherever it was shown.) At any rate, in a fascinating article on Griffith's sources in art history,

Bernard Hanson has observed cross-references both major and minor between *Cabiria* and the Babylonian sequence of *Intolerance*. To begin with, both films concern themselves with a city besieged, the former with Carthage under Roman attack in the third century B.C., the latter with Babylon under siege from the Persians in the sixth century before Christ. Beyond that, the great courtyard setting that is the most spectacular (and thanks to the often-reproduced stills, the most familiar) of the *Intolerance* sets is an expansion of a similarly designed, painted and decorated setting in *Cabiria*. Griffith even insisted on including large elephants as features of the decor—they were said to be some 30 feet in height—even though his researchers could find no evidence that pachyderms were ever a significant part of this civilization's iconography. The point was that they had been used on the *Cabiria* sets, and Griffith liked them.[6]

The staging of the siege sequences in both pictures, mighty forces assaulting mighty battlements, is also similar (and there are, indeed, film historians who believe that Griffith did not improve upon Pastrone's work with this material). As for minor matters, Hanson observes that in both Pastrone's and Griffith's courts the highly sophisticated residents are in the habit of keeping exotic, and sometimes dangerous, animals as pets, that in both pictures the heroic central figure is seen attended by a faithful and hugely strong retainer, dubbed Maciste in the Italian work (and so popular in that country that a number of sequels placing him at various other interesting historical intersections were made) and called The Mighty Man of Valor in *Intolerance*, where he was played by Elmo Lincoln.

Griffith was no plagiarist; his work is too strong and singular to support the notion. Still, some of his original dissatisfaction with *The Mother and the Law* must have stemmed not merely from the invidious comparison he made between it and *Birth* but from the equally invidious one he made between it and *Cabiria*. When he realized there was a way to rescue the film he had already shot, by combining it with something that would both constitute a response to his foreign rivals and drive home still more powerfully his moral about the dangers of meddlesomeness, it must have seemed one of those happy moments where improvisation turns into inspiration.

Still, it must not be supposed that the intensity of feeling that went into the creation of *Intolerance* was generated solely by competitive impulses or by Griffith's need to proselytize for free speech on the screen. It is obvious that some of the early filming on *The Mother and the Law* had a powerful effect on him, most particularly a trip Griffith, Bitzer and Karl Brown made to San Francisco to research prison conditions in the city jail there and at San Quentin across the Bay. The darkness and stench of the first made its impression on the men, especially when they contrasted it with the comparative airiness of San Quentin, and its splendid view of the surrounding area. The main, grisly business here was to get a clear understanding of the living conditions of a condemned man and, more important, to obtain step-by-step details of the process by which, finally, he was put to death. The warden himself conducted them on their tour. He even sprung the gallows trap for his visitors, and its clang, echoing in a bare room, as it banged against the side of the gallows platform after its release, would re-echo in Brown's consciousness for the rest of his life.

The trip was a sobering experience, and Griffith's realization of ritualized death in the finished film remains to this day as powerful as any such sequence ever done in the movies—precisely because the detailing is so lavish, so profoundly felt. That was true of everything else about the so-called "modern" story. When it came time to reproduce a city jail cell on the studio stage the workmanship was so realistic that Lillian Gish, seeing it for the first time, had to turn away from it. "Well, that's life," said Griffith briefly but soberly. When the company went on location in the poorest sections of Los Angeles to film sequences like the police raid on a house of prostitution and the battle between strikers and national guardsmen, Brown thought there was a new dimension of realism in Griffith's work, a brutality that he had not observed before. He also remembers Griffith seeing, on location, a Mexican mother bringing her crippled daughter up on a homemade wheeled stretcher to watch the movie people at work. Griffith drew George Siegmann aside and spoke quietly to him. The assistant disappeared and returned with a heavy-laden canvas bag in which were kept the silver dollars used to tip people on location. Griffith took the bag, and while the rest of the company was occupied with making its next setup, went to the child and outlined her entire body in silver dollars. There was no explanation; indeed no words were spoken across the language barrier separating director from mother and child.

Obviously the whole story of *The Mother and the Law* evoked for Griffith his past struggles, reminded him of the stratum of life from which he must have believed, at times, he would never escape. Perhaps, having achieved success, he perceived past moments when he might have taken turns that would have mired him more deeply, perhaps permanently, in this terrible hopelessness he was now recording on film.

But the San Francisco trip might have been productive of something more than the emotional tone of *Intolerance*'s modern sequence. It might, as well, have shown him the way to realize the spectacle sequence he had been yearning to make. For on the trip back from San Quentin the three filmmakers caught a glimpse of the newly risen spires for the San Francisco Exposition of 1915. They were, well, Babylonian or anyway, vaguely Asiatic, in spirit, reflecting an interest in Orientalia that had crept into American popular culture, via Europe, at this time, and which seemed refreshingly nonpuritanical to many people. Certainly, the fair was a flight of architectural fantasy bound to inspire a director now in search of pictorial grandeur. Griffith ordered the car stopped and Bitzer to take some pictures of the Tower of Jewels, the fair's most aspiring structure. These shots were taken with mattes in place, that is to say, part of the negative was left unexposed, so that other elements could be combined with the tower later.[7]

Whether or not his brief view of the exposition abuilding planted the germ of an idea in Griffith's mind, or fertilized one already growing there, we cannot be certain, but when he came to make his Babylonian story, the presence of the fair so nearby was a great convenience for him, because it had attracted to the West Coast the artisans and craftsmen he required to realize his overarching vision of Babylon. With the fair completed, some of them were available to execute Griffith's vision.

Because of the vast construction effort it required, the Babylonian section of *Intolerance* was filmed last, and research and building appear to have consumed most of the summer and early fall of 1915. Joseph Henabery, the actor who had played Lincoln in *Birth* and was to play several roles in the new film while serving as an assistant director, was an important figure in this effort. Griffith had had occasion to notice his passion for accuracy of detail in his preparations to play Lincoln and when the first version of *The Mother and the Law* was screened, Henabery pointed out that the priest accompanying Bobby Harron to the scaffold was wearing clerical garb of a kind worn only in France. Griffith quickly ordered the scene reshot, and after Henabery pointed out some other inaccuracies, he was ordered to take over research work on the picture.

He bought a huge number of books, so many that using them in order to answer efficiently the kind of quick questions Griffith was always asking ("Now, what kind of chariot would we use for the year of Belshazzar's Feast?") became impossible. Over the business office's objections, Henabery started buying two copies of each volume so that he could cut the illustrations out of them and paste them in a scrapbook.

Illustrations were arranged by subject matter—armor, chariots, cooking utensils and so on—and material that was unclassifiable (including reproductions of some nineteenth-century paintings of Biblical scenes that manifestly suggested staging ideas to Griffith) was thrown in helterskelter. At first, according to Henabery, Griffith didn't think much of this idea, but when he saw how quickly his assistant could respond to his queries by flipping through the book, the director took to toting it around himself on his rounds—no easy burden since eventually it came to weigh upwards of eight pounds. For an amateur, Henabery did his work well. The sources he went to were the best that scholarship had to offer at the time, and, eventually, it would pay off in unexpected ways; Griffith, for example, was able to obtain for the souvenir booklet sold at the film's first-run engagements endorsements of the picture's historical accuracy from noted students of Assyrian culture.[8]

Not that Griffith was imprisoned by historicism. In several instances, he chose to follow not scholarship but scholarship once removed in envisioning the past, by using familiar academic paintings of Old Testament scenes as guides for his own visualizations. Resorting to the scrapbook, Hanson traces direct influence on *Intolerance* to three such works: *Fall of Babylon* by Georges Rochegrosse (1891), *Belshazzar's Feast* by John Martin (1821) and *Babylonian Marriage Market* by Edwin Long (1875). None were precisely imitated (as Griffith had attempted to do in the "historical facsimile" shots in *Birth*), but there is reason to believe that the first of these paintings, the *Fall*, Griffith had actually seen, for it appears that it hung for a time—it is now lost—in Louis Martin's restaurant, which was a popular dining spot in New York in this period. Designed by Henry Erkins, who specialized in exotically atmospheric restaurants, the establishment was done up in the Babylonian manner, and three of Erkins's renderings of it are also to be found in the scrapbook, so they, too, had their influence on the look of the finished film.

All this suggests that Griffith, though concerned about historical accuracy, and eager to overpower the audience with spectacle, was equally careful not to too radically disorient them visually. Perhaps he sensed, even as he conceived his "fugal" form, that cutting back and forth between its four stories would be confusing enough. He would, therefore, give them firm links between the popular visual culture they had been unconsciously absorbing all their lives and this radical departure in film form that he was planning.

Questions about the overall look of a shot or a sequence were solved by Griffith "with a single decisive stroke," as Karl Brown put it. "People believe only what they already know. They knew all about how people lived, dressed, and had their being in Biblical times because they had been brought up on Bible pictures, Bible calendars, Biblical magic-lantern shows, Christmas cards, Easter cards, pictures of every incident with which we were concerned. Never mind whether these pictures were accurate or not. Follow them in every detail because that's what the people believe to be true, and what the people believe to be true *is* true—for them—and there's no budging them."[9] Psychologically Griffith was quite right on this point—and historically he did not do so badly. Most of the popular artists who specialized in Biblical scenes in the nineteenth century were at some pains to be archeologically correct in their details, and in matters of ritual Griffith kept at hand the Catholic priest who had lent his vestments for the reshooting of the prison scene, as well as a rabbi, Isadore Myers, the father of Carmel Myers, a young actress who began her career as an extra in the picture. When it came to doing the Huguenot story, Griffith was equally unconcerned with slavish accuracy, though here he resorted not so much to a visual tradition as to the traditions of eighteenth-century French theater, the conventions of which, as Hanson points out, had generally been taken over by filmmakers dealing with French subjects no matter what historical epochs they had under consideration.

If this implies that Griffith's treatment of the Christ story and the Huguenot episode was far more perfunctory than his work on the modern and the Babylonian stories, it is not accidental. Indeed, the Judean Story was presented as nothing more than three tableaux—the miracle at Cana, the incident of the woman taken in adultery and the Crucifixion—and although all were well shot there is nothing very inspired in Griffith's handling of these sequences. As for the French story, it has a truncated feeling about it, as if, perhaps, Griffith shot more of it than survived the final cut. Basically it is the story of an aristocratic protestant family who are repeatedly shown in scenes of ordinary domestic tranquility, their concern with the growing intolerance shown them and their coreligionists by the Catholic court somewhat overshadowed by their preoccupation with their plans for the wedding of their eldest daughter ("Brown Eyes," played by Margery Wilson) to the stalwart Prosper Latour (Eugene Pallette). The innocence of their activities is contrasted to the intrigues of the court, where Catherine de Medici (almost comically overplayed by Josephine Crowell in a mistaken performance) persistently pressures her son, Charles IX, to sign the order for what came to be known as the Saint Bartholomew's Massacre. This occurs on the eve of the wedding and what suspense this portion of the film generates concerns Pallette's efforts to fight his way through streets crowded with the king's rampaging soldiery to rescue his fiancée and her family. All, including Pallette, are eventually killed.

One feels the director's distance from these people. After all, he knew the people and the milieu of his modern story intimately and over the long months of research and construction on the Babylonian sequence he obviously developed a strong feeling for that time and place (and for its showy cinematic possibilities, which galvanized him), while he had plenty of conventionalized art (and feelings) to help him deal with the Nazarene (as the titles identified Christ). But these Frenchmen—they did not strike a chord with him, and his handling of them is very like, but distinctly no advance over, his handling of the Camerons in *Birth*. They are seen as purely innocent victims of large historical forces, living in complete withdrawal from the events of the day, with no ideological passions beyond a mild devotion to worshipping their God in their own way, though they, like Christ, are more clearly victims of the title emotion than either the Babylonians or the modern citizens, whose stories are more richly developed.

In any event, the French and Judean stories gave him something to do while he was awaiting completion of work on the sets for his Babylonian story, which remain to this day among the most remarkable ever devised for a motion picture, equaled in their massiveness in the American film perhaps only by Douglas Fairbanks's *Robin Hood* battlements in 1922. At the time there was simply no precedent for construction on this scale in this industry. According to Karl Brown, the unsung hero of this effort, not mentioned in any previous accounts of *Intolerance*'s filming, was a man named Walter L. Hall. Where he came from (and where he went after this film) is not specified. But he looked, according to Brown, like the young Winston Churchill, and had an almost supernatural skill with a pencil that fairly flew across the cardboards on which he made, without benefit of T-square or compass or even, it seems, a ruler, the designs for the Babylonian set that slowly arose on that historic empty lot across from the studio where the Camerons' Piedmont had lately stood. Hall had a genius for extracting a significant detail from one part of Henabery's research, blending it with another from somewhere else and creating something theatrically satisfying yet entirely practical for Huck Wortman to build.

The secret, the man who was surely the movies' first production designer claimed, was all in "perspective," and he held forth on this subject so extensively that he came to be known around the studio as "Spec" Hall. He affected great unhappiness in his labors ("the most demanding, miserable work a man can do") and yet claimed he had no need of the money it brought him. No, it was something he had a gift for, had been unable to prevent himself from developing and now could not escape. "Why do you do it?" Brown once asked, and the poor man cried, "Because I must, can't you see that? Because I *must*!"

His labors were immense. For he not only executed the grand designs for the Babylonian sequences, but all the set decorations as well— statuary, friezes, wall paintings and so on. He interrupted his toil only when his adolescent daughter visited the studio, leaping from his drafting table to the window to check that she was not falling into bad company among the raffish show folk as she wandered the lot.[10]

Wortman and his crew placed their executions of Hall's grand designs on the empty lot across from the studio according to a ground plan staked out there by Bitzer and Griffith months before. Los Angeles had never seen anything like the huge ramparts that began to challenge the sky at the corner of Sunset and Hollywood. They may have been as much as 150 feet in height (Bitzer's estimate), and they were wide enough (and strong enough) for a chariot to be raced along the top. Large signs proclaimed the picture's working title, still *The Mother and the Law*, and the name of this strange enterprise's proprietor, D. W. Griffith, to passersby. Sometimes a large balloon, moored to the set, was sent aloft to call further attention to these unprecedented doings.

As they worked, the story that they were finally going to tell took shape in Griffith's mind. It was not, in essence, a very complicated tale; its power would all derive from the manner of its telling, and from the overwhelming nature of its settings. Griffith presents the Babylonians as a happy and peace-loving people, presided over by a king more interested in archeology than the affairs of state, a prince (Belshazzar, played by Alfred Paget) who is preoccupied with his love affair with the Princess Beloved (Seena Owen). He, in turn, is loved from afar by the Mountain Girl (Constance Talmadge, in her first important role), who, in *her* turn, is loved by a functionary of the temple priests, the Rhapsode (Elmer Clifton, the assistant director, who would soon begin making pictures on his own). Belshazzar orders the introduction of a new god, Ishtar, devoted to love, into the city's religion, thereby offending the high priest (Tully Marshall, a stage actor new to the West Coast, who would have a long, villainous career in silent and early sound movies). The Priest conspires with Cyrus the Persian to attack the city. In the first great assault on it the invaders are repelled, but not for long. Prematurely celebrating the victory at Belshazzar's famous feast, the court is distracted and priests open the city's gates from within, allowing the Persians an easy victory, despite the Mountain Girl's discovery of the plot and her wild chariot ride to try to warn the Babylonians of it. She arrives too late and is killed in the fighting—one of the rare Griffith rides to the rescue that does not result in a rescue. Belshazzar and the Princess Beloved commit suicide rather than permit the Persians to capture them.

There are no particularly memorable performances in this section of the film. Talmadge made a strong impression, but hers was one of those jumpy performances that Griffith often imposed on his ingenues, very tomboyish. There is no doubt that the great performance in this portion of the film was a directorial performance. Once again Griffith had huge forces under his command, and once again his mastery of them was singularly calm. "That is very fine," he would say when something pleased him and that phrase, spoken so quietly, so authoritatively, was the highest praise his coworkers could expect, and it was enough. Indeed, Griffith's steadfastness, his care in presenting nothing but the quietest, most serenely confident air in public, despite the complexities of this enterprise, and its costs, mounting in unprecedented fashion, is one of the salient motifs in everyone's memories.

Billy Bitzer, for example, would remember that when rehearsals ran long, and repetition would begin to take its toll on actors and director alike, Griffith would simply stroll away, leaving an assistant in charge. One day he followed Griffith to his office and discovered him stretched out on his couch, mulling over his staging—and, more important, allowing his actors time to work out their problems by themselves. On the stage he was approachable but carried with him always that slight air of isolation from which his authority derived. He always lunched alone, studying the notes he had made for the afternoon's shooting; then he would arise, put the notes—all the script he ever had—in his pocket and never refer to them again.

Bitzer, too, was allowed his freedom during rehearsals once he had chosen his angles. He was usually not sent for until Griffith was ready for camera rehearsal and the timing of the scene, which was Bitzer's job. Once when he forgot his pocket watch, Griffith stopped work and sent someone to buy the cameraman that innovative timepiece known as a wristwatch, which Bitzer apparently thought sissified, and wore only under grumbling protest. But he had little choice about it, since Griffith had simply taken his old pocket watch—and never returned it. Bitzer's riposte was to bring a darkroom timer to the set one day, the loud ticking of which caught Griffith's attention. "Is there a clock around here? I hear ticking." Informed of Bitzer's ploy, Griffith made no outburst. "Of course," was his bemused comment. "Sounds good."[11]

In short, one searches the memoirs in vain for any outbursts of temperament. Those were for others. And a certain weariness did creep into the attitudes of Griffith's people as the production crept slowly on, the months turning into more than a year of shooting. Even *Birth* had not prepared them for anything like this and their inner clocks were still attuned to spending no more than a few weeks on a film. Hearing someone on the set one day wonder aloud if this picture—whose dimensions no one had any clear idea of—would ever end, Griffith commented quietly: "I don't see why everybody is in such a hurry to get through. We'd only start another one."[12]

One suspects that Griffith was so happy in this element he had created for himself, so delighted with the leisure the mounting of the production gave him to permit inspiration to come to him, that he saw no reason—beyond money, which was supremely uninteresting to him just then—to hurry. And surely after the lifetime of haste he had endured, after all those two- and three-day Biograph productions, this expanse of time was something for him to revel in. For despite the vastness of his enterprise, he was actually working as few moviemakers ever have, that is to say as a novelist or a poet does, with his general theme sketched in but with the creative centers of his intelligence, and his freely associating, freely roaming unconscious responding to it with stroke after stroke of apt improvisation. His film was growing as a work of art should—not by filling in an outline, but organically, taking on a shape dictated mainly by its own inner necessities.

People remember him working twelve- to sixteen-hour days, even when he was not actually on the stage directing, and surely his abstemious habits and his interest in physical culture were never more valuable to him than they now were. Some of his training methods were conventional: he ran, he worked out in the morning with Indian clubs, he occasionally paid boxers to spar with him. On the other hand, he embraced some odd, faddish habits for various brief periods. For a time he took to shaving his head because he had heard a theory that this would prevent baldness. For similar reasons he took to wearing a straw hat with wider than usual mesh because he thought sunlight encouraged hair growth. Finally, his belief in dancing to promote fitness remained unabated, and since attendance at dance halls provided an opportunity to observe ordinary people going about their ordinary occupations, he derived double benefit from these outings, which were a favorite Saturday night diversion. A couple of years after this, Griffith would ask an interviewer to: "Note the fighting peoples of the world. They are dancers, every one of them. All the conquests have been won by dancing people, and all the great achievements have been wrought by nations that dance."[13] He seems not to have noticed the fact that the terpsichorean urge is near universal and the quotation is typical of the rather grand rationales he liked to offer in public for most of his activities. But there can be no doubt of his devotion to dance as diversion and as an aid to fitness both mental and physical.

Just who his favorite dancing partner was at this time it is impossible to say. It is odd that having used Lillian Gish so extensively in *Birth*, all he could find for her was the role of the woman tending a cradle, always titled with the line from Whitman ("Out of the Cradle Endlessly Rocking") and used as a device to link the four stories of *Intolerance*. Gish was apparently cheerful about the situation, availing herself of the opportunity to learn a great deal about film production while undistracted by a taxing role. This is particularly remarkable in that her sometime rival, Mae Marsh, had the best role she ever had under Griffith's guidance. Indeed, the fact that he did such extensive reshooting on her section of *Intolerance* may betoken the renewal of something more than a purely professional regard for her. So does the fact that she alone dared to break the long-standing rule of addressing the director formally in public where it was always "Mr. Griffith." Just once she was overheard to call him "Griff," and his outrage is the one show of temper—"Jovian"—that anyone has recorded during the shooting of *Intolerance*.[14] But it passed quickly, and Griffith remained a determined champion of Marsh's potential for stardom, leading to quarrels with Aitken, who could not see it, and to Griffith's engaging in more than cursory supervision of her debut film for the Triangle program, *Hoodoo Ann*, a strange and interesting tale about a hexed orphan, which was made in 1916, the story of which he wrote, and which bears evidence of his directorial hand.

In any event, his emotional climate was obviously warmed not only by the trustworthy production team that he had developed over the years, but by the enormous success of *Birth*, which, despite its controversies, continued, as he worked on this new picture, to confirm his own most confident estimates of his talent. Psychologically, he could not have been in better condition to use the great set now nearing completion, and the improvisatory genius he poured into the shooting of the Babylonian sequence was at a level he would never surpass. People not directly concerned with its construction had not been permitted to peek behind the wooden wall that surrounded it at street level and no one among his co-workers knew precisely what use Griffith was going to put them to. And they just kept growing. Every once in a while Griffith would stroll over to inspect Huck Wortman's handiwork and then make a casual inquiry: How about a new wing here? Could we add a little height there? And, generally, the construction boss was able to oblige him.

Bitzer would claim that one of the more spectacular improvisations began as a joke. After conferring with Griffith it was often his task to relay instructions to Wortman and one morning he inquired with ostentatious innocence if it would be much trouble to run a ramp sturdy enough to support a chariot and horses up to the top of the battlements and whether that structure could be sufficiently reinforced so that the rig could be galloped full tilt along it. Wortman didn't understand, according to Bitzer (who was not above improving on a story), that his leg was being pulled and, a little later, when Griffith appeared, Huck inquired just how many horses would be hauling the chariot so he could make the appropriate calculations. "Say, Billy, that would be a good idea," Griffith responded. "Would there be too much vibration for your camera?" Bitzer would come to rue that attempt at a practical joke, but a memorable shot was in the making from that moment on.[15]

Nature, however, almost prevented it—and all the other Babylonian shots—from ever being made. For by the time the sets were ready in the early fall of 1915 the season of the Santa Ana winds, on-shore airs that emanate in the desert around Los Angeles and thus reverse the prevailing wind pattern, was upon the filmmakers. Brown would recall being pressed into service to attach hawsers—ropes of the same size used to moor ships—to key timbers at the top of the set and then stretching them to railroad ties, which were then buried in the earth around the set ("dead men," they were called) to secure it against the elements. Bitzer claims to have been routed out of bed several times to help batten down Babylon. Wortman and the others remained convinced that damage that could not be accurately measured had been done the set by the Santa Anas, and their justifiable insecurity lent an element of danger to the set's use in the weeks to come.

For example, when it came time to take that shot of Belshazzar racing his chariot across the battlements, rallying his forces by exposing himself to the slings and arrows of his enemies, it required perhaps a dozen men to tug and haul the chariot up the zigzag ramp Wortman had constructed out of camera range. When they got it in position, they found the horses very nervous, for when they stepped on the pathway Wortman had made they sensed what he knew in his bones as well—that it was a wobbly structure that might not bear the stress of their gallop. The camera position was in a tower and Bitzer and Brown were required to perch perilously near its edge to handle their machines. Leaning out to check their lens settings took nerve, but not as much as just sitting still and cranking once the horses and vehicle were sent flying forth.

Griffith signaled George Siegmann below to set his besieging army into motion, and then the charioteer was told to go. The entire structure swayed but it held, and Griffith ordered a second take—"a little faster, if you can." Wortman hurried up to protest, but he was ignored and the wranglers, true to the code of their trade, refused to show fear as they unhitched the trembling animals and followed the chariot, once again hand-drawn, back to its starting position. While this was going on, Brown "studied Griffith as though I had never seen him before. He was leaning casually against a parapet, his cheap straw hat shoved back on his head, his mouth slightly open in a grin of purest delight. The man was actually *enjoying* the situation."[16] Needless to say, the horses and their glorious cart came at the camera again, this time with a verve that satisfied Griffith. The walls of Babylon absorbed their pounding without harm. The film was perfectly exposed, a point the nervous cameramen reassured the director about without spot-checking their aperture plates (dust on them meant a scratched negative and a ruined shot), so anxious were they to be done with this business. One almost feels that neither men nor machinery nor, for that matter, animals would have dared deny Griffith's will at this juncture.

And so it went. Did he desire a herd of elephants to serve as mounts, battering rams and power for movable siege towers for the attacking Persians? Somehow they were rounded up—despite a certain confusion when it was discovered that male and female elephants were not amenable to taking direction when they were mixed, by assistants who did not know much about handling them. Did Griffith one day decide that it would be a very nice effect if one of Babylon's towers should crash to the ground at the height of the assault? Very well, Huck Wortman would rig it so that canvas and wood looked like stone and mortar going down. And fix it so that it fell all around the cameraman, a quaking Karl Brown, who remained somehow unscathed. Well then, how about a night shot of the battle? Griffith one day decreed that such a thing would be "very fine." Bitzer rigged the whole set with magnesium flares and got a wondrous effect. Did the hundreds of extras supposed to be attacking the walls quail when the defenders hurled all-too-realistic rocks down on them? Then there was always someone like the young Sidney Franklin, later to write, direct and produce, most notably at M-G-M, to come off the short films he and his brother were making for Triangle, to rally the troops, and to get himself knocked out when his shield proved no defense against a rock hurled from those heights (the brave "general" saw his "troops" turn tail when he went down, but there were always others to carry on). Did Griffith require men to leap from the walls (into nets out of camera range, of course) and did no one volunteer? Very well, how about an extra five dollars, double the day's pay, for leapers? In a moment he had too many and was forced to cry a halt. "Stop those crazy fools. I haven't enough nets—or enough money." One of the leapers was Woodbridge Strong Van Dyke II, later to be better known as "One-take" Woody Van Dyke, director of *Trader Horn*, *The Thin Man*, the first Johnny Weissmuller *Tarzan* picture and other solid entertainments of the 1930s. One of his hobbies, as a youth, had been stage makeup, and his friend, Walter Long, the character actor, convinced Griffith that his young friend could help him solve the problem of creating a convincing makeup for the Babylonian king. Van Dyke was summoned from the "mourners' bench," the resting place outside the casting office where actors waited, often in vain, for a call, and the young man quickly provided an excellent makeup, for which he was rewarded by a Griffith snort and a hasty exit. Van Dyke thought he had failed, but in fact he had succeeded—Griffith was merely angry that his staff, which had labored fruitlessly on this problem for days, had been shown up by this young stranger.

Van Dyke thus made the team but was almost fired when, trying to earn an extra fifteen dollars driving a chariot in a charge, he upset it and almost ruined a take, then regained favor by devising a way of massproducing beards for extras (crepe paper on wires that could be hooked over the ears, which produced some comic moments when the players, between shots, would push these contrivances up on their foreheads and use them as visors to shield them against the sun). Eventually, he joined von Stroheim, Franklin, Clifton and the others as one of the assistants handling the extras in big scenes, and became, as well, Griffith's chairboy and gofer.[17]

Despite the magnitude of the Babylonian sequence and the necessity it imposed on him to concentrate on the technical and logistical aspects of moviemaking, it must not be supposed that Griffith ignored what had always been his strongest suit as a director, the almost hypnotic control he exercised over performers. Part of his magic, especially with actresses, was in his voice; he could, it seemed, get a player to register any emotion he wanted simply by talking her through a close-up. But there was more to the matter than that. He was a quick, clever, manipulative psychologist, very often a kind of emotional prankster as he worked with his players to get the effects he wanted.

A typical case? A journalist, working incognito, got herself hired as an extra on *The Mother and the Law* and observed Griffith trying to get just the smile of delighted recognition he wanted out of Marguerite Marsh—Mae's older sister—when she saw her lover making his way toward her across a crowded ballroom floor. It was just before lunch when they were working on the scene, and Marsh was distracted as a long morning's work neared its end. Griffith observed her loss of energy and urged her to wake up. "Just think," he joked, "you are going to have a nice lunch presently, paid for by the firm." His pleasantry was rewarded with a smile and he said, "Save that for the picture. That is exactly the expression I want when you see your lover coming to ask you for a dance." When the setup was ready, Griffith began, as customary, to talk her through the scene. "You seem a bit impatient. You are looking about to see why he doesn't come for you. Now you see him." At which point he cried, "Steak." Which of course drew a huge smile from the girl.[18]

Nor was he above more elaborate stratagems. According to Bitzer, he deliberately started a romance between Seena Owen and George Walsh (Raoul's brother, who had a small role in the film) because he wanted his actress, whose gifts were limited, to bring more emotion to her role of the love-enthralled Princess Beloved. Then, when it seemed to Griffith that the affair was going all too well—that Owen was literally waxing too fat (and happy) for the role—he informed her that Walsh was toying with her. Then he ordered Walsh to stay away from the stage when she was working, insisting his attentions were distracting. As a result the actress pined away her excess poundage, forlornly wandering the lot hoping Walsh would again notice her.[19]

Around this time a young actress named Juanita Horton talked herself into the studio to seek a job and found herself being interviewed by Frank Woods. During that talk Griffith noticed her and quizzed her on her motives. Her answer was innocently frank: her family was poor, she needed a job during school vacation, and "Mama said I wasn't trained to do anything, so there was nothing left for me but acting." Griffith suppressed his laughter and, though she had worked in other studios, told her to report to him after lunch for a test. In it she was forced to improvise a scene on one of the Babylonian stages in front of the more experienced professionals assembled there. She was supposed to be a slave girl, playing with a pet beetle at Belshazzar's feet: "Watch it run away, go get it and bring it back . . . it's a pet. Play with it. Now put it back in the cage. Look up at the Prince . . . you adore him . . . he's like a god." There was no beetle, and no cage, only Griffith's voice to take the girl through her test. Young Miss Horton passed and became better known under the name the studio gave her, Bessie Love. Eventually Griffith would see to it that she got leading roles in the Triangle program pictures.[20]

Gods have a right to their jests, their games, and Griffith's co-workers, having granted him that status, granted him those privileges as well. They have been claimed ever since by directors, and never denied them so long as, like Griffith, they exercised them in good spirits, without screaming or sadism.

"A delightful guy," Allan Dwan would later summarize Griffith, in a phrase remarkable in the Griffith memoirs for its lack of awe, its suggestion of ordinary humanity. Dwan continued: "Always pleasant, always a little reticent—I never saw him in an angry mood—and he had a good sense of humor." This point Dwan has buttressed in several interviews with an anecdote that finds Dwan and Douglas Fairbanks sitting on the steps of a bungalow, deep in conversation about a picture they were planning, Dwan illustrating some point by scratching a diagram in the dirt at their feet, only to look up and confront, in close-up, the glaring face of an unleashed lion. The two men froze in terror—until Griffith appeared around a corner, seized the beast lightly by his mane and said something like "Come, little pussy-cat" and walked the aged and entirely docile creature away. Dwan never doubted that the boss had set up the whole gag, borrowing the big cat from the *Intolerance* set, where he was to be observed as a court plaything, in order to startle a star he had trouble relating with and a favored young director he knew would appreciate the gag.[21]

No one seems to remember just how many weeks they were on the walls of Babylon, but it seems to have been early winter before Griffith at last decreed that he was finished with them. But he was not yet finished with the picture. Shots of the Persian army on the march had to be taken, and these were done near San Pedro, along the seacoast. Each morning for several weeks a huge army of extra players had to be rounded up, made up and costumed at the studio and then transported to the Dominguez Slough—one of many freshwater ponds that had been created by the subsidence of coastal land in the area south of Los Angeles—which doubled as the Euphrates River. The means of transport was the interurban streetcar system that formerly linked the cities of the area, before the freeways displaced it. What a sight it must have been—hundreds of Persian soldiers riding the streetcars to and from work. And what a logistical effort for Siegmann, Erich von Stroheim, Van Dyke and the others captaining this mob.

While this work was going forward, the Walls of Babylon came tumbling down, so that something even grander could be erected on their foundations. This would be Belshazzar's court, vast, open to the sky, its walls, if anything, higher than the battlements it was replacing. It was, and remains, one of the most extraordinary examples of the set decorator's art ever created—a forecourt, broad steps leading up into a platform area that stretched back some 300 feet, its sides lined with elephant-surmounted columns, every inch of its walls intricately painted. It would require weeks to complete and impose a hiatus on the production which would delay completion of principal photography until the early summer of 1916.

This had no effect on Griffith's mood. There was plenty to occupy him, not the least of his chores being to attend to completion of financial arrangements for this monster he was creating, but it seems that at this time there was, for him, nothing that could disturb his equanimity.

His sense of well-being derived from *Birth*, for all the time *Intolerance* was shooting the earlier picture was playing with unprecedented success, evidence of which was delivered almost weekly to Griffith, constantly buoying him. By the end of 1915, the producer's gross on the film came to $1,802,792.93, of which profits in the amount of $337,559.24 had accrued after distribution, exhibition and negative costs had been deducted. Under his contract, Griffith was entitled to a share of these profits, of course, but even before he received them, he had collected, throughout the year, royalties taken off the top of the picture's gross. These amounted to $140,243.09, but dividends from Epoch as well as from the other companies with which he had royalty arrangements, plus his Triangle salary, swelled his income for the year to $250,431.34, on which his income taxes, for this first year in which they were levied, amounted to just $7,585.24—laughable by modern standards, the beginning of a lifelong irritation to Griffith.[22]

These financial results encouraged Griffith to make a very simple equation: big pictures equal large successes. What he saw no reason to consider was another equation: large risks can also equal larger losses. But why should he? His own limited experience had shown him only the bright side of these matters and, indeed, the comparatively limited experience of the rest of his industry at this early stage reinforced this belief. This is not to imply that money was particularly significant to Griffith. His wants were simple. The only serious drain on him in these days was the 15 percent of his income that he had to turn over to Linda under the terms of their separation agreement. He was also helping to support various relatives back in Kentucky (he had bought a house for his mother in La Grange, near his birthplace, but she would die in the early winter of 1915, an event that does not appear to have unduly unnerved Griffith). Yet there was no sudden surge of ostentation. He continued to live as he had lived, this lifelong creature of hotels and restaurants, dressing with a certain theatricality of style, being driven about in excellent cars, but in no sense indulging himself materially as others, suddenly striking it rich in Hollywood, would so frequently do. In time to come, Griffith would regret not paying more attention, at this time, to his personal finances, regret that he did not begin building, as he might have, the kind of fortune that such contemporaries as Chaplin, Pickford and Fairbanks were starting to accumulate. But the thought simply did not occur.

The money, as he saw it, was but the tangible reward, and belated at that, due his genius. Therefore he could think of nothing better to do with his gains morally, or for that matter, practically, than to reinvest them in that genius. Such it seems was the euphoria of this year that it never occurred to him to think that *Birth* might be a once-in-a-lifetime phenomenon, or to remember what he knew as well as anyone—that show business is not the most stable of enterprises. He thus established yet another motion picture precedent, for he was the first, but by no means the last, creator of a huge film success to believe that he had lifted himself above the ordinary vicissitudes of his trade.

Over the years a double myth has grown up about *Intolerance:* that it was unimaginably expensive to produce and that its exorbitant costs, combined with its lack of success at the box office, encumbered Griffith with debts from which he never recovered, his career with a burden that dragged him to ruin. Neither is true.

Financing *Intolerance* was as easy as paying for *Birth* had been difficult. Curiously, the Wark Producing Corporation, the independent company controlling *Intolerance,* did not officially come into being until December 1915, during that period when the Babylonian sets were being rearranged and Griffith was free to journey East. Since the heart of the new film, *The Mother and the Law,* had begun life as a Majestic feature, it had to be purchased from that entity, which received Wark shares for it. These, in turn, Griffith and Aitken then bought back for Wark for $121,414.07. This wink-of-the-eye shuffle seems to have been financed largely out of monies Roy Aitken ($24,300) and Griffith $31,500) paid into Wark in return for stock, and by a straight, unsecured loan of $60,250 which Griffith made to Wark at the time it was incorporated. In theory they were getting a bargain. Aitken ended up with 750 shares of Wark's stock, Griffith 150 shares. Likely Aitken would have taken more, but he transferred 300 additional shares to Triangle, in return for money that company had already advanced the production. Thus 1,200 of Wark's total outstanding shares, numbering 1,500, were committed as the company was formed. The remainder were used to back certificates of indebtedness, which were sold to investors for $1,000 each. These certificates were to pay their holders interest of 6 percent a year after two years, and were guaranteed redeemable at $1,100 in five years. But it was not these modest, seemingly certain returns that attracted investors. What interested them was the chance to obtain stock of seemingly unlimited earning potential in what promised to be a new *Birth.* Griffith himself, through one of his several corporations, took 35 of these certificates in addition to his other investments in Wark, and the Aitken brothers put another $24,000 out of their personal funds into the certificates. It is a measure of Griffith's confidence that he permitted Lillian Gish to invest $3,000 in *Intolerance,* having refused her mother's offer to put money into *Birth.*[23]

With most of its production cost charged off to Majestic and Triangle (and those concerns compensated on paper, in paper), with $300,000 cash in hand from certificate sales, *Intolerance* would go to market fully financed, contrary to myth. The apparent source of the oft-repeated notion that the picture cost in the neighborhood of $2 million is an article that appeared in the *Scientific American* in its issue of September 2, 1916, as the picture was opening. Among other absurdities the piece listed an expense of $360,000 for costumes and uniforms for 18,000 soldiers. It solemnly noted that this and similarly inflated figures "were not compiled by a publicity agent, but by Mr. Griffith's auditing department. It is a well known fact that 'Intolerance' cost approximately $1,900,000." Of course what happened was that the publicists, creating a "cast of thousands, cost of millions" campaign, had got the auditors to cook up fraudulent figures for the scientific journal's reporter.

Actually there exists in Griffith's papers a very precise production accountant's statement, drawn up sometime after the picture was finished, previews had been held and release prints struck. This document shows that the negative cost of the picture was precisely $385,906.77, the largest single item being for set construction, with salaries running a close second. It was not cheap by the standards of the day, but it was a far cry from being a multimillion-dollar production, and it is obvious that between the Griffith-Aitken investments and the money raised through sale of the certificates of indebtedness *Intolerance* went forth with its bills paid in full, and with reserves sufficient to pay for prints and exploitation.[24] Nor can it be said, considering the amounts that were flowing into him from *Birth* and from salary, that Griffith's commitment to the production placed him in imminent danger of penury. In all—counting the $35,000 in certificates that his D. W. G. Corporation held—his investment in *Intolerance* at this point amounted to $126,750, or roughly half his 1915 income. It was a substantial statement of belief in his own vision, but considering that Griffith's income would remain at something close to its present level for more than a decade, it did not represent a ruinous commitment on his part. Nor did the loans he made to the corporation over the next few years, before it was dissolved in bankruptcy. One of them was made to settle unspecified debts, probably incurred in promoting and distributing the film; another was to meet the guaranteed interest payments on the certificates of indebtedness when they fell due one year. In all, these further loans, never repaid, amounted to another $139,000. Clearly he lost heavily on this dream and there came a time in Griffith's life when he could have used it, but it had nothing to do with the failure of his studio later, and, given his income level over the next fifteen years, it represented more inconvenience than disaster to him.

These troubles, of course, were far in the future as 1915 turned into

1916, as Belshazzar's court turned from vision into reality. And Griffith was finally ready to begin shooting on this wondrous stage. The first revelation of what his artisans had wrought remains one of the greatest single shots in the history of motion pictures. The camera beginning on a high angle, moving down and forward until, at least as originally planned, it came to a close-up of two doves hitched to a tiny jeweled chariot, plaything of the Princess Beloved. The camera crane had not been invented then, and Griffith and Bitzer went aloft in a balloon, hoping it could be winched down at a steady enough pace, and without undue swaying, to make the shot successfully. But it did not work, and it was Allan Dwan who applied his training as an engineer—he was a graduate of Notre Dame—to the problem and devised the solution. This consisted of mounting the camera on an open platform elevator that was, in turn, mounted on a narrow-gauge railroad flatcar, with tracks leading into the set. As the elevator was lowered workmen propelled the railroad car slowly forward and thus, in a matter of an afternoon, the screen's first crane shot—and still one of its most effective—was taken. It did not quite reach the doves, but its length and smoothness were exemplary.[25]

It would form, eventually, the nucleus of everyone's memory of the film, a shot that summarized its virtues—technically innovative, confident in manner, bold in its aspirations, sweeping in its effect. Indeed, the entire Babylonian sequence, however feverishly melodramatic its story, suggested imagistic possibilities on a grand scale that no previous film had proposed. For the grandeur of the overwhelming sets simply awed people who were serious about the movies' potential for theatrically unprecedented spectacle, and Griffith unfolded a sufficiency of wonders within them—love goddesses being worshiped, marriage markets in progress, decadent revelry of all sorts.

On the other hand, he was not as sure with the Babylonian court as he was with his battle scenes. The fine things mix with static, and operatically stagy, moments throughout, and it appears that Griffith paid less attention to nuanced performance here than was his custom elsewhere—or perhaps believed that a naturalistic approach on the part of his actors was inappropriate to his material. There are times when he seems at a loss to fill interestingly the vast spaces he had caused to be created for this royal household to occupy, and sometimes it appears that the director, no less than the rest of us, is simply dumbstruck by the magnificence he had ordered up, his inventiveness overtaxed. The thought seems to have occurred to Henabery as well. At one point, fearing the incohesive quality of what he had seen shot, he pressed on Griffith some novels he had come across in his researches about this period, thinking they might suggest some ideas to the director. But after browsing them, Griffith returned them by way of an assistant, to whom he made the quietly withering comment: "Well, I thought until yesterday that maybe

Henabery was right. But now I know he's all wrong."[26] In other words, this was, as if there could be any doubt of it, Griffith's picture—its mistakes as well as its glories.

And, in the end, what's wrong with the Babylonian sequence indeed pales in comparison to all that is right with it. In the end, all doubts, all questions are simply overwhelmed by our sense that we are in the presence of an artist who is, as never before or later, simply drunk on the power of his medium and his own powers over it. His intoxication is not wild, not in danger of causing him to fall down and make a fool of himself. It is the kind of intoxication that frees one of inhibitions, that gives one a sense of mastery over self and world, that is liberating to experience and liberating to behold, because, in the end, it carries away both he who is possessed by it and those who are in his presence—past hesitations, past flaws that might otherwise make us stop and think. Finally, one simply surrenders not so much to what is visible and concrete in work of this kind but to the almost palpable spirit animating it. If, that is, one is open to such unspoken messages. The trouble with works like *Intolerance* is, alas, that not everyone is capable of responding to them: they remain imprisoned by the literal and cannot hear the unplayed music of the thing.

Something that would affect his future as profoundly as the need to go on recapitulating the experience of directing great enterprises occurred when Griffith was master of the revels in Belshazzar's court. That was his meeting with a young woman. It was his profound interest in, belief in the spiritual values of, the dance that led to this meeting. Ruth St. Denis, that pioneering figure in modern dance, had come to Los Angeles in 1915 and had opened a school there. St. Denis was, in fact, out of much the same theatrical tradition that had formed Griffith. She had danced and choreographed for Belasco, and there was always something melodramatic in her mode of expression. Moreover, like Griffith, she was working new territory with precious little precedent to guide her, there being no American dance tradition, beyond the folk, for her to draw on. Griffith attended recitals at her school and was sufficiently impressed by what he saw to send some of his actresses there to study movement. It also occurred to him that the St. Denis dancers were ideal for the terpsichorean sequences of the Babylonian story—a dance of the god Ishtar's priestesses and, of course, the dance that is one of the features of Belshazzar's feast. In due course, a group of St. Denis's pupils were hired.

Among them was a young woman Griffith had first observed at her studio. She was Carol Dempster, the fourteen-year-old daughter of a Great Lakes ship captain who had tired of that occupation and moved his family from Duluth to California. She had been spotted by St. Denis in a school production and she was to graduate from the choreographer's first Los Angeles class and tour briefly with her, before returning to Los

Angeles and beginning her career first as a small parts player with Griffith, then as the star of most of the films he made in the years between 1920 and 1925. She was a mildly attractive young woman, and thanks to her dance training, she moved well. But there was something angular about her features, something thin and pursed about her mouth, something veiled about her eyes, that did not generally photograph well. There was something angular about her personality, as well; there are no warm reminiscences about her among the other Griffith players (as there are even among the young actresses who were at various times rivals for his favor), no warm memories of her among moviegoers of her time. Her reviews, too, would be at best reserved. And what Griffith saw in her he never confided to anyone. But this meeting, in the spring of 1916, was as significant as anything that happened to him that year, for assuredly her presence in major roles in major films in the years to come would have an effect on their success, and it would be a negative one.

It is doubtful that their love affair began at this early date—though not impossible, given Griffith's obsession with pubescent females. But Carol Dempster had been noted. As for the work she had been engaged to participate in, it is almost impossible for modern eyes to evaluate, for what is more ludicrous than recent avant-gardism that has yet to be draped in the kindly veil of long historical perspective? It seems that both St. Denis and Ted Shawn, her partner and husband, were present on the set when the dances were filmed, and for a long time it was believed that St. Denis herself served as lead dancer, but toward the end of her life she denied ever appearing before the camera in this film, and the extant, imperfect prints of *Intolerance* have not yielded up, to dance experts, any definitive images by which to resolve this question. It seems likely that Griffith's faithful staff pianist and occasional choreographer, Gertrude Brombeck, might have served as the dancers' captain.

Shooting on *Intolerance* ended not long after this, though there was some additional photography during the postproduction period. Very likely the epilogue—in which airships are seen bombing New York, soldiers are seen killing and maiming one another, and all this destruction is brought to a halt by the appearance of a sky full of angels, after which a title, "And Perfect Love shall bring peace forevermore," hammers home the message—was done after principal photography was completed. At any rate, Griffith appeared one day at Bitzer's bungalow office inquiring of the cameraman whether he had gone to Sunday school and if he remembered certain Biblical verses about shining throngs of angels appearing on earth to sing God's praises. That was the image he wanted for the end of the film, and once again Bitzer found himself ordering telephone poles planted in the studio yard, ordering wires strung from them and getting the costume department to run up angel wings and robes. Once again comely young ladies—some 75 of them—were hired to hang, suspended in midair in burlap loops covered by their costumes yet attached to these wires, to get the desired effect. Once again their giddy spinnings and the hot sun took an unpleasant toll among them—and Griffith, forgetting his inspiration, almost ordered Bitzer to stop the elaborate preparations for the shot until he was reminded that it had been his idea in the first place.

Titling, too, proved a problem. The job went to Anita Loos, whom Griffith summoned to his side one summer's afternoon, and asked to return to the studio that night to view a first cut of the picture. She believed she was the first person, aside from Griffith, ever to see a fully assembled version of *Intolerance,* and she recalls thinking, when the lights in his projection room came on at the end, that "D. W. had lost his mind." She added: "I sat a moment in stony silence, which I could only explain to the Great Man by telling him that I had been moved beyond words. Actually, he was so absorbed in his film I doubt he realized my bewilderment."[27]

The problem she had with the film was the same problem others had with it—even after her clarifying titles had been added to it. That was the lack of anything but thematic unity to bind the four stories together. Obviously titles would help stress this unifying factor and provide transitional pauses to allow audiences to catch their breath and adjust their perceptions. There was also historical background to be provided and, said Griffith, if she could find any way to inject some humor that would be most gratefully received. It was a large job, and Loos spent weeks in the projection room running the film over and over again. By and large she did a good job, though particularly in the Babylonian sequence there is an uncertainty of tone that is occasionally jarring—quasi-Biblical diction in one title contrasting with near-slangy modern locutions in another. Mostly, though, the titles seem perhaps a little less high-flown than those of *Birth.*

Even so, after the first preview, once again at Riverside, California, this time on August 6, 1916, Henabery, who rode to the preview in Griffith's chauffeur-driven Fiat with Bobby Harron, Mae Marsh, Lillian Gish and Griffith, found himself confused and disappointed by what he saw. He was quite unable to join in the excited gabble on the ride back and next day, when Griffith asked him what he thought, the assistant found fault with the titling—too much in some places, not enough in others. In particular he felt that the relationships between some of the characters was insufficiently explained. Griffith at first rejected the criticism: "You don't know what you're talking about." But after lunch Griffith approached him again, listened again to his criticisms, then summoned Frank Woods and informed him that Henabery was right—with the result that this versatile man was now assigned to write some supplementary titles, revamp others.

Nor was that the end of his services to the picture. Griffith took it East, showed it to his associates there and wired back to Los Angeles requesting Henabery to shoot some inserts for Belshazzar's feast. He wanted, he said, nudes. Obviously the feeling among the promoters was that the picture needed some pepping up. Henabery did not agree; Frank Woods thought he ought to do what the boss had ordered; Bitzer simply said he would shoot anything Henabery set up. So he compromised. He looked again at the John Martin painting of the feast and arranged his people in attitudes borrowed from it—and with bits of gauzy drapery strategically placed on his players. Griffith meantime had recruited, according to Henabery, some prostitutes to pose for his camera back in New York, their attitudes being somewhat more flagrantly sexual than those Henabery coached. This material was edited together by Griffith in New York, but it was Henabery's master shot that was used, and when Griffith returned his oblique comment on the matter was: "You know, it's a strange thing when your assistant shoots better scenes than you do."[28] A little later, at Griffith's insistence, Henabery was given his first full directorial assignment. Griffith was, in an offhand, even rather secretive way, a generous man. And never an envious one. He was too secure in himself, by now, to be prey to that emotion.

3

And so, at last, it was finished. And rushed into release. The New York opening occurred just a month after the first preview in Riverside, and once again the Liberty, where Birth had opened, was crowded with a fashionable audience. Once again there was a full orchestra and an elaborate score concocted by Breil with Griffith's help. Once again there was a lavishly produced program, containing among other items Griffith's helpful and disarming explanation of his film's unusual construction: "The purpose of the production is to trace a universal theme through various periods of the race's history. Ancient, sacred, medieval, and modern times are considered. Events are not set forth in their historical sequence, or according to the accepted forms of dramatic construction, but as they might flash across a mind seeking to parallel the life of the different ages . . . switching from one to the other as the mind might do while contemplating such a theme."[29]

The Times review was, at best, mixed, and not at all acceptant of Griffith's rationalizations. Ever since Birth, its anonymous critic said, the question of whether that film was an accident or whether Griffith was "a new master of the cinema" had interested people "who study the personalities that manipulate the puppets of stage and studio." The verdict on *Intolerance* was that he "is a real wizard of lens and screen." And despite the film's "utter incoherence, the questionable taste of some of its scenes and the cheap banalities into which it sometimes lapses" it was judged "an interesting and unusual picture." Special praise was awarded "the Stupendousness of its panoramas, the grouping and handling of its great masses of players."[30]

There is something *pro forma* in this praise—as if the reviewer could offer nothing less to a figure of Griffith's stature. For he went on—ludicrously—to term "The Mother and the Law" section "a lurid modern melodrama in the prevailing mode of the screen," and to suggest that the French drama and the Passion "do nothing but add to the general confusion and might well be eliminated." Though obviously impressed by the splendors of the Babylonian story—the siege and fall were "masterpieces of the cine"—he enigmatically ended his piece with the remark that "they are so splendid it seems a pity the story was not deleted." In other words, it seems this anonymous fellow would have been content with a two-reeler consisting merely of the most arresting shots of the Babylonian sequence, a sort of historical newsreel.

Nor was this the only such opinion. Alexander Woollcott, writing a few days later in the *Times*, opened his essay thus: "Unprecedented and indescribable splendor of pageantry is combined with grotesque incoherence of design and utter fatuity of thought to make the long-awaited new Griffith picture at the Liberty an extraordinary mixture of good and bad. . . ." He rightly suggested that not all of the four stories bore very close examination as examples of "intolerance," stating, indeed, that only the two least-developed ones actually stood up to analysis in this light—Christ and the Huguenots having actually been martyred for holding ideas at variance with those of the majorities in their societies. The longer, more carefully detailed stories were not, he argued, such good examples of the great theme Griffith pretended to be examining, and the point is generally valid. Unstinting in his praise of the Babylonian sequence ("The imagination and personal force represented in such an achievement suggests a man of stature. . . ."), he guessed correctly that Griffith had arrived at his unifying thematic idea only after he had begun shooting, though he guessed wrongly that it was this sequence which had gone before the cameras first.[31] The damage was done, though. After opening week, most considerations of *Intolerance* would labor under the necessity of countering reviews of this mixed and hesitant character.

Reviewers with a somewhat better background in the recent development of cinematic storytelling techniques—especially as practiced by Griffith—were at pains to point out that *Intolerance* represented not a radical and confusing departure from current practices but a logical development—a development on the grand scale, really—of the technique of crosscutting between parallel stories (or parallel events in the same story) that Griffith (and others following his lead) had been working with for much of the last decade. The review in the *Boston Evening Transcript*, for instance, noted the roots of many of the ideas, themes and images of the film in such earlier Griffith works as *The Musketeers of Pig Alley*, *Judith of Bethulia* and *Home, Sweet Home*, to name only the most apt of the illustrations adduced to make the point—which was obviously designed to assuage fears that the new picture might prove "too difficult" for the humble movie audience, as well as to answer the doubts of earlier critics.

A somewhat bolder defense of the film was offered by Vachel Lindsay, in the course of reviewing Hugo Munsterberg's pioneering psychological study of "the photoplay," as he called it. Lindsay felt that the interweaving of the stories gave a kind of unspoken significance to each of them that they would not have achieved standing alone. He wrote: "Babylon is shown signalling across the ages to Judea. . . . And in like manner the days of St. Bartholomew and of the crucifixion signal back to Babylon sharp or vague or subtle messages. The little factory couple in the modern street scene . . . seem to wave their hands back to Babylon amid the orchestration of ancient memories. The ages make a resonance behind their simple plans and terrible perplexities. The usual shallowness of appeal of private griefs and loves as shown in the most painstaking intimate films, their inability to arouse complete responding passion in the audience, is thus remedied. The modern story is made vibrant by the power of whirling crowds from the streets of *Time*." (Lindsay's italics.) As usual with Lindsay, his poet's intuition served him well in evaluating Griffith's work, in finding in it certain qualities that were not apparent to those who, as Lindsay said, were incapable of estimating a film "in any but a nickelodeon way."[32]

And yet, despite this, one still cannot help but think that the discomfort this film caused those who could not see beyond the conventional was not entirely misplaced. One of the film's most enthusiastic critical advocates was Julian Johnson, the responsible and responsive critic for *Photoplay* in a time when that journal was a more or less sober chronicle of motion picture activity. The power and the daring of the film quickened his pen, and by and large his lengthy review—responding not just to what he saw, but to the ambition that lay beneath the cascading imagery of the film, propelling viewers past its flaws—was everything Griffith might have hoped for. Or almost everything. For even this intelligently enthusiastic writer reiterated the wish that "Mr. Griffith had worked out a whole evening of his great Babylonian story. Sticking to this alone he would have added an art-product to literature as enduring as Flaubert's *Salammbô*." And he added, in what he obviously thought was a *sequitur*, "If I may predict, he will never again tell a story in this manner. Nor will anyone else. The blue sea is pretty much where it was when the sails of the Argonauts bellied tight in the winds of a morning world, and so are the people who live in the world. Still, we wish to follow, undisturbed, the adventures of a single set of characters, or to thrill with a single pair of lovers. Verily, when the game is hearts, two's company, and the lovers of four ages an awful crowd."[33]

In this review we begin to understand why *Intolerance* would prove to be a popular failure, despite initial success at the box office that was comparable, for three or four months, to that of *Birth*. Through the years Griffith's defenders have insisted that the failure of the film was in no way its author's fault. It has been said, for example, that America's increasing preoccupation with the war in Europe cut into the attendance of the film, particularly since its overall message was pacifistic, and that the nation's severance of relations with Germany, on the last day of February 1917, and the official declaration of war in April harmed it commercially, but receipts had begun to fall off well before that; there is no evidence that people generally were staying away from movies because of their preoccupation with the war or politics (1916, of course, was a Presidential election year). Nor is it really possible to say that people were daunted by word that the picture was difficult, hard to follow. On the whole, the less sophisticated reviewers away from the eastern cultural centers were burbling in their enthusiasm, content to stress the notion that a master of spectacle exceeded his previous triumph in this realm. There was little, in print, therefore, to stay the mass audience from turning out for *Intolerance* as it had for *Birth*, and the notion that reviews, or events, conspired in their blindness to deny Griffith a triumph commensurate with the risks he had taken simply does not stand up to scrutiny.

The simple fact is that *Intolerance* did not have, as they now say in the trade, "legs," that is, staying power. It caused its stir in that small, still-forming community that was serious about the artistic potential of film, and that group's interest radiated outward into those circles in which being culturally *au courant* is a significant value. But once they had seen it, there was no breakthrough to the larger audience, which breakthroughs tend to be based, not on promotion, advertising or reviews, but on word of mouth, which, in turn, is usually based on developing a strong sense of identification between the people of the screen story and the people of the audience. The trouble with *Intolerance* at the popular level is that it kept interrupting one narrative with another, spoiling the identificatory impulse just as it started to build in one story or the other. In short, a vital emotional connection was missed. And if people could not fully articulate the vague sense of unease that they felt when they left the theater, they did vaguely communicate their dissatisfaction with the picture, despite all the compensatory suspense and spectacle Griffith provided them. The large audience was not so much confused as distanced by the director's work. *Intolerance* was for them what it remains for many to this day, despite its high historic importance in film history, an easy film to respect, but a hard film to cherish.

The crowded quality of the canvas Griffith provided, his failure firmly to isolate faces in that crowd, should not be seen merely as heroic commercial indifference or miscalculation, an easily forgivable error by an artist with his mind on loftier matters. It was the reflection, on a simple level, of a far more profound intellectual and esthetic failure. The best analysis of where Griffith went wrong on this more complex level is in Eisenstein's essay "Dickens, Griffith and Film Today." Despite the Marxist—and chauvinistic—underpinnings of his argument, the Soviet director cast a shrewdly practical eye on Griffith's strengths and weaknesses, particularly as they were demonstrated in *Intolerance*. Noting that Griffith's basic editorial style in all his films stressed tempo—the sheer force of ever-quickening pace as he approached the climax of his stories, usually with extensive crosscutting between contrasting elements within them— he observed that what he called "relentlessly affective rhythm" was usually absent from Griffith's work. This rhythm, Eisenstein thought, arose out of some controlling conceptual unity, in turn based on some powerful ideology—in his case, he insisted, Marxism, but probably any strongly held personal view of the world would do. Out of this, quite naturally, there would arise unifying images and symbols, items that might have helped, in the particular instance of *Intolerance*, to unite the four stories organically through visual analogies. What the Russian had in mind were what he liked to call "montage tropes," juxtapositions of two or more images to create a meaning larger than the sum of its parts, the equivalent, in imagery, of a figure of speech. This is the sort of thing at which Eisenstein himself was supremely gifted as a director, and it was from such visual metaphors that works like *The Battleship Potemkin*, the next great advance in the spectacular cinema, derived their uncanny power. But as Eisenstein wrote: "Griffith's cinema does not know this type of montage construction. His close-ups create atmosphere, outline traits of characters, alternate in dialogues of the leading characters, and close-ups of the chaser and the chased speed up the tempo of the chase. But Griffith at all times remains on the level of *representation* and *objectivity* and nowhere does he try through the juxtaposition of shots to shape *import* and *image* [Eisenstein's italics]." As the Soviet director notes, the only thing remotely resembling this sort of image-making in *Intolerance* is the recurring shot of Lillian Gish rocking the cradle, which does not really work as a satisfying linking device. Neither it nor anything else in *Intolerance* provides a "fusion" of the four stories in "a single imagist generalization," a "unified, powerful, generalized image" of what the director means to say about "intolerance."[34]

We need not insist on a Marxist or any other ideological interpretation of Griffith's theme to feel the lack of a truly thoughtful underpinning to Griffith's drama. Nor need we imagine that the general public actively missed such a controlling principle. Rather, it is that all of us, sophisticated and unsophisticated alike, sense it when works of art do not exhibit a strong emotional connection between the artist and his material, the kind of connection Griffith could not help but make with *The Birth of a Nation,* for example. The connection he made with the Babylonian sequence, which had more to do with technique and ambition, does not carry with it this charge. It occurs only in the modern story, where Griffith's simple compassion for his characters and his hatred of the forces oppressing them does deeply inform the work and carry us along on the strength of his emotions. Indeed, except when we are being intermittently overwhelmed by the Babylonian sequence, we find ourselves longing to get back to the Dear One and the Boy, annoyed by distractions from their story.

And we can blame no one but Griffith, finally, for this failure, just as, finally, he must accept the blame for the racist implications of *Birth.* His fatal flaw as an artist was his intellectual shallowness, his headlessness about what he was saying (and not saying) thematically as he told his stories. It would be a constant and growing problem in his work in the years to come—his confident belief that he was dealing with great themes, his utter failure to do so at any but the most primitive and sentimental level. For as the cinema in general grew more intellectually advanced, more capable of dealing subtly with ideas, or at least with subtly developed views of human nature, Griffith's cinema began to seem underdressed, its melodramatic essence almost nakedly exposed. As a result it began to seem more obviously "old-fashioned," out of date, particularly to the intellectual trend-setters.

At this stage of Griffith's career, this issue is not yet a crucial one. The richness of his film, its position as a summarizing statement of all his—and others'—developments in technique to this time, what it suggested about the possibilities for a further broadening of the screen's scope, were enough to override doubts, to carry the day with people who cared about the art of the film—and to ensure *Intolerance's* continuing position in the history of the medium as one of its noblest, and for various reasons, inimitable, experiments.

Nor can we yet say that *Intolerance* marked an irrevocable turning point in Griffith's career, an experience that would turn him forever away from work in his best vein, that is to say, the intimate drama. If he deliberately buried in *Intolerance* one of his finest works of that kind (*The Mother and the Law*), we also know that throughout his career he would be drawn back to these smaller, more naturalistic stories, caught endlessly in conflict between his natural affinity for this kind of filmmaking and the seductive but inflationary demands of spectacle. We now know that it is almost inevitable for movie people, having known the heady experience of a surprise success of immodest proportions, to try immediately to top themselves. The temptation is almost irresistible. Since Griffith's time we have seen men as diverse as David O. Selznick, Orson Welles, Francis Ford Coppola and Michael Cimino fall into confusion, bombast, self-delusion as, in the wake of movies like *Gone With the Wind, Citizen Kane, The Godfather* and *The Deer Hunter*, they succumb to the spell of their own temporarily inflated reputations, believe there is no limit to their power to translate their visions into films, and then compel awed attention to those films. As he pioneered so many other things, Griffith between *Birth* and *Intolerance* was pioneering this near-megalomaniac syndrome also—and with the same disappointing results that others would discover in time to come, when they exceeded the medium's limits, the audience's limits, their own limits.

But contrary to the conventional wisdom about Griffith's life and career, *Intolerance* no more broke him spiritually than it did financially. Seeing that it was going to be a financial failure, and perhaps sensing as well that what people were praising, and what history would best remember about his film, was not the work itself but the unprecedented effort that went into it, Griffith set about converting it from what he had hoped it would be, a turning point in film history, into something it also was not quite, a turning point in his personal history, that moment in his personal mythology at which visionary genius was thwarted by an uncomprehending world. In her autobiography Lillian Gish quotes a letter she says she received from Griffith in which he told her of wandering through darkened theaters, barking his shins on the empty seats. "I don't know where to go or where to turn since my great failure," she claims he wrote.[35]

It is a line that nearly everyone who has written about Griffith has followed, but his behavior in the months that followed the release of *Intolerance* was not that of a man lost and crying out in the wilderness. The royalties from *Birth* were still flowing in, and there were other prosperous contracts (including the one with Triangle) still in force. Beyond that, as we would now say, he remained eminently "bankable." Other studios and distributors continued to woo him with undiminished fervor and his satisfying activities as perhaps the most prestigious public spokesman for the motion picture industry continued unabated.

It is true that right after the film was released Griffith promised that he was "going to some lonely spot where I can be all by myself and rest. I am going to do a lot of thinking."[36] It is also true that he gave out an interview in which he said that *Intolerance* would be his last picture. He said that the kind of battle he had been forced to fight when *Birth* was released "makes it impossible to ask investment of the tremendous sums of money for a real feature film with the result dependent on the whim or the lack of brains of the captain of police." He observed that inexpensive films, the equivalent of the old ten-twent-thirt melodramas, could perhaps be produced without undue official interference in their exhibition, but these, naturally, did not interest him. On the other hand, large-scale endeavors calling vast attention to themselves created too "stupid, cruel, costly" battles with the censors. He said in this widely quoted interview that he would go back to the theater because "I believe only the stage can tell the whole truth."[37]

But this mood, a combination of exhaustion and his continuing outrage over censorship, soon passed, especially when he saw that *Intolerance* would cause no controversy beyond the esthetic. By December, when a reporter asked him if he was really contemplating quitting the movies, he was able to say that he was only thinking about that among other options. "I have been tempted greatly by Rome," he said. "But when I think of the troubles and the terrible financial risks of putting on Babylon . . . I feel like saying, 'get thee behind me Satan.' "[38] But his very lightness of tone indicated he was not seriously thinking small, that he was still looking for something on a scale suitable to his new status.

While he looked he wandered, overseeing openings of *Intolerance*, being ceremoniously received by his old ally in the fight against censorship, New York's Governor Whitman, for whom he supervised a short campaign film, continuing to lobby and lecture in Washington (and elsewhere) against censorship, appearing before Chicago's suffragettes, who pleaded with him to make a film about the fight for women's rights (he pretended interest, but nothing came of it). Along the way, he found time to continue his squabbles with Aitken. When the financier let Mae Marsh slip away to Samuel Goldwyn (still called Goldfish at the time) Griffith fired off a telegram suggesting "YOU ATTEND TO MANAGING THE TRIANGLE WHICH IS CONCEDED TO BE THE WORST MANAGED BUSINESS IN FILM HISTORY. . . ."[39] Not long thereafter he would claim that the use of his name as supervisor of Triangle releases that he did not actually direct was done without his knowledge; that all his energies had been absorbed by *Intolerance*, which is not quite true, there being plenty of evidence that he participated as planner and trouble-shooter on a number of the program features.

Still, that public declaration of his lack of interest in the routine Triangle pictures (in an interview granted a very young Louella Parsons, then working in Chicago) was a signal to Aitken that Griffith had lost what little confidence he still had in him. By the spring of 1917, he would have signed with one of Aitken's bitterest rivals, Zukor, and, more significantly, he would be embarked on yet another large-scale production, a film that was, in its way, as important in his career, and certainly in the development of a sense of his own greatness, as either *The Birth of a Nation* or *Intolerance*. In short, the commercial failure of Griffith's "Sun Play of the Ages" in no sense diminished his celebrity or sobered his increasingly grand public manner or stayed him from pursuing whatever creative visions suggested themselves. On March 17, 1917, just weeks before the United States entered World War I, Griffith sailed for England and into the closest encounter of his life with the shaping forces of modern history. It was an encounter he undertook with the fullest confidence.

CHAPTER TWELVE

"A Drama of Humanity"

DOCUMENTATION on the point is sketchy, but it seems clear that some-time in the early winter of 1916–17 Griffith was approached by the British War Office Cinematograph Committee with the idea of producing a feature about the war—most particularly about its effect on ordinary citizens. Implicit in this offer was the possibility that men and matériel would be placed at Griffith's disposal for the more spectacular battle sequences; better still, there was the possibility that he would be allowed to go to the trenches and obtain documentary footage there.

The offer could not have been more timely. On the basis of early box office returns, he had passed the fall of 1916 savoring the prospect that *Intolerance* would be another great commercial success. By the beginning of the new year, however, the drop in its business began to look irreversible, especially since Griffith deepened the problems his mixed reviews and often mystified audience response presented him by hesitating too long before taking the picture out of its expensive road show engagements and placing it in wider general release. This practice of limited release at advanced prices, so successful with *Birth*, so satisfying to his increasingly imperious ego, which demanded that a Griffith picture be treated as something special—an event—would betray him now and in years ahead. The financial records of this period show, week in, week out, dwindling but still good ticket sales being offset by the cost of employing full orchestras in expensive theaters on these road show engagements. Receipts were further diminished by the limited number of times the picture could play (twice a day) under this policy.

There was obviously a temptation to put all this behind him and begin looking to the future. This was particularly so given Griffith's sense that the time had come to part company with Harry Aitken. The financial pressures under which Triangle had been laboring had obviously con-

340

tributed greatly to the strains between them during the production of *Intolerance.* These pressures had not diminished with its release. Very simply, Aitken's backing was insufficient for the ambitious production schedule his three principal producers had been promised. Sennett and Ince were as restive as Griffith by this time. The Aitken brothers' story in this period is of a desperate scuttle not only to find more investors but to retain the stars their various companies had under contract. Each time one of these came up for renewal, however, the competition, often led by Adolph Zukor, who had been the first to raise the stakes in the star wars when he gave Mary Pickford first a $100,000 a year contract, then (in 1916) a $10,000 per week contract (plus perquisites), countered with a better offer.

At one point in 1916, Harry Aitken had convened a meeting at his Culver City lot during which he invited Zukor and the Jesse L. Lasky–Sam Goldfish partnership to join with him in creating what would have been the first great consolidation of motion picture power. His competitors declined, though Zukor and Lasky (without Goldwyn) did, indeed, join forces a little later. Thereafter Aitken went to distributors and to Wall Street for more financing and obtained it only by surrendering, bit by bit, operating control of this company. By 1918, Triangle was in bankruptcy, suits and countersuits between various principals were in the courts, and the Aitken brothers had passed from the stage. They retreated to Waukesha, Wisconsin, whence they had come, made a modest living distributing *Birth* and dreamed of a remake. The handsome classical colonnade they had erected to form the Washington Boulevard boundary of their studio still guards the M-G-M lot. It is their one monument.

About his partners' fate, however, Griffith cared little. When his old suitor Zukor, whose Famous Players company was flourishing, approached him with an offer of a generous production contract with his Artcraft subsidiary, he quickly acquiesced. The arrangements were similar to those the director had enjoyed with Triangle. He would be free to make a "big picture," a right he would immediately exercise in order to complete the film the British government proposed, with his own company handling the initial road show release, Zukor getting general release rights in return for financing. But he was obliged to personally direct six smaller features, not to cost more than $175,000 apiece, while overseeing the rest of his company's output. The difference, of course, was that Zukor was both better financed and better organized than the Aitkens. In later years Harry Aitken would claim that, in a last attempt to retain Griffith, he had offered him a block of Triangle stock, equivalent to his own holdings. Wisely, Griffith declined; within a year the paper would be worthless. He did, however, delay making a public announcement of his deal with Zukor until the day he sailed for England aboard the *Adriatic.* Before leaving, he presented Lillian Gish and her mother with a package wrapped in old newspapers, not even tied with a string. He said it was all that he had in the world—hardly true—and asked them to place it in safekeeping for him. They assumed that it was bonds and cash and placed the bundle in a safe deposit box for him.

If, then, there were sound business reasons to leave town for a while, there was an equally excellent excuse for his choice of destinations, for *Intolerance* was about to premiere in London, at the famous old Drury Lane, which had never shown a picture before playing *Birth* in 1915. If his discussions with the British government did not work out, this grand occasion provided a more-than-adequate rationale for the trip. Personally, of course, he had every reason to look forward to the journey. There could be no question of his reception as a figure of world stature. *Birth* had been a great success in London ("loathsome black horrors," an obviously titillated Lady Cynthia Asquith wrote in her diary; "I am most haunted by the black hands coming through the door of the besieged cottage"[1]). Griffith had reason to expect her class—the political, social and intellectual elite—to turn out for him, which they most splendidly did.

One gains a sense from his remarks throughout this period that Griffith, given the warrior lineage he was so prone to exaggerate, felt an obligation to study the Great War at close hand. It is too much to say that he felt guilty about pursuing his own preoccupations since the start of that war. But he was, by common consent, the world's pre-eminent director of military spectacle, and he had not yet addressed himself to what was, by increasingly common consent, the largest and most brutal war of all time. One cannot help but think that Griffith had been up to now well out of it. From 1915 onward, most movies about the European conflict had stressed the need for preparedness (*The Battle Cry of Peace*, *The Fall of a Nation*, with a typically inflammatory script by Thomas Dixon), and even pacifistic works like *Civilization* contrived to be anti-German. These were the sort of ludicrously "important" statements that it is best for any director to avoid, and that was particularly true of Griffith, with the bombastic and self-important side of his nature now increasingly at the ready.

Nevertheless, one likes to think there is some truth in the story that Griffith had sketched an outline of a contemporary war drama over two years before he sailed for Britain. His first (and entirely official) biographer, Robert E. Long, who was one of Griffith's publicists when he wrote a pamphlet-size life of his employer in 1920, has Griffith reading a news account of French families being driven from their homes as the war came near in December 1915, and "even in the midst of his most active work, over and over again recording in his mind the incidents of the news report." According to Long, Griffith was so taken with the idea that he kept working at it nights, even on into the dawn's early light, while shooting *Intolerance*, "adding a touch here, an elaboration there. . . ."[2] Long's account is plausible, if only because stories of families dislocated by war and its consequences—as his had been—always touched Griffith. He was, indeed, filming such a story—the Huguenot section of *Intolerance*—as he sketched this one.

His remarks upon landing in Britain indicate that Griffith felt he was, however belatedly, arriving where he belonged: "In one way, this is indeed a great day to be alive. In another terrible. It is terrible when you see the things you must see and feel the things you must feel. [But] it is the most terrific moment in the history of the world. We used to wish that we could have experienced the days of Caesar and Napoleon. And now incomparably greater times are taking place all around us."[3]

The interview rings strange to modern ears. The notion of World War I as a heroic or romantic enterprise was soon to be shattered by those of the English and French literary generation who survived the slaughter on the Western Front and began writing their grim and disillusioned memoirs and novels almost as soon as they were demobbed. From their writings has grown the now unquestioned view of "The Great War" as an event that put an end to the sentiments and sureties of the Victorian Epoch, and as *the* event against which the spirit we think of as "modernism" formed as a reaction. Henceforth every great artist, including those of the cinema, would begin to experience personal, social and cultural life as a kind of chaos, to find themselves and their world in a state of perpetual disintegration, with such renewals as they discovered tentative and temporary, anguished and ambivalent.

Given his nature, Griffith would have been incapable of picking up such clues as might have been available to him about this fundamental change in perception. And, of course, his hosts—official Britain—had every reason to avoid bringing it to his attention. What they had in mind was for him to make a picture that would aid their extensive efforts to draw America into the war, a picture that would stress the sadistic brutality of the German enemy but would not, of course, hint at the mass stupidity and unredeemed horror of trench warfare.

In short, Griffith had arrived at the very event that would undo the cultural consensus that had formed his sensibility and informed all his work. But he would emerge from this encounter essentially oblivious to the nature of the war and to the effect it was having on the young generation that bore its brunt. Worse, his reception in Britain would have the effect of further aggrandizing himself in his own eyes and drawing him still further from the best sources of his art.

2

The London premiere of *Intolerance* was a great success, perhaps not least because it took place on Saturday, April 7, one day after the United States had entered the war. To some degree, Griffith was the symbolic recipient of British gratitude for this desperately desired intervention. In his curtain speech, Griffith was typically false-modest, promising "to do better next time" if his audience "did not like it." He also played gently on the sentiments of the crowd, which included the likes of Sir Thomas Beecham and Sir Johnston Forbes-Robertson, the actor, as well as representatives of the hereditary peerage, confessing, "This is my first visit to England, but with what little I have seen I am already very much in love with this land my forefathers left many years ago." He said the first girl he had ever fallen in love with was English—Em'ly in *David Copperfield*, which he claimed (untruthfully) he had to steal away to the garden to read since his parents disapproved of books "as a recreation for children." He concluded, to cheers, by saying: "But upon account of one other thing I am prouder to be upon this historic platform. The decision of Mr. Wilson to enter the great struggle now progressing is now known and I am happy to think my country will soon be taking part with yours in this great fight for freedom."[4]

The gross for the premiere was $500 higher than any that had ever been recorded for a single motion picture showing in England, and the next week Griffith was able to cable home: " 'INTOLERANCE' RECEPTION GREATEST IN DRURY LANE HISTORY. CHEERS AND APPLAUSE AFTER FIRST ACT LASTED SEVEN MINUTES. EVERYONE CERTAIN IT IS TREMENDOUS TRIUMPH. SPLENDID ADVANCE BOOKINGS AND SUNDAY NEWSPAPER REVIEWS PRAISE IT UNANIMOUSLY."[5] That praise, however, was tempered, as it had been in the United States, with reflections that perhaps Griffith had tried to do too much, that, putting it nicely, there were more wonders in *Intolerance* than could be comfortably encompassed in a single viewing. And again, as at home, business declined rapidly after the surge of the opening weeks.

Griffith, of course, was preoccupied with matters more pressing than box office receipts at the Drury Lane. And, as was becoming increasingly the case with him now, a certain mythomania accompanied him on his rounds—and in his later recollections of them. Various sources have him in Paris the night before the *Intolerance* opening, then rushing back to London and trying to enlist. Still others have him consulting with "the gifted men of England"—Barrie, Wells, Shaw, Bennett, Galsworthy, Chesterton—as to what his contribution to the war might best be, with them advising him to enlist his genius in the cause, producing "a drama of humanity, photographed in the battle area."[6] Still others speak of

Lloyd George summoning him to 10 Downing Street and urging him to make a film that would "make up America's mind to go to war for us"— a request obviated, of course, by the events of April 6.

More likely the matter was simpler than that. Lord Beaverbrook, the press lord who was to become a lifelong friend, had recently taken over the cinematograph office and doubtless he initiated the invitation to come to Britain. It is also reasonable to surmise that from the outset he had more in mind than a simple documentary, that he wanted a large and spectacular Griffith production, something with great mass appeal. It is also likely that the visit had as its purpose completing arrangements for a fictional feature, not initiating them, and that Griffith's introductions to literary England and to the Prime Minister, as well as his presentation to Queen Alexandra, which he "again and again" told a hagiographer was "my greatest moment,"[7] were all arranged by Beaverbrook in his role of a good host seeking a favor.

Mostly all this went splendidly. Shaw turned a little cranky, according to Griffith, when in the course of trying to press a manuscript upon him that the writer thought was suitable motion picture material, he also began lecturing Griffith on what was wrong with American films. Griffith claimed he left this luncheon as quickly as possible to avoid an argument. But Lloyd George, another humbly born man who loved hobnobbing with the celebrated, lingered over breakfast with him, delaying a cabinet meeting so that they could finish their conversation. Whether it was at this meeting or at one of the others Griffith enjoyed with the Prime Minister it is impossible to say, but at some point Lloyd George proposed that Griffith could do a great wartime service by taking seriously Winston Churchill's ideas for film scenarios. It would occupy the author of the Dardanelles disaster with another sort of authorship and still his criticism of the conduct of the war. One also cannot pinpoint the date of a reported exchange between them about what the politician called the "mediocrity" of the American mind, to which Griffith replied that, after all, our civilization was based on English culture and that we had to work within the limits thus imposed. In any event, it is obvious they liked each other, and before leaving for home Griffith recorded a scene of him shaking hands with the Prime Minister outside 10 Downing Street. It was used as a prologue to *Hearts of the World*, with a subtitle claiming the director was being wished well as he set forth to make his movie.

As for his meeting with Alexandra, Griffith would recall a certain nervousness at the encounter, but he found her graciously pleased to put him at ease by touching his sleeve and seeking his opinion on the state of the British film industry. At this time he began meeting a number of titled and socially prominent women who would later join with the Dowager Queen to appear before his camera in footage that was, in its way, more unprecedented than anything he shot at the front.

All this attests to Griffith's stature. No other producer or director—for that matter, few stars—could have commanded the kind of reception he was accorded in wartime Britain, which had preoccupations far greater than the comfort of film folk. He was right to look back on his wartime visits to England as the pinnacle of his public life.

After the *Intolerance* opening he was given passage to France on a British destroyer and taken up to the lines, where photographs, both still and movie, were taken of him in the trenches. These were shot so as to give the impression that he was visiting the most forward positions. But Kevin Brownlow reports that the footage of Griffith that still exists in the Imperial War Museum archives is unconsciously comic in effect.

"The center of Ypres by 1917 has been so heavily shelled that the cathedral-like Cloth Hall has been blasted to a slender Islamic minaret. The other buildings, too, have been knocked into such extraordinarily delicate fingers of stone that there seems no way for them to remain vertical. Into this chilling scene steps a tall, jaunty figure in a smart tweed suit of English cut, a bow-tie—and a tin hat. It is David Wark Griffith, recorded by a British official cameraman on his tour of the front."

It is, says Brownlow, like a scene from H. G. Wells's *Time Machine*. "Griffith, dressed for a grouse shoot, appears to be on a thoroughly pleasant afternoon outing in the midst of the bloodiest war in history." There follow various surrealist bits: Griffith tagging along with a group of surly-looking French *poilus* to a half-finished trench they are working on, peering in to watch them, then comically miming their digging motions; Griffith stumbling into a heavily shelled dugout, stumbling over some rubble, disappearing, then emerging to signal "cut" to the cameraman; Griffith and party entering a trench, alleged to be but 60 yards from enemy positions, the rest of the party pretending to duck as a shell is supposed to come in, but Griffith remaining imperiously, and heroically, upright, his dignity—and his image—intact. At various points in the unedited footage, says Brownlow, one can observe the participants standing stock still, awaiting the call to "action" before beginning their carefully planned activities.[8]

Griffith, of course, had a different tale to tell when he returned to the United States and began recounting his war stories to the press. Whether these adventures occurred on this preliminary expedition or later, when he actually shot a few moments that would be included in *Hearts of the World*, is unclear, but there is no doubt Griffith tended to exaggerate their extent. The basic story on which he embroidered various details at various times has him inspecting a trench in company with a British officer who was wearing a new and shiny pair of boots he did not want to muddy by going down into the trenches. Strolling along the top of the parapet, the two men attracted the attention of German observers, who lobbed a shell in their direction. It landed, according to Griffith, some 20 yards from him, but proved to be a dud. It, however, encouraged his escort to dive into the trench. In some versions of the story the dud was but a prelude to a bombardment that lasted the rest of the day. In others another officer came along and threatened to arrest Griffith on the ground that he might be a spy since he wasn't in uniform. In all versions Griffith recorded gratitude to the enemy, for the trench in which he sheltered was a German trench, recently captured by the Allies, and was, as he put it, dug deeply and well, providing, as he thought, better protection than the French and British emplacements.[9] It is the repetition of this incident, however varied his versions of it, that leads one to think that, at least once, Griffith was actually under fire somewhere near the front lines. But, as we shall see, he was never able to convert his observations into anything more than anecdotes; no vision of the singular and unprecedented nature of this war ever emerged from him.

Still, it would do for his purposes, and immediately upon his return to London he set production plans in motion. A cable was dispatched to Lillian Gish and, accompanied by her mother, she sailed for England aboard the *St. Louis,* an American ship bearing an early contingent of doctors and nurses to the war zone. On May 28, Dorothy Gish, Bobby Harron and Billy Bitzer followed aboard the *Baltic.* One of their fellow passengers was General John J. Pershing, on his way to prepare the way for the American Expeditionary Force, which he would command. He recognized Dorothy Gish and confessed that he was made nervous by the need to appear before newsreel cameras and she agreed to coach him in camera manners. With Bitzer she spent a cheerful afternoon photographing the general.

Griffith, meanwhile, had not been idle. Using government cameramen, he shot on the Salisbury Plain, where there were large British encampments, and he also used Lady Ripon's estate at Coombe Hill, Kingston, as well as the Army and Navy Hospital for footage that showed a number of aristocratic ladies setting aside their lighter occupations in order to do war work. It was in one of these sequences that the Dowager Queen made a brief appearance before Griffith's camera. More than one of these ladies had hopes of screen careers developing out of this work. Elizabeth Asquith, for instance, had heard from Augustus John, before Griffith arrived, that he might be doing *Morte d'Arthur* and judged it might be "just my chance," to turn her "medieval type" to account. Similarly, Lady Diana Manners, with whom Griffith was so smitten that he offered her a contract, found that she could never quite tell this "oddly reserved American" that she "very much wanted to tour America as an actress." (She did, in Max Reinhardt's *The Miracle,* for five years.)

Alas for careerism amongst the titled classes! It is dubious that Griffith ever even intended that they appear in the major work that he was beginning, the film eventually entitled *Hearts of the World.* More likely, he was shooting for a project called *Women and the War*, which never materialized. This footage, together with other odds and ends, reached the screen in a later, more modest Griffith film, *The Great Love*, their example of devotion to the cause inspiring its hero to greater exertion. But the film has been lost, and all that remains of it are a number of publicity stills attesting to the presence of the great ladies, most of whom were great beauties, working for the visiting celebrity.

When his principals and his cameraman arrived, however, Griffith got down to more serious work. It was not just a matter of shooting, it was a matter of study as well. For in the wartime capital the little group of Americans found an emotional intensity, generated by a population caught up in great and terrible events that they had not observed anywhere before. Lillian Gish's account of these days carries a sense of excitement, and of tragedy observed, that is quite striking.

London was under attack from the air, by both dirigibles and conventional aircraft, much of the time Griffith and his company were there. Since the group was quartered in the Savoy, hard by the Thames, they were often in a position to see the enemy as the Germans flew up the river toward their targets, and more than once they were able to inspect the damage. Once, after a night raid, the cries of the wounded rose to them from the street, where a bomb had demolished a tram. During a daylight raid they were able to see where the bombs had struck and to arrive on the scene where a nursery school had been hit, killing close to a hundred children. All, including Griffith, wept, and Lillian Gish would recall him saying, "This is what war is. Not the parades and the conference tables—but children killed, lives destroyed."[10]

Griffith encouraged the Gish sisters to observe life closely as it was being lived under wartime pressures and dangers in London. "It's only in wartime that emotions are off-guard," he told them, and they spent hours at Victoria and Waterloo stations, where the troops began their journey to the war, and through which the wounded passed on their way to hospitals and homes in England. The poignancy of the departures, the horror of many of the returns, were memories they would not shake. On one stroll Griffith spotted a young Londoner swinging along with a remarkable stride, loose-shouldered, something carefree and defiant about it, and the director and his star followed the chap for something like an hour, until Lillian was sure she could imitate the walk and demonstrate it for Dorothy, who indeed used something quite like it in her role of the Little Disturber in *Hearts*.

It is not entirely clear how much of the film Griffith shot in England made it into the finished version of *Hearts of the World*. We know that Griffith shot peaceful exteriors for the prewar sequences of his film by doubling such English villages as Stanton, in Worcestershire, and Shere, in Surrey, for Ham, where he worked later in France and which, since it had been shelled, was used for a few exteriors in the wartime portions of the story. But matching sets were built for additional photography in California the following fall and early winter and it is difficult to tell the real from the mock settings. In Stanton another famous life crossed Griffith's when Noël Coward was engaged, at a pound per day, to appear as a village youth pushing a wheelbarrow in a scene with Lillian Gish. The experience left little mark on Coward, he would later write, "beyond a most unpleasant memory of getting up at five every morning and making my face bright yellow, and a most pleasant memory of Lillian, Dorothy and Mrs. Gish, who were remarkably friendly and kind to me."[11] Still, his youthful image survived Griffith's final cut, and that is more than one can say for the material he so famously shot in France.

Indeed, the question of how much time Griffith actually spent in France, working on his film, is the most vexing problem it presents. Certainly it was not the "seven months" that the newspaper stories all mentioned when he returned to the United States. Nor even the vaguer "months" Lillian Gish suggests in her autobiography. Such records as there are indicate that Griffith returned to France for no more than two weeks in the fall of 1917, and despite Gish's insistence that her sister and her mother, as well as Harron, made the trip, there is no other evidence that they did. Bitzer says flatly that neither he nor the others went with Griffith, though Bitzer says he traveled by himself on a flying trip, to get some aerial footage around Le Bourget, which he was supposed to supervise but not take, but which he ended up shooting after all when the French pilot mistook some signals and headed skyward with the cameraman clinging to a perch on his wing. There is also no definitive evidence in the *Hearts* footage that survives (it was presented in varying American, British and French versions and was also shortened for general release after its road show engagements and changed again, to be less anti-German, after the peace) that Griffith and his actors shot for any length of time in France. Since Lillian Gish has often somewhat embellished the facts about Griffith's activities, and has some interest in maintaining the most heroic possible version of Griffith's wartime activities, it is hard to credit her tale of lengthy toil within range of the guns. Yet one cannot dismiss, entirely, the richly detailed accounts of her wartime trip to France, not only in her autobiography but in the 1932 *Life and Lillian Gish*, a biographical enterprise in which she obviously fully cooperated— even to the extent of providing diary entries to the writer, Albert Bigelow Paine (who was also Mark Twain's biographer and literary executor). She recounts how Bitzer had to be left behind because of the suspiciously Germanic name (Johann Gottlieb Wilhelm) on his passport; how she helped Griffith to obtain the necessary papers for the rest of the group by charming an official at the American embassy in London whose wife had taught her Sunday school back home in Ohio; how the ship carrying them across the channel was turned back three times by the threat of mines en route; how they arrived in Paris at night and Griffith insisted on immediately touring the city, which was blacked out, on the ground that never again would there be an opportunity to see it by moonlight, since the lights would be turned on again after the war; how, that evening, at Napoleon's tomb, Griffith confessed that perhaps he had been "stretching my talents" in *Intolerance*. It is certain that Gish and Griffith attained Paris and lingered in its environs long enough to do some shooting. About the rest of the party's presence there one is necessarily much less certain.

One's doubts stem largely from the fact that the only scene in *Hearts* (or any of the other films Griffith carved from his wartime trip) in which both France and a leading player are unmistakably recognizable involves Gish and Gish alone. It would have been unprecedented for Griffith to have taken his other principals to such a singular location and then not employ them. Beyond that, anecdotes about the others are vague in both Gish books; the vivid incidents and all the dialogue in direct quotation belong to Gish and Griffith exclusively. It seems possible she might have invented companions in order to protect propriety—not that one suspects its opposite, given that these were public people engaged in a highly public activity in highly public, officially sanctioned capacities. Still, it was a time when respectable young women did not join 42-year-old men on foreign travels, even on serious business, without at least nodding at convention. But whatever her feelings about Griffith, the film makes his infatuation with her clear. In *Birth* she was very much part of an ensemble; in *Intolerance* she was a mere symbol; but here her story is central, and the camera caresses her as never before.

Ham, on the Somme, the only certainly identifiable French location in the finished film, had been overrun by the Germans early in the war and had been retaken later. According to Gish, they were once nearly caught in a rolling barrage, and she also reports that Griffith claimed that on a separate expedition with his cameraman two of their guides were killed and a group of men they were supposed to meet were "obliterated" by shelling (this story, however, appears in no other account of Griffith's journey to the war). There are, as well, tales of motor trips through ruined fields and burned-out orchards, of sheltering from artillery fire in the basement remains of shelled homes, of the constant rumble of the guns, night and day, worse to Gish, in its constancy, than the sudden alarms caused by the air raids on London.

They sailed from England within a matter of days after their return from the war zone and landed in New York on October 16, after an uneventful passage home. By early November all were assembled in California with others of the Griffith company, including George Siegmann, once again playing the heavy, and Ben Alexander, later to find a larger fame as Sergeant Joe Friday's sidekick on "Dragnet," who was to play a child who never ages in the drama that covered more than four years in a French family's life. Also present for minor roles were such old Griffith hands as Adolphe Lestina, Kate Bruce and Josephine Crowell.

On his way to the Coast, Griffith paused to acquire some footage of the German army in action that had been in the possession of a Captain von Kleinschmidt, who had used it in lectures before America's entrance into the war and who now stood accused of espionage. Griffith spent the considerable sum of $16,000 on this material, then was warned against using it by Banzhaf, his attorney, who apparently feared legal and public relations repercussions, should it be discovered that money had changed hands between Griffith and the alleged "spy." Other footage was purchased from a short-subject producer, but it is curious, given the British War Office's interest in the project, that he was not given access to its rich library of captured footage. Perhaps he did not discover his need for this material until he returned to the United States and it was too late to ask London for assistance.

Griffith's other major acquisition during his New York stopover was Erich von Stroheim, just then at liberty and gathering his forces for the assault on Hollywood that would shortly turn him into a legendary figure. He had, of course, been an assistant and small-parts player on *Birth* and *Intolerance*, then had received his first screen credit as an assistant director when he worked with John Emerson on the *Macbeth* which Sir Herbert Beerbohm-Tree had made for Triangle, and which Griffith had "supervised" from as great a distance as possible. Von Stroheim had stayed with Emerson as an assistant and sometime actor, the while receiving other roles in the cycle of anti-German films that gathered continually mounting force during the war years. He played the heinous Hun in such epics as *Sylvia of the Secret Service* (with Irene Castle in the title role), *For France* (his first large role) and *The Unbeliever*, among others. Then, so the story goes, he moved back East, to work with Allan Dwan as an assistant and as an actor on Douglas Fairbanks's *His Picture in the Papers*. He was dispatched to acquire some explosives needed for an action sequence. He could not, apparently, resist employing his deepest Germanic accent and his most hatefully imperious manner in dealing with the clerk selling the munitions. The clerk called the authorities the minute von Stroheim left and they made an embarrassing scene for him at the studio. Fairbanks, who might normally have been amused by the episode, was passionately committed to the Allied cause, and when work on the picture was completed he fired von Stroheim.

There followed a period in which a disheartened actor was reduced to cheap lodgings and a deep depression, even pawning his overcoat to survive. It was at this time, with idle hours to fill, that he first read Frank Norris's *McTeague*, the novel that would form the basis for his masterpiece, *Greed*. Then, however, a doctor friend of his noticed a newspaper account of Griffith's return and suggested von Stroheim go see his old mentor. The actor was, he later claimed, reluctant to do so, given his unhappy frame of mind, but the good doctor prepared a mysterious injection for him (doubtless some primitive form of speed) and it put a definite spring in von Stroheim's stride. He appeared at Griffith's New York office and did a very smart click of the heels and his most courtly bow. "For you, Mr. Griffith, I would work for a ham sandwich a day," von Stroheim said, and Griffith that night sent him on to Hollywood. With his organizational skills and his knowledge of European military customs, "Von" was just the man Griffith needed to help move his complex production along at the pace he and his business associates knew was required if it was to get into release before the market was entirely saturated with war films.[12]

In Los Angeles, confusion was more than usually rampant. Griffith intended to use his old Fine Arts studio as headquarters, it having apparently passed from the Aitkens' control into other hands. But word of his plans had not passed to the studio's new managers and they forbade Griffith's crew access to the lot for a time. At first the company was confined to the old Babylon set, still standing on the backlot across the street. It was in the forecourt of the mighty temple that small sets for the village interiors were built, to the specifications of a new designer, Charles Baker, a calm and gifted Englishman with a Cockney accent. According to Karl Brown, trenches (with rain pipes) were eventually dug on this lot, and a French street, matching the English streets on which Griffith had already shot, was also erected—this behind the temple set. Film was eventually supplied by Famous Players–Lasky, which would handle the picture's general release. Some material was shot on that studio's ranch, as well as on other Los Angeles locations.

Griffith, now smart in the tweedy English tailoring that he had learned to favor in London, was never more serene and confident, according to Brown. Yet he drove his people hard. Gish speaks of working until midnight on Christmas Eve and all day on Christmas. She and her family could not find time to gather around their tree and open their presents until almost New Year's, such was the pace of production. Still there was time for those small bits of perfectionism that were a Griffith trademark; it is said that he insisted that his players speak French—even if it was only nonsense French—when they were before the cameras, in order to confound the lip readers and add to the authenticity of their playing. And, it seems, everyone worked with a happy will. Only von Stroheim had cause for disappointment. For reasons never made clear, the role of the chief Prussian villain went to Siegmann, despite at least implicit promises that the eager von Stroheim would have it. He was seen actually to shed tears over this rejection when he sought consolation from friends on the lot. Of course, Siegmann was a reliable heavy, and one used to long parts. Or perhaps Griffith thought von Stroheim already over-exposed in what was to become for him virtually a patented role. Maybe he simply did not want his invaluable assistant distracted from his duties as a commander of extras by the demands of a long role. In any event, von Stroheim did not suffer for long; he went directly from this picture to *The Hun Within*, where he was once again the lead villain, menacing Dorothy Gish. It appears Griffith, supervising this picture, which was directed by his old friend Christy Cabanne for Zukor's program, gave von Stroheim the role as compensation for his *Hearts* disappointment. When it was finished "Von" went on without pause to a job as an assistant, and as a Prussian officer, in *The Heart of Humanity*, a near-plagiarism of Grif-fith's film, but one in which some authorities hold that the battle scenes, supervised by von Stroheim, were superior to Griffith's. More important, the picture was made at Universal, and von Stroheim used the opportunity to ingratiate himself with that studio's boss, Carl Laemmle, thus gaining the opportunity to direct his first film, *Blind Husbands*, based on a sce-nario he had been trying to sell for three years.

Griffith was able to begin editing shortly after the first of the year, with the picture scheduled for release in the early spring. The work on which he so engaged himself, with his customary concentration, is, of all Griffith's major films, perhaps the most difficult to evaluate. As William K. Everson notes, it is in plot and overall structure remarkably similar to *The Birth of a Nation*: ". . . the same family structure, the same separa-tions and reunions, the same editing patterns. . . ."[13] As almost anyone seeing it now and comparing it with actual footage from World War I will note, the picture has about it an air of unreality that is strangely dis-quieting. If, to be sure, the matching of his California footage and his English, French and purchased footage is quite seamless, if we feel no dislocations in the shifts from scene to scene, or shot to shot, we also do not feel ourselves firmly rooted in French soil, either. Moreover, in the combat sequences we do not gain any realistic sense of this war as it was actually fought. For Griffith, war had to be an enterprise of sweeping movement, and he seems not to have recognized, even after firsthand inspection, that World War I was, singularly and tragically, exactly the opposite—a war of stalemate and attrition. Curiously, the war he "fought" on screen was the war that many of the generals on both sides of the real thing kept fantasizing, and trying to position themselves for, a war in which a dramatic breakthrough, some bold and dashing stroke, would put an end to agony and waste.

Griffith seems to have recognized that this was not his kind of war. In a famous interview he granted in early 1918 to another friendly journal-ist who would soon be in his employ, he made the oft-quoted statement that "viewed as a drama, the war is in some ways disappointing." And again: "Promoters often boast of having made motion pictures for which the settings and actors cost a million dollars. The settings of the picture I took cost several billion dollars. . . . I think I will be able to make good the claim that I will use the most expensive stage settings that ever have been or ever will be used in the making of a picture." To have been as close as Griffith was to this war and to permit himself to sound so callous in quotation speaks volumes about how fame can lead to disastrous self-absorption and to the inability to perceive common reality. When one contrasts the general blandness of his view of this war with his impassioned defense of the Southern cause that he had mounted for *Birth*, it says something, as well, about the flaws in his nature.

To be sure, his callousness was somewhat mitigated by some of the other material in Harry C. Carr's article. When, for example, he claimed that he had found himself saying, "Why, this is old stuff. I have put that scene on myself so many times," he was referring not to combat but to sequences of departure and return, of loved ones caught up in the anxiety of leave-taking, or in the terrible mixed joys of welcoming home a wounded soldier and, of course, the more terrible sight of "women coming away from the government offices, stunned with grief, a little paper in their hands to tell the worst that had happened." Undeniably, he had previously done scenes of that character. And, undeniably, too, combat itself was not photogenic in the traditional sense. On this point, surprisingly, Griffith was more acute than his film indicates. The battle he claimed to have witnessed "looked like a meadow with two ditches in it and some white puffs of smoke and no signs of human life anywhere," and he added: "A modern war is neither romantic nor picturesque. . . . Everyone is hidden away in ditches. As you look out across No Man's Land there is literally nothing that meets the eye but an aching desolation of nothingness—or torn trees, ruined barbed wire fence and shell holes. . . . There is nothing but filth and dirt and the most soul sickening smells. The soldiers are standing sometimes almost up to their hips in ice cold mud. . . . It is too colossal to be dramatic."

Doubtless to justify the choices he had made for his film, he went on to point out that "the closer you get to the front, the less you know what is going on," and there is some truth in that observation, some truth in the notion that the overall shape of the drama, the coming of crises and their resolutions, was better perceived at headquarters, where information was collated, the changing disposition of all the troops more or less known. It is also true that such flow and movement as a camera might be able to record—such spectacle as this war offered—was better observed a few miles back, where one might film men and matériel moving forward, the casualties being brought back.[14]

But spectacle is, of course, only one dramatic form, and not generally the most subtle or interesting. Griffith had long ago demonstrated he was capable of another, more intimate and more humane form of drama. And it is that which he might have found had he approached this war without preconceptions, without a need to capitalize yet again on his reputation for, and commercial success with, moviemaking on a large scale. And if his head had not been so thoroughly turned by, and if he had not felt beholden to, official London and its official, and highly unrealistic, views of what this war was. We were, after all, only a few years from such theatrical successes as *Journey's End* and *What Price Glory?*, both as melodramatic as anything Griffith might have wished for, yet still a great deal more realistic than anything he managed, and reflective too, of the disillusionments that any perceptive artist, coming as late to the war as Griffith did, should have been able to sense.

Indeed, there is some evidence that he did see more than his film or his public utterances convey. Besides the infamous Carr interview, he gave another one that must be weighed in the balance. This occurred earlier, and was not timed, as Carr's was, to promote the film in the month of its release. It was given to Mae Tinee of the *Chicago Tribune* as he passed through that city on the way back from the war to the studio in Los Angeles. She inquired of him if, after a time in the trenches, one "grows used to the fear . . . sort of—well—comatose. . . ?"

"No," he replied, "not that. But the people over there become great actors. They talk and laugh and act much like the people over here, but it is acting, for the Great Fear is over everybody and everything."[15] So, he did see and sense more of the reality of this war than he usually let on. But there is a sadness that his huge effort could not have reflected more of the spirit of this interview.

There are mitigating factors. The treatment accorded him in Britain might well have addled even a less impressionable and ambitious man. And we can reflect that while the war was going on few popular artists of any calibre were immune to the call of a patriotism that required a blind faith in the justice of the Allied cause. And if *Hearts of the World* measures poorly against even our most rudimentary understanding of the historical events that it seeks to capture, as well as against the sober literature (and films) that later sought more honestly to invoke the Great War, it is still a reasonably good Griffith film, more assured than *Birth*, more controlled than *Intolerance* and perhaps somewhat more deeply felt than the later historical spectacles, *Orphans of the Storm* and *America*.

The two families destined to be separated by war in this film are both American in origin, living side by side as expatriates in a little French town on the eve of the war. Gish plays the only child of one family, Harron one of several sons of a none-too-successful painter. Again, as in *Birth*, the scenes of domestic tranquility are lovingly done, and are intended to form a vivid contrast to the carnage that is to come. In this Eden, only

Von Strohm—perhaps the name was suggested by von Stroheim's—a German "tourist" (Siegmann), suggests the fragility of everyone's contentment; he is altogether too devoted to his notes and his snapshots—clearly a spy (though there are no obviously significant military installations hereabouts). Most of the early portion of the film belongs to Dorothy Gish, as "the Little Disturber," a hoydenish street singer from Paris, bent on winning Harron away from Lillian Gish. Griffith permitted her to overplay, as he did every young woman he cast in what was, for him, a stock part. On the other hand, Dorothy Gish was by far the most naturally charming of his comediennes, and this role established for her a screen character on which much of her subsequent career would depend. There is a good-natured quality, quite unstrained as compared to some of Mae Marsh's efforts in a similar vein, that preserves her likability even when the story requires a certain improbability of behavior.

In any event, she switches her attention to another comic character, one Monsieur Cuckoo (Robert Anderson), and, on the eve of war, the Boy and the Girl (as the subtitles identify them) are about to be married. He, however, opts to fight for his adopted land ("any country worth living in is worth fighting for") and joins the French army. While he is away, the village is shelled by the advancing Germans and his father and the girl's mother and grandfather are killed. In shock, the Girl, clutching her wedding dress, wanders the battlefield, in what is, perhaps, the film's most compelling sequence, a splendid mad scene, in which Gish's fragility and her very subtle playing stand in moving contrast to the horrors she confronts. She comes upon the Boy, seriously wounded and unconscious, and they pass what should have been their wedding night together, in silent stillness. When she wanders off seeking aid, the Red Cross arrives and takes her lover away, and upon her return, she presumes him dead. Now she returns to the village, shelters in its inn (which is managed by a German sympathizer) and there is nursed back to sanity by the Little Disturber.

Thereafter, alas, the film begins to deteriorate to melodrama of a creaky and unpersuasive sort. The German advance having encompassed the village, its citizens are put to work as slave laborers, and the Girl, unable to do the heavy work in the fields, is beaten by a particularly nasty enemy sergeant. Even Gish found this sequence overblown, and she claimed that despite padding worn under her costume, the enthusiastically wielded knout bruised her flesh (though in the sequence as shown in surviving prints the blows appear to be few and held carefully in check). But there is yet more suffering to endure. The Boy's mother, despite the determined support of his three young siblings, dies of exhaustion, and it is only thanks to a reunion with the Girl, who steals food from the inn for them, that her children survive.

Meantime, the Boy, now recovered, volunteers for duty as a spy behind German lines. Disguised as a German officer, he spends two rain-filled days in shell hole, before he judges the time right to signal for a French attack. The sequence, Griffith claimed, was based on a true incident, and it must be said that it is the only portion of the film that gives one something like an authentic sense of modern warfare's terrors. Once he has completed his assignment, the Boy makes his way back to the village, still occupied by the Germans, and is there reunited with the Girl at last, but almost disastrously.

For they are discovered in the Girl's room by the same German sergeant who had previously administered the thrashing to Gish. Now as the Boy struggles with him, the Girl stabs him from behind and he staggers out, falling at the feet of Von Strohm. The sergeant has breath enough left to tell Von Strohm of the lovers' presence. Since he has lusted after the Girl since before the war, and had made an earlier attempt at rape (she was rescued by some German officers, one of whom thanked God the war had not turned everyone into beasts), he rushes to consummate, at last, his dreadful desire, this despite the fact that French troops are counter-attacking.

By this time the Boy and Girl have retreated to the attic, and the Boy promises to kill his lover before letting the German have his way with her. Crosscutting between the frightened youths, the sadistic German and the now rapidly advancing French column proceeds in the accustomed Griffith manner. The fate worse than death, or perhaps death itself, is avoided when the Little Disturber, observing the situation, tosses a hand grenade at Von Strohm just as he is about to burst through the door and just before the French arrive.

In bare outline the film, perhaps, sounds even less persuasive than it is on the screen, where Griffith's touches, and the good playing of his actors, ground the piece in a certain believability. Especially in this latter regard *Hearts* represents a continuing advance in Griffith's technique. Then, too, the cutting in the latter portions of the film rushes one right along, past various points of disbelief and clichés that verge on the ludicrous. Yet, the outlining is not unfair, either. It does suggest how wedded Griffith remained not only to the conventions of the rapidly expiring stage melodrama but to his peculiar views of human sexuality. To put the matter simply, the special horror of the Great War is not adequately symbolized by a case of rape narrowly (if suspensefully) averted. In considering this film it is hard to escape the feeling that just as Griffith had, at this time, reached the heights of his useful fame—that is to say, a fame that would help him to advance his work rather than separate him from the roots of his talent—so, too, one feels he is beginning to reach the end of his vision.

One has to be careful in making this point. In the fourteen years left to him as an active filmmaker he would offer at least four films that would summarize his virtues more clearly than anything he had accomplished up to this point, one of which would be, arguably, his finest sustained performance on a large scale. There would also be, very shortly, a film that would, stylistically, break fresh ground not only for him but for movies in general. There would be, right up to the end, even in his lesser works, bursts of pictorial beauty, honest observation and nostalgic charm which are both entrancing and disarming. Still, one is left with a sense that the essential flaw of *Hearts of the World* was the manifestation of an essential flaw in Griffith. The heart of *his* world was to be found in his obsessed sexuality, where there was no persuasive middle range between brutality and simpering blandness. In the end, no matter what their ostensible subject, no matter what other excitements and delights his pictures offered, he was usually manipulating his material as he did the stuff of his war film, in order to get at this, to him, mesmerizing matter. From this moment on, and with growing, impatient certainty, one feels his obsession limiting his vision, preventing it from reaching out toward a sustained and sensitive contemplation of the complexities of the male–female relationship in particular, the life of modern times in general.

3

This failure did not affect Griffith commercially or in the eyes of the reviewers. He had, yet, a few years of grace left to him, and *Hearts of the World* was in no sense a commercial failure. Indeed, its world premiere at Clune's in Los Angeles was as triumphant as any previous Griffith opening night had been. It appears, if we are to follow Karl Brown's account, that once Gish and Harron had been rescued, the shots of the advancing French were blended with sound effects of thousands of marching feet, at first a whisper in the distance, then growing louder and louder, with the sound of martial music now joining them. There must then have been some sort of dissolve, and then images of *American* soldiers began to pass beneath the window where Griffith's little band of survivors huddled. Now the pit orchestra was in full cry, joined by the thunderous theater organ, in "Over There." "The soldiers kept marching past that window, young and clean and incredibly fine after what we had seen of Siegmann and his hoglike Huns, and there seemed to be no end to them. On they came, more and more and more of them, and still more as the curtain closed and the picture was at an end."

It was, obviously, a great *coup de théâtre*, more evidence, if any is needed, that on the simplest level, Griffith was a highly skilled showman, capable of attacking an audience's emotions with the most direct of assaults. His last-minute work suggests a brilliant improvisation by Griffith, designed to relate his film to the immediate events of the day, and the immediate emotional concerns of an American audience much preoccupied by this nation's entrance into the war. According to Brown, there was no applause after the lights came up. "The people simply stared at one another, stunned by the experience. No elation. More of a grim setting of jaws and squaring of shoulders . . . a sober and determined crowd, unlike any I had ever seen before. Their blood was up and they didn't care who knew it."[16]

Whether this ending was retained for Griffith's road shows of the picture or for Zukor's release of it as a program feature is unknown. What is known is that the reviews were somewhat reserved. Brown's statement that "the general opinion, expressed in terms of hurt indignation, was that Griffith had botched his picture abominably" can in no sense be proved by consulting the newspapers of the day. Nor was there any general indignation over the fact that he had done "a made-to-order, government-sponsored, paid-in-advance *propaganda* picture" (italics his).[17] Propaganda was more or less what people expected of popular artists of this time, and it was held against none of them in a year in which anyone with a German name was held in suspicion, where German customs and tag phrases were being dismissed from ordinary usage. Only in the White House, where again Griffith arranged a special screening for the President, his family and aides, was there open criticism of the film. Mrs. Wilson was apparently horrified by the scenes of German brutality and expressed her feelings to Griffith, who later wired her that he had spent "a sleepless night and troubled day" trying to think why the film had so affected her. He pointed out that the public is "a very stolid, hard animal to impress" and that it was necessary to hit hard to capture its attention. Nevertheless, he said he would eliminate a couple of scenes—possibly this is where Gish's beating scene was truncated—so as not to offend "the refined and sensitive spirits such as yourself. Otherwise I shall be a very disappointed, broken individual, for my hopes and my work and prayers have been so bound up in this that, unless it is pleasing in your household, I feel everything has been in vain."[18] This screening, however, took place more than three months after the Los Angeles opening, and it did not reflect, or by contrast, influence, any of the film's reviews.

The more important critics remained committed to the position most of them had taken at the time of *Birth*, namely, that Griffith was a genius, and they continued to express faith in his talents. The worst they did to this latest work was damn it with faint praise. "It succeeds in its ambitious aim," said the *New York Times*, which took that aim to be making "the war a big reality, to bring as much of it as possible within the four walls of a comfortable Broadway theater. . . ."[19] If the anonymous reviewer could not seem to work up much enthusiasm for this venture, he dutifully reported a high degree of it among other members of the first-night audience.

This enthusiasm was translated into good box office receipts. When its initial release was completed, *Hearts* had turned a profit of something over $600,000—very respectable, though, of course, Griffith did not see all of that, by any means. It is also true that the picture might have done a bit better in its final subruns—and abroad—if public gatherings had not been sharply curtailed by the outbreak of a worldwide epidemic of influenza in the fall and winter of 1918–1919—and if the Armistice hadn't intervened. But the film was no disgrace in the marketplace, and if there were any intellectual regrets about it among its principals they surfaced later. Lillian Gish, for example, says "I don't believe that Mr. Griffith ever forgave himself for making *Hearts of the World*. 'War is the villain,' he repeated, 'not any particular people.' "[20] She speculates that such later works as *The Greatest Thing in Life*, with its emphasis on the brotherhood of man, and *Isn't Life Wonderful*, with its sympathetic portrayal of the hardships endured by German civilians during the war, may have been at least partially motivated by a need for atonement.

But in 1918, Griffith had no time for any regrets, if any indeed touched his consciousness. War or no war, he had a contract with Zukor to fulfill—and a sense, shared by everyone involved in the movies at that time, that the industry was moving rapidly toward new and more sophisticated levels of economic development. In the circumstances one had to tend to one's own interests, an activity that required quick, shrewd and daring judgment. This was not a realm where Griffith was greatly gifted, but he plunged into it as determinedly as he plunged into the process of making films under his Artcraft contract.

D. W. Griffith at the height of his powers—and power. The year is 1920. The place is White River Junction, Vt. The occasion is location shooting for his great hit *Way Down East*.

Fatal excesses: *Above*, Albert Grey, Griffith's brother (and always misguided business associate), breaks ground for the new construction required to turn the Flagler estate on Orienta Point, Mamaroneck, N.Y., into an overlavish film studio. The aerial view shows the site after Griffith had finished the conversion. Within five years it would destroy him economically. Still, he enjoyed playing Lord of the Manor, as when he greeted his thirty-two-year-old admirer Abel Gance, after the American premiere of his *J'accuse* in 1921. The Frenchman perhaps spoke for his generation when he said of this occasion, "Only one opinion mattered to me and that was Griffith's." The master approved his disciple's work and helped him to obtain American distribution of his antiwar film.

Griffith never learned to drive, but splendid chauffeur-driven cars were a personal trademark—like his custom tailoring from Bond Street and his love of dancing. This auto dates from the Mamaroneck period, as does the production still below. Griffith, seated before the camera, is trying to instill the proper jolly mood for *Way Down East's* sleigh-ride scene.

A study in contrasts: Lillian Gish, as Anna Moore, the plain
country lass, is glamorously transformed for her introduction
to Boston society in *Way Down East*. Lowell Sherman as Lennox Sanderson, the wealthy wastrel who seduced her by means
of a mock marriage, awaits her at the foot of the staircase.

Night shooting at Mamaroneck. It was into these entirely authentic snows that Anna was cast after her shameful secret—she had borne Sanderson's child out of wedlock—was discovered. Gish, working in the thinnest of costumes, fainted from exposure to the blizzard gales but carried on.

A revolution on film: Griffith, in straw hat, mounts the guillotine platform to direct the climactic scene for *Orphans of the Storm* in 1921. This was undoubtedly the most expensive single sequence he attempted after the Babylonian glories of *Intolerance*. It is said that if it had rained this Sunday he could not have completed the scene; there was no money to recall the extras for another day of shooting.

A star is created: Griffith's passion for Carol Dempster was an indulgence almost as costly to him as his studio. The public was far cooler in its response to her than the besotted director. She was rarely as winsome on screen as in the portrait below. With Neil Hamilton she played the secondary love interest in *The White Rose* (*above right*) in 1923, and gave perhaps her best performance, again opposite Hamilton, in *Isn't Life Wonderful*. Griffith took them to Germany to shoot the latter film in 1924.

Paradise lost: With his studio shuttered and his company near bankruptcy, the salary Griffith could command as a director for hire kept the firm out of receivership from 1925 on. *Sally of the Sawdust (opposite top)* starred W. C. Fields and Dempster, and it made money. *Abraham Lincoln (opposite bottom)* was Griffith's first sound film. Made in 1930, it starred Walter Huston. Its box office receipts failed to match the critical acclaim it received.

The Struggle: Griffith's last film, in 1931, was appropriately titled. Despite location shooting, rare in these early days of talkies, this lugubrious tale of a drunkard's downfall—the film was both underfinanced and not fully thought out—brought the director's career to a sad end.

A leftover life: Sixteen years remained to Griffith after his last film. In 1936, when he was 61, he married Evelyn Baldwin, 26, in Louisville. Their marriage endured for a decade, and not entirely unhappily, either. Still, Griffith found it hard to settle down to domesticity. He always liked a night out with one of the boys, like Woody Van Dyke (*below*), once one of his assistants, now a reliable director of M-G-M entertainments like *The Thin Man* and *San Francisco*.

Outside looking in: Griffith visits Lionel Barrymore and Lillian Gish on the *Duel in the Sun* set in 1946. Both, of course, began their film careers with him. The director, King Vidor, left, went into movies following Griffith's example.

Old men can't always forget: Montages of stills from his films decorated Griffith's den in the little Beverly Hills home he shared with Evelyn. This picture is from "A day in the life of . . ." newspaper feature done on him the year he died.

CHAPTER THIRTEEN

"Wound Round with a Woolen String"

THE year between the release of *Hearts of the World* in April 1918 and the release of *Broken Blossoms* in May 1919 was among the most significant of Griffith's life, for the events of that time would, in large measure and in ways that neither he nor anyone else could foretell, shape much of his future as an artist and as a force in the motion picture industry. As important, the consequences of his actions in this year would also shape his own sense of himself and his accomplishments for the remainder of his days. It is not too much to say that some of the unhappiness that attended his later years was made in this moment, when, ironically, his power and prestige were still at their height.

The questions before Griffith in 1918–19 were economic, artistic and personal. In general, they were of the sort that any successful man of his age (he would turn 44 in January 1919) might ask himself as he looked back on what he had already achieved and looked forward toward consolidating those gains and capitalizing on them still further. In Griffith's case this issue was compounded by the fact that the motion picture industry itself was in an analogous phase. It, too, was reaching toward maturity, toward the dimensions and the structure that would pertain almost until our own time and that, indeed, are still perceptible in the so-called new Hollywood of the present day.

Griffith was well aware of these developments. In 1918 he was in business with one of the chief architects of industrial change, Adolph Zukor, and by early 1919 he would join forces with two of Zukor's principal rivals, and was concerned about what he should be doing to maximize his profits. "What seems to be your opinion as to where the money is," he inquired of his youngest brother, Albert, who was managing the road show engagements of *Hearts* at the time, "in the big picture . . . or the program? Of course, there is a terrific gamble with the big picture."[1]

The trouble was that he had no time for thoughtful contemplation of his future. The present was too much with him. In the year prior to releasing *Broken Blossoms* he would personally direct no fewer than six films, while supervising perhaps an equal number in Dorothy Gish's comedy series (also for Zukor). Beyond this, Griffith would make a one-reel short in aid of a Liberty Loan drive and would agree to serve as chairman of the Motion Picture War Service Association, which entailed public appearances at a variety of bond rallies and charity meetings. In fact, the gala at which this organization was formed must rank as one of the great social occasions of early Hollywood history. Almost all the prominent film folk were present, and they raised $32,750 for war-related causes, mainly through the simple expedient of autographing their tickets to the affair and then auctioning them off among themselves. Griffith, for example, sold his to Mary Pickford for $2,500, in turn purchasing Mae Murray's for the same amount. (The top price for an autograph was $2,600, paid by Chaplin for his own signature, after a spirited bidding war with Griffith, who insisted that Charlie do his famous walk as part of the deal, with Chaplin refusing until he had won—after which he delighted the crowd with a demonstration of that jaunty stroll.) The evening ended with a series of tableaux (featuring the likes of Bobby Harron, Sessue Hayakawa and Wallace Reid) and some smart close-order drill by members of the Lasky Home Guards, under the command of the resplendently uniformed Cecil B. DeMille.[2]

As if all this were not enough to preoccupy Griffith, he now renewed his relationship with the young Denishawn dancer Carol Dempster. Over the course of the next year and a half she would progress from dancing in the prologues he sometimes staged for the important engagements of his films to secondary roles in the pictures themselves, then finally to starring parts. Within a short time she would supplant Lillian Gish in both his professional and his private life. Not that either woman ever publicly admitted that her relationship with him was anything but professional. Nor would Griffith, until many years had passed, preferring that peculiar blend of courtly discretion and guilty feelings that ruled all his connections with women. Still, the arrival of Dempster in his life and on his lot was an event bystanders could not ignore. This was trouble in paradise, and the memoirists and interviewees, usually silent on the subject of Griffith's romantic doings, speak quite frankly of the stir that Dempster created in their little world—generally not to her advantage. He seems to have been more visibly smitten than he ever had been before, and, of course, the films of the next years speak eloquently of his passion for this rather plain and usually inept actress. Whatever happiness we may imagine her bringing him in the years they were together, the cost of her presence at the center of his work for close on seven years was exorbitant.

Not that Gish was quickly set aside. She would actually do her best work for Griffith in the next three years. Rather—and rather unpleasantly—he would resort to his practice of encouraging professional rivalry between leading ladies. There was always competition in his organization for his favor, among the men as well as the women, but Griffith seems to have taken particular and perverse pleasure in encouraging his leading ladies to battle for his professional attentions. One of his press agents at this time was a bright, cheeky man named Gerrit Lloyd, who, perhaps because he too was of Welsh descent, enjoyed Griffith's confidence and a degree of intimacy with him longer than anyone else who ever worked with him (he would advance, eventually, to scenario writing, with screen credit on three of Griffith's last five films); he would comment (in a series of remarkable letters addressed to Barnet Bravermann, the director's would-be biographer) that "DW got a kick out of having Gish and Demp[ster] bitter rivals for him. When one turned a neat trick on the other he would burst out with a roar of laughter."[3] Clearly, in terms of personal relationships, these were not Griffith's finest hours—or months. But the habit of near-Jovian manipulativeness is powerful in the directorial temperament, and Griffith was at the height of his powers (and power) just now. He cruelly stretched out the struggle between his once and future favorite—or anyway, did nothing to alleviate it—for some three years.

Of course he had other distractions. His largest problem now was to fulfill his arduous Artcraft contract in a year's time. That he did so, and in so doing made two of his finest small works as well as another picture that many consider to be among his greatest—and is, certainly, among his most influential—is a tribute both to the fecundity of his imagination and to that remarkable energy he could always summon in those days to drive himself on. What he did, in effect, was rekindle the old Biograph spirit, which permitted him to shift rapidly from subject to subject without loss of concentration.

One suspects that a certain sense of relief attended his work on these projects. His advance from Famous Players was $175,000 for each film and with the endless need for product in the Paramount exchanges, there was a steady pressure on Griffith to turn them out as rapidly as he could. There was no room for indulgence in them, and there is no record that he entertained any fancies about expanding any of them beyond their natural proportions. He would later say that he undertook them in order to earn the wherewithal to finance larger films, but there seem to have been no specific plans in that regard. Rather the Artcraft contract represented an attempt to mark time—and test the wind—in a profitable manner. This was hard work, but it contained no element of anxiety. And Griffith's best work in this series has about it a relaxed and easy grace, even a certain wry and gentle humor, that is only intermittently present in his other long films and would almost entirely disappear from his later pictures.

The subject matter of the Artcraft films breaks down into convenient categories. Three are distinctly war films, designed in part to use up footage that was left after *Hearts* was finished; two (and these are the best of those it is still possible to see) are simple exercises in nostalgic recall; one is, of course, the singular *Broken Blossoms*. The first of them to go into production, and into release, was *The Great Love*, a story Griffith had conceived the previous fall as a way of deploying not only his battle footage but the material, of infinitely greater value to him, that he had shot in England with the Dowager Queen and the ladies of society. His conception was fleshed out by his old scenarist-colleague from Biograph, Stanner E. V. Taylor, who was to work with him on several of these Biograph-like films, and it was surely in work before *Hearts* went into release.

The Great Love tells a fairly simple, straightforward story, in which a highly idealistic lad named Jim Young (appropriately from Youngstown, Ohio), played by Robert Harron, fired by stories of German atrocities, goes to Canada, enlists in the British army, and while training in Britain, observes the scenes that Griffith's cameras had earlier caught—the whole of society dedicating itself to the Great Cause. Wounded at the front, he returns and meets one Susie Broadplains (Lillian Gish), the daughter of an Australian clergyman, who is also finding maturity as Jim is, through dedication to something larger than herself—patriotism. Alas, having received an unexpected inheritance, she finds herself pursued by an esthete and womanizer called Sir Roger Brighton (Henry B. Walthall, returning briefly to Griffith's employ). Against her better judgment she is attracted to him, but in the end he is revealed to be a traitor, and Gish and Harron are reunited by bonds not merely of love but of exultant patriotism.

The film is impossible to re-evaluate, because it is one of two lost Griffith Artcraft features. The original negative was permitted to deteriorate and no prints have yet been recovered anywhere by archivists. It is obvious that Griffith's Sir Roger was at least suggested by a real Sir Roger—Casement, that is. He was the one-time British consul who, after the war began, attempted to raise funds for an Irish legion to fight on the German side and also attempted to secure German support for a rising in Ireland. When he was sentenced to death, a tide of sympathy for him was stemmed when the authorities circulated what were purported to be, and might actually have been, entries from his diaries indicating he was a homosexual. Griffith would assuredly have heard discussions of this notorious case when he was in England, but could not, of course, have portrayed an overt homosexual on screen. Obviously showing him as an excessively refined aristocrat who yet had a taste for innocent young females was the next best thing in decadence.

The film was indifferently received. Griffith himself sent out a letter contradicting Famous Players publicity which referred to the film as his "greatest." He simply said he didn't think it was. The *New York Times* did speak of the "deftness" with which Griffith linked fact and fiction in the film and if there were occasional missing links, and if obvious theatrical devices sometimes obtruded themselves on the general documentary air, still "his degree of success becomes much more prominent than the relatively small measures of his failure."[4] Its anonymous critic also found Gish and Harron more effective than they had been in *Hearts*. On the other hand, some reviewers found the picture overlong for the story it had to tell (a damning criticism that, since surviving records indicate it was somewhere between five and seven reels long, that is, an hour to an hour and a half in running time). Others found Walthall somewhat over-melodramatic, and still others perceived its resemblances to Griffith's old Biograph mode, a view that was not meant as praise, implying regression rather than the prime American virtue of onward and upward progress.

If there was satisfaction for Griffith in *The Great Love* it lay in the fact that it enabled him to pay his wartime social debts. In the press book for the film he comments: "I never really knew the meaning of the word 'graciousness' until I went to England and began to produce my picture-plays over there." He speaks gratefully of the nobility and the socially prominent who "although they are directing and supervising the affairs of the empire . . . gladly took the time to assist in the making of the picture." This act, he asserts, reverting to a theme that often preoccupied him in these days, the need to make the motion picture socially respectable, was "an honor paid the photodrama which could not be equalled."

All of which could not have been more handsomely put. The trouble is that Griffith was doing something of a sleight-of-hand trick. He had promised his subjects that they would be appearing in a film whose proceeds would go to charity, a term that, even broadly defined, did not include the coffers of Adolph Zukor and D. W. Griffith, and he had come back from England publicly proclaiming the altruism of his overseas venture. But there is no record that a single penny derived from his war films was ever diverted to charity, not even the proceeds of a premiere. Of course, a sophist might argue, so firmly was Griffith enlisted on the side of the Allies, that all the war films served the cause in the largest propagandistic sense.

If one must perforce remain somewhat ambiguous about *The Great Love*, there can be no ambiguity at all about the next film Griffith placed in production, *A Romance of Happy Valley*. It is one of the most fully realized of his films, and one for which, even today, so modest and unassuming is it, no explanatory apologies need be made. It is an extraordinarily simple tale of a young man named John L. Logan, Jr. (Robert Harron), a passionate inventor, who feels he must leave "Happy Valley" in Kentucky to make his way in the larger world. His particular passion is the creation of a toy frog that can actually swim, and if that obsession

seems a pale substitute for the faithful love offered him by Jennie Tim-
berlake, his rural sweetheart (Lillian Gish), it is not hard to accept youthful ambition as a convention to part young lovers for a time—especially
since both confidently expect that it will be only a matter of months before success crowns his labors. In fact, though, some seven years pass before John achieves the success that will permit him to return home with
his pride intact. But all that, anyway, is just an excuse for Griffith to
study, with comic sympathy, two ideal types—the dedicated creator and
the faithful helpmate, with the poverty endured by the former related
with reminiscent passion by the director. It is true the film ends with a
burst of belated melodrama—John's parents have fallen upon evil times
economically, and when their son returns unannounced his father, who
has been contemplating a robbery, is led to believe that he may have
murdered not only his intended victim but his son as well. Still, things
are made to work out satisfactorily and even if the conclusion is strained,
the clever intricacy of its plotting carries one heedlessly along. Indeed, by
the time the melodramatics start up, the firm's simple charm has long
since won one over.

The sweetness of having the villagers pray in their church that young
Logan be spared the sinfulness of New York's ways, the comic spectacle
of Gish hugging a scarecrow that is wearing one of her lover's old coats as
a way of showing how much she misses him, her nightly peek under the
bed to be sure no evildoer is there, the manfulness of Harron's endurance
in pursuit of his vision—all of this is managed with a gentle irony Griffith
had not employed since the short features he made before *Birth*. We have
no trouble believing his press release statement that making this picture
"was like a holiday to me." And we can accept his rationale for it without
wincing: "It appears to be the pleasure of most of us to associate drama
with persons about whom we know very little. Yet it is true that most
wealthy persons lead the most prosaic and uninteresting of lives, whereas
the doings of our friends in denim and calico [are] aswarm with the most
amazing romances and tragedies and dramas of every kind."

But the picture is more than merely charming. It works so well because it is so strongly felt, and it is strongly felt because it is one of Griffith's most autobiographical films. It opens, in fact, with a careful reconstruction of the toll road, with its gate and gate house, that ran past the
old Griffith farm, and we cannot doubt that his boyhood memories supplied something more than the film's Kentucky setting; it doubtless supplied character types and bits of behavior for his players as well. More
than that, Harron's character seems in many respects to be a projection
of the youthful Griffith. Had not Griffith himself not set forth from similar innocence, in similar innocence, to make his mark in the world? And
had not success eluded him for far more years than he thought it should
have? Indeed, Griffith seems often to have thought himself as much an

inventor as an artist. When he was living on the poverty line with Linda he once toyed with a scheme of canning and marketing a meat pie of his own devising. Later, embittered by his lack of lasting economic success, he would speak wistfully of the riches that might have been his had he been able to patent such technical devices as the close-up and the fade-out and the iris. Finally, there can be no doubt that Griffith entertained, besides that most basic of American fantasies, which holds that it requires only one good idea to make one rich, yet another that is almost as powerful. That is, the fantasy of returning home in triumph, showing the dubious neighbors of youth that one's own more elevated evaluation of one's talents was all along correct. In later years, when he was no longer permitted to make films, Griffith would return to Kentucky and there attempt to disport himself as a great man, hoping his reputation had not suffered here as it had in the movie world, and found himself welcomed.

There is another, less happy, autobiographical note to the film. In Gish's character here, as in the subsequent and similar *True Heart Susie*, which Griffith made a few months later, he achieves a rare fusion of feminine characteristics. She has the spunk, pluck, humor and capability that we associate with the young women more often played by her sister, Dorothy, and by Mae Marsh in his films. And though childlike, she is not quite the idealized virgin of the other roles she had herself played for Griffith. To put the matter simply, she is in *Happy Valley* a believably attractive young woman, perhaps closer here than elsewhere to the real Lillian Gish whom Griffith doubtless loved after his fashion. But when Harron is in New York, the temptress who attempts to lure him away from his work, and his devotion to his sweetheart back home, is none other than Carol Dempster, making her debut in a credited screen role, a few months before she was to turn eighteen. It is a very small part, the sort of thing producers are always giving to aspiring girl friends, yet the coincidence is excruciating: Harron in a role that is clearly an autobiographical projection, Lillian Gish finally playing a woman something like her own capable and faithfully supportive self, and Dempster, the newcomer, trying to lure the hero from his true path. That she is seen to fail in the film is less significant than the fact that she is trying.

A *Romance of Happy Valley* was shot in the summer of 1918, but it was set aside for a time so that Griffith could get on to his next war film. It was perfectly clear, now, that the conflict would soon end, rendering virtually valueless the material Griffith had acquired abroad, and so he turned immediately to *The Greatest Thing in Life*. When *Romance* finally went out to the theaters the following January it was received with the same respectable but somewhat muted reviews as the other pictures in the series. And since it too was "lost" until a print was recovered in the Soviet Union in the late sixties, its reputation has only lately begun to grow.

Unfortunately, *The Greatest Thing in Life* still remains in the limbo of the lost. And, according to Lillian Gish, this is a tragedy, for she feels that if modern audiences could see the picture it would do much to correct what she insists is the false impression of Griffith as a racist, which *Birth* revivals reinforce. It is possible, for this picture, which at one time during production bore the title *Cradle of Souls*, concerns itself not only with the racial issue but with simple snobbism as well. In it, Harron plays a rather superior young southern gentleman named Edward Livingston, who patronizes—in both senses of the word—a young French-born cigarette-counter saleswoman, Jeanette Peret (Lillian Gish). She is repelled by his manner—and does not know that he has befriended her ailing father and paid for their passage home, where he hopes to regain his health. Livingston follows, but his manner still offends Jeanette, who instead marries a decent, unromantic grocer, played by David Butler (who would have an extremely long if not greatly distinguished career as a comedy director, working especially with Bob Hope and Doris Day in the forties and fifties). The war begins, however, and serving with the American army, young Livingston learns to respect people as individuals, without regard to their former stations in life. Jeanette's husband dies in the course of preventing her rape by a German officer, naturally, and the lovers are at last united. The crucial scene occurs when Livingston, wounded in battle, is rescued by a black soldier, who is himself wounded in the effort. They tumble into a shell hole together. When the Negro feels his life beginning to fade, he calls out for his "Mammy," asking for a kiss, which Livingston, cradling him in his arms, bestows upon him in his final moment. Gish, who suggested the title under which the film was released, claims that when audiences saw this dramatic and touching scene they were "tense and quiet." Many reviewers mentioned the sequence favorably ("possibly one of the finest things ever presented on the silver sheet" said one trade paper[5]), but again the querulous note that Griffith seemed to be doing no more than repeating himself crept in here as it did in so much of the comment on the Artcraft series.

One critic, in the *Washington Herald*, went so far as to guess that Griffith was not actually directing the pictures and attributed *The Greatest Thing in Life* to Bitzer, causing Griffith to inquire in a letter to the editor, "Why this slander? He is a good, true man."[6] But such light spirits aside, the Artcraft series' overall critical reception reinforced Griffith's determination to abandon these modest ventures: there was in epic films not only the possibility of a greater fortune but a continuation of the huge acclaim he had previously enjoyed as well. At the time, reviewers and public alike were still too close to the Biograph films to appreciate that Griffith was, at least in some of these "short story" films, broadening and deepening the good qualities of his earlier work, giving freer rein to his singular blend of realism and lyricism, gently and unassumingly stated.

Several of the reviews mentioned a new technique revealed in this film and one of the negative notices claimed that *The Greatest Thing in Life* had but one novelty to offer, "a sort of idealized close-up—with hazy, dreamy outlines, singularly suited to Lillian Gish."[7] These odd bits of soft-edged photography were inserted here and there in Bitzer's characteristically sharp-edged work at the behest of their subject. Whether, as she would claim, Griffith just happened to notice her passport photograph and appreciate the cinematic possibilities of its style, or whether she insisted on his hiring the author of that portrait, Henrik Sartov, to help her present a more glamorous image, it is impossible to say. But she was in her early twenties now, old for a Griffith heroine, and Bitzer was becoming more difficult for everyone to deal with, as his sense grew that his contribution to Griffith's reputation was insufficiently appreciated. Anyway, Sartov made his motion picture debut on this film, and his influence, as the pioneer of diffusion in cinematography, not merely on Griffith but on the way actresses, especially aging ones, are filmed, is incalculable.

He was, according to Karl Brown, "a strange little man, balding in front and fuzzy at the back . . . frightened and futile, perhaps because he lived in constant fear that someone might discover his secret and put him out of business by doing the same thing . . . only faster and more professionally. His secret, of course, lay in his lens, an extremely long-focus instrument that, to employ successfully, he had to back far, far away from his subject." One day Brown got a close look at it, and discovered that it was nothing but "a yellowed old spectacle lens . . . full of all the bad faults that optical scientists had been working for decades to eliminate." It could, to be sure, form an image, but only at its center. The rest "splayed out like a raw egg dropped on the kitchen floor." However, if you stopped down the exposure the aberrations were more sensed than seen and the lady at the center came out "pure peaches and cream."[8]

Sartov would develop his technique beyond this relatively crude point in the years to come, eventually employing a series of filters, mounted in front of an apparently normal lens, which were capable of providing as much or as little diffusion as a scene (or his subject's ego) required. But what was a mere "gimmick" to the technically minded Brown was a revelation to the movie world, and Sartov would, like Dempster, make steady progress in Griffith's little world, eventually sharing photographic credit with Bitzer and finally supplanting him. If the lovely Lillian Gish thought she required Sartov's services, how useful he must have seemed when Dempster was on the set.

In this complicated year, however, improvisations of all kinds were necessary. There was, for instance, a need for personnel to staff the little series of Dorothy Gish comedies Griffith was committed to overseeing. And then there was the Bobby Harron problem. He was under threat from the draft, and there was a lively correspondence between Griffith and various government officials in which he argued that the young actor's work in films represented a significant contribution to the war effort, a correspondence that did, in fact, result in at least a *de facto* deferment. And also resulted in a measurable growth in Harron's range. From being merely an agreeable juvenile presence he was developing into a gifted comic actor. Still, he could not do it all, and with the threat of military service hanging over him, Griffith felt obliged to reach out toward another young actor, Richard Barthelmess.

He was himself the son of an actress, and as a youth he had brushed lightly against Griffith and his people when they were at the Biograph on Fourteenth Street. He would later remember seeing members of the company lunching at a nearby restaurant. Now, after a couple of years at Trinity College, he was beginning to establish himself as a leading man in films, primarily opposite Marguerite Clark. Acting on a tip, he had, the previous year, raced to catch Griffith at Grand Central Station as he was leaving to complete *Hearts* in Los Angeles and applied for a job with him. Griffith had then asked Dorothy Gish and Harron to catch Barthelmess in a Marguerite Clark picture then playing, but they had reported back that he seemed too short—not that one might expect from a rival like Harron a very flattering report on another male performer of similar type. But in 1918, Barthelmess was working in Fort Lee with another leading lady, Madge Kennedy, under the direction of Chet Withey, a frequent Griffith assistant, and Withey advised writing an application letter to Griffith on the Coast, which Barthelmess did. Later that summer, working with Clark in the Adirondacks on a picture directed by Marshall Neilan, Barthelmess received a telegraphic inquiry from Griffith about his age, height, draft status and current salary. Neilan advised raising the latter by a fictional $50, and Griffith hired Barthelmess to come to the Coast on a seven-week guarantee to appear opposite Dorothy Gish in the second of her comedies. (The quality of the first, *Battling Jane*, had incidentally concerned Griffith, and he wrote in a telegram to Banzhaf: "MY OWN OPINION THIS RATHER ROUGH BUT DIFFERENT AND SEEMED TO PLEASE THE AUDIENCE AS WE OFTEN OVERESTIMATE THEIR INTELLIGENCE. THE NEXT PICTURE IS MUCH BETTER CLASS WITH GOOD SETS AND ON A MUCH HIGHER PLANE. . . ."[9])

Barthelmess was very much the sort of actor who pleased Griffith— mannerly, even-featured, competent, rather bland and unexciting. But he fitted in comfortably with the "large happy family" at the studio, "more like a club than a factory,"[10] with everyone down to the wardrobe mistress encouraged to attend filming and offer suggestions. Griffith advanced Barthelmess very rapidly, once again demonstrating that he feared male actors who gave off a profound sexual charge. Indeed, Barthelmess would go directly from his first Dorothy Gish film—they were budgeted at less than $25,000—into a Griffith-directed film, a small, quickly made picture, the last of Griffith's war pictures, yet one that would have, in its way, far-reaching consequences for its maker.

The film was known as *The Girl Who Stayed at Home*, and it was the first of the Artcrafts not to star Lillian Gish. It was made at the height of the flu epidemic—Barthelmess remembers Griffith wearing a gauze mask over his face when he was on the set—when Lillian Gish was stricken with the disease. Griffith could easily argue that budgets and schedules forced him to press ahead, with Dempster in a role that was clearly meant for Gish, and he did so. Director and star made the most of the opportunity, Griffith even inserting into the film a modern dance "specialty" for his protégée which can best be described as ludicrous.

He was, however, blind to all of Dempster's shortcomings. She was, as Karl Brown put it, "narrow-faced with close-set eyes . . . and there was a little protruding bump at the tip of her nose," which he recalled Griffith bewailing: "To think that perfect beauty can be marred by one little bit of misplaced flesh. What a shame, what a crying shame. Other-wise . . . perfection."

She was clearly not an actress to Brown's taste—and he was but the first of many to reach that conclusion. He also found himself aptly wondering, ". . . why play kindergarten teacher to this inexperienced snip of a girl who might be very good to her mother but who had no business being thought of in the same reverie with Lillian Gish . . . ?"[11]

But playing kindergarten teacher was precisely the point. Griffith had always loved the role, and succeeded in it, with his female stars. By now he felt that no matter how unpromising the clay he could mold it into something splendid. And there was another factor involved here, namely, a strong identification with the problems Dempster had with the camera. Griffith was, of course, a striking-looking man, but certainly not conventionally handsome, and he might have felt his failure as an actor had something to do with that. If he could take a woman who bore a certain resemblance to him and make the public accept her, he would not only prove his present power but gain a certain balm for his own past slights. Once Lillian Gish asked him why he kept trying with Dempster, despite the public's antipathy to her, and he replied, "You don't know what it is to have a big nose."[12]

In any event, Dempster's first starring film, *The Girl Who Stayed at Home*, tells the contrasting stories of two brothers, Ralph and James Grey (Barthelmess and Harron respectively), as they confront war service. The former is a serious and upstanding youth, who on a trip to France before the hostilities meets and falls in love with the daughter of a comically unreconstructed confederate expatriate. The older man is once again played by the Griffith veteran (and Louisville compatriot) Adolphe Lestina, the girl by Dempster. Ralph's brother is everything the

Barthelmess character is not, a lounge lizard who affects a peculiar, and highly humorous, "killing slouch," a weird walk variously described by critics as a crablike scuttle and an attack of stomach cramps. At any rate, Harron's is a likably comic performance and appreciated because it grows organically from character and story; there had been some criticism of the comedy turns and bits that Griffith was wont to drop into his pictures willy-nilly to lighten them. There was also praise for the actress, new to Griffith, who played opposite Harron. Identified in the titles as "Cutie Beautiful," she is, as well, the title character, "the girl who stayed at home." She was played by Clarine Seymour, small, dark, vivacious, who had been working in short comedies for Hal Roach, among others. Of all the Griffith actresses she was the one who might best have been able to play a flapper convincingly—something that might have been enormously helpful to him in the years to come. Her sudden death, and Harron's in 1920, would be a double blow to him. For the moment, however, they simply stole the picture away from Barthelmess and Dempster, who gives a fussy, jumpy performance, doubtless reflecting her own, and her director's, anxiety that she make a strong impression. Before the picture ends, army service (and the steadying love of Cutie Beautiful, whose morals are better than her ragtime manner) makes a man out of the Harron character, and, having survived a rape attempt—the rescuer is again a German officer again proclaiming that the war hasn't made beasts of everyone—the Dempster character is reunited with Barthelmess. Happy endings all around.

On the whole, critics found this the slightest of Griffith's war films (as surely it was), although some, like the *New York Times* man, found it, astonishingly, superior to *A Romance of Happy Valley*, precisely because of its mood shifts and intricacy of plotting. There was also, surprisingly, some protest over its failure to attribute universal beastliness to the Germans—even though it was not released until the spring following the armistice. There was, surely, something too casual about the film's structure, that lack of firm sense of intent that inevitably discomfits an audience almost subliminally. The hasty charm of individual moments cannot quite compensate for that. And, of course, the film's underlying social purpose, which was to help rally public support for the draft (Griffith had shot some documentary footage of Secretary of War Newton D. Baker and of various selective service officials, which was included in the film), was irrelevant by the time the picture reached the theaters in the spring of 1919.

Still, considering the pace at which Griffith was working, the picture was not at all bad. And Griffith continued to be modest enough about the Artcraft pictures, making no great claims for them and insisting they be understood as nothing more than entertainments. But unceasing toil must take its toll, and around the time he was working on *The Girl Who*

Stayed at Home he wrote his friend, and occasional backer, the New York theater owner and producer Morris Gest, that "I haven't got time to think over propositions for a big picture." As he put it, mixing his metaphors, "I have been all wound round with a woolen string of work for this Artcraft program" and "I don't see my way out of the woods of these six pictures." In the letter he alludes as well to the ravages of the flu epidemic, which besides disabling Lillian Gish, had caused many theaters to shut their doors in October and even led to a cessation of production on some lots. The epidemic, he confessed, had hurt receipts on *Hearts* (in which Gest had money): "Hit us just when we were starting to go strong."[13]

The pace and pressure of nonstop production, the distractions of the world and of the heart, all of these would have been sufficient excuse for Griffith to content himself with the simplest and most routine productions. But all his Artcraft films (and not a few of the Dorothy Gish comedies) went over the budgets that were based on Zukor's advances, with Griffith finally putting up, out of his own pocket, close to $135,000 all told, to pay for the overages.[14] All of this makes it the more remarkable that he would pause, gather his forces and create a film that was not only utterly distinct from the others in style, tone and quality, but, in fact, distinct from any other film that he or anyone else had yet produced. Indeed, it is not too much to say that in the six decades since it was produced there have been few films that followed the poetic and tragic model of *Broken Blossoms*.

2

It was Mary Pickford who first directed Griffith's attention to a volume of short tales called *Limehouse Nights* by the English writer Thomas Burke. He might well have found it himself, the book having been a bestseller, but she obviously recognized that the writer and the director were kindred spirits. Both were drawn to poverty as a setting, to melodrama as a structure and to a prose style they thought of as poetic but others might well regard as merely empurpled. At any rate, Griffith read Burke's book, which was published in 1917, and found himself particularly engaged by the first story in it, "The Chink and the Child." The reason is not hard to discern. Once again an innocent child-woman (in the book she was only twelve) lives in dire fear of an animalistic older man—in this case her father, a prizefighter named Battling Burrows, who, having sired her illegitimately, ragefully resents her presence in his life, administering savage beatings to her for offenses that are minor and, in some cases, imaginary. In the Burke story, Lucy's protector, the "Chink" of the title, meets her in a whorehouse, where she has been taken by a friend after her father has locked her out of their home. In the tale the "Chink" is a frequenter of opium dens and gambling rooms, but her plight touches the better side of his nature, and their relationship, of course, remains utterly chaste. After her friendship with the Chinese is discovered by her father and he beats her to death, the Chinese gains his revenge by inserting a venomous snake in Burrows's bed.

Griffith retained the essence of the story (and some of its prose for his titles), but there were substantial changes, particularly in the character of the Yellow Man, as he was carefully identified in the film, where he is given a fixed address—he keeps a shop—and a more generally idealistic nature. He is presented, in fact, as a devoted follower of Buddha, come to the West as a sort of missionary in reverse, to teach the gentle ways of his religion. The refinement of his sensibility in the movie version makes the contrast with the stupid, violent and deeply prejudiced Burrows the more vivid. He is intended as an example of Eastern virtue, and, implicitly, as a living criticism of Western values. Griffith even invented a little scene in which a missionary (in Griffith's terms yet another "meddler" or "uplifter") bound for the Far East, "to convert the heathens," presses a tract on the Yellow Man and an ironic title has him say of the Christian: "I wish him luck."

Beyond this the film as a whole is still another plea for understanding amity among the peoples of the world. Even without the existence of *The Greatest Thing in Life* to buttress the case, we can perhaps stipulate that Griffith's prejudice did not extend beyond blacks and that it was mostly quiescent when the possibility of sexual congress across racial lines was absent. In this connection it is interesting to note that a scene in Burke's story, where the "Chink" kisses Lucy and she eagerly, if innocently, responds, is not present in the film. Nor is the mild, but palpable, erotic charge of the story ever visible on screen: at most the Oriental is seen in genteel longing for a love he knows to be forbidden. Only in the sadism of Burrows do we sometimes scent a trace of the psychosexual. There is one other significant change in the translation of story to screen in the Yellow Man's murder of Burrows. Instead of the rather elaborate and preposterous business of the snake—Griffith's loathing of reptiles was fanatic and, on location, he set men to work clearing the area of snakes— a direct confrontation is set up.

But it is Griffith's manner of retelling this story, not his comparatively minor tamperings with it, that imparts to the film its singularity. And Lillian Gish's remarkable performance as Lucy is what, in the final analysis, makes it unforgettable. Between them, they transform what might have been no more than a melodrama into a film that, as a result of pace, visual design and touching performance, strikes a note of genuine tragedy. And herein lies an irony, for it appears that Griffith toyed with the notion of giving Gish's role to Dempster.

While Gish was still recuperating from the flu, Griffith began rehearsing Dempster in the part. The authority for this remarkable information is the ubiquitous Harry Carr, who told it to Adela Rogers St.
John, who did not retell it until after Griffith's death, in an article in
which she placed a large portion of the blame for his decline on Dempster.[15] Yet it fits: the coincidence of Gish's illness and the rise of Dempster's star, as well as the fact that a more closely involved observer than
Carr or St. John, namely Richard Barthelmess, testifies that Griffith began working on the film before he had definitely decided on its casting.
Barthelmess asserts Griffith was also rehearsing with George Fawcett, an
older character man who had been with him since *Intolerance,* in the role
of the Yellow Man. It was Rose Smith, now working with her husband,
Jimmie, as a cutter, who proposed Barthelmess for the role. "With all
modesty," says Barthelmess, "I can state that after having watched Fawcett rehearse . . . I merely went into rehearsal myself and copied every
mannerism that Fawcett had given the part. I couldn't have done better,
as Fawcett was a fine actor."[16] He adds, however, that Griffith took him
to Chinatown in Los Angeles on several evenings so that he could absorb
the atmosphere.

Gish says her recovery was hastened by messages of love from the
studio. It may be that it was also spurred by the thought of another actress making off with a role Gish was obviously born to play. Be that as it
may, Donald Crisp, another old Griffith favorite, was cast for the third
major role, that of Battling Burrows, and a rehearsal period of some six
weeks ensued as the sets were built. With Charles Baker serving as the art
director, though that credit had not yet been invented, the process now
called storyboarding, in which shots are sketched out before shooting begins, was employed, as it had been on *Hearts* and several of the other Artcraft films. Indeed, Baker, an equable Englishman with stage training,
whose delicate ink and wash drawings are repeatedly praised by Karl
Brown, appears to be one of the unsung heroes of this film. For one's first
impression and one's final analysis both lead inescapably to the conclusion that, more than any other Griffith film, its force derives from its
visual rather than its dramatic qualities.

One can trace its overtly stated themes and ideas backward and forward in Griffith's work. But neither before nor later did Griffith do such
a fully realized mood piece. The darkness of the Limehouse streets, lit by
the occasional gas lamp, the mist and fog swirling in, the pavements glis-
tening with damp, remain indelibly in mind, the work of but a comparatively small number of shots. And the contrast between the squalor of
Lucy's hovel and the elegance of the apartment above the Yellow Man's
shop, which becomes her refuge, enforces the contrast between his values
and her father's as no amount of melodrama can. Indeed, given the slow
pace of the film, and its relative lack of action until the climax, it is the

sense not of pace but of place—explored at leisure and with due attention to detail—that holds one enraptured. For this, praise must as well be extended to Sartov, who has a "special effects" credit on the film (though the one true special effects shot, a miniature, the Thames as viewed by night from Limehouse, was executed by Karl Brown, borrowed back from the army, after he had been drafted, for the job). Sartov's contribution was also obviously larger than his cophotography credit implies. For neither before nor after did Bitzer shoot anything that had the quality of *Broken Blossoms*. A visual contrast is enforced; everything involving Burrows is shot in almost documentary style, while everything involving the Chinese rescuer is diffused, softened.

The whole enterprise may be regarded, in fact, as one of those lucky congruences of talent and timing that have been responsible for not a few films that rise above modest origins to attain memorability. The very efficiency with which it was made attests to that. According to Lillian Gish, shooting consumed only eighteen days, apparently without a break and with considerable night work, necessitated by the fact that Crisp, who was directing a film at another studio at the time, could work only after normal hours and on weekends. Barthelmess says, "The whole experience was a most pleasant one," although he adds that "Griffith was a hard taskmaster . . . not always too kind in his criticism of his artists in order to bring out an emotional quality which was necessary to the scene."[17]

The picture's most memorable moment, the closet scene, might have been achieved in this way. It comes after a sequence in which Burrows, informed of his daughter's hideaway at the Yellow Man's, goes there, violently vandalizes the apartment and then drags his daughter home. Escaping him briefly, she locks herself in a closet to avoid his brutality, but while she grows more and more hysterical, he finally succeeds in breaking down the door to administer the beating that kills her. In her fluttering panic, her desperate turning in that claustrophobic space, there is something of the quality of a trapped animal. It is heartbreaking—yet for the most part quite delicately controlled by the actress. Barthelmess reports that her hysteria was induced by Griffith's taunting of her. Gish, on her part, claims that she improvised the child's tortured movements on the spot and that when she finished the scene there was a hush on the stage, broken finally by Griffith's exclamation, "My God, why didn't you warn me you were going to do that?"[18]

No matter how it was achieved, the result is memorable, one of the privileged moments of Gish's career. Her work becomes the more astonishing when one recalls that she was a 23-year-old woman playing a girl whose age was advanced for the screen only to fifteen. She had, she says, almost turned the role down because of her age and had been anxious enough about this problem to visit orphanages in order to study the ways of adolescence. There is no question but that intelligence, craft, study and intuition combine. The latter quality contributes another invaluable image to the film. She says that one day in a rehearsal of a scene where Crisp throws a spoon at her and criticizes her for never smiling, she instinctively pushed the corners of her mouth up into a smile with her fingers, a typical gesture of a child younger than Lucy falsely obliging, yet mildly defiant. Griffith loved it, insisting that Gish repeat the gesture at various points in the picture. It forms a kind of counterpoint to its over-all grimness, while suggesting with poignant simplicity Lucy's lost child-hood. Gish points out that it also became a kind of trademark for her, symbol of a brave yet endlessly beset girl. The editor of a film magazine once said that "an optimist is a person who will go to the theater ex-pecting to see a D. W. Griffith production in which Lillian Gish is not attacked by the villain in the fifth reel." One newspaper critic actually proposed creation of a Society for the Prevention of Cruelty to Lillian Gish, and by 1926, James R. Quirk, the influential editor of *Photoplay*, was writing: "In the last twelve years she has been saved just in the nick of time from the brutal attacks of 4,000 German soldiers, 2,000 border ruffians and 999 conscienceless men about town. Someday I hope the American hero breaks a leg and fails to get there before the German sol-dier smashes in the door."[19]

This time, however, there was to be no reprieve for Miss Gish, no reprieve for anyone. At the end of *Broken Blossoms* all three of its prin-cipals lie dead, and when the death of Burrows is reported to the police, one of them looks up from the newspaper report of war casualties that he has been reading and says, "Better than last week. Only 40,000 casual-ties." It was uncharacteristic of Griffith to give such a context to a film, and uncharacteristic of him to strike a note of irony quite as precise and well placed as this one. Of course, the complete devastation with which the picture concludes is without precedent in the Griffith canon, prob-ably without precedent in any major film by anyone else up until this time. One of the useful qualities of the multilevel film, especially as Grif-fith worked, was that he could balance the tragedy that overtook some characters by permitting others a happier fate. There was no possibility of that in a film as concentrated and intimate as *Broken Blossoms*.

But if it is what is uncharacteristic about this film that gives it its dis-tinction, it is what is all too characteristic of Griffith that presents the modern viewer with certain nagging doubts about it. To begin with, deli-cate as the Gish and Barthelmess performances are, Donald Crisp strikes one as entirely out of control. His is as shamelessly villainous a perfor-mance as one can find anywhere in silent film—and this is a realm where the competition throngs. It is not just a matter of redeeming qualities be-ing absent from the script; there is the broadness of his playing as well. Such eye-rolling; such grimacing; such monstrousness. Crisp, of course, remained a familiar figure in films, and one need only think of the soft-spoken intelligence of his work in other pictures to realize that he was capable of something more subtle than he offered here. The miscalculation of his performance seems to be a director's error as much as it is an actor's flaw. There are even moments, alas, where Gish's performance is more intense than it strictly need be. In the climactic beating, for example, her writhings sometimes seem excessive in comparison to the strength of the blows we see landing. And then there is the matter of the titles. Even the most passionate of *Broken Blossoms* defenders are uncomfortable with them. "Oh, lily flowers and plum blossoms! Oh, silver streams and dim-starred skies!" cries the heart of the Yellow Man as he bathes the face of his poor tortured love. And that says nothing about "all the tears of the ages" rushing over his heart when she dies. We are back again at "the opal gates of death" which opened for Mae Marsh in *Birth*. And, of course, we are here quintessentially back at Griffith's obsession with death and the maiden, not to mention the blossom of innocence broken and trampled by male brutality. One would admire the film more, somehow, if another director, one who had not so fervently worked this emotional territory for so long, had made the film. And one cannot help but think, perhaps a bit unworthily, of another strange coincidence between biography and fiction. It does not seem entirely accidental that Griffith for the first time actually kills the Gish character at just the moment in his personal history where he was toying with another commitment that he knew carried the potential of killing their relationship. Indeed, while *Broken Blossoms* was before the cameras he was momentarily distracted by preparations for the Los Angeles opening of *The Greatest Thing in Life*, for the prologue of which George Fawcett served as director. With an eye to promotion, Griffith featured the stars of his next release, *The Girl Who Stayed at Home*, in this enterprise. Clarine Seymour appeared among the Followers of Modern Dance in one episode (one of her partners being a dancer who had drifted to California in 1918 to work in almost invisible roles in minor films, one Rodolfo Di Valantina, shortly to become better known as Rudolph Valentino). In another segment Carol Dempster, appropriately, was to lead the Dancers from the Land of Shadows.

None of this should detract too much from Griffith's achievement in *Broken Blossoms*. The largest sadness it presents, in retrospect, is that it became, in the context of Griffith's career, a singularity, a signpost on a road not taken. It turned out to be a transitional film, not for him, but for movies as a whole; perhaps to put it cynically, the first memorable European film made by an American. For what one sees in it now besides a willingness to embrace a tragic vision on film which the Germans in particular would soon bring frequently to the silent screen, are the beginnings of a *mise-en-scène* that would be explored, with increasing vividness, in the decade ahead, by the likes of Pabst, Stiller, Von Sternberg and others, re-emerging in the United States in the sound era, in the genre now identified as *film noir*. Perhaps what was required to make still more effective use of the visual and emotional values Griffith explored was a more cynical view of life, and a less guilty view of the sexual equation than he was capable of taking.

Be that as it may, Griffith himself hesitated over the film. Several weeks after photography was completed, Lillian Gish asked how the editing was going, and he replied: "I can't look at the damned thing; it depresses me so."[20] One suspects that there was more operating here than gloom, that Griffith might have been genuinely amazed and puzzled by what he had wrought and what its effect on his public might be. It might well have been that he feared for the commercial fate of such a grim motion picture. But the working out of the public fate of *Broken Blossoms* would be delayed for some months, not because Griffith, or anyone else, was inordinately concerned about recouping the cost of so inexpensive an enterprise, but because it was to become a bargaining chip in the large industrial drama that would for the next two or three months command Griffith's most intense interest—and that of just about everyone else who had a large stake in the well-being of movies as a commercial activity.

3

Griffith might have been oppressed by work on his films in this year, but he was not unaware of what his backer, Zukor, had been working to create over the past few years—which was nothing less than a film monopoly— the equivalent, in this new field, of United States Steel or Standard Oil. In 1916 his Famous Players–Lasky corporation had managed to absorb, over the protests of its principal, W. W. Hodkinson, the nation's largest exhibition chain, Paramount (though it would be some years before that subsidiary would supplant its corporate conqueror's name in first position in movie advertising and title sequences). At the same time, Zukor had just about finished brushing off the Aitken combine, which had been a potentially powerful competitor. Now doing a $25 million annual business as a large and well-financed vertical trust, containing all the elements required to bring a film from conception to consumption, Famous Players stood alone in size and power. It was perfectly clear that if Zukor continued unchecked he could achieve imperial sway over the industry, with smaller competitors in production, distribution and exhibition allowed to exist largely on his sufferance.

Thus, in late 1917, a new concern, First National, was formed. The idea was Thomas Tally's, the pioneer Los Angeles exhibitor. It consisted of having the new company act as a purchasing agent for independent productions on behalf of exhibitors in 26 key cities. Well financed and aggressive, in 1918 it lured Pickford and Chaplin to its side with rich deals that promised them a higher percentage of the grosses than Zukor was willing to offer, and it was making overtures to Griffith as well.

By late 1918, however, a new threat began to be perceived. If, somehow, Famous Players–Lasky and First National should merge—and rumors of that possibility persisted—then the remainder of the industry would be faced with a force even more potent than the Famous Players–Lasky–Paramount combination, perhaps more so even than the late unlamented Patents Trust. For between them, these two firms controlled almost all the first-run theaters in the major cities. If they came together, they had the resources, if they so chose, to snap up such smaller independents as might try to continue to produce or market films. More alarming to Griffith, such a company could easily begin dictating terms to the major stars and directors, forcing them to work for far less than they were able to command now with their guarantees and percentage deals. Indeed, in a little more than a decade most of the big names (and for that matter, just about everyone involved in making movies) would be salaried contract workers, bereft of profit participation and of any great say in what they would do as they toiled under the oligopolistic conditions imposed by Paramount and its half-dozen major competitors who survived the period of industrial consolidation that the 1920s represent in the economic history of American film.

Of all the people prominent in movies at this time, Griffith had perhaps the liveliest fear of such an eventuality. The emerging stars had all done very nicely working for others. Their fame and their wealth had grown steadily, and as long as they continued to draw, they had no reason to worry about money. Griffith, on the other hand, felt that his career had very nearly aborted as a result of the constraints Biograph had placed on him. Nor had things been much better with Triangle. The struggle to make *The Birth of a Nation*, the film that had given those who had reluctantly followed him riches beyond compare, was still fresh in his mind. If *Intolerance* had represented a setback financially, it had certainly not set back his reputation. And now, as 1918 drew to a close, he could perhaps discern that *Hearts of the World*, though a comparatively minor success in the marketplace, was still going to net him about as much as his long, hard labors on the Artcraft series would. In other words, he believed his financial future and his reputation lay in having the freedom to make what he liked to call "big" pictures.

And, of course, there were other satisfactions as well in making films on that scale; the reward of fame, of adulation as a combination producer-author that quite literally no other director of the time (excepting perhaps the onrushing Cecil B. DeMille) enjoyed as they worked, virtually anonymously, on one program picture after another. Finally, there was a sense that D. W. Griffith could not seem to be going backward, that he could not long continue to make little films the critics and public often seemed to indulge rather than admire in the unstinting manner he had recently enjoyed. None of this would he be able to enjoy if he were forced back into the role of an employee.

In January 1918, interviewed by *Theater*, he had let himself go on this subject, imagining, for instance, Milton taking *Paradise Lost* to a theatrical manager and trying to interest him in a stage version. "Or supposing the impossible, that you had secured a production, of what manager would you expect a performance that would contain any of the poetry, any of the soul of your work?" By contrast, he observed, the motion picture had taken the works of Milton, Browning and the other immortals, "has deemed none of them too 'highbrow' and has 'got them across.' Perhaps the production was not always perfect, or wonderfully artistic, but the big idea was still there, still intact, and it reached the hearts of the spectators. The motion picture is doing daily more than the stage of today can think of doing." As for the stage director, why, he "will throw up his hands in dismay" when he begins to learn the many difficulties that can go wrong on the technical side of things as a film is converted from raw stock to projectable print.

By now, significantly, Griffith felt it safe to lean back and venture an uncharacteristically modest, but entirely correct and gracious thought: "I do not 'teach' the players with whom my name has been linked. We developed together, we found a new art and we discovered the possibilities of that art, we learned together."[21] That, too, was important to him as he sensed the wind of change rising, the need to keep his ensemble together, truly the only family he had ever known in his adult life. The need for "the good companions" (to borrow Priestley's apt title from his theatrical novel) that he treasured was very strong in him, the better side of his paternalism.

He hated even to loan them out to another director and, a little later, when Mickey Neilan sought to borrow George Fawcett for a small, good role, Griffith refused him, writing jocularly that he wanted to get all the drawing power out of his stock company for his own pictures—"God knows they need it badly enough!"—and then adding: "Let you young peppy birds go out and train the other fellows and don't try to rob the nests of the poor old hens and roosters staggering sadly toward the grave."[22] Underneath the joking tone was a realization that he had to hoard to himself all the advantages he could. He perhaps overvalued his stock company, but he did not underestimate the peril he was approaching. If he gave too much of himself to one of the emerging giants, or if they were to achieve dictatorial status in the industry, he would no longer be able to function without stint among the admiring friends whose support was more important to him than he usually admitted.

But what, exactly, was he to do? In the fall of 1919, worrying over the release of *The Greatest Thing in Life* ("a sure fire picture" he thought "not to be compared with *Great Love*"[23]), he ventured the opinion that First National "exhibitors get more out of these pictures than the Art-craft." On the other hand, his brother Albert, whom Griffith forced to adopt a pseudonym (Albert Grey) but whose inept counsel would ill-serve Griffith at every turn in the years ahead, was convinced that Zukor, having lost Pickford to First National, would want to keep Griffith, but was nevertheless advising an independent course. He thought Griffith should avoid entangling himself with either Famous Players or First National, and sell his program pictures directly to the theaters at higher prices and without distribution fees. How he was to accomplish this was something of a mystery. For one thing, Albert, whose previous business experience was as a soap salesman, envisioned Griffith continuing at his present killing pace, turning out program pictures at the rate of one every two months, and using them to help defray overhead so that Griffith could do a special every year or so. For another, he offered no sensible opinion as to how Griffith would distribute—even on a states' rights basis—without a set of exchanges or how he would get important play dates with the major theaters in the key cities controlled by the two concerns that were powerful enough—even if they did not merge—to shape any independent producer's destiny.[24]

Of course, any rationale for an independent course—however thoughtless—was bound to go down well with Griffith, as Albert well knew. But Albert had his own interests to attend. He was a self-aggrandizing and essentially foolish man in thrall to the delusion that he could hold his own in the marketplace against the likes of Zukor while building his own satrapy within Griffith's organization.

Here was yet another problem for Griffith—the lack of first-class business advice. Just as he would not tolerate strong leading men in his pictures, he would not tolerate knowledgeable and decisive legal and financial advisors around him either. His attorney, the loyal and gentlemanly Banzhaf, was capable of efficiently carrying out Griffith's instructions, and was not actively wrongheaded, like Albert, but there is in the records not one instance of his disputing Griffith, or of presenting him with information or insights that might alert him to hidden perils. Years later, Griffith's accountant, J. C. Epping, would write: "A clever, strong, combative lawyer would have been of much greater benefit to him. That he should fear such a lawyer . . . was an unfortunate idiosyncrasy . . . Mr. Banzhaf was too cultured, admirable and conscientious a gentleman to be such a counselor. . . . Mr. Griffith needed a lawyer of very keen mentality and capacity of correct appraisal of the men he was dealing with and their motives."[25]

So, distracted by his work, quite literally ill-advised, Griffith and his people talked to both Zukor and First National about his future and then, in January 1918, began to explore an even more exciting possibility. The idea originated with two associates of Zukor's, Hiram Abrams, a distributor from New England who had been running the Paramount chain after Zukor had taken over, and B. P. Schulberg (father of the novelist, Budd), who had functioned as Zukor's publicist, sometime scenarist and general personal assistant from the early days of Famous Players. They felt themselves shunted aside by Zukor as his corporation grew and were, of course, eager to be their own bosses. Schulberg's son, in *Moving Pictures*, his memoir of growing up as the movies grew up, says that the idea of combining the five biggest names in movies at that time (besides Griffith, they were Pickford, Chaplin, Fairbanks, and the western star William S. Hart) in a company they would control (but which its originators would manage) came to his father in a late night meeting with Abrams, though Abrams would claim otherwise when they had a falling out. But which of the two conceived the idea is less important than the fact that United Artists (as the new firm would be called) was a grand design whose time had come. Schulberg even created a manifesto—"89 Reasons for United Artists"—which he took to California with him, along with his family, early in Jaunary 1919. Most of the industry's leaders were assembling there for a convention of First National's exhibitors at the Alexandria Hotel, which was to early Hollywood what the Beverly Hills Hotel now is, home away from home for visiting Eastern moguls as well as a meeting place for everyone with deals to make or rumors to spread. When Chaplin met with First National's leaders he was dismayed by their coolness to his plea for a relatively modest additional advance to ensure the quality of his films, despite the fact that *Shoulder Arms*, his sweet spoof of army life, was currently a hit in the theaters. Similarly, Douglas Fairbanks, who had been financing his independent productions through Famous Players–Lasky, was finding Zukor uncharacteristically reluctant to discuss arrangements for the future, after his contract expired. They, like Griffith, were ready for a new approach to their careers.

It appears that Chaplin was the first of the big five to be approached with their plan by Abrams and Schulberg, and he liked it well enough to take it to his pal, Fairbanks. He, in turn, had no trouble enlisting Mary Pickford's interest. They had become lovers and, indeed, late in 1918, Fairbanks had announced his separation from his first wife because of this affair. Griffith and Hart were then brought in to explore the plan. Meantime, if Chaplin is to be believed, a female "detective" was engaged to solicit the attentions of a First National executive. After three nights of "dates" (which Chaplin, another Victorian sensibility who lived to outlive his historical moment, insisted were entirely chaste) she reported that merger was imminent. Thereupon, again according to Chaplin, all the potential partners engaged a center table in the Alexandria dining room, there to ostentatiously talk business. The idea was that the mere sight of them in earnest confabulation might scare the opposition into delaying *their* merger, which would obviously have to take place without the services of the movies' biggest names. Chaplin insists that at that point none of them intended to form a company of their own. His implication, however, is that once the group was seen together events took on a momentum of their own, with the heads of studios calling Chaplin and friends to offer their services to the fledgling corporation.

It is a curiosity of the memoirs of United Artists' star-founders that none mention Abrams and Schulberg. They must claim credit for business genius as well as performing genius. In any event, the events surrounding the creation of this new firm are somewhat more prosaic than Chaplin allows. One by one all the principals came quite quickly to the conclusion that freedom and profit might best be served by creation of the new distribution entity, basically a servicing rather than a producing or financing organization, and after a night meeting at Fairbanks's home, an agreement in principle was made, with, it seems, Charlotte Pickford, Mary's mother, sitting in for the star who was home, ill with the flu. By the next afternoon, however, Fairbanks had taken the agreement to her, and on January 15, 1919, she placed her signature on it, completing the first phase of organization.

Rumors about the new entity abounded, of course. The news was too big for anyone to keep to himself, especially the ebullient Fairbanks. But it was not until February 5 that the official announcement of what was at first called the United Artists Distributing Association was made to the press. In part this delay was occasioned by the need to sell out the organization's progenitors, Abrams and Schulberg. In the course of his work on behalf of the Liberty Loan drives, Fairbanks had become friends with William Gibbs McAdoo, President Wilson's son-in-law and his Secretary of the Treasury. McAdoo was a lawyer and a self-made man who had thus far neglected to make a fortune of his own. He had earned only about $12,000 a year in government, and now that the emergency was over, was eager to find lucrative employment. Fortuitously (or perhaps not) he was vacationing in Santa Barbara at this time (Fairbanks, in a typical gesture, had sent a brass band to welcome McAdoo at the Los Angeles railroad station). It was only natural for Fairbanks to apprise his distinguished new friend of the United Artists discussions, even more natural for him to propose McAdoo as president of the new concern. Of all the movie people, Fairbanks at that time had the shrewdest sense of the power of stardom. He wanted to tighten the loose ties that had been bound, during the war, when Washington had discovered what a useful propaganda adjunct film was, when the movie people had come to enjoy close alliance with the political power elite. He was aware of how a name like McAdoo's could add social and economic respectability to the

movies. And he was right. The formation of United Artists was front-
page news in such establishment organs as the *New York Tribune*, with
the leads featuring McAdoo's name, and his successful personal solution
to the postwar unemployment problem, above the descriptions of the
new company function and the names of the founders.

But this was a bitter blow to the men who had thought up the idea
in the first place. At a meeting in Santa Barbara, McAdoo—who also had
an offer from Carl Laemmle at Universal—turned down the United
Artists presidency and proposed his long-time press secretary, Oscar Price,
for the post, with himself taking on the title of general counsel at a fee
falsely rumored to be $100,000 per year, but still very agreeable. In short,
he collected the big movie dollars without having to sully himself by daily
association with this raffish crew. In the circumstances he thought it pre-
sumptuous of Abrams and Schulberg to get 20 percent of the company.
Two percent would be more like it, with that going to Abrams, the knowledgeable (and often abrasive) expert in distribution, the only movie business man in the new firm's operating hierarchy. Schulberg was offered a
post as Abrams's assistant, on a salary, with no share in the business. This
left him in a worse position than he had been in with Zukor, where at least
he held a small amount of stock in Famous Players. He came to believe
that his friend Abrams had conspired with Fairbanks and McAdoo to
ease him out, a charge Abrams denied, and there was a lawsuit over the
matter that was finally settled out of court in 1922. Griffith regretted
Schulberg's disappearance and even intervened to try to get him to take
the assistantship that was offered him. In later years he would speak
warmly of Schulberg, who was, like himself, largely self-educated yet well-
spoken and, at least by movie standards, quite literate.

There was a warning in this, if Griffith could have seen it. He was not
present at the Santa Barbara meeting, and it seems he was but cursorily
consulted about it. In the counsels of the company, Fairbanks, in league
with the lady who would soon be his wife, and his best friend Chaplin,
constituted a majority. United Artists would always reflect the desires of
this threesome far more than it would Griffith's. In any event, preoccupied with his own creative problems, he would, in essence, give them
and their management his proxy—and then complain bitterly about their
policies.[26]

The basic trouble was that the UA proposal, tempting as it was,
placed a severe financial strain on Griffith. It called for each of the principals to subscribe to 1,000 shares of common stock at a price of $100 per
share, with the company having the right to require them to pay on demand, every 30 days, 20 percent of their subscription for the first five
months of the company's existence, in order to finance start-up costs.
Moreover, as a sort of performance bond for each of the nine films each
agreed to provide the company, these shares were divided into nine blocks

(eight containing 111 shares, one containing 112) which were placed in an escrow account, controlled by Dennis F. ("Cap") O'Brien, attorney for Pickford and Fairbanks, and soon to be the most powerful voice in the firm's operations. He would return one block of stock to them as they turned over each of their films for distribution. That meant, of course, that the partners could realize no dividends until they made the pictures.

This would have posed no problem if they had all been able to start delivering films to UA immediately. But only Fairbanks was free of previous commitments. Pickford and Chaplin both owed films to First National, with the former unable to make a film for United Artists until 1920, the latter not working himself free until 1923. In this connection, the developing reluctance of William S. Hart to commit to the new combine was a serious blow, for he was free to start producing for it immediately. Curiously, the austere—if sometimes personally cruel—western star might have had more of the true spirit of the artist than any of them. He was comfortably off, and as much a loner as the character he played on screen. Huge wealth did not interest him, and neither did complicated business arrangements requiring constant tending. He just wanted to be free to pursue undistracted his vision of the West, a vision very much informed by his sense that what he was celebrating was fast disappearing. He did not withdraw entirely from the discussions, but his name did not appear in the public announcement of the new company's formation, either. In the spring he was still discussing with its management the possibility of releasing through UA, but he finally renewed his contract with Zukor, who gave him sufficient production funds and a promise of all the creative freedom he needed.

As for Griffith, precisely a week after he signed the agreement in principle to form the new corporation, he signed a three-picture deal with First National, even though he still owed Zukor two films on his Artcraft contract. The First National arrangement called for a $50,000 advance on signing, a payment of $92,500 upon starting his first film, $125,000 upon starting each of the next two—and payments upon the completion of each which brought First National's cost for each film to $285,000.[27]

Griffith would claim he needed this First National money to finance his forthcoming obligations to United Artists, and that is probably true. At the moment he had just enough coming in from *Hearts* and his Artcraft deal to finance the remaining pictures he owed Zukor. Without dipping into his personal resources he could not fulfill his obligation to the UA stock subscription or finance films for the new firm to release. His inability to comfortably manage the latter feat would, indeed, condition all his relations with UA. Heretofore he had been able to finance his pictures on the advances paid him by distributors. But the UA agreements would specifically state that the principals had to supply films to the new company at their own expense. To do this Griffith would have to set up a new corporation, in which he would attempt to capitalize on his name and his pictures' reputation for profitability. But that would take time, and he could not hope to keep his actors and staff together—and, as he was beginning to hope, own a studio of his own—without being uninterruptedly in production on some basis. Since the majority of his new allies were still under obligation to First National themselves, it also occurred to him that, if he started immediately supplying films to UA, he and Fairbanks would be carrying most of the company's burden alone for at least a year. Finally, it may be that Griffith did not entirely share their dream and wanted to make certain United Artists was truly a going concern before he entrusted all his work to it. To put the matter simply, and for all the idealism of their first press releases, all concerned were doing their best to protect themselves, as we would now say, on the downside.

Still, they proceeded to sign the contracts that bound themselves to one another on February 5, 1919. They released a statement that read, in part: "We believe this is necessary to protect the exhibitor and the industry itself, thus enabling the exhibitor to book only pictures that he wishes to play and not force upon him . . . other program films which he does not desire, believing that as servants of the people we can thus best serve the people. We also think that this step is positively and absolutely necessary to protect the great motion picture public from threatening combinations and trusts that would force upon them mediocre productions and machine-made entertainment."[28] For his part, McAdoo, who in the end settled for a $50,000 yearly counsel's fee (plus 1,000 shares of United Artists stock), also issued a statement stressing a populist view of the founders' motivations: "They have determined not to permit any trust to destroy competition or to blight or interfere with the quality of their work. They feel it is of the utmost importance to secure the artistic development of the motion picture industry and they believe that this will be impossible if any trust should get possession of the industry and wholly commercialize the business."[29]

A cynic may have a chortle or two over that last phrase, but the talk of trusts and the necessity to resist same was not entirely a press agent's fiction. A 1927 Federal Trade Commission investigation concluded that Famous Players–Lasky had, indeed, been maneuvering for a merger with, or a takeover of, First National in this period. Though his scheme was rebuffed, and though it is impossible to say how much the formation of United Artists, by focusing public attention on the matter, helped in the fight against this scheme, Adolph Zukor continued to wage the war on other fronts, acquiring, over the next decade, most of the First National theater chains piecemeal.

4

After the heady days of January and February, when all the United Artists could feel that special satisfaction that derives from taking charge of one's own fate, or at least enjoying the illusion of doing so, Griffith, in particular, found himself with a great deal of unfinished business to attend. He still owed Zukor two pictures, and now he owed three more to First National, in addition to which he had agreed to begin turning films over to UA for distribution "no later than Sept. 1, 1920."[30] As it happened, he had two scenarios ready to shoot, but he also had a completed film in his vaults, *Broken Blossoms*, and by this time he surely understood that he had made something that was, by the standards of the day, extraordinary.

Griffith therefore premiered this extraordinary film in an extraordinary fashion. He had scheduled a D. W. Griffith repertory season at a New York legitimate house, the George M. Cohan, the main purpose of which was to present some revisions of previous work. He had carved two program-length features out of the best material in *Intolerance*, *The Fall of Babylon* and *The Mother and the Law*, and he had a revised, "peace" edition of *Hearts of the World* ready as well. A new film, especially one as radically different in tone and style as *Broken Blossoms*, would illuminate, and be illuminated by, this context.

Contrary to the generally accepted story, releasing the film in this manner was not a desperate expedient for Griffith, an answer to Zukor's rejection of *Broken Blossoms* as too poetic and too gloomy. Griffith had a contractual right to designate one of his Artcraft films a special and handle its initial run as a limited engagement with advanced prices. It may be that Griffith was counting on strong reviews and a good response from the sophisticated New York audience to still such concern as Zukor had about the film. But given its low cost, and the generally good results he had enjoyed with the other Griffith Artcraft releases, these cannot have been very serious. And once the film opened to the least ambiguous acclaim any Griffith picture had ever enjoyed, Zukor found himself in a bidding war to handle *Broken Blossoms*' general release. It was a war he pursued vigorously—with no hint of the philistine contempt for the film that has been attributed to him by Lillian Gish, among others.

Even before the official opening, it became clear that the film had a singular emotional power. After an early screening, according to Lillian Gish, Morris Gest was discovered throwing and kicking chairs, yelling and generally behaving like a maniac. The gist of his message was that the film was the greatest thing ever seen on Broadway and that ticket prices instead of having a three-dollar top should be scaled to $300. (It was, incidentally, at this screening that some blue stage lights were accidentally left on, bathing the picture in a rather exotic glow; Griffith ordered the effect retained.) On opening night, the response, as seemed so often to happen with Griffith films, was a reverential hush before the applause and the cries for an appearance by Griffith broke out.

But there was nothing hushed about the reviews. The *New York Times* called it "a masterpiece in moving pictures," "not a movie melodrama with an unhappy ending—but a sincere, human tragedy." Beyond that, it praised Gish for her success in a role "so difficult as to be beyond the reach of almost any actress whose name comes to mind," and noted that "many of the pictures surpass anything hitherto seen on the screen in beauty and dramatic force."[31] Julian Johnson, in *Photoplay*, went further. *Broken Blossoms*, he said, "is the first genuine tragedy of the movies," because its outcome "seems foreordained, the drums of doom are sounding from the first steps of the pageant." And justifiably he praised Griffith's willingness to explore new territory. "The extraordinary part of Griffith is that he has never ceased to be a pioneer. He continues to advance. He dares to present novelties of form and novelties of material. He does not always get away with it, but he keeps right on. . . ."[32]

It is difficult to find major reviews of *Broken Blossoms* that did not follow this line. It is true that people made joking plays on the title ("Busted Buds") and after the picture went into general release *Photoplay* printed a gag going the rounds in which a provincial theater manager exclaims to a producer, "I always heard that Griffith was so much." "Well, isn't he?" inquires the producer. "Say," comes the reply, "those close-ups in *Broken Blossoms* were so out of focus when I started to run the print that I had to cut most of them."[33] Only *Variety*, then, as ever, resolute in casting a shrewd commercial eye on all things, faulted the film. "Draggy," was its opinion, reporting that after the premiere "none could be found, other than the usual assortment of sycophants, who was prepared to give it as his opinion that the picture would prove a money-getter. The majority connected with the selling end of the industry shook their heads dubiously."[34]

For a rarity, however, the commercially minded had underestimated the public. Buoyed by the New York notices and by the excellent grosses of this "platform" engagement (as it would now be described), *Broken Blossoms* went on to generate profits—if not grosses—in excess of any Griffith film other than *Birth* before it and *Way Down East* after it. Thus, commercially as well as artistically, *Broken Blossoms* represented, in the long run, a broken promise. If, somehow, Griffith could have pursued the spirit that was moving in this film, if he had sloughed away the melodramatic residue still present in its dramaturgy instead of reinforcing it in his future productions, if the austerity of its design and structure had guided him, his fate—if not commercially, then as an artist—might have been very different. Under pressure, however, he reverted to the material he knew best and what experience taught him erroneously was "sure fire" with audiences—theatrical melodrama.

And he was under pressure. He had to move on as quickly as possible. Meantime the question of *Broken Blossoms'* general release went unresolved until August. Zukor was willing to make a special arrangement with Griffith for it. Knowing the latter's need for immediate cash, and estimating their combined gross to be around $600,000, he proposed not releasing the film until they had realized three-quarters of that figure ($450,000) in exhibition contracts theater owners could not cancel. Based on the division of profits pertaining in their Artcraft contracts, this would have netted Griffith a more or less immediate $250,000, with more doubtless to come.[35] United Artists, however, was desperate for product. The company's first film, Fairbanks's *His Majesty, the American,* was due for release in September, but he could not get another film ready until the end of the year. By that time UA would have sixteen exchanges open with almost nothing to do for almost three months. Thus Griffith had a strong incentive to distribute *Broken Blossoms* through UA. Zukor, despite his reputation for ruthlessness, always had something of a soft spot for Griffith, and he permitted him, finally, to buy out Artcraft's interest in the film for precisely the sum he had estimated it was worth to Griffith— $250,000. This was a large sum compared to the $80,000 the film's negative had cost to create, but it was scarcely exorbitant—about what Zukor thought Famous Players might realize at the minimum by releasing it, and only $28,000 more than the price he would have been obliged to pay for it under the terms of his contract with Griffith. He would have been justified asking a sum closer to his maximum expectations, especially since he was turning the picture over to a company that had been formed largely in an attempt to thwart his own interests.

In August, the UA board (composed of the principals' lawyers) voted to borrow the money to advance Griffith to purchase the film, accepting from him a presonal note for that amount, and insisting that 80 percent of the film's rental deposits be set aside for application, if needed, against the bank loan.[36] As it happened, it was unnecessary. By late January, *Broken Blossoms* had returned $454,711.50 to the distributor, only $9,000 less than the phenomenally popular Fairbanks film had grossed with a month's head start on it in the theaters. In the end, the picture would return in the neighborhood of $700,000 to United Artists.

The *Broken Blossoms* opening was followed, at a distance of only two weeks, by the opening of Griffith's penultimate Artcraft production *True Heart Susie,* which he had somehow managed to complete during the winter. Critically, it was smothered in the excitement surrounding *Broken Blossoms,* though it seems to have performed as well as any of the other Artcraft productions in its program release. But it is unfortunate that this pastoral romance, so similar in spirit to A *Romance of Happy Valley*, and no less charming, was largely ignored at the time. It is the last film in which Griffith draws directly upon his warmest memories of a bucolic childhood, and the last of his looks backward at a fast-vanishing America without the intervention of subplots, chases, sexually imperiled heroines and the rest of his beloved melodramatic contrivances. It also includes a performance by Lillian Gish that is among her finest, and different from her work in *Romance* because it is more overtly comic, at times gently parodying those conventions of girlish innocence also beloved by Griffith. She gives a certain tartness to a role that is always dangerously close to excessive sweetness.

The basic story, Gish has said, was suggested by the romance of David Copperfield and his faithful Agnes. The setting here is Pine Grove, Indiana, essentially indistinguishable from Griffith's Kentucky, just across the Ohio River. The introductory shot, like that of *Happy Valley*, is from a high angle, but instead of showing a toll road, symbolic, as it were, of life's highway and the costs of setting forth on it, as the earlier picture did, this time we see two modest, pleasant houses confronting each other across a country road—separated but not impassably so. In one lives Susie May Trueheart, in the other, William Jenkins (again Robert Harron). Establishing sequences show them as childhood sweethearts, though they never openly acknowledge anything more than friendship. When it is time for William to consider college, Susie sells her beloved cow, among other possessions, so that she can secretly subsidize his ambitions. The sale of the cow is one of the film's sweetest, and most memorable, sequences, for Susie obtains a written promise from the purchaser that he will provide "a good home" for the animal, and she actually kisses it goodbye.

William's commitment to the ministry is doubtless sincere, but he possesses an eminently distractable heart. When, after graduation, he returns to Pine Grove to take up pastoral duties there, he finds himself fatally drawn to the town's new milliner, Bettina Hopkins (Clarine Seymour, in effect repeating her role in *The Girl Who Stayed at Home*). The word "flapper" might not yet have come into currency, but Seymour was creating a transitional figure somewhere between the earlier "vamp" and those bouncy girls with bobbed hair who eventually became prime symbols of rebellious youth in the 1920s.

By contrast, Gish, for all her sweetness, is seen as rather repressed, unable to express her feelings truly unless she is alone and, more than that, safe behind the sheltering walls of her home. Indeed, as John Belton has pointed out in an excellent analysis of this little film, much of its design implicitly stresses this point, with Harron's character (and family) seen in the open air, moving more or less boldly through the world, while Gish and her people are seen in more confined circumstances. As things

work out, William marries the milliner while the faithful Susie uncomplainingly serves as one of her bridesmaids.

Bettina, of course, is totally unsuited to life in a parsonage, where
William devotes some of his time to work on an inspirational book. She
takes to running about with a fast set (among whom is Carol Dempster in
a small and quite unshowy part). Out with this crowd, Bettina is caught
in a heavy storm, falls ill and eventually (as a subtitle has it) ". . . dies
as she had lived—a little bit unfaithful." Susie knows the story but keeps
it from William, who vows that he will never marry again. His ignorance
and naïveté are, however, unbearable to Susie's aunt, and she tells the
young man what he ought to have realized for himself long since, namely,
that Susie Trueheart bears an uncannily apt name. He goes to her and
finds her at a window of her house, watering flowers. She hides shyly behind the watering can, and William must reach awkwardly through the
window to embrace her. The shot, of course, is reminiscent of the famous
welcome home in *Birth*, but with the action reversed; this time the embrace promises a drawing out rather than a drawing in. Yet, as Belton
says, "the composition—combining male and female, exterior and interior—reflects a new stability and balance in their union."[37] As a fillip, it
should be noted that by this time William's book had been published to
considerable acclaim, fulfilling again the Griffithian dream of worldly
success crowning the triumph of true love.

Finally, it should be observed that in this film Gish plays on the
screen a role that seems to predict the role she was now beginning to be
forced to play in real life—the faithful and, it would seem, quietly suffering, woman whose love is not so much spurned as taken for granted by a
man romantically overwhelmed by another woman. Their exclusive professional relationship nearing an end, and their personal relationship in
turmoil, Gish would nevertheless take up a Susie-like role in Griffith's life,
patient, discreet, and above all loyal. In the years immediately ahead, she
would work for Griffith whenever he needed her, and she would never,
over the course of a very long life, mention Dempster, except in the most
carefully neutral terms, or criticize Griffith publicly. She would become,
instead, the fiercest defender of Griffith's flame, insisting on the greatness
of his work and his spirit against all criticism, in the process perhaps exaggerating both to the point where he became an almost inhuman paragon of creative and personal virtue.

Whatever else he was, Griffith was a paragon of energy. And it may
be that his capacity for hard work, for undertaking more than he, or any
other man, could possibly handle successfully (or even rationally), contributed to the terrible financial miscalculation he was about to make.
Not to mention the romantic one now reaching a crisis point.

For with *Broken Blossoms* successfully launched, Griffith entrained
for Los Angeles, determined to discharge the last of his obligation to Art-

craft and to begin satisfying First National as well. He paused briefly in Columbus, Ohio, where a large gathering of Methodists had convened, and arranged to produce a documentary film about the conference, which he intended to give to the church for nonprofit use. His mother had been a member of this sect and he dedicated the film to her memory.

Also on his mind at this time was the need to have a studio of his own. Despite the fact that his name was now up over the gate at the old Fine Arts lot, it was what it had always been, a cramped rental facility that suited neither his status nor his ambitions. After all, his UA partners all had lots of their own. Besides, for reasons he never made clear, he was determined to move his operations back East. It was, of course, closer to the theater, and he still thought of himself as a man of the theater. And, of course, United Artists was being managed from New York. Then, too, a major new studio, the first significant production facility to be built in New York since Biograph had constructed the studio he had only briefly used, was going up in Astoria, Long Island, to house Paramount's East Coast production. It might have falsely signaled to Griffith a general move back to the place where movies had begun. Finally, *Broken Blossoms* had been entirely shot on stages, the first long Griffith film not to employ locations extensively, and he might have felt that the need for a wide variety of outdoor settings was now diminishing. It has, in fact, been argued that the film's largest unintended effect within the film industry was to show other producers what could be accomplished within the controlled environment of a stage, leading to a general retreat from location shooting that was not arrested for some thirty years. Be that as it may, over the early summer of 1919, telegrams flew back and forth across the country as, from a distance, Griffith supervised the search his brother and Banzhaf were making for a suitable venue for him near New York.

Not that he could devote more than passing attention to the problem. There were pictures to be made. The two scenarios readily at hand were once again the product of Stanner E. V. Taylor—a western eventually called *Scarlet Days* and a rural melodrama called *The Greatest Question*. Neither would turn out to be among D. W. Griffith's most distinguished works.

Indeed, *Scarlet Days* is, arguably, the worst feature-length film he ever made. If it has any abiding interest at all it lies in factors surrounding its production, not in the production itself. To begin with, it provides a notion of the rather casual manner in which Griffith worked with his associates in devising original screen material. For it seems one Alice E. Phillips of San Francisco advanced the claim that it had been plagiarized from a story she had submitted to the Griffith organization. In replying to this unfounded charge, Taylor wrote that sometime in December 1918, Griffith had asked him to turn his thoughts to a western and that "two weeks later while returning with Mr. Griffith from a visit to some auto races I outlined the plot I had conceived . . . and a few days later at his request [I] reduced it to writing."[38] Subsequently, Harry Carr contributed to the story, too, for he had apparently held a number of "table talks" with Griffith about the legendary Southern California bandit Joaquín Murietta, a sort of Robin Hood figure (at least as his story had come down) who was then enjoying a certain vogue among movie people (Douglas Fairbanks was among them). They liked the feeling that they were treading on romantic historical ground. At any rate, Griffith changed the time and date of Taylor's story from Arizona in 1849 to California in 1875 and incorporated some incidents from Carr's Murietta yarns in the picture.

The film actually has very little to say about the Murietta character, who appears under the name Alvarez. It is mostly about Nell, a "dance hall" woman (the traditional movie genteelism for prostitute) played by Eugénie Besserer (who would achieve her immortality as Jolson's mother in the first talkie, *The Jazz Singer*), and her relationship with her daughter, played by Dempster. The latter has been kept in the East, at a fashionable boarding school, unaware of just how her mother earned her tuition. While the girl is journeying West for a visit the mother gets into a brawl with another "hostess," who dies of a heart attack in the course of the fight. The mother is falsely accused of murder, however, and is saved from a lynch mob, composed of friends of the late "Spasm Sal," by Alvarez. Frustrated, the proprietor of the dance hall (Walter Long, at his greasiest) leads a bandit band against the cabin where Nell (the Besserer character) and her daughter are, and they are saved only when the much-wanted Alvarez gives himself up to the sheriff as a distraction. In due course, however, he is himself rescued from jail by his fiery mistress, Chiquita, who is played by Clarine Seymour with frequent broadly comic displays of Hispanic "fieriness" (she butts at things, like a goat, and even includes a goat among her targets).

The picture plays the way a synopsis of it reads—as a very strained concoction. The location work was done in Tuolumne County, California, and a few critics commented approvingly on its fresh look. But this scenery is just scenery to Griffith, or perhaps to Elmer Clifton, who functioned virtually as a codirector on this film. In any event, Griffith was unable to make the connection between landscape and character which he so successfully managed in films like *Happy Valley* and *Susie*. Indeed, as his relatively few westerns for Biograph indicated, the broad vistas of the American West rarely moved him as they did so many other directors. He never rejoiced in the sense of discovery that animated this great film form, from the days of Hart to the days of Ford. His sensibility was very much rooted in the gentler and more enfolding ground of his native South and his adopted East. It may be that the emptiness of this film, all story and movement but no characters who were not clichés, offers as good a clue as any about why he was now so anxious to relocate in a place more psychologically congenial to him than California.

Of the picture's many failures, none is more apparent than that of that gentle WASP, Richard Barthelmess, as the dashing bandit, Alvarez. With his hair plastered down and a goatee and a mustache plastered on, he cuts a rather ridiculous figure, the more so when it is recalled that another actor, much more suited to the role, was available, and had even been seriously considered for it. This was Rudolph Valentino. Griffith would later claim that he first met him at a spaghetti party at the home of Elmer Clifton, his assistant, and that he had told him he might become a star if he lost 25 pounds. But apparently Valentino was slender enough, and appealing enough to win his job as a prologue dancer at the premiere of *The Greatest Thing in Life*, as well as a caddish role in *Out of Luck*, one of the Dorothy Gish series. Griffith wandered on to one of that picture's sets one day and suggested a nice bit of business to Valentino— biting one of his victims' pearls to see if they were genuine. It was Dorothy Gish who recommended him for the Alvarez role.

By this time Valentino was something of a familiar around the lot. Barthelmess would recall him as one of the young people enjoying "an extremely happy existence" making movies in Los Angeles at the time. "We worked long hours," he said in 1945, "very often at night and on Sundays, but we would find time maybe to go horseback riding and have a picnic at night or go to the old Ship Cafe at Venice . . . [a much-favored hangout for the movies' younger set in the early days] or to the old Vernon Country Club on the outskirts of Los Angeles."[39] Valentino was, by repute, an amiable and even rather passive individual off camera— Griffith's sort of temperament—and it appears that the director liked him in his rather distant way. Since Valentino physically suited the role of Alvarez much better than Barthelmess did, it is puzzling that Griffith did not use him. But one rather suspects Griffith of backing away from the strong sexual appeal of an actor who singularly combined the exotic and the boyish.

In later years Griffith would, in fact, admit that he had made a mistake. At the time, he had told Dorothy Gish that "women are apt to find him too foreign-looking," but in that very same year Valentino played a professional co-respondent in *Eyes of Youth* with Clara Kimball Young, the role that brought him to the attention of June Mathis, the Metro scenarist and story editor, who proposed him for *The Four Horsemen of the Apocalypse* which, in 1920, made him a star—a star whose career, incidentally, was marked by a succession of portrayals of romantic outlaws not so very different from the one he might have played in *Scarlet Days*. "Well, I was wrong in that," Griffith told Lillian Gish. "Now they apparently like these foreign fellows. . . . Maybe they're changing."[40]

Maybe they were. And maybe this casting error was an early sign of Griffith's inability to keep up with social change in a decade that would seem to contain nothing but that quality.

But if Valentino was missed, it must be admitted that Carol Dempster appears to somewhat better advantage in *Scarlet Days* than she does in many of the other Griffith films. Her slightly stiff manner rather suits the character of a young woman brought up in the genteel world of eastern boarding schools suddenly cast up in a rough frontier world. One suspects that some of her awkwardness in Griffith's films resulted from attempts by her director to force her into the Pickford-Marsh-Gish mold, which went against her type. She was mature for her years in manner, and there was something no-nonsensical about her. It would be four years later, too late in her career, and his, that Griffith gave her a role that suited her and in which she was highly effective.

This summer, however, her abilities as an actress were subject to less discussion in the Griffith company than was the simple fact of her disturbing presence there. For this we have the word of Ralph Graves, then a young juvenile, later a leading man whose career dwindled into low-budget action pictures when the talkies arrived. In 1919 he was hired as a sort of standby for the restive Harron and he had his first Griffith role in *Scarlet Days*. Cast as a young Virginia gentleman prospecting for gold far from home, he was Dempster's love interest in the film. And as a newcomer who passed fairly quickly through the Griffith camp, he was also a fairly objective observer of its oddities. Though finding Griffith "slightly illiterate" and a bit of a "humbug," he also describes him as "likeable" especially if you did not let him awe you. Literate or not, he had in Graves's view a "profound," instinctive "sense of beauty." This combined with his capacity for "indefatigable" work had obviously, until now, been more valuable to him than the genuine literary sensibility that he lacked. There is something cool, bracing and believable in Graves's descriptions, as there are in Karl Brown's, qualities not always present in the feminine memoirs.

Graves is, in fact, the only source for a summary of the company's mood in the summer of 1919. "An uninteresting lot . . . rather dull little people with pretty faces," is his blunt description of his colleagues among the actors, and he says Dempster's replacement of Gish as Griffith's favorite "created quite a flurry. It denoted a change of viewpoint as well as a change of attention on the part of Mr. Griffith. Dempster's entry created jealousies and factions, as well as a feud among the staff members. . . ."[41] Graves stayed out of all that and it is also clear that Gish herself maintained a cool façade. She must have felt that just as Dempster could never replace her professionally, she could not do so personally, either. She would therefore continue to work, outwardly imperturbable, for her mentor and wait in vain for his romantic fever to cool.

She did so until 1922—not perhaps the confidante she had been, but still a voice of conscience, and her strategy might have worked had not Dempster proved to be a young woman of remarkable tenacity.

Still, the gradual loss of Gish's idealistic influence on Griffith is clear, and must be regretted almost as much as her gradual disappearance from his films in the years immediately ahead. Griffith himself, in his last sad years, came to recognize this fact. Adela Rogers St. Johns had recorded encountering him, somewhat tipsy, more than a little self-pitying, in Musso and Frank's Grill on Hollywood Boulevard sometime in the 1940s. When the conversation turned to the old days he whimpered, "I never had a day's luck after Lillian left me." It was an astonishing admission, and St. Johns claims she replied, "But . . . D. W. . . . Lillian didn't leave you! You chucked her out for that mediocre girl. . . ."[42] The truth is perhaps not quite so melodramatic as this exchange indicates. Griffith's luck did not entirely run out until another decade had passed, and he can scarcely be said to have melodramatically cast Gish aside. The business was somewhat more delicately managed than that. Yet the fact remains that a fine actress, one who was perfectly suited to Griffith's sensibility, and perfectly pliable to his command, did begin, in this summer, a process of disengagement. What this process cost Lillian Gish is perhaps best summarized by the fact that though the next picture Griffith made (the last at his California studio) starred her, she had no recollection of its contents or of the events surrounding its making when it was run for her in 1964. There is one entirely undescriptive sentence about it in her autobiography. Clearly she had blocked it, and the moment of its making, out of memory. Yet, if it is a failure, *The Greatest Question* is not without interest. In its modest way, it represents an attempt, however flawed, to preserve some of the spirit of the pastorals while grafting on to the basic form material Griffith judged to have larger and more pressing interest for a contemporary audience.

Basically it is the story of a sweet child named Nellie Jarvis (otherwise known as "Little Miss Yes'm"), played by Lillian Gish. The daughter of itinerant peddlers, as a very young girl she sees a husband and wife commit murder, a scene she blotted from memory. Later, after both her father and mother have died, she is taken in by a kindly couple, the Hiltons, who have two sons, one of whom (Ralph Graves) goes off to war, the other of whom (Robert Harron, in his last role under Griffith's direction), becomes Nellie's good, shyly loving friend. In order to help the Hiltons, who are quite poor, she hires out to the Cains—whom she does not recognize as the very couple who committed the murder she witnessed a decade earlier. The husband has lascivious designs on her; the wife (played rather too sweepingly by Josephine Crowell) is nothing less than a sadist. By this time, the Hiltons' elder son has died in the war (in a rather spectacular scene, the submarine on which he is serving must dive and he is left on deck) and despair is added to his family's growing destitution. It is at this point that Griffith introduces his newsy topic, spiritualism. For the Hiltons visit their son's grave and he appears reassuringly to them—a vision that restores their wavering faith. Thereafter, oil is discovered on their land, their remaining son rushes off to tell the good news to Nellie, arriving at the Cains' dismal home just in time to rescue her from—what else?—a beating and an attempted rape, both occasioned in part by a restoration of Nellie's memory of the dark deed she had earlier witnessed. The picture ends with a festive dinner and a confession of love by the young people, who nevertheless decide to wait until they are more mature before marrying.

In its way, the film is as busily overplotted as *Scarlet Days*, and its references to spiritualism are both awkward and perfunctory. They were used to sell the picture to a mass public which, for a brief moment, was much intrigued by the claims made on behalf of the spirit world by Sir Oliver Lodge, the distinguished British physicist, who gave it a certain scientific credibility, and Sir Arthur Conan Doyle, Sherlock Holmes's creator, both of whom had lost sons in the war and believed they could get in touch with them through mediums. Griffith, however, makes no attempt to delve at all deeply into this matter, which might actually have made an interesting film subject. It is one more distraction in a film that needed less, not more in the way of contrivances. Griffith might also have spared his audience yet another sequence in which Lillian Gish is once again placed in sexual peril. (Says Graves, "He enjoyed scaring the little boys and girls during rehearsals by giving a first-class imitation of how the paleolithic man enjoyed a little woo. . . . Always, a nasty heavy who coveted the whispy carcass of the ethereal Gish or the light fantastic . . . Dempster. Mr. Griffith enjoyed giving a demonstration of how this part was to be portrayed [while] the little heroine stood by in great awe and wonder. . . ."[43])

Yet for all of this William K. Everson is right to call *The Greatest Question* pictorially superb, ". . . with some of Griffith's best use of landscape for lyrical and dramatic symbolism." Again, the outdoor settings evoke those of his boyhood, while Gish, in her brave, best moments evokes something of Pickford's tragic slavey in the remarkable *Stella Maris* made a year earlier by Mickey Neilan. In short, and unlike *Scarlet Days*, there are moments of true feeling and honest memory illuminating the picture.

Still, one must not claim too much for the film. As Everson concludes, "like so many 1920 films [the picture was actually released in November 1919] it is a kind of transition film from Victorianism to the coming sophistication."[44] It is an appropriate summation, for as he finished it, Griffith was preparing at last to make a transition of his own, from what he saw as employee status to what he saw—erroneously—as full independence, producing what he liked, when he liked as the sole master of his own fate. For in mid-August the long-discussed, long-delayed deal was finally struck by his agents and a few weeks later, he set forth for the East and the realization of his cherished dream, a studio of his own, housing a production company that was entirely his, with which to succeed—or fail—as he would.

CHAPTER FOURTEEN

A Man's Estate

"HE loved beauty," Lillian Gish said, many years later, when she was asked why D. W. Griffith had chosen so expensive a site for the first, and last, studio he would ever own.[1] And, assuredly, it was beautiful, perhaps the most imposing combination of grounds and structure anyone has ever employed for the manufacture of motion pictures (only Pinewood, in England, compares). The Henry Flagler Estate, 28 acres on Orienta Point, near Mamaroneck, about an hour out of New York City, was nothing less than a robber barony; the sometime residence of a man who was one of John D. Rockefeller's most prosperous associates in the creation of Standard Oil, a pioneer of the Florida land boom, something of a decadent and something of a recluse, which was part of this isolated property's appeal for Griffith. Built on a thumb of land stuck into Long Island Sound, the estate contained, in addition to the main house, towered and turreted, a smaller but still quite lovely servants' residence, a summer house, a gate house, a gardener's cottage, stables, a dock, a narrow beach, a small forest, extensive orchards and gardens which, in time, supplied fruits and vegetables for the commissary—the only known economy in the Griffith operation.

The basic cost of this grandeur was high, but it was not exorbitant. Perhaps because takers for such a place were necessarily rare, its $375,000 cost was actually less than some of the larger commercial properties Griffith's people considered on his behalf. And, through McAdoo's intercession with a friend in real estate who by coincidence controlled the property, favorable terms of purchase were arranged. The truly damaging costs would come in converting a residential site to industrial purposes.

But as Griffith kept making clear in letters, price was no object. To be sure, for a successful man, newly wealthy, the place suited his new sense of himself, but he also wanted something that could be quickly converted to his use—he dared not be out of production too long—and that was a specification Orienta Point seemed to fulfill; local building codes were easier to satisfy than those of New York City. Moreover, it occurred to him that he could live as well as work on the estate. He had been living in hotels since separating from Linda, but as the Gish pastorals show, and as we might guess were true of a man of his age, his thoughts were turning more and more to the past, to the last real home he had ever known, the farm in Oldham County. He felt the need to root himself again. And in plantationlike splendor.

But there was more at work here than nostalgia for a past that never was. Like everyone in the first generation to gain substantial wealth and fame from the movies, Griffith was groping for a way to live, and a way to present himself to the world, when there were no appropriate models available to guide him in this enterprise. No show people had ever had to deal with celebrity (or money) at the levels this new technology (reinforced by the other new communications technologies, ranging from tabloid newspapers to inexpensive mass magazines, to—soon—radio) imposed on them. Griffith's partners in United Artists were leading the way in literally reinventing fame's rules and regulations at this time. Whether one is talking about the Beverly Hills life-style—the town grew up around Pickfair—or the crowd of functionaries they employed to ease their passages through (and around) the world or their determination to treat (and be treated) as equal members of the traditional social, political, industrial and intellectual elites, one is talking about a kind of public life unprecedented for performers.

The trouble was that the traditions they were establishing were not really appropriate to Griffith. For one thing, though he was certainly famous enough, he was not a generally recognized public figure. He could still pass anonymously through a crowd if he so chose, and generally he did. As Gerrit Lloyd said, he was not comfortable with strangers, especially if they were people of accomplishment. "You must remember that Griffith is not a ready man with quick reactions," the press agent wrote. "It takes a certain measured interval for his brain to function, and to cover that moment he was embarrassed and constrained . . . a groping man trying to orient his interest."[2] It was at such moments, Lloyd said, that Griffith evoked his grand, haughty manner, the manner of the old-fashioned matinee idol, very much at odds with the new celebrity style of a Fairbanks or a Chaplin which was much more democratic and relaxed in tone—an implicit denial of "genius" as opposed to the old-fashioned assertion of it.

Lloyd, in another letter, traced this style back from Griffith's friend John Barrymore through the Booth family to Garrick, but its exemplars are of less significance than the fact that, as a young actor, Griffith had obviously envied the style and wished to emulate it. Now, at last, he had the chance. And his choice of a headquarters was conditioned by this need. For it must be remembered that among the great actor-managers the tradition of owning an imposing country estate, a sequestered retreat from the rigors of the road, was a powerful signal of status. Junius Brutus Booth had his Arcadia farm near Baltimore. James O'Neill had his seaside retreat at New London, made gloomily famous in later years by his son's *Long Day's Journey into Night*. William Gillette had his eccentric's castle in Connecticut in which to rest from his labors as Sherlock Holmes. Real estate of this character was as much a part of theatrical success, as Griffith had been given to understand it, as an orotund vocal manner or the sweeping gesture with a cape. He intended to work, not rest, in his great new pile, but he liked the swimming and the boating the sound offered, and it was as isolated and as impressive as anything his sometime betters had ever enjoyed, and he intended, when he finished converting it, that it be every bit as luxurious as their vacation homes.

Finally, the property appealed to the secretive side of his nature. Lloyd believed, with some justification, that Griffith and his managers systematically drained off fairly large sums of money from what was at this time in the process of becoming a publicly held company and that this money ultimately found its way into Griffith's pockets. Probably it was used to cover gambling debts and to give money to the director from which Linda could not extract her percentage. More important, though, for a man who "became affected, wily, secretive" around women[3] Orienta Point afforded him, as Lloyd said, a place where "he could carry on his affair with Dempster in secrecy and freedom."[4]

And, it seemed, he could certainly afford this new—and only—luxury in his life. For as he prepared to move in, neither he nor any reasonable man saw any likelihood that his status or income was likely to decline in the years ahead—not with the entire industry he had helped found obviously standing on the brink of economic maturity, not with *Broken Blossoms* making a small fortune in the theaters and United Artists giving off at least a rosy promise.

According to an undated financial report drafted late in 1919, Griffith pictures, beginning with *Hearts of the World* and ending with advances in hand or unquestionably due on the First National releases, had earned a total of $8,596,431.73, of which $3,445,346.06 found its way back to Griffith's privately held corporation. These figures represent the takings from all six Artcraft releases, the first of the Dorothy Gish series and *Broken Blossoms*. They also appear to include receipts from the road shows of some of these productions that Griffith's organization had handled itself. There was reason to suppose that yet more money would be derived from the last subruns of the Artcrafts, new Dorothy Gish releases and, of course, from the share of profits that would be due as the First National releases went into the theaters and—as everyone confidently expected—moved into profit. A few months later, when a prospectus offering stock in a new publicly owned D. W. Griffith corporation was printed, the grosses over this period were stated to be in excess of $9 million, profits more than $4 million, and there is no reason to think the claim greatly exaggerated. Besides, as the prospectus pointed out, the new distribution arrangement with United Artists would permit Griffith to realize 80 percent of a picture's domestic receipts, instead of the 70 percent that was then the standard in the industry.[5] On the basis of past performance there seemed no reason at all for Griffith to suppose the money would not continue to roll in as it had in the past, perhaps at even more gratifying levels. Therefore there was no reason for him not to indulge himself in living and working like the American industrial prince he seemed on the verge of becoming.

And yet, even before he signed the papers on the Flagler estate, warning signs appeared that a more prudent, or less willful, or less distracted, man might have noted. Griffith had sent his redoubtable construction boss, Huck Wortman, to New York ahead of him to begin planning the conversion, so that work could begin the minute the title changed hands. A month before that happened, Wortman reported the estate lacked an adequate electrical power supply and that the cost of remedying this defect would be high, for access to the property was via a private road, householders on which were not enthusiastic about heavy duty lines being strung past their windows. The cables could be buried, of course, but still permissions would have to be obtained, and installation would be expensive. No matter, Griffith said, and ordered that a generator be purchased so that the studio could be electrically self-sufficient. In the long run the generator proved inadequate, despite an outlay of around $40,000, and cables had to be strung anyway over more land acquired for that purpose. But that was only the beginning. The private road still had to be widened to permit access for trucks, while the mansion itself had to undergo almost complete renovation; the huge kitchen and a second dining room were converted into a small indoor stage and the bedrooms upstairs were turned into a wardrobe department, dressing rooms and offices. The camera department was in the basement, while Griffith took over the banquet room for his office, as well as one of the smaller outbuildings, close to the water, for his residence—the first house he had lived in since he was a boy. The servants' quarters, close to the mansion, were turned into a commissary, with living quarters for Griffith's Japanese driver and his wife, the cook, occupying the second story.

Significant new construction was also called for. A large, glass-roofed stage had to be built adjacent to the main house (it was connected to it and the commissary by covered passageways) and a laboratory had to be built as well. And this says nothing of the need to equip the place with the manifold hardware of film production—lights and cameras, the raw material for the sets, editing room paraphernalia, costly processing equipment for the lab. And its isolation, far from the region's commercial center, naturally increased the cost of everything. By September, long before anyone could hope to do any work at the studio, intercompany correspondence indicates a pressing shortage of cash to carry on the work.

Griffith could not even realize the modest personal saving he might have by living in the studio. While it was being readied he took quarters at the Claridge Hotel on Broadway and 44th Street in the city and he kept rooms in one theatrical district hotel or another throughout the time he had the studio. Orienta Point was just too remote from the city and the artistic, intellectual and social life he had hoped not just to enjoy but to profit from professionally when he moved his headquarters back to the East.

On this point we have the persuasive testimony of Raymond Klune, who began his career as a studio manager (he later oversaw all physical production for David O. Selznick and M-G-M) with Griffith. Hired when he was only fifteen to assist J. C. Epping, he would later observe that at least half the million dollars the Griffith Corporation realized from its public sale of stock in 1920 would go into capital improvements on the studio, some of which Griffith had previously advanced his own money to pay for.[6] To put the matter simply, there was probably capital enough on hand to comfortably pay for the creation of the seigneurial studio or to finance new productions without undue strain. There was not enough to do both.

Ironically, the first film to be made largely (but still not entirely) at Mamaroneck was directed not by Griffith but by Lillian Gish. It was one of her sister's little comedies, *Remodelling Her Husband,* and according to Lillian, she was pressed into service because Griffith had other uses for Dorothy's usual director, Elmer Clifton. Indeed, he did. For Griffith had decided to do his next two films virtually simultaneously in Florida and would require Clifton's aid even more than he usually did, especially since one of them would star Dempster, the other Clarine Seymour, about whose relationship with Griffith there have long been rumors, even hints of scandal. Whatever the truth of their personal relationship, there can be little doubt that, true to his habit, he was using Seymour as a professional threat to his new leading lady, her rivalrous presence a threat to Dempster's security in her new role as court favorite.

Meantime, obviously, he had found a neat way of occupying Gish in a remote and gainful way. She was not the first woman to direct a movie (Lois Weber, who made a number of successful films, many of which took up women's issues, had begun directing in 1912), and she was not the only female director of this era (it has been estimated that twenty-six women directed pictures in the period between 1913 and 1927). But it was still rare enough for women to be given this responsibility, so the work was balm for her ego, if not for her heart. Moreover, Griffith asked his once and future leading lady to oversee the studio's construction—on the ground that men would work more willingly for an appealing woman. That matter settled to his satisfaction, he decamped with most of his company for Fort Lauderdale. Besides its calming effect on his emotional life, there were other advantages to be found in the South. He hated working in the cold, he loved exploring new locations, and he could ask his contract players to double in the two films (the casts, except for the leading women, were virtually identical). And there was double start money, too, from First National, a not inconsiderable consideration in his strained financial circumstances.

The films themselves are among the weakest in the Griffith canon, and there has been some speculation among Griffith's more devoted apologists that Elmer Clifton might have done more than merely assist on the first of them to go into release, *The Idol Dancer,* a tale at once ludicrous and lugubrious, which Stanner Taylor had adapted from a magazine story. Yet Griffith initially thought well of it, "a sure fire big picture, with lots of action and a new environment," as he wrote to a First National executive.[7] Aside from such novelties as palm trees, grass skirts and white sand beaches, it is actually full of classic Griffith themes and touches, leading one to believe it is almost entirely the work of his hand. Its awkwardness may be ascribed to the same lack of feeling for tropical landscape that Griffith felt for the West and, later in his career, for other exotic locales, in which he communicated a sense of being a tourist rather than a feeling of being fully at home in them.

The story has Barthelmess, attempting something other than his usual mannerly characterization, playing a drunken beachcomber on "a Romance Island under the Southern Cross," as a subtitle has it. He becomes the rival of the local missionary's invalid nephew (Creighton Hale) for the affections of the half-caste daughter of the resident trader. She is White Almond Flower, in whom mingles the blood of "vivacious France, inscrutable Java and languorous Samoa," and she is played by Seymour with energy, good cheer and no rooted feelings whatsoever. There is, of course, a Griffith brute lurking in the hibiscus, with one lustful eye fixed upon the girl, another upon an invaluable string of pearls in the possession of her father. Like others in his line, he is able to heat up the motley crew of natives in order to launch an attack aimed at both prizes. These natives are not different in character from the blacks of *Birth* (though the role of the Ku Klux Klan is this time played by other natives, Christian converts who are loyal to their minister and who, instead of riding to the rescue, paddle to it in their canoes). Also as before, the decent people are at the climax surrounded in a small, cramped house, fighting desperately for time in hopes of a rescue. There is, finally, as there was in the slave quarters sequences in *Birth,* and as there was more recently in *The Greatest Question,* a certain amount of what can only be described as "coon comedy," in which an ignorant follower of the missionary good-heartedly apes the ways of his betters but succeeds only in parodying them at a loss of his own dignity. At the end, the missionary's nephew having been eliminated by a satisfactorily brave death in the siege, White Almond Flower confesses her love for the beachcomber, agrees to wear civilized clothes, and they are seen to throw the idols that symbolize the forces that have kept them apart—his booze bottles, her graven image of the native god, before whose larger statue she had earlier been seen dancing—into the sea. "Not convincing," said the New York Times when the film was released, and in the mildness of that condemnation there is charity.[8]

The other Florida production, based on a magazine story called "The Black Beach," known as "The Gamest Girl" during work and finally released as The Love Flower, was marginally better, if only because it was simpler in structure and less offensive in some of its attitudes. Basically it is a tale of motiveless relentlessness. A trader named Thomas Bevan (George MacQuarrie, the missionary of the previous film) has incurred the enmity of a police detective, Matthew Crane (Anders Randolf, The Idol Dancer's heavy), for a minor crime committed half a world away. The policeman has pursued the trader to the West Indies, arriving there in time to learn that Bevan has killed his wife's lover and fled to Monokai, another "Romance Island" in the South Pacific, and continues—no explanation offered—in his chase. Enter Barthelmess on his sailboat, a young adventurer in the Robert Louis Stevenson mold, who encounters Crane and unwittingly (and improbably, considering how wide the world is) conducts him to Monokai, where Bevan and his daughter, Stella (Dempster), have found a peaceful haven. No fewer than three times does Stella attempt to kill the implacable policeman as she tries to prevent him from reaching her father. He does, however, find him, there is a fight on the edge of a cliff, both tumble into the sea and Crane believes Bevan must have died in the struggle. So do Stella and her lover, but her father, being an expert swimmer, has swum away under water, leaving Crane to make his way back to civilization, where he makes out a report indicating the criminal is dead. Under an alias, Bevan can now resume life without fear of apprehension for crimes that were, after all, morally unassailable. The young lovers, naturally, get to live happily ever after as well. The response of the New York Times to this film was of a character that would increasingly plague Griffith. For it noted that if it had been produced "by any of a hundred inconspicuous directors, the chances are it would be universally judged a 'pretty good melodrama,' but coming from Mr. Griffith, from whom the public has been encouraged to expect something exceptional, its shortcomings are not easily overlooked."[9] Among those, surely, was the performance of Dempster, who was accused of being "sugary and kittenish"—in other words, doing a Lillian Gish imitation, and not for the last time.

Curious, this. For Griffith has now worked with her enough professionally to sense what her natural range was. The personal qualities that had drawn him to her in the first place were clearly quite the opposite of Gish's, and one would have thought that if he truly cared for her he would have emphasized those. Early in their relationship Griffith had asked Bitzer what he thought of Dempster and the cameraman had astutely replied: "The new type. Full of pep and built for speed," a summation Griffith had agreed with, noting her athletic qualities, not only as a dancer but as a swimmer. She was also a forthright sort of woman. A little later Bitzer overheard her talking with Griffith on the back lot and she dared to address him as "David." Unlike Mae Marsh, she got away with it.[10] Bitzer's wife would recall that Dempster could actually get him to unbend to the point where they would play a game of tag, chasing each other around the lot—"very undignified."[11] He would have served his purposes and her career better had he used her as a "new type," but aside from a few swimming and diving sequences, which showed Dempster's aquatic skills to advantage, she was both miscast and misdirected in the film.

The story of its production turned out to be more interesting and adventurous than anything placed on the screen. Fort Lauderdale, in those days, was not a resort capital, nor did it present much in the way of photogenic scenery, after one had exhausted the possibilities of swamps and coconut groves. Griffith sent scouts to Cuba and to the Bahamas to search out more attractive locations, and one of them returned with the word that everything the picture needed was to be found near Nassau. The problem was transportation. The one steamer that regularly plied the route between the mainland and the island was laid up for repairs, and Griffith's company idled until a young sailor suggested a yacht that might be chartered to make the run. This character had it in mind, according to Bitzer, to use Griffith's charter fee as a down payment on purchasing the craft, called the *Grey Duck*, for rum-running.

It was a trim and well-appointed boat, about 100 feet in length, smartly painted and well trimmed in mahogany. Bitzer would later estimate that it could carry perhaps fifteen or 20 people comfortably, but even leaving behind Kate Bruce, his elderly character actress, and Barthelmess and his mother (who were inseparable and were scheduled to join the others later, after the regular boat was restored to service), there were 37 on board when it set out from Miami.

The run should have taken only about a day, but according to Bitzer, the vessel was undermanned by an inexperienced crew, and captained by a young and untried skipper. Toward nightfall, it became clear that they were off course and that prudence dictated finding safe anchorage in the Berry Islands group the *Grey Duck* was just passing. Next morning, though, a storm was visible at sea, and Griffith decided to order the boat to ride it out in safety, even though food was running low and most of the fish that were driven in from the sea by the bad weather proved inedible. Still, there was water and even home brew available from the island's few residents, and the mood aboard remained larky.

Not so on shore. The storm was of near-hurricane force, it had been tracked by the Coast Guard as being directly in the *Grey Duck's* path, and there was fear that the boat had been lost. Boats and planes were sent forth to look for the ship, and Barthelmess, his mother and Miss Bruce chartered a former minesweeper to join in the search. The weather was so bad, however, that their captain elected to steam directly for Nassau, where his little party anxiously settled to await news of their missing co-workers. Meantime, of course, the search for Griffith and his group had become something of a newspaper sensation, so much so that, after their safe return, suspicions that the whole incident had been arranged as a publicity stunt were bruited about.

Actually, however, lack of food and adequate sanitation quickly turned the adventure into a substantial discomfort, and when the party discovered the *Grey Duck's* usual master sheltering in another boat on the same island, he was prevailed upon to attempt to finish the voyage, and they put out to sea, only to be turned back again by high seas. Bitzer claimed that in the course of this failure people fell to their knees to pray and that Porter Strong (who was Griffith's best male friend at the time among the acting company, and a specialist in blackface roles) was seen wielding a straight razor rather uncomfortably near the throat of his terrified pet parrot. He was dissuaded from silencing the bird, the *Grey Duck* put about, and the next morning, when the weather finally cleared, the boat was finally able to complete its passage to Nassau. Sunday morning church bells were ringing as it entered the harbor, and a picture exists of Kate Bruce welcoming Griffith, who looks rather splendidly storm-tossed in slicker and nautical cap. He had, naturally, behaved with his customary calm authority, and Dempster was apparently a cheering and confident presence, too. Later, in dispatching a gracious wire to Navy Secretary Josephus Daniels, thanking him for sending out planes and submarine chasers in search of the *Grey Duck*, Griffith termed the five days in which they were missing "a most distressing experience" and one in which "we were in some peril." "It was only by the grace of God that we reached the Bahamas in safety," he said.[12] The location work proceeded without incident, and Griffith returned to Mamaroneck to find progress having been made on the studio, though he was still, frustratingly, unable to put it to full use.

He rushed through postproduction on *The Idol Dancer* and *The Love Flower*, now more than ever determined that, henceforth, he would concentrate his best efforts on projects that would match in impressiveness not only his new studio but his sense of himself and his place in the world. He would make definitive film versions of works he believed to be the theatrical and literary "classics" of his time, works that he had long admired and had, as well, held unquestioned sway over the general public for as long as he could remember. As an actor, he had wanted to play in these works. At Biograph it was the melodramatic spirit of these pieces that he had imitated, while chafing at the limitations of money, time and film length which prevented him from approximating their full impact. Now, it seemed, his moment was at hand; the failed actor's largest ambitions would at last be realized.

Latter-day commentators have implied that the groundwork for his precipitate financial decline was laid here, that this material was "old fashioned," and that embracing it showed that Griffith was "out of touch" with his public. But the point is dubious. Griffith's public, any moviemaker's public, is not primarily the critics and tastemakers of New York, who would increasingly find his work in the twenties wanting when compared with films being imported from Germany and—later—the Soviet Union, or for that matter, with the pictorially, editorially, sexually and socially more sophisticated work that began to come out of Hollywood later in the decade. With this group, Griffith would suffer particularly because so much of his earlier reputation had been based somewhat erroneously on his innovativeness, which, of course, lay much more in the realm of motion picture technique than it did in the realm of social or psychological acuity. But these people were distinctly a minority. Griffith's audience was a much vaster and less-demanding one. And their mood was slow to change. They still admired traditional theatrics, still thought as well of grand old stories as Griffith did.

In any event, as Griffith contemplated the directions he might take in the months before the decade turned, the shape and tone of things immediately to come, now so clear to us, looking back, were by no means clear to anyone in the movies or, for that matter, elsewhere in the culture. For instance, when the statistics gathered for the census of 1920 were analyzed, it was reported that the country had urbanized, that as of that year more Americans lived in town than in the country—the first time since we began counting that the balance had tipped in that direction. But somehow the Census Bureau counted every hamlet with a population above 2,500 as an urban area, although most American cities, even today, with populations as high as 50,000 and 100,000 remain repositories of traditional values, and that was certainly even more true of such small cities in 1920, when, taken together with the substantial remaining farm population, they constituted a majority, the very majority, indeed, on which H. L. Mencken made his fame by excoriating in this period. These were the people who, whatever was going on in intellectual circles, put Harding, Coolidge and Hoover in the White House. You could not go broke underestimating their sophistication. Or so it seemed.

The most cursory glance at the commercially successful films of the decade—many of them critically well received, as well—reveals among them almost all the popular classics of the late-nineteenth-century stage and literature, highly romantic and highly melodramatic, receiving either their first production, or their first feature-length production: *Daddy Long Legs, Pollyanna, Dr. Jekyll and Mr. Hyde, Treasure Island, Little Lord Fauntleroy, The Prisoner of Zenda, The Trail of the Lonesome Pine, The Hunchback of Notre Dame, Romola, The Three Musketeers, The Phantom of the Opera, Peg O' My Heart* and so on and on. There was no reason for Griffith not to contemplate doing material of this kind, and no reason to suppose that the commercial failure that would attend him in this decade could be blamed on his being "out of touch" with public taste. Far from it; many men, many film companies, made fortunes by being precisely as "out of touch" as he was. And whether you were P. C. Wren or Rafael Sabatini, it was obviously possible to go on creating hugely successful new works that employed variations on the old formulas at great profit to yourself and to the great pleasure of your public.

It would have been convenient for his admirers if Griffith had not aligned himself, now that he had some power, with gentility and cultural conservatism. It would have been better for his reputation, then and later, if he was going to go broke, that he do so heroically, following an esthetically radical course, leaving behind him some masterpieces in which the eager student could find the first traces of the modernist spirit, rather than masterpieces (which, indeed, he once or twice managed to make in this era) that depend for their appeal on their crystallization, in images, of the past.

When a cultural sharpster might have been reading *Jurgen*, Griffith was in touch with the General Lew Wallace estate about the screen rights for *Ben-Hur* (the asking price, alas, was a million dollars!) and engaging in mutually flattering correspondence with H. Rider Haggard about acquiring one of his novels. When he might have been snapping up *Winesburg, Ohio*, or even *Main Street*, he was buying the rights to Joseph Hergesheimer's much different view of small-town life, *Tol'able David*, not to mention his exotic romance *Java Head*. And he would leave it to someone else (Thomas Ince) to be the first to bring O'Neill to the screen (*Anna Christie* in 1923, starring Griffith's discovery, Blanche Sweet). Of course, he had little choice in the matter. For better or worse his taste and his talent were fully formed, and so was his character.

The perils and potentials of being able to exercise his taste to its fullest were illustrated by his first major purchases for production at Mamaroneck. Both were plays of long-standing popularity, both were hugely expensive to acquire and to mount. One, long since forgotten, was *Romance*. The other, the source of what is, arguably, Griffith's most nearly perfect expression of his spirit and sensibility, was *Way Down East*. Ro-

mance was written in 1913 by the American Edward Sheldon, who despite being blind and bedridden, enjoyed a long career in the popular
theater and an even more remarkable one (considering his circumstances)
as friend and correspondent to a huge circle of literary and theatrical
friends, most notably John Barrymore. The story of an affair between a
high-spirited Italian opera singer and an English clergyman, recollected
by the latter after he has risen to a lonely bishopric, and learns of her
death, it had an obvious appeal for Griffith in his nostalgically ruminative
mood. Only a minor success in America, it had become an enormously
popular vehicle for Doris Keane and her husband, Basil Sidney, in England. They held the rights to it, and they were not disposed to dispose
of them cheaply. Indeed, Griffith entered into a contract with Keane that
was, as far as can be ascertained, unprecedented for its day, she receiving
a total of $150,000 in advance and 50 percent of the picture's gross after it
had earned its first million dollars. Here was another Griffith innovation,
a huge price plus points for what he thought was a property whose reputation would precede it to the theater.

The advance to Keane represented more money than Griffith had at
the time, but he was so determined to make the picture that he talked his
United Artists partners (including McAdoo, who was scarcely a plunger)
into helping him secure a bank note for $350,000 to defray acquisition
and production costs. Each of them, Griffith included, deposited personal
notes for $70,000 to the lender as collateral. They received no interest for
this gesture, although Griffith agreed to let their joint enterprise take a
distribution fee of 25 percent, five points over its normal charge for this
service, for handling the production. Before the picture was completed,
the sum of the personal notes was reduced, though United Artists itself
had to dip into its thin trickle of cash flow to meet further charges on the
work as it went over budget.

Curiously enough, having gone to all this trouble, Griffith turned
direction of the piece over to his assistant Chet Withey. Perhaps as preparations for production proceeded he sensed that the film was somewhat
lacking in cinematic values. Or perhaps Keane and Sidney were so proprietary about it that he did not wish to confront them with the extensive
changes that were needed to transfer this stage-bound work to the screen
and decided merely to provide them with a competent technician and depend on their reputation, and the play's, to bring the virtually unadapted
film success at the box office.

It did not work. Reviewers complained about the picture's heavy reliance on subtitles to carry the story, and about its lack of cinematic movement and pictorial qualities as well. "The screen of 1920 may be this,
that or the other," wrote the man from the *Boston Evening Transcript*,
"but beyond peradventure it has left such a photoplay as this . . . far
behind."[13] Far more damaging to Griffith than notices of this quality was

Romance's dismal performance at the box office. It returned only a little more than half its cost to United Artists, which meant Griffith had to make good the bank loan, and that put him in financial trouble right at the start.

Doubtless he had counted on profits from *Romance* to finance future ventures. Instead, it forced him to undertake new borrowings to finance new pictures. And since he did not have a line of credit with the banks—as the major producers had, or shortly would have—he had no option but to put up as collateral his personal property, his personal interest in previous films and, most damaging of all, mortgages on the negatives of each unfinished film. This meant that the very considerable cash flow each of them generated (overall, according to Klune, profits and loses on individual Mamaroneck films were mostly modest, and roughly canceled each other out) could never be used to finance future production; it was always being diverted to debt service.

In other words, if Griffith had been financed as he had been in the past, by distributors' advances, or if United Artists had possessed a solid line of credit at a bank to finance its partner's films on gentle and forgiving terms, Griffith would not have been under the terrible financial pressure that developed between 1920 and 1924. His studio might not have set any records for profitability, but it might have been able to bump along the bottom edge of solvency, preserving his treasured independence. In lieu of UA financing he might have used the capital he had raised by his stock offering for production, but that was all used up in the expensive conversion of the millionaire's mansion into a film studio. Now his only hope was to produce cheaply and quickly, using the cash flow from one production to finance the next—which proved impossible. Griffith could still shoot fast, but the habit of frugality, the old discipline of his beginnings, was now anathema to him.

All of this might have become clearer sooner, in time for his course to be changed, had not Griffith been blessed, immediately after the *Romance* fiasco, with his last major box office success. Indeed, one suspects that one of the main reasons he detached himself from *Romance* so quickly was that this new project ensnared him entirely. It was, of course, *Way Down East*. And though it may seem odd to regard this hugely profitable film as his one masterwork untainted by either dubious moral implications or wildly wayward esthetic choices, as a mixed blessing, so it proved to be. For the profits it generated temporarily covered the problems inherent in the Griffith operation, preventing him and his associates from seeing them clearly or addressing them properly until it was too late.

Way Down East was first performed, in a version considerably different from its final form, at Newport, Rhode Island on September 3, 1897, the work of an inexperienced writer named Lottie Blair Parker, who brought her script to William A. Brady, the producer-writer, who, in turn, engaged an actor-manager named Joseph R. Grismer to help him and Mrs. Parker make something salable out of what Brady saw held the germ of a good idea. The three collaborated on several versions of the play (with Grismer gaining a coauthor's credit and a meaty role as the villain). They also suffered through several cool receptions before a production that Brady mounted with Florenz Ziegfeld enjoyed a mild success in New York. It was not until 1899 that the play, in its final form, was copyrighted, and when it was Brady emerged with all rights to English-language productions of it. Very shortly it became a staple for road and resident companies throughout the United States, and Brady estimated that he earned some $200,000 in royalties from it, Mrs. Parker contenting herself with whatever money Brady had paid her to buy out her interest, plus the rights she retained to foreign-language productions.

Brady understood the commercial as well as the sentimental power of the piece and was not about to surrender it cheaply to the movies, even to a friend like Griffith. The price they finally arrived at was $175,000, breaking the record-setting price Griffith had just paid for *Romance*. Nor was that the end of his story costs. Mrs. Parker had to be paid $7,000 for her rights to the non-English speaking territories, and Griffith engaged a playwright, Anthony Paul Kelly, to prepare a scenario of which Griffith in the end used very little. That cost him another $10,000. These preproduction charges set the pattern for the picture; *Way Down East*, which contains no spectacular settings, no mobs of extras, no overpaid stars, nothing of the sort that usually runs the cost of a movie up, turned out to be the most expensive film Griffith had made to date.

Mostly what he paid for was the passage of time, time for the seasons to turn, time for the elements to produce some of their more wondrous effects. He would have to hold his company on call and tie up his studio for better than six months—far longer than his usual production schedule—with interest charges mounting up on the extensive borrowings the production required. But it was worth it. One of the distinguishing qualities of the film, perhaps the most significant factor in permitting it to transcend the limits of its primitive genre, derives from his careful rooting of his characters in their environment, from the manner, as well, in which nature's moods seem to reflect their emotional weather. These were qualities no amount of stage machinery could produce, and it may be that *Way Down East* represents the culmination of the process, stretching back almost to the beginning of the movies, by which film, possessing a superior technology, finally rendered its rival obsolete: the triumph of optics over mechanics.

Griffith did not tamper with the basic story he had spent so much to acquire. In the film as in the play Anna Moore (Lillian Gish) is a "down east" country lass—the phrase refers to that portion of Maine which lies geographically east of Boston—who comes to the Hub to seek financial aid from rich relatives. They treat her condescendingly, but she meets and falls in love with Lennox Sanderson (Lowell Sherman, who made a career out of playing overhandsome cads and weaklings). He arranges a mock marriage to trick the girl into sleeping with him. He also insists that their "wedding" be kept a secret, so as not to anger his father and cost him his financial support. When she becomes pregnant, she, of course, insists that their marriage be revealed, whereupon Sanderson then tells her the truth—and deserts her. She returns home, but her mother dies, and she takes refuge in a rooming house, where she bears her child—very realistically by the standards of the time, too much so according to some moralistic critics, and some censorship boards. The child sickens and dies and it may be that the emotional high point of the film is Anna's vigil with him—in which she baptizes him (no minister is called) before death comes.

Thereafter, Anna wanders the roads until she comes upon the Edenic farm of Squire Bartlett and his family. There, after convincing the stern but essentially benevolent owner of her worth, she finds both work and warmth, winning the love of the son, David (Barthelmess). Unfortunately, the Bartlett farm is quite close to the Sanderson estate and the dastardly Lennox, now enamored of a Bartlett cousin, Kate Brewster, who the squire hopes will marry David, finds Anna's presence an uncomfortable reminder of his past and he keeps asking her to leave. She refuses, but when her former landlady, visiting a nearby small town, sees Anna, she tells her story to Martha Perkins, the village gossip, who retells it to the Squire, who orders Anna from his home, in the theater's classic casting-out scene, inspiration since of a thousand cartoons and parodies. Lennox happens to be present, taking dinner with the Bartletts, and before Anna exits into the ferocious blizzard that has blown up, she denounces him as her seducer. David believes her story and rushes out to find her.

There ensues one of the most remarkable sequences in film history, in which the hysterical Anna, blinded by her emotions as much as she is by the storm, wanders through the gale and then on to a frozen river, where at last she collapses. In the morning the river ice begins to break up and, still unconscious on her ice floe, she is carried perilously close to the edge of a falls, from which, at the last possible moment, she is rescued by David. The sequence is extremely long and extraordinarily vivid, so suspenseful that one scarcely heeds a few moments of rather inept effects work. The picture ends with forgiveness all around. And a triple wedding that includes, besides Anna and David, Kate and an eccentric professor to whom she is inexplicably drawn as well as Martha Perkins, of all people. Forgiven her almost death-dealing gossip, she marries a comic rustic who has been fruitlessly pursuing her for 20 years, too shy to speak his love. Martha is not only a vital link in the film's main story but a link as well to its busy comic substructure which draws on the theatrical tradition of rural comedy for characters and situations—perhaps a bit tiresomely so.

It is the ability to show real sleigh rides and spacious barn dances, to place Gish and Barthelmess in a real blizzard, and on a real river as the winter ice breaks, that gives the film an insuperable advantage over the stage. Whatever reservations one entertains about the motives and psychology of these characters, whatever strain has been placed on credibility by the coincidences on which the story so heavily depends, they are (almost literally) blown away by the storm sequence, so powerfully is it presented. But there are other advantages in the motion picture adaptation. Perforce, the stage play was bound close to the Bartlett farm. The film opens with crosscutting between the farm, and its orderly moral universe, and Anna's adventures in the unsettling environments of road and city. Before she knows of the peace that awaits her, when she returns to the country and its values, *we* know it, and the contrast makes her situation the more poignant. But there are still more, and subtler advantages to contemplate in the screen adaptation. In a body of work rich in such imagery, there are few sequences more poignant than Griffith's handling of the death of Anna's child, or her lonely and pathetic wanderings afterward on the road that will take her to Squire Bartlett's. And whether he is showing us Gish's touching encounter with someone else's baby or simply a kitten falling asleep in the warmth generated by the Squire's hearth, the power of the screen to inform the heart without lecturing it, is brilliantly, and unassumingly, employed.

But the film represents more than a tribute to the fast-vanishing theatrical tradition to which Griffith owed an allegiance, though that doubtless accounts for his failure to trim some of the more dubious comic conventions of the play. The film's homage is really to the moral universe he had inhabited when he was growing up. Lillian Gish has written that "we all thought privately Mr. Griffith has lost his mind" when he purchased this "horse-and-buggy melodrama,"[14] but until he had completed his work with it, no one could have guessed the depth of his intentions. For he must have sensed that the play's hokum now had an endearing, nostalgic quality that sophisticates could comfortably indulge while the unsophisticated could still relish it, and that this would give the film a wide appeal that the simpler, more straightforward *Romance of Happy Valley* and *True Heart Susie* lacked. It would, in effect, help sell a vision that went beyond superficialities of plot, went to the simple heart of a simpler time in which all the troublesome ambiguities he was now encountering in his work, his financial affairs, his personal relationships— indeed, just by living as an adult in a changing world—were simply nonexistent.

In the best of the latter-day analyses of the film Stanley Kauffmann speaks correctly of the "utter seriousness with which Griffith took the whole project."[15] In fact, one responds so warmly to the picture in part because of the habits Griffith for once did *not* indulge. The slapdash quality that attended the production of the two films that immediately preceded it as well as the work on some of the Artcrafts is not in evidence here. Neither is the pseudopoetry or the grandiosity that marred so many of his "big" pictures. Also missing are the bestial males acting out of Griffith's rapacious fantasies. Lennox Sanderson may not be morally superior to the other Griffith villains, and by modern standards his lounge lizardry may have an unintentional comic quality, but he at least has a human face, and we can understand how the other characters in the film might be disarmed by him. Even the cruelly unforgiving behavior of Squire Bartlett when he discovers Anna's "sins," so at odds with his kindly—if wary—manner earlier (and so at odds, too, with the character of the actor playing the part, Burr McIntosh, that he kept apologizing to Lillian Gish for what the script called on him to do), becomes acceptable. We understand him to be something more than human, to be the very symbol of the moral code on which order in the little universe of the film depends for its happiness.

Some part of Griffith's "seriousness" about the work perhaps derived from an identification he must have felt with the patriarchal Bartlett character. The Mamaroneck studio was very much his squirearchy, and within that remote world he functioned very much as the squire did, as *pater familias*, moral arbiter, supreme ruler. Billy Bitzer's widow would tell an interviewer Griffith was "always strutting around with his parrot nose . . . snooping around with this nose . . . it never missed a thing. There wasn't a corner of the studio he missed."[16]

Griffith had never asked so much of his faithful film family as he did on this picture. Even for him the rehearsal period was a long one—some ten weeks, mostly spent in the public rooms of his hotel in the city. Among other delays there was a wait for a blizzard to blow up and, when it finally did, the company worked day and night at Orienta Point, knowing this one brief moment was the only one they were likely to have in which to make the film's vital storm sequence. The blizzard's power, of course, was heightened as it blew in from Long Island Sound and across the unsheltered point. Gish was required to work in a costume consisting of a thin black dress and a skimpy shawl. And she had not only to fight the howling gale; she also had to sink exhausted into freezing snowbanks. Ice formed on her face while Griffith himself suffered from frostbite. A nurse was present, and since one of Gish's faints was the real thing, this turned out to be a wise precaution; the actress had to be taken back to the studio via sled to recover. Mostly, however, it seemed to her that the brief comfort of coming in out of the cold only increased the agony of going back out to face the elements. So she and the rest of the crew huddled around a bonfire between takes, hoping the cold would not freeze the oil in Bitzer's camera, which could cause delays rendered the more agonizing by anxiety over whether the work could be completed before the storm abated.

But if work in the blizzard was painful, much of it on the ice floes was genuinely hazardous. In modern times principal actors would not have been used in many of these shots. But though stunt doubles were occasionally employed, and some shots, in which the unconscious Anna floats near the edge of a falls, just before David rescues her, were made later in the spring, on a mild river near a minor falls in Farmington, Connecticut (the ice floes being made of plywood), most of the sequence was done in early March at White River Junction, Vermont, with Gish and Barthelmess doing much of the stunt work themselves. The company arrived before the ice in the river broke, so they had to saw and blast chunks of ice loose for their shots. Gish claimed that she was on the ice twenty times a day for something like three weeks, and even if memory has somewhat exaggerated her ordeal, it was surely not a brief one. She deepened it by suggesting she let one hand and her hair trail in the river when she collapsed on the ice. Her hair froze stiff and she has written that the hand she immersed in that bitter stream still pains her when the weather turns cold.

At another point during one of the numberless takes required for the river sequences, as the current gathers speed, Barthelmess, hampered by a raccoon coat and heavy spiked boots, must leap from floe to floe trying to reach her before she is carried over the falls. There was nothing like a Niagara (an insert shot of which was placed—rather ineptly—into the sequence to build menace) near White River Junction. Still, Gish was being carried at ever increasing, and quite unexpected, speed toward dangerous rapids as the actor made his way to her. Directing from a bridge over the torrent, Griffith shouted to him to pick up his pace, but the command was lost in the roaring of the water. Barthelmess himself, however, soon saw Gish's danger, and racing toward her, leaped onto a piece of ice too small to bear his weight. The look of panic on his face as he starts to sink, then heaves himself onto a sturdier bit of ice is utterly real. And there are similar fearful moments—clearly not acting—as he carries Gish to safety across the highly untrustworthy ice. The effect of these shots in the final film is to break through fictional conventions and send a clear signal to the audience of the dangerous trouble taken on this film. They may therefore represent a poor choice esthetically. But they are also undeniably thrilling as documentary footage, and Griffith was justified in surrendering to their undeniable impact.

Not everyone was as resolute as Barthelmess was. Griffith, finished with principal photography, left a second unit behind at White River Junction, under Elmer Clifton's command. It was to make long shots of the ice breaking when the spring thaw finally arrived. Doubles were to be used in this work, and a telegram from another assistant, Leigh Smith, attests to its rigors:

MR. CLIFTON PROVED HIMSELF A HERO TODAY. ALLAN LAW [A STUNT DOUBLE] WENT YELLOW. CLIFTON DOUBLED FOR LAW ON THE MOVING ICE IN THE MIDDLE OF THE CONNECTICUT RIVER AND WAS RESCUED BY BEING RAISED TO A BRIDGE BY ROPES. HOPE CLIFTON'S WORK SHOWS ON SCREEN. STOP. KNEW CLIFTON WOULD SAY NOTHING HIMSELF SO AM SENDING THIS WIRE.[17]

Sure enough, Clifton's telegram the next day merely reported that they had "worked like beavers" for five hours photographing the ice as it went out. He had 2,000 feet of film, he said, and was planning to send a house into the maelstrom the next day and perhaps get shots of Gish being caught in it, too. He begged Griffith to look at the footage as soon as possible so he could reshoot if need be. But, as Smith had predicted, and true to the masculine code of the time, no mention was made of Clifton's services above and beyond the call of directorial duty.[18]

In his reminiscences Barthelmess would also say nothing about the dangers he faced on this film, although when he spoke about it with Gish later, both would wonder whatever possessed them to take such risks for a mere movie. But, of course, they were young and ambitious and knew no better. Besides having faces then, they had character, too. Independent observers record Gish laughing as she got up from the snowbanks into which she staggered on the blizzard night-shoot. Later she would tell a journalist that she had been more chilled when she had to work outdoors one night in a Pacific Coast fog on *Broken Blossoms*. But she was, and remains, an iron-willed, supremely disciplined actress, proud of her strong constitution and the cheerfulness with which she had accepted the rigors of her profession. In accepting the hardships of *Way Down East* it helped that, despite her doubts ("I wondered how I was going to make Anna convincing"), she also understood that this could become one of her great roles. Her victimization here is not by violent assault, but by desertion and rejection, the consequences of which are suffered inwardly. Hers is one of the great lonely performances. If in some respects similar to the comic and tender explorations of a similar emotion in the earlier pastorals, the difference here is that she has a context supporting a richer evocation of the trials of a loving heart. Here, too, she could, as never before, follow the advice Griffith was always giving young actors, which was merely to think an emotion, not try too hard to demonstrate it physically. This she did superbly. And, for once, Griffith allowed her to do so without inordinate flutter, perhaps because he saw that the storm surrounding her at the end conveyed her inner turmoil better than any pantomime could.

In later years, the sequence would, in fact, come to be regarded as exemplary, a pioneering demonstration of how the movies could, more easily and often more powerfully than any other fictional form, obey the famous Jamesian dictum that "landscape is character." When he gave his ground-breaking theoretical lectures on *Film Technique and Film Acting* in 1926 (published in book form in 1929), V. I. Pudovkin, the great Soviet director, said, excitedly: "First the snowstorm, then the foaming, swirling river in thaw, packed with ice blocks that rage yet wilder than the storm, and finally the mighty waterfall, conveying the impression of death itself. In this sequence of events is repeated, on large scale as it were, the same line of the increasing despair—despair striving to make an end, for death, that has irresistibly gripped the chief character. This harmony—the storm in the human heart and the storm in the frenzy of nature—is one of the most powerful achievements of the American genius."[19]

Yet wonderful as this sequence is—and in its simplicity and power, its lack of elaborate contrivance, it stands alone among the several great climaxes of Griffith's work and has, indeed, few rivals anywhere in the cinema—one does not wish to isolate it from the rest of the film. However minor and silly some of the comedy of the preceding passages is, however improbable the psychology and sense of the world the major characters (aside from Gish) exhibit, that conclusion depends for its power on something more than the weather. It completes, transcendently, a dramatic and moral arc, forms an emotional consummation that is, perhaps, richer, more subtle than it at first seems. One has to search it out amidst the old-fashioned dramatic trumpery; yet it surely derives, as Kauffmann argues, from the fact that *Way Down East* is rooted "in the myth that underlines much of melodrama: moral redemption by bourgeois standards." He continues: "It has been suggested that Anna is a secular saint, truly good, suffering for the sins and blindness of her fellows, finally undergoing an agony that reveals her purity. She is betrayed in her trust, she goes through travail, she labors in humility, she declines happiness because she is unworthy (refusing David's love), and she shows that death holds no terror for her. At last she achieves heaven—*on earth*."[20]

A tragic coincidence may have contributed to the film's "seriousness." Clarine Seymour had been scheduled to play the secondary role of Kate Brewster, David's intended, who instead falls in love with the eccentric visitor, Professor Sterling. She rehearsed with the company at the Claridge and she was present at the studio when the blizzard sequence was shot. But she fell ill sometime in early April, just as the company was about to embark on the film's extensive interior work, as well as the outdoor sequences that required good weather. These included all her major scenes, and she died of a rather mysterious affliction, given various names in various sources, in a hospital at New Rochelle on Sunday, April 19. She was only 21.

It would be too much to say that her death deepened Griffith's or anyone else's dedication to *Way Down East*, but surely the parallel between her untimely death and the terrible crisis Anna endures in the film was not lost on the people making it. It can also be said that her absence affected the quality of the finished product. Her replacement, Mary Hay, was an attractive and competent young actress but rather too straight to be entirely persuasive as someone enamored of the eccentric professor. Seymour's giddy good nature would have been much more effective in the part, though Hay was persuasive enough for Richard Barthelmess, who married her shortly after the film was completed.

As for Griffith, he never brought a higher measure of energy or concentration to any film. And he never risked more, financially. Consider: to buy the rights to *Way Down East* he had borrowed $175,000 from the Central Union Trust Company, putting up as collateral 80 percent of his personal interest in the film. Then on April 23 he borrowed another $150,000 from another bank, the Guarantee Trust Company, putting up as collateral his personal interest in five of the six Artcraft pictures, plus *Hearts of the World*. A month thereafter, he had to put up the negative for *The Love Flower* in order to receive a $315,000 loan at 6 percent in order to buy the rights to the film from First National so he could then turn it over to United Artists for distribution—his contribution to peace among the partners and to the company's continuing need for product. But that was still not the end. In June, just as plans for incorporation and the public offering of shares in the D. W. Griffith Corporation were coming to fruition, he borrowed another $200,000 from the Central Union, this time putting up his rights in the four latest Dorothy Gish comedies, his remaining 20 percent interest in *Way Down East*, plus a $150,000 life insurance policy he held. His exposure at this point thus amounted to $525,000, most of it attributable to production costs on *Way Down East*. Adding in loans that were still outstanding on *The Love Flower* and *Romance*, it is clear he had managed to run up close to a million dollars in debt during the first six months of 1920, retirement of which was entirely predicated on the performance of his pictures at the box office.

And then, in June, just about everything else he had was placed in the hands of the Chicago firm of Counselman & Company, which was handling his corporate underwriting. This included: all the physical assets of his studio, 300 shares of United Artists common and preferred stock, contracts with artists (valued, very generously, at $250,000), all his extant distribution contracts, his mortgaged rights in *Hearts*, the Artcrafts, the Dorothy Gish pictures, the First National releases, and all

other films then in production, plus "good will," which was also generously evaluated. Thus virtually everything Griffith had was, in effect,
twice encumbered—first to pay for current production, then to establish
the corporation. Just to service production debt all his pictures had to
turn at least a modest profit. If they did not, creditors obviously had recourse to the films themselves, which meant, in turn, they would be attaching the corporation's only real assets. It also meant that Griffith himself could, in the worst imaginable case, be rendered penniless.

To be sure, he had received, in return for the assets he had placed
with Counselman, all the Class B stock of the corporation—375,000
shares of it plus a note for $150,000 giving him a claim against his own
corporation for money he had advanced it during the period he was awaiting flotation of the public stock issue. But that issue, which was to consist
of 125,000 shares of Class A stock, to be sold at $15 a share, had a prior
claim on the company's assets—up to $25 per share in the event of volun-
tary liquidation, up to $20 in the event of bankruptcy. At either figure,
the pay down on the Class A stock would require far more than the company had in realizable assets, particularly since the only truly valuable
property among them, the films themselves, were already pledged to the
banks as loan security. Worse, Griffith was obligated to pay a dividend
of $1.50 per share per year on the Class A stock, a feat he never fully ac-
complished. Indeed, to keep the company afloat in the years ahead, Griffith deferred much of the $200,000 annual salary to which he was con-
tractually entitled, leading him, in the end, to sue his own concern for
back pay. To put the matter simply, and mildly, if *Way Down East* were
not a hit, his company would be out of business almost before it started.

He was thus under tremendous pressure, as he ended his shooting and
began editing, titling and scoring, not only to finish as quickly as possible,
but to make the picture as good as possible. As was his wont, he pursued
his postproduction work long into almost every night, right up to the day
of the premiere. Others might fall asleep as he screened dailies, but never
Griffith, and his colleagues, according to Carr, were always hearing his
voice drifting across "a chasm of sleep." "Do you like the second shot or
the fifth best?" The questions were particularly insistent on *Way Down
East*, with Carr claiming there was 80,000 feet of film, the result of mul-
tiple camera coverage, to select from for the 12,000 feet used in the final
negative. Even allowing for a press agent's exaggerations, there was, undoubtedly, a huge amount of film to go through. Title writing took place
at a long table Carr claimed had once been used by Flagler for his board
meetings, with Griffith, as he did on the set, lighting innumerable ciga-
rettes, taking a puff or two on each, stubbing it out, until, as Carr put it,
"the place looks like a jury room."

Of course, there were previews; there always were with Griffith films.
In this case they were held, in August, in Middletown, New York, and

Kingston, New York. "The try-out of a Griffith picture is always great fun. He gets his staff into a flock of automobiles and we go trundling upstate to some queer country town, where we fill the hotel. Wondering crowds stand around the street corners to see him pass. You scatter around through the audience and hear what people say. Then the local manager comes up full of mysterious importance and we are all invited up to the Elks Club to a midnight supper of lobster a la Newburgh—and other things. . . . Coming back from the tryout, Griffith always tears the picture all to pieces. . . ."[21]

Griffith was more than usually concerned about the verdict the public would shortly render on *Way Down East*, so much so that, just before the film opened in New York, he drafted for publication in the newspapers a "Letter to the People, Whose Servant I am." Its purpose was to explain to them why a film lacking "massive or spectacular effects" and "depending upon . . . tears, comedy and human interest" entirely, could be so costly. He points to the huge crew and the two months of time required for the ice sequence, observing, quite correctly, that "we have attempted nothing that seemed so impossible as the photographing of this elemental, resistless force." He notes the time taken to wait for the seasons of the year to change and the multitude of details attended to "in securing proper atmosphere." In effect, he says, all this may not look expensive at first glance, but "we have spent many months of work, night and day, and a total expense of over eight hundred thousand dollars." This, he adds, is "the plain truth, that despite its simple settings, it is the most expensive entertainment that has ever been given since Caesar plated the arena with silver for the citizens of ancient Rome. We know that million dollar productions have been often advertised. This is not my line—the press department would doubtless claim it a two-million dollar production, but I am telling you the simple truth. If you are interested enough I will gladly furnish you Price, Waterhouse Company's audits."

For once, Griffith was not exaggerating. The cost of the production is roughly correct and, for that matter, setting aside World's Fairs, it is hard to think of any entertainment since Roman days that had cost more. His style throughout the letter was modest to the point of diffidence, much in the manner of his opening-night curtain speeches. But his underlying anxiety surfaces very clearly at the letter's conclusion: "We know all of this expense and time has nothing to do with the value of the story, we merely use it to say we have done our best. The dice of Fate are lifted, and when we throw it [sic] it is for you, oh masters of the game, to say if we win or lose."[22]

It is likely, however, that all his anxiety about *Way Down East*'s reception had been mostly driven from his mind on the night of September 3, 1920, when *Way Down East* premiered at the 44th Street Theater in

New York. For on the previous evening Bobby Harron had shot himself in circumstances that have never been adequately explained and now lay close to death in Bellevue Hospital.

The facts in the case are simple enough. Harron, now 26 years old, had been visiting his parents in Los Angeles, where he had bought them a home, and had returned to New York for the premiere. By ominous coincidence, he checked into the Seymour hotel. At some point, so the story goes, he had bought a revolver from a man who needed money, had carelessly stuffed it in the pocket of a dinner jacket and forgotten it. As he unpacked in his room the gun had fallen from the coat, struck the floor and discharged. At the hospital, after an operation, a priest who had been a friend since childhood found him and asked him if he had intended suicide and Harron swore not. After he died police and the press accepted the story of accidental death, but one must wonder; it seems more than a trifle strained.

There were reasons why Harron might have felt despondent. Though there had been no open breach with Griffith, and he was still under contract to the Griffith company, it must have seemed to him that he had been supplanted as its leading man by Barthelmess (although, in fact, the latter would make no more films for Griffith either). Nor could he now go back to playing juveniles. It is true that Griffith had made a loan-out arrangement to star Harron in four low-budget comedies for the Metro company. The first of these $25,000 films, five reels long and entitled *Coincidence*, had been completed. It was very much a second-string affair, directed by Chet Withey and photographed by Louis Bitzer, Billy's nephew. The contrast between the little picture on which he had been working and the preparations for launching the most expensive of all Griffith's productions must have been particularly poignant to Harron, who had, after all, literally grown up in the business with Griffith and had appeared in all of his major films prior to *Way Down East*. It might also have become clear to him at this time that Dorothy Gish, with whom he had been in love, and who was at the moment touring Europe with her mother and Constance Talmadge (and her mother), was now thoroughly enamored of James Rennie (they would marry the day after Christmas of this year). It may be, too, as rumor has long had it, that he was troubled by homosexual tendencies he could no longer deny. In short, there was every reason for an impressionable and not very worldly young man to have felt severely cast down, perhaps to the point of self-destruction.

In any event, Griffith and his staff set about putting the best possible face on the situation. Harron's mother and sister were sent for, but he died on September 5 while they were en route from the Coast, and Griffith, a priest and some other friends met them at the station, took them to a hotel and then broke the news to them. Lillian Gish later took them home to her rented house in Mamaroneck, where they stayed until well after the funeral. On that day work would be suspended for fifteen minutes at most at the film studios as a memorial to Harron.

Billy Bitzer would stoutly maintain that given his religious convictions, Harron's death could have been nothing other than an accident. Yet the tone of his remarks seems to belie that protestation. The end of an era, he called it: "With Bobby's passing, some thread of unity seemed to leave us. A feeling of guilt lay heavy on all of us. It was a falling away and a breaking up of our former trust and friendship . . . it was never the same again."[23] Guilt, trust, friendship betrayed—the words and the emotions connected to them do not apply to accidental deaths. The sense of family that had attended Griffith's work from Biograph days was fading and he would not be able to maintain it amidst the pressures of the new movie world. More than he knew, or anyone else knew, *Way Down East* was a culmination, not only of the kind of movie he had made best, not only of his aspirations for the movies, but of a method of work as well.

Meantime, the show had to go on. And on opening night Griffith was in his box, always unlit, always equipped with a set of buttons that enabled him to signal, via cue lights, to the conductor in the pit and the projectionist in the booth keeping them synchronized. In those days projector speeds could be varied, and chases were usually sped up as they passed through the machine, romantic and tragic passages slowed down. And, building on the lucky accident of *Broken Blossoms*, Griffith was also experimenting with the play of colored light on the screen, attempting to enhance the mood of different scenes with different lighting effects—not too successfully, it would appear. The audience, by all reports, was whistling, stamping and cheering by the time the ice floe sequence had unreeled, and Alexander Woollcott, writing anonymously in the *Times*, while allowing that the opening night audience was undoubtedly composed of "well-wishers," had to concede that "any audience would have cheered it, and all audiences will." He had his reservations about "the familiar tricks and puppets of rural life as it is understood in our theater," and about Griffith's excessive use of animal and flower symbolism as well as about the score, laden with painfully familiar themes taken from the likes of "Jingle Bells" and even "Little Brown Jug." But the acting, he thought, was excellent, and that climax. . . .[24]

Over at *Life*, the humor magazine, which had a stake in sophistication, Robert Benchley was hilarious: "It seems hardly fair to Anna to revive the old scandal just as it was beginning to be forgotten, and it is certainly not fair to the public to revive the old comedy scenes just as we were congratulating ourselves that a few slight scars were all that were left on our memory." But even Benchley had to concede grudgingly that "some remarkably beautiful scenery and snow effects . . . make the whole picture worth sitting through." Still, he continued, "The whole problem of the drama, after all, is whether or not Anna was worth it. A straw poll taken in this department shows an overwhelming sentiment in the negative. Number of votes cast, one; number in favor of saving Anna, none. Number in favor of letting her ride over the falls, one. . . ."[25] But Benchley's jocular sentiments were distinctly in the minority. Most reviewers were unstinting in their praise.

One of the most interesting reviews appeared in *Exceptional Photoplays*, a publication of the National Board of Review, which has previously been encountered in this chronicle as the National Board of Censorship, functioning at the center of the *Birth of a Nation* controversy. This new journal represented an attempt to provide a more intellectual criticism than the general press of the time provided the slowly growing number of people who took movies seriously. Its reviews were anonymous, the product of a committee that drew its membership from the liberal community, a group that as a whole took surprisingly little interest in a medium that was an inherently populist medium—unless of course, it offended one of its principles. One of the few exceptions to this rule was Alfred B. Kuttner, early proselytizer for the psychoanalytic movement and friend of Walter Lippmann. In his review of *Way Down East* he was far more tolerant than his colleagues of the play's dated conventions and its general air of quaintness. Instead of trying to show his sophistication by disdaining and distancing himself from them, he acutely noted that when a melodramatic work "succeeds in maintaining itself in the national repertory for a great number of years, it is safe to assume that the human appeal of the characters or a touch of real poetry in the story rises above the conventional effects at which melodrama usually aims." In this case, he went on, "There is a real and unaffected poignancy about the betrayal of a young and ignorant girl by a sophisticated seducer which can easily be brought home to vast audiences. Here the moving picture has the advantage over the play. For photoplay art has resources which permit it to soften the crassness of melodrama and to disguise its shopworn qualities. The silent drama leaves our imagination more free, and the girl's misery which is none the less real for being one of the oldest stories in the world, can still be brought to us with artistic freshness."

This was, in its way, an important statement about the nature of film. It recognizes that movies are not just photographed stage plays, even when they *are* photographed stage plays, that they have resources, not always clearly defined or even consciously recognizable, which are, or can be, of a transforming nature. It also recognizes that there are, or can be, values in a popular screen work that simple people can sometimes recognize more readily than literary people can. Clearly, Kuttner's interest in psychology had introduced him to the concept of the archetype. And though he was not, perhaps, saying anything that Vachel Lindsay had not said before, he was saying it in a comprehensible form, not poeticized or a trifle hysterical as so much of Lindsay's writing was. Beyond that, there is something refreshing in the piece's refusal to strike attitudes, its willingness to accept the film on its own terms. Kuttner's reservations are largely of a technical nature, and it is only at the end that he gently notes a certain regressiveness about the picture. "Mr. Griffith cannot touch any story without putting his stamp upon it. His version of *Way Down East* will travel far and long. When it has travelled long enough he may perhaps again find courage to try his hand at another *Broken Blossoms*."[26]

Still, Kuttner isolated the appeal of the film better than anyone else at the time. By taking an old but well-liked work, allowing the new medium to freshen it without distorting it or losing its basic value as a simply unbeatable entertainment, Griffith had made a film that was irresistible on almost any level on which it was approached. A simple comparison merely with his own work shows that. Though it traffics in many of the same values as the Gish pastorals of the previous year, its scale transforms it into a major work, while unlike that other minor candidate for designation as a masterpiece, *Broken Blossoms*, it avoids poetical and "prettifying" excess (the word is Gilbert Seldes's). Yet among the long films, it avoids the moral blindness of *Birth*, the structural imbalances of *Intolerance* and the simple failures to understand observable reality that marred *Hearts*. And, of course, it was unmarked by the cynicism, or perhaps more properly the attempts at cynicism (a manner Griffith was quite bad at), to be found in some of his other work of the time.

To some critics *Way Down East* might be old hat, but it wasn't to Griffith and he brought authentic feeling, authentic emotion to it, as he did to all his best work. He liked and believed in these people, liked and believed in the conventions through which they were seen. In short, this may well have been the film he had been aspiring toward since Biograph days, the perfect matching of man and material on a project that lay at the dead center of his range. There is an ease to the film, a comfortable stride to its pace, even a certain control in its titling that make it a delight for a modern audience to watch. By dropping back in time Griffith here frees us from the discomfort we often feel in the presence of an old-fashioned sensibility working in an inherently modernist medium. For once, we can relax and have a good time with him, enjoy him enjoying his confidence in himself and his material.

And so the picture went forth. And it did travel "far and long." Two statements, perhaps, indicate as well as anything the breadth of its appeal. One was a letter from John Barrymore, then at the height of his powers, to Griffith. Having seen *Way Down East* twice he wrote that "any personal praise of yourself or your genius . . . I would naturally consider redundant and a little like carrying coals to Newcastle," but not "having the honor of knowing Miss Gish personally," and fearing direct address might be considered "impertinent," he asked Griffith to tell her that "her performance seems to me to be the most superlatively exquisite and poignantly enchanting thing that I have ever seen in my life." He had seen Duse and Bernhardt on the stage and thought Gish matched them "for sheer technical brilliancy and great emotional projection, done with almost uncanny simplicity and sincerity." It was, he said, "great fun and a great stimulant to see an American artist equal, if not surpass, the finest traditions of the theater."[27] What music for the movie people! Greater respect than that from one's peers cannot be hoped for and Griffith quoted from the letter in his advertising campaign.

But more useful than that was the outpouring of praise from people who did not ordinarily have much to say about the movies, except perhaps to condemn their pernicious influence on public morals. Typical of this support from quarters previously unheard from was a lead editorial in the *Omaha World-Herald*, when *Way Down East* reached that hinterland. It began by saying the motion picture had, at birth, come "into the hands of those who were striving not for the best art but for the most dollars." Yet despite this "debasement" here was *Way Down East*, and here was the man who made it. "David Wark Griffith is not merely a keen businessman exploiting 'the movies.' He is a man of culture and refinement and ideals—a true and a great artist. He is a man of vision and convictions—a great preacher. And he has shown us, in this 'simple story of plain people,' how the screen can be used. With true art of a high order of excellence, not alone to entertain the people but to serve them. He has made the combination of beauty with truth. He has put art to its loftiest practical use as the handmaiden of simple goodness. He has given us a foretaste of what 'the silver screen,' in its free and unimpeded development, under the hand and inspiration of genius, can and will become even within the lifetime of men and women now in their youth."[28]

There is much more in this vein. But the editorial voice from the heartland illustrates the rich lode Griffith had tapped and the predominant mood of the nation at the time, a mood greatly at variance with the general impression we carry of that historical moment. It was, of course, one that everyone was anxious to exploit, Griffith not least of all. It is an irony that the success of *Way Down East* would lead to the first serious rift between Griffith and the other United Artist principals over the division of the spoils, a rift that would never fully heal in the years ahead.

3
——

The problem was that both parties saw *Way Down East* as an answered prayer. Griffith's interest, as he saw it, lay in holding on to the picture as long as possible, showing it at advanced prices in the key cities under the auspices of his own organization. His theaters were scaled to a two-dollar top, far higher than the ticket price even in first-run houses when a picture was released in the customary way. And, of course, he did not have to give 20 percent of the grosses to UA as a distribution fee. On the other hand, United Artists was still desperately short of films to release and it, too, was short of cash. The partners felt, as well, that they had treated Griffith generously in the matter of *Romance*, which had failed so dismally at the box office (its losses represented close to half the corporation's losses for the 1919–20 fiscal year). Moreover, they were fearful of establishing a precedent under which Griffith would hold back his best films and permit UA to distribute them only on their second runs or in the least desirable territories while lumbering the company with full responsibility for items like *The Love Flower*.

The pressure from the company began to build in the fall, when it became clear that *Way Down East* was going to be a large success—and that Griffith was not turning it over to UA. Banzhaf was questioned on the point at the November 5 UA board meeting. By December 6 the UA minutes would note that "a general discussion was engaged in by all present relative to the devising of some method that would procure from Mr. Griffith the immediate marketing, through the United Artists Corporation, of his picture, 'Way Down East,' and if that were not procured, some business arrangement with Mr. Griffith by which the United Artists Corporation would share in the receipts derived from 'Way Down East' because of its claim upon Mr. Griffith for the right to market that picture."[29]

This last was a debatable point. Like all the UA principals, Griffith had the right to draw an advance of up to $200,000 against his eventual share of the monies realized when any given picture went into distribution. But he had not availed himself of this opportunity in this case, obtaining all financing from outside sources. From the start he obviously intended this picture as a "special," meaning he was not legally bound to turn it over to UA for distribution. Morally, of course, that was a dubious position for a principal in a company that was struggling to establish itself.

It appears that Griffith was willing to let Banzhaf and Epping discuss UA's handling the picture when it came off its road show engagements, despite some hesitation on the matter, based on a growing belief that Abrams was marketing the films of Pickford and Fairbanks more aggressively than he was Griffith's. This might not have been true. Abrams's compensation derived very largely from his percentage of sales, and it was in his interest to get the best possible price for all the partners' pictures. It is likely that Griffith's brother Albert, ambitious to head a full-scale distribution service for Griffith, was the source of this poison. It is also likely that Abrams was forced to take pretty much what he could get for *Romance* and *The Love Flower*, and that deals for those less-desirable films compared unfavorably with the deals he could make for the better Pickford and Fairbanks releases—but try explaining that to Griffith!

Still, a crisis might have been avoided if Griffith had not run short of cash around the first of the year. He had devoted much of the fall to personally opening *Way Down East* in a number of its more important and successful engagements outside New York. Receipts from these were slow in arriving and anyway had to be applied to the loans outstanding on various productions as well as to studio overhead. Besides, *Way Down East* had been a mighty effort and Griffith was tired. With his remaining reserves of cash and energy he decided to do something more modest for his next release. Returning to Thomas Burke and *Limehouse Nights*, he found two stories he thought could be combined in a single scenario that could be made inexpensively at Mamaroneck. He did the writing himself, went into production on the film he called *Dream Street* in the late fall— and found himself running short of cash in January.

He had the option of shutting down until revenues from *Way Down East*, which was returning as much as $48,000 a week, replenished his treasury, a matter of a couple of months at most, or he could get a rela- tively small loan—$65,000—for a short term and keep going. He did not want to lay off his employees and he did not want to go back to the banks for such a small sum. So he asked Banzhaf to see what United Artists could do to help out. A loan against the heavily encumbered *Way Down East* negative was ruled out because of the banks' prior claims on it and because UA had no stake in it. There was also reluctance, perhaps based on the *Romance* experience, to lend Griffith money on an unfinished pic- ture. But Banzhaf and some of UA's New York executives came up with a plan by which Canadian receipts for *Way Down East* could be used to guarantee the advance. When this idea was communicated, via Cap O'Brien, to Pickford and Fairbanks on the West Coast, they asked that Abrams be permitted immediately to start selling the film in Canada for regular runs.

This outraged Griffith. He not only distrusted Abrams's ability to get top dollar for the picture; he also feared that an immediate selling effort would vitiate the profitability of his first-run bookings there. He apparently fired off an angry wire to Fairbanks, threatening to keep *Way Down East* out of UA's hands entirely. The exact wording of the threat is lost, but Fairbanks's hot response is not:

> THIS RECENT ACTION OF YOURS WITH 'WAY DOWN EAST' IS MOST
> UNFAIR. STOP. IT SEEMS TO ME THAT IF YOU HAD APPLIED A SENSE
> OF JUSTICE TO A MATTER WHERE HONOR HAD SOMETHING TO DO
> WITH IT, YOUR ASSOCIATES WOULD HAVE GOTTEN A BETTER DEAL.
> I SEND YOU THIS TO LET YOU KNOW HOW I FEEL AND THAT IT MIGHT
> HAVE SOME EFFECT ON YOUR FUTURE.[30]

While Griffith brooded on that one, Banzhaf sent a milder wire to O'Brien insisting that "CLIENT WILL POSITIVELY NOT CONSENT" to a change in the deal as originally worked out, adding "ANY CHANGE WOULD BE GREAT EMBARRASSMENT TO ME AND IMPOSSIBLE TO CONSUMMATE."[31] His client, unfortunately, was in a bad temper (rather rare for him) and of a mood to vent his spleen. In and of itself, the Canadian squabble was minor, but as a symbol it was not. His partners were great stars; their names on pictures virtually guaranteed their profitability. But the Griffith name, though famous, guaranteed nothing at the box office. Each new film had to be sold on its merits, and Griffith was convinced that the road show engagements, besides carrying the hope of immediate profits, generated more significant attention from reviewers and the word of mouth endorsements from audiences that helped build the take when the picture went into ordinary release. Beyond that, he was cross because he had been at some pains to fulfill his UA contract, while Pickford was being slow off the mark and Chaplin had yet to deliver a single film to the company.

Thus he sent a long wire to Fairbanks claiming that receipts on *The Love Flower* had been "absurdly low," while Pickford's *Suds* and a Mack Sennett pick-up, *Down on the Farm*, were garnering large advances prior to their release. This was galling to his pride as well as his pocketbook, so he wrote:

> KNOWING WHAT I CAN DO WITH MY OWN PICTURES WITH MY OWN HANDLING AND HAVING GOOD PROOF OF WHAT THE BOOKING OFFICES [THE UNITED ARTISTS EXCHANGES] CAN DO WITH MY PICTURES WOULD LIKE VERY MUCH TO WITHDRAW ENTIRELY FROM THE UNITED ARTISTS. STOP. DON'T MEAN THIS TO ANSWER YOUR ANTAGONISTIC WIRE BECAUSE LIFE IS TOO SHORT TO FIGHT AND SQUABBLE AND DON'T SEE WHY IT COULD NOT BE DONE AND EACH GO OUR OWN WAY AND STILL BE GOOD FRIENDS AS BUSINESS IS ONE THING AND FRIENDSHIP ANOTHER. IF I AM TO GET NO MORE RETURNS FOR MY WORK THAN I HAVE RECEIVED THROUGH UNITED ARTISTS' EFFORTS HAD BETTER FOLLOW CHAPLIN PRECEDENT AND DO NOTHING AT ALL. . . . AM SURE SOME GOOD PRODUCING COMPANY COULD BE PROCURED TO TAKE MY PLACE. AM WILLING TO MAKE ANY ARRANGEMENTS THAT YOU MAY CONSIDER ALONG THIS LINE AND IN A GENEROUS FASHION. . . .[32]

Into this widening breach Little Mary bravely and sensibly stepped. A wire from her to Griffith, which might have crossed Griffith's to Fairbanks, pointed out that the losses on *Romance* had so depleted the UA treasury that it held insufficient funds, at the moment, to pay her and Fairbanks monies owed them out of collections on their films. As a result, she said, they were having a difficulty financing new production for the company, but were "ASKING NO SPECIAL CONSIDERATION OR GUARANTEE

FROM UNITED AND ARE LIVING UP TO THE SPIRIT AND LETTER OF OUR CON-
TRACTS." She added, however, they would be willing to consider an ad-
vance on *Dream Street* "PROVIDED THAT IT BE REGULARLY SOLD BY UNITED
AS SOON AS POSSIBLE AND WITHOUT OTHER CONDITIONS THAN THOSE SPECI-
FIED IN YOUR CONTRACT. . . ."[33]

Here was an out. They could all pretend that the Canadian plan
was a foolishness their advisors and functionaries had come up with while
the artists themselves were otherwise engaged. Griffith leapt at it. He
said the Canadian loan plan "WAS A MATTER THAT MR. EPPING AND MR.
BANZHAF HAD TAKEN UP. . . . IT WAS THEIR IDEA, NOT MINE. AS FAR AS THIS
IS CONCERNED CAN SEE THE JUSTICE OF YOUR WIRE AND BELIEVE YOU ARE
ABSOLUTELY RIGHT SO HAVE NO HARD FEELING CONCERNING THIS. . . ." Still,
he would not back off his assertion that his pictures were being sold short,
and he did not withdraw his threat to leave United Artists. He did con-
clude, however, with placatory compliments: "HAVE NOT SEEN YOUR LAST
PICTURE BUT HAVE HEARD GOOD REPORTS. HAVE SEEN *Mark of Zorro*, HOW-
EVER [it was Fairbanks's first period adventure], WHICH I THOUGHT EX-
TRAORDINARILY GOOD."[34]

This brought a stern but fair-minded response signed by all three of
the other UA principals. They noted that some of Fairbanks's contracts
for *His Majesty the American* were less remunerative than some of Griffith's for *Broken Blossoms*, but that he had not complained. Moreover,
they observed that Griffith had the right to okay all contracts Abrams
made. They then passed on to their most pressing concern. "WE HAVE BEEN
INFORMED AND BELIEVE THERE IS AN ORGANIZED EFFORT AMONG YOUR EM-
PLOYEES AIMING TO INFLUENCE YOU AGAINST UNITED ARTISTS AND TO MAKE
REQUESTS THAT NONE OF US HAVE MADE UPON UNITED ARTISTS." They also
claimed that some of his people had visited UA exchanges and threatened
that no more Griffith pictures would be released through the organization. "THIS INFLUENCE," the wire continued, "IS SEEKING TO PREVAIL UPON
YOU TO EXHIBIT YOUR PICTURES IN MANNER IN WHICH YOU ARE DOING WAY
DOWN EAST." The reference, of course, was to Albert, who was constantly
out and about on his selling missions, in whose character there certainly
was the ability to make idle threats and who surely was opposed to the
United Artists deal. The West Coast crowd could not forbear to point
out that Wark Productions, formed to produce and distribute *Intolerance*, had this very month gone into bankruptcy, an event that had not
helped Griffith with his stock issue in the new company (and which, incidentally, belies the widely held belief that Griffith went broke paying off
the *Intolerance* debts; he tried hard to reduce them, but in the end simply
walked away from them). Be that as it may, Fairbanks, Pickford and
Chaplin calmly informed Griffith, in conclusion, that they were going to
live up to their UA contracts and that they expected him to do likewise.[35]

Their wire closed the incident, and Griffith proceeded to complete his film. But this brisk exchange illustrates most of the issues that went into the making of Griffith's economic tragedy. Neither side was entirely wrong in evaluating the situation. The needs of United Artists were real and from its point of view it was entirely correct in attempting to make Griffith live up to his obligations to the firm. In due course, if he could have held out a few years longer, until the company was functioning at full speed, it would have been the best distributor for the kind of films Griffith wanted to make, films that required a certain amount of special handling. But he was right that, at the moment, United Artists could not offer him what he required, though he was focusing on a minor issue when he criticized the prices Abrams was obtaining for films.

The real problem was more complex, a reflection of the rising costs of producing long features and of the motion picture industry's coming to maturity as an economic entity. The major producers—companies like Famous Players–Lasky, Fox, Universal and (soon) Metro-Goldwyn-Mayer—were now cranking out so much film that they could practice block booking. They could offer an exhibitor a full year's programs, right down to the short subjects, which they could sell to him well in advance of delivery, using the 25 percent advance it was customary to exact from the theater men to help finance these still uncompleted films. The exhibition contracts were also handy sources of collateral for short-term production loans, looked on most favorably by the banks, which saw that under this system risk was spread over many films, with profits almost automatic over the long run. The exhibitors naturally complained about being forced to take the good with the bad in these packages, but block booking, together with the theater chains the majors owned and operated, brought national organization and steady economic growth to what might now justifiably be called an "industry." Indeed, when after a decade of litigation the producers agreed, in 1948, to divest themselves of their theaters and end what was left of a diminished block-booking system, these actions, as much as the advent of television, permanently destabilized movie economics.

But UA, in the early twenties, stood very much outside this system. It owned no theaters and it did not have enough films to offer them in blocks. This meant its producers had to finance each film individually, something most banks were reluctant to do. And selling them one by one made for an extremely slow and erratic cash flow, which meant that Griffith, whose resources were less than those of his partners, could not depend on current revenues to finance future production—the very situation he had found himself in on *Dream Street*. Abrams tried to compensate for this defect by attempting to collect full payment in advance from exhibitors for the artists' pictures, but that caused bad feeling among customers, to the point where the president of an exhibitors' association wrote to Griffith complaining about Abrams's aggressiveness.

In short, United Artists was a good idea, the time of which had not quite arrived for its other owners, and would never arrive for Griffith. The company itself would enjoy only two marginally profitable years between 1919 and 1929, and would not start to turn steady, if generally quite modest, profits until the 1930s, after Joseph Schenck had taken over its presidency and brought in enough independent producers to assure a good flow of films through the exchanges. Thus its dividends were of no significant help to Griffith when he most needed them, while its lack of access to finance was always a detriment to him. Had he stayed with Zukor, or found someone of similar caliber who could have assured him of steady financing, he might have avoided the debts that eventually crushed him.

But this is not certain. Even if Albert had not been present to urge him on, Griffith still would have loved road showing, with its gratifying opportunities to earn a star's portion of applause, attention and, occasionally, profitability. Nor does one imagine even the indulgent Zukor unprotestingly financing his expensive taste in projects or his wasteful work habits. And it is possible no one could have withstood the overhead charges his studio imposed on his productions or dealt with the simple fact that Griffith had become by this time a compulsive gambler. According to Raymond Klune, Griffith frequently gave him as much as $5,000 to bet on the horses and the same wildly plunging spirit now attended his movie enterprises. There was no one in the organization with the strength or the prestige to stop him. In the end, the question of whether his arrangement with United Artists was good or bad for him must be regarded as moot. He was the most significant author of his own destruction.

4

Even with a success like *Way Down East* working for it, the corporation's need for money was insatiable. According to its projected budget for 1921, it could not expect to have any cash balance accruing from the picture until mid-March; meantime it would require anywhere from $46,000 to $101,000 per week to keep the studio open and functioning.[36] And given the visibility of *Way Down East*'s success, and the need to dispose of some 25,000 shares of class A stock that remained unsold, it could scarcely skip payment of its first dividend. The books for 1920 were thus made to show a profit of $217,246.54 and a dividend of a dollar per share, 50 cents less than originally promised, was declared, payable March 4.[37] With these demands on its resources outstanding, it is scarcely surprising to find Griffith going to one of his banks for another $50,000 for *Dream Street* less than two months after he had secured his advance for the picture from United Artists. A little after that this loan—secured in part by *Way Down East*—was increased to $250,000, partly to help finance Griffith's next project, the superproduction that was eventually released as *Orphans of the Storm*. Once again, United Artists had to help out, agreeing to pay $10,000 a week for 22 weeks, directly to the bank out of its *Dream Street* receipts, with another $10,000 a week for 13 weeks going to the Griffith corporation. There was, of course, no certainty that *Dream Street* would generate that kind of revenue at the box office, but in return for this favor Griffith, acting as usual against his brother's advice, granted UA the right to distribute, through a new overseas subsidiary, both *Dream Street* and, far more significantly, *Way Down East*, in the British Isles.[38]

Luckily, *Dream Street* did not perform badly at the box office, in the end losing only about $150,000. This is somewhat confounding to latter-day viewers of the film, who find it one of Griffith's feeblest efforts. As indeed it is. Essentially a triangle, in which the brothers McFadden, Spike and Billy (respectively Ralph Graves and Charles Emmett Mack), vie for the affections of Gypsy Fair, a music hall dancer played in her "hippity-skippity" manner (as a contemporary critic put it) by Carol Dempster. Spike, who eventually wins the girl, begins his courtship by trying to force his attentions on her. Billy is throughout "a creep," as scholar Arthur Lennig bluntly describes him, a weakling and a lurker in the shadows unable to declare his love for Gypsy Fair. Their stories at first meander, then rush to a preposterous conclusion. Early in the film the girl, whose father has been blackmailed into serving as a police informant, seeks to free him from this bondage by betraying to the police a gambling den owned by one Sway Wan, a Chinese who is also infatuated with her (he is, as well, a voyeur and another potential rapist). After her father dies, the story's emphasis switches to the brothers. Billy kills an intruder in their rooms but allows the police to believe Spike was the murderer. The latter escapes from jail only to be recaptured believing that it was Gypsy Fair who betrayed him this time, although in fact it was Sway Wan who did so. At his trial Billy finally comes forward with a confession and is let off on a plea of justifiable homicide. Whereupon Spike and the dancer marry, but permit Billy to settle in with them. A child quickly follows, but man and wife become successes on the stage and Billy also succeeds, as a composer.

The tale is, of course, preposterously strained, and none of its principal characters is very appealing in deed or manner. It was a defect Griffith apparently sensed, and he did what he could to compensate for the weaknesses of his scenario. An elaborate Limehouse Street was built at Mamaroneck and he pumped plenty of fog into it, trying to recapture the picturesqueness of *Broken Blossoms*. It and the other sets give off a somewhat expressionistic air, though probably not intentionally. Griffith might have heard of *The Cabinet of Dr. Caligari*, made in Germany the previous year, but since neither it nor *The Golem,* which together created the vogue for this style, was released in the U.S. until after *Dream Street* was finished, the look of the film was probably dictated by a desire to economize—and, perhaps, to find a way of blending the realistic portions of the film more comfortably with some highly stylized sequences Griffith worked up. (That Griffith was aware of the reviving German film industry's potential as a rival is indicated by a wire to his brother, when he was on a selling trip to Europe this spring: "IF GO BERLIN BE CAREFUL OUR PICTURES NOT SHOWN DIRECTORS OR PRODUCERS. DON'T WANT EDUCATE THEM FURTHER."[39]) In these he set to wandering about his Limehouse set a Preacher of the Streets (played by the elder Tyrone Power) who represents good, and a Masked Violinist (Morgan Wallace) representing evil. Their appearances at various moments in the film dictate the responses of the characters to various situations, suggesting a certain determinism in human behavior. Recourse was also had to a third, inanimate symbol, which Griffith explained in an interview: "The evening star hangs over the little characters of that story and seems to guide them. There is constant reference to that star. It tells them if they can walk in the streets among men and still keep their faces turned towards the stars, the going will be a little easier." (In the same interview, incidentally, he said there would be no peace in the world, no League of Nations "until we stop referring to our fellow man as the Wop, the Chink, the Hun . . ."[40] when in *Dream Street* he presents a Chinese villain in the most stereotypical terms, and even has Dempster tell him, after he is beaten up following the attempted assault on her, that that will teach him not to bother white girls.)

Griffith's symbolic characters are innovative and they might have worked dramatically had he not backed them up with literal visions of heaven and hell, complete with angels and some devils desultorily pitchforking sinners. If imagery of this kind was discomfiting in *The Avenging Conscience, Birth* and *Intolerance,* it is risible in a less-primitive movie age, in the context of a film that, at best, can aspire only to a certain realism. In his defense it should perhaps be noted that throughout the twenties films that pretended to a certain elevation of tone often resorted to this kind of thing. In this very year, for example, the hugely successful *Four Horsemen of the Apocalypse* literally depicted the doomy riders galloping about through cloudy mists, scythes at the ready, not to mention a rather comical dragon snortingly symbolizing war's hellishness.

Griffith betrayed his insecurity about *Dream Street* in various ways. For example, he tried a new method of titling, in which one character's line of dialogue would fade out to be replaced by another's reply—an attempt to find an improved visual equivalent to the rhythms of speech. And, after opening the picture at New York's Central Theater, he moved it over to Town Hall, where it played on a program that introduced "Kellum Talking Pictures" to a not very interested world. Except for one se-

quence in which Spike sings a love song to Gypsy Fair there was no attempt to give the illusion of speech within the film, but there were short
subjects—an Irvin S. Cobb monologue (in Negro dialect), a song, and,
leading off the evening, Griffith himself on film, talking: "In the center
of the silver sheet a dot appeared, spread and David Wark Griffith's features, animated, looked out upon the Town Hallers. He did more. He
spoke lines. They were 'The Evolution of Motion Pictures.' " Griffith
briefly praised "the sensitive mechanism, so marvelous and accurate" that
enabled Orlando E. Kellum to synchronize sound with the lip movement
of performers—essentially it consisted of carefully cued phonograph records. Some observers praised the invention's audibility, others the excellent synchronization. But there was much criticism of the "metallic"
quality of the sound and it was said "the scratching of the needle could
be heard throughout the auditorium."[41] So destructive to mood was the
tonality of the sound system that general doubts were expressed as to the
value of talk in dramatic films. Said one notably near-sighted reporter:
"For short subjects—campaign speeches, etc.—the talking movies may
enjoy some popularity. But, at best, they are only a novelty and there is
not the slightest chance that they will 'revolutionize' the motion picture
industry . . . they will do more to drive audiences out of motion picture
theaters than bring them in."[42]

As always, Griffith was pressing against the technical limits of his
medium. Then, too, there was publicity value in the novelty, and that was
important to him as well. He had hired Harry Reichenbach, a famously
colorful press agent of the time, to promote the film and he had turned
the length of Forty-third Street, from river to river, into "Dream Street"
by erecting signs so labeling it at every intersection. And the block between Broadway and Sixth, where Town Hall stands, was decorated with
American and Chinese flags, a not entirely tasteful choice given the character of the picture's Chinese villain. He had a streetcar advertising the
film clanging up and down Broadway and each night fiery lights shone
from the top of the hall to attract the multitudes.

The reviews tended to concentrate on the photography—it was the
first film on which Sartov had sole credit, Bitzer having been put on detached duty to work with the sound engineers—and the atmosphere. One
paper charged Griffith with administering to the "nine-year-old mind of
the audience," a phrase it put in quotation marks, indicating that this
cliché has a longer history in discussions of the movie than one might
have supposed. Another, when the picture finally arrived in Minneapolis,
waxed ironic: "When Mr. Griffith adds colored pictures of hell, including graceful young women in flaming draperies, and blue skies in which
the evening star stands for 'the eternal' his profundities overwhelm. And
what is the symbol whereby the stage dancer's dress is flame red, while
everything else is in the customary black and white? Is this a symbol of

fire, a symbol of passion or a symbol of screen trickery?"[43] Still, everyone was quite tolerant, and a notice in a magazine quite fairly summarizes the general reception for *Dream Street*:

"It is not fair to judge a Griffith picture on its plot. Griffith does not believe in plots [a remarkable statement, that], he believes in pictures. . . . By an adroit use of lights, by clever settings, and by skillful handling of his players, he can make you laugh, cry and get all excited over the silliest kind of wish-wash, clap-trap situations. The master magician of the movies hypnotizes you, and while you are spellbound by his pretty pictures, he slams at your head an outrageously absurd and sentimental melodrama."[44]

However misguided some of his choices of material—like *Dream Street*—Griffith gave his audiences good weight for value, and he gave of himself without stint. "It's so much more fun to give the best that you have in you," Griffith told an interviewer in May 1921. "At the end of my career I want to be able to feel that I had at least attempted to make a decent job of things."[45]

5

In this effort factors beyond the economic pressures that were piling in on him more and more forcefully almost every day were at work. He could no longer operate solely on instinct, not with pictures costing what they now did. Like everyone else in the business, he was now compelled to try to outguess the audience, determine their mood and their standards. Sometimes he was optimistic about them: "I find that the more thought I give to a picture, the better the public likes it. All opinions to the contrary, the public does like clean pictures, it does like pictures which have been carefully worked out and it does like ideas." Moreover, he added, this demand "is going to increase as time goes on."[46] That was the spring of 1921. By the fall, however, he was saying: "It will be several decades yet before producers can make motion pictures that do not also classify as entertainment for every grade of intelligence. America has no sincere or even conscious interest in art. It is first and almost completely interested in industry."[47]

The statements indicate honest conflict. He did aspire to what he thought of as art, though perhaps one might better use that old genteel phrase "the finer things." But he also had to survive and nowadays that meant providing entertainment for "every grade of intelligence"—a task rendered more difficult in his case by the fact that his name had become a brand name, and he could not turn out a vast range of products, as a studio could, without diminishing the value of that name. Neither could he repeat himself. He had to keep looking for material that offered at least superficial novelty or significance of some kind, even if it was only the significance of scale. His dilemma was illustrated by the choice he had to make, in the spring of 1921, between two projects. He had the possibility of exercising the rights to Joseph Hergesheimer's novel *Tol'able David*, which he had acquired for Richard Barthelmess. But now, acting on Lillian Gish's advice (she noted the play had never failed, and also noted capital parts in it for her and her sister), he entered into negotiations for *The Two Orphans*, that venerable (1874) classic of the melodramatic stage. Once called by Daniel Frohman, the producer, "the perfect play," it had become the chief support of Kate Claxton, the actress who had played the leading role as a young woman at the American premiere (McKee Rankin, for whom Griffith worked in stock, had been in that company, too). She subsequently acquired the rights to the American adaptation of the Adolphe d'Ennery-Eugène Cormon success and went on to establish what most authorities believe to be the record for the most performances in the same role.

Both the novel and the play offered Griffith good prospects. But both had their disadvantages, too. *Tol'able David* is a rural romance, in which a plucky and good-natured boy, suspected of cowardice, triumphantly (but with due modesty) endures various tests (including a final confrontation with three bullying brothers) and asserts himself as a man of character and strength. It is, obviously, the kind of material Griffith was good with, but he had never placed a male at the center of one of these pictures (and rarely enough at the center of any of his pictures) and that might have disquieted him somewhat. Nor did the novel contain a really spectacular conclusion—the fight against the brute brothers being a rather small-scaled bit of action compared to the climax he had created for *Way Down East*. Clearly he felt *Tol'able David* might suffer not only by that comparison but because its overall tone was not so very different from his great success.

In contrast, *The Two Orphans* had not one but two imperiled heroines, was by Griffith's lights a "classic," offered him a certain novelty in that he had never attempted its time and place (France, just before, and in his adaptation, during, the Revolution) and enormous possibilities for spectacle. It would cost more, to be sure, but it had, as he saw it, a potential for profit at least as great as that of *Way Down East*. In the end, he decided to go with it.

Because there was no role in *Orphans* suitable for Barthelmess, he formed his own company, bought the rights to *Tol'able David* from Griffith (for $7,500), and with Henry King directing his first important film, from a scenario by Edmund Goulding (who would himself go on to a career directing "women's pictures"), he would enjoy an enormous success with it (when he screened the picture for his mentor, Griffith embraced and kissed Barthelmess at the end). Dempster, too, was absent from the studio during most of the time *Orphans* was before the cameras. Griffith arranged a loan-out for her—the only one of her career—and she was playing opposite John Barrymore in *Sherlock Holmes* while Lillian Gish played her last role for Griffith.

Griffith needed to concentrate all his energies on this mighty prospect, for he never undertook a film that caused him more problems than the one that was finally released as *Orphans of the Storm*. This title change is typical of those problems. For it turned out that the rights he secured from Claxton for $5,000 down and another $5,000 payable later were virtually valueless. The copyright on the version of the play that she had spent her life appearing in had expired a few years earlier and she did not control rights to the French original. These were claimed by William Fox, who had made an *Orphans* film in 1915 based on them (and had, indeed, paid Claxton a small settlement for infringement on *her* rights, which she had sold to yet another film company for its 1911 version of the play). The upshot was that Griffith had to pay Fox $85,000 for his rights in order that the latest and grandest production of the piece could play abroad, where, just to complete the picture of confusion, a recent Italian adaptation was also in the marketplace, and a similar German film had to be bought to keep it out of American theaters. The bargain Griffith must have thought he was getting turned out to be no bargain at all.

Not that Griffith was in a mood to stint. In the original play the French Revolution is little more than a rumor of unrest, casually mentioned at just one point in the drama. The playwright's attention was concentrated on a theme he recurred to time and again, and which was, in any event, one of the central preoccupations of popular fiction of every sort in the nineteenth century, the lost child. Gilbert and Sullivan satirized it in *The Pirates of Penzance*, Oscar Wilde in *The Importance of Being Earnest*, but it was a serious matter to nearly everyone else, this matter of the aristocratic foundling, forced to endure, often without being aware of his or her previous status, the most terrible and demeaning reversals of fate until some distinguishing mark he or she carries is discovered late in the last act and a restoration to rightful place is effected.

Reduced to its essence, that is what *The Two Orphans* is about. But Griffith, writing under the *nom de screen* he had employed on *Hearts of the World* (Gaston de Tolignac) and clearly inspired by *A Tale of Two Cities* and by Carlyle, was determined to bring the Revolution to center stage. By so doing, he further complicated a plot already so convoluted that it almost defies description and, in its reliance on coincidence, utterly defies belief. The two orphans in question are Louise (Dorothy Gish), the daughter of an aristocratic mother, put out for adoption as a baby because she is the product of a less-than-aristocratic liaison, and Henriette

(Lillian Gish), daughter of the family that takes Louise in. The two girls could not have been closer had they been blood kin, and when a plague kills Henriette's parents and blinds Louise, Henriette sets out for Paris with her to find a cure for the latter's affliction.

In the city Henriette is abducted by a dissolute nobleman, the Marquis de Praille, and Louise, abandoned, falls into the hands of the wicked Mother Frochard, a sort of female Fagin, one of whose sons quickly develops an unseemly passion for the blind girl, the other of whom is devoted and seemly in his behavior. Meanwhile Henriette, forced to appear at a fete (worse than death?) with De Praille, is humiliated by him and his friends and is rescued by the Chevalier de Vaudrey (Joseph Schildkraut), who is the nephew of the Countess de Linières, Louise's natural mother. She, in her turn, has married the prefect of the Paris police, who knows nothing of his wife's past and has a scheme in hand to make a prosperous marriage for De Vaudrey. Henriette's appearance in his life makes this match even less appealing to him. Later, discovering Louise missing, Henriette appeals to the Countess for help, and as she does so hears the girl singing in the streets as Mother Frochard has forced her to do. Louise disappears before Henriette can reach her, the prefect trumps up some charges against her and jails her to keep her away from De Vaudrey. For good measure he imprisons him, too, hoping to break his resistance to the arranged match.

Now, however, revolution breaks out, Henriette is freed from the Bastille and is reunited with her would-be lover when he breaks free of prison. He, however, is denounced to a revolutionary tribunal by an old enemy of his family and he and Henriette are reincarcerated. By this time Louise has been released from her bondage by the good brother Fouchard and they are in the courtroom where—so near and yet so far—Henriette recognizes her sister, but cannot reach her before she and De Vaudrey are sentenced to the guillotine. Luckily, she had previously made friends with the moderate Danton (ludicrously identified in a title as "the Abraham Lincoln of France") and there is a typically Griffithsian ride to the rescue by him and his followers. Marriage, reunions, forgiveness and the restoration of Louise's sight all follow.

If the picture was busy it was also big. Griffith literally covered half his studio's acreage with huge sets, representing among other locales the Royal Palace, Notre Dame, Versailles, the Bastille; and on the days when his streets had to be filled with mobs, extras, literally by the truckload, were brought in. A huge effort at historical authenticity as to costumes and props was made, with even a Harvard professor put on as a consultant in these arcane matters. Yet, for all that, the shooting, for the most part, went smoothly over the summer. Bitzer was by now openly resentful of Sartov, even to the extent of refusing a request for advice on the ground that he would not help a man who was trying to take his job away from him. And Dorothy Gish was heard to murmur, in comic resentment, that Schildkraut was prettier than she was (and, in terms of costuming and hairdressing, he was, though he was also a bit of a stiff on camera) and not much liked by the cast and crew for trying to upstage Lillian Gish. But if nothing else, experience had given Griffith a facility with this kind of moviemaking. He kept things functioning smoothly, and he managed his big scenes with dispatch, and with a quality he had not previously attained in comparable sequences. His camera positions are more vivid, his cutting crisper than it ever had been. In *Orphans* he might be said to have fully established all the conventions by which spectacle has ever since been staged. This is the more remarkable in that, attempting to economize everywhere he could, he shot less coverage than usual.

It was at this time that Abel Gance, the French filmmaker, met Griffith, whose welcome to his young admirer bespeaks his graciousness under pressure. Accompanied by the Gish sisters, he attended the American premiere, in a hotel ballroom, before an invited audience, of Gance's antiwar drama *J'accuse*, beating a quick retreat at the end of the film, without giving a response to the anxious Gance. The next day, however, Griffith called, according to Gance's biographer Kevin Brownlow, to say that he had been too moved to speak, even claiming he had suspended shooting on *Orphans* that morning because he had been so emotionally devastated. This seems a typical Griffith exaggeration, but he invited Gance to Mamaroneck, where Gance confronted the representations of revolutionary Paris that Griffith's new art director, Edward Scholl, had designed. It was on this trip that Gance conceived his vast *Napoleon* film, and seeing the period that had attracted Griffith's attention, was concerned the American might be thinking of a similar project. Griffith claimed, again falsely, that he had toyed with such a film but would leave it to Gance. This flattering deferral to Gance's gift, and grand passion, was accompanied by practical assistance. Griffith was instrumental in arranging for United Artists to distribute *J'accuse* in the United States.

Gance apparently got no hint from Griffith of the difficulties under which he was laboring, but they must have been truly frightening, as costs mounted even above the level of *Way Down East*'s. There was a Sunday, for example, when hundreds of extras had been recruited—and had to be paid—and the threat of rain put the work in jeopardy, with no money on hand to call the people back. The corporation's papers make it clear that while the film was before the cameras, and with one large note still outstanding, Griffith could borrow no more from the Central Union Trust Company, the bank with which he had the closest relationship. Early in August he was forced to take a loan from the faithful Epping, who somehow had $158,000 of his own money on hand, to keep the company shooting. Less than a week later Griffith was cabling Emile Wertheimer, the English distributor with whom he had successfully worked in the past, looking for more. He could not entirely hide his desperation:

HAVE A REAL CHANCE FOR YOU AND PARTNERS. HAVE SIXTY-FIVE PERCENT OF TWO ORPHANS FINISHED WITH OUR MONEY. NEED THREE HUNDRED FIFTY THOUSAND FOR COMPLETION EXHIBITION AND PRINTS. IF YOU WILL ADVANCE THIS WILL ALLOW YOU TO TAKE OUT FIRST RECEIPTS OF WORLD RIGHTS . . . UNTIL YOU ARE FULLY PAID. WILL TAKE OUT OUR SHARE AFTERWARDS THEN GIVE YOU TWENTY-FIVE PERCENT OF THE ENTIRE PROFITS LIFE OF PICTURE AND WILL ARRANGE FOR YOU TO HANDLE UNITED KINGDOM ON EQUITABLE BASIS. ENOUGH OF PICTURE PUT TOGETHER TO ASSURE IT WILL BE ONE OF MY MOST SUCCESSFUL BOX OFFICE ATTRAC- TIONS. WILL RANK WITH WAY DOWN EAST AND BIRTH AS HAS BIG HEART INTEREST AND STORY. VERY ELABORATE PRODUCTION WITH ALL STAR CAST. THIS IS A REAL OPPORTUNITY. ANSWER CONFIDEN- TIAL. KINDEST REGARDS.

GRIFFITH[48]

It was indeed "a real chance." And it is a measure of Griffith's need that he was willing to give up so much for his finishing money. The sur- render of first returns meant abandoning hope that *Orphans* could help to finance future production in the near term. And the surrender of UK and other foreign rights meant risking the wrath of his United Artists partners, who needed Griffith's films for their newly opened foreign opera- tion. In the end, however, Wertheimer and friends passed on this large and risky investment, but they were able to help out by purchasing the UK rights for $93,000 promptly delivered. In return Griffith surrendered 75 percent of his profits there until the debt was repaid and agreed to a 50–50 split of all subsequent profits, the deal being obviously nowhere near as good as the 70–30 split Griffith would have received from United Artists in the United Kingdom if he could have avoided this commitment. But the money helped tide him over until he repaid his previous Central Union loan, at which point he got a $340,000 loan against the now-com- pleted *Orphans* negative, with which he paid back Epping, who held the previous lien on that precious 13,500 feet of film.

In this period, curiously, a form of salvation was offered to him. William Randolph Hearst sent his chief editorial advisor, Arthur Bris- bane, to Griffith with an offer to direct Marion Davies in *When Knight- hood Was in Flower*. Implicit therein was the opportunity for Griffith to amalgamate with Hearst's Cosmopolitan Pictures corporation. "It would have made him a major," Raymond Klune would later say. Certainly it would have relieved the immediate financial pressure, enabling the Ma- maroneck studio to turn out the three pictures a year Klune felt were required to justify the overhead it imposed on Griffith.[49] Of course, it might not have worked for long, a partnership between two imperious egos like Griffith's and Hearst's, but in retrospect there are certain attractions in the arrangement. Supervising a picture or two a year for Davies, who was more gifted, particularly as a comedienne, than people have allowed themselves to think because of her allegedly scandalous life, would not have been any more arduous than trying to make a star out of Carol Dempster. And Hearst was at the time anxious to have Davies appear in historical and romantic pictures of the kind that suited Griffith's temperament. But, of course, prudence, not to say prudery, dictated avoiding an alliance with Hearst and Davies. Griffith had his reputation to consider. And his need for independence, though that was surely as compromised by his debt load as it would have been by doing a few pictures for Hearst. What he did to alleviate that load was no worse, in the last analysis, than what he would have had to do for Hearst.

The publisher's overture was rejected in a wire that made too many excuses. Or perhaps just the right amount of them, considering the power of the Hearst presses:

> HAVE JUST HAD TALK WITH MR. BRISBANE. AM IN THE MIDDLE OF MY MOST EXPENSIVE AND EXTRAVAGANT PICTURE "THE TWO ORPHANS" IN WHICH I HAVE INCORPORATED BIG HISTORICAL PAGEANTS SO DO NOT EXPECT TO FINISH BEFORE FIRST OF YEAR AFTER WHICH MY DOCTOR SAYS I MUST GO SLOW AND HAVE MADE ARRANGEMENTS FOR TWO SMALL PICTURES. . . . AT MR. B'S SUGGESTION HOWEVER WOULD BE VERY GLAD TO TALK IT OVER WITH YOU WHEN YOU RETURN TO NEW YORK AS I CONSIDER THIS ALWAYS A GREAT PLEASURE ANYHOW SHALL LOOK FORWARD TO IT. THANKS FOR YOUR MANY FAVORS. ASSURING YOU OF MY DEEPEST APPRECIATION OF YOUR KINDNESS. . . .[50]

Rushing, Griffith was able to get *Orphans of the Storm* ready for holiday season openings in Boston three days after Christmas, in New York on January 2, 1922. On the whole the reviews were favorable. The *New York Times* actually saw the film as a return to form. Its anonymous reviewer may have sniffed that it was, at heart, just a melodrama, but he conceded that "one surely felt that Griffith was himself again. All of his old power to make moving pictures with life in them, to put the point of meaning into them and the fire of continuous action was evident once more."[51] Hard to say where this critic might have been when *Way Down East* opened.

Over at *Life*, Robert E. Sherwood thought the picture "in many ways the best thing he has ever done, and that, it need hardly be explained, is saying a great deal." He noted that there was "a definite Griffith tradition in the movies," a blend of unsullied love contrasted with base and degenerate passion, suspense promoted by "obvious but nonetheless efficacious tricks," railings against intolerance and oppression (in this case Griffith was at pains to draw parallels between the French and Russian revolutions, not at all above enlisting his picture in the anti-red crusade then sweeping the country), beauty, sordid tragedy and "above all, the usual Ku Klux Klan climax." If all these qualities were present and accounted for once again, he thought "pictorially and dramatically," *Orphans of the Storm* was better than any competing film. Like others in the more sophisticated segments of the press, Sherwood could not resist comparisons to *All for a Woman*, with Emil Jannings as Danton, and *Passion*, the Ernst Lubitsch film about Madame Dubarry and, in general, he found Griffith's picture superior to the German films. "Monte Blue [Griffith's Danton] has it over Emil Jannings as Mr. Khayyam said, like a tent."[52]

At the Chicago premiere the usual cheers went up when the picture was finished and, as usual, Griffith allowed himself to be dragged, all modest protest, onstage, where he made the usual self-effacing speech, "tears in his eyes and in his throat." He reiterated the analogy between Lincoln and Danton and claimed the former had inspired the film. A journalist, carried away by the occasion, exclaimed in print: "If Griffith has been great before, he is even greater now!" and asked, rhetorically, "Is he then the Great Emancipator of films?"[53]

And so it went across the country. There was even a private showing in Harding's White House after he took office in the spring. So the picture, seemingly so remote in its setting and themes from contemporary realities, did profit somewhat from Griffith's careful positing of an anti-Bolshevist, anti-anarchist theme; he, like many others at that moment, seemed to think that Bolshevism and anarchy were identical ills. He was at pains to point that moral in the film's press book. In the figure of Robespierre, the deepest-died blackguard in his piece, he found the sort of figure he had for years loathed—the single-minded and inhumane "reformer." As Griffith put it, he led, "as so often in history," a fanatical minority of "think-as-I-think men . . . [who] stamped out with the guillotine all who opposed them. . . . And the leader of the slaughter was that conscientious public servant Robespierre—the advocate incorruptible—the patriot who scented the Republic's danger so keenly that in every opponent he discovered a traitor and marched him to the axe forthwith." Griffith did not see any Robespierres in the United States. The attorney general who had so recently organized the raids on alleged radical organizations, A. Mitchell Palmer, was not mentioned. No, the directional finger pointed elsewhere. "Russia has been much like that. The people seem to win, but a fraction of fanatics defeats their will to govern."

Of course, with a $950,000 investment at stake, one does what one can to attract the populace. And if anti-red preachment did not get them, perhaps Billy Sunday would. The evangelist issued a strong endorsement of the film, which Griffith repeated in huge ads. "God help our girls in this age of danger," the evangelist thundered. "War leaves its traces on hearts, minds and morality," he said, and then, somewhat tortuously, pointed the analogy between the sorrows of girlhood unprotected from "the dreadful power of a people broken loose from all restraint," as Griffith showed them on the screen, and those of modern girls "not orphans in fact, but in spiritual neglect because fathers and mothers do not understand the world's hideous dangers" as they might be found "even today in the world's great and cruel cities."[54]

In justice to Griffith, it must be said that a position as a defender of faith and morals was forced on him as *Orphans* went into release. While he was still shooting his film the Fatty Arbuckle scandal broke, and as the picture began to open across the country, the murder of William Desmond Taylor, the director, whose name was linked in the press with two female stars, Mabel Normand and Mary Miles Minter, occurred. Thus, wherever he went, Griffith, as a leader of the industry, was asked about the moral standards of his colleagues and he hoped, to the *Chicago Tribune*, that "people would not get the wrong idea about the motion picture life and social ideals."[55] As for himself, he told another reporter, "I believe deep down in their hearts every man and woman is clean—wants to see clean things. I refuse to produce an underwear ad and label it a motion picture."[56]

All of this, in some measure, worked for the picture—the beloved old story, the impressive spectacle Griffith had added to it, the reviews, the publicity. *Orphans of the Storm* made money—but not enough of it, and not quickly enough. For Griffith, if he was to continue operating at his new standard, needed not just a modest success, but a huge one. Early in 1922 he caused to have distributed to his stockholders a balance sheet for the year ending December 31, 1921, showing a loss of $112,853.70, though in an accompanying letter he observed that there was actually on hand more than $1.2 million in cash. What the board was doing, he said, was depreciating all current productions at an accelerated pace in order to preserve this sum until *Orphans of the Storm* "which had received the same favorable reception as that given *Way Down East* by the press and motion picture public" could be placed in general release the following fall, after the "dull season."[57]

There having been a short, sharp depression, with general economic conditions remaining uncertain, the explanation was plausible. But Griffith was actually setting up his stockholders for a disappointment when the fiscal year ended six months later, for he knew he would need most of those reserves to meet the corporation's debts and to finance production in the interval ahead. Only if the financial showing of *Orphans* in its road show engagements was at least as spectacular as *Way Down East*'s had been, could he hope to pay even a partial dividend. But it was not. Most of these expensive-to-mount engagements did not cover their costs, and Griffith and Albert Grey persisted with them far too long, delaying the picture's entrance into general release, where profitability finally lay.

One can perhaps see in retrospect why there was measurably less enthusiasm for *Orphans* than there had been for *Way Down East*. Edward Wagenknecht, one of Griffith's most determined critical apologists, has called *Orphans* "a practically perfect film . . . a prime example of how good a film could be,"[58] citing in particular the masterful composition of its shots, the brilliance of its editing, and the relative lack of excess that had marred some of his other spectacles. But still it somehow fails to engage us very profoundly. The sense that clings to us as we watch *Birth*, that we are in on the discovery of a medium's possibilities, is, obviously, missing. So is the sheer self-intoxication that keeps *Intolerance* fresh. Nor is there anything here as powerfully affecting as the mad battle-field wanderings of Gish in *Hearts*, or the vigil with her dying baby in *Way Down East*. And *Orphans* lacks that film's originality in attempting to meld the quotidian with the spectacular. Somehow, for all its graces and facility, one keeps one's distance from *Orphans*.

William K. Everson has commented on its absence of both a strong villain and a powerful hero. For the former we have vile De Praille, but he disappears after his threat to Lillian Gish's virtue is turned aside. Thereafter, we have Sidney Herbert's Robespierre, a broad but still rather chilling portrayal of the puritan in power by an actor who physically suits the part splendidly. Even so, he is rather an abstract figure, just because there is nothing personal in his menace. Everyone, in his view here, seems tainted by original sin. On the other side, the noble De Vaudrey is almost as much a victim of circumstances as the two orphans are, and is therefore hard to identify with emotionally, especially in Schildkraut's rather priggish performance. That, of course, might not have been entirely his fault. For once again one must confront Griffith's inability to create a persuasive hero. We see that beneath his wig and his knee britches he is yet another spiritual descendant of the Little Colonel, personally honorable and brave but essentially a boy who handles events as he handles women, by attempting to charm rather than conquer them. Since conquest for Griffith always involved brutal dominance, he could never conceive of it occurring as a result of intelligence, wit or simple, nonrapacious forcefulness. This being so, he could not conceive of confronting that other difficult mistress, history, in these terms either. And since his views of women were similarly stunted, it must never have occurred to him to have either of the Gishes function as savior of the two of them. This left him, finally and unsatisfactorily, with Danton, obviously a historical figure Griffith admired, but one whom he did not flesh out adequately in human terms. In the film he functions more as a *deux ex machina* than as a fully realized heroic figure, a functionary of the plot but never a servant of the viewer's imagination.

One is tempted to say that in *Orphans* Griffith never quite bridged the distance between his subject and his sensibility, never quite achieved full emotional engagement with the place, period and personages of this story. In the final analysis it is precisely that engagement that made *The Birth of a Nation* what it was. And it is what has made that very short list of memorable movie epics—Eisenstein's *The Battleship Potemkin*, Gance's *Napoleon*, Lean's *Lawrence of Arabia*—what they are. Without that passion, derived from a sense of standing on some native psychological ground, the epic deteriorates to spectacle—and fairly empty spectacle at that.

But there is more to Griffith's failure with *Orphans* than that quite obvious point. The epic is, in essence, a masculine form. Its central convention requires a heroic figure set in opposition to huge historical forces, a figure who, after trial, and even temporary defeat, comprehends them, tames them, bends them to his will. Or dies trying, thus rescuing spiritual victory, an exemplary martyrdom, from the contest. Of the great works in this form perhaps only *The Battleship Potemkin* flouts this rule. Eisenstein, working at the height of his youthful powers (and revolutionary ardor), was able to present a collective hero, a mass of people, responding to, acting upon, a noble idea set in careful, deadly opposition to the ignoble reality of Czarist governance. But, of course, Eisenstein's singular capacity for imagistic intensity and, again, his passionate involvement with events he had lived through, enabled him to work at a level impossible for Griffith to attain.

This was partly because of the inherent nature of his material. *Orphans* is not at heart an epic; it is, in essence, a tale of female victimization, not so very different from *Way Down East*. Griffith had saved, freshened, cinematized that story with the spectacle of the blizzard and the perils of the icy river. Why not have the French Revolution serve the same function here? Or, to go back a little further, he had turned *The Mother and the Law* into something grand by grafting onto it the other stories that composed *Intolerance* as it was finally released. Maybe the technique would serve him again here.

But *Way Down East* worked because the original stage play had been built to the same climax as the film. It required no wrenching about to bring its principal characters to their climactic (and climatic) final peril. *Intolerance*, magnificent as it is as pure cinema, fails dramatically precisely because there is no inherent connection between its spectacle and its human story. It, finally, is the operative analogy to *Orphans*, not *Way Down East*. For the French Revolution is like the fall of mighty Babylon: once it appears on screen it is so compelling that it becomes the only worthwhile subject for the filmmaker. And try as he would, Griffith could not make a persuasive linkage between the play's characters and the events he was trying to impose them upon. Indeed, the plot he was given was in itself so busy, and his characters have so many obligations to it, that there is no time for them to indulge any emotion to any depth. In these circumstances, the revolution cannot be meaningfully grappled with by Griffith's people. At best, they can manage to stay just a step or two ahead of it until the last timely rescue frees them from their frantic scurryings.

So *Orphans*, however handsome and adroit it was in some respects, must be judged a failure, because it does not make those nearly subconscious connections between a work and the basic emotions of large numbers of people. It attracted enough of a crowd to pay for itself, eventually, but it was not a strong enough hit to give Griffith what he most desperately needed at this point, an opportunity to pause, reflect, regroup, rediscover his basic strengths and their application to changing times. Instead, he remained strapped to the wheel of his debts and the picture marks the moment when Griffith's claims to leadership in his art and his industry lost their validity. From here on he would be a follower, and often a rather desperate one at that.

CHAPTER FIFTEEN

Gold-Plating
the Woolworth Building

"DESPITE fame and friends, he spent Christmas alone, his only gift being a cigar from a *Post* reporter who took pity on him." Thus, D. W. Griffith on December 25, 1921, awaiting the world premiere, in Boston, of *Orphans of the Storm*, scheduled for three days later. The scene was not untypical of Griffith when he was between pictures; the anonymous hotel room, the self-imposed loneliness; the gentlemen of the press in flattering attendance, encouraging him not merely to speak about the work at hand, but to generalize about the state of the motion picture art and its future.

On this topic Griffith adverted to a theme that was much on his mind at this time, the growing power of the movie star, gained at the expense of the people who actually created films. He said, according to the next day's report in the *Boston Post*, "there are two classes of picture fans; the unthinking class who worship the star, and the thinking class interested only in pictures that reach an artistic standard and known not for the actors, despite their valuable contribution, but for the director."[1] He was, it seems, entirely unable to acknowledge and act upon the obvious, which was that his name and fame were no longer able to compete effectively against the rapidly growing box office power of star performers.

He was approaching a moment when such an acknowledgment was vital to the survival of his studio and of his own creative independence; the history of the next three years, indeed, revolves around this point. His name, not that of his players, continued to dominate the advertising campaigns for his pictures, while publicity—by the ream—focused on his "genius." It was he, often unaccompanied by his players, who as each film went into release, gave the press interviews and trouped the country, making personal appearances on its behalf. And, it must be said, the press, especially outside New York, remained loyal, by and large, to its earlier estimates of him. At least until the middle of the decade, Griffith's reviewers were patient with his failures and eager to praise, even to over-praise, his partial successes.

The last four films he would make for his own corporation were a disparate (not to say desperate) group—a comedy-mystery, a romance that contained what seemed to him, at least, a sensational element, a last reversion to spectacle, a final attempt at realism—each of which repre-sented an earnest effort to catch the shifting wind of popular taste. His most important star, Gish, had now finally had enough. She decamped first for independent production, later for a long-term contract at M-G-M, neither very happy experiences, though some of her work, in films like *La Bohème* and *The Scarlet Letter*, was memorable. As compensation, Griffith did cast about for some players who had some publicity value—an actor enjoying his first large Broadway success, one of his own former stars still well loved but now in need of a comeback, a rising young British matinee idol, and, latterly, two men who had attained full-fledged Broad-way stardom but were not yet the movie stars they would become. The only things he could not bring himself to do were the two things he most needed to do—end his efforts to make a star of Carol Dempster, and en-gage genuine movie stars, people who might have, by their presence, brought his movies in from the margin to the center of prosperity. For the irony of these years is that Griffith did not fail by much, that almost to the end there was cause to hope that his enterprise might turn the corner and achieve, if not great riches, then that degree of stability that would have allowed him to continue functioning autonomously.

But neither of these courses was open to a man of Griffith's tempera-ment. His female performers he had always seen as extensions of his will, whether they were his lovers or not, and he could not believe it was be-yond him to put Dempster over on the public. After all, he had, as he saw it, done the same for other women when his fame and power were far less than they were now. Of course, besotted as he was, he could not see that Dempster was scarcely a Pickford, a Marsh or a Gish, or how misplaced and self-defeating his love for her was. As for hiring other players, male as well as female, whose names were as important as his, that, too, was out of the question. There was only one star at the Griffith studio, and that was the man whose name appeared above all the titles.

One is compelled to believe that this reluctance to engage the great names was partially motivated by fear of his ability to control stars who were not of his own making. For example, his friend John Barrymore had been appearing in films off and on since 1914, achieving greatness in the new medium with his *Dr. Jekyll and Mr. Hyde* in 1920 and confirming that status with almost yearly screen appearances thereafter in pictures not inherently more distinguished than Griffith's. Romantic, virile, humorous, he was what Griffith needed, and precisely the sort of talent he had come back to New York to associate with. Their acquaintance was marked by mutual respect and, as we have seen, Barrymore had even taken on the thankless task of acting opposite Dempster. Moreover, the combined status of actor and director might well have had extraordinary power at the box office. But Griffith made no overtures to him.

Indeed, around the time of his Christmas musings about the nature of the film audience, Griffith was toying with a curious theory about how, in the future, the public might begin to recognize people such as himself as nothing less than heroic figures. "Your hero is yourself," he declared, "so the national hero becomes the one who expresses in the highest degree the achievement the people of the nation would like to achieve individually."

He noted a shift in that national spirit. Where once we had been a "fighting people," making heroes of our most potent warriors, now, despite having just fought a great war, he observed no soldiers in the current pantheon. They had been replaced, he thought, by industrialists, with Henry Ford being perhaps the most admired contemporary figure. If we could, in such a comparatively short period of time, make such a substitution, was it not possible to predict that in another fifty or a hundred years, "America will awaken to an appreciation of art"? He thought so; at which point, he predicted, the artist would replace the industrialist as the popular hero. Indeed, he thought, "Perhaps motion pictures will do more to stimulate this interest than any other force."[2]

He made it clear that so far as his own field was concerned, he was not talking about mere actors assuming the heroic role. Rather, he imagined men like himself taking that part. In this, he was prescient. For by the time a half-century had passed, and the *auteur* theory had passed from the minds of the French *cinéastes* who concocted it into the general consciousness of a public that had, indeed, begun to conceive of artists—and not just filmmakers either—as heroes, certain directors were seen in just the light he had predicted. By the 1960s many were casting themselves in what they took to be the Griffith mold, as lonely visionaries, fighting the brutal commercialism of the studios, with their crass indifference to highly original ideas, to esthetic innovation and singularity of expression. Historically, they and their supporters would look back on Griffith (and his sometime assistant von Stroheim and his latter-day admirer Orson Welles) as being among the first martyrs to the forces they now saw oppressing them. That there had been a powerful element of self-destructiveness, or anyway, of blindness to the legitimate interest of others, in all these cases was not often spoken of when this history was invoked. Nor are the names of film artists every bit as gifted—one thinks of men like Hawks and Hitchcock in this regard—who managed to create highly individual statements while existing comfortably within the status quo. In any case, whatever credit posterity has granted Griffith as a heroic and tragic victim, it came far too late to do him any practical good.

There is some evidence, however, that even as Griffith expounded to the anonymous reporter in his Boston hotel room about the nature of the film audience, he and his associates were trying to come firmly and practically to grips with the distressing realities of his present situation. That month, for example, Banzhaf had quietly let it be known that the Flagler estate was once again on the market. The asking price was $500,000, which, could it be obtained fairly quickly, would net the Griffith corporation a tidy—indeed, rescuing—profit on its two-year-old investment. Then, too, closing its books for the year, Griffith's financial managers decided that instead of paying a dividend on shares they would write off all the company's previous productions, even though *Orphans* and *Way Down East* both had considerable earning power left in them. This they did—adding in some other properties and buildings—in the amount of $1,646,951.68, producing a net loss on the year's operations of $170,349.64. By in effect retaining earnings they improved the condition of their working capital. Now, if the master could be induced to make a modest, prudent little film, something not much grander than a program feature, and if he would stay close to a budget of around a quarter of a million dollars, then 1922 might prove to be a year of consolidation, from which the company might emerge in more stable condition.

On the surface, in the short run, Griffith seemed content with this course. He would do his best to oblige his counselors. He tried to purchase rights to a hit play, Mary Roberts Rinehart's *The Bat*, which along with *The Cat and the Canary* had established a vogue for haunted-house mysteries on Broadway. But when he found its price to be $150,000 and that its author and producers were insisting on a clause in the contract prohibiting the film from release until the Broadway run was completed, he sensibly decided to pass on the property. Instead, encouraged by Gerrit Lloyd, he set to work on a script of his own, borrowing *The Bat*'s generic conventions. (His pseudonym this time was "Irene Sinclair," perhaps to be understood as the sister or the cousin or the aunt of the "Roy Sinclair" who had scenario credit on *Dream Street*; the lesson he should have learned was to stay away from the works of the Sinclair family.) The film's working title was "The Haunted Grange," its setting was to be a country house outside Louisville and production was scheduled for the spring.

In short, all was proceeding sensibly, at least for the moment. But Griffith continued restive with his chronic illness of the ego, his continuing sense that small films, unless he could find a way of imparting some true stylistic distinction to them, as he had with *Broken Blossoms*, represented regressions for him.

This impulse, conventional economic wisdom to the contrary notwithstanding, may not have been entirely wrong. There were distinct limits on what small films could make; none, really, on what a successful spectacle could take in. And in the Griffith scheme of things, overhead and promotional charges on any film, large or small, tended to be similarly inflated. Therefore a case could be made that, for Griffith, big gambles were the best gambles, that if he could just make one more success of the magnitude of *Way Down East* he could break out of the debt cycle that was dragging him down.

To do that, however, he would have to change at least some of his ways; he would have to hire proven stars in order to mitigate some of his risks and he would have to exercise caution and discipline in his road showings. Above all, he needed to pause in his ceaseless labors, regroup and rethink present practices and future plans. That consuming energy of his, that constant need to be up and heedlessly doing, which had served him so well in the past, was now a destructive force in his work. If he was going to plunge, he had to learn to think carefully before doing so.

But that, above all, he could not and would not do. Aside from a few ocean voyages to Europe on business, there is no record of any vacations for him. He leaped from one project to the next, and even when he was not working eighteen-hour days, his restlessness drove him through the days and nights without pause. He was, in these years, a considerable man-about-town. He loved opening nights and ringside at Madison Square Garden, he loved the nightclubs and speakeasies where he could dance or laugh at the lunacies of, say, Clayton, Jackson and Durante, or Jimmy Savo. With an ermine-clad Dempster on his arm, he was seen everywhere in New York—the older man doing his best to show the younger woman a good and glamorous time. If he stopped at all it was to drop in at Albert Grey's home in New Rochelle for rambling midnight conversations about the movies—his own and others'. Sometimes he sought out the company of Molly Picon, then a rising young star of the Yiddish theater, and her producer husband, Jacob Kalich, whose work and values Griffith much admired. He loved the cooking at their apartment almost as much as he loved the sentimental comedy at their theater.

It was more typical of him to be dreaming some large dream. And to be trying to do something to realize it. Thus, as he was seeming to agree to a period of retrenchment, and preparing to start *One Exciting Night*, he suddenly found himself in thrall to another grand scheme—perhaps the grandest of all his grand schemes—and he took a month off to pursue it. The idea was for nothing less than a "History of the World," to be brought to the screen in the form of eight or ten thematically linked features, each ten or twelve reels long, each costing, he estimated, between $1.5 and $2 million to produce, each preaching in some degree, a pacifistic message. Its genesis was doubtless H. G. Wells's *The Outline of History*, which had been published with enormous success in 1920, and which was indeed one of the works that helped shape the intellectual spirit of the decade. Its appeal for Griffith was obvious, for in his attempt to compress the entire history of the world into a few hundred lively, prejudiced pages—putting his highly personal stamp on history, as it were—Wells had done what Griffith had done most notably in *Intolerance*, but as well, of course, in his other, less far-reaching spectacles. Then, too, his mind, with its boldness and idealism, was bound to appeal to Griffith, and in April he sailed for Britain to attend the opening of *Orphans* there, and meet with the writer as well as with Beaverbrook and his wealthy friends to seek backing for the project.

The idea was not entirely impractical, however grandiose the conception. Griffith could not help but be aware of the sudden growth of pacifistic sentiment, particularly in the United States since the war had ended. *The Four Horsemen of the Apocalypse* caught this spirit and had been a popular success. And the previous fall, the American Secretary of State, Charles Evans Hughes, had electrified the world when he opened the Washington disarmament conference with a detailed plan for scrapping two million tons of battleships either in commission or under construction, naming the very names of the vessels he proposed to scuttle, including his own government's ships. (At the time, Griffith proposed to the Secretary of the Navy, among others, using the ships to make a naval spectacle, concluding with their sinking.) Perhaps the world was ready at last to accept what it had not accepted in *Intolerance*—a large film, complicated in structure, infused not just with the passion for peace but with Griffith's idealism for his medium, an idealism that was in danger of being lost in the growing preoccupation with his studio's economic survival.

Both points were important to him. All his spectacle films had, to greater or lesser degree, demonstrated a failure to resolve a basic conflict in his attitude toward war. On the one hand, he idealized the heroic virtues; on the other, he could not resist contrasting these with sentimental chromos crudely poeticizing a rather soft and simple-minded vision of peace and brotherhood. Rarely in a significant artist is the contrast between the masculine and the feminine sides of his nature (or, if you will, the pull of his father's legend vs. the softer reality of his upbringing as his sisters' pet) so vividly presented. Rarely is there so little consciousness of this dichotomy's existence. One likes to think Griffith saw in the mood of the moment a chance finally to settle this matter.

In the longest of the several interviews he granted after his return in May, he gave full vent to his idealistic impulses. He conceded that his "History" would "have to contain a romantic theme to hold the attention," and promised as well that it "will be brutal, more brutal than anything I have yet made." But these concessions were for the greater good. He wanted to make a film, he cried, thumping on his desk for emphasis, that showed war caused by a handful of leaders who, seeking personal glory, arouse the masses to "a false fervor in which they do not think for themselves." They are stimulated, he said, "by the picture of men going into war with bands playing and flags flying. The glory of war! Ask some of our boys who were over there about the glory of war! Glory to hell! There is no glory in war." No, he said more quietly, "Every war has meant a great loss, paid by the masses. When the masses can be made to understand this, talk of glory will fall on deaf ears." That was where his vast movie could play a role, since "the motion picture is the esperanto of expression . . . the one language the entire world understands." Perhaps his film "may not prevent all wars of future generations," he modestly conceded, but he did envision this eventuality: "When a war looms, let the government show just a few reels of this film. Then war will not come." If such a showing stopped just one conflict, he thought, it would justify his efforts.[3]

Just why he imagined the government leaders he had just excoriated as the creators of war would pause on the brink of a war to show a pacifistic film to the very people they were whipping up, and thus undermine their own schemes, he did not explain. But one frequently gains the impression from Griffith's more impassioned interviews and public appearances of an actor being carried away by a role he has created for himself. On the other hand, there was a certain commercial sense operating in him also. Two years later the first of the great antiwar plays, *What Price Glory?*, would appear on Broadway, to be followed in due course by Raoul Walsh's popular film version. Thereafter, scarcely a year went by without some play, novel or film attracting wide patronage with a message similar to the one Griffith proposed. One thinks of *The Big Parade*, *All Quiet on the Western Front*, *Journey's End*, and so on into the late thirties, a virtual subgenre catering to the general antiwar sentiment of the time.

Despite his assertion that "financiers of England have offered to back the project with great sums," and despite Wells's agreement to serve as chairman of a board of historians who would outline the project and then serve as consultants on its historical accuracy once it was in production, nothing more came of it, at least in part because Griffith was so heavily pressed by the demands of his studio. He was scarcely back in the country before he had to begin production of *One Exciting Night*. Again, a large loan was obtained, this time for $267,500, from the faithful Central Union Trust, with the negative pledged for security, along with such foreign receipts on *Way Down East* and *Orphans* as were unencumbered and whatever might still dribble in from the studio's other productions.

The leads were assigned to Dempster and to Henry Hull, whom Griffith had known as a child actor in Louisville and who was now playing the lead in *The Bat* on Broadway. (Hull would go on to a long career as a reliable character actor in films, continuing to work into the 1960s.) The story once again involved a foundling (Agnes Harrington, played by Dempster), whose adoptive mother is being blackmailed by one John

Rockmaine (Morgan Wallace) to force Agnes to marry him. She, however, favors John Fairfax (Hull), and joins him on a party at a disused country estate he owns. In his absence, it has been employed as a hideout by a gang of bootleggers, and just before Agnes, Fairfax and friends arrive the gang's leader is murdered, and some loot he has been trying to make off with hidden by his killer. A Scotland Yard inspector living nearby investigates, with his suspicions centering on Fairfax. There is much groping through the darkened house by various interested parties, as the money and the killer are searched for, while the latter, of course, attempts to protect himself. It ends with Rockmaine exposed as the criminal, with Agnes discovering her true identity and, predictably, the inherited wealth that goes with it. Before things are set to rights, Griffith employs many of the conventions of the "haunted house" genre—sudden scary noises (generated by the orchestra), clutching hands, masked characters appearing and disappearing through hidden passageways and panels, that sort of thing. One of the less happy conventions he embraces is that of the Negro servants who are quakingly, eye-rollingly, convinced that ghosts are present. Once again, they are played by white actors, among them Porter Strong, blacked up.

Shooting and editing proved uneventful. Principal photography was completed on schedule, on budget. Gerrit Lloyd would later estimate that, left in its modest original form, it might have made as much as a half-million dollars—enough to finance the next production without resort to the banks. And, indeed, it was cut and previewed and ready for release when Dempster was overheard complaining to Griffith that the picture lacked "a big Griffith finish." By which she actually meant that she had no compelling climactic scene comparable to those Gish had enjoyed in her major films. Griffith took this matter seriously. A day was spent in conference about the addition of a storm sequence. The audience will expect it, Griffith argued, while Lloyd and the others urged restraint. At the end of the day Lloyd remembered being "worn out" from the discussion, but felt "I talked him out of it, and really talked that time." Alas, Griffith spent the evening with Dempster and the next morning when Lloyd came to work, he found crews preparing the ground for the storm scene.[4] Griffith's publicists would later claim that, as he had in *Way Down East*, Griffith had taken advantage of a passing inclemency, sending cameramen out into a hurricane that brawled its way up the Eastern Seaboard on June 11 of that year, and maybe a few shots were picked up in this way, but basically the sequence is composed of crude but expensive trick shots made, according to one interview with the director, "under the glare, literally, of every high-powered, portable light that could be hired between Boston and Philadelphia, with enough airplane propellers to equip a squadron—flaying the flooded hillside and struggling actors." But, of course, for shots where trees appeared to fall on or near an actor, lightweight fakes had to be used. Since there is a corollary to the old moviemaker's dictum "a tree is a tree" which holds that "a cardboard tree is a cardboard tree," the fraud is painfully apparent.

"Does it surprise you to know that the storm scene alone . . . cost about four times as much as *The Birth of a Nation* in its entirety?"[5] Griffith inquired of a reporter, permitting himself, as usual, the impressing exaggeration. But even at twice the cost of the earlier film, the sequence was wildly overpriced. And, indeed, it cost around $250,000 directly. Indirectly, it cost around the same amount, for once it had been added to the film Griffith insisted on road showing, which generated losses in that range. Thus, instead of generating a quick half-million in profits, *One Exciting Night* generated a quick half-million in deficits, the long-term effects of which were disastrous. Lloyd believed these doomed the company, describing them as "the real crusher" in the Griffith firm's business history. "After that he was digging money on any terms wherever he could get it."[6]

The picture itself bore much evidence of Griffith's insecurity about it. Overexplained by an excess of titles, its opening sequences so clearly laid out the characters' motives that there was little possibility for surprise later, and Griffith kept inserting obvious clues about the mystery, so that the simplest viewer could track it (though his characters kept losing its thread). After release, perhaps realizing his mistake, he was more than usually severe with it, chopping some 2,000 feet out of the film, in this process rendering some passages not teasingly mysterious but annoyingly incomprehensible.

In his remarks to the press as the picture went into release Griffith was far more modest—almost apologetic—than he usually was. It was as if he was making a plea for sympathy. To be sure he suggested to one interviewer an analogy with *Macbeth*, but the New York program carried a foreword in which "The Management" disarmingly observed that "Mr. Griffith has departed from the heavy and the spectacular to tell a modern story of mystery . . . to follow the example of the story tellers of old in giving you a story of entertainment." The only pretentious note was an observation that Griffith had made an effort in the latter part of the drama "to follow the old Greek unity with the events and action occurring in one night, and as nearly as possible in the exact time it will take for these events to happen." In a personal note Griffith called the film *"a little romance*—just a little mystery" (his italics) and added, ". . . we shall feel amply rewarded if it serves to make you forget your own little troubles for at least a few minutes."[7]

This is a line he continued to follow in interviews. To a reporter from the *New York Tribune*, for example, he claimed only to like "several things about it," repeating the modest hope that "it will take people out of themselves during the few minutes they are seeing it." He added, somewhat defensively, "Perhaps this picture appears like a hasty work. It is the exact opposite. There is no more difficult thing than to put mystery and suspense on the screen."[8]

On the whole, the press bought Griffith's disarming manner. The *Times*, for example, though dubious about subtitles "that try to make a rampant melodrama into an allegory, or something" liked "the simple mystification and highjinks without an overlaid purpose" and called it a "hilarious thriller." Paul Gallico, before he turned to sportswriting and sentimental fiction, reviewed it for the *Daily News* and found himself remembering "the good old-time hokum serials" and calling the picture "a treat." Like several other reviewers, Robert E. Sherwood, writing in the *Herald*, was of a mood to indulge the director's slumming: "Mr. Griffith often has to devote his attention to pictures like this, because it is an open secret that some of his more ambitious offerings have not been quite as profitable as they might be." But he added the hope that *One Exciting Night* would make enough money to pay for another *Broken Blossoms*. Only Quinn Martin in the *World* was thoroughly devastating. "Tedious and involved and rambling" was his judgment, bearing no mark "that would tend to identify it with the maker of 'Way Down East' or even 'Broken Blossoms.' "[9]

This essentially generous pattern was repeated in reviews around the country, with two points of particular interest arising. One was the praise generally lavished on Porter Strong's "spook" comedy sequences. There is not the slightest evidence that anyone was offended by it. On the contrary, everyone seemed to think him extremely skillful and risible. But if there was a reluctance to abandon a long-standing affection for this deplorable stereotype, there was a concomitant eagerness to see in Carol Dempster's performance the outlines of a new kind of heroine, a modern girl who, if not quite a flapper, was at least able to avoid Victorian swoons in the face of danger. "The picture is a great tribute to the new woman, the woman of our day, from seven to seventy," Sylvia Cushman had written in the *Boston Telegram* when Griffith opened the picture there two weeks before bringing it into New York. "The type that develops the body and mind; while at school takes up athletics, imitating and equalling the man."[10]

Despite its strong candidacy as Griffith's poorest feature, receipts from the film were by no means negligible. But with the storm sequence and heavy road-showing and promotional expenses added, the total cost of the picture was set down on at least one set of studio books at the near-incredible sum of $928,594. For that kind of money, Griffith could easily have made a spectacle.

But even had he stayed close to his original budget, there is evidence that operating as an independent, Griffith could not any longer make

and market program pictures at prices competitive with the work of more
heavily industrialized studios. His old colleague Frank Woods provided
him with all the information he needed on this point—had he been willing to pay attention to it. Trying to attract independent producers to
their distribution network both at home and abroad, United Artists had
set up a subsidiary known as Allied Producers and Distributors, which in
due course agreed to handle, among other films, those produced by a
company calling itself Associated Authors. Its principals included Woods
and two other well-known screenwriter-producers. Attempting to secure
Griffith's support, Woods sent him a well-reasoned and detailed memo
regarding production costs, which gives us a good idea of industry standards at the time. (His letter, incidentally, shows that he knew Griffith's
helter-skelter manner of dealing with paper work, for it begins with the
stark admonishment: "This letter is important. Read it and don't leave
it lying around.") Budgets for the Associated Authors productions, all of
which were to be program features, were to range from $65,000 to $75,000
apiece, which, according to Woods's calculations, meant that they could
undercut the typical Paramount budget on similarly modest films by
$15,000 to $25,000. In other words, he was saying that an efficiently managed studio could turn out pictures on the scale of *One Exciting Night*
for $100,000 or less. Even Paramount's "Specials" or "A" pictures were
costing, according to Woods, around $150,000, or a little more than half
of Griffith's original budget for *One Exciting Night*, a little more than a
quarter of what he ended up spending on his negative.[11] In short, by
developing industry standards, Griffith had been over budget before he
went over budget. For *One Exciting Night* had to bear alone his studio's
entire overhead and exploitational expenses for the year. There were no
other pictures to share these burdens with it, as there were at the burgeoning major studios.

   This point cannot be stressed too strongly. Maybe Griffith's films of
this decade, even the best of them, do not compare well with the works
of men like Eisenstein, Gance, Murnau, Vidor, Lubitsch, all of whom, in
their best films, worked at levels of technical and intellectual sophistication that were to Griffith's new work what *Intolerance* had been to his
competitors. But for the ordinary filmgoer his films were generally more
than acceptable. And when even films as weak as *One Exciting Night*
did reasonably well at the box office, and when his more imposing works
grossed as well as Pickford's and Fairbanks's big films (which by and
large they did), then one must argue that Griffith's problems generally
lay on the cost side of the ledger, not on the receipts side of it. And that
brings us back to our starting point. Given the fact that beyond a certain
level his costs were irreducible, given the fact that none of his films, large
or small, failed by much, given the fact that even without marquee names
his pictures, overall, did roughly as well for United Artists as those of his

partners did, one can only speculate what might have happened if he had added to his pictures the one element his partners—and his competitors—automatically brought to their productions, namely, genuine star presences.

His casting for his next picture, which he turned to without pause once *One Exciting Night* had been launched, was at least interesting: it took for its subject matter and setting material that Griffith genuinely cared for, and it was more coherently thought out, more simply felt and in most respects more confidently and interestingly photographed than its immediate predecessor, or its immediate successor. Apparently the idea for the picture had begun to nag at him while he was working on *One Exciting Night,* for pasted to the back page of a scrapbook containing press cuttings about *Dream Street* there are a number of news clippings dealing with the transgressions—mainly sexual—of clergymen, which is what *The White Rose* is about. "Pastor Father of Child of 17-Year-Old Girl, Jury Decides and He is Jailed," reads one of these preserved headlines. "Suicide of Woman Causes Wife to Sue Minister for Divorce," says another. And the lead of a third item read, "The Rev. Henry Brockman, Lutheran minister, under arrest for white slavery, shot himself dead in Iron River, Mich. . . ." Clearly, Griffith was arming himself for yet another attack on moral hypocrisy. He saw in this subject a chance for a little genteel sensationalism. After all, in the better circles anticlericalism, especially directed toward ministers to the small-town boobocracy, was very much in fashion. One can imagine clippings of the sort Griffith assembled serving as the basis for a scathing essay in Mencken's *Mercury.*

So, once again, "Irene Sinclair" took pen in hand to scratch out the brief outline from which Griffith worked, and Huck Wortman was dispatched to Louisiana to scout locations. Meantime, Griffith was casting a wider-than-usual casting net. Mae Marsh had been on his mind since April of 1921, when he sent this telegram to her:

JUST SAW THE GREATEST PERFORMANCE EVER SEEN ON ANY SCREEN. THEY ARE REISSUING THE BIRTH OF A NATION FOR THE CAPITOL AND FOR THE FIRST TIME IN YEARS I SAW THE WHOLE PICTURE CLEAR THROUGH. THE BEST PERFORMANCE OF WHICH I SPEAK IS THAT OF THE LITTLE SISTER PLAYED BY MISS MAE MARSH. THE SCRUB LADIES ARE WASHING THE TEARS OUT OF THE AISLES YET. THIS GOES FOR EVERYBODY WHO SAW IT. COULD NOT HELP TELLING YOU ABOUT IT. ROSE AND JIMMIE [SMITH—HIS CUTTERS], MR. BANZHAF, MR. SUTCH [HERBERT, AN ASSISTANT OF MANY YEARS' STANDING] AND MISS WEINER [AGNES, HIS DEVOTED SECRETARY] WANT TO GET IN ON THIS. NEVER REALIZED BEFORE HOW GOOD IT IS—MEANING YOUR PERFORMANCE. . . .[12]

The wire was doubtless gratefully received, for after she left Griffith first for Goldwyn, then for free-lancing, Marsh's career had declined. Only rarely had anyone found the spunk, humor, and vulnerability that Griffith had brought out in her, and a few months after his telegram she invested in a show she hoped to bring to Broadway and wired him, charmingly, asking him to attend a dress rehearsal, saying: "EVERYTIME I MAKE A MOVE OR CHANGE THE EXPRESSION OF THE PAN IF THERE IS ANY LEFT TO CHANGE I ALWAYS SAY I WONDER IF MR. G. WOULD THINK IT OK. . . ."[13] There is no record of whether or not he accepted her invitation, but it is clear that the idea he now began developing must have been written with her in mind.

For the leading role opposite her he chose a man as little known to him as Marsh was well known. Griffith had been introduced to Ivor Novello by a drama critic with whom he was lunching in the Savoy Grill, when Griffith was in England on his history project. Novello was a young Welsh playwright and songwriter, a sort of minor Noel Coward, sharing that gifted man's sentimentality but not his wit. He had already written the song for which he will doubtless be forever remembered, "Keep the Home Fires Burning," but not yet the string of light romantic musicals that would make him a considerable figure in the West End between the wars. He had the kind of chiseled good looks that appealed to Griffith, who seems to have seen in him another Barthelmess. In fact, he was a homosexual, and thus had even less romantic rapport with his leading ladies than Barthelmess. Still, at the time he had made a couple of minor films and fancied his possibilities as a movie star, and so after their first meeting secured an interview with Griffith, who might have been impressed by the fact that the actor, whose real name was Davies, was Welsh. Anyway, the director promised to keep him in mind, and he kept the promise. Novello, for his part, broke a contract with a British film producer to take the job that Griffith offered him late in 1922.

The location to which he reported in February of 1923 was New Iberia, in the Bayou Teche region of Louisiana, where a splendid manor house had been secured to serve as the home of Joseph Beauregard, the character Novello was to play. Later on, the company would move to the New River, near Fort Lauderdale, Florida, and to rented studio space in Miami for interiors. The result was a strikingly beautiful film (Bitzer, Sartov and a new man, Hal Sintzenich, all worked on the photography) mistily backlit in many sequences, full of moss-hung and exotic foliage.

It must be said that Novello's stiffness and reserve before the cameras were well suited to his role of Joseph, a divinity student and scion of an aristocratic family who decides to see a bit of the world between graduation and taking up his first parish. Though titles describe him as a man "given the power to lead us upward" out of "unrest, hatred, greed," Novello seems more possessed by withdrawn gloom than by moral fervor.

On his modest travels he meets Mae Marsh's character, yet another of Griffith's orphan children, named Bessie Williams, but known as Teazie, for her cheerful, childlike ways. She looks back somewhat to the comically restless Clarine Seymour role in *The Girl Who Stayed Home*, although Teazie is only pretending to be a flapper. She has been told that she must imitate this style if she is going to attract a man, and, because she is an innocent, that imitation can be based only on what she had read and heard. Joseph, alas, is not worldly enough to tell the difference between pose and reality. Still, they fall in love. And they sin. But he is so guilty about this lapse from ministerial decorum that he departs hurriedly, not knowing that she had become pregnant. Even so, his sexual transgression weighs heavily upon him and he takes to preaching guilt-ridden sermons while pursuing his chaste love affair with Marie Carrington, a woman of his own class, played by Carol Dempster.

In later years Dempster would allow that she was always "opposed to the fluttery Griffith heroines,"[14] and she appears grateful here to sink into what amounts to a secondary role and one in which little is required of her dramatically (though Griffith continued to favor her in the two-shots and to give her more than her share of the close-ups). She, in her turn, is loved by John White, a grocery store clerk and a dreamer of large dreams. He is played by Neil Hamilton, a young actor who had been doing bits and posing for advertising illustrations until he answered a Griffith casting call. He would, in the next two years, become the studio's leading man, with highly ambiguous results. Here his character owes much to those that Bobby Harron played in *True Heart Susie* and *A Romance of Happy Valley*. He is a writer (*Life from a Grocery Store Window* is the title of the book he scribbles away at) and must go out into the world in order to achieve the success that will render him worthy in his own eyes, and, in this case, those of the woman he loves.

In the meantime, Griffith has carefully contrasted the false piety of the preacher with the truly Christian spirit of the black people who take Teazie and her baby in when everyone else rejects them. Once again the leading players are whites in burnt cork, but many of the extras and small-parts players are blacks, and a story in the film's press book summarizes Griffith's attitudes toward them—and, perhaps the nation's—chillingly: "It took lots of patience the first day, but in the ensuing days the colored people were on hand early and eager to work. 'Dat man sure can handle us folks, and he treats us right,' said one lanky Negro who registered quite comically in the film. Being a southerner and having been reared among numbers of Negroes, Mr. Griffith knows the little tricks of cajolery and patient thoughtfulness necessary to keep the Negro in good humor and responsive to calls upon his intelligence."[15]

Still, these characters are peripheral to Griffith's main concern, which is Teazie's search for acceptance and reconciliation with her lover. In due course, baby in arms, she appears in Beauregard's neighborhood, now haunting his life as previously her memory had haunted his conscience. There is a great melodramatic moment when, standing on a dock, she is powerfully tempted to hurl herself and her baby into the water, ending her travail, and it is a tribute to the delicacy of Marsh's playing that she makes this scene, indeed the entire concluding passage of the film, as persuasive and touching as it is.

This is particularly true given Griffith's characteristic failure in the film's early reels to establish her character effectively. Once again, he imposed on an actress that weird jumpiness that was his way of establishing girlish innocence. From this ludicrousness, Marsh had a long way to come back. And she had precious little help from anyone. Technically, Griffith's direction was regressive. His staging of the actors, whether in repose or in motion, was often awkward, his camera often too distanced and objective, as if he were more interested in the handsome lighting and background than his people, and his cutting was more than usually uninteresting. Finally, Novello cannot come up to any of the large emotions required of him as he renounces Dempster and accepts his responsibilities for Teazie and their child, though the director almost literally turns away from him, especially when he is working with Dempster—concentrating his camera on her reactions rather than his anguish. Perhaps Novello simply could not realize the heavy emotional demands of the scene, or maybe Griffith could not bear to take them away from his lover, but for whatever reason they are never as powerful as they should have been.

Still, the production of *The White Rose* represented for Griffith a happy time. Only one peculiar incident marred work, namely an appearance by Griffith in New Orleans for the local premiere of *One Exciting Night*. After the picture was shown, Griffith launched into an impassioned defense of *The Birth of a Nation*, claiming he was proud of the controversy it had stirred, and, according to an undated and unidentified clipping found among his papers, citing it as a force counteracting the "unfair and prejudiced" histories of the Civil War and Reconstruction imposed on all the nation's school children by "Northern brains and capital" as well as laws passed in Washington that "hurt the south." It was an uncharacteristically immodest curtain speech by Griffith, perhaps stirred by the warmth of the welcome he had received in Louisiana, and by his own pleasure in being back on what looked to him like native ground after so long an absence.

But the occasion was wrong. "As he continued a strange change took place," the newspaper report continued. "The applause diminished perceptibly. Men looked at one another with some surprise. It had been a long time since talk of this kind had been heard in New Orleans. The Spanish-American war and the world war have done so much to eradicate any sectional differences that have existed that it seemed rather strange to drag out dead and bygone hatreds at this time, men whispered to each other." The anonymous reporter might have exaggerated on that point, and he did concede that Griffith continued to receive some evidence of approval as he meandered to his conclusion, making, among other dubious claims, one that the Volstead Act (prohibition) was a delayed result of the Civil War. In the end he cried, "If this be treason, if this be treason, then it is. So help me God!"[16]

It may be that Griffith had been drinking on his private train on the way in from his location, for it was assuredly during this year that he began to abandon his former abstemious ways. Now, two or three times a day, according to his associates, he was calling his little brown pot of "tea" to be delivered to the set with everyone understanding there was something more potent than tea therein.[17] Or it may be that he was simply overtired and overexcited, a hardworking man given a night's surcease from his labors and as a result abandoning his usual thoughtful calculation when he appeared in public. But that was the only untoward incident on this production.

For the most part Griffith appears to have been in a particularly easygoing frame of mind, warmed perhaps by a sense of coming home to native, southern ground. In Louisiana he was the house guest of Weeks Hall, the gracious owner of The Shadow, the plantation house, built in 1830, that was Griffith's principal location. A few months later he would write "the longest personal letter I have ever written since I went to work" to Hall, with whom, in the long southern evenings, he had obviously been more than usually open and intimate. "I have no more pleasant recollections in all my life than the time I spent with you," he said. "I have never known more thoughtful hospitality than that which I enjoyed at your hands."[18]

When the company moved on to Florida, they found themselves being received by vacationing notables including President and Mrs. Harding, who were cruising the inland waterways in a houseboat, and James M. Cox, the man whom Harding had defeated for the presidency in 1920, as well as that elder of Democracy, William Jennings Bryan. On a less grand note, Griffith acquired a raccoon as a pet and even brought it back to the studio with him. For a time he kept a supply of peanuts in his pocket and laughed loud and long at the creature's comical efforts to cadge them. Epping was along on the trip and wrote back to Banzhaf: "Mr. Griffith looks like a million dollars: I have never seen him look so well in years."

Epping himself was in a chipper mood. He felt that whatever damage *One Exciting Night* had done, the previous year's strategy of consolidation and conservatism had paid off. Accounts payable, many of them representing the heavy (and losing) expenditures on road-show presentations, had been reduced by around $150,000 since the first of the year, and $100,000 had been paid on the Central Union Trust loan, reducing total indebtedness to that institution to the neighborhood of $550,000. But he felt something like three-quarters of that figure could be retired by the fall, using only receipts now coming through from other productions, which meant that when The White Rose "begins to earn revenue it will represent practically an entirely free and clear asset of the Corporation of a very substantial cash value." This was, as he pointed out, a first for the corporation, and, after "the severe uphill battle" represented "substantial progress, which in the future, will become accumulative."[19]

To be sure, there were some small clouds in the Florida skies. Linda Griffith was claiming that her 15 percent of her husband's earnings should be calculated on his gross, not on his net after taxes, and was threatening court action, while a corporate stockholder who had the good fortune to be an elderly widow was talking fraud and threatening to sue because she had not received the regular dividends to which she was entitled. But it was possible to silence both matters with the outlay of a little cash. In short, if Epping and Banzhaf could keep Griffith to the relatively frugal ways he had followed on The White Rose for a bit longer, there was every reason to believe that Epping's optimism was plausible. Neither of them could, of course, see into their employer's restless mind or anticipate the quite unreasonable, ultimately devastating, events of the months to come.

3

The first problem was Griffith's dissatisfaction with The White Rose once he returned to Mamaroneck and started going over his footage. His response to it may be gauged from his passing remark to Weeks Hall after the film was in release: "I do not think that the picture we made did amount to very much." Later, in interviews, he referred to it as a pot-boiler, and even his publicity for the New York premiere, once again at advanced prices for reserved seats, seemed intended to disarm criticism rather than to encourage enthusiasm. The program contains a note insisting that "One or two human beings could be far more interesting than a thousand remote persons carrying unfamiliar spears,"[20] and arguing that if the trend on the stage was to take intimate drama more seriously than spectacle (Anna Christie and Lightnin' were invoked to bolster this point), a similar trend would soon be discernible in film.

As it turned out, this rationale was unnecessary. The critics were more than kind to The White Rose. The Times found the story "rather worn and thin and much drawn-out," but praised Marsh and "photography that smites the eye constantly." On opening night, indeed, "there was applause for the beauty of the scenes."[21] In the *Herald*, Robert E. Sherwood simply wrote, "We fell for it with a dull, sickening thud. If there were any dry eyes at the Lyric Theater we were in no mood to observe them, for we were having troubles of our own."[22] At the *World*, Quinn Martin, so dubious about *One Exciting Night*, said Griffith "has aimed straight at the heart and he has hit his mark."[23]

All in all, then, a modest success could be expected, especially when the troubles Griffith and his associates had expected from state and local censorship boards did not generally materialize. It is true that one or two localities objected to illegitimacy as a subject—conveniently ignoring its centrality to the beloved *Way Down East*—and a handful of clergymen protested the portrayal of one of their own as "A Fallen Man," as some of Griffith's ads referred to Novello's character. But care had been taken to obtain endorsements from several ministers as well as from social workers and reformers, so no harm was done at the box office. Indeed, the picture returned to the studio, as its share of rentals, almost twice its production costs, and a gross roughly comparable to that of *One Exciting Night*. But as always, the receipts were slow in arriving and there were once again large losses from exhibitions under Griffith's own auspices. Naturally, the overhead kept running. What might have been a modest success for a larger studio, or for someone operating on a different scale than Griffith, turned out to be, at best, a break-even venture.

Seen purely in terms of Griffith's work *The White Rose* is quite creditable, a tender working out of some of his preoccupying themes, in a film that is cinematographically more than usually handsome. It does, however, have an air about it that leads one to group it with earlier works; it comes as something of a surprise, upon seeing it, to realize that it was made and released as late as 1923. And when one notes that it preceded by only a couple of months Chaplin's first United Artists release, *A Woman of Paris*, a rather rude awakening occurs. For this film, which Chaplin wrote and directed for his longtime leading lady, Edna Purviance (and in which he appears only in an uncredited bit), takes up a similar theme, the loss of a young woman's innocence, but with an astonishing difference. For in retelling the story of a country maid whose village lover, a painter, is prevented by his family from joining her on their planned elopement to Paris, and of her subsequent acceptance of the role of a rich man's mistress, there is scarcely a sentimental or moralistic note. Rather, Chaplin's instrument is the most delicate and worldly irony, put with a sly wit that is literally unprecedented on the American screen. The picture was not, by any means, an immediate popular success; it grossed in about the same range as *The White Rose*. But it was an enormously influential film. Among sophisticated viewers and filmmakers it established a vogue for the dry, wry comedy of sexual manners. Ernst Lubitsch, the master of the form, always credited Chaplin's film for showing him his path, and his first picture in this vein, *The Marriage Circle*, followed in 1924, to be followed, in turn, by dozens of other imitations over the next few years. From this point onward Griffith's approach to material of this kind would appear out of date—and as the years went on, not merely to the sophisticated, either.

For the moment, however, he was occupied with another kind of comedy. In late May and early June of 1923, Griffith was under the distinct impression that he was about to go into production with a picture tentatively entitled "Black and White." The story, concerning a young mystery writer who dons a blackface disguise in order to gather evidence that will prevent a man falsely accused of murder from being executed, was the product of Anthony Paul Kelly, the playwright who had worked on the scenario of *Way Down East*. He had discussed the idea with Griffith at least a year earlier and had been encouraged by the director's response. From the start, it was conceived as a vehicle for Al Jolson, the cantor's son who had risen out of vaudeville and the nightclubs to Broadway stardom as a blackface singer and comedian, and Kelly acted as an intermediary between him and Griffith. This, of course, was precisely the sort of enterprise Griffith would have been well advised to avoid, but he had an obvious (if, to the modern observer, misguided) affection for blackface and Jolson was the acknowledged master of that curious art. Then too, brother Albert, the self-appointed business realist in the Griffith organization, was more than usually active in advancing the project. Besides, Griffith intended only to supervise the picture, once again turning direction of an outside star to a minor craftsman, in this case one Jack Noble, who had worked in a variety of genres and styles. This might well have been a factor in the unhappy events that were to follow, for Jolson was obviously insecure about his film debut.

For a time, all went well. Jolson approved the final draft of the story and, since he had never made a film, and was concerned about his appearance on camera, both with and without his famous makeup, contracts were held up until a screen test could be made. It was run off at the Lyric one afternoon in early June, and Jolson and his entourage appeared satisfied with it. Within a couple of days a verbal understanding was reached between Griffith and his associates and Jolson and his, among whom was Nathan Burkan, Chaplin's lawyer and representative on the United Artists board. The latter agreed to draw up papers calling for a $15,000 salary and a 25 percent share of the profits for Jolson. Production was scheduled to begin June 22, when Jolson's current show, *Bombo*, ended its run and the star had taken a week's rest. During that time set construction began. Jolson reported for rehearsals, his contract still unsigned—though the Griffith corporation had executed the document—and worked with apparent contentment for a week, during which time Griffith shot some costume tests, which on Thursday he ran for the star. No complaint was raised by Jolson, who said he would report for more rehearsals the next day.

But he did not. In fact, he was not heard from until Sunday, June 24, when Griffith received a radiogram from the S.S. *Majestic*, steaming toward England, which read, in its entirety: "ORDERED BY MY PHYSICIANS TO TAKE OCEAN VOYAGE IMMEDIATELY OWING TO MY NERVOUS CONDITION REGRET THIS MORE THAN WORDS CAN TELL WILL SEE YOU ON MY RETURN JOLSON."[24]

On July 3, Griffith, Grey and Banzhaf arranged a meeting in Burkan's office, where Burkan said that he regarded Jolson's contract as binding, even though it had not been signed, and that he believed the performer liable for damages. Griffith claimed the corporation was out of pocket $75,000–$80,000 for sets, salaries and sundries, but allowed that he would settle for half that amount. Burkan said he could make no commitments until he had talked to his client, and there the matter was left for the moment.[25]

Except in the busy mind of Albert Grey, who now proposed to go ahead with the picture, using another star. If after all it could somehow be finished, a dead loss might be recouped and there was always the possibility of profit. An agreement was made with Grey by which the studio agreed to subordinate its debt to whatever he borrowed (up to a limit of $65,000) to complete the work. Out of that sum he agreed to pay the studio $1,000 a week for rental of space on the lot. Lloyd Hamilton, then starring in a series of two-reel comedies, but with little feature experience, was engaged for the Jolson role; a new partnership was formed between Albert and an outside backer, with Albert personally responsible for a production loan obtained from the Manufacturers Trust Company.[26] The resulting picture, only five reels long, was released by W. W. Hodkinson under the title *His Darker Self* but did not reach the theaters until the following March. It received few reviews and little publicity and Hodkinson was able to obtain only scattered and minor play dates for it.

No money was ever returned to the Griffith corporation, and Grey was eventually forced to mortgage property in New York and New Rochelle, with Griffith himself pledging his California property, in order to prevent the bank from obtaining a summary judgment against his brother. In 1927, Griffith was forced to dip into his own pocket to pay the last $15,000 due on Albert's note.

But this misadventure does not end with Grey's humiliation. Burkan backed off his earlier opinion that Jolson was liable for the costs incurred as a result of his broken verbal agreement and the Griffith corporation sued the star for costs and damages in the amount of $751,000. The case did not go to trial until September 1926, by which time the company was a debt-ridden shell. Griffith was an appealing, informal witness.

When Burkan asked him why he had not had his own people draw up the contract instead of leaving the task to Burkan, Griffith drawled, "I thought you had more brains than some of my associates, Mr. Burkan." One exchange was particularly telling. Burkan: "Now, Mr. Griffith, do you mean to tell this court that you went ahead producing a picture without a contract?" Griffith: "Well, I had the word of men of honor. In the country I came from, that's enough. I have made verbal agreements with some of the biggest stars in the country and none of them have ever gone back on their word."[27]

Still, Burkan and Jolson were effective in their own cause. Burkan's argument was that Jolson was not a contract jumper in the usual sense, leaving one employer to go to another for a better deal. No, "He did not go into pictures for anybody else; he had stayed out of pictures all this time because the man realized from what he had seen—a test made by the greatest director in the world . . . that he did not have the screen personality that is so essential to success. . . ."[28] Jolson testified that he had thought himself "terrible" and "rotten" in his tests, but could not argue Griffith and his associates into abandoning the project. It seems likely that what terrified Jolson was not so much his appearance but the fact that the silent screen denied him the use of the most potent weapon in his performer's arsenal, his singular singing voice, and that his hopes that pantomime and physical comedy would compensate for its absence were dashed by the tests, which were probably quite static, designed as they were mainly to demonstrate costume and makeup alternatives. After all, Jolson would not hesitate over films when the time came to achieve his niche in history as the star of the first talking (actually singing) picture, just four years later. Indeed, Griffith's attorneys tried to get the case reopened later when they discovered that Jolson had made a Vitaphone short, in which he sang, between the time he walked out on Griffith and the time the case was brought to trial, a fact that Jolson conveniently omitted from his testimony. Nothing came of this, however, the court perhaps understanding that silent and sound films are virtually different mediums, and that Jolson's willingness to appear in the latter had little bearing on his unwillingness to appear in the former. Thus the jury's original verdict, in favor of Griffith, but awarding his corporation only a token $2,671, was allowed to stand. Coming so soon after Griffith's other, more serious financial troubles, it did nothing to enhance his reputation for practical acumen.

4

That dismal final outcome was three years in the future in the summer of 1923. But surely Griffith's troubles with the Jolson picture confirmed for him the wisdom of avoiding star performers. Surely it reinforced, as well, his impatience with modest projects that had no rationale other than their box office potential. He could argue, with some justification, that the Jolson venture was more troublesome and time-consuming than a spectacle, and for him obviously nowhere nearly as satisfying. And now another big picture was taunting his imagination.

Its genesis is obscure, though sometime in the early summer Will H. Hays, one-time congressman from Indiana, later Harding's attorney-general, now head of the Motion Picture Producers and Distributors of America, whose major task was to clean up the industry's image in the wake of the Hollywood scandals, got in touch with Griffith about doing an uplifting and educational feature about the American Revolution. He was acting at the suggestion of the Daughters of the American Revolution, precisely the sort of group whose favor he was interested in currying. Of course, the subject had interested Griffith since his playwriting days and the moment of its presentation to him was propitious psychologically, since he was looking for a subject that offered him some scope. It must have occurred to him as well that he could count on substantial assistance in marketing the film not only from the DAR but from other patriotic groups as well.

His first impulse was to use the story of Nathan Hale, the school-teacher-spy, as the basis for his film. He inquired into the copyright status of Clyde Fitch's old play on the subject, and at the same time he exercised the option he held on Novello's services, asking him to play Hale (a costly move since in the picture he finally developed there was no part for Novello, who eventually sued to collect the fee to which Griffith had obligated himself). In July, it began to seem to Griffith that the Hale story did not offer him enough scope to support the kind of epic drama he felt increasingly compelled to make. As a consequence, he acquired, for $12,500 (and 5 percent of the profits) a revolutionary war novel called *The Reckoning*. In the bargain he acquired the cheerful services of its author, Robert W. Chambers, a dauntingly prolific popular novelist who had, since the turn of the century, churned out one commercially successful historical romance after another, most of which took their themes from the American past.

The screen story he and Griffith concocted is a very curious one. Chambers's novel was mainly about the comparatively minor theater of war in New York State, where, historically, Captain Walter Butler, an Indian agent for the king, stirred members of the Iroquois nation to a series of vicious raids on settlers loyal to the revolutionary cause. But this was the stuff of an action picture, not of epic cinema, and again Griffith was determined to expand his basic story so that it could encompass material that was part of every school child's iconography of the Revolution—Patrick Henry's speech, Paul Revere's ride, the Minutemen of

Lexington and Concord, the Battle of Bunker Hill, George Washington at Valley Forge.

To link this material with Chambers's fiction, a remarkably far-darting and highly coincidental romance had to be invented. It involved Nathan Holden (Neil Hamilton) as a dispatch rider for the Boston Committee on Public Safety—an occupation that gave him an excuse for galloping hither and yon, as Griffith (more than history) dictated—and Nancy Montague (Dempster), the daughter of a rich, sternly Tory family. They meet in Virginia, when Holden comes there carrying messages from the northern patriots; meet again when he returns on a second mission to the South. Thereafter, Griffith manages to get the entire Montague family to Lexington in time to witness the end of Revere's ride and the legendary battle on the green. (Holden's arm is jogged while the fight is on, and a bullet from his gun wounds Nancy's father, complicating the plot not quite as much as the fact that her brother, played by Charles Mack, sneaks off to fight for the rebels and is killed at Bunker Hill.)

Later, the Montagues are maneuvered into Chambers's basic tale via a visit to a relative in the Mohawk Valley. By this time Nathan is with Washington at Valley Forge, and the general, by a lucky happenstance, sends him north with Morgan's Raiders to help put down the Indian up-risings. Nancy's father, not apprehending Butler's vileness (as played by Lionel Barrymore, he is one of Griffith's more persuasive heavies), has betrothed her to him. A warning by Holden makes no impression on Montague. It is only when he discovers that Butler is the moving force behind the massacres that Montague learns his true nature.

But too late. By this time Butler had taken over the Montague farm as a headquarters, where one night a scene taken almost directly out of War, Griffith's old play, is enacted. For Nathan, on an espionage mission, overhears Butler's plan for another raid. He also sees his beloved Nancy brought to him so that he may have his terrible way with her. Once again, the hero is forced to choose between duty and love. Shall he race away with the intelligence that will warn of the impending attack or shall he stay to defend the honor of the woman he loves? He chooses duty, but in this instance Joseph Brant, the Indian chief, intervenes, informing Butler as he is carrying Dempster upstairs to her dread fate that his Indians can-not be held back, that their attack must begin this very night. Thereafter father and daughter Montague escape, and Morgan's Raiders, riding to the rescue in typical Griffith style, encounter Butler and his force, killing the former and routing the latter. Holden is accepted as the heroic and splendid fellow that he is by father and daughter Montague.

In the original release print, it required fourteen reels to tell this tale—meaning it was as long as Intolerance and longer than any other Griffith picture—though the running time was cut considerably after the opening. It also required a vast expenditure of money, for Griffith not only planned battle scenes as extensive as any he had previously done, but he also wished to shoot as much footage as possible on the historical sites of the events he was recounting. As well, there were painstaking reconstructions of the English Parliament in debate about the colonies, the Virginia House of Burgesses in pre-revolutionary session and so on. By the time Griffith began taking scenes in August, it must have been clear to everyone in the organization, if not to him, that Epping's hopes of solvency, just a few months earlier, were doomed. Indeed, by September, Epping himself was advancing $47,500 to cover production costs, and some of the other older loyalists had agreed to deferred salaries—to a total of $32,385—adding their names to the distinguished roster that included Elmer Clifton, who had been owed $27,300 since *Way Down East,* and Mae Marsh, who had deferred almost $10,000 of her *White Rose* salary.

By October, Griffith's associates were back at the Central Union Trust, requesting a new loan that would bring their company's total indebtedness to the bank back up to $500,000. This time, the bank was not as pliable as it had previously been. To be sure, the corporation had adhered closely to its repayment schedules through the years, but it is also true that it seemed never to be able to clamber entirely out of debt. What had begun as a series of discreet loans had turned into what amounted to a line of credit. But that was something the bank had never intended to establish and its questions were getting harder and more detailed, Banzhaf's answers at once more wheedling and more inflated in his predictions of good things soon to come. In the end, the money was obtained, but it is also clear, from subsequent events, that this source was dry from this point on.

Still, the work proceeded. And, as usual, Griffith was all serenity on the set. Through the late summer and early fall he led his cast and crew up and down the Eastern Seaboard, reconstructing the events attendant on the authentic birth of a nation. The first scenes shot were of Paul Revere's ride, for which an Irish hunter, Laugh-A-Ballagh, was hired, a horse so spirited (according to the publicity) it threw nine riders before one Harry O'Neill got the part of Revere by staying on him. At any rate, it required two weeks of shooting on the back roads and in the countryside around Mamaroneck before Revere's ride—often singled out in the reviews as the movie's high point—was completed. Thereafter, the company moved to the area around Somers, New York, for various battle scenes, including Bunker Hill, for which an entire infantry regiment was borrowed from the U.S. Army, outfitted with period uniforms and drilled in the formations and tactics of the time. As usual, Griffith, who had four credited cameramen on the film, worked quickly. The records indicate that he finished with the troops in less than a week and had all the rest of the battle footage completed in another week. There was one rather poignant moment when Griffith, complimenting a soldier on his performance, asked him where he had learned to die so persuasively. "In the Argonne" came the regular's quiet reply.[29]

The company moved on to Lexington for the completion of Revere's ride and for some principal scenes to be used in conjunction with the Lexington and Concord battle sequences made later at the studio. Among other moments filmed there was the departure of John Hancock and Sam Adams for Burlington to escape arrest. It was pointed out to Griffith that historically the former's wife had told him not to forget to bring along a salmon for their supper, so Griffith, always a stickler for that kind of historical detail, ordered up a large and smelly fish for John Dunton, playing Hancock, to carry in his lap. Another historical society onlooker reminded the director that however late the hour, children would have been awakened by the arrival of Revere with his alarm, and so children's costumes were sent on from the studio. Meantime, Gerrit Lloyd was placed in charge of the leaves. Historically these events had occurred in spring, but now it was fall, and fallen leaves had to be raked up and kept out of shot. It was not a task Lloyd considered in keeping with his dignity. And when the wind rose, his neat stacks would blow past the camera, while Griffith cried, "Leaves, leaves" and Lloyd scurried to retrieve them.

While he was in Boston, Griffith also took shots at the Old North Church, which required careful rewiring for his lights, of the signal lanterns—"one if by land, two if by sea"—that warned Revere of the Redcoats' plans before he set forth on his ride. Thereafter he and the company moved on to Virginia for scenes at the Westover and the King Carter estates, and to Yorktown, where the battlefield was employed as a location. After that it was on to Fort Myers, where elements of the Third Cavalry were dressed in buckskin in order to play Morgan's Raiders. They were commanded, in the film, by Jonathan M. Wainwright, then a major, later to be in command at Corregidor when it was surrendered to the Japanese in World War II. The rest of the picture was completed at Mamaroneck, with the exception of the Valley Forge sequence. For this Griffith waited until the snow had fallen there while he was in post-production.

His leading man, Neil Hamilton, would later recall the pleasures of working with Griffith on the film. For example, Charles Mack came to him one day and said, "It gets my goat, always having to do things his way. Let's do something our way for a change." Whereupon he and Hamilton worked out some piece of business and performed it in rehearsal. Griffith's comment was a question: "Mr. Hamilton, are you having a fit?" It was one of the several occasions when Griffith told him, "Remember, you don't have to do anything—movies are the science of photographing thought," one of the most often-quoted of his dictums.

The only time Hamilton remembered Griffith raising his voice was when he overheard Mack and Hamilton discussing someone who, at age 45, they regarded as old. Griffith was himself 47 at the time.[30]

And for the first time, perhaps, feeling it. In his letter to Weeks Hall, he made a quite uncharacteristic confession: "I feel tonight, after a terrifically hard day, that I would be much happier at anything else than directing pictures. I feel myself caught in a net of circumstances. I feel myself always bayed by those hounds of circumstances, driving me on to be up and doing, though in my saner moments I know it is absolutely unimportant whether I am up and doing, or whether I am sitting still and doing nothing."[31]

Still, weariness was not allowed to show. For private circulation Chambers, the scenarist, drafted a little satirical playlet, which bore the film's working title (and eventual subtitle), *The Sacrifice*. It is a giddy, almost surreal bit of comedy, which portrays in splendidly heightened terms the serene inefficiency of Griffith's working methods. In it we find Griffith ordering John L. E. Pell (who had credit on the film for "Historical Arrangement," meaning he found the correct locations for the scenes and authenticated historical details) to "find out for me how many buttons Sam Adams wore on his underwear." Calling for his Hepplewhite blackjack (with which to belabor Chambers) and ordering an assistant to tear up all of Chambers's manuscript "except the preface, and send that to Harold Bell Wright to revise." In the script overeager assistants are to be found gold-plating the Woolworth Building just in case Griffith decides he needs it. ("Don't let them run the elevators—that isn't historically accurate," says Griffith.) They also propose that a whale attack Washington as he crosses the Delaware, and doing a five-camera setup on an insert shot of a historic clamshell Griffith likes. At one point he cries, "If we can get rid of that cheap novelist we may make some progress. Why, I haven't shot half a million feet yet, and there are ten reels we haven't touched." At another moment he calls for a blindfold and shears, crying, "I'm going to shut both eyes and cut 50,000 feet out of the first part," at which the assembled staff cry out in delight, "That will put a kick into it! That will put the Griffith touch into it!"—both, obviously much discussed and much desired qualities on this lot.[32]

This little piece is, perhaps, the only truly funny evocation of life at Mamaroneck, and one that somehow seems to capture, better than anything, the spirit of the place—Griffith's amiable egotism, the whimsicality of his working methods, the utter loyalty of his staff, and, of course, the unchanging lunacy of motion picture production. It also says something about the unique relationship Chambers enjoyed with Griffith. Ten years older than the director, entirely secure in himself, he had a warm affection for Griffith, unhesitatingly expressed. "In my life I have known two or three people who it is *always* [italics his] a pleasure to see. Mr. Griffith is one of them."[33] His feelings were reciprocated: Griffith genuinely missed him when the picture was finished. One cannot help speculating how the director's career might have been changed, or at least eased, if he had enjoyed the friendship, and the advice, of someone like Chambers—a literate, sensible, worldly man who had also tried to use popular forms for serious purposes. And one who was unafraid to speak his piece yet had to be treated as an equal.

The Christmas season passed with Griffith toiling fifteen and sixteen hours a day, cutting and titling *America* (while Chambers occupied himself novelizing his scenario, so different from his original novel that he had no qualms about self-plagiarism, only about quality—"If this be literature make the most of it!" he wrote to Griffith). Rushing toward his preview date of February 21, 1924, the director had no time even to buy Christmas presents as the negative cost of the picture rose and rose— to $623,357.49 as of the first of the year.

More money was obviously needed and this time the bank got "cold feet." The quotation is from a letter by Pat Powers, the legendary buccaneer of the motion picture's early days, not, perhaps, the sort of man Griffith might have chosen to do business with. At this point, however, he had no choice in the matter and as Powers was later to tell it, he "stepped in behind the bank and advanced the money which enabled Mr. Griffith to finish the picture." This amounted to $259,000, secured by second liens not only on *America* but on many of the studio's previous films as well. It was, for Powers, a fairly risky venture, though as he laconically put it later, "Everybody got his money."[34]

At the same time, Griffith and Hearst were back in touch again. This time they got to the point of drafting contracts for Griffith to direct a screen version of J. M. Barrie's turn-of-the-century romantic comedy *Quality Street*. The publisher's Cosmopolitan Pictures eventually offered him $150,000 to direct plus 10 percent of the profits up to $500,000, 25 percent thereafter. It was a sum that would have tided the studio over until *America* began to return profits. Once again, for reasons unrecorded this time, the deal fell through, though in a short while something very similar would have to be worked out elsewhere in order to keep afloat. For as *America* neared completion it was becoming vividly clear to everyone in the Griffith organization that unless it proved to be a mighty hit, some alternative to the business methods they had been using would finally have to be embraced. The strain on Griffith, on everyone, was just too wearying.

Even Griffith began to acknowledge this fact publicly. In one or two pre-release interviews he let slip the suggestion that if *America* was not a success his company would be in jeopardy. These hints of doom were mostly drowned out by the thunderous publicity to which *America* opened.

The reviews in New York were, however, mixed. There was strong support from the Hearst press, with the *American*'s Rose Pelswick actually bursting into rhyme for her review,

> I got up and cheered as those
> armies appeared, and was
> swept right along in their swing,
> Or was vibrantly stilled at the
> action that thrilled, with a
> thrill that few pictures can bring. . . .[35]

Thus she began, and gushed on for many more such lines. Even a few critics under no editorial guidance about where their patriotic duty lay joined in. " 'See *America* First' is the best slogan in motion pictures today," wrote Don Allen in the *World*.[36] But many of the reviews were far more reserved. Sherwood in the *Herald* gave a very fair summary of what amounted to the prevailing view among his colleagues. He praised the spectacle and feeling of the film's first half, but then he wrote, ". . . the general trend of Mr. Griffith's spectacle is down-hill. The later reels are incoherent and wearisome and the finish extremely flat."[37] There was a variety of explanations for this, but basically the criticism was a compound of two disappointments. There had been an unrealistic expectation, based on advance publicity, that Griffith was undertaking a panorama of the entire revolutionary saga, an expectation which the first half of the film had actually quickened, with its many, and well-realized, historical reproductions. There were far fewer of these in the picture's second half, as it more closely concentrated on the melodramatic doings of his fictional principals, and that disappointed, especially since they were involved in a part of the war isolated from its main currents. Even Louella O. Parsons, not yet the powerful gossipist she was to become, raised this point. Though elsewhere in her piece she did her best to follow the Hearst line, she could not help admitting that "when our emotional spree is ended and we sit down with the calm light of reason to analyze this latest Griffith picture, we suddenly remember our history. We recall some of the dramatic incidents . . . that led to the freedom of the colonies, and we are surprised to find some of our school day impressions of American history missing." She noted, ironically considering the film's origins, the absence of Nathan Hale as well as Lafayette, Ben Franklin, and John Paul Jones, among other figures, from our national hagiography.[38]

These complaints, whether voiced at Sherwood's level or at Parsons's, were justified. Once Griffith removed his main characters from the context of great events, where in the early reels they had attained a certain dignity as, as it were, foreground observers, they diminished into stock figures moving in over-familiar melodramatic situations. There was also, here and there among the critics, a certain reserve about Griffith's handling of his big scenes—the chases and battles, of which, until now, he had been regarded a master. That, too, seems justified, for as the *New York Post*'s anonymous reviewer said, they were "not nearly so effective as those of 'The Birth of a Nation' "—now ten years past.[39] The critics did not tax him with this point, but the fact was that other directors were bringing more sophisticated techniques to bear on the problems of staging spectacle.

The year before Douglas Fairbanks's *Robin Hood* (directed by Griffith's former assistant, Allan Dwan) had set a new standard for splendor and wit in this realm, while the work of another Griffith-trained director, Elmer Clifton, had given *Down to the Sea in Ships* power, coherence and, in its seafaring sequences, authentic thrills, which *America* did not contain. And however preposterous its religiosity, DeMille's *The Ten Commandments*, released just before *America*, had a crude force and popular appeal that Griffith's picture could not match with the general audience. And this says nothing about the style of *Rosita*, the historical romance Ernst Lubitsch staged for Pickford in his first American film. Then, in the period between *America*'s premiere and its general release, James Cruze's majestic *The Covered Wagon* (photographed by Griffith's sometime camera assistant Karl Brown) quite outdistanced Griffith's film in the realm of domestic historical spectacle, after which Fairbanks returned with *The Thief of Bagdad* offering wonderful charm (and special effects) in a picture of great scope. It, too, was directed by a former Griffith aide, Raoul Walsh. In short, members of a new generation, who had learned from him, were now beginning to surpass Griffith. Compared with their work, there is something perfunctory, cramped, and distinctly unfelt about *America* (although it must be admitted that the best surviving print of it is the English version, re-edited to answer objections that it was anti-British, which got it temporarily banned in the United Kingdom in 1924). It bears little evidence of emotional involvement by the director and offers nothing in the area of craft and technique that he had not previously surpassed.

In the weeks and months that followed its release, Griffith supported his road showings of the film—they once again proved unprofitable—with endorsements from prominent citizens, and the press weighed in with articles and editorials that had the not entirely exhilarating effect of making the picture sound as if it were good for one, like medicine. For example, the *Daily News* in New York editorialized: "Some of the 'intelligentsia'—of which clan, by the way, the Chicago youths Leopold and Loeb are members in good standing [the reference is to the homosexual child murderers, one of the great newspaper sensations of the day]—will give no thanks for the picture. To them, any evidence of patriotism, of single loyalty to one's country, is merely evidence of mental weakness."

The paper also grumbled that "Pink Pacifists won't like the picture because it depicts battles and men and women being killed." But "denatured" Americans of this sort were, to the paper's mind, a minority. The vast majority, it felt, could not see it "without a thrill of pride." And it hoped every boy and girl "old enough to have studied our history ever so little" would be given the opportunity to see us vivified on the screen.[40] In June, as the Democrats arrived in New York for their nominating convention, a writer for the *New York Commercial*, a business journal, proposed that the delegates might profitably attend *America* as an inspiration for their labors, since it was so powerful a weapon against the "Radicalism . . . gnawing at the very foundation of American institutions."[41]

There was more of this sort of thing as the picture opened across the country. But the editorial huffing and puffing served the purposes of Will H. Hays, looking for middle-class respectability for the movies, far more than it did Griffith. Over the years, perhaps, *America* made back its cost, but with virtually all the initial cash flow it generated diverted to the lenders, its immediate effect on Griffith's fortunes was negative, not positive. In April he was forced to borrow again from Epping in order to meet bills for the film's promotional expenses. By June, United Artists was reporting advances for the general release of *America* as less than $250,000—as disappointing as the road show grosses had been. And now, with the corporation falling behind in its scheduled repayments of its loan, the Central Union Trust was growing threateningly restless.

5
—

So it was clear, very early on, that *America* was not going to be the hit Griffith required. That meant that if his company was to survive at all, it could do so only in greatly reduced circumstances. The studio would surely have to go, and plans for large-scale productions would have to be held in abeyance. All Griffith could hope to do now was a series of small pictures. But now coincidence came into play. The five-year contracts all its founders had made with United Artists in 1919, the contracts that guaranteed the company exclusive distribution rights to their productions, were about to expire. And Griffith was just one film away from fulfilling the minimum number of films (nine) all had agreed to supply. His partners—everyone connected with United Artists—were anxious to keep him producing at his accustomed pace. His pictures had made little for Griffith, but for UA they had generated almost as much rental income as Fairbanks's had, a million dollars more than Pickford's had, and ten times what Chaplin's single release had, and were vital to its cash flow.

But when it was proposed that all four of them extend their contracts for another three years, under essentially the same terms and conditions, Griffith balked. His interests were not theirs.

Early in 1924 he was entertaining several prospects, most of them vague. The most concrete, the one that could be trusted, was from Adolph Zukor, who, sensing the weakness of United Artists, approached all its founders at this time. At this point his Famous Players–Lasky company was unquestionably the most powerful in the industry and he was in a position to offer the "Big Four," as the trade press constantly referred to them, an honorable way out of their difficulties. It is true that in 1923 their company had shown its first modest profit, but it was not enough to offset the losses on its previous year's business, and prospects for this year did not look bright. He could give them everything they needed: steady, comfortable financing, outside the implacable clutches of the banks, lavish road showings of their "specials" (they had all eventually followed Griffith's lead on this practice, though, sensibly, they did not use the technique as extensively as he did), and first-class general distribution, broader in its coverage, and at better prices, than Abrams could arrange for them. Everything, that is, but full creative independence. And on this point they were all more than a little sentimental. Chaplin, in particular, saw no reason to abandon it; he had little trouble financing his relatively modest and infrequent productions out of his own pocket. Fairbanks and Pickford, reports indicated, were tempted, at least briefly; their films were costly, their production schedules tightly filled. They might justifiably consider it a relief to set aside the wearying problems of finance and rely on their star power to ensure creative control of their films under the Zukor banner. Not knowing how deep Griffith's difficulties were, or the pleasant regard in which he and Zukor held each other, industry gossips said, ironically, that he was the least likely of the Artists to succumb to Zukor's overtures. And he kept his own counsel.

But there was no quelling the talk of disunity among the Artists and after the company's annual meeting on March 28, 1924, it was thought wise to put out a press release, signed by all the principals, indicating they intended to renew their production contracts with the firm for three more years. Griffith had no intention of actually doing so, but he was not yet able to decide on an alternative, so he allowed his name to be used on this undertaking, which he understood not to be legally binding, in order to keep peace among his associates.

That done, he left on April 15 for a trip to Italy to investigate the most curious of the propositions that had been placed before him, a tentative offer by a consortium of Italian bankers to make pictures in their country. With Mussolini in power, and the restoration of that nation's former grandeur on everyone's mind, the revival of its motion picture industry seemed a logical step. Before the war it had been the most

ambitious of the European industries, with a particular taste and apti-
tude for historical spectacle. (It will be recalled that the international
success of these films had quickened Griffith's desire to do something
similar and led him first to *Judith of Bethulia*, then to *The Birth of a
Nation*.) There was, then, a superficial logic to linking his name and skills
with that of this possibly reviving industry. The titles he bruited about
before sailing included *Faust, L'Aiglon, The Last Days of Pompeii*, and
Antony and Cleopatra.

He was out of the United States just over three weeks, which means
he was in Italy for about a week. But he was treated as a great dignitary,
escorted everywhere by Fascist honor guards, and he returned to the
United States burbling with enthusiasm for what he had seen. "Mussolini is a great man," he declared to reporters who met him when the
Homeric docked in New York on May 8, "with the allegiance of youth
behind him. He could do great things. Who knows but that he may be a
Napoleon who'll sweep the world." He found Italy prosperous, full of
"hustle" and "mad about Mussolini." He added, "I believe that anything
may happen as a result of this fascism. I should like to put into a film the
remarkable spirit of the fascisti."[42] In his defense, it should be noted that
Griffith was neither the first nor the last foreign observer to return from
Italy with glowing reports of a new spirit in these early days of fascism.

In any event, he was preoccupied less with politics than with practical concerns, and about those he was less than optimistic. He found
film facilities in Italy inadequate to his purposes, especially in the electrical end of things. There was, to be sure, the promise of a new studio
that would have everything he needed, but it was not yet ready. And even
if it was rushed to completion he was concerned, he said, about the problem of directing casts and crews that would, perforce, be multilingual,
which he was not. He was concerned about achieving his effects when
they had to be filtered through a translator. Finally, though the meetings
with the Italian bankers had been, he claimed, promising, he had to await
a visit from a delegation of them to the United States for final negotiations. Nothing more was heard of them or their proposition, and it is
likely Griffith left Italy with but few hopes for his future there.

If Griffith's predictions about Mussolini's future were wildly inac-
curate, his thoughts on the future of the movies, delivered in the pages
of *Collier's*, which appeared while he was still abroad, were at once
strangely prescient and remarkably shortsighted. As usual, he talked of
the movies becoming a powerful force for peace, but, more interestingly,
he predicted that the directors, actors and technicians of the future
would be trained in their arts and crafts by the colleges. He also foresaw
improved color technology and its widespread employment, as well as the
wide screen with projected images both larger and of better quality than
were presently available. He foresaw, as well, the five-dollar admission

charge to first-run theaters, the showing of films on planes, trains and ships, and some means of showing films and even librarying them in the home, though he did not call the former television or imagine the VTR and the cassette as the instruments of satisfying the latter prophecy. The one thing he did not see was the thing that arrived first, the thing he had, indeed, experimented with in *Dream Street*, namely, talking pictures.

"I am quite positive that when a century has passed, all thought of our so-called speaking pictures will have been abandoned," he wrote (and the style of the piece indicates that it received only the lightest attention by a publicist-ghost). "It will never be possible to synchronize the voice with the pictures." This was wishful thinking on his part, an expression not just of his belief in the poetic potential of the screen, but of his reverence for the stage, which he seemed always to wish would retain its pre-eminence as the medium for the spoken word. He was sensitive to the charge, especially prevalent in conservative intellectual and middlebrow circles, that movies were doomed to be a second-class medium, inherently inferior to the stage. By proposing that they develop along their own path, he seemed to imagine (correctly as it turned out) that film might eventually establish its own conventions and be judged on its own terms, without reference to the theater. At any rate, he argued for *Collier's* that even if it proved technologically possible to achieve sound pictures it was pointless, "because the very nature of the films forgoes not only the necessity for but the propriety of the spoken voice. Music—fine music—will always be the voice of the silent drama. . . . We do not want now and we never shall want the human voice with our films."[43] He was writing, of course, less than four years before the debut of *The Jazz Singer*. Which does not necessarily invalidate his point, or should one say his idealism?

We can be sure that having taken care of the future of the movies, Griffith devoted a good deal of time aboard ship to contemplating his own future. The conclusions he reached were startling, for within a month after returning home, operating with more-than-usual stealth, he completely reversed the course of his career. On the face of things nothing appeared to change. He quickly arranged to purchase a short story he could film on a modest scale over the summer, completion of which would fulfill the last of his obligation to United Artists. The only thing slightly out of the ordinary about this project, initially called (with unconscious appropriateness) "Wrong Receipt," later to be known as "Dawn," and finally released under the story's original title, *Isn't Life Wonderful*, was that it would require extensive filming abroad. That, however, might have commended it to Griffith, who had good reason to want to leave town at this season. For on June 10 he entered into a secret agreement with Adolph Zukor's Famous Players–Lasky corporation to direct pictures for it. It was the third time in his career that Griffith had sneaked into a long-term commitment, and when the news broke it would confound not only the industry but his United Artists partners as well. Their surprise and outrage would be a measure of just how successfully he had concealed his troubles from outsiders. The radical nature of this new course was testimony to the sudden increase in pressures on him in the spring of 1924.

In June it became clear to Griffith that with receipts from *America* falling below expectations, his corporation would not be able to meet scheduled payments on its Central Union Trust and Pat Powers loan. Under the terms of that agreement (which were formally enforced on June 24), the bank could require Griffith to turn over to it, immediately upon receipt, all monies deriving from *America* and the five other pictures on which it held a lien. Moreover, the Griffith corporation could make no outlays to anyone, for anything, without prior approval by the bank. Even his United Artists stock, under this agreement, had to be surrendered to Powers as surety that his secondary loan would be repaid after the bank was satisfied. This was bankruptcy in all but name. Over the summer Griffith sold the studio sailboat as well as $2,000 worth of the mineral company bonds he had acquired so long ago—and received dunning letters from a mechanic who had done some repairs on his car. But the deepest significance of the bank's action was this: no funds whatever were available to begin production on the film he owed United Artists.

Thus the irresistible attraction of Zukor's offer. Famous Players agreed to guarantee a $250,000 loan Griffith was able to secure from a new bank, the Empire Trust, thus enabling him to go ahead with his ninth UA film—the one that would discharge his contractual obligation to that firm. Equally important, two-thirds of the large salary Griffith would be drawing from Famous Players would be diverted to his company, which, skeletonized, with virtually no operating expenses, could use these funds to reduce its debts. In the end, he committed to Zukor for four films, the director's compensation to be determined by the size of each film's budget: "small" pictures would bring him a fee of $100,000, commencing on the first camera day; "big" pictures would bring him $200,000. He was entitled to 20 percent of the profits on each picture, but if he went over budget without getting prior written agreement, he would be penalized 20 percent of the overage. Since it was contemplated that he would make two "big" and two "small" films, the potential takings on this deal were $600,000 plus percentages. With two-thirds of that total due to go to the Griffith corporation, it can be seen that, with sale of its real estate and the collection of money due it on the pictures still in United Artists release, there was potential here for a return to corporate solvency.

There was also, alas, a potential for bad feelings. Griffith's corporation would need a steady flow of money in order to keep up with its debt schedule, and that would mean, as things worked out, that Griffith had to continue going from picture to picture without pause, taking whatever script Famous Players handed him. There were also potentials for squabbling and bitterness elsewhere in the agreement.

But those problems were in the future. For the moment, the main issue, and it was a lively one in the mind of his advisors, was preventing United Artists from discovering Griffith's impending defection. If it did so, the company might hold up the Griffith corporation's share of receipts on the eight films that it was handling. If that happened, the creditors could throw the company into receivership. Griffith's people perhaps exaggerated the danger, but they were also feeling guilty: Griffith had signed that statement of intent to renew his contract, which certainly gave the Artists a moral, if not an enforceable legal claim on his loyalty. It was only a matter of time, they knew, before the truth willed out. But they would play for every day of it they could get.[44]

In these ambiguous, difficult and shaming circumstances, it is all the more remarkable that Griffith was able to undertake a film that would turn out to be arguably the finest film of this period, unarguably a film that would justify his struggle to maintain his independence, since it was the first Griffith picture since *Broken Blossoms* that it was impossible to imagine a studio financing sight unseen. For *Isn't Life Wonderful* is a stark, highly realistic monochrome about ordinary, middle-class people coping with the effects of the postwar inflation and depression in Germany, small in scope, sober in intent, entirely lacking in glamorous appeal.

How Griffith came across the original story, which was contained in a collection by Major Geoffrey Moss, entitled *Defeat*, is unknown. Moss, an upper-class Englishman who had served four years in the trenches during the war, had written a slightly racy novel about decadent high life in Vienna—it was called *Sweet Pepper*—and then gone to Germany to oversee construction of a yacht he had ordered. There he had time to observe the effects of the victorious nations' punishing economic policies on people he regarded as innocent victims of the conquerors' vengeful spirit. As he later said, it offended his essential Britishness, that is, his sense of fair play. And so he wrote his book of thematically linked, somewhat sentimental tales, as a form of protest and a cry for justice.

Their appeal for Griffith is readily understandable. He obviously analogized between the treatment of Germany after this war and the treatment of the South after the Civil War. He knew something about the oppressions of the victorious, or so he thought, and he certainly knew something about the bitterness of a poverty for which the individual feels blameless and which he can do nothing, through his own efforts, to lift. Here, in short, was something with which he had a powerful and basic

emotional connection. Beyond that, the story itself cried out for a reversion to the simplicity and directness of his old Biograph manner. Any inflation, esthetic or economic, would have been inappropriate.

The story he told was, indeed, as simple as any contained in the Biographs. A family, consisting of a father who is a professor, a grandmother,
an aunt, a son named Paul (Neil Hamilton), recovering from the effects
of being gassed in the war, another named Theodor (Frank Puglia), who
works as a nightclub waiter, and Inga (Dempster), an orphan who has
been raised by the family and loves Paul, ekes out a subsistence livelihood
in Berlin. Their only hope is a small plot of land Paul acquires, on which
he intends to raise potatoes and build a shack in which he and Inga can
live after they are married. There is a family celebration when he brings
home the first samples of his crop. But when he and Inga harvest and
start to bring home a wheelbarrowful of the potatoes, they are mistaken
for hoarders and profiteers by a crowd of idlers, two of whom set out to
steal the food from them. After a chase, Paul is beaten and their wheelbarrow stolen. When Inga discovers that he has not been killed in the
attack, she insists that since they still have each other, life must be wonderful after all.

It required a certain indomitability to bring this material to the
screen. But for once Griffith was operating with discipline and frugality.
The picture has seven major characters, all of whom are well and believably played, but Griffith worked it out so that he had only to take
three of them (Dempster, Hamilton and Puglia) with him to Germany,
employing the others in the family scenes that he would shoot later on
the Mamaroneck stages. He took just one cameraman with him and, as
a wedding present, paid the passage for Hamilton's new bride. This little
unit shot street scenes in the oldest, most picturesque quarters of Berlin,
as well as in the suburb of Kopenick, with other excursions to nearby for-
ests and plains for the chase and farming sequences.

This material has a poignant realism about it that had not been
present in Griffith's work in this decade. The harshness of the conditions
he observed firsthand while making the picture obviously moved him.
Each morning, for instance, the lobby and stairs of his hotel were
crowded with actors importuning him for work, and, as he had in his
earlier days, he found himself observing ordinary people, studying their
faces, absorbing the tone of their talk—and employing them as atmosphere. Very simply, he had traveled thousands of miles to find himself
in touch, not with the exotic, but the familiar—the long-buried roots of
his experience as a child and as a young man, the methods and materials
that had given him his first success as an artist. In *Isn't Life Wonderful*
he somehow made it back to his best, his truest self.

There is the simple, affecting joy in the family when a hen starts lay-
ing, or the gift of a sausage arrives to cheer them. There is a lovely Grif-

fith touch when Dempster stuffs paper in her mouth to puff out her cheeks, to prove she is not losing weight by surrendering her rations to her sickly lover. The picture's most memorable scene finds her in a butcher shop queue watching the sign advertising prices being changed at intervals while she waits to get in. Each new rise increases her anxiety, and she counts and recounts her money, hoping an inflation that heightens almost by the minute will not place the items she wants beyond her range before she gains the shop door. The situation, the imagery, take us back to *A Corner in Wheat*. Even that Griffith staple, the chase, profits from a reduction in scale and an increase in feeling. There are no troops of horsemen here—just a frightened couple trying to escape a mob and, in particular, two peculiarly determined pursuers, with the ironic strength of the episode deriving first from the contrast between the natural beauty of its setting and the deadliness of the action, second from the fact that pursued and pursuers are equally victims of a fate they do not deserve and might better be leagued against, as their common interests—class interests, if you will—dictate.

Even the material Griffith shot later, when he was back home—sequences of the family at home—matches the tonality of his Berlin footage. The humor (mostly supplied by Lupino Lane, playing an acrobat who has attached himself to the family) is unobtrusive and very occasional, the interaction of the family members tender and muted. And the work of Dempster and Hamilton is exemplary. Her plainness suits this role, and playing a character not unlike herself—plucky, awkward and sensible—Griffith for once had the wit not to try to turn her into an imitation Gish or Marsh—she is believable and touching. Hamilton, too, is persuasive in a role that suited his natural unassuming decency better than his previous efforts as a rube romantic or a dashing revolutionary hero. He would go on, almost immediately, to a rapid succession of leading roles in the waning days of silent pictures, then to character leads, secondary leads, occasional villainies in sound pictures, before he was brought low by alcoholism. From this he fought back bravely working on the stage, in B pictures and latterly as a character man in all sorts of film and television ventures, finally attaining a certain fame as the constantly befuddled police commissioner on the *Batman* television series. A gracious, intelligent man, he was asked, late in his life, what he thought had gone wrong with Griffith in the twenties, and he rose from his chair, paused dramatically and said, "We failed him—his men; we weren't strong enough."[45] In that he was partially correct. But properly cast, as he was here, he did not fail Griffith or himself.

Part of one's regard for this picture derives not from what it included, but from what Griffith managed to leave out. It is a relief, for example, to see a Griffith heroine assaulted not for her virtue but for a hoard of potatoes. It is a relief to see Griffith's humanism stated not in large visual flourishes, but through looks and gestures and attitudes. And it is splendid to see him substituting thought and discipline and a firm sense of goals and priorities for his reliance on the stroke of expensive genius, to see him, as it were, addressing us in an earnest whisper rather than a shout.

It is especially admirable that he was able to do so at this time. For he was unable to put his anxieties behind him when he left the country, and the cable traffic between him in Berlin and Banzhaf in New York was outraged. Rumors of Griffith's desertion of United Artists began to circulate almost as soon as he left town. To counter them, United Artists executives pointed to the March 28 statement of its principals' intention to renew their production contracts for three more years. Privately, to Banzhaf, they suggested that the statement could possibly be construed as binding; anyway, the company was going to behave as if it were. When Griffith heard this, his usual control deserted him and he cabled Banzhaf: "IF BY ANY CHANCE ARTIST'S LETTER IS BINDING IT IS A MOST STUPID AND FATAL MISTAKE STOP AT THE TIME AND AFTERWARDS YOU ASSURED ME LETTER MERELY FOR PRESS PURPOSES AND NOT AN AGREEMENT. WHAT ARE YOU GOING TO DO. CABLE GRIFFITH."[46]

To this Banzhaf replied:

YOU AND I KNOW PUBLICITY STATEMENT WAS NOT INTENDED AS CONTRACT ALTHOUGH ARTISTS CONTEND OTHERWISE STOP I MAINTAIN IT IS NOT HOWEVER LEGALITY CAN BE DETERMINED AFTER DELIVERY OF PRESENT PRODUCTION WE MUST NOT ROCK BOAT AT THIS TIME BECAUSE ALL PAYMENTS FROM UNITED WOULD CEASE IF THEY BELIEVED RIGHT SUCH BELIEF AT THIS TIME WOULD BE FATAL TIME ALONE WILL ANSWER QUESTION OF STUPIDITY. BANZHAF.[47]

Thereafter, their trans-Atlantic conversation softened to a business-like murmur, and they resolved to make no further statements in public, or to United Artists representatives until Griffith's return, when he could talk to Hiram Abrams about it. United Artists by that time had agreed to make advance payments against bookings of Griffith's current films up to $250,000.

When he finished in Berlin, Griffith returned by way of London, where he showed censors a recut version of America, called Love and Sacrifice, in hopes of getting the ban against it lifted—an effort in which he initially failed. Back home he plunged into completion of principal photography and postproduction on Isn't Life Wonderful, while United Artists spokesmen insisted that rumors of any producer-partners leaving the company were totally false, designed to run up the stock of an unnamed rival, and, indeed, Famous Players–Lasky's stock had risen marvelously on the strength of these reports.[48] Griffith, in his turn, asserted to a trade journal reporter that his signature on the March agreement "means nothing," since he signed as an individual, not as an officer of his corporation, and that he indeed had an agreement with Zukor that he intended to honor as soon as he had completed his present film.[49]

He thereupon retreated to Mamaroneck and left Banzhaf to try to resolve the situation. His mood, as he worked on the film, was confident. "I think I had very good luck . . . in Germany," he wrote to Charles G. Dawes, the Illinois banker, then campaigning for the vice presidency on Coolidge's ticket. The letter, which is an apology for (typically) mislaying a letter of introduction to Hjalmar Schacht, the financial "wizard" who later served Hitler well, takes an obvious pride in the fact that "I lived among the ordinary people of Germany and met thousands of them." It also shows an acute understanding of political conditions there, which Griffith observed to be prerevolutionary but subject to amelioration, if the onerous burdens of the peace treaty could be lifted, thus undercutting "the hard work that has been done by our Russian friends." He added, ominously, and correctly, "Germany must be restored or else Europe is lost."[50] Nothing Griffith ever said shows him to be so intelligently in touch with practical politics, and that reinforces one's sense that somehow this project pulled him out of that state of withdrawal and mild megalomania that had grown in the Mamaroneck years, though his failure to make contact with the German filmmakers who were establishing new standards for the art demonstrates his resentment and envy of the innovators who were challenging his position. The fact that he was unable to sell his film in Germany—it was too depressing according to distributors there—perhaps says something about the quality of his portrayal of the society he found on his travels.

Alas, he needed a Schacht, not a Banzhaf, to extricate him from his difficulties with United Artists. Throughout this period the other Artists and their advisors were attempting to lure Joseph M. Schenck into their combine. A Russian-Jewish immigrant, he had risen with his brother Nicholas from drugstore ownership to control of the Palisades Amusement Park in New Jersey, moving from there into motion pictures. They became aides to Marcus Loew, the pioneer theater owner, whose company would eventually control M-G-M and of which, from 1927 to 1951, Nick would be chairman. Joe had left in 1917 to produce Fatty Arbuckle comedies and then would produce the films of his wife, Norma Talmadge, her sister Constance (Griffith's "Mountain Girl" in *Intolerance*), and their brother-in-law Buster Keaton, who was married to the youngest Talmadge, Natalie. Schenck was an honest and well-liked motion picture figure in those days; besides being in a position to supply a large number of films to the Artists' exchanges, he also had access to bank financing. And if the Artists were to offer him the chairmanship of the company, he was more than eager to buy in, providing the financial and producing acumen Abrams, essentially a salesman, lacked. He would, in fact, turn the company around within a couple of years and it may be assumed that, had he taken an offer to join the company which had been made to him in 1920, Griffith's career might have been very different.

Even now, Schenck tried to be helpful. Before the official announcement of his connection with United Artists there was discussion of his stepping in to secure loans that would relieve Griffith of his most pressing obligations and place him "in such a position that he would not have to worry about finances. . . ."[51] Later, with Griffith still tied up on *Isn't Life Wonderful*, the other Artists convened in Los Angeles to make their final arrangements with Schenck, at which time they put forward, to Banzhaf, a good news–bad news proposition. They told him they would, if necessary, go to court to enforce their rights to Griffith's services under the March 28 agreement, which the rest of them were now about to formalize fully in order to assure Schenck that Norma Talmadge and other stars and producers he hoped to lure into the fold would remain in the best of company. On the other hand, their terms were not onerous— one picture a year from Griffith would satisfy them. And at their November 12 meeting, Schenck assured Banzhaf that he would personally finance Griffith's first picture for UA distribution. Better still, he planned to set up a new corporation, the sole function of which would be to finance, as needed, pictures produced for the company's distribution in the future; he further guaranteed that he would personally retain controlling interest in this new entity so that no outsider could gain control of United Artists through this concern.

Banzhaf liked this plan. He was confident that he could win a legal test of the vexing springtime folly in which he had encouraged Griffith. But he did not want to do so if there were a gentlemanly and profitable way out. It was at just this delicate moment that Albert Grey blundered in, with a wire to Banzhaf saying that if United Artists wanted to retain Griffith, it would have to loan his corporation $650,000, wiping out its entire indebtedness. Banzhaf was outraged. United Artists had advanced more money on distribution contracts than it had taken in, and could at any moment cease weekly distribution to the Griffith Corporation of current receipts until the advances were covered. If that happened, the banks, receiving nothing, could foreclose. "AFTER LAWSUITS, BANKRUPTCY AND RECEIVERSHIPS NOTHING WOULD REMAIN EXCEPT DISGRACE,"[52] he desperately wired.

It was madness. Griffith should never have permitted his brother to intervene. He must have known that Albert had been trying for five years to isolate him, not only from United Artists, but from all sensible business advice in order that he, Albert, could take command of his fortunes. At this point, he was doing nothing less than blocking an admittedly belated, but nonetheless promising, rescue attempt, one that might have preserved Griffith's independence after all. Perhaps the younger man had an unconscious desire to wreck his brother's career. Or maybe the captaincy of a derelict ship struck him as better than no captaincy at all. Or perhaps he was simply an idiot.

Even so, both Schenck and Banzhaf tried to get through to Griffith. The former proposed ignoring Grey's wire "without prejudice" and requested Griffith wire him directly regarding his needs. Banzhaf supported him with a statement that if Schenck were given time and direct access to Griffith even a loan of the magnitude Albert mentioned might well be arranged. But Griffith, preoccupied with his new film, and having little relish for conflicts among his associates, even less for implicit criticism of his brother, cut off all further discussion. "THIS SITUATION VERY COMPLEX AND IMPOSSIBLE TO MAKE ANY DECISIONS BY WIRE," he informed Banzhaf. And that was that.[53]

A couple of weeks later, Griffith turned *Isn't Life Wonderful* over to United Artists, and it went directly into general release on December 1, with the ads carrying an unpromising subtitle, "A Romance of Love and Potatoes." Even so, Griffith's reviews were as fine as any he had received in recent years. "Through countless deft and effective touches in this simple yet deeply stirring narrative, Mr. Griffith again proves himself a brilliant director," wrote Mordaunt Hall in the *Times*.[54] "Impressive in its stark simplicity," said the *Morning Telegraph*. "If you have a soul alive to the suffering of a man and a maid, 'Isn't Life Wonderful' will thrill you."[55] "The most convincing 'bit of life' it's been our good fortune to see," chimed in the *World*.[56]

Some of the out-of-town papers were less enthusiastic, mistaking realism for the merely old-fashioned, but the trade reviews were, in their way, the most interesting. There was a general recognition that the picture was distinctly unglamorous, not to say downright gloomy. But they urged exhibitors to make special efforts with the film. At least two of them ran editorials. The *Exhibitor's Trade Review*, for example, wondered, "Can the American people be made to appreciate a picture created as a work of art, with the ordinary petty box-office angle subordinated?" It hoped so, and urged exhibitors to get behind the film or stop complaining about "factory grade" stuff.[57] *Motion Picture News* also did a lead editorial, in which it compared the picture to Robert Flaherty's great pioneering documentary, *Nanook of the North*, released two years earlier. "To put it simply, Mr. Griffith put his camera on his shoulder and went forth to photograph a story right where the story happened. . . . And the result is impressive realism. . . . Every good writer writes his stories just this way. There is no other way—to make them ring true." It is amusing, in a way; by going back to his beginnings, not so very many years ago, Griffith was getting credit for daring and innovation, with his work being used to criticize studio-made "artificiality." How quickly the movie world had turned. *Motion Picture News* not only begged theater men to "take pains—extra pains" with films of this sort, but urged pro-

ducers to embrace the semi-documentary as an alternative to the insipidity of the average program picture.[58] It was advice that would be
taken with admirable artistic effect, and little box office success in the
late years of the silent era, in works like Von Sternberg's *Salvation Hunters* and Karl Brown's *Stark Love*. Once again, Griffith had initiated. Only
this time there were no tangible rewards for his pioneering.

Isn't Life Wonderful did not harm his cause, but it did not help it
either. He had no choice but to effect a compromise between his moral
obligation to United Artists, and his legal obligation to Famous Players.
That end, and the end of his independence, came quickly. On January 2,
1925, papers for the sale of the basic Mamaroneck property of twenty-
eight acres were signed. A real estate developer who wished to subdivide
the land had been found, and he agreed to pay $485,000 for it over the
next four years. Another thirty acres, those acquired to bring industrial
strength electrical power into the studio, remained unsold for some years,
and all the outbuildings were torn down, with only the Flagler mansion
left as a reminder of great wealth and great dreams of it. Eight days after
that deal was done, Griffith executed a memorandum of agreement with
United Artists. Under its terms he was required to make one more picture for its immediate distribution and place his UA stock in escrow, with
Cap O'Brien exercising his voting rights. Once his deal with Zukor was
completed, he could regain the stock by distributing through the company he had helped found. Ten days thereafter the ever-obliging Zukor
agreed to let United Artists distribute the first of the films he was financing for Griffith, who was now, at last, free of his freedom. And free, perhaps, to speculate on what it had been worth.[59]

On the economic level his failure was bitter. Far from achieving the
enterpreneurial independence and wealth that he had dreamed of, Griffith was in far worse condition than when he had started, with two-thirds
of the salary he was about to start earning going to discharge his company's debts, much of the deferred salary that company still owed him
seemingly uncollectible. In later years he and his supporters would allow
it to be understood that these losses were the price an artist had paid to
pursue his visions. But that is no more than a saving lie. Only three of
the films Griffith made for release through United Artists were truly
singular works, and all of them were producible through conventional
means. What studio would have denied him *Way Down East*, so suited
to his gifts and such a time-tested, consumer-tested work? As for *Broken
Blossoms* and *Isn't Life Wonderful*, "difficult" as they seem, we have
seen that the leader of the commercial film world, Adolph Zukor, was instrumental in financing both of them. The other spectacles, too, so like
so many other popular films of the time and so much in the vein for which
he had gained his bankable fame, would surely have found corporate
favor. And the others? Some of them he would have done well to be

dissuaded from making. Some might have been none the worse, and less damaging to him, had they been produced under the tight fiscal control of a studio. Indeed, when Griffith himself looked back on these years he did not mourn the things he had left unsaid, some great or passionately felt work that he had been denied the opportunity to make. No, he seemed to mourn only the fact that while other picture people were making fortunes he was losing one, though it never seemed to occur to him that it was his own inability to sacrifice some of his seignorial status and manner—at least in the short term—that prevented him from realizing his dream of wealth. Indeed, even operating as he did at Mamaroneck, he needed only a little more discipline and shrewdness—and perhaps a little luck—to have it all. Thoughts of F. Scott Fitzgerald, and of the life he recorded in another mansion, on the other side of Long Island Sound, occur. For now, not-quite-consciously (but not-quite-unconsciously, either), Griffith began turning his life into a legend, the sort of heroic (and tragic) artist's saga he had talked so earnestly about with the reporter in Boston two years earlier. This required of him now a will to fail as powerful as his will to succeed had been. But he was entering into a situation that would give full range to that impulse. If he could not fulfill the bright side of the American Dream he would, instead, act out its equally well-known dark side. One must never forget that he was first and foremost an actor forever in search of a great role for himself.

CHAPTER SIXTEEN

"Saintly Showman"

"THE time has come when, for the good of motion pictures, you should take an accounting of yourself." With that blunt, if belated, advice James R. Quirk of *Photoplay*, then the most influential motion picture journal for the general audience, began "An Open Letter to D. W. Griffith," which was the lead article in the December 1924 issue of his magazine. It was an odd little piece, but it set the tone for much of the criticism that would attend Griffith for the few years of creative life that remained to him.

Quirk was of the opinion that "your very habits of life have made you austere. You literally have withdrawn from contact with things about you. You have created a wall between yourself and the outside world. You have made yourself an anchorite at Mamaroneck." The result, he said, was "puritanical repression," which, in turn, caused Griffith's pictures to "shape themselves towards a certain brutality because of this austerity." Speaking either paradoxically or out of both sides of his mouth, Quirk told Griffith, "Your refusal to face the world is making you more and more a sentimentalist." And, besides, it was making him "deficient in humor."

His advice? "I am not recommending that you acquire puttees, a swimming pool or a squad of Jap valets. Nor am I suggesting that you pal around with Elinor Glyn. Yet, if I had my way, I would imprison Cecil B. DeMille at Mamaroneck for a while and I would loan you his Hollywood trappings, each and every one of them. . . . You must sacrifice yourself for the good of pictures. Let someone else take charge of your soul for a year or so. Faust tried it—and had a good time."

The only DeMille-like "trapping" that would have done Griffith some good was a contract like that of his rival's, which gave him far more creative independence within Zukor's empire than Griffith obtained, but with solid financial backing as well for a production unit with which studio executives dared not trifle. "Jap" valets Griffith did not need. Nor did he need this piece, which was probably inspired by an advance screening of *Isn't Life Wonderful,* which, of course, might have been understood by a not-very-astute critical mind as rather more brutal than most films of the day (though surely not more so than *Greed,* for example, which had preceded it to the screen by only a few months) and, perhaps, in its concluding passages, as too sentimental for its moment (though surely not more so than many previous Griffith films that had been warmly praised). But it seems more likely that an establishment-apologist like Quirk—the survival of his magazine depended, to a degree, on the indulgence of the studios—was writing a coded approval of Griffith's Famous Players–Lasky contract, by this time fully discussed throughout the industry.

But it is neither Quirk's motives nor his crocodile sympathy for a man he must have known was in the painful process of being forced out from behind his "wall" at Mamaroneck that detains us now. Rather, it is the fact that his is the first substantial, general assault on Griffith to be found in a significant national periodical. He had, naturally, received his share of bad notices over the years, but this was the first important piece to question the governing principles of his work. From this moment on, critical fashion would shift decisively against Griffith. And we are talking not just about the printed word; we are talking, as well, about talk—in that small circle of intellectually influential people who took film seriously, and in the motion picture industry itself. Among these groups, where once, it seemed, Griffith could do no wrong, now he could do no right. Even when they were forced to admit that something of his had pleased them, there was an element of grudging surprise in their words.

It was extraordinarily cruel, this sudden and massive turnabout. The man was, after all, fifty years old and he had just suffered a bitter (and embittering) blow in the loss of his studio. Moreover, he had a right to think that, if he so chose, he need do nothing more to secure his reputation and his place in film history. One can well understand the air of befuddlement that attends so many of his public utterances from this time onward—and the occasional self-abasements as he attempted, not very cleverly, to woo back his supporters.

He could not see it at the time, but he was being victimized by the fact that film was, at this point, an art without a history, therefore in many observers' minds not yet an art at all. It was, perhaps, a fad or a phenomenon that had the potential of becoming an art, and everyone who proposed himself to be an artist, was under an implicit obligation to keep contributing to this development, through technical innovation, through the expansion of the medium's range. This demand arose particularly from journalists and (later) historians of liberal, technological or Marxist biases, who "embraced a theory of Progress in contradistinction to all other arts," as Andrew Sarris has written. "By their standards, the cinema does not rise or fall, as do all other arts, in relation to the artists involved. Instead, the cinema is subject to a certain mystical process of evolution by which Griffith's Babylonian crane shots are on the bottom rung of a ladder that mounts to Eisenstein's Odessa Steps." If one combines the demonstrable fact that Griffith had long since made his great technical contributions with the equally demonstrable fact that the innovative impetus had moved to Germany, to Russia, to younger men everywhere, and then observes that at the more popular and commercial levels fashions had distinctly shifted—whether for better or worse, may well be debated—one can see why, and with what justification, people started thinking of Griffith as old-fashioned, out of step.

That does not, however, explain the continuing cruelty and contempt that has been visited upon him and his late work by film historians in the years since. Considering the pace of innovation from 1914 to the establishment of the first set of generic conventions for the sound film approximately twenty years later, it is ridiculous to ask one man, no matter how gifted, to partake of them all or even approve of them all, let alone take the lead in establishing them all. Griffith obviously had his limitations and if there are no masterpieces among his last eight films, little innovation and much imitation, only two or three are out-and-out disgraces. And in thinking about them all, it is well to bear in mind Sarris's dictum that "the cinema of Griffith is no more outmoded, after all, than the drama of Aeschylus."[1] Early work or late, it is all of a piece, bound to the conventions of the artist's formative period, and it requires only an acceptance of these as the givens of his sensibility to appreciate properly and criticize fairly. Just as one must avoid pitying him—he and his loyalists have done all that is needed of that—one must also avoid patronizing him—his less-feeling critics have done all that is needed of that. At all events, it was a saddened, more than usually distant man, perhaps more defeated in spirit than he yet knew, who moved from his own studio to Paramount's East Coast facility in Astoria, Long Island, to take up work under his new contract, where he conducted himself with an honorable professionalism, doing his best within the limits of what can only be described as a disheartening situation.

2

Griffith's first film at his new headquarters, the one that United Artists would release, was, happily, a project he had wanted to do within his own organization—an adaptation of the recently successful Broadway musical comedy Poppy, with a book by Dorothy Donnelly and music—naturally irrelevant to the silent screen—by Steven Jones and Arthur Samuels. What was not irrelevant to Griffith was its setting in the hard-scrabble world of small-time carnivals, which took him back to his own trouping days, and a sentimental plot line involving these favorite conventions of his, an orphan girl and a long-lost fortune. Then, too, he acquired along with the rights to the play, its star—W. C. Fields. For him, too, Griffith felt an affinity. His background had been, if anything, more marginal than Griffith's, and he, too, had spent many a long year in the lower reaches of show business before attaining stardom as a featured performer in every edition of the *Ziegfeld Follies* from 1915 to 1921. After a brief stint with *George White's Scandals*, Fields had felt ready for a book show and full stardom, and *Poppy* had been his chosen vehicle. And a perfect one, at that, for in the character of Professor Eustace McGargle—juggler, boozer, confidence man and victim of the fates—he had found the outlines of the screen character he would, after the coming of sound, make immortal, in among other vehicles a remake of this very film.

The terms of Griffith's contract permitted him, on all of his Famous Players productions, his choice of two stars (as well as a cameraman and an editor among other key functionaries), so naturally Carol Dempster got the lead and the title role when the picture was renamed *Sally of the Sawdust*. Griffith's second choice, for the romantic lead opposite Dempster, was also unwise as it developed—a young Theater Guild leading man, who commuted daily from Griffith's set to Broadway, where he was playing in *The Guardsman*. He was Alfred Lunt, and he was so (justifiably) distressed by his performance that he made only one film thereafter (of *The Guardsman* coincidentally) and told later inquirers that he could remember almost nothing about the experience. Fields, however, entirely enjoyed the filmmaking process and Griffith as well. He would go immediately from *Sally* to a second film under his direction. In an interview later that year he said: "I consider Griffith one of the finest men I ever knew. He is marvelous to work for, most inspiring and encouraging. And poor! He cares nothing for money, lives only to make pictures. But if ever he goes broke, everyone who ever worked for him in pictures will go back and work for nothing—and I'll be there to lead 'em on."[2]

Would that that had been true! Still, there can be no doubt of Fields's sincerity. For around the same time a *New York Daily Mirror* feature writer named Dorothy Herzog printed a blind item claiming that Fields had, as a matter of "conceit," doubled his salary demands between *Sally* and his second Griffith picture, *That Royle Girl*. This brought a letter from Fields claiming that her informant had not given her "the whole unvarnished" in the matter. Yes, said Fields, "I did boost the bad news almost double" for the second film, but only because he had cut his price almost in half in order to do *Sally* "because I knew I would get the benefit of the masterful direction of D. W. Griffith, whom I consider the most patient and greatest, the most helpful to any artist, ham or hamess of any director living." He went on to call Griffith a "lovable great artist," a "generous and unselfish character" and to add, "Any and all success I had in *Sally of the Sawdust* is due entirely to D. W. Griffith."[3]

That success was substantial. In his first large screen role, Fields worked at several disadvantages. For one thing, he wore a mustache, which gave him a slightly sinister air. For another, of all the voices in the world for which written titles cannot adequately substitute surely Fields's drawl—conniving, wheedling, airy, and paranoid—is it.

Then too, though Dempster is given plenty of time for her tedious specialty dances, Fields, who really did have a great specialty, namely, his wondrous juggling routine, which he always did without patter, meaning that its essence could have been conveyed splendidly on the silent screen, is one time cut off before it can fairly get started (though it appears Griffith shot his whole marvelous cigar box routine) and another time is but briefly glimpsed from a distance, with the heads of extras preventing us from seeing most of what Fields is up to. Still, something of his essential comic character does come through: the habitual delicacy of his gestures, for example, and his singular humors—the cowardice masked by bravado, the sudden rages cooled by hasty second thoughts. And there are some nice little bits: a peanut wagon that he is tending converts at a touch into a mini-bar serving bootleg liquor to the thirsty, for example. And then there are those moments when Fields and Dempster (who plays his ward) are penniless on the road, looking for carnival work. We see them riding the blinds, for instance, as Griffith more than once had, and we see Fields crawling into a baker's oven, in search of warm sleep, as Griffith claimed he once did. In this case, however, Dempster, not knowing that her guardian is in the oven, innocently pumps the bellows, raising the temperature and toasting him uncomfortably.

The story, which had Fields trying to restore the orphaned Dempster to her wealthy grandparents, who had ordered her mother never to darken their door again after she fell in love with a circus performer, might have had an antique air, but it would have been serviceable enough had it not been needlessly attenuated. Part of the problem lies in Griffith's undiminished desire to give excesses of screen time to Dempster, part of it lies in her performance, which consists again of a desperately jumpy attempt to mime young adolescence. Dempster was only 23, to be sure, an age at which Pickford and Gish could still manage assignments of this sort, but she now looked older than her years. In her romantic passages with Lunt, neither her director nor her costar was helpful. The latter, despite what he was to become in the next three decades, was unarguably the least persuasive of all Griffith's hopeless leading men—stiff and sexless. But almost every shot in which he appears with Dempster

favors her, which means he does not have even a fighting chance to establish his character—that of the wealthy scion of a family who are close
friends of Dempster's unknowing grandparents and disapprove his flirta-
tion with the circus waif. There is, though, one curious scene, a masked
ball to which Lunt invites Dempster in which she appears elegantly
gowned and coiffed, her only such moment in films. Transformed, she is
almost unrecognizable. It may be, as Anthony Slide has written, that her
métier might have been society romances, or Norma Talmadge roles, as
Gerrit Lloyd kept urging Griffith to put her in. Be that as it may, we get
from this sequence some sense of what Griffith saw in her—the capacity
for a kind of cool elegance that, alas, never found a natural place in his
films.

Finally, it must be admitted that Griffith's awkwardness and un-
familiarity with comedy is all too evident in *Sally of the Sawdust*. Fields
is so good that he almost manages to disguise the fact that he could have
been better had Griffith known how to stage and cut comedy, and if many
of his scenes did not simply trail off or trail on past their point. This is
particularly evident in the climactic chase, where he escapes from some
bootleggers who have mistaken him for an accomplice who has betrayed
them, bucketing through open country in an open Ford to try to save Sally
from the law, which has arrested her (and placed her on trial in her grandfather's court) because she assisted him in a three-card monte game. The
sequence is too long for the amount of comic invention it contains—more
frantic than funny.

Yet with all that admitted, *Sally* is an agreeable film, good-spirited
in its mild little way. And perhaps the inevitable comparisons to the work
of Chaplin or Keaton or Lloyd are invidious. Voiceless, Fields was not
yet their peer, or even fully himself. But if we read the picture as neither
a vehicle for him nor for the director's lover, but for what it is at its best,
an affectionate recollection by Griffith of his own early show business
days, it exercises a certain hold on us.

As it did on its contemporaries. The reviews were, for the most part,
more than indulgent. "Among the finest of all motion pictures yet made,"
asserted the *World*. "A glorious experience," said Mildred Spain in the
News. "You'll regret it all your life if you miss 'Sally of the Sawdust,'"
said the lady from the *Graphic*. It is true that the word "hokum" came
up in several of the notices, notably that of Richard Watts, Jr., in the
Herald Tribune, but even those who refused to surrender entirely to the
sentiment of the film, or disliked seeing Griffith pander quite so openly
to mass tastes, stressed its broad audience appeal.[4]

Later that year, however, a small New York theater, the Fine Arts
Guild, presented a series of revivals, including among them *Broken
Blossoms*, to which Robert E. Sherwood betook himself. He still re-
sponded favorably to the film, but commented on its heavy reliance on

subtitles, Griffith's use of pictures "merely as illustrations for the text." Then he added: "Unfortunately, while Chaplin, Lubitsch, Vidor and many others have moved ahead with the times, Griffith has stood still. He has never learned that a movie camera can speak for itself." This, he said, was "cause for lamentation, for Griffith was the first heroic figure of the movies," demonstrating, in his early days, "an amazing degree of imagination and an admirable courage." But then, devastating with historical appreciation, Sherwood concluded, "In summoning that essential nerve, Griffith made advance atonement for all the crimes he was subsequently to commit in *Dream Street* and *Sally of the Sawdust*."[5] The statement was more sophisticated than Quirk's, but one can discern in it the new critical line on Griffith beginning to solidify. Within a couple of years no film critic with the slightest pretension to elevated standards would be able to ignore it.

There was one level on which *Sally of the Sawdust* was unquestionably an exemplary production—if belatedly so. That was the economic level. Produced under studio control, released at regular prices, and featuring Fields, who if he was not yet the movie star he was to become, was still a well-known theatrical figure about whom there was considerable public curiosity, the picture was brought in on budget and eventually returned to Zukor's concern a profit that exceeded $200,000—even though the release was handled by another company.[6] In short, even with a picture that was not his strongest, but produced with self-evidently sensible methods, Griffith had finally made his first quickly and distinctly profitable picture since *Way Down East*.

He had no time to relish this rare experience. Two weeks after he turned *Sally* over for distribution he was on the set for the first camera day of *That Royle Girl*, a film that turned out to be as troubled as the previous one had been pleasant. It was the story of a Chicago "jazz baby" who works as a modiste, is in love with a rather slippery bandleader, but is also an idealist, often communing with the spirit of Abraham Lincoln by visiting the Saint-Gaudens statue of him in Lincoln Park. When her lover's estranged wife is murdered, he is accused of the crime, and Joan Daisy Royle pluckily sets about obtaining evidence to clear him. This involves undercover work in the underworld against the deadline imposed by his execution date. Improbably, she falls in love with the district attorney who has been in charge of her lover's prosecution, and the ending finds the bandleader marrying a chorine and Joan Daisy and the D.A. also marrying.

The picture appears to be as unsuited to Griffith's talents as anything since *One Exciting Night*, although about that one cannot be entirely certain, since no print of it is known to exist. Griffith, however, had no doubt on the point. He described it as "a lame idea," adding, as he later wrote Zukor, "I begged Mr. Lasky to let me out of doing this picture, as I did not think I could make the right kind of picture out of it."[7] Based on a novel by an undistinguished popular writer, Edwin Balmer, which had been purchased by the studio in manuscript, before its last chapters were completed, *That Royle Girl* had resisted several attempts at adaptation, and several other Famous Players directors had resisted the project. Lasky, it seems, initially promised Griffith that he too could pass on it if he insisted, but then reneged on that verbal agreement, putting pressure on Griffith, through his "supervisor" (the early term for "producer"), William LeBaron, to accept the property.

All concerned were caught in an unhappy situation none of them had made. Committed to providing a weekly change of bill for one of the nation's largest theater chains, Famous Players had to complete the equivalent of a double feature every week—over a hundred films a year. This relentless demand for product often and perhaps necessarily overrode nice questions about the quality of that product, and Lasky, in charge of East Coast production for the company that still bore his name, often had to abandon his customary amiability to fulfill that demand. As for LeBaron, "clever and smiling," as he was described, he was a former newspaperman, and, in later years, Paramount's executive in charge of W. C. Fields. He was also typical of a new breed of literate (or at least semi-literate) cynics attracted to, and recruited by, the movie companies as they matured economically and found that they required a new layer of what we would now term "middle management" to oversee their day-to-day affairs. LeBaron did not need to humiliate Griffith, but to discipline him in the new ways of industrial efficiency. He was also a man on whom the pressure to deliver the pictures in his charge on time, on budget, was intense, and had understood there was no reason to fret unduly over a modestly budgeted programmer like *That Royle Girl*. Good, bad or indifferent, it would be swept out of most people's memories in a matter of days by the unending flood of film rushing through the world's theaters. His interest was to push it quietly into that stream and avoid any trouble or expense that might bring Mr. Zukor or Mr. Lasky out of their offices sniffing or snorting.

As for Griffith, he was once again the victim of a shabbily drawn agreement. His salary represented his old organization's only unvexed cash flow. It needed its share of his pay check arriving steadily to meet its obligations, but it came in only when he was actually at work on a picture. He had been assured that among the advantages of working for a large and efficient operation like Famous Players was a story department that would have on hand at any given moment a selection of suitable projects for him, so that he could, if need be, go from picture to picture without delay. This proved to be far from the case; when he needed something to follow *Sally* immediately there was nothing available except *That Royle Girl* and his choice was to wait patiently (and salary-less) or make the best of a bad thing.

Trying the latter course, the studio was generous with him. Dempster was again given the lead and Fields's demand for a larger fee was met so that they could reconstitute the father-daughter relationship that had worked successfully in their previous film. This time they were supported by two male stars who, if they were not of the first rank, were at least known to movie audiences—the dashing Harrison Ford and the reliable James Kirkwood, whose association with Griffith of course dated back to Biograph and whose son is the well-known contemporary playwright and novelist. Again, location shooting was permitted, and Griffith's Chicago exteriors may have lent at least a little verisimilitude to a rather strained story. Then, at some point, whether in story conference or after Griffith had begun principal photography is unclear, the need for a strong finish was urgently borne in on both Griffith and his supervisor. Griffith reverted to that favorite device of his, a cataclysmic act of nature—this time a cyclone that strikes the roadhouse lair of the gangster-murderers after Dempster has tracked them there, literally blowing them away. It was, he later explained, "the only elemental thing I could use that could carry on and culminate the fury of life in Chicago—the vortex of disordered . . . humanity. . . . I wanted the picture to make a shell hole somewhere. . . ."[8]

It did—in his budget. Intended as a "small" production, meaning, under the terms of his contract, that it could cost only $250,000, he estimated that his cyclone would add $200,000–$250,000 to *That Royle Girl*'s budget. That, of course, required executive approval, which Griffith claimed he received from LeBaron and from Walter Wanger, then beginning his long career as a production executive as one of Zukor's assistants. Unfortunately, the sequence added nothing to the value of the picture—both reviews and internal corporate correspondence indicate that the miniatures employed in it were notably unpersuasive. Worse, it created a breach that would bring Griffith's relationship with the studio to a premature end.

The problem again lay in Griffith's contract. Remember that after costs were recouped, he was entitled to 20 percent of a film's profits, which in the case of *Sally of the Sawdust* had amounted to something over $40,000. Remember, too, that as a defense against his profligate ways the studio had insisted on a clause charging him 20 percent of any amount that he went over budget on any given production. By a strange coincidence the share of the overage on *That Royle Girl* chargeable to Griffith was about $50,000, so for the year Griffith's gains and losses roughly canceled each other out. Banzhaf argued that he interpreted the contract differently, that its intention was to treat each film discretely, but it is hard to see how, under that view, Famous Players could ever have recovered its penalty payments unless it docked Griffith's salary. Griffith himself argued that since he had received executive approval of the additional expenditures they were exempt, under another cloudy contractual clause, from penalties. To this claim the studio replied that he should have obtained these approvals in writing. In all, it was a nasty wrangle, and since the Griffith corporation had been counting on the *Sally* percentages to meet its debt payments while Griffith was between pictures, the company was again in danger of default and required yet another loan to keep it out of bankruptcy.

In the meantime, *That Royle Girl* was released and suffered almost immediate failure. Even the usually sycophantic Grey had urged that the cyclone sequence be shortened because it "looks artificial," that Dempster spent too much time mooning about the Lincoln statue, that she "fights entirely too much" in an "exaggerated" fashion that costs her sympathy, and that she had far too many close-ups.[9] Some of these criticisms were apparently answered in Griffith's final cut, but there was no saving an enterprise that called for a lighter approach than the floridly sentimental attitude Griffith apparently brought to the subject of flaming youth.

The *New Yorker*, in its first year of publication, and trying hard to establish its reputation for sophistication, commented: "Mr. David Wark Griffith, saintly showman . . . is indisputably the grand master of moral-istic-melodramatic balderdash. He has the corner on treacle, mush and trash and automatically is out of our set." It added that if W. C. Fields continued with him "he will surely be fired by Mr. Ziegfeld as being no comedian."[10] Not all the reviews were so devastating, but there was no disguising that Griffith, who was giving out interviews decrying the scanty attire in which women were sometimes seen in public, was neither a Von Stroheim nor a Lubitsch when it came to sex (or even mere sexiness)—and that Dempster was not Clara Bow, either.

But if *That Royle Girl* added nothing to Griffith's prestige within the studio or with the critics and the public, it was not, commercially speaking, a disaster. Once again, had Griffith not added his storm scene the picture would have turned a modest profit. As it was, it lost only about $180,000,[11] washing out the studio's profits from *Sally*, but, it would seem, causing no great alarm in the executive suite. For, as the year turned, Famous Players was in the process of turning over to Griffith a long-cherished project, intended by the studio to be one of its major productions of 1926.

It was *The Sorrows of Satan* and, in some respects, it must have seemed to Zukor and his associates an ideal project for Griffith. And so it might have been had it been made a little earlier. The title was a famous one, for the book of that name, by Marie Corelli, became when it was published in 1895 the greatest best-seller England had known until that time. Taken together with her numerous other works, it served to make this eccentric and ignorant woman the world's best-selling author during the late Victorian and the Edwardian ages. In general, her novels combined simple-minded religiosity, simpering romanticism and a full-blown style that it pleasured the critics to twit for several decades. Reclusive, vindictive toward the many enemies she made (and imagined), she also maintained a Venetian gondola near her home at Stratford-Upon-Avon, and liked to be swept along Shakespeare's river in it when she was not permitting her tiny self (she was not more than five feet tall) to be drawn through the streets of his town in a pony cart.

Besides being her most famous work, *The Sorrows of Satan* was also quite typical of her production. The title figure grieves because he finds it so easy to corrupt men and women here below, yearning to find someone who will resist his blandishments because, as the author interpreted a Scriptural hint on the point, God would reward his fallen angel with an hour in heaven for each potential sinner who refused him, grant him full pardon should the world finally reject him entirely. Satan presents himself in disguise to one Geoffrey Tempest, a struggling writer too pure in his ideals to achieve worldly success, just after the author has been relieved of his poverty by receiving what he is led to believe is a bequest from his uncle, but is, of course, the devil's bribe. Lucifer, in the form of Prince Lucio de Rimanez, presses his services on him as a guide to worldly pleasures, and arranges a match between him and one of the tempter's handmaidens, an indolent and lascivious society woman. Tempest abandons most of his ideals, but when he meets Mavis Claire, a writer as idealistic as he once was, a great struggle for his soul ensues. Finally, on shipboard, the Prince reveals his true identity and asks Geoffrey to curse God and commit himself to evil. Geoffrey refuses, the prince is whisked skyward for his promised hour of paradise, and after a shipwreck Geoffrey is returned to London, to poverty, but also to Mavis.

A modest version of this story had been made earlier in London (it starred Gladys Cooper), but Famous Players had pursued remake rights since 1918, not securing them until after Corelli's death in 1924, "the longest negotiation in film history for author's rights,"[12] according to John Cecil Graham, the Famous Players representative in London who had doggedly pursued the matter for six years. Considering that the book was in its sixtieth printing when its author died, it might also be considered that Graham got a bargain when he paid a mere $35,000 for the novel.

Part of the delay in coming to terms with Corelli stemmed from her disapproval of Cecil B. DeMille as director for the film, despite his conviction that this was a ripping yarn, very much his sort of thing. One source credits his defection from Paramount at this time to his disappointment over not being assigned to *Sorrows* now that the author's death had removed the last bar to his heart's desire. One rather imagines there was more involved in that decision but even more enigmatic is the corporation's obsession with the novel's screen possibilities. What might have looked like sure-fire commercial potential in 1918 cannot have seemed nearly so promising by the mid-twenties. Still, the long-sought dream was now within grasp and it is always hard to step back from such culminations. And, initially, Griffith was drawn to some aspects of the material.

Geoffrey, the writer, for instance, obviously resembles those dreaming scriveners and inventors, striving to fulfill themselves in an indifferent world, whom Griffith had so sympathetically portrayed before. And, indeed, his depictions of idealists in their garrets are among the most successful passages in the final film. Then, too, *Sorrows* gave Griffith splendid opportunities for those symbolic representations of heaven and hellishness, that he favored. Finally, there were plenty of highly melodramatic confrontations and some strong romantic possibilities in the story, especially as it was finally adapted for the screen.

Yet from the start Griffith had his hesitations as well. He knew perfectly well the standing of Corelli's reputation among serious literary people and at one point remarked on the "pitiful waste of time" filming a work of hers represented when of Conrad's work only *Victory* and *Lord Jim* had been filmed.[13] Beyond that, he must have felt that given his own current reputation for datedness he could ill afford to be associated with an artifact like *The Sorrows of Satan*.

Still, Famous Players persisted—and insisted there was nothing else for him. So from the time *That Royle Girl* was launched until March 1, 1926, when the first camera turned, Griffith struggled with his employers over the *Satan* script. On one point there was general agreement—that romance was to be stressed, the metaphysical de-emphasized. To this end, the character of the female writer was introduced at the beginning of the story rather than halfway through, as she was in the novel. Another significant change was in the character of the other woman, who was represented on the screen as an exotic Russian princess rather than as an Englishwoman, perhaps as a competitive response to the arrival and popularity in the United States of such foreign temptresses as Pola Negri and Garbo (whose first American film, *The Torrent*, was released in 1926). On these matters disagreement was minimal, and there was no great resistance when Griffith insisted that this be a "big" picture, not only as that term was employed in his contract, but in the way it was handled; once again he was aiming for a road show release. He succeeded in getting the original cost estimate raised from $550,000 to $650,000 (of which his fee would be $200,000). He also argued, perhaps paradoxically, that some of Corelli's more astonishing visions of the struggle between the forces of light and darkness be visualized on the screen, not left to the audience's imagination. "Hokum" they might be—but amazing they might also be, and he obviously hoped that his special effects would wow audiences into a suspension of disbelief, rewarding them for the advanced prices they would be asked to pay.

This dispute was not resolved before principal photography began. Obviously the Famous Players people hoped when the picture was assembled the love story would carry it without resort to the additional expense that effects would entail. After more struggles they gave Griffith a strong cast. As Tempest, Ricardo Cortez (despite his stage name he had actually been born in Vienna and grew up in New York) was recruited. A Latin-lover type, he had been the studio's second-string Valentino, but loaned out to appear opposite Garbo in *The Torrent* he had been effective, as he was to be in this film. Dempster automatically got the role of Mavis, and suitably cast and discreetly directed, she was also excellent. Lya de Putti, a Hungarian actress who had just had a large success in E. A. Dupont's internationally acclaimed German film *Variety* (opposite Emil Jannings), played the *femme fatale* with notable lightness. Finally, as Lucifer incarnate, Adolphe Menjou essentially brought over from *A Woman of Paris* his characterization of a boulevardier whose suave and witty worldliness seduces the audience as subtly as it does the other characters. There was a self-amusement about his ostentatious charm that saved it from cynicism. In all, *The Sorrows of Satan* offered perhaps the best ensemble-playing of Griffith's films in this decade. Perhaps precisely because the story was, putting it mildly, improbable, he strived for a certain underplayed naturalism, and obtained it.

But perhaps the most striking quality of *The Sorrows of Satan* is its *mise-en-scène*. In the entire Griffith canon there is no other film that looks like this one. It is obviously influenced by the expressionism the German cinema had made fashionable at this time, and there is a richness and sophistication of design about it that is altogether unique in Griffith's work. Particularly memorable (despite deep cuts made in it by the studio) is a prologue in which the heavenly war of the angels, leading to Lucifer's expulsion, is strikingly shown. There is also a very fine later sequence in which Tempest decides to join Menjou in his wanderings and the coughing and sputtering of his car coming to life seems to drown out Mavis's cry of warning and despair—even though this is, of course, a silent film. There is a perfectly timed overhead shot, quite uncharacteristic of Griffith, and a peculiarly memorable image of the devil's shadow looming huge and menacing above the writer. That shot, lingering so powerfully in memory, is emblematic of a film to which Griffith throughout brought a vision that was entirely new to him, a film from which it sometimes seems all gray tones have been eliminated in favor of starkly contrasting blacks and whites, in which there is a crispness of editing (and a relative paucity of subtitles) that is, again, quite unlike his usual manner.

It can, of course, be argued that Griffith's style here was mere stylishness, an attempt to catch up with the parade of foreign legionnaires that had so bemused the better critics and the advanced public in recent years. Doubtless he did want to show them that he could do that sort of work too when he felt like it. But he had long since shown, in enterprises as diverse as *Intolerance, Broken Blossoms* and *The White Rose,* that he was capable of a larger variety in his visual repertory than he was sometimes credited with. Then, too, if a certain faithfulness to Corelli's plot, characters and morality was an imposition of this project, he was under no compulsion to find the visual equivalent of her childlike and burbling verbal manner. Perhaps he could disguise or minimize the dated quality of his material by being as *au courant* as possible in the manner that he retold it.

If this was indeed his strategy, then the studio's failure to let him film some of the material he wanted to do was a mistake. Particularly at issue were a transformation scene in which the Prince de Rimanez would shed his urbane garb and manner and take on the classic lineaments of his true Satanic self, and Corelli's "ship incident" (as it was referred to in story conferences), in which after Tempest's refusal of a formal pact with him, the Devil ascends to heaven for his promised hour of bliss. This last, Griffith thought would make a spectacular climax for the film, despite the costly difficulty of the special effects work. He was in this, as in his other disputes with management, seeking transcendence, a film that would rise above its silly source to achieve the visionary, and he was, in this instance, going about it in the right way. This time he was not looking for it in a single storm sequence, but in a series of unbalancing, mystical incidents that taken together would have given his film a quality quite unlike anything anyone had so far tried.

That vision was not fully realized. Principal photography had gone smoothly enough, but Griffith hesitated over the editing, even demonstrating signs of panic as he pulled things out and pushed them back in, refusing to show his cut of the film to Zukor and the other Famous Players executives, until on June 29, Walter Wanger addressed a memo to a staff lawyer stating, "Will you please write a letter to Mr. D. W. Griffith for Mr. Adolph Zukor, stating that he expects to see *Sorrows of Satan* on July 15 as promised. This is to be a very friendly but firm letter."[14] It was friendlier, anyway, than any of the correspondence that would ensue between Griffith and his employers, who now entered upon a period in which they groped desperately—and recklessly—for ways of "improving" the film at the stage when it is always most difficult and expensive to do so, in postproduction, when the principals have scattered to their next assignments, the sets have been struck and retakes are expensive if not entirely impossible to do.

The picture was first shown to Zukor at his lavish Mountainview

Farm in Rockland county (which, along with the Paramount building now nearing completion in Times Square, was the visible symbol of his rise and his industry's rise; in a little more than a decade the net worth of Famous Players had increased from a few hundred thousand dollars to, at the end of 1926, $149 million). Besides a swimming pool, a golf course and a working dairy farm, which contributed much of its product to a local orphanage, there were naturally screening facilities on Zukor's 1,000-acre country premises, and Griffith was forced to show his picture at a weekend gathering where business and pleasure were mixed—not perhaps the best of circumstances for a film like *The Sorrows of Satan*. On the whole Zukor and his guests seemed to like what they saw, but there were some criticisms from the tiny, whispery-voiced mogul. He thought, for example, that more suspense and menace were required in two places: in the temptation of Tempest by Lucifer and his climactic return to Mavis after he has finally rejected that temptation. More of a struggle—of conscience in the first instance, for life itself in the second—was wanted. There was also a spot of bother about an orgy sequence, which was moved from early in the film to later (and was finally removed altogether if one can judge from the surviving print). All of this Griffith agreed to work on.

At which point bright Walter Wanger, not long out of Dartmouth, began taking a very active hand in matters. He sent a copy of the Corelli novel to Norman Bel Geddes, then regarded as the most visionary of Broadway designers, and asked him to write a scenario for the final sequence and design a spectacular setting in which to stage it. A script and some charcoal renderings of the set were completed by the protean Bel Geddes in 36 hours and with Lasky's approval and the acquiescence of LeBaron, who was in charge of physical production at Astoria, Bel Geddes was set to work, in secret, shooting this sequence. Griffith did not find out about it, apparently, until it was finished, and such was his desire to please, he received it most politely, though he insisted on reshooting the reshooting. He used the set to make his marvelous prologue, and it would seem employed some of Bel Geddes's footage in it as well. He also used, if Bel Geddes's account of the incident is to be believed, a considerable portion of his scenario in redoing the ending.[15]

This along with some other retakes he did not complete until September, when Cortez and an important supporting player could return to work. This version was then shown to Wanger, LeBaron, Forrest Halsey, the screenwriter, and Julian Johnson, the sometime film critic, now working for the studio and assigned to write titles for the picture. They professed to see a vast improvement, and Griffith took this cut to Upper Montclair, New Jersey, for a short preview run. The audience reaction was poor, however, and someone informed Zukor, who came out with Lasky to see it. They, too, were unimpressed, and Zukor now reversed himself, taking the position that Griffith should have left the picture substantially as he had shown it to him in July. Griffith did not inform him of the extent of the meddling that had gone on without Zukor's knowledge—in the long wrangle that followed he never did name names or even mildly criticize any individual, only the general process by which the studio executives operated. Instead, he restored the film to a condition very close to its original form, and invited Zukor to view it—which Zukor refused to do. At this point, Lasky, however, accepted this version but indicated that some final changes would be made by his production department. Griffith was told not to participate in this process (Lasky said "they got results in their own way," Griffith would later recall).[16]

It was this version, very much a corporate version, that appeared in New York in mid-October, with Griffith now being blamed by Zukor for changes he had not participated in making and had himself disliked when he saw them. The charitable explanation for this irony is that the pattern so familiar in corporate life, of underlings overresponding to a chief executive's desires, had asserted itself. The less-charitable explanation is that Griffith was the victim of complex maneuverings within the Famous Players hierarchy. At the time B. P. Schulberg, having returned to Zukor's side, was in charge of West Coast production, and there was a powerful rivalry between him and Lasky in New York, with Schulberg's pictures turning out to be more profitable and Griffith's film the most expensive and worrisome on Lasky's schedule. As *Sorrows* started to look like an impossible commercial proposition, the conspiracy took root to blame Griffith for all the errors committed in its name. When, a couple of months after it was released, the Astoria studio was briefly shuttered, Griffith's film was mentioned in press reports as a significant cause for suspension of operations there.

For the moment, however, one can but admire Griffith's patience and honorableness in dealing with Zukor's corridor politicians. Indeed, he had been given the impression there was good reason to hold his tongue and his temper. For all during the summer he was encouraged to "play with" *Satan*—the phrase is surely one a young executive, not an aging and fairly desperate director, would use to describe the work Griffith did in that period—Zukor had been talking with him about the final picture due under his contract, and proposing that he undertake yet another, larger project under a separate pact. The former was to have been *The White Slave*, Griffith's cherished adaptation of a disreputable melodrama in which Dempster was to have costarred with Richard Dix. The latter was to have been a biography of Florence Nightingale. In conversation Zukor promised various improvements in Griffith's arrangements with Famous Players. These included forgiveness of the $50,000 penalty on *That Royle Girl* and a $25,000 raise for doing *The White Slave*. In addition, he agreed to have his story department start work on the script immediately so that Griffith would not have to idle without salary after work on *Satan* was completed. He even agreed to pay the director $6,000 a week, his regular big-picture salary, every week he had to wait for a new script should he sign to do *Florence Nightingale* or some other picture after *The White Slave*. Albert Grey, who was present at these meetings, was even moved to reduce these terms to a memorandum of agreement and offer it to Zukor for signature on August 30.

Given the tenor of these contacts, and the fact that no bad temper was ever visible in Griffith's dealings with other studio executives during this troubled time, it comes as a shock to find Zukor maneuvering for a termination of his contract with Griffith just a couple of months later. It comes as a shock, that is, until one consults the final production costs and the record of the first month's receipts during the New York road show engagement at the George M. Cohan theater. The first of these is perhaps the more astonishing; the picture's negative cost was $971,260, more than $300,000 over the original budget. As Griffith pointed out, much of this expenditure was out of his control. Some $264,000 was devoted to story and other preproduction costs, and there was probably another $100,000 wasted in "playing with" the picture after he had finished his first cut. He observed, for example, that an original estimate of $25,000 for miniatures rose to more than $55,000.

Such exculpations were wasted on Zukor. His response to Griffith's long, polite and painstakingly detailed letter was curt, cool and dismissive. "The facts as you state them and the explanations you give are different from what I know them to be," he wrote, adding that if Griffith had left the picture as Zukor had originally screened it, "we would have had a different story to tell. . . ." The only aspect of Griffith's letter to which he responded favorably was a suggestion that perhaps they should "agree to disagree." Zukor concluded: "You mention at the end of your letter that we should endeavor to dispose of our differences amicably. I am very much in favor of doing so in the hope that I may retain the high regard in which I have always held you."[17]

The implication that Griffith must have been lying, that he had far exceeded Zukor's demands for revision, makes it clear that Zukor knew little about the summer's frantic activities and that his aides concealed from him their role in permitting—indeed, encouraging—the picture's runaway costs. It even appears that they went on to sabotage the crucial New York opening as well. It would not have been the first or the last time a motion picture company's executives deliberately harmed one of their firm's productions in order to turn their judgments (and their errors of commission and omission) into self-fulfilling prophecies.

For as it turned out, the New York reviews were not at all bad. Indeed, Mordaunt Hall of the *Times* wrote that in handling the film's many mood shifts "Mr. Griffith reveals himself as a master, and . . . he had made a photodrama that excels anything he had done in recent years."[18] In the *Sun*, John S. Cohen wrote: "Boasting of no literary values, but of many cinematic ones, 'Sorrows of Satan' is something to see." Its director, he said, "when he chooses to use it, had the most remarkable cinematic mind in the profession . . . for he has changed his technique to meet the changing standard of cinema supervision." And he added, "He handles light and shade even more imaginatively than that master of them, Victor Seastrom," citing the Swedish director whose production of *The Scarlet Letter*, starring Lillian Gish, had been a critical success a couple of months earlier.[19] The other general circulation dailies were, for the most part, equally enthusiastic.

Still, the opening-night audience, according to Cohen, who seems to imply that it arrived primed to scoff, was restlessly disapproving and distinctly unappreciative in its comments as it filed out. Weaknesses in the presentation—a dull score and poor projection, much too slow in the climactic passages—vitiated the experience. The trade paper and fan magazine reviews, always attuned to industry gossip and in some instances purchasable, were weak, stressing not the visual beauty of the film, nor Griffith's demonstration that he was more than capable of keeping up with the times, but rather emphasizing the "old-fashioned" quality of the story, though there was, justifiably, praise for Dempster, for only the second time in her career given the chance to exercise her gift for sober and mature roles.

In short, the word was out; *The Sorrows of Satan* was a disaster, and never mind what the critics said. Within two weeks, well before Griffith and Zukor began exchanging correspondence, the trade press was reporting that the failure of *Satan* was going to lead to Griffith's forced departure from the company. The source of these rumors can only have been the second-level executives leagued against Griffith, for Zukor was by nature a secretive man and Griffith had every reason to put as good a face as possible on the matter so as not to harm his film further.

Indeed, on November 29, Griffith responded to Zukor's invitation for discussion of an "amicable settlement" by noting: "The thing that I regret most in this matter is the unfortunate publicity which immediately seeped through your Company relative to our dispute, which . . . gave the picture a very serious set-back and took away whatever chance it had of being a Broadway success." Even at this late date Griffith offered to recut the film, restoring it to its original form, for the general release scheduled for early 1927.[20]

By now though, it was too late to do anything for *The Sorrows of Satan*, or the regrets of D. W. Griffith. He had been thoroughly victimized both in production and in the launching of his film, and the reviews could not counteract the generally negative atmosphere surrounding it. And now a second set of figures—the New York grosses—dealt the final blow to Griffith. In the first week at the Cohan, it took in only

$8,460 and continued at about that level for the next four weeks, with exhibition expenses exceeding grosses over that period by $65,359.38. It must be observed that even if the studio had been fully confident of the film it might still have fared badly, for the competition as it opened in New York was powerful. *Ben-Hur* and *The Big Parade* were still running, and John Barrymore's *Don Juan* with its novel music and effects sound-track was a more recent hit, along with Garbo's second picture, *The Temptress*. Famous Players itself had a good new road show attraction in the Ronald Colman *Beau Geste*. All these films had a stronger, simpler, more direct popular appeal than *Satan*. They required no explanations, critical or otherwise, to bring the people in.

If, as it seems, very little blame can be attached to Griffith for this failure, the fact is inescapable that he had been something less than his own best advocate in a difficult situation. His confidence had deserted him; that arrogance any artist requires to defend himself and his work was simply not to be summoned up when he most needed it. One need only contrast his high-handed manner with the Aitkens, even with United Artists functionaries in the more immediate past, with his passivity in response to the machinations of Lasky, Wanger and the rest of the production people, his obsequiousness in his relationship with Zukor, to see the point.

"He wasn't the same person," his cameraman, Hal Sintzenich, would recall of their days on the Famous Players Astoria lot.[21] Even a stranger noted the air of displacement and defeat about him. "I never saw him dressed in anything but a high, stiff collar, a gray felt hat, high shoes with brass hooks and pulling loops at the back, and one of a succession of suits none of which could be less than fifteen years old, and all of which were woefully out of style," Norman Bel Geddes would later write. "He looked like a hard-up, itinerant school teacher. His face was grave. When he smiled it was with the benign rigidity of a stone buddha. . . ."[22]

It is possible that Griffith could not help himself, understandable enough in the wake of his own studio's failure. But it is also possible that the old actor had found a tragic role that he rather enjoyed. He had understood, and wanted everyone to understand, that his fight for autonomy had been a heroic and lonely stand against all the trends of his industry. Now, he seemed to be attempting to turn his defeat into martyrdom, shaping a legend he could live with, one that could live on after him.

This thought is not entirely speculative. For during the entire period he was under contract to Famous Players, there had been a steady pulse of publicity about his debts, and his losses, a constant attempt to enlist sympathy for him. It had begun in September 1925, with an article entitled "What Will Griffith Do Now?" by Gerrit Lloyd. Written for a fan magazine, it described him, in a very strained metaphor, as "The big bull elephant of films," a creature "sagacious, determined and courageous" now walking "a trail paved with mortgages . . . heavy laden with debt. . . . His savings from all his vast works . . . sunk to the boundary posts of a small California ranch" (which Griffith, indeed, managed to retain almost to the end of his life).[23] The following June the endlessly loyal Lillian Gish added her voice to that of the press agent. In London she gave interviews which were relayed home, and she was more than outspoken about his plight. She exaggerated outrageously. "He is as poor as a church mouse," she cried, "as poor in fact as on the day he started producing." She described his contract with Famous Players as "selling himself to a film trust," his lot with the company that of "making pot-boilers for the mob and asking himself whether each scene will please the mob taste. In other words this great artist is going through a most humiliating experience." But, of course, she portrayed him as bravely soldiering on. "When I last saw him he told me: 'I have fifty bosses now, Lillian, but I am at least paying my debts.'"[24]

This chorus of pity reached its peak when Griffith added his voice to it. In an interview headed "He Might be the Richest Man in the World," he laid claim to such inventions as Bitzer's fade-out and Sartov's soft-focus photography and said that if he had patented them the royalties would be worth millions per year. Conveniently ignoring the fact that cameramen had devised them, he also asserted that he had not protected these advances in part because he "wanted to help the business." Setting that aside, he proceeded to rewrite more recent history. "I'm not a bad businessman, honestly I'm not. I was never in difficulties until I turned my business over to others. In California in the old days, when I both directed and managed, I got along all right. It was only when I came to Mamaroneck and turned over my business handling to others that I became involved." He blamed the failure of his studio on "bad management" and "bad releasing contracts" (though, in fact, his UA contracts were more favorable than he could have obtained elsewhere), then made the astonishing claim that he was not earning "a cent" for himself (although his one-third of the Famous Players contract had netted him well over $100,000 at the time of the interview), and that he was working for his stockholders, claiming to have earned enough, so far, to pay back over a third of their investment. But like the claim that he had paid back the investors in *Intolerance,* this was a fiction. He was working to avoid bankruptcy, to be sure, and doubtless harbored hopes that one day he might restore his and his stockholders' company to functioning status. But the fact remains that his investors never saw another penny's return on their equity.[25]

Griffith's condition at this time enlists sympathy, of course. And he (and Gish) may perhaps be forgiven for resisting recognition that the industrializing process had gone too far in the film business ever to be reversed. And for resenting the niggling, self-protective interference of small, conscienceless spirits, entirely without artistic gift, in his work. Yet one cannot help but reflect on the vagaries of the narcissistic personality as well. Griffith, the product of cold and distant rearing, was almost classically of this breed, thus subject to those swings between grandiosity and self-pity that are characteristic of it. Now, in the deepest trouble of his life, facing a situation that would depress anyone, the impulse to sorrow for himself was irresistible. And, of course, it added impetus to his downward course.

This was not, of course, readily apparent to most observers. Indeed, to some it seemed his recent record was not at all bad. One of his pictures had made money, another had shown him quite capable of working in a fashionably up-to-date manner. There were yet people in the film business convinced that he could still work profitably—if not quite as the leader he had once been—and were thus willing to give him a comfortable corporate home. One of them would now step forward with a generous offer, permitting him a dignified exit and promising possibilities for the future.

CHAPTER SEVENTEEN

At the Crazy Hotel

In May 1927, D. W. Griffith returned to Los Angeles. He returned in style, and he returned to stay. He engaged a suite at the Biltmore downtown. His splendid car, one of the legendary Hispano Suizas, was shipped West by rail along with four trunks of clothes. Seven boxes of books and papers were sent via steamer through the Panama Canal to his new offices at the United Artists studio (formerly the Pickford-Fairbanks lot, latterly Samuel Goldwyn's headquarters) on Formosa Street. If he was a man "toiling in chains," as Beaverbrook's *Daily Express* had headlined Lillian Gish's account of his present state, their links were forged of velvet.

During his troubles over *The Sorrows of Satan*, Griffith had approached Joe Schenck, offering to produce and direct something for Norma Talmadge, a notion to which Schenck had responded with his characteristic hustler's eagerness. Ultimately, nothing came of that plan, but as word of Griffith's troubles with Famous Players spread, Schenck took the opportunity to resume the suit for Griffith's talents which had been rejected two years earlier. His initial admiration for Griffith was as strong as Zukor's had once been, though Schenck had a temperament that made it far easier for him to express his feelings. Both men were small and unhandsome—Schenck even had a congenital cast in one of his eyes—and seem to have seen in Griffith's bearing, his courtly manner and his dignified reserve, Wasp qualities that they, as immigrant Jews, rightly or wrongly envied but could not emulate. Correspondence shows that Schenck, unlike Zukor, had a powerful impulse to take Griffith into protective custody, saving him from his own impracticalities and from the sharpsters of the business, by lifting from him the burdens of commerce so that he could concentrate on his art.

When Schenck proposed the first of several generous, long-term offers to Griffith, the latter's gratitude was boundless:

WHATEVER HAPPENS AND I MUST FRANKLY ADMIT THAT I AM IN A
QUANDARY . . . I WANT YOU TO KNOW THAT I AM ABSOLUTELY
SINCERE AND I BELIEVE THIS FROM THE BOTTOM OF MY HEART
THAT I AM CERTAINLY THANKFUL FOR HAVING LEARNED TO KNOW
YOU AS YOU REALLY ARE AND I HOPE AS LONG AS I LIVE TO HAVE THE
FRIENDSHIP OF JOE SCHENCK AS ONLY A REGULAR FELLOW COULD
SEND A WIRE LIKE THE ONE YOU SENT. . . .[1]

Indeed, it would appear that Schenck's manifest eagerness to acquire Griffith's services actually weakened his bargaining position over
the five-month period in which Griffith contemplated his next move.
There were other possibilities, including a very serious one set forth by
the independent group, financed by Pathé, that included DeMille: they
hinted at the possibility of setting Griffith up in a new company of his
own. This was particularly attractive to Griffith because, reversing his
previous prejudice—on the basis of his experiences with the Aitkens' Triangle program—he was now interested in doing supervisory work, especially if he could have a group of directors and actors under personal contract to him so that he could loan out their services. At this point,
observing the success of former employees, ranging from Pickford and
Sennett to Barthelmess and Hamilton, he was often heard to regret that
he had not signed them to long-term contracts permitting their mentor to
participate in the latter-day profits accruing, as he saw it, from the tutelage he had provided.

Schenck was having none of that. His task as he saw it was to discipline Griffith's talent, not to overindulge his weaknesses, which as
Schenck saw it were largely entrepreneurial. It took until mid-April to
settle Griffith's Famous Players contract and come to terms with
Schenck. Zukor was as generous with Griffith's leaving as he was with his
coming. In return for his company surrendering all rights to the films
Griffith had made for the studio, it agreed to pay off the remaining balance and interest on the old loan for *Isn't Life Wonderful* (close to
$100,000), forgive almost $35,000 in advances it had made against Griffith's salary and make a cash payment of $15,000 upon his signature of a
release of contract.[2]

The Schenck deal, in turn, was generally more sensible than the
Famous Players contract had been. Griffith's salary would be less—
$80,000 for "ordinary" pictures, $140,000 for "special" productions payable at a rate of $5,000 a week—but his profit participation on the total
of five films he agreed to make was improved, and so was his cash flow.
When he was between pictures he would receive a weekly salary of
$1,000, in return for which he agreed to consult and supervise on other
films at the company's discretion. This arrangement eliminated one of
the most troubling aspects of the Famous Players contract, as it permit-

ted Griffith to wait for, or develop, material he thought was right for him free of the pressure to start work in order to get paid. Schenck and Griffith also addressed the other area of contention that had developed at Famous Players, cost overruns. The arrangement they arrived at was much clearer, and involved no economic penalties for Griffith. The "ordinary" productions were budgeted at $400,000 or less, "specials" at figures to be mutually determined over $400,000, but there had to be a written agreement as to which category a film fell into before production began. Even if, somehow, an ordinary film turned into a special when it went over budget, Griffith's compensation would not and could not rise with the costs. Indeed, once a picture exceeded its budget, Griffith had only two options; he could turn it over to the studio to finish as it saw fit, or he could draw an additional $75,000—but not a penny more—to try to finish it as he wanted. He would be charged no penalties in the latter event, but neither would he be able to hover endlessly and expensively over a film, trying to cure its problems.

By industry standards, these limitations were not onerous; Schenck wanted Griffith present on his West Coast lot to keep not a wary eye on him but an avuncular one. And, given the relatively modest scale of his operation, that was something he, unlike Zukor with his vast empire abuilding, could do without resort to underlings—at least at first. As for Griffith, there was one other boon that was specified not by the new contract but by an older one. The price of buying his way out of his former arrangement with United Artists had been surrendering control of his stock in the company, to be regained only when he again started releasing through UA. Schenck was UA's president and all his Art Cinema productions went out through the Artists' exchanges. Griffith's corporation would be regaining one-fifth of its shares every time he finished a picture and have them all back in hand when he completed his obligation to Schenck.[3]

All in all, Griffith had done well for himself and he seemed to appreciate it. The United Artists lot, small and unstructured, perhaps reminded him of the old Fine Arts studio of a decade earlier, and his relationship with Schenck, at least in its first two years, was quite unstrained, almost collegial. And with "Joseph," as Griffith habitually addressed him, acting as an honest broker between the United Artists founders, much of their former tension was eased, and Griffith, Pickford and Fairbanks found themselves meeting on a basis more pleasant than it had been in years. His manner appears to have been cooperative, energetic and a little more than usually detached.

But if there is a sense of renewed possibilities, of modest cause to hope in Griffith's life this spring, there was also an ending to be endured. Carol Dempster had come West, too, and taken quarters on Elm Drive in Beverly Hills, some distance from Griffith's downtown hotel. There was obviously a certain estrangement between them, and even though she was no longer bound to Griffith by written contract, she obviously hoped he would use her in his Art Cinema productions. It is by no means certain, however, that he shared that desire. It may be that Dempster's talent was one of the indulgences Schenck intended to deny Griffith for his own good, but it seems more likely that Griffith intended to use Schenck's lack of enthusiasm for her as an excuse to rid himself of her.

This is contrary to the accepted interpretation of this passage in Griffith's life, which has the younger woman deserting the older man as his career falters and he cannot support her ambitions any longer. Yet there was no breach in the relationship between Griffith and Schenck at this point. The tone of their correspondence through 1927 and 1928 remains entirely cordial, as it surely would not have if the producer had forced an unwanted separation between Griffith and Dempster. Beyond that, the record of Griffith's mood and behavior at this time does not suggest a man grieving over a lost love but rather a man working hard at a fresh start. Finally, there is documentary evidence that as Dempster "aged" (she was all of 24 now, Gish's age when Dempster replaced her), Griffith's always roving eye had begun to fix itself on another young woman and that his feelings toward Dempster were now more guilty than grieving. If there was remorse, it came later, and perhaps as something of a surprise to him.

Griffith's first weeks on the Coast, however, were dominated not by his relationship with his sometime star, but by his relationship with his new employer. Schenck had unwisely decided to try to make a feature out of *Topsy and Eva*, a vaudeville act in which the Duncan sisters, Rosetta (who blacked up for the Topsy role) and Vivian, did a comic turn based on the Harriet Beecher Stowe characters. Lois Weber, the pioneering female director, had originally been engaged to direct but quit when she learned that she would not be permitted to make something more than an extended, not very tasteful, joke out of the material. Del Lord, a Sennett director, replaced her, but "made a mess of it," according to Raymond Klune, who had come West with Griffith. So, at Schenck's urgent request, Griffith "shot quite a few additional scenes and recut the greater part of it, and from the comments I have heard, improved it to a rare degree." As a matter of fact, Klune wrote Banzhaf, "J.S. made the remark that the picture is now worth $300,000 more. (It must have been worth about 40 cents before.)"[4] As was frequently the case, Schenck's enthusiasm had run away with him. The picture contains, according to Thomas Cripps, a good performance by the distinguished black actor Noble Johnson, as Uncle Tom, but is otherwise not a tribute to Tom, but shows ". . . a pathetic, regressive burlesque of [Griffith's] racial views."[5]

This overstates the extent of Griffith's responsibility for the finished product, but one can scarcely overstate Klune's good cheer over the way things were going on North Formosa Street. The only problem he saw was that Linda Griffith—or rather her lawyers—had been heard from anew, now that Griffith was once again employed, pursuing back alimony, and, perhaps, the notion of a lump-sum settlement that recurred, off and on, in the course of their seemingly endless saga of fiscal torment. Once again, Griffith was sulfurous about the matter, threatening to declare bankruptcy in order, finally, to escape her clutches. But Klune, who, like the rest of Griffith's financial advisors, had been all through this before, calmed him and, in his report to Banzhaf, turned briskly to the subject of Griffith's first feature for the Art Cinema. "It is supposed to be an excellent story," he chirped. "Work will start in about 2 weeks. He is making tests now." And then he added, "Not of our friend either." (Italics his.) In short, Dempster was gone—and with no regrets that Klune felt impelled to mention.[6]

Just when she departed Los Angeles cannot be said. She appears in the records just one more time, and then for the record as it were. On October 30, 1928, Klune addressed a letter to Miss C. M. Conway, the Griffith corporation's bookkeeper, setting forth the following information: In 1926, when Griffith and Famous Players began negotiating a conclusion of their contract the latter endeavored to sign Dempster to a contract at $1,250 per week. Griffith countered with an offer of the same figure for each week she actually worked, $500 for each idle week. Miraculously she accepted this less lucrative offer. Even more remarkably, "Mr. Griffith . . . never advised the Corporation of the existence of this verbal contract . . . but, however, admits that it is a definite commitment of the Corporation, made by himself as President. . . ." Since she had not worked in the two years since this agreement was reached, Conway was now directed to set up a new entry in her journal, "Non-Production Expense (Idle Time Talent)" in the amount of $52,000 (or 104 weeks at $500 per week) and begin sending checks to Dempster at her residence, the Plaza Hotel in New York.[7]

It was clearly a payoff, heart balm to use the old-fashioned word, though the sum of the settlement strikes one as quite reasonable. In any event, this belated settling of accounts, over a year after they had broken up, is the strongest possible evidence that Griffith was the moving force in dissolving their relationship, for if she had left him he surely would have felt no compulsion to aid her. If he had regrets, they did not surface until the summer of 1929, when Dempster married Edwin S. Larsen, a New York banker, with whom she was to enjoy a long, prosperous and happy marriage, deliberately far removed from the public eye. Griffith, it appears, was astonished by this turn of events and might well have given people the impression that his heavy drinking at the time was an effort to drown his sorrows, though, as we shall see, there were other reasons for him to take to the bottle around that time. As for Dempster, she made no public comments about her past prominence or her relationship with Griffith. Except this, recorded many years later: "I just never think about my days in pictures. I am always surprised that anyone remembers me. It was so long ago. So many of my movies were so sad. Maybe my fans would like to know that in real life Carol Dempster had a happy ending."[8]

At the time of their breakup, however, Griffith, as usual, had ample opportunity for romantic distraction. Around the time he was making *The Sorrows of Satan,* he had met Evelyn Baldwin, who would become his second wife a decade later. About seventeen at the time, she accompanied her mother to a charity function at the Astor Hotel in Times Square, where Griffith was living. At the party a man they did not recognize kept walking back and forth in front of them, staring at Evelyn. Finally he spoke to her: "You're Little Nell," he said. "I'm thinking of Dickens' Little Nell." Whereupon, having caught their attention, he introduced himself. It was Griffith, of course, explaining that he was contemplating a film of *The Old Curiosity Shop* and thought Baldwin looked just right for the role. A relationship of sorts developed from the meeting, of what intensity one cannot be certain. According to the lady, "he would call us occasionally when he came back to New York."[9] But it appears that as early as 1927 something a little less casual than that had grown between them, despite the discrepancy in their ages (he was now 52). For example, it is clear that Griffith shot a screen test of Baldwin, for on May 27, 1927, her mother, Sarah, wrote to Griffith reporting that she had shown the test to a plastic surgeon who had apparently been consulted about a nose job. He said "the required change can be effected in perfect safety, with very little inconvenience and with about a week's seclusion." She added a P.S. "Evelyn says: New York is bleak and dreary without the voice she loves to hear."[10] This was a condition she grew accustomed to, for aside from one six-month stay and several briefer trips, Griffith did not return to the city until 1931. In the first 18 months of his contract with Schenck he worked almost without cease, and completed three films.

2

Whatever pressures the waning days of his relationship with Dempster had placed on him were now lifted. So were those that had been generated by the struggle to keep his corporation functioning. It was still a drain on him—basically, he turned $1,000 a week over to it—but his labors continued to buy him the silence, however sullen, of his creditors. Above all, Schenck was in these days confident, reassuring. To put the matter simply, Griffith had, for the first time in this decade, breathing space.

And he needed it. Everyone in the picture business did in 1927. For the time of the great transition was at hand. *Don Juan* with its synchronized score had been a financial success. And a series of Vitaphone shorts—the series that had caused Jolson to recover from his camera-shyness even as he was going to court with Griffith to claim near-terminal affliction with the disease—had generated high, sometimes controversial, interest when they played the 100 or so houses then wired for talking pictures. Already the leading theater chains had met in secret conclave to agree not to use the Warner Brothers' pioneering system; already Zukor, who had participated in those meetings, was scurrying around behind his competitors' backs to see if he could break that agreement and induce the Warners to give his theaters an exclusive option on it. He failed, but only because the Warners were greedier than he was. Still, not to worry, both sides had a reason to be confident about their possibilities. Zukor and the other chain magnates had some 200 alternative systems, many of dubious patent lineage, but some of greater technological sophistication, to choose from. As for Warner Brothers, their system, though primitive (it depended on phonograph records that had to be fussily cued up in the theaters, rather than on a sound-on-film technique which eliminated many problems and would eventually carry the day), was in place; in April of 1927, a month before Griffith arrived in Los Angeles, his old nemesis Jolson had taken up labors on a specially refurbished stage on the old Warner lot on Sunset Boulevard on that historic, if dreadful, work, *The Jazz Singer*. It would premiere on October 6, 1927, a little more than three months before Griffith's first film for Art Cinema opened.

Still, in the summer of that year sound was only the cause for a certain anxiety, not yet of panic. Indeed, there was considerable sentiment for the view that the talking picture would remain what it was for the moment, a novelty that, often as not, annoyed movie patrons at least as much as it pleased them. The hiss of the recordings, their unnatural tones, their habit of falling out of synch, frequently led to complaints from the customers and to the oft-expressed opinion among the better critics and the leading filmmakers that no technology as tinny as this one, so prone to break the carefully wrought mood of a sophisticated silent film, could possibly endure for long.

And sophisticated films had become. Not just the self-consciously ambitious ones either. By this time it seemed that almost every director with aspirations beyond that of grinding out routine program pictures had taught himself what amounted to a new film language. What had begun as, perhaps, a regional dialect in Germany had become, by this time, a new international language. Lighting aimed now toward a much more modeled effect and sets were being designed by trained art directors, who were (to put the matter simply) building mood and character right into them. The camera, too, had become much more mobile, prowling these imaginary structures restlessly in search of the arresting image. They were craned and tilted up and down, they hung from the rafters and crouched on the floor, or rolled along on dollies next to the actors, in order that the audience might see as they saw. Cutting, too, grew more lapidary, more suggestive. In effect, the two-dimensional picture plane of the screen had been broken, and audiences were now being drawn into a third dimension. That illusionary dimension—depth—often implied another, psychological one that transcended, or tried to transcend, the purely behavioral. The attempt now was not merely to "photograph thought" but to suggest, through a variety of symbolic and technical means, the unconscious dimension. Another way of putting this is to say that Europeans in particular were attempting to bring to the screen at least some aspects of literary and artistic modernism. King Vidor, who with *The Crowd* in 1928 was to prove himself to be the greatest American-born director of the brief high-silent period, would later recall that it was not just the films arriving from Berlin, the impact of which was larger and more immediate than that of the Russian and Scandinavian movies, that influenced him, but expressionist and cubist painting. Surely, too, the effects of still photography as practiced by the first generation of camera artists—Stieglitz, Steichen, Weston and the rest—were beginning to assert an influence on the movies.

All of this became particularly clear in 1927 when F. W. Murnau, director of the much-admired *The Last Laugh* (and prior to that a brilliant retelling of the Dracula legend, *Nosferatu*), completed his first Hollywood film, *Sunrise*, for William Fox. A near-tragic romance, it contrasted the glamour (and the corrupting pull) of the city with the simple verities of countrified domesticity, both of which are shown in the most delicately heightened realism—expressionism that is not quite expressionism, if you will. The picture was a revelation (and unlike many influential silent films, remains so today) in that it demonstrated that, under subtle control, the techniques thought to be "experimental" could be employed not merely on obviously novel works, like Fritz Lang's masterful *Metropolis*, which arrived in the U.S. at this time, but to refresh and transform the basically banal material of popular romance.

In any case, this picture, which wrapped in mid-June of 1927, was as much the talk of Hollywood as *The Jazz Singer* was, for the word drifting off the Fox lot was that Murnau was doing right here, at the very center of the commercial industry, a film every bit as "artistic" as any of the imports that were causing such a stir among critics and informed audiences. It is a measure of Schenck's regard for Griffith that he hired one of *Sunrise*'s cameramen for his first Griffith film. Karl Struss, who would share the first Academy Award for cinematography with his co-worker on *Sunrise* Charles Rosher, reported to the United Artists lot the minute Murnau's film finished, and there he would stay as long as Griffith stayed, with the rehired Billy Bitzer working under him, and distinctly in Struss's style, which owed a great deal to the latter's parallel career as a distinguished salon photographer whose work had appeared in Stieglitz's *Camera Work* as early as 1912.

Nor was this the end of the pains to which Schenck went to ensure that Griffith might see his return to Hollywood as something of an artistic rebirth as well. He hired the first great American production designer, William Cameron Menzies, to create a style for Griffith's first Art Cinema project that would set it apart from his past work. Menzies had done *Rosita* for the Pickford-Lubitsch odd couple, the marvelous fantastic voyage that Fairbanks had undertaken in *The Thief of Bagdad*, and *Gone With the Wind* was in his future. For the first of his four assignments with Griffith, he would create a massively brooding, darkly romantic vision, that was indeed entirely without precedent in the director's canon. In fact, with Struss, he would provide whatever lasting interest there was to *Drums of Love*, as their first collaboration with Griffith was eventually called.

The subject matter of this enterprise also bespeaks Schenck's ambitions for Griffith, for it was a reworking of the romance of Paolo (Malatesta) and Francesca (da Rimini), immortalized by Dante and the subject, over the centuries, of operas, painting, poetry and drama—most recently a five-act tragedy by the American playwright George Henry Baker, written in 1855, but in revival a vehicle for Otis Skinner which Griffith surely knew at least by reputation. Its literary credentials were excellent and its reputation in traditional "cultural" circles impeccable. Indeed, one rather expects that they were too much so for Schenck, Griffith and the film's adapter, Gerrit Lloyd. Though for reasons clear only to them they agreed to change the story's setting from Renaissance Italy to Portuguese South America in the eighteenth century, they still treated it with a stately, not to say ponderous, reverence that is almost unbearably dull.

The essential elements of the classic triangle are, of course, preserved. A beautiful blond princess, here called Emanuella, is for political reasons betrothed to an ancient rival of her family, here known as the Duke Cathos de Avilia. Never having met him, she does not know—and no one bothers to inform her—that he is very much older than she, and as a title identifies him, a "super-dwarf" (actually a hunchback). He sends his handsome younger brother, Count Leonardo, to claim her. Something like love at first sight smites the younger pair, and this is something the older man, despite his mature charm and intelligence ("Forgive me, but so much love has been stored up in this old hulk—and now I know it's all for you"), cannot overcome. Emanuella and Leonardo are observed at their trysts—after the duke is called off to war, leaving his "most precious possession" in his brother's trust—by Bopi, the Duke's malevolent jester, who informs his master, who, in the first version of the story that Griffith shot, kills them, more in sorrow than in rage.

Griffith lingered, and lingered, over this not entirely novel or greatly edifying situation. His characteristically quick rhythms slowed to almost ceremonial pace. Perhaps he, too, was awed by his story's distinguished lineage or by Menzies's great sets. Perhaps he was slowed by the fact that *Drums of Love* reverses his former treatments of beauty and the bestial. When Emanuella first encounters the duke one half expects him to turn out to be Griffith's typically, and grotesquely, lascivious threat to youthful female innocence, and is surprised to find him develop, instead, into a model of sorrowing civility. More likely, he knew from the start that he was treading on dangerous movie ground, a tragedy that required him to kill characters with whom the majority of his audience was supposed to identify, and was concerned to overwhelm their resistance to this end by calling attention at every moment to the sobriety of his portentous art.

To this end, the picture is burdened with "touches" of the most obviously ironic sort. Some of them—like Emanuella's wedding night, in which she is seen backlit in her white dress in the gloomy bridal chamber, pleading in vain to be permitted to delay consummation for another night—are at least visually striking. Others are close to the risible. Among them one might number a shot of Emanuella reading Tennyson's "Camelot" (as *The Idylls of the King* are here identified so no one can miss the analogy) as she contemplates yielding to Leonardo. A candle flickering out, a doll representing the duke blowing over when she finally makes her decision to yield, are the not very subtle symbolizations of subsequent events. Later she is seen tucking a crucifix out of sight in her bodice, so it will not remind her of the moral obligations she has set aside in her passion.

There are also quite a large number of rather obvious glass or matte shots as they would now be called, in which painted background and live actors are melded not on the stage but optically, on the film negative itself. Some extraordinarily fine and virtually undetectable work of this kind had been accomplished before this date, but Griffith—if we are to believe a rationale offered by a publicist—was seeking not the real, but the unreal, a three-dimensional effect akin to that of some antique sketches he happened to see one day. The result, whatever the intention, is visually jarring.

But it may be that the largest factor in undoing the picture is an unintentional effect of Griffith's casting. As his young lovers he chose, or had chosen for him, Don Alvarado, yet another Valentino impersonator, but one of small grace or skill, and Mary Philbin, an ingenue whose best previous work had been as the singer beloved by Lon Chaney's *Phantom of the Opera* and as object of Conrad Veidt's affections in *The Man Who Laughed* (his tragedy was that his mouth was twisted permanently into the rictus of laughter). Indeed, this rather cool and stiff actress might have got the part with Griffith because she was identified in the public mind as the permanent romantic victim of the touchingly damaged. In this case, done up in a blond wig, she was playing opposite yet another highly accomplished actor, Lionel Barrymore, who given a chance at a Chaney-like role, made the most of it, in a subtly dominating performance that has the effect of drawing all sympathy toward him. Thus, in the ending as originally made, it is perhaps not so much the death of the lovers, an uninteresting couple throughout, that disturbed audiences, but the fact that it is Barrymore's duke who having won their hearts must now yield to the dictates of "honor" and put them to death. One does not want him to do so, and does not totally believe him capable of the act.

The film did not open in New York until January 24, 1928, before the usual "celebrity-packed house," with Morris Gest once again prowling the lobby of his Liberty Theater, fussing over the comfort of David Belasco, Max Reinhardt and the rest of the show folks and literati, while the uninvited gathered in the drizzle outside to catch a glimpse of them. The reviews were almost uniformly respectful but unenthusiastically so. Quinn Martin of the *World* was entirely typical when he wrote that "I had not seen in all my days before the cinema screen episodes photographed in so altogether exquisite a fashion," but also called the picture "at times lazy and noticeably lacking in spirit and pace." He found himself wondering "what may be the effect on forthcoming audiences of so altogether unhurried a method. . . ." In the *Telegram*, Leonard Hall crudely, but with admirable forthrightness, summarized not only his feelings but those of the majority of his faintly praising colleagues when he wrote: "Reviewing a Griffith picture is like nothing else in the experience of an American picture fan. For, after all, D. W. has been our first and foremost, our best beloved, our pet genius whom we could always count when the great lords from overseas—the Murnaus, the Lubitsches and the Stillers—arrived with their great bags of tricks to show us how it is done. And that's why it's so tarnation sad when the Grand Old Man turns out a 'Drums of Love.'"[11]

Despite the fact that Schenck stood solidly behind the picture—"You too will find it Griffith's greatest," ran the headline in one ad—returns on the New York run were not many or happy, and Griffith addressed himself to the problem not one of the reviews mentioned, namely, the film's tragic ending. It was obviously impossible to lift the mood of gloomy foreboding that hung over every shot in the film, nor was it possible to avoid an unhappy finish of some sort. But the ending he concocted was in better keeping with the Duke de Avilia's character as Barrymore portrayed it than the previous one had been. Now, confronting the guilty lovers, the older man finds that he cannot bring himself to wreak vengeance upon them. Instead, when his jester (overplayed, incidentally, by that usually reliable character actor, Tully Marshall) reminds him of the debt he owes to honor, the duke stabs his tormentor and is himself stabbed in return. As he lies dying, his brother and wife beg forgiveness, which he nods, and a title has him say: "Only blood could wash this from the honor of the Avilias. It—it—is best that it should be my blood." As the lovers fall to their knees, praying for Heaven's forgiveness, one cannot help but agree with him, for this ending completes the arc of the duke's character, as Barrymore played him, far more logically than its predecessor did. Since it is every bit as lugubrious, however, it is hard to see how it answered the objections of the sales department, and, indeed, it appears not to have improved the film's box office prospects in the slightest. An attempt to get the New York critics to re-review the revised film failed, and without the guidance of the opinion leaders, the out-of-town reviews were far harsher than the first notices.

As the picture went into general release in the spring and summer of 1928, reports from the theater owners were dismal. Here and there audiences actually laughed at the excesses of passion demonstrated in the picture. By summer, Klune was advising a new Griffith employee, Ed Lindeman, who had been put on to represent Griffith's interests with the United Artists sales department, that it was all right to allow UA to force *Drums of Love* on theaters that were expressing interest in the next Griffith production, which, for some reason, everyone expected to be a big hit, but not to allow them to shift their payments from the old picture to the forthcoming one. His largest hopes now lay with foreign distribution of the film, he said, but he still wanted every penny that could be realized on *Drums of Love*, hoping against hope for profit and the Griffith Company's percentage thereon.[12]

There was no break between the *Drums of Love* revisions and Griffith's next film. In manner, style, approach, *The Battle of the Sexes*—which is as careless in the making as *Drums* was careful—represents a veering contrast to its predecessor. Though Schenck has been blamed for this choice of projects, it is by no means certain that he imposed it on a reluctant Griffith. Relations between the two men remained mutually admiring. While he was at work on *Battle*, Banzhaf wired him for instructions as to what, as a director of United Artists, Griffith wanted to do about a raise Schenck was asking to compensate him for the increased duties he had undertaken since the sudden death of Hiram Abrams the previous fall. Griffith's reply was to vote for it: "HAVE NEVER MORE WILLINGLY AGREED TO PAY ANYONE SO WORTHY OF IT."[13] Beyond that it must be observed that the contrast between this film and its predecessor was not more vivid than some of those that are visible in Griffith's record as an independent. It was not more startling, for example, than the difference between *Way Down East* and *Dream Street,* or *Orphans of the Storm* and *One Exciting Night.* We may also suppose that Griffith had a certain sentimental regard for the film's source, which was his own previous movie of the same title, the first of his films for Reliance-Majestic after leaving Biograph in 1914. Finally, he perhaps saw in the story line a chance to make a guardedly autobiographical statement. This need to impose upon what at best might have been a comedy of (slightly dated) manners surely accounts for the faltering tone of the picture, which teeters sometimes on the brink of farce, sometimes on the brink of tragedy, but only rarely evokes any emotion but discomfort.

The story is, so far as one can tell (the earlier version of *The Battle of the Sexes* having been lost), much as it was before. A married man (Jean Hersholt, halfway between the evil Marcus of *Greed* and his kindly Dr. Christian of latter-day radio) is seduced by a younger woman (Phyllis Haver, in the kind of flapper role she specialized in) who, with her boyfriend (Don Alvarado again), intends to work a badger game on the older man. His wife discovers his infidelity and is driven to the edge of suicide. Her rooftop contemplation of this act, complete with fantasies of it, is the picture's most powerful, if inappropriate, scene. Their daughter, the pert, pretty Sally O'Neil, confronts the golddigger in her apartment, threatening to kill her, but "Babe" the accomplice (described in one memorable title as "perfumed ice"), intervenes, and when the girl's father enters later he discovers her and "the wrong answer to a maiden's prayer" (to borrow another title) in what seems a compromising situation. When he begins a moral lecture, his daughter tells him he has sacrificed his right to judge her. This brings him to his senses, and later we find daughter informing mother, "Mumsey, Mumsey, Daddy's gotten over his sick spell." After which, he contritely concedes: "I've had a bitter, bitter lesson, Mother. Can you forgive me?"

Despite the film's overt moral, Griffith's sympathy for bourgeois values strikes one as *pro forma.* In the early passages one feels almost as if some reels from a W. C. Fields comedy have been mixed into *The Battle of the Sexes,* so awful are the children, so constricting the life of the Hersholt character's family. All Griffith's sympathy, even when there are elements of satire in it, lies with the older man. There is, for example, as much pathos as there is comedy in scenes where Hersholt, who always plays in a befuddled and victimized fashion, is seen working out in a gym, or donning a corset in a vain attempt to reduce his waistline to youthful proportions. And there is really nothing funny at all about a scene in which he is seen rolling $20 bills into his lover's hair and she is observed stealing more while he is thus distracted.

At some point in contemplating this picture, the thought inescapably occurs that in its projection of its central character it is not as far as it seems from *Drums of Love.* Their situations, their characterizations

could not be in greater contrast, but they are both the middle-aged victims of younger people and their vigorous passions, both, finally, the ob-
jects of the director's pity. The raging masculine beast that Griffith has
recognized in himself and had turned loose in so many of his earlier films
has become, in these late works, a rather threadbare tiger, forced to confront and accept a dismally declining lot.

As, perhaps, Griffith himself was, not merely in the agreeably passive gratitude with which he served his savior Schenck, but in his relationships with women as well. In New York for the *Drums of Love* premiere,
his nephew Willard, now also in his employ, had introduced him to a
very much younger woman named Hazel, with whom, obviously, he had
undertaken what he understood to be a casual affair. Money appears to
have changed hands—the lady was not well off—and now she was writing
him, thanking him for his "assistance," asking for more ("I guess you'll
have to be my guardian or something—will you?") and hinting that she
would not entirely mind a healthful trip to the West Coast.[14] Griffith
sent a check, but obviously suggested that she not think of him as a permanent source of help. He had, in one way or another, always paid for
the favors of young women, but now and in the future—always excepting
his relationship with Evelyn Baldwin—there would be a nakedness in his
need, and often in the nature of his transactions, with the "Hazels" and
the "Babes" and the "Lillians" (no Gish, she), that is hard to reconcile
with his public image at the time, or for that matter with his historical
image.

As for the film itself, it carried high hopes into its initial New York
engagement. "Let me tell you that they love it," Klune wrote to Lindeman of reaction around the studio. "It has been a long while since I can
remember having anything to do with such a well-liked picture."[15] And
when a print was sent to United Artists New York headquarters, the sales
manager, Al Lichtman, though he had some criticisms about pacing and
an anticlimactic ending, fairly burbled telegraphically: "I LIKE PICTURE
VERY MUCH THINK IT WILL PLEASE ALL CLASSES OF PEOPLE SHOULD PROVE
BOX OFFICE WINNER . . . EVERYBODY HIGHLY PLEASED AND BELIEVE SHOULD
MAKE GOOD PROFIT. . . ."[16]

Griffith himself had some doubts about the synchronized music
track, which he felt fought the mood of certain scenes, and was ambiva-
lently concerned with the film's effect on his reputation. On the one hand
he was quoted as saying, "Here I promise one picture with real entertainment," while brother Albert was reassuring United Artists executives that
it would prove he did not make pictures exclusively "for the critics and
the highbrows." All well and good, and Griffith was indeed concerned
that the film not be oversold, as his previous effort had been ("we certainly cannot advertise it as a great production or as one of Griffith's greatest," he advised). But on the other hand he also thought that a compari-

son with, perhaps, Chekhov's short stories was not entirely out of order, and he wondered if a guiding hint along those lines might not be dropped to some of the better critics.[17]

If it was, it had no discernible effect, for it is impossible to find a Griffith film that was more catastrophically received by reviewers. Richard Watts, Jr., spoke for the vast majority when he described *The Battle of the Sexes* in the *Herald Tribune* as "a badly acted, unimaginatively directed and thoroughly third-rate sex drama."[18] "A little more pretentious, perhaps, than its predecessors, a whole lot drearier, and tricked out here and there with evidences of distinctly bad taste,"[19] added Katherine Zimmerman in the *Telegram*. Even tabloids like the *Mirror* and the *Graphic* were contemptuous, while *Variety* was typical of the trade press: "Patrons lured to this one by the Griffith bulbs are slated for disappointment, almost shock."[20]

Resort to the ironic might have given this film a wry and worldly unity of tone, permitting Griffith to tell his story in an even voice, obviating the need for his inappropriate descents into the near farcical in recounting the husband's transgressions, the ludicrous melodrama of the daughter's activities. It was juxtaposition of all these rather desperate attempts to give dramatic life to his film that in turn gave rise to questions of "taste"—and to the movie's wild mood swings, which caused so many of the reviewers to suggest—quite correctly—that it was amateurishly out of control.

With this otherwise gratefully forgotten movie we come close to the heart of Griffith's problems in this endless period when he groped for something to say and the means of saying it. We have seen, in both *The Sorrows of Satan* and *Drums of Love*, that with the assistance of *au courant* craftsmen he could find visual styles that were comfortable for him, yet satisfying to those who demanded new levels of "modernity" in screen imagery. We have seen, as well, that whenever he worked with material that was distant in time or space from contemporary American reality the strengths of his sensibility—its forthright sentimentality, its black-and-white morality, its romantic-nostalgic feeling for the past and even for the old-fashioned dramatic conventions—were acceptably, if not excitedly, received by critics and his audience. It is only when he imposed that sensibility on modern stories, modern settings—in *One Exciting Night, That Royle Girl*, and now in *The Battle of the Sexes*—that his work appeared at painfully obvious disadvantage to his competitors. In other words, Griffith, no less than an actor, needed to be type-cast, steered toward his strengths.

Whether Schenck had the temperament or the time for such an effort is obviously an open question. Whether Griffith, battered by the ill fortune of recent years, and eager to keep heedlessly busy, could have stopped to think or to accept counsel that called attention to his limits is also a question. And, as it happens, a moot one. For even before post-production work on *The Battle of the Sexes* was finished, it was "definitely decided that we are going to do *The Love Song*." It was, said Klune, "a very fine story, and should be a real Griffith picture." He expected that it would be ready to open by the end of the year.[21]

Circumstances were pushing Schenck, who was, in turn, pushing Griffith. The scenario, based on a story by Karl Vollmoeller, the German author of *The Miracle*, Max Reinhardt's international stage success, was the work of Sam Taylor, a rising star among writer-directors of comedies. Cowriter and director of some of Harold Lloyd's most successful features, he had gone on to more sophisticated, if not necessarily better, things with Schenck and Talmadge. Now he was about to move still further up the Hollywood ladder by writing and directing Pickford's hugely success-ful *Coquette*, to be followed by adaptation and direction of Pickford and Fairbanks's first talkie, *The Taming of the Shrew*, which owes most of its posthumous fame, alas, to the credit Taylor received on the early prints: "By William Shakespeare. Additional dialogue by Sam Taylor." He was apparently too preoccupied either with these weighty ventures or their important stars to undertake production of the film that was eventually released as *Lady of the Pavements*. And so, Griffith was prevailed upon. And for some reason accepted the assignment.

Schenck gave him Lupe Velez, who had scored a hit opposite Fair-banks in *The Gaucho* that year, as his leading lady. She might not have been his type, but she was good copy—"Whoopie Lupe" as the headline writers styled her, though not yet the "Mexican Spitfire" of the B-picture series she was doing at the end of her life. To play opposite her, Griffith was assigned William Boyd, a DeMille discovery, a stolid, popular lead-ing man, but not yet what he was to become either, namely, Hopalong Cassidy. His third star was Jetta Goudal, a statuesque French actress who had emigrated to the United States after the war and pursued a minor, short-lived career on stage and screen.

As for the story: "When you learn that a haughty and faithless countess, told by her indignant fiance that he would rather marry a woman of the streets, plans vengeance by plotting to make him fall in love with a cabaret performer disguised as a girl from a convent, you probably can figure out fifteen minutes after the film opens how everything is going to work out. . . ."[22] So wrote Richard Watts, Jr., when the film opened in New York, having premiered in Los Angeles, and contrary to the usual practice with Griffith pictures, having opened in various key cities across the country, supported by Velez's personal appearances on stage with it, which she would repeat in New York. Schenck was clearly hoping to get some money out of the picture before the New York reviews could harm its repute.

In fact, however, these notices were not horrendous. "Indifferent" would be a more appropriate word. The film was praised, legitimately, for its handsome photography and sets—it may, indeed, be the slickest Griffith production next to *The Sorrows of Satan*—and, again correctly, criticized for a rather bland and suspenseless working out of the plot. Griffith really had no taste for the kind of refined social cruelty that is central to the plot of *Lady of the Pavements* and, of course, no understanding of life in diplomatic circles during the Second Empire. It is certainly true that the film's liveliest passages take place in The Smoking Dog café, where the Velez character makes her living as a singer, not in the ballrooms and boudoirs of the upper orders. Whether this is because Griffith was more comfortable in these environs or whether Velez, whose stock-in-trade, a manic energy, simply compels the kind of attention that neither Boyd nor Goudal could attract, it is impossible to say.

The New York opening offered a new kind of humiliation for Griffith. For the first time he was treated as a vehicle director. In part because of her personal appearances, in part because of her then current affair with Gary Cooper, in part because of her general, good-time-girl reputation ("Spies report that 'Whoopee Lupe' has threatened to paint the town red before she goes back to Hollywood"[23]) she dominated the reviews and the feature stories. Watts, for example, did not get around to mentioning the name of the picture in which she was starring until he was two-thirds of the way through his review, so entranced was he by her on-stage performance, which consisted of songs, stories and impersonations of, among others, Gloria Swanson, Dolores Del Rio and her costar Goudal. "It is something of an indication of the new star's value that she receives so much space in the review of a photoplay directed by the distinguished D. W. Griffith," he wrote. Others did not bother with even that much of an apology for mentioning her director only in passing. It is poignantly ironic that, after fearing for so long the presence of stars in his films, it was a minor phenomenon like Lupe Velez, not one of the great ones, who delivered this blow to his ego.

It hurt. He had invited Molly Picon and Jacob Kalich to a preview and they "were terribly disturbed at the complete indifference of all those assembled. . . . After the picture was over, he took us to Lupe Velez and introduced us to her and as we left the theater his only remark was, 'No brains, no brains.' " Then, taking Kalich by the arm, he said, "Come, let's go back to your world, people are kinder there." As was their wont, the two men sat up over a bottle of slivovitz until the small hours, talking about religion and mysticism. Before he left, Griffith—perhaps rendered self-pitying by drink—signed a guest album for Miss Picon. He wrote, "There is no more," and signed it "D. W."[24]

3

But there was more. And at least in its promise, not all of it was as gloomy as Griffith's mood on this occasion. In fact, by dint of his labors, continued collections on old films, and stringent economies, D. W. Griffith, Inc., was, as of December 31, 1928, substantially out of debt, except for $3,000 still owed the Shubert theater chain, probably for some test engagements that year of a version of *Way Down East* with a sound track added. Though no profit had accrued to the company from this experiment, or ever would, it was financed by the purchase, at bargain rates, of a block of United Artists stock which it held, by Griffith for $25,000, stocks that would prove vital to his future well-being, as it turned out. Finally, Banzhaf reported a confidential advisory from the Treasury Department that it would shortly be refunding taxes overpaid by the corporation as far back as 1921. In the event, the rebate would be only about $38,000, but, miraculously, it was intelligently invested (by Klune, in the face of history's worst bear market) and it would, despite the crash of 1929, throw off dividends and provide some of the capital that helped the company to make one last, ill-advised attempt at independent production. That, however, was in the future. For the moment, Griffith could compliment himself on what he had accomplished in four years of contractual servitude. He might not have added anything to his reputation or his personal fortune, but he had rescued his company and his name from the disgrace of bankruptcy. He could afford, now, to pause, rest and contemplate the inevitable—his first sound production—in some leisure. Or so it seemed.

He came East with Schenck in January 1929 and he would stay at the Astor in New York until well after *Lady of the Pavements* had opened—roughly six months in all. It was during this period that his relationship with Evelyn Baldwin ripened (though there were several more casual liaisons as well). At the same time, and despite or because of Linda's pending legal action over her neglected alimony payments, he also sought a *rapprochement* with her. He found in her a surprisingly supportive consultant regarding his plans for the future. Alone of those who could catch his attention, she appears to have had some sense of how the contradictions between his gifts and the current movie climate might be resolved. She saw that he could not go on lurching after the latest fads and fashions. Nor were some of his former themes and preoccupations still viable. But his historical imagination, especially when it was directed toward the American past—that was a different matter. There had always been, and there still was, a steady interest in historical sagas. They would not go out of style until our own time. And besides, his name was favorably associated in the public mind with work in this vein. As she would say to him a little later, when events had proved her correct, "You are America's film historian through blood, tradition and poetic feeling."[25]

With this assessment he seemed to agree. For though he sent on to Schenck a number of ideas, including *The Cradle of the Deep* (a bestselling autobiography in which the young author, Joan Lowell, claimed—exaggeratedly—that she had spent the first seventeen years of her life at sea without schooling or the other amenities of childhood) and an unproduced play variously called *Commonsense Bronson* and *Commonsense Brackett* (which he thought "could be made the first pastoral, on the order of *Way Down East*, since the inception of talking pictures"), and though it was briefly thought he might be asked to do the screen adaptation of *Journey's End*, it was historical material that fired his imagination. He talked of an epic about the rise and fall of the Confederacy, a history of Texas and a story called *The Pioneer Women*, which Schenck unenthusiastically optioned for him.

But the months dragged on, and no conclusion was reached. There were problems on both sides. Schenck genuinely feared and disliked talking pictures and seems to have been rendered uncharacteristically indecisive when confronted with them. "Talking doesn't belong in pictures," he was once heard to decree. He also groused, not entirely inaccurately, that "the trouble with the whole industry is that it talked before it thought."[26] He was not a comfortably literate man, and the process of making decisions in this brave new world, a process that involved the evaluation of literary properties and the detailed analysis of long scripts, put him off. Nor had he been much encouraged by a radio broadcast, a year earlier, in which all the United Artists stars (Fairbanks, Pickford, Barrymore, Dolores Del Rio, Talmadge, Gloria Swanson and Griffith—who gave a seemingly self-contradictory talk on "love in all its phases, eschewing the sex angle completely") gathered behind the locked doors of Pickford's bungalow on the lot to prove to their not completely breathless fans that they could all speak if need be. Because the press had been excluded from the premises, rumors of ghost voices abounded, and at some of the theaters where the regular schedule was interrupted so that patrons could hear the show, moans and boos were heard, admissions had to be refunded and the pictures people had paid to see hastily switched back on.

On his part, Griffith now set aside the theoretical objections to talking pictures which he had so recently stated, and voiced public enthusiasm for the opportunities presented by the new technology. In an interview he gave to a trade journal he predicted, accurately, that 30 years hence the only place silent pictures would be shown would be in special screening rooms, museums in effect, where "People will laugh . . . and say, 'And that's what papa and mama thought was real entertainment. . . .'" Very simply, he noted what all the critics of the talkies had failed to mention, which was that they actually did offer the potential for expressive possibilities that the silent film, for all its sophistication, could not match. Perhaps this potential was not yet visible—or more properly, audible—but it was there, and it did not necessarily have to detract from the glories of montage and *mise-en-scène* which had evolved so quickly in the silent era. As he put it: "Imitation of stage technique will kill the talking picture if it is continued. . . . The dialogue picture can only succeed . . . when [it] is essentially a silent picture with the addition of dialogue. When this is done successfully you will see the greatest entertainment the world has ever witnessed." But, he continued, "We must preserve all the speed, action, swirl, life and tempo of the motion picture today. Add dialogue to that and, boy, you will have people standing in their seats cheering."[27]

To Griffith, as he considered it in the abstract, sound was no different from what the movies themselves had been when he came into them. It presented the director with an opportunity to invent a new set of storytelling conventions by which, if he was good and lucky, he could impress some part of his sensibility on the new medium. And the sound film was just that—essentially a new medium, not merely the old one enhanced. A couple of months after this long interview, when a reader wrote the *Sunday World* claiming, "You will never see a man of the good sense and artistic appreciation of D. W. Griffith falling for this new and artificial piece of machinery," the newspaper asked him for a response. It was simple: "I am nutty over talking pictures. . . ."[28]

This opportunistic enthusiasm for any and all new technologies was one of Griffith's most agreeable, and American, characteristics. Remember that even before he had found any esthetic justification for sound, he had experimented with it in *Dream Street* as well as with color and wide screen techniques. In fact, just weeks after expounding so cheerfully on the future of talkies, he was participating in an experiment with a far wilder dream—television. On February 3, 1929, he traveled to the studios of WGY, the General Electric company station in Schenectady, to read a fifteen-minute speech on the subject of success in the movies. He told his familiar stories about the rise of people like Pickford and Valentino from obscurity to fame and added one about Lupe Velez arriving in Los Angeles with $20 in her pocket and becoming a star in two years, thus plugging his latest film. He concluded with a recital of the communications miracles of recent times—films, radio, talking pictures and now "this last miracle of miracles," television, which he said ought to make everyone "deeply thankful that we live in this grand and glorious age and in this grand glorious country. . . ."[29] It required the signals of three facilities, one long wave and two short wave, to beam Griffith's voice and image across the continent, but, sure enough, it arrived there. The next day's *New York Times* reported on its front page (along with news of a

similar transmission from America to England by the Marconi company)
that according to Gilbert Lee, an amateur experimenter in Los Angeles,
"the speech was heard clearly throughout a fifteen-minute period and
that during the first few minutes Mr. Griffith's eyes, nose and mouth were
clearly identified in the reproduced television image."[30]

But if Griffith was intellectually up to the challenge of any and all
new technologies—rather more so than most people—spiritually and psychologically the task of working with them in his own medium was clearly
daunting to him. Given a chance to rest, he became aware of the toll the
decade had taken on him, and though he could play a confident confidence game when an interviewer was present, the first long pause he had
taken since he had gone to work for Biograph over 20 years before did not
refresh him. On the contrary, it seemed to make him anxious and restless,
a condition that steadily worsened as Schenck rejected one proposal after
another for his next film.

Relations between the two men remained polite, but it is clear that
the producer was losing confidence in Griffith, since overall his films,
which by Schenck's estimate averaged a gross of about $625,000 apiece,
were no more than break-even propositions. Still, as Tino Balio observes,
this was better than Schenck's brother-in-law Keaton's films did (an astonishing fact, that, considering the quality of that work), not to mention
those of John Barrymore and Dolores Del Rio. Moreover, the distribution fees Griffith's films generated contributed greatly to the turnaround
Schenck effected at United Artists (which showed major profits—of $1.3
and $1.8 million—for the first time in its history in 1928 and 1929).[31] But
that was not enough for a high roller like Schenck. He operated on the
abiding principle that has guided movie magnates from the beginning
until the present moment, which is that modest profits do not compensate one for the immodest risks and the immodest troubles any major
film creates.

As for Griffith, his long stay in New York made communications
with "Joseph" difficult, and even when the producer was in New York it
appeared that he was dodging the director, though he might simply have
been too busy with his multitude of responsibilities. As a result of the
pressures on him, Schenck began layering assistants around him, which
must have caused Griffith to fear (rightly as it turned out) that he was
in for a repetition of his experience at Famous Players. Then, after *Lady
of the Pavements* opened, he was taken entirely off salary, even his $1,000
a week consulting fee stopped, on the ground that he was not in Los
Angeles, which was the only place he could usefully render the service
specified. This, of course, deepened his anxiety, especially since Linda—
despite her friendly attitude toward Griffith personally—was beginning
to ask Banzhaf just when they might expect their percentage of Griffith's
income to start flowing in again. The lawyer also reported regular ques-

tions from Griffith corporation shareholders about Griffith's plans. There was, still, a steady stream of inquiries from other producers wondering if Griffith might be free to undertake assignments from them, but that would have necessitated an open breach with Schenck, probably accompanied by lawsuits and other public signs that Griffith was once again in trouble. Worse, such a course would jeopardize Griffith's United Artists holdings, which, since Schenck's advent, were rising mightily in value. In all, his lawyerly advice was to get back to work. Indeed, he pointed out that if he had held to his old work patterns, Griffith might have made one, possibly two, pictures during the time he was lazing about in New York.[32]

All very reasonable and businesslike. But callous as well. Griffith was now 53 years old. He had suffered a long season of debilitating financial and artistic reverses. He had labored unceasingly for years, struggling up from poverty, carrying Bert Banzhaf among many others along with him. Surely he was entitled now to a period of personal retrenchment and reflection. No? Very well, he would drink some more. Only an alcoholic haze, apparently, could dim his misery. And that, too, harmed him in Schenck's eyes. Surely reports of Griffith's drunkenness reached him; surely they deepened his sense that Griffith was no longer worth the troubles he caused. In any event, at some point in this period his attitude toward Griffith began to change. There was no longer any warmth in his courtesy. There was a hint that he would not object if Griffith cared to resign.

Whether Griffith—or Schenck—clearly understood what Schenck was thinking is hard to say; Griffith himself was not good at sly maneuver and was not quick to recognize it either. But Schenck's coldness he could read, and in this last spring of the decade Griffith's drinking passed from the heavy to the alarming category; he was getting started on his depression a few months before the nation as a whole got started on its.

Still, he was prevailed on to get back to the Coast, get back in personal touch with Schenck—and get back on the wagon. This last desire caused him to detour on his way West and stop off at Mineral Wells, Texas, for a cure. He took up residence in a hostelry referred to variously in telegrams addressed to him there as the Crazy or Krazy Hotel—no ironies intended. Apparently he liked it, for he returned there at least once in the future—and had "crazy water," the spa's mineral water, shipped to him on both coasts. Apparently his rest accomplished what everyone hoped it would do for him, for he returned to Los Angeles "a prohibitionist" as Evelyn lightly phrased it in one of the many sweetly yearning letters she wrote to him during this period.[33] She was not yet 20, but there is a maturity mixed with the girlishness of her letters, and an obviously uncomplicated love for him that must have been—should have been—heartening to him. She made not a single demand on him, preferring instead to dwell on her adventures studying acting and dancing (Griffith, without prompting from her, set up an interview for her with Belasco from which nothing came) and on her fond memories of their good times together. Even when she heard he was keeping company with other ladies she took a humorous and unthreatening tack. ("What's this I hear about you running around with a beautiful brunette? I 'keel her!! And you too!! I'll do it with my little hatchet. . . ."[34]) Above all, she was everlastingly confident and supportive about his work. ("I am praying for you every day, that you will keep well, and that your next picture will be a marvelous success. But whether it is or not, I know it will be very good. Your worst would be a thousand times better than anyone else's best, and that is no exaggeration."[35])

She would have found few on the United Artists lot that summer who would agree with her. At the studio there was only evasiveness about the next film, and a continuing unpleasantness about Griffith's compensation. By now it seems that Schenck was definitely trying to drive Griffith into breaking his contract, but that he was still not ready to face the public consequences of doing so himself, knowing that Griffith and his corporation would have sued, and probably won, since he had committed no breaches of its terms.

In any event, sometime in the late summer or the early fall, Griffith finally came up with an acceptable idea, a biography of Abraham Lincoln. His admiration for his subject dated back to boyhood, when he was imbued with the not uncommon southern reverence for the magnanimity and wisdom of the man who had defeated the Confederacy, a view of him that had of course informed *The Birth of a Nation*. What turned Griffith's thought to Lincoln at this time is not known, though it is almost certain that he must have read the first two volumes of Carl Sandburg's hagiographic biography, dealing with "The Prairie Years," which had been published to considerable popular success in 1926. For immediately after Schenck gave him tentative approval of the project—he apparently agreed with Linda that if Griffith had any remaining commercial viability it was as a maker of historical spectacle—Griffith got in touch with the poet, who had also reviewed films among his other duties as a writer for the *Chicago Daily News*, offering him a modest fee for a week or two's consultation on the screenplay, the first unsatisfactory draft of which he and Gerrit Lloyd had worked out.

The poet, who was at work on the concluding volumes of his biography and had conceived a powerful proprietary interest in Lincoln, wanted a deeper involvement than that of a consultant. He wired:

KEENLY INTERESTED IN SEEING LINCOLN PICTURE DONE WHICH WILL BE A SERIES OF PERSONALITY SKETCHES SETTING FORTH HIS TREMENDOUS RANGE OF TRAGIC AND COMIC. . . . KNOW ALMOST

PRECISELY WHAT IS WANTED FOR HISTORIC ACCURACY WOVEN WITH
DRAMATIC INTEREST. . . . ALL PAST PRESENTATIONS HAVE FAKED
HOKUM WHILE NEGLECTING ESTABLISHED AND ENTERTAINING DRA-
MATIC VALUES OF LINCOLN. . . .[36]

Ultimately, Griffith would follow Sandburg's advice; his *Abraham
Lincoln* would be a highly episodic work, alternating anecdotal incident
and great historical moments. But Sandburg would not contribute to it.
Despite an offer to cancel a number of his recital engagements and to
bring with him to the Coast a collection of books, pictures and notes
about Lincoln which he claimed was "the most compact and human ever
assembled," his asking price of $30,000 was too stiff.

Schenck was determined to keep the price of the picture down. Indeed, he insisted that although the film was to be budgeted as a "special,"
Griffith's salary should be calculated as if it were an "ordinary" picture,
meaning that Griffith was taking a $60,000 pay cut to do the film. Worse,
Schenck asked Griffith to forego his $1,000 a week consultant fee while
the picture was in production and to permit him to charge against his
salary the $1,000 per week he had been receiving since returning to the
studio on July 20. No question about it now: Schenck was doing his best
to drive Griffith into quitting, though he continued to insist that it was
hard times, and the poor returns on Griffith's first three pictures, that
were forcing him to seek these adjustments.

Griffith was outraged. He wanted to quit, sue—and try to raise
$500,000 in order to finance the production himself. There were panicky
bicoastal consultations, into which Epping, who had resigned as the
Griffith corporation's treasurer, was called. Thanks to Griffith's hard work
and Klune's good management the per share value of his corporation's
stock had risen from nothing to about $4.00, which meant that if borrow-
ings could be avoided and Griffith kept working and especially if its now
increasingly valuable United Artists holdings could be retained, the possibility of an honorable liquidation, with shareholders getting at least some
of their money back, was suddenly a real possibility. The consensus, therefore, was to try to reach a compromise with Schenck.

After several weeks of hard bargaining, one was worked out. Art
Cinema abandoned its demands for salary reductions and deductions,
Griffith agreed to allow his consulting fee to lapse after nineteen more
weeks, and both sides agreed to let the fifth picture called for by the original contract slip into limbo: if they mutually agreed to make it, all well
and good; if not, no breach of contract would be implied. As Klune reported, "it took a good deal of patience on the part of Mr. Griffith" to
reach this arrangement, "and he well understood its complications." As
Klune put it: "It, of course, is now obligatory for him to make a knock-
out picture. If he does, he won't need to worry about a contract because

I believe Art Cinema Corporation will be first in line to be after him. On the other hand, if he doesn't make a good picture, the attitude which was so clearly expressed during the last two weeks will be expressed again, to a much more disagreeable extent I am afraid. . . . Mr. Griffith fully realizes what we are doing and is more determined than ever now that 'Abraham Lincoln' shall be a great picture."[37]

As was, and is, so often the case, the film's fate might already have been predetermined by the studio. Whether consciously or unconsciously, Schenck and his henchmen might have decided that if he could not be gotten rid of cleanly, a dirty job would do—by politely sabotaging his last-chance production. But he had a worthy star, Walter Huston, new in Hollywood after a long vaudeville career and a short Broadway career (notably in *Desire Under the Elms*), committed to the project. The next task was to produce a satisfactory final draft script. Rupert Hughes, the popular novelist, who had many years of screenwriting experience, turned him down, on the ground of his preoccupation with the biography of another president, George Washington, and so, on the very night that Klune was recounting the final outcome of the autumn's economic drama, Griffith entrained for New York and conferences with Stephen Vincent Benét, the 31-year-old poet whose long epic *John Brown's Body* had just won the Pulitzer Prize, and which Griffith had admired sufficiently to contemplate trying to film.

Benét, his wife and two children had been leading a rather rootless existence after some expatriate years in Europe and were anxious to buy a house, which the fee Griffith and he finally settled on—$1,000 a week for twelve weeks—would help them to get, so he signed on and returned with Griffith to the Coast, working on the screenplay in Griffith's drawing room on the train. Benét had written advertising copy in the course of his career, and a play with Griffith's sometime business associate, William Brady, so he was under the impression that he could handle anything Hollywood could throw at him. Besides, he and Griffith got on splendidly, with Griffith taking his young collaborator around to visit the great movie colony homes and along with him—and a couple of girls—when he went dancing. There was also a banquet in Griffith's honor at the Hollywood Roosevelt, where Benét was amused to find himself introduced as the latest in the long list of Griffith "discoveries."

Meantime, he wrote—and rewrote. "I think we're about through & then Mr. Griffith has a new idea. The trouble is—he's generally right," he wrote in one letter to his wife. Somewhere along the line they managed to produce a draft that Benét thought was acceptable. But, he quickly added, "I'm damn sure they won't use it but will try to cheese it up with love interests and Negro comedy characters—but when I've presented it to them, my literary conscience will be clear."

The film, he correctly predicted, would turn out to be a "half-baked opus, neither one thing nor the other—and then they'll wonder why it failed." As a sympathetic observer, not involved in the desperate politics of the production, he saw that "there is a tragedy going on here—D. W. G.'s." But there was nothing he could do about that, and he did not apparently understand any more than Griffith did just how much malice was involved in the hazing they and their script were undergoing. It may even be that the executives they reported to did not understand it either. Men like Schenck, when they lose interest in a director or a project, do not necessarily order man or work to be subverted. Rather they create around them an aura of anxiety which their courtiers, ever sensitive to such moods, pick up, magnify and communicate. They can fuss the life out of a creative enterprise without ever once raising their voices, and that was what was going on now.

Toward the end of the remarkable series of letters he wrote home about his adventures in Hollywood, Benét summarized as follows: "Nowhere have I seen such shining waste, stupidity and conceit as in the business and management end of this industry. Since arriving, I have written four versions of *Abraham Lincoln*, including a good one, playable in their required time. That, of course, is out. Seven people including myself, are now working in conference on the 5th one, which promises hopefully to be the worst yet. If I don't get out of here soon I'm going crazy. Perhaps I am crazy now. I wouldn't be surprised."[38]

His, and Griffith's, chief tormentor was a "Yale man [and] a son of a bitch." This was John Considine, Jr., who also claimed attendance at Stanford, Oxford and Heidelberg, though no one mentions a dueling scar. He was a Walter Wanger type, with good manners and an ingratiating line of literary chat, which led to his assignment, through the years, as a staff producer on a number of up-scale films at a variety of studios. He had, in fact, made F. Scott Fitzgerald's first stay in Hollywood a misery and was remembered by the able and civilized husband-and-wife writing team of Frances and Albert Hackett, whose first producer he was, as "that dreadful man."[39] At Art Cinema, he was apparently attempting to mediate between several factions, and might have been under more pressure than Benét could discern. But Klune's blunt memory—"Considine bullied Griffith"—agrees with Benét's contemporary impressions and with what is known of the producer's style of working. It was his habit to read scripts with a blue pencil in hand, scratching out line after line as he read, never realizing that some of what he was cutting was necessary to set up subsequent events he had not yet learned about. And at some point it was his pleasure to leak word of changes he had ordered Benét to make to *Variety*, implying that Pulitzer Prize winners had a lot to learn from the movie professionals about script writing. Benét, normally the most agreeable of men, was so outraged that he threatened to sue for libel, and

Considine quickly sent off a wire retracting his careless statements to the paper.

Typically, when the long anguish was finished, and the last draft turned in, Considine told Benét the script was the greatest he had ever read—"No thanks to him," commented Benét—and offered to extend his contract so that he could stay on for rewrites after shooting began. Benét turned him down, and also turned down Griffith's offer of a deal to help him develop his idea about a history of Texas, which was now apparently focused on the stand at the Alamo. But he left consoled: "On the whole," Benét wrote his wife, "I don't think it will be such a bad show when Griffith gets finished with it. Not as bad as we thought for a while."

And he was right. It was by no means a "bad show." But the principal photography, which began February 24 and continued for eight weeks, was characterized by Griffith as a "nightmare of mind and nerves" in a letter to Schenck that might not have been sent to him in the form in which it is preserved.[40] At any rate, by mid-May Griffith was back at the Crazy Hotel, recuperating. Supervision of the first cut was left to Considine, who wired him: "THE PICTURE SHAPED UP MARVELOUSLY IN CUTTING AND IN MY OPINION COMPARES VERY FAVORABLY WITH YOUR BEST AS WELL AS WITH THE OUTSTANDING PICTURES OF TODAY STOP I HONESTLY BELIEVE THAT WE WILL ALL BE VERY PROUD OF THIS ONE STOP." He promised Griffith an opportunity to add scenes if he thought that advisable after seeing his cut, though he felt that would not be necessary. Anyway, he unctuously added: "THE MAIN THING FOR YOU NOW IS TO GET PLENTY OF REST WITHOUT WORRYING ONE BIT. . . ."[41]

Griffith's withdrawal at this stage, however necessary to his well-being, was fatal to his future involvement with the picture. Further suggestions were listened to politely, but largely ignored, and Griffith, unwilling and perhaps unable to fight, returned only briefly to Los Angeles, leaving quickly for New York without seeing the picture as it was finally dubbed and scored. This, and all the rest of the fine tuning, was left to Considine. In his defense, it may be suggested that Griffith might not have been able, physically or psychologically, to undertake this work. He did do a few retakes, but it appears that his major activity in this period was overseeing a trailer he had been asked to prepare for a new version of *The Birth of a Nation*, to which music and effects had been added by the Aitkens. He recruited Walter Huston to appear with him in it. Got up in dinner jackets, they appear somewhat awkwardly, especially Griffith, as fine gentlemen settling down in a library for a little talk about history, truth and other elevated subjects. Huston presents Griffith with a cavalry sword, like the one Jake Griffith carried during the war, and in the course of their conversation Griffith admits that the film is a little one-sided in its approach to historical truth, but asserts autobiographical license in telling a tale that sprang out of him and which he had been preparing himself unconsciously to make since he was five. The piece is ambiguous and defensive, all too uncomfortably aware of the criticism that had been heaped on the film since its release. And it appears to have done small good. *Birth* did very little business when it entered the theaters later in the summer, though some of the retrospective articles about it were properly appreciative of its historical significance in the development of screen narrative.

Griffith was not, of course, present for the first preview of *Abraham Lincoln* in San Diego, but Considine was able to report that it was a "GRAND SUCCESS AUDIENCE THRILLED . . . AND HELD ALL THE WAY THROUGH. . . . CAN'T TELL YOU HOW OFTEN THEY APPLAUDED FROM START TO FINISH HAVE NEVER HEARD SO MUCH APPLAUSE AT END OF ANY PREVIEW." He added, not unintelligently, that for it to be a success the interest of "the flappers" would have to be captured, and to that end urged Griffith to propose an ad campaign that would suggest that by seeing the film they would discover "some startling truths about Lincoln's private life"—an utterly amazing proposal given the nature of the film.[42]

Griffith did not see a finished print of the picture until the first week of August, and then called Considine with suggestions for some rearrangements, notably of two early love scenes between Lincoln and Anne Rutledge. Considine wired back with far too many excuses about why this could not be accomplished before the film's opening on August 25. There was, however, no open quarrel between the two men, and Griffith went manfully about his promotional chores for the picture. There were the usual outlandish claims for himself—that he had read 180 books about Lincoln, for example. On the other hand, he was generous in his praise of Benét's work, suggesting that some of the future of talking films depended on recruiting writers of his caliber to work on them. He also gently followed Considine's line; "Abraham Lincoln is not to be thought of as a statue," he told one reporter. "There has been such a tendency to place him on a pedestal that the human side of his character has been overlooked. . . . Lincoln was a complex, many-sided personality with all the characteristics of the average man in addition to his rare genius."[43]

Perhaps because they felt guilty about their dim view of his recent films, perhaps out of knowledge of the troubles now afflicting his career, perhaps because critics, like everyone else, are always pleased to welcome the errant back to the true path, and perhaps because they apprehended the geunine merits of the film, the New York press gave his film superb reviews. Watts: "a handsome, dignified, and frequently moving photoplay, which is never cheap or maudlin, and which often succeeds in being genuinely distinguished." Gerhard (*Evening World*): "Reverting after all these years to his beloved Civil War theme, David Wark Griffith . . . takes his place in the van of present-day leaders." Martin (*Morning*

World): "Mr. Griffith was in every way at his best." There was high praise, as well, for Huston's performance ("Beautiful, tender, humorous and entirely touching," as Watts put it), even from those who had reservations about other aspects of the production, and Benét, too, came in for a full measure of encomia for his writing.[44] All in all, it was a triumph, and one that was supported in the trade press and by a number of earnest editorials of the kind that *America* had received, urging the film on the public as a patriotic duty. Despite the hard economic times, it should have been a larger commercial success; at the very least it should have restored the industry's confidence in Griffith, and more important, his confidence in himself. It is a measure of the toll that recent years had taken, and of the battering his sense of self-esteem had taken during this production, that he could not convert this *succès d'estime* into a lasting comeback.

It is also odd that the picture's reputation has suffered a decline in recent years, particularly among Griffith specialists. Perhaps because of a desire to rescue his next and final film, *The Struggle*, from the calumnies heaped upon it, there is a need to make invidious comparisons between it and its immediate predecessor, as well as a need to prove that in this period contemporary critics were suddenly struck blind on the subject of Griffith. But if *Abraham Lincoln* is no masterpiece, it is also quite an engaging film; and considering what talking pictures had been up until that moment, one can easily understand why contemporary critics were so taken with its pictorialism, its moments of near lyricism.

To be sure, Griffith's *Lincoln* was hardly a penetrating psychological portrait. It might, in fact, have been called something like "Beloved Moments with Mr. Lincoln," as it was essentially a compilation of the most familiar "humanizing" anecdotes about him—the stuff of schoolbook histories—and inescapable historical highlights. In retrospect, Lincoln scholarship having proceeded apace, the film looks naïve and sentimental, but not more so than the later films with which it must reasonably be compared, John Ford's *Young Mr. Lincoln* and John Cromwell's *Abe Lincoln in Illinois*, both released in 1939. The former is more comic adventure than history, and a rousing entertainment, but scarcely deeper than the Griffith film. The latter, based on Robert E. Sherwood's play, is almost lugubriously sober. Neither is actually more watchable than Griffith's work, and if Henry Fonda's performance in the title role for Ford is as good as Huston's it is not better—and both are infinitely preferable to Raymond Massey's for Cromwell, which is congealed by portents of tragedy to come. No, what Griffith, Benét and Huston were after, and got, was a sort of folk epic, rather Sandburgian in tone—and, it must be said, quite handsome to look at.

On this last point, the first critics were correct in their praise. If the film was more sound-stage–bound than Griffith would have liked, the obvious falsity of some of the settings actually worked for the picture, imparting a stylized quality to it, lifting it out of the merely realistic toward the mythic level. And the scatteration of action scenes—notably one of Sheridan's ride—and of semispectacular ones—Lincoln's nomination—hinted, as Rouben Mamoulian's *Applause* and Vidor's *Hallelujah* the previous year had, that the range of the sound film was greater than had as yet been apprehended, that it might encompass something more than backstage musicals and drawing room dramas, for the most part taken over directly from the theater. For whatever else it was, and was not, *Abraham Lincoln* was surely the first major historical film of the sound era, a beginning of an attempt to reclaim the past for the movies.

It had its defects, of course, most notably a lack of real sting, whether dramatic or comic, in its individual scenes. There was a serious bit of miscasting in having Una Merkel, essentially a comedienne, play the tragic Ann Rutledge (though there were strong compensatory bits from such old Griffith favorites as Henry Walthall and Hobart Bosworth, and such newcomers as Jason Robards, Sr., and Cameron Prudhomme). And there were strange lazinesses, such as having Lincoln, called upon to make a speech at Ford's Theater, rise and begin, "Again I say . . ." before launching into a reprise of the Gettysburg Address.

But all that aside, *Abraham Lincoln* is a more than creditable Griffith performance, infinitely more entertaining than any of his other films for Schenck, and more intrinsically interesting than anything he had done since *Isn't Life Wonderful*. Considering the circumstances in which it was made, it is even a remarkable film, for it implies that if he could have found a way in the late twenties to make pictures on themes and in a manner that drew on his strongest feelings, his fate might have been different; that if he could have found the heart and the support to go on with that effort in the thirties, it might well have been happier.

But Griffith appears to have found only small consolation in his reviews. What counted now was what counted with Schenck and the rest of the moguls, and that was the box office, where as "Joseph" informed him, business was "very spotty." "In some towns it is doing very well—in others it is doing very badly."[45] Griffith thought he knew why. In one of the scripts he and Benét had worked on, they had created a pair of fictional foreground observers, young lovers, whose story paralleled that of Lincoln. In the end the young man would have turned out to be the sentry whom Lincoln famously pardoned from a sentence of death for falling asleep at his post. The pardon is in the film, naturally, but as just another proof of The Emancipator's saintliness. Looking back in the fall of 1930, Griffith thought this approach "would not have hurt the main story concerning Lincoln," but would have served, as the story of the Camerons had, in *Birth*, to place great events in human perspective, and provide the film with the suspense that the simple retelling of history, the outcome of which is known to everyone, can never do.

Who can say? Perhaps he and Benét did not work this approach out persuasively. And it might well be that Considine and the other studio politicians were awed by the film's subject matter and afraid to permit Griffith and Benét such license. In any event, Griffith was still bitter about interference from the studio staff, and undertook to lecture Schenck on it out of his "very real friendly feeling toward you." He advised Schenck, if he was too busy to act as his own production chief, to appoint a single deputy with full decision-making authority to act for him instead of permitting several factions to contend for that authority, with a man like Considine trying to please them all. "I do not believe it is possible to get good results from a director . . . when [he] has to work trying to please two or three factions. No great book or play was ever written by but one man. . . . Certainly no Dickens or Shakespeare or Thackeray, or even the second class ones, were ever successful by any endeavors other than their own."

This was the lesson that Griffith took from *Abraham Lincoln*, from all the experiences of the past five years. Henceforth, somehow, he would try to be his own master. He had, he said, several offers but was "in no hurry in the matter of production." He would wait, he said, until he had the material to make a really successful and profitable picture. And with that he signed off from Schenck, and from moviemaking as an industrial process, "With best wishes for your health and the fair measure of content given to any of us poor humans. . . ."[46]

CHAPTER EIGHTEEN

"No Casting Today"

"I PASSED him on the street the other afternoon and I didn't stop to talk because, somehow, there's nothing one can say these days to D. W. Griffith while big electric signs flash the title of his new ignominious effort." The prose is sob-sister stuff, there being nothing the press likes better than the fake-tragic contemplation of those it has helped to make mighty brought low. Needless to say, when Julia Shawell, the "Getting Personal" columnist for the New York Graphic, the most sensational of the tabloids, encountered Griffith a few days after the opening of what neither of them imagined would be his last picture, The Struggle, it was "a rainy and bleak twilight." Needless to say, she had just emerged from Carnegie Hall, where "another gray-haired" master (Toscanini) was touching upon the sublime as he led the New York Philharmonic triumphantly through a Brahms symphony. Needless to say, she could not help but reflect, "however cruel . . . the musical world may be to artists, it cannot be nearly so heartless as men like Griffith are to themselves."[1]

Yet the image of Griffith scurrying through the rush-hour crowds shamefaced and unseeing—because he did not want to be seen—rings true. For The Struggle, whose marquee lights would go out within a matter of days, was not even interestingly "controversial," or the kind of work that a friendly critic might argue would find an audience after the passage of time had brought historical perspective to it. No, this film, which seems to have started out to be an antiprohibition tract but ended up looking like a temperance drama (more than one critic compared it unfavorably to Ten Nights in a Barroom), was an unambiguous critical and commercial disaster. Griffith collected for it a set of notices that were not merely the worst of his career but may well be the worst that any director of his standing and past achievement has ever had.

The beating was savage and remorseless. "A shiftless and pitiably stupid homily which, esthetically and financially, should be an embar-

560

rassment to all concerned," wrote *Time*, dismissing it in a 21-line paragraph.[2] "The crudest talking picture that has yet been manufactured," said the *Herald Tribune*, while the man from the *World-Telegram* called it "a major tragedy of David Wark Griffith, once the outstanding figure in motion pictures." The civilized John S. Cohen of the *Sun*, noting the film's debt to scenes and situations Griffith had been using since his Biograph days, called it "Mr. Griffith's own antique show," but concluded with only a mild irony instead of a denunciation: " 'The Struggle' is not one of the works by which Mr. Griffith will float on the wings of posterity."[3] That was probably the kindest thing anyone said about the film at the time.

In the face of notices like these, and of box office returns so wretched that the picture was pulled from the Rivoli and then quickly, almost slyly, peddled by United Artists mainly in the small towns, Griffith took to his rooms at the Astor and settled down for some serious drinking, a state that continued, it would seem, until late January. These benders had become, and would continue to be, his response to all rejections, personal or professional, though it would not be until his last two years that his alcoholism would be almost constant. The evidence is that when he was not depressed his drinking was moderate and his moods for the most part agreeable.

For the moment, however, he had to confront the undeniable fact that the failure of *The Struggle* meant not only the end of hope for D. W. Griffith, Inc., but the renewal of the old, debilitating battle with debt, for he had borrowed in excess of $200,000 in order to finance a negative that cost around $300,000 and would return only about $100,000 to him. This time, he could now see, there could be no hope, however vague, that the company would be restored to healthy functioning; he and his associates would henceforth merely be trying to bring it to a point where it could honorably close its books for good and perhaps salvage a few dollars for its founder. Moreover, given his consistent record of box office failure, he must also have seen that henceforth a return to studio employment or access to independent finance, except that which always exists at the farthest, lunatic fringe of the film world, were no longer realistic options for him. If there was ever a moment in his life when a long, drunken withdrawal was justified, this perhaps was it.

But if his despondency was explicable, the choices that had led him to that state are not entirely so. Why, one is compelled to ask, why this particular film at this particular time? It is true that for as long as Griffith had lived prohibition had been a controversial subject in the United States, and that the passage of the Eighteenth Amendment had done little to still that controversy. It is also true that by 1931 sentiment for repeal had intensified, as the social consequences of prohibition had become clear and painful to a developing majority. In the broadest sense,

The Struggle might have seemed newsy to him, a contribution to a debate he had wanted to join since the mid-twenties, when he was in touch with leaders of the repeal movement, offering arguments against prohibition that were very like those put forward finally in his film, and which were in line with his lifelong distrust of reformers.

It is obvious, too, that his personal interest in the problem of alcoholism had grown more powerful in recent years. When he had written to the repeal leaders he was not more than a social drinker. Now he was something considerably more than that, and given his abstemious Methodist background, he was a guilty and self-conscious drinker, one who must have devoted at least some sober thoughts to the question of how he had become what he had become. What he would not do, as the film makes painfully apparent, was to come to grips with the more profound social issues presented by prohibition, the more profound psychological issues presented by the alcohol addict. Indeed, the picture is, as we shall see, irresolute to the point of absurdity on the latter question.

Pressing thoughtlessly ahead on the film, without resolving his feeling on the subject at hand, meant that he was also unable to develop a plot and characters capable of persuasively advancing his argument, or for that matter, being persuasive at any other level. He was unconsciously, but surely, forging the disaster that was to ensue. And, of course, ignoring his vow to Schenck of the previous year, that he would undertake no new project until he had patiently developed a story in which he was totally confident, patiently cultivated backing that would see him comfortably through production.

It would be convenient to argue that he needed money and could not dally long over such niceties. But that was not the case. If he could scarcely be accounted rich, he was not personally desperate, either—he took only a $16,000 fee against 40 percent of the profits for this film. His corporation was in a similar straitened but not miserable position. There were not, as there had been in the past, any pressing demands from his stockholders to keep busy. Indeed, with dividends from Klune's investments and the United Artists stock coming in, and with the depression trending toward its depths, the argument of prudence, of a conservation of limited resources until times were better, could easily have been invoked to answer any questions.

No, it seems that this time the compulsion to produce came only from within himself, from his own restless need to busy himself, buttressed now, perhaps, by a fear of idleness, and the troubles it led to—the drinking and the womanizing. (Earlier this year he had been subjected to a great deal of unpleasant publicity as the result of the latter weakness; a Hollywood extra girl had sued him for damages she calculated at precisely $601,000, claiming he had attacked her when she went to his apartment to discuss a "screen test," and only her own bad reputation prevented her from collecting.) So there was a need operating here that went beyond neediness. But there was also no more capacity now than there had ever been to confront himself or the realities of contemporary life. Once again he would speak his mind in the borrowed tongue of antique melodrama. Indeed, it could be argued that *The Struggle* was a little anthology of all the weaknesses his work had exhibited in the past.

The screen treatment that he scratched out was based largely on his memory of an old play, Augustin Daly's *Demon Drink*, the copyright for which, though it had been taken out in 1879, was still in force. Luckily, however, the novel on which it was based, Emile Zola's *L'Assommoir*, was unprotected in the United States, and so Griffith felt free to engage writers to turn his idea into a finished script. For this task he summoned Anita Loos, asking her to bring her husband, John Emerson, into the collaboration. The wit that he had been the first to appreciate had become public knowledge, public property, with the publication of *Gentlemen Prefer Blondes* in 1925, so it was hard for Anita Loos, hard for anybody, to understand why he wanted her for this project. She would recall, however, that he opened their first meeting with a recital of his troubles, with particular emphasis on the ingratitude of his family, many members of which were receiving now, as they would for years, support checks from him. When he turned to business the story he told her was *"Ten Nights in a Barroom*, practically," and she withdrew from the meeting without committing herself. "I knew how bad it was," she would later recall, but she also recognized that by this time "I was the only writer he had any connection with," and, almost as an act of charity, she and Emerson took the job at a minimal fee—$5,000 plus 5 percent of the Griffith company's gross. They would have to work in haste, however, for they were booked to leave for Europe in a few weeks and so would not be available for lengthy rewrites or for consultation during shooting.

In later years Miss Loos would claim that all along she had hoped to inject some conscious comedy into the film: "I thought we might save it by kidding it; I thought we could take the edge off the soap opera." But, she recalled, perhaps because he was temporarily under the sway of the naturalist esthetic as well as a naturalistic novelist, Griffith kept advancing a theory "that everything in life was completely unmotivated . . . that people don't have any reason for anything they do." Loos thought this was nonsense, especially when the work in hand was the creation of a dramatic structure, where motive is everything.[4]

But in the end, the film reflects a good deal of Griffith's theory. For in tracing the step-by-tiny-step decline of Jimmie Wilson, from his first drink to street begging to the D.T.s, no irresistible reason—no major tragedy or disappointment—is ever given for his increasing resort to alcohol, and the imbalance between cause and effect in his story is one of the major reasons why laughter rises unbidden as the movie proceeds. Jimmie is seen taking a drink because he is worried about his hospitalized daughter, because he doesn't want to wear a tie his wife has given him and he dislikes to an awkward social occasion, because a friend loses a job. No reason, psychological or otherwise, is adduced to explain why these perfectly acceptable reasons for taking a fortifying shot or two must, in Jimmie's case, turn into the beginnings of a near-fatal addiction. Nor does Griffith make the case against prohibition that he intended to make. His position, as stated in a prologue, was that when alcohol was sold openly, on licensed premises, it was a natural and pleasant part of life, with no glamour attaching to it. To illustrate this point he showed a sunny beer garden, populated by cheerful middle-class people quaffing light wine and beer. Prohibition, by criminalizing drinking, imparted to it an air of evil excitement that, he argued, led the impressionable to experiment with harder and headier brews, and he seems to imply that poor Jimmie, like poor Griffith, might have been spared the worst degradations of alcohol if he had been able to drink in pleasanter surroundings, without the bad influence of lowlifes to lead him on to perdition.

The point is, obviously, a dubious one—alcoholism was scarcely unknown before prohibition—and in any case it is quickly abandoned as Griffith concentrates on the picturesque horrors of Jimmie's descent. Of all the films in which he sought to illuminate a large historical or intellectual theme with a small-scale human drama none so abruptly abandons the pretense of concern with the general issue that was on his mind. And none is so careless about working out the human story. If one could take *The Struggle* seriously on some level, one might well conclude that any device, including prohibition, which prevented others from falling victim to Jimmie's fate would be worthwhile. For he finally reaches a hallucinatory stage where he is unable to recognize his own child—and Griffith reaches a stage where he must resort to that most dubious of his own devices, namely, the locked room, the frightened girl and the brutal male, all self-control abandoned, threatening her life. It is *Broken Blossoms* all over again, though this time the child is rescued. And with his wife faithfully nursing him back to health, there is recovery and reformation for the male. In fact, like so many Griffith heroes, Jimmie has been working on an invention, adoption of which at the factory where he has worked restores him to prosperity and self-esteem at the end of the film.

Many excuses beyond its narrative and structural weaknesses have been offered for *The Struggle*'s dismal reception—though those weaknesses would have been sufficient to doom any film. Casting was one of them. Loos, for example, had at one point proposed Jimmy Durante for the lead, thinking that his somewhat grotesque presence might make the melodramatic excesses of the film more real and, perhaps, turn it into—what? Rude expressionist poetry perhaps? The Felliniesque as we might now think of it? The idea was too desperate to be practical, especially considering the time it would have required to write a script to support an interpretation of that sort, and the extraordinary demands it would have placed on Griffith's talent. Anyway, Griffith's reluctance to cast powerful stars in his films was now reinforced by budgetary considerations. For $500 a week he could obtain Hal Skelly, a former vaudevillian who had scored a Broadway success playing a comedian undone by drink in *Burlesque*. He was bland, in the way Griffith liked his leading men to be, and he could do victimization, though he proved incapable of bringing any other coloration to the part. Opposite him Griffith cast Zita Johann, a young actress who had made her Broadway debut jointly with Clark Gable in *Machinal*, had enjoyed good notices in a Philip Barry play, *Tomorrow and Tomorrow*, had just had an unfortunate experience with M-G-M (she had won a contract but no roles) but still was anxious to break into movies, and so was available at an economical rate. The rest of the cast, which included Evelyn Baldwin in a small part as Jimmie's sister, was composed of unknowns, badly chosen because, in Loos's opinion, "he had deteriorated." She remembered as "one of the most pathetic moments of my life" a casting session in his room at the Astor when Griffith enthusiastically brought in a little girl to play Skelly's daughter, entirely unaware that she was dressed in a style some thirty years out of date—"so out of it, so corny."[5]

But if the picture's problems began with script and casting, they did not end there. As Evelyn Baldwin was to remark later, "Everything went wrong that could go wrong."[6] Just as shooting began, it became necessary to increase the production loan that had been negotiated with the Federation Bank and Trust Company from $75,000 to $200,000 and that, it seems, forced Griffith to scrimp and wriggle in order to keep going until the new funds were in hand. At roughly the same time a deal to rent a stage at Paramount's Astoria studios fell through and Griffith had to take his company to the drab, badly equipped studios of something called Audio-Cinema, Inc., in the Bronx. And in those dismal surroundings, it became necessary to force the pace of his inexperienced people, because Skelly had a booking in London and could work for only a month. Baldwin remembered him as "high-spirited" while he was working, but John Houseman, who was married to Johann at the time, recalls things differently. "It was an unhappy engagement; during which she found herself working in outrageous conditions with none of the charismatic inspiration that Lillian Gish and so many others had found in earlier films with the Old Master. She would return late at night, green with exhaustion from chasing Skelly from saloon to saloon in pouring rain—drenched, shivering, wind-whipped and deafened by the old-fashioned wind machines—and sit hunched before our midsummer fire, drying out and mumbling bitterly through her tears that she should never have done the lousy picture and that she was ruining her career and her health."[7] The latter, of course, recovered, and the former never amounted to much anyway; she did a handful of pictures, among them Howard Hawks's *Tiger Shark* and the female lead in a minor horror classic, *The Mummy*, as well as some more stage work. But it might be recorded that her exertions contributed to such small distinction as *The Struggle* had. Lacking funds for elaborate sets, Griffith was forced to take to the streets, and his authentic locations were, indeed, uncommon in the early years of sound production, when recording out of doors was thought to be impossible, a difficulty he solved, with his usual technological daring, by resort to a parabolic microphone an inventor had brought to him.

He was rewarded for his troubles by a posthumous irony. The critics of the time, now used to elaborate artifices of the studio-made film, found Griffith's Biograph-like realism "old-fashioned," and that was insensate of them. But the esteem in which some Griffith supporters have come to hold the picture (a "true Griffith masterpiece," according to Anthony Slide) is equally ridiculous. The claims advanced for it are based largely on the grittiness of its appearance. Carried away by that, and by the contrast between it and other American films of the time, Arthur Lennig, for example, has written, "The film was honest and sincere . . . and very unHollywoodish; it has no false glamour, no 'beautiful' people, and no consciously artistic lighting and photography." All of which is true enough, and perhaps admirable enough, but these virtues cannot compensate for the absurdities of dialogue that is banal, a story and characters that are but pale reflections of things Griffith himself had done with more conviction before. And the argument that "soap opera . . . is actually closer to what real life is than many a more sophisticated form" is an absurdity.[8] Griffith had no gift for the forced psychological perspective or the conventions of staging and manner that give soap opera its archetypal characters and its situations their telegraphic immediacy, hence the form's strangely seductive power to compel attention. The issue, all along, was the one Loos was groping to formulate but for which she never quite found the right words. It was not self-satirizing humor that Griffith needed but a recognition that broad-stroke melodrama is always rendered absurd when it is played within the realistic conventions of the sound film, together with a recognition that moral earnestness cannot redeem this fundamental flaw. Only the flat understatement of neorealism, determined underplaying, something along the lines of *Isn't Life Wonderful*, might have saved the film. But, of course, in the context of his career and film conventions at this time, that, too, was out of the question.

When he got into the cutting room with his film, he apparently sensed its inadequacies. An assistant director on the film, Jack Aichele, would later recall for Griffith biographer Robert Henderson the picture's editor, Barney Rogan, telling him that Griffith worked frantically on the film, cutting and recutting, resorting to the out-takes in search of the salvation that is almost never to be found there, in the meantime throwing out sequences that had looked good to Aichele on the set.

But it was hopeless. All Griffith could do was brazen it out and hope for the best. The ad campaign featured a racy come-on, "A Man of Steel . . . in a Melting Pot of Pleasure," and the press book offered theater owners the opportunity to buy, in gross quantities, berets emblazoned with the legend "D. W. Griffith's The Struggle" with a place to add in the name of the theater in which it was playing. One does not imagine that the Advertising Cap Company did very well with the item. But Linda Griffith had her hopes. "DEAR DAVID," her opening night telegram read: "I SEND YOU ALL GOOD WISHES FOR A GREAT SUCCESS TONIGHT."[9] And William Randolph Hearst, himself a relentless teetotaler, was steadfast: "HAVE REQUESTED PAPERS TO DO EVERYTHING THEY CAN TO HELP PICTURE,"[10] he wired. Griffith arranged an opening night of "due pomp," as Mordaunt Hall put it in the next morning's *Times*. Al Smith was in the audience, along with Nancy Carroll, the actress, and "the distinguished aviatrix Ruth Elder." Who was not in his accustomed place on stage at the end of the screening was D. W. Griffith. There had been the odd snicker or two, and, it would seem, a certain restlessness in the audience. So Hal Skelly, whose admiring loyalty Griffith had commanded as he had so many other performers in the past, was pressed into service, and Hall reported him "very busy" as he directed a follow spot this way and that in the audience, picking out prominent guests for introduction, trying to distract people's attention from their host's absence, trying to turn discomfort into occasion.[11]

2

Griffith could walk away from the Rivoli Theater and, with the help of his bottle, try his best not to look back. But it was not possible to walk away from the complexities his last film had added to his already vastly complicated financial life. It would require almost two years to sort them out, some 20 months of threats, disagreements and general unpleasantness on every hand. The strategy in this battle for Griffith's survival with some measure of financial dignity was devised by his cousin, the Honorable Woodson R. Oglesby, sometime congressman, full-time lawyer and wizard of financial maneuver. In a letter introducing him to his fellow United Artists stockholders, Griffith described him as a man who "showed more sense than yours truly and saved his 'jack.' He has retired to one of those little million dollar cottages at Lenox, Mass. To walk through it twice supplies all the exercise you could possibly need. Mr. Oglesby has consented to give up his time, his golf and other demure entertainments to try and straighten out our tangled affairs, merely through friendship."[12]

This friendship was real, and at this difficult time the warmth with which his kinsman and fellow Kentuckian received him into his home on frequent visits provided Griffith with good cheer and a measure of hope that was reflected in the genial tone he took in describing Oglesby and his family. In the early thirties, particularly in the summertimes, Griffith spent a good deal of time at his cousin's estate, where he was always given a three-room suite with private bath.

But the crucial if belated addition to Griffith's life was provided by Woodson's clever tenacity in practical affairs. Described by Griffith as "a dead pan Louis" with "that same cold exterior that most of the Oglesbys preserved—a hard outside, and like most of them, with a heart as big as a motor truck inside."[13] Oglesby, unlike Banzhaf, had no desire to be liked by Griffith's associates in the motion picture business. That, combined with his objectivity of mind, strength of will and weight of reputation permitted him to carry through his plans for his cousin's salvation no matter how the people he was negotiating with squawked and squirmed. He was also someone Griffith, that secretive and mistrustful man, would listen to and follow.

Oglesby's plan for his cousin's financial salvation was in design simple and blunt, in execution remarkably complex. He wanted to liquidate Griffith's interest in both his studio and United Artists, but on terms that would realize a goodly sum of money, enough for Griffith to live on in comfort for the rest of his life. There was a solid basis for hope in this regard. Raymond Klune would recall later that "I used to hide money from him" first at Epping's bidding, then on his own authority, to keep up payments on an annuity that Epping had insisted on taking out for Griffith's benefit when the corporation was founded. By the 1930s, according to Klune, it was capable of paying out $30,000 a year to Griffith in semiannual installments.[14] It also seems likely that the cash value of several other insurance policies the company had carried on him, at the insistence of lenders (on several occasions they had also proved useful as collateral as well), reverted to him when it went out of business. The problem now was to add to this nest egg.

To that end, Oglesby proceeded on two fronts simultaneously. The more complicated one, technically, involved Griffith's relationship with the company he had founded. In early 1932 Griffith was in debt to it for more than $79,000, mainly as the result of advances he had taken against his percentage of *The Struggle* (some of which had been for the benefit of Brother Albert and his ne'er-do-well nephew Willard, recently added to his entourage). Although the company had turned over its share of that film's $100,000 gross, it still owed the Federation Trust $145,000 in principal and interest on *The Struggle*'s production loan. Since the bank had gone into receivership before the picture had gone into release, there was no hope of refinancing this debt, and, it would seem, small hope of recovering the collateral Griffith's corporation had put up in order to obtain the loan. This last was of great moment to Griffith, for in addition to the mortgage on the Mamaroneck land (just recently defaulted by the real estate developers who had purchased it) it consisted of 500 United Artists shares he had owned personally but had surrendered to the company in order that it might, in turn, use them to secure the Federated loan. If these went, his last substantial bit of wealth would go.

And they would have if Wood Oglesby had not noticed something interesting on the Griffith corporation books. Griffith's original employment contract had stipulated an annual payment of a $200,000 salary for a term of ten years. But Griffith had waived his claim to a large unpaid portion of this money—$334,550—when the studio was in trouble. Remember, too, that during the years with Famous Players and Art Cinema he had passed through to the company a large percentage of his fees from those concerns, by Oglesby's reckoning $596,574, or close to half of the $1,209,558 he had earned. This had been set up as a loan and now, said Oglesby, it was time that it be repaid.

But, of course, there was no way that so large a sum could be repaid. Very well, said Oglesby, my client will resign his presidency and sue for what is owed him. And, on April 15, 1932, at the same meeting at which the corporation voted to sell back to United Artists the last few UA shares it held (proceeds from which were applied to the Federation loan, reducing it to the neighborhood of $95,000 plus interest) Griffith's resignation was accepted. On May 27 he commenced suit against D. W. Griffith, Inc., for recovery of back salary.

It was on the face of it an amazing situation. But it was also a sham. The suit was intended from the start to be purely *pro forma*, a means by which a friendly figurehead, one Robert E. Lent, who had replaced Griffith, could divest the company of its last remaining assets, but in an unquestionably legal fashion, so that no stockholder could question the propriety, the necessity, perhaps even the justice of so doing.[15]

Thus, miracle of miracles, Griffith's suit, which was brought in Westchester County, away from the eyes of the New York press, was settled out of court on June 29, 1932, just a month and two days after it had been instituted. Under the terms of the settlement Griffith abandoned his claims to back salary and surrendered to the corporation his millions of shares of worthless Class B stock in it. In return, the corporation handed over to him its mortgage on the Mamaroneck property and its rights in the films he had made and, most important, returned to him title to the 500 shares of United Artists stock that had been used as collateral in financing *The Struggle*.

Since money was still owed the Federation Bank and Trust, Griffith personally assumed responsibility for that debt. He was, therefore, still exposed. That, however, was a condition Oglesby now moved to rectify. He began, with Griffith's help, a campaign to harass United Artists, his idea being to have Griffith make such a nuisance of himself that the company would be glad to buy out his remaining UA shares at an inflated price. That these shares, for the moment, resided in the vaults of the Federation Trust need not concern us at this time, for it was largely to regain them that Oglesby was maneuvering.

His first ploy with Schenck was to pretend anger when, also in April of 1932, Schenck asked for authorization to make secured production loans out of United Artists' surplus at his own discretion, without consulting his board or the principals they represented. This was necessary, he said, because in these trying times banks were not inclined to undertake risky loans to movie companies. This Griffith well knew; three banks had passed on *The Struggle* before the luckless Federation Trust had accepted the risk. But Griffith, that grandly imprudent man, now suddenly became the soul of prudence. He thought that UA should conserve its cash resources, awaiting the day when, he predicted, the banks would force distributors to consolidate, thus eliminating the duplication inherent in competing sales and exchange systems. Better yet, why didn't United Artists just divide up its surplus among its stockholders—he estimated that would come to around $325,000 apiece—and quietly fold its tent.[16]

Outrage! "You understand that a corporation cannot be dissolved merely because one stockholder wishes to withdraw therefrom, and particularly a corporation such as ours that has many contracts for the distribution of photoplays which have yet many years to run," Schenck replied. "It is the duty of the directors and the stockholders to protect the finances of the corporation so that [it] is able to carry out its anticipated obligations and also the business for which it was organized."[17]

Outrage in return! Griffith accused the company of paying "grossly inflated salaries to officers, in-laws and protégés of certain stockholders" (as if he had not been guilty of the same thing), of inflating charges to outsiders for rental space on the UA lot, which was still owned by Pickford and Fairbanks, of making interest-free loans to favored producers (a reference to funding the company had provided Gloria Swanson for two pictures, one of which turned out to be almost as disastrous as *The Struggle*) and, reverting to his old complaint, of dumping his films at disadvantageous prices.[18]

A little later Oglesby weighed in with a letter of his own, following a meeting with Cap O'Brien. In it his, and Griffith's, motives are finally made clear; they have all along been setting up what amounted to a blackmail situation, in which the threat of a suit, charging malfeasance by the officers and directors of the company, would be withdrawn if Griffith's stock were taken up at, say $500 a share. In the same letter Oglesby indicated that he already had an offer of $325 a share from an unnamed party—almost certainly Samuel Goldwyn, who was then releasing through the company.[19]

Schenck was inclined to brazen the matter out. "In my humble opinion, Mr. Oglesby is a bluff," he replied to O'Brien's report on the matter, later adding that Griffith was "just an ungrateful fool being led by Oglesby."[20] But in his way Oglesby, the country boy who made good, was just as tough and tenacious as the immigrant lad who had made good. When he got no response to his suggestion for a buy-out, he referred to a verbal offer Schenck had made to him, calling for a partial liquidation of the company's surplus. Oglesby now accepted it in principle but conditioned acceptance on closing down the company's system of exchanges and letting someone else distribute its product. This, Oglesby estimated, would save three or four hundred thousand dollars a year, and permit distribution of, say, $56 a share.[21] This was far less than Griffith needed at the moment, but it was also far more than Schenck was willing to pay. As Oglesby surely knew, Schenck was not about to destroy his distribution system. But this further demonstration of true grit on Oglesby's part helped motivate the UA people to rid themselves of this troublesome man and his annoying client. As did Oglesby's cool appearance on Griffith's behalf at a formal meeting of his corporation's stockholders in Delaware on February 7, 1933, where he blandly testified as to the propriety and mutual advantage of the settlement the corporation's new officers had made of Griffith's claims for back salary.[22] He won unanimous approval for what was, in effect, the total destruction of whatever stockholder equity was left in the company. That week, a reporter for a trade journal happened to pass Griffith's headquarters at 1619 Broadway and observed "this significant message lettered neatly and prominently in gold on his office door: *No casting today.*"

Now everything was in place for a move toward a final settlement with United Artists. It took two months to work out the precise terms, but on April 19, 1933, Griffith and United Artists concluded their relationship forever. On that date, out of the surplus Griffith had claimed to be so concerned about, he was paid $200,000 for his 500 shares of stock ($100 per share less than Oglesby's original price) plus $2,000, an amount equal to the interest on the production loan to Swanson which it had waived when reaching a similar settlement with her. Just why Griffith's ego required this trifling bit of equity with that hard-pressed lady it is hard to say. In any event, Griffith took payment in the form of a check for $104,580, the exact amount still owed to Federation Trust, which Griffith immediately endorsed over to it, a series of thirteen promissory notes totaling $97,000 and $419.44 in cash, which he pocketed, apparently not caring about the 56 cents that disappeared somewhere in the paper shuffling.[23]

Griffith used some of the proceeds of the notes to pay off a lab bill for prints for *The Struggle* which amounted to some $16,000, and to aid in briefly reacquiring a half-interest in the Mamaroneck property. His partner in this transaction was Woodson Oglesby, acting in the name of his children. The book value of the property was a little more than $3 million, the amount still owed on the Edgewater Point real estate company's original mortgage. This document had been acquired by an agent of Oglesby, who bought the land at a foreclosure auction for $5,000. Now Oglesby agreed to pay Griffith $151,000 for his share of the property. Fifty-six thousand dollars of this was in cash, another $5,000 came as Griffith's share in the proceeds of the sale of a small parcel of the land, and $63,000 was covered by the return of the remainder of the United Artists promissory notes, which Griffith had allowed Oglesby to use as collateral for a loan to lift the tax liens on the property. Oglesby also agreed to pay the balance owing Griffith on this transaction—$27,000— as he disposed of the property later. One of his sales techniques, it was later revealed, was threatening to sell to blacks, thus causing other property owners to pay inflated prices "to protect" their holdings; he and Griffith were sued over this matter in 1939—a nice irony for the man who made *The Birth of a Nation*.[24]

That aside, Oglesby did well for his cousin, and it is obvious that he put himself at significant risk to do so by purchasing this property in bad times. Just how much Griffith netted out of these maneuvers is, finally, impossible to say, just as it is impossible to determine precisely what other resources he might have had to tide him through his last years. One suspects they were larger than he admitted. For besides the windfall his cousin engineered for him, it must be remembered that, even allowing for the salary he forgave his corporation, he did lay hands on something like a million dollars over a period of ten years, and that he had hardly started the 1920s penniless, considering what he had made on *Birth* and from other salaries before the corporation came into being. It must also be remembered that his personal habits, aside from his gambling, were not spendthrift, and that he was in the habit of tucking large amounts of cash aside in odd corners. Recall the mysterious newspaper-wrapped bundle he pressed on the Gish family before his departure for Europe and *Hearts of the World*. And the oft-repeated story of the small, forgotten fortune— around $20,000—found by auditors in the safe of the Alexandria Hotel in Los Angeles after it went bankrupt in the 1930s appears to have been true, too. Finally, there were delayed benefits from the Oglesby transaction. He received, for example, $24,000 as his share of the sale of *Way Down East* to a small distributor who re-released it in the 1930s, and there was also, perhaps, $15,000 from the English producers who purchased the rights to remake *Broken Blossoms* in 1935, plus, probably, a portion of a director's fee for him, too. All in all, and despite his almost constant protestations of poverty hereafter, Griffith had come out remarkably well. If he had not laid the foundations for a great show business fortune as Pickford, Fairbanks and Chaplin had done, he would henceforth want for little. Considering that this extrication was accomplished in the worst year of the Depression, the first year of Franklin D. Roosevelt's presidency and the year of the bank holiday, one can only stand in awe of Woodson Oglesby's tenacity and sagacity.

One may, perhaps, spare a bit of that awe for the legend of D. W. Griffith's noble insolvency in the cause of art. If it was in part self-generated, it has, through the years, been reinforced by defenders of the faith like Lillian Gish, who added to it an element of moral suffering on her mentor's part as he contemplated the fate of those who had staked money on their faith in him. In her autobiography she quotes Griffith agonizing in terms that would do credit to a nineteenth-century melodramatist over what he should do to protect his stockholders after his withdrawal from his Art Cinema contract. "These are people who saw and loved my pictures," she has him saying, "and because they believed in them they have invested all their savings. Hard-working men. Widows with children. How can I let them down? It keeps me awake at night. . . ."[25]

But this is pure invention on someone's part. Griffith's position, as quoted by Epping, among others, was always that people who bought stock of any sort were knowingly placing their money at risk—that was the way of things in business—and he had small sympathy for their complaints when things went wrong. Nor is there any evidence that he spared a thought for anyone but himself during Oglesby's lengthy and questionable maneuverings. His only known sacrifice in that period was to move out of the Astor into less-expensive digs at the Park Central Hotel on Seventh Avenue between Fifty-sixth and Fifty-seventh streets, but with his valet and general factotum, Bob Greathouse (at one time one of his road show managers), still at his side. And with money to maintain his car, to continue his regular excursions to nightclubs and roadhouses up the Hudson to conduct himself as he always had, with a certain public flair.

One does not begrudge him. Far more than most, his company had been the extension of one man, one talent, and the risk of betting on a one-man enterprise should have been clear to the majority of those who chose to invest in his corporation. Moreover, he cannot be said to have spared much thought for his own financial security as he worked his sixteen-hour days on his films, driving himself relentlessly through the months and years without surcease, trying to make a go of things. Indeed, if he had dared pause to think, the reputation of his later work might stand higher than it now does. In short, there is adequate justification for close, belated attention to his own economic welfare in this period, but none in imputing to him larger-than-usual concern for his fellow man.

3
_____

Not that Griffith was immune to the hardships of others. If he had any inclination to turn his back on the harshness of the times, his friends and family were ever-present reminders that others were far less fortunate than he. He was the sole support of his sister Ruth and her daughter, also named Ruth, in California, a major contributor to his sickly brother William's welfare back home in Oldham County, and among his regular visitors to the suite at the Park Central were Billy Bitzer, very much down on his luck, brother Albert and nephew Willard, all of whom required frequent handouts. In a letter to Ruth Griffith, with whom he was cheerful and funny in a way that he rarely was with anyone else, he described the scene in his suite one winter's day when Albert and Willard dropped in to thaw out. "They were only partially welcome as both of them made a dive for the radiator and as I had been using it for a pleasant seat before they came, we had a scramble—the radiator not being long enough for three people to sit on. And Albert hasn't lost any flesh." A paragraph in the same letter attests to the settlement—alas, temporary—of one of his largest problems:

"Now don't get excited about this news I'm going to impart to you. It is possibly the most tremendous event that has ever happened in our lives. I am having the statement I am about to make sworn to before a Notary, so you will surely believe it. I am almost afraid to tell you for fear it will react too fiercely on you. Wonder of wonders! Believe it or not! Truth, after all, is stranger than fiction!

"WILLARD! WILLARD!! HAS GONE TO WORK!"[26]

His elation did not last long. "Damn Damn dear Willard," as Griffith once addressed him, eventually became a sort of transcontinental moocher. Griffith received cheery, chatty notes from all over, but all of them ended the same way, with an ingratiating plea for assistance. Griffith was beset on every side. One month Linda would be off on a cruise to Mexico (on his money, of course) and thanking him for the flowers he had had delivered to her cabin; a few months later there would be a letter full of barely suppressed fury over his lack of recent support ("It is beyond my comprehension that you continue to show no appreciation whatever of my self-effacement through the years").[27] When Bert Banzhaf died suddenly in 1934, Griffith found himself paying for his funeral expenses, though their business relationship had ceased by then.

Since Griffith was nearly always impossible to reach by phone or mail (the letters and messages were always piling up in his pigeonhole behind his hotel's front desk) and he despised correspondence in general ("Don't write and they won't have anything on you," he once advised Bitzer), the hotel lobby often contained a few former employees or old acquaintances looking for a job or a handout. There were, at one point, so many of them that he ceased to take his afternoon strolls in Central Park or down Sixth Avenue in order to avoid encountering them. If he did go out on an errand (he particularly enjoyed getting a soda at the drugstore fountain across the street) he would affect a great bustling haste in order to have an excuse for giving the importunate a short answer. Or he would have Miss Baldwin accompany him, so that he appeared lost in his attentiveness to her. Once, in his rush, he slipped, fell and broke his leg, which, according to Bitzer, Baldwin rebroke when she accidentally bumped against him when he was in traction in the hospital.

His was obviously a much-shrunken world, and Bitzer's portrait of it enhances the sense we have of him as a man passed by. He tended, indeed, to rise late (a room service waiter generally delivered his breakfast around 11 A.M.) and then Greathouse, who has been described as "Mr. Griffith's Gangster," would arrive to get his marching orders for the day. On his round of errands Greathouse generally paused to chat with show biz pals, mostly from the business side of films, and would return with news of how the new pictures were doing, who was up, who was down, on which intelligence Griffith doted. As the day wore on the small circle of friends and relatives would gather for gossip, reminiscences and schemes for the future. In the evening Griffith would order his car and he and Baldwin would head out for dinner or dancing, the theater or the movies.[28]

Yet this portrait of a limited life is in some measure deceptive. For one thing, freed of his economic struggles, and the demands of production, Griffith—as his letters show—was relaxed and chatty, enjoying himself. For another he was by no means confined to New York and his hotel. Bitzer says he particularly loathed the winters there—in part because of the case of frostbite he had acquired on *Way Down East,* which of course was painful when the cold came to the Northeast. He had enough money to motor South, to Virginia or to Florida, to escape the inclemency. Finally, he did not believe that he was retired or futureless. Like anybody else who had been in show business for any length of time, he knew how rapidly fortunes could rise and fall and rise again. Indeed in the winter of 1933, in the period when Wood Oglesby's assaults on various corporate treasuries were reaching a climax, Griffith was beginning what he hoped would be a new career—as a radio personality.

He signed to do two fifteen-minute network broadcasts a week. The sponsor was Hinds Honey and Almond Cream, a hand lotion. The salary was $450 a week, the show's title was "Hollywood as Griffith Knew It," and his duties were light but pleasant. He would share some of his memories with a writer, who would then gently and romantically fictionalize them. On the air Griffith would engage in a scripted conversation with the announcer-host leading into and out of these little playlets, pointing their moral or putting them in historical perspective. On the whole, the reminiscences were reasonably accurate, although of course certain dialogic liberties were taken with them, and on the whole the press was quite kind to the enterprise, speaking enthusiastically of the naturalism of the acting on the shows, for example, and praising Griffith's manner as well. Floyd Gibbons, one of the premier radio announcers of the time, even wrote him a fan letter.

Griffith himself waxed enthusiastic about the medium's possibilities in interviews, claiming he was "cuckoo about radio," for instance, and describing it as "a marvelous medium," requiring "no tricks" for success. Of course, he said, venting the weariness and cynicism he often affected in these years, it could not possibly be considered an art, any more than the movies could be: "The life of a broadcast is about as permanent as a whiff of smoke, it fades in a moment. The life of a film is at best five years. For that reason neither . . . may be called an art." But still he admired the craft and skill radio required, and it is obvious that he saw in the brevity of the typical radio show of the moment an analogy with the brevity of films when he first entered them. Perhaps, he implied, he could do for the new medium what he had done for the old—show the way to longer, more complex dramatic structures. "Right now I have under consideration a dramatization of a picture story I once made called 'Intolerance.' . . ."[29]

That was pure fancy, of course, and his show was canceled after 13 weeks. But it brought him out of his hotel room and gave him a touch of his old-time celebrity (as well as a chance to perform a little). Best of all, it established for all to see that he was healthy and competent and able to work in a disciplined fashion. Given the tales that had circulated about his drinking, this was important to his hopes for a comeback, which he was now pursuing actively, promoting ideas of his own, seeking literary and theatrical properties he might produce, and making himself available to others who had ideas for films he might make.

Among the more interesting of his schemes was one to return to the legitimate theater as a producer-director. He had taken an option on three plays, plus the future output of one Walter Charles Roberts, a drama teacher at Ithaca College. The play Griffith felt was most promising was a comedy called *Damn Deborah*. It was about a woman who disguises herself and serves in the army for a couple of years. Griffith was shrewd enough to offer it to a young actress who had just made her debut as a leading lady on Broadway. She met with Griffith and allowed that doing the play with him would be a "grand experience." But Katharine Hepburn also thought the "play and the part have too much the quality of *Warrior's Husband,*" the work in which she had made her first large theatrical success.[30] She had been the key to his hopes for the production—there were not too many actresses who could convincingly do male impersonations (she would prove her skill in this realm on the screen in *Sylvia Scarlett* three years later)—and little more would be heard from this project.

As to films, many people came and went through Griffith's life in this period, singing many a strange song, all of them notable for their lack of connection with the commercial realities of the moment. In fact, of Griffith's ideas and of the ideas that were presented to him, the only one that showed the slightest awareness of current social conditions and current fashion in artistic and intellectual circles came from Linda Griffith. While in Mexico, she had encountered a Vassar graduate who told her about an experimental play by Hallie Flanigan, then teaching at the college and shortly to become head of the Federal Theater Project. It was called *Can You Hear Their Voices?*; it was a sort of precursor of her Living Newspaper experiments and had enjoyed a certain success in avant-garde theaters both in the U.S. and abroad. She sent a copy to Linda, who transmitted it to Griffith, with this endorsement: "It is tremendously pregnant for the present disturbed world conditions and I feel something could be done with it for a movie. It has IDEAS, and someone with ideas has got to come along if the movies are to be saved for they are dying of dry rot."[31] Well, not quite, perhaps, but again, it was, ironically, Griffith's estranged wife who continued to believe in Griffith's capacity for breaking new ground, perhaps even recalled, as he might have, how vividly and poignantly his first films had expressed the social reality of ordinary people in troubled times.

Doubtless the suggestion seemed impractical, and anyway Griffith's only known attempt to contribute to the great nationwide debate on social policy in the early thirties was to haul out his old article on the injustices of the income tax, refurbish it and send it around to several publications. In it, he argued, perhaps presciently, that artists and inventors, creative people generally, were unfairly treated by tax laws that favored the rich, particularly in regard to their capital gains. The press was as uninterested in Griffith's views on this matter as he was in Hallie Flanigan.

No one else presented Griffith with anything as interesting as Linda's idea. Some Italians approached him as they had before, apparently taking at his word his previously expressed desire to do a biography of Mussolini. There was also talk, through intermediaries, of his undertaking a biography of John D. Rockefeller, with special emphasis on his philanthropic activities in the realm of public health. And someone from the Julius Rosenwald Foundation approached him about doing a film on Negro life in America, apparently not knowing or caring about *The Birth of a Nation*'s reputation among blacks.[32]

Certainly the gentlemen from the foundation were unaware that *The White Slave*, which had once been announced as his final Famous Players film but had of course been canceled when his contract was canceled, was still very much on his mind. He controlled the rights to the old play on which the film was to be based, and he wrote to both Winfield Sheehan, head of production at Fox, and Carl Laemmle, Jr., serving in the same capacity at Universal, offering it to them. To the former, astonishingly, he wrote that this play "has some very tremendous situations, as I don't think there is anything calculated to raise the gooseflesh on the back of an audience more than that of a white girl in close relations to negroes."[33] How dismaying! Almost two decades after *Birth* he had still learned nothing from its reception. Or perhaps was incapable of learning from it.

But if it was not clear before, it becomes self-evident at this late date; with Griffith we are dealing not so much with racial prejudice, but rather with a deep and permanent sexual obsession. Indeed, the thought recurs that blackness was almost incidental to the obsession, a convenient visual aid in symbolizing the ugliest and most rapacious of male impulses, but not perhaps to be taken personally by blacks. As he had proved in so many films after *Birth*, color was not entirely necessary to the working out of his great, sordid theme, that theme that thrilled him to the deepest, darkest (and entirely unacknowledged) recesses of his being. In any event, he could no more abandon it in his work than he could abandon the pursuit of underage girls in life. It is saddening and infuriating, for one is hard pressed to think of any other major figure, in films or for that matter in any of the arts, who so single-mindedly kept circling back on this particular pathology. And to find him still in thrall to it when he needed to prove that he could move on to other matters is particularly distressing.

Nor was *The White Slave* the only evidence of his curious concern. Throughout this period he kept proposing a sound remake of *Broken Blossoms*, even at one point taking it to Paramount (as Famous Players had now officially become), obviously hoping Zukor, who had thought so well of the film a decade before, would have the same enthusiasm for a new version. Nothing came of that, or attempts to interest other backers in it. But then in 1934 and '35, a deal began to come together in England,

and in May of the latter year Griffith, accompanied by Greathouse, sailed for London, a suite at the Dorchester and work on the script, in the employ of producer Julius Hagen and Twickenham studios. Whereupon, something went wrong, though it is hard to say just what.

The only full-scale account of the incident appears in a memoir by Rodney Ackland, a screen-struck playwright of no great distinction. An admirer of Griffith's work, he laid siege to him at the hotel, passed a vetting by Greathouse and wormed his way into Griffith's confidence and into a promise that he could write the screenplay. It is at this point that the persuasiveness of his tale and his obvious need for self-aggrandizement come into conflict. He says that at the time he began chatting Griffith up, the only thing that was firm about the production was the casting of Dolly Haas, a winsome young actress then married to a Twickenham supervisor named Hans Brahm, in Lillian Gish's old role. According to Ackland, neither the script nor the casting of the Richard Barthelmess part was set. Enter, at this point in Ackland's story, Emlyn Williams, the Welsh actor and playwright, then enjoying his first large West End success in *Night Must Fall*, the well-remembered thriller that he starred in and wrote. He was, says Ackland, a friend of his and also a Griffith fan, and the next thing he knew, Griffith, who had enjoyed the play, suddenly decided to cast Williams in the role of the saintly Chinese *and* let him write the screenplay, too. The bitchy implication is that Ackland's friend Williams eased him out of his writing assignment. This seems unlikely; it seems much more plausible that Williams, by this time, had won both jobs on the strength of a well-publicized success and that Griffith was more than happy to endorse Williams, who was Hagen's choice for both jobs.

Still, at this point Ackland's account starts to regain plausibility. For his portrait is of Griffith at his most vague and grandiose, enjoying his genius's perquisites at one of the world's great hotels, and muddling the best thing about *Broken Blossoms*, the perfect simplicity of its allegorical statement about innocence and evil. He proposed, for instance, a subplot that would somehow express the necessity for maintaining Anglo-American friendship, and wrote a scene in a pub, involving an American journalist, an English sailor, a poet and a prostitute, that included some flowery speeches not just on that theme but on that other Griffithian favorite, the brotherhood of man, as well. It puzzled Ackland, though clearly Griffith felt a need to pad his short and simple story. "I want to hear words, words," Griffith roared at another point. "I want words to come from the screen, beautiful words, like Shakespeare, like the Bible, so that moving pictures will *mean* something at last!" This, too, rings right. He would have wanted something like that, the man who once aspired to write poetic drama, and he would have thought that a sound adaptation of the most famously "poetic" of his silent films would be the place to attempt to do with dialogue what he had always tried to do with titles. He would, he implied, teach the new medium to stretch itself as he had the old.

Or anyway prepare the excuse of aspiration if he failed. And one has to believe that he was getting ready for that eventuality. That, anyway, is one explanation—the other being sheer hubris—for the self-destructive events that now followed. For one day a young woman presented herself in the Dorchester lobby asking to see Griffith. Greathouse was sent downstairs to interview her and returned saying she was an aspiring actress, about eighteen, who had worked in a laundry in Paris, saving what she could out of her salary in order to make an assault on show business. Hearing Griffith was in London, she had made her way there, but in the process her pittance had been lost or stolen. It was a story that couldn't miss with Griffith, and when she stood before him recounting it, tears that Ackland judged would be highly photogenic slid down her cheeks, and Griffith needed to see no more. "I must have her for the Gish part," he cried, and forthwith ordered a room booked for her at the hotel and spent the next week "coaching" her.

But, of course, another actress had already been signed for the part, as the director well knew, and he was in no position to impose his "protégée" on the producers at short notice. He brought her in and did a reading with her of the closet scene; it was judged ludicrous and he was fired.[34] He made a drunken phone call to Gish, blubbering of his desperate need for her. Soon thereafter he was on the boat home. The film was made by Haas's husband, his first solo directorial assignment, and after a name change (to John Brahm) he went on to a minor directorial career, most notably handling a pair of moody Victorian thrillers, *The Lodger* and *Hangover Square*. His *Broken Blossoms*, however, was a critical and commercial failure.

As for Griffith, this project represented his last realistic chance for a comeback during this period, and his behavior in England represents a model, unfortunately, for his response to such subsequent opportunities as were presented to him. At some point he would always manage to demonstrate his imperiousness and impracticality (and unexpressed fear) and succeed in turning the opportunity aside, even when it was presented in good spirit, by people whose motives were of the best.

For the moment, however, there would be no more opportunities in pictures; it would be four years before another presented itself. And so Griffith restyled himself. He was a writer now, he said. After he returned from England he told Frank S. Nugent, the *New York Times* film critic who would later turn screenwriter, that he had two plays that he was working on, one of which he had conceived thirty years earlier, but "never had time to do. . . ." "You know," he mused, "I never went into the movies to stay. I went there just to make money so I would have time to write." No, he didn't care to discuss their themes. No, there were no concrete plans for their production. The important thing, he said, was getting them done, getting them out of his mind.[35]

4

He was not being entirely misleading. Over the next few years he would write a good deal—working on the plays, on some poems (very much in his youthful manner, they might have been revisions of earlier works) and finally on an autobiography. All these he would abandon at some stage prior to completion, as if he were afraid of finishing anything, afraid that in confronting a final draft's inevitable lack of perfection he would also be forced to confront his own inadequacies—and the end of whatever fantasies of a continuing creative life he still maintained. Writing in these years was, for him, like a return to filmmaking, more useful as a dream than as a reality. He had his excuses, and they are perfectly reasonable ones. He had turned 60, and after a life sentence of hard labor he had a natural impulse to enjoy his parole, which he had sufficient resources to do in a modest way. There was a powerful impulse to restore his Kentucky roots, to enjoy the company of old friends and relatives in Oldham County and in Louisville. He had returned there in 1934, for sister Ruth's funeral, and found them welcoming, unquestioning and deferential. He felt free to be easy and lazy with them, and from 1935 to 1939 the little house he owned in La Grange—once occupied by his mother, now lived in by his brother Will and his family—was his legal residence, though he kept quarters much of that time in Louisville as well, since he still enjoyed his night life and the sense of a city abustle around him. He wandered a great deal in these years, in near-untraceable patterns—south to Miami and New Orleans, and west to Los Angeles. This was particularly so after the spring of 1936, when, at long last, he finally resolved the long anguish with Linda—and took a new bride.

In the end, that resolution was surprisingly simple. At the time of Ruth's funeral he had met a shrewd, distinguished and cultivated Louisville lawyer named J. Ballard Clark, who hinted in response to a question that it would not be difficult for Griffith to obtain a divorce from Linda in Kentucky, in such a way that she would not find out about it until it was an accomplished fact. Sometime in late 1935, after his sojourn in England, Griffith returned to Louisville with that goal in mind.

Clark's plan, like that of Oglesby for getting Griffith safely out of his economic entanglements, was in its essence simple, but required some maneuvering. To obtain a divorce under Kentucky law, Griffith had only to prove that he had been a resident of the state for five years and that he had not cohabited with his wife for a similar period of time. The fact that he had been the legal owner of the La Grange house for longer than that, and that he could prove that he and Linda had not lived together since 1911, qualified him on both counts. On December 26, 1935, preliminary papers were filed without publicity in La Grange with a judge who was a friend of Clark's. Under his guidance, the good old boy network then set up a conspiracy of silence around the plan, which required nothing of Griffith but a modicum of patience—no more than a couple of months of it, which, considering the quarter century of guilty irresolution that had attended his relationship with Linda, was little enough to ask. He passed the time happily. (There are reports of him in an Ohio River gambling casino, two chorus girls from the Gaiety Burlesque theater in Louisville on his arm, ordering champagne; giving out interviews to local newsmen; generally playing the great man taking his ease.) Of course, the deviousness of the plot appealed to his secretive side, and he appears to have taken something like a small boy's delight in it.

Finally, on February 28, 1936, a Friday, Clark was informed that his hand-picked judge was ready to sign the final decree. Only then did the story reach the newspapers (the *New York Times* carried a small item in its next day's editions), but by then, there was nothing Linda could do about it. Griffith had wanted to have Evelyn present the day the decree was handed down and marry her immediately—"he was as ardent as an 18-year-old," Clark would recall—but the attorney insisted he wait until the divorce could be officially recorded, which could not be done until Monday, March 2.

Sometime over that weekend Evelyn and her mother and Evelyn's sister arrived in Louisville, sometime on Monday Clark had a copy of the divorce documents sent to Griffith by messenger, and sometime on that same remarkable day Donald Crisp reached him from Hollywood. The Motion Picture Academy wished to present him with a special award for his contributions to the industry. Could he fly out in time to accept it at the annual Academy Awards banquet the following week? No, but he and his new bride could catch a train and arrive in time.

The news put Griffith into an uncharacteristic dither. He ordered a dinner for 50 from his hotel's catering manager, then changed it to ten. And before the ceremony he found it necessary to have one or two fortifying drinks in the bar downstairs. Nonetheless, he was retrieved from the Bluegrass Room by a newspaperman friend and he presented himself in perfect dignity in a small public room on the Brown Hotel's mezzanine floor at 8 P.M. There, with his brother Will and Ballard Clark at his side, David Wark Griffith, 61, and Evelyn Marjorie Baldwin, 26, were joined in holy matrimony by the Reverend W. R. Johnson, the Methodist minister from La Grange. Sometime later, on one of his visits to his office (Griffith liked to drop in of an afternoon for a leisurely chat), Griffith would suddenly kiss Ballard Clark on both cheeks and say to that startled man, "I love you." He would also suggest that he might have a great and prosperous career as a divorce lawyer if he cared to join the movie colony in Los Angeles.[36]

In this judgment of the lawyer's skills, Linda Griffith would certainly have bitterly concurred, had she been able to contain her outrage at the way she had been outmaneuvered. A year later, in an effort to gain a last measure of revenge against Griffith, she sued him for $50,000 in unpaid alimony in New York, at last making public the indiscreet letter admitting his affairs that Griffith had feared for so many years. He countersued for $500,000, charging he had been defamed by her, but the suit was dismissed and Linda was afforded a judgment that proved to be uncollectible, as Griffith avoided service of it by never again coming to New York. (His chauffeur would recall driving him East for business meetings in later years, but stopping in New Jersey, where his associates would meet him.) Just weeks after Linda's suit was tried another suit, brought by one of the Griffith Corporation's creditors, threw the company into receivership, and Griffith bought the rights to the few films it still controlled for $500, acquired some of its furniture and entered a bid for the last parcel of land it held at Orienta Point.

These sadnesses, however, were a year off. For now all was happy confusion with him. In the Griffiths' haste to catch a train for Los Angeles, their baggage was sent to the wrong station in Louisville, but such was his prestige locally that the train was held some 45 minutes until the luggage arrived. And the awards ceremony proved to be wonderful in Evelyn's eyes. "This was all quite new to me, and to meet these Hollywood people *en masse* . . . was quite a thing, but I was quite touched with the way they greeted him. When his award was announced, the entire room arose like a sea and cheered."[37]

Neither she nor Griffith knew they were being used, albeit as gently as possible, as innocent instruments in a political war. The Academy Award ceremonies that year were under threat of boycott from the Screen Actors Guild, the Directors Guild and the Writers Guild, embryo labor unions struggling, so far without success, to win the right to represent their members as bargaining agents with the studios. By boycotting the Oscar ceremony they felt they might call attention to their cause and taint the publicity value of the awards, thereby harming the studios in the only place that matters, their treasuries. The president of the Academy that year was Frank Capra, who believed, perhaps naïvely, that the Academy could be, if it was not yet, the keeper of an idealistic flame in an industry not notable for that quality—and as part of his campaign to get members to ignore their unions' pleas not to accept any award, nor even to grace the ceremony with their presences, he conceived the idea of the award for Griffith. He was an authentic admirer of the man and thought he deserved this recognition, but he also thought sentiment and curiosity about him might help override the boycott. Griffith, if he knew about Capra's scheme, would not have cared; he was developing into an anti–New Dealer, anti-unionist anyway—his old instinctive populism long since blunted—and, anyway, what a treat for Evelyn!

Later, Capra would credit his presence as a major contribution to the evening's success, and Griffith appears to have had an excellent time. Old colleagues like Crisp and Wally Walthall (who would die just weeks later) were on hand, and both his citation ("For his distinguished creative achievements as director and producer and his invaluable initiative and lasting contributions to the progress of the motion picture arts") and his ovation clearly moved him, for the press reported him gulping back tears as he declared his pride in being a member of what he described as the finest industry in the world. Then, as now, Academy ceremonies tended to run on, and it was at one A.M. that Griffith was called upon to present the major awards (to Bette Davis, for best actress in *Dangerous*, to Victor McLaglen for best actor in *The Informer* and to *Mutiny on the Bounty* for best picture). The most notable absentees, demonstrating their union solidarity, were John Ford and Dudley Nichols, the screenwriter, both of whom won prizes for their work on *The Informer*.[38]

The Griffiths stayed on in Hollywood for some time, and among the pleasures of the visit was a day on the set of *San Francisco*, the mighty M-G-M epic about the earthquake and fire that had propelled Linda into Griffith's arms. Starring Clark Gable, Spencer Tracy and Jeanette MacDonald, the picture was almost entirely the product of Griffith's protégés; it was produced by John Emerson, written by Anita Loos and directed by his old assistant, Woody Van Dyke. In the press Griffith had been lavish in his praise of Van Dyke's *The Thin Man*, claiming to have seen it four times. After welcoming them, Mrs. Griffith later recalled, Van Dyke kindly engaged Griffith in a private conference about how a scene should be staged, and had him call "Action" to start it, "Cut" to end it. In its way, it was as fine a tribute to Griffith as the Oscar ceremony, and during their later stay in Hollywood, "One Take" Van Dyke, who was one of the busiest and most commercially successful directors of the day, generally made an effort to keep up with Griffith and to draw him back a little bit into the social life of the movie community.

The Griffiths left Hollywood for a stay in Florida late in the year and then returned to Kentucky, before circling back to Los Angeles, where in 1938 Griffith was made the Directors Guild of America's First Honorary Life Member. On this visit, too, Capra invited them to the set of *Mr. Smith Goes to Washington*. But Kentucky remained their base until 1939. The summers they passed in the La Grange house, most of the winter months in Louisville, sometimes at the Brown, but at least once in a small house, not far from the center of the city. They kept two Persian cats—they would have cats in varying numbers throughout their married life—and Griffith's day often began with a stroll to a restaurant called the Sweet Shoppe, where he would buy coffee for his cronies and hang about gossiping until he made his way to Ballard Clark's office in the late afternoon. In the evenings there was dancing and gambling and the movies. Evelyn was not always on his arm on those occasions, for he had rediscovered the delights of male companionship, especially when his destinations were not of the most elegant. There were also grander occasions— the State Fair, for example, or the Kentucky Derby, where Boyd Martin, the *Courier Journal*'s well-known drama critic, would recall seeing him in a dapper gray suit set off by a purple hat and tie. "On any other man the purple hat and flashy car would have seemed odd, but on the angular frame of the great D. W., with his air of arrogance and greatness, it somehow looked just right." Here, on home ground, D. W. Griffith was clearly still a celebrity.[39]

The car of which Martin speaks was a Mercedes, which Griffith had acquired after he and Evelyn returned from Los Angeles, along with the services of a kindly young black man, Richard Reynolds, as chauffeur-mechanic. Car and driver had as their chief function taking Griffith and his bride on leisurely motor trips through the South. The first of these, Reynolds would recall, was to Miami, for a stay that stretched on for some five months, probably in the winter of '36–'37. Reynolds, who would stay with Griffith into 1941, particularly remembered the drive home from Florida, through the Smokey Mountains in the spring, with Griffith pausing to savor the beauties they encountered along the route, "with no hurry as long as she was enjoying herself." He would add: "I know he got a great pleasure out of it—you could tell by his disposition, expressions on his face, and the lovely conditions between the two individuals."[40] "He was interested in showing me what America was like," Baldwin would later recall.[41]

Back home, Griffith's major preoccupation was his writing. It was probably at this time that he made his final assault on the plays he had talked about earlier. The first of them, *The Treadmill*, is a grand allegory, dominated by its symbolic title instrument, on which humanity, urged on by such religious figures as Christ and Buddha, exhausts itself in meaningless labor, while caged monkeys watch and cynically comment. "My God, every time it goes forward one step it goes back another," says one of the simians. At various points Adam and Eve, demons from Hell, preachers, corrupt businessmen and other symbolic figures step forward to demonstrate the waste of our days. In opposition to them Griffith offers idealistic lovers—a poetic lad and his girl friend, who grow up as the play wends on, making naïve and florid speeches about the power of love.

This sort of fake-profound, fake-simple poesy alternated with slangy vernacular, very much in the mode of *The Fool and the Girl* and, for that matter, *The Struggle*. But some of the stage pictures Griffith imagined were quite spectacular. Evelyn, who sometimes spelled the professional secretary he brought in to take dictation—often for sessions that would last eight or ten hours—would recall, ". . . he used pictures better than words, he dictated pictures." There were also some passages that have a certain verbal energy, even passion, about them. One recalls, in particular, an exchange that might have been taken over from one of Thornton Wilder's plays, in which the central couple, now grown elderly, debate life's meaning. She allows as how "each generation might be building a stairway up to where you can get to understand things," but admits that it may require a thousand years just to make a step or two toward those heights. Maybe she is right, her companion says, but "I sure would just like to know what it's all about. People just livin' and just dyin' and don't seem to amount to nothin' anyhow." Still, he concedes that her idea "gives you a little push to keep on hoeing." Whereupon she speaks Griffith's mind of the moment: "Well, it seems to me that after you lost your money and finally got down to this little garden . . . you slept better at night and seemed to be better off all the way around." "Yes," he says, "I certainly feel better since I really got down to work."[42]

But Griffith's work, this writing, was damnably hard for him. He could not sustain the pitch of his sometimes intense enthusiasms for very long. "He'd work on a thing for a month and then he'd not see an end to it and set it aside," his wife would later recall, and the heavily reworked manuscript of *The Treadmill* offers ample testimony to his inability to solve the problems it presented him. One of his old difficulties arose: the play is simply too abstract and too emotionally empty, and far too large a vehicle for the small and simple ideas he wanted it to carry. Nor did he ever work out a coherent narrative line, or characters of sufficient complexity, to sustain an audience's interest in it. Finally, he was more than usually debilitated by cynicism. All the revisions in the manuscript bespeak the romantic idealist coming to grips with the failure of his hopes, the meaninglessness of the human endeavor. And that, of course, makes sustained literary effort a hellish enterprise. Boyd Martin spoke to him sometime during this period and recalled him summarizing his life thus: "You cannot improve upon what was once written about a man; he was born, he grew up, he slept a little, he ate a little, he laughed a little, he loved a little—and then he died." But what about your career as you look back on it? Martin persisted. "I am much more interested in whether the plumber will be at the place . . . in La Grange in the morning," Griffith replied.[43]

But if this project discouraged him, another seemed to energize him. Its dimensions were vague. Evelyn would remember it as "this book on Kentucky," which he told her could be the basis of a great film or play.

He was, by her estimate, supporting, or at least giving handouts to, perhaps 30 of his relatives, and he was quite regularly seeing almost as many of them at Sunday gatherings around the area. But "research" gave him an excuse to get out and about even more. Reynolds, who drove him all over Shelby and Oldham counties, for interviews in aid of this project, said, "Farmers and old timers who would sit around in the courthouse yard reminiscing about the old days . . . they knew how he came up and how they came up . . . and he got a great kick out of talking to them about the old times."[44]

If the material he gathered on these expeditions informed anything he tried to write, it was probably his second play, which he called *The Musquito* [*sic*]. It is set in his home county, many of its characters bear the names of Griffith relatives and its central figure, named John, is obviously a projection of Griffith—a young man who in the first act aspires to be a famous writer and in the last act, like so many Griffith heroes before him, returns home having attained that goal. Stylistically it is touched by expressionism (there actually are mosquitoes on stage and they function significantly in the working out of the plot); structurally it shows an attempt to bring cinematic technique to the theater. But this play is, if anything, more awkward and less persuasive than *The Treadmill*. Still, it does have a certain autobiographical interest. For one thing "John's" father is seen to be quite mad, suffering from what can only be advanced syphilis. Naturally one wonders if Roaring Jake's erratic behavior in his late years can be traced to a similar source, and if Griffith perhaps only discovered this fact in talking with old-timers during the period when he was writing. Then, too, Griffith here writes openly about his marriage by giving John a wife with whom he has not lived for decades but who refuses to divorce him. Finally, he speaks of his reputation as a womanizer, when he has another character accuse John of having had "more love affairs than most anybody in this county. . . . Oh, I know, I've read and heard"—to which Griffith's surrogate enters a modest demurral, incidentally. This character, to whom John responds very warmly, is, interestingly, a young girl of about Evelyn's age, in the play the daughter of one of John's contemporaries. Still, Griffith backs away from a true confrontation with himself, and seeking to bring the piece to a happy conclusion, has John's father bitten by the mosquitoes, inducing a fever which allegedly burns away his venereal disease and restores him to the sort of loving relationship with wife and family that Jake Griffith never enjoyed.[45]

Doubtless work on the play—and especially the "research" for it— helped fill the empty hours and discharge some of his restlessness. One can scarcely regret it. What one does regret is Griffith's failure to come to grips with an autobiography. The thought of doing one had apparently never occurred to him previously. Or, if it had, his secretive nature had caused him to reject the notion out of hand. But early in 1938 events conspired to turn his thoughts in that direction.

Griffith had been interviewed during one of his early visits to Kentucky by a young newspaperman named Jim Hart, who later moved on to Chicago and Hearst's *American* there. At some point one of his editors happened to mention Hart's acquaintance with Griffith to Fulton Oursler, the well-known journalist, who at the time was editor of *Liberty*. He in turn said his magazine might be interested in a piece reflecting Griffith's views on present-day Hollywood if Hart could get around to it. Shortly thereafter his paper was struck by the emerging Newspaper Guild and Hart returned to Louisville, where he contacted Griffith regarding Oursler's proposition.

Griffith liked the idea. Pieces under his by-line had appeared in the magazine before, and he also associated its name with that of the New York theater where *Birth* had first played and thought the congruence a lucky omen. So he and Hart set to work, with Griffith dictating "discursive" notes, which included this bitter passage (as later rendered by Hart): "Hollywood today is a sterile film Detroit with emotions as standardized as automobile parts. We have moving pictures that do not move. Activity is mistaken for action; sex for love; and sound effects for suspense. If history remembers at all the people responsible for such an assembly line, it should only be for the vandalism they have wrought in a medium that could have ranked with art and literature."[46]

This sort of thing went over well with readers of a magazine like *Liberty*, and its editors thought it would go over still better if these and other similarly critical remarks could appear under Griffith's by-line. Since the first draft had consisted mainly of quotes from him, this required only the excision of a little introductory material and Hart's name, which he readily agreed to do. With this mild success behind them, and with quite a few autobiographical notes already made by Hart, the two men agreed to attempt a book.

Griffith disliked desks, formality; they would work, he decreed, in surroundings "that evoke creation." He also found Hart's pad and scratching pencil a distraction. The writer would have to remember whatever Griffith said as best he could and they would correct whatever Hart managed to get down later, when it was typed up. They worked either sitting on the porch of the La Grange house or in the lobby at Brown's or occasionally at a nearby lake where, after a relaxing swim, they would lie side by side on the grass, with Griffith chain-smoking and selectively recalling his past. For the most part Griffith kept their appointments reliably (though he did once or twice break one of them in order to go drinking with a police reporter friend). But Hart, who was a shrewd and

practiced newsman, understood that he was not getting from Griffith anything like a full story. "Gradually I began to realize that he was not
dictating pages, but was rehearsing and directing scenes out of his past.
If the 'scene' didn't fit, he would alter or delete it."[47]

What Griffith wanted the piece to fit was a mythic tale, the main
thrust of which was well summarized by the working title Griffith proposed, "D. W. Griffith and the Wolf." The wolf was poverty and Griffith meant to imply that from start to last his life had been conditioned
by the omnipresence of this gray and skulking menace. This was, at best,
a partial truth, obviously, and the skimpy manuscript, only some 25,000
words long, and breaking off after the premiere of *Intolerance*, must at
best be regarded as veracious only in the poetic sense. Hart recognized
this, but he was functioning as no more than a secretary and copy editor;
only occasionally, "when the manuscript read like *True Heart Susie* or
The Adventures of Frank Merriwell" could Griffith be persuaded to re-
cast his story, though even then he would "have a small tantrum over
the deletion of a single pet cliche or prosy sentence." The habits of hokum
and secretiveness were simply too deeply ingrained in Griffith for him to
break now, and Hart was treated as so many of Griffith's subordinates had
been treated in the past, with politeness, with measured camaraderie, but
with no genuine respect.

The result is a manuscript that is like the worst of Griffith's movies—
deaf to both objective and subjective truth, deaf even to its own vul-
garities, self-parody of the cruelest kind. And Hart knew it. As a gentleman Griffith could be excused for not wishing to recount his romantic
feelings for Lady Diana Manners or his refusal to say in public what he
told Hart in private, that Lillian Gish was "the only woman in his life
for many years." But even the material that he could safely have spoken
of honestly he did not. As Hart says, the thing does read like cheap
popular fiction, or even a silent picture scenario, though done in the false-
modest tone of Griffith's old curtain speeches.

Finally, the evasions and prevarications became too much for Hart,
and he proposed that Griffith cease dictating and let him work up the
book from his notes, submitting his work to Griffith for his approval when
it was finished. This Hart apparently attempted to do, but he was interrupted by the start of World War II. He was also put off by Griffith's
wish that what he had given Hart not be published until after his death.
Later, Hart might have been deterred in a plan to turn autobiography
into biography by fear of Seymour Stern, an "official" competitor who for
several decades fought off all efforts to intrude on what he came to regard
as his exclusive territory. In any event, Hart was not writer enough or
historian enough for the enormous task of sorting out truth from false-
hood in the story Griffith told him.

Be that as it may, Hart's memoir of this ultimately unhappy collaboration reinforces the impression of a man who finally had the leisure but not the will to face himself. At one point, for instance, Griffith happened to be reading a newspaper column by Arthur Brisbane and remarked that he would himself like to do a column. Did Hart know anyone at the syndicates? He did, and under the impression that Griffith meant to comment on film, offered their joint services to several firms, all of which replied with interest. But when one sent a representative to Louisville to confer with Griffith he broke his appointment and was finally run to ground in the bar of the Seelbach Hotel, where he announced that he had no intention of dealing with show business. World affairs were what he wanted to write about, he declared firmly. Whether this perversity was his way of again pushing aside opportunity or whether he really fantasized himself a molder of political opinion, it is impossible to say.

His only true service to history during this time was his agreement to deposit his papers, and copies of all his films that he controlled, with the Museum of Modern Art's small new film department, a considerable coup for its curator, Iris Barry, and that then struggling institutional stepchild. She had been cultivating this ground since 1936, when she presented retrospective showings of *Intolerance* at the time Griffith received his honorary Oscar, and the receipt of his material, the museum's first large gift for its film archive, and the attendant publicity, helped convince people that popular movies were worthy of appreciation and preservation. The large retrospective exhibition of Griffith's work, which Barry staged in 1940 (it coincided with the museum's first large-scale exhibition of the work of another Welsh-American vernacularist, Frank Lloyd Wright), helped to extend its range into areas previously unexplored by museology, while the monograph she prepared for that exhibition was the first serious attempt to gain an overview of Griffith's work. Once again, and once again without quite consciously knowing it, Griffith was pioneering. And paying the price of being first on the field.

So much has developed from that first retrospective of an American filmmaker's work. It is not too much to say that the notion of film as a fit subject not just for museum exhibition, but for scholarship, begins with this event. And whatever one thinks of the academicizing of film, of Ph.D. programs in their history and esthetics, of doctoral candidates charging about collecting the old-timers' reminiscences, of retrospectives and festivals and lifetime achievement awards, one cannot help but believe Griffith's later years would have been much happier if he could have spent them in the company of serious younger people respectful of his achievements, eager for his opinions and his memories, as later generations of directors have, to the enhancement of their self-esteem, and of the historical record.

5

Instead, he got a job which turned into another disappointment. Hart has given the impression that it came as a response to publication of the *Liberty* collaboration in June of 1939. He thinks it reminded producer Hal Roach of Griffith's existence and caused him to press employment on the director, who was now 64. But both Mrs. Griffith and Roach himself remember the circumstances differently. She recalled Griffith simply deciding to return to the Coast to look for work, and Roach remembered being moved at the sight of Griffith at loose ends in Los Angeles, "not doing a damned thing . . . one of the great geniuses of the business."[48]

Roach had been in movies almost as long as Griffith but had been much more successful in maintaining his independence. He had been a gold miner and a mule skinner before drifting into the movies as an extra in 1912. Tough and shrewd, blunt and hearty, he founded his fortune as Harold Lloyd's first partner, and unlike his great rival, Sennett, he survived the transition from silent to sound production and the diminution of the market for short comedies in part because he had a good story sense, in part because he had a comedy team in Laurel and Hardy who were, if anything, more adept in talking pictures than they had been in pantomime.

Now, however, Roach's modest studio in Culver City was branching out. He had enjoyed a considerable success with the sophisticated *Topper*, starring Cary Grant and Constance Bennett, and presently had an extremely sober adaptation of John Steinbeck's novel *Of Mice and Men* in production. He also had a notion for another large-scale project, *One Million B.C.*, which was frankly inspired by Griffith's old one-reeler *Man's Genesis*. He had long admired Griffith—he remembered visiting the *Intolerance* set several times—and when Griffith's troubles in the twenties became public knowledge, Roach had wired him an offer of a contract to direct short comedies, even though "he didn't have a funny bone in his body."[49]

His little operation was, of course, ideal for Griffith. Essentially a two-man operation (Hal Roach, Jr., was in business with his father), it was in no sense an industrial organization. It was, in fact, about the only kind of place that Griffith might reasonably have expected to work, since all the other studios were yet more hierarchical in structure than they had been in his last days with Schenck. Here he could have direct access to his employer and here, too, he would feel few pressures upon him, for Roach wanted to use him only as a consultant and general assistant on *One Million B.C.* Contrary to the impression Griffith gave people at the time, Roach had no firm plan to let Griffith direct the film, a job he and his son would undertake in due course. All he ever said to Griffith, he later recalled, was "D. W., I need somebody to help me with the picture. Would you like to go on the payroll?" It is possible, of course, that he implied a possibility of directing if things worked out well between them in preproduction. It is also possible that Griffith read more into the offer than was intended. "I think he was confused at the time," Roach would say. "He was disillusioned with things."

Roach would say after the fact that Griffith's name should never have been mentioned in connection with the picture, meaning that his intention was simply to have Griffith do a quiet job behind the scenes and collect his paycheck without fanfare. In this, however, Roach was being duplicitous. He understood the dignifying value of Griffith's name in connection with this project, and his publicity department set up a number of interviews with him for the press, one of which was with Herb Sterne, a publicist and free-lance journalist who was to become perhaps Griffith's closest friend in his last years. He would recall that the studio gate guard did not know Griffith's name and that he found him tucked away in a small office. But on at least one occasion Griffith and Roach were interviewed jointly and were elaborately collegial with the reporter. "It's a screwy idea," Roach opined of the film. "I concur in the sentiment," murmured Griffith. "Mr. Griffith is producing, I'm only directing," Roach said. "He worked on the script; a lot of the ideas are his; he's casting the picture." Replied Griffith: "The picture is, of course, Mr. Roach's—he is directing. He selected the story in the first place. I am here merely in an advisory capacity. I give what help I can."[50]

This help was not inconsiderable, and at the early stages of the film it was crucial. Lewis Milestone, who was directing *Of Mice and Men*, asked him what he was doing on the somewhat raffish Roach lot. Griffith quite shrewdly replied: "Hal Roach remembers me from the old days. His analysis was that each time I made a movie I brought out a couple of stars."[51] In fact, the first task Roach assigned him was, "Find me a girl," by which he meant a leading lady. Afterward he observed Griffith, who clearly found the job congenial, chatting it up with extra girls around the lot. A bit after that he came to Roach and announced simply, "I've found the girl. Come on out and I'll show you." With that, he took the producer to the back lot, where he introduced him to a pretty blonde whom he instructed to take off her shoes and run to some telephone poles a short distance away. This she did "very well and gracefully," as Roach remembered. Since the picture consisted very largely of a tribe of cavemen scampering away from enemies both human and animal (the last being prehistoric monsters), it was perfectly clear that the leads had to be athletic as well as handsome in their bearskin briefs. Griffith then directed Carole Landis's screen test (it was silent) as well as a love scene opposite an amiable if leaden young Roach contract player, Victor Mature, with whom Griffith felt a certain rapport, since he was from Louisville, too. Both were hired, and Griffith was proud of his contribution to their casting.

What else he did on *One Million B.C.* is problematical, though it appears he worked with the effects department, supervising the trick shots (lizards were shot so that they resembled prehistoric creatures and integrated, by process photography and mattes, with the actors). But he complained as time passed that no one seemed interested in listening to his advice and opinions (there were differences with Roach, Jr., in particular). Richard Reynolds, his chauffeur, would recall Griffith saying as they headed home from the studio, "These young whippersnappers don't know what they're talking about, they don't even know the technique . . . they try to ignore me . . . but I really know. I was born with it, I started it, I invented it. . . ."

He did not quit, and he was not fired, either. He served out his time. He became friends with Milestone, who found him most encouraging. He never drank and with Milestone at least, never discussed his troubles. He did not gossip, preferring to talk not about actors and actresses but, as Milestone would recall, about "the boys and girls in the laboratory," praising them for the technical magic they were performing on the film. He was "the first man to see *Of Mice and Men*," when Milestone finished it, and after his job came to an end he wrote to Gish: "I used my six months to good advantage—studying the so-called 'new technique.' I was interested to see that many of the best directors, Frank Capra and Lewis Milestone in particular, are getting back to the old silent technique, merely using dialogue to heighten the effect. They are getting away from the 'talkie talkie' pictures. . . ."[52]

Griffith was both right and wrong. It is perfectly true that by the middle of the decade the camera had almost entirely won back its freedom of movement and its freedom to go anywhere and observe anything, indoors or out. It is also true that many an effective sound film included some sequence that was, in its essence, a silent sequence, something as fluid, as free in its use of visual symbols, and as free of the need to express itself in dialogue, as any of the older films had been. But the true glory of this decade's work lies precisely in the talkiness of the talkies. The dialogue supplied for them by the New York playwrights and novelists who came West for the money and left behind a convention as powerful in its way as Shakespearean verse—namely fast, smart, tough, urbane conversation—determined the shape and pace of thirties movies more than any other factor. We associate this manner primarily with the briskly bantering comedies that may be the great glory of the American screen in the later half of the decade, but its influence was felt in every sort of film with a contemporary setting—gangster movies and romances, detective stories and international intrigues, even occasionally in the better musicals. And this dialogue, staged as rapid, frequently overlapping crosstalk, imposed upon the film itself a rhythm that was for the most part quite different from that of the silent picture. In a way the talkies of this first decade were more duplicitous than the silents. They did not announce themselves openly as poetic fantasies; despite premises that were as fantastic as any previously seen on film, they had, precisely because they could speak, a more realistic air about them. And this new manner was not of a kind that the slow-spoken, essentially humorless Griffith would have found congenial even if he had been younger and more adaptable. One has to believe that, except in very special circumstances, he was now unemployable as a director. And, perhaps deep in his heart, grateful not to be asked back into this quite changed world.

This does not mean that he might not have been employable in some other capacity, perhaps somewhat along the lines in which Roach had used him, though at a more dignified level. Elder statesmanship might have been something he would have been good at, given the chance. He had the bearing for it, the presence and the voice. But Hollywood had yet to conceive of itself as a cultural institution. It still defined itself by the industrial ideal; it rather liked thinking of itself as tough and unsentimental, a maker of products—a Detroit of the mind, as Griffith had said. So there really was no place for him, except as an object of distant pity.

6

The most persistent impression of the years that followed—and Griffith had almost eight more years to live—is of an old man, drunk and mumbling (and occasionally declaiming) about his past glories as he staggered about the night streets of Hollywood, getting into arguments in the bars, occasionally making indecent propositions to the women he encountered. There is a certain irresistible dramatic logic in this image of the once great and powerful man in pathetic decline, acting out his own variant on the most basic and potent of the movies' self-referential myths, the *What Price Hollywood?–A Star Is Born* myth. It is, however, an image based to a large extent on guilty rumor—the movies have always employed large numbers of people anxious to believe the worst about the ways of their world—and on a single interview Griffith was tricked into giving less than a year before he died by a journalist named Ezra Goodman. He had trouble peddling his concoction to the better journals but finally placed the piece in *PM*, the short-lived, left-leaning New York tabloid, which had a natural interest in demonstrating how America in general, its business institutions in particular, treat the individuals on whose broken lives fortunes are built. The editor who finally took the Griffith story knew what he had, it was indeed "a juicy piece of Sunday copy—a yarn about a great man down on his uppers," as Goodman later characterized it, and once it was in print it was freely quoted in the more genteel press. And Goodman himself used an expanded version of it as the introduction to his stupefying book, *The Fifty-Year Decline and Fall of Hollywood*, the title of which, since it was published in 1961, implies that the place had entered its decay before it was actually established as a production center.[53] But this story is hardly the whole story of his last years, however artfully it suits one's sense that life, and especially the life of the artist, ought to imitate the conventions of art. On the contrary, though Griffith lived his last decade in a kind of limbo, it was a not entirely unpleasant limbo—only an unproductive one.

Aside from one notable adventure, when Griffith took Evelyn to visit Hearst at the San Simeon "ranch" (as movie people always seemed to refer to it), their life together seems to have been singularly bereft of glamour. That trip, however, would loom large in Evelyn's later memories. There must have been 50 guests present the weekend they spent there, with the Griffiths assigned one of the lavish cottages; and though the meals struck Evelyn as "rather stuffy and formal," she found Hearst, whom she saw through Griffith's respectful eyes, to be a fascinating figure. On Monday, Griffith decided that they should press on to a fashionable fishing resort along the Rouge River. Evelyn had never fished before and was dismayed to find the other guests equipped with all the proper Abercrombie and Fitch gear. The best she could manage was a riding habit, but she was thrilled to land three steelheads, while all Griffith caught was an old boot.

There is no record of other outings as memorable. During their first year or two in Los Angeles, they often went to the shore to watch the sunset over the Pacific. Two or three times a week they would go to the movies. Once they signed up for a course of dance lessons at an Arthur Murray studio, but after Griffith's lifetime experience with the avocation, his style turned out to be too set and singular to be changed. On Sundays they would occasionally gather a small group and head for Griffith's ranch, now being productively worked as a fruit farm. A picnic would be brought along and sometimes a copy of a play from which each member of the company would choose a part to read aloud.

They also moved around a good bit, living in small sublet houses in Coldwater Canyon; on Canon Drive in Beverly Hills; in Westwood; in hotels when, because of the wartime housing shortage, they could find nothing to rent. They finally settled down on Peck Drive, also in Beverly Hills, for the last years they were together. By that time they had nurtured a small circle of friends. Some of them were Griffith's "children"—

Mae Marsh, for example, Woody Van Dyke before his untimely death in 1943, even Mickey Neilan (though Griffith tended to see that sometime boy wonder on his own, since he was now very much down on his luck, drinking, living in a cheap Hollywood hotel, driving a cab, picking up occasional work as an extra). Evelyn would remember a night at Neil Hamilton's, where she was embarrassed because she did not know how to play poker. Griffith pretended he didn't know how either so that she would not be deserted for the evening (though one of his proud memories was playing at the White House with President Harding and his cronies, with the Chief Executive taking over his hand for him and stopping a string of losses at an unfamiliar game).

Among his old friends, Lillian Gish was perhaps the most loyal and eager to try to help find Griffith something useful to occupy himself with. She had been startled and alarmed by news of Griffith's marriage, but she developed a fondness for Evelyn and when she returned to Los Angeles to make a couple of pictures in 1943—her first after a decade of stage work—frequently joined in the outings to the ranch or arranged small dinner parties that included the Griffiths. One time, at Garbo's request, she brought the actress and Griffith together at one of these parties, although the meeting was not a success. Garbo, according to Gish, gave Griffith the impression she was not so much interested in meeting him for himself, but because she had heard that he bore a resemblance to her discoverer, mentor and lover, Mauritz Stiller, and this hurt Griffith's feelings.

But if the encounter with Garbo was not a great success, there were new acquaintances who became, at least for a time, friends. Herb Sterne, the publicist he had met at Roach's, was helpful in keeping Griffith ("the idol of my youth") abreast of the latest news of the town, and since he was working at the time for Preston Sturges, he brought the two men together, and Griffith became a staunch, public admirer of the great writer-director's comedies. He was quoted as saying *The Miracle of Morgan's Creek* was the funniest film he had ever seen. And, of course, there were still thoughtful people who sought Griffith out to pay homage to the influence he had had on them through his work.

Among these were Jean Renoir, the great French director, who contacted Griffith almost as soon as he took up his wartime residence in Los Angeles. He had loved Griffith's films since he was a very young man, before he began to direct. In particular, he found silent close-up to be the "marvel of marvels," and in his autobiography he speaks of how some of them—of Gish, of Pickford, of Garbo—"are imprinted on my memory for life" because of what they revealed "about the inward life of the idealized woman." He found Griffith, as he says in his book, "a very well-preserved elderly man," entirely capable physically and mentally of directing, which made his bitterness about not being able to do so understandable and poignant to Renoir. He and Evelyn were frequently guests at Renoir's table, and Gish also included the two directors at dinners at her house. Evelyn would recall being present at the home of Charles Laughton, who had starred in *This Land Is Mine*, one of Renoir's American films, when Renoir married his script girl and longtime companion Dido Freire in 1944. Renoir himself liked to recall the time he gave a dinner party to bring Griffith together with his old assistant von Stroheim, who had, of course, given what may have been his greatest performance in Renoir's *Grand Illusion*. Asked many years later if the two men had enjoyed their reunion, Renoir laughed and said, "No." His largest memory of the evening was of von Stroheim drinking too much Scotch and getting sick.

In the course of this interview Renoir was both more open and more subtle about Griffith than he was in his autobiography. He said he felt Griffith was "overplaying" the role in which he had cast himself, that of the great man in decline. He also felt that in his reminiscences Griffith placed too much emphasis on his technical contributions to the movies, not enough on the poetic qualities of his work. This was a highly intelligent observation. Griffith was indeed tiresome in these years with his obsessive talk about the technical devices he had pioneered. It was as if he despaired of trying to explain his claim on history to those who did not remember or could not understand the poetry of his best work.[54]

But Renoir, that gentlest of ironists and most humane of men, regarded that idiosyncrasy as perhaps inevitable in the case of someone like Griffith, and he made a singular observation about him: "He had the naiveté of the authentic great man." This was, he said, "an indisputable characteristic" of great artists: he had observed it in von Stroheim, in Chaplin—and perhaps in himself. "To succeed in his enterprises Griffith has to transform reality, and build around him the Griffith world, a nonintellectual world of feeling and sensation." But immersion in that world, of course, left him defenseless in the real world, and "disgusted to see the movies in the hands of men less gentlemanly than himself."[55]

Renoir's view of Griffith helps to explain not just the bitterness of these years but his lost and befuddled air as well. He seemed to know, without ever openly acknowledging the fact, that even if he could get a job in pictures it would not solve his essential and essentially insoluble problem, which was reclaiming that lost world of the imagination, that lost kingdom where he had been able to project a kind of subjective idealism that he had not even been able to consciously define. At the heart of every artist's life lies the impenetrable enigma of creation as he practices it, and somehow one feels that Renoir, a fellow artist, a greater and more conscious one, came as close as anyone to glimpsing and measuring Griffith's secret.

Unable to see him as Renoir did, the well-meaning Griffith loyalists never stopped working in his behalf. Herb Sterne, for example, put together a Griffith retrospective at a local art gallery in the winter of 1943, hoping the publicity would remind Hollywood of Griffith's existence. Renoir, Dudley Nichols (who had written the Laughton film), René Clair, Harriet Parsons, Louella's influential producer-daughter, turned out on opening night, and the showings ran on for seven weeks, with excellent coverage in the press, but they generated no job offers. Later, there was a similar series at the University of Southern California, with gratifying results for Griffith's self-esteem, but again generating no response from the studios.

In these years, various possibilities continued to offer Griffith brief flickers of hope. One of the liveliest of these was the revival of a suggestion that Gish had made some years before, a screen adaptation of a play about Lizzie Borden in which she had briefly appeared on Broadway, 9 Pine Street. Sterne succeeded in interesting Preston Sturges, then Paramount's hottest director, in producing, Dudley Nichols in doing the screenplay. By now Gish was unsure if she was still right for the central role, but out of loyalty to Griffith she kept those doubts to herself. A meeting of all the principals was arranged, and once again Griffith appeared late "stinking drunk and abusive," as Sterne later phrased it. "Why do you people think I want to make a picture?" he snarled. "Why do you think it's worthy of me?" "This antagonized Preston—the world isn't large enough for two egos like Preston's and Griffith's," as Sterne said, and nothing further came of this idea.[56] Both Sterne and Gish recalled the possibility of doing a low-budget adaptation of a Gene Stratton Porter story for Monogram, on poverty row, but that hope was also turned aside by Griffith.

Then, in 1945, Griffith succeeded in writing a screen treatment based on his experiences trouping with the Twilight Revellers so many years earlier. The outline was rather good and so unlike Griffith's usual style that one suspects a ghostly hand in the final draft. In it Griffith moves beyond pure autobiography to add some interesting elements: a drama of generational contention between the company's star-manager and his son, the juvenile, a love story between the latter and the ingenue. Most important, he moved the little company west, on the trail to Texas, where they encounter Indians, who rob them of their costumes and very nearly take their lives before a last-minute rescue. If that scene seems familiar to some moviegoers it should, for it was shot, with only small variations, by George Cukor in his 1960 film about a theatrical troupe working the West, Heller in Pink Tights. Cukor was not, of course, a plagiarist. He had cherished the hope of doing a story like this before meeting Griffith and he nursed it in the years afterward. It may even be that he suggested the notion of the Indians clad in the finery of Richard III grotesquely threatening the actors, for Joseph Jefferson recounts such an incident in his autobiography, which Cukor knew. On the other hand, Griffith had probably read that work, too.

It is no matter, really. It is important only to note that this late in his life Griffith was capable of writing something as professional and entertaining as this genially hokey and nostalgic treatment. Whether this was because of Cukor's helpful interest or the fact that he was drawing unpretentiously on his own memories and feelings for the old days in the theater, it is hard to say. But Cukor spoke of him later as "a prodigious worker, very gentle, very patient, charming but remote," and never in any sense out of control as a result of drink or anything else.[57] If their collaboration never amounted to much more than a few pleasant meetings, it might have been because their natures were antithetical. Though not himself a witty man, Cukor, as his films attest, liked wit and quickness, a brisker kind of literacy than Griffith commanded. Curiously, the script on this theme that he eventually shot was cowritten (with Walter Bernstein) by Dudley Nichols, his last work before his death.

After this there was nothing else for Griffith professionally, although Cukor would correctly remember talk of an attempt to make a film biography of Griffith's life, a project conceived and advanced by Lillian Gish, who was inspired, apparently, by the success in 1946 of *Night and Day*, a life of Cole Porter as ludicrously fictionalized as Griffith's life would have had to be in those days. If Griffith, who would shortly be calling his own autobiographical efforts "lousy," paid more than distant attention to this idea—and to the notion of having Grant, that least grandiloquent of actors, play him—it is not recorded. (*Silver Glory*, as Gish called this project, was eventually done on television in 1951, with John Newland in the role.) For at this point Griffith was greatly distracted: his marriage was beginning to visibly unravel, in the process loosening Griffith's grip on himself.

What went wrong is difficult to say. Perhaps Evelyn said it all when she remarked that "he was not a family man, he was a loner," which meant, among other things, that he was erratic in his habits. He liked to eat at odd hours and increasingly he liked to go out without her, in search of male companionship—and possibly female as well. This most basic of the tensions between man and woman—the tension between the former's desire to roam, the latter's need to nest—he could not do much to mute, and Evelyn, as she would later admit, was too young to understand all this and deal with it effectively. "I should have tried to adjust myself better," she would say later. Their differences began to reach irreconcilable levels sometime in 1946, when Evelyn's mother, who had frequently visited them, became ill at her home on Long Island. Evelyn felt she had to journey back to be at her side, and Griffith was childishly resentful. He had never liked Mrs. Baldwin, perhaps being jealous of her continuing hold on her daughter, which Sterne described as being "right out of a

Griffith picture." She was sanctimonious, and given to saying long graces before dinner, which Griffith would try to drown out by ostentatiously rattling the silverware. More infuriating was the way the two women would shut him out when they were together. Sterne would remember Mrs. Baldwin endlessly brushing Evelyn's hair as they murmured and laughed together while Griffith fumed, ignored. He took Evelyn's return to the East as an affront, an act of choice between her mother and her husband. And left to his own devices, he went on a monumental spree, one so serious that Sterne took it upon himself to call Evelyn and urge her hasty return. "She really laid me out—'My mother's dying; I've been through all this before; he'll have to take care of himself'—and hung up."

When she finally did return, the scenes between Griffith and Evelyn were quite awful. Again Sterne was involved in one of the worst of them. This time it was he who received the panicky phone call. It came late one night, it was from Evelyn, and she was in hysterics. Griffith was in the Beverly Hills jail, arrested as a common drunk. There now ensued, almost literally, a scene out of *A Star Is Born*. Sterne roused himself, went to the jail and found Griffith too drunk to be moved. He returned with Evelyn at seven-thirty the next morning when Griffith was somewhat sobered and managed to get him out before the newspapermen arrived to see if the night's haul had included any celebrities. As the desk sergeant handed back his watch, his wallet, his walking stick ("which he handled like a French marquis") Griffith looked at Evelyn. "I know what you've been doing all night," he said.

"Don't tell me . . . ," Evelyn started. Then stopped. And then slapped him hard across the mouth. Within a very short while they had separated. And Griffith had moved into his final haunt, the Knickerbocker Hotel on Hollywood Boulevard. In 1947, Evelyn Griffith received a settlement from her husband (it involved among other things, the sale of his ranch, with the proceeds going to her) and in November of that year, with Griffith supporting her plea ("I'm a bachelor at heart"), she received her interlocutory decree. She returned to New York, found work as an executive secretary and eventually remarried—happily. "David's ideal of womanhood was that of the child-wife—frail, delicate, compliant, loving," Lillian Gish would later write. "He idealized womanhood on the screen, but when he had to live with it he could not make the adjustment."[58]

Or maybe he just decided that it was time, at last, to let go of all pretense, to start to act out the last act of the legend he had been shaping for so long. For it was at this point that the reality of Griffith's life began to provide the raw materials for the tragic image that almost everyone has of his last years. All coherence vanishes from the accounts of his activities. He kept close to his rooms and to himself, emerging mainly to eat—and to drink. It is only in restaurants and bars that people seemed to encounter him. Ciro's, the Trocadero, the Brown Derby on Vine Street—these were on his rounds. He was not always out of control. He was even capable, at times, of self-irony, especially with Herb Sterne: "Herb, I like you because the only thing you ever ask is, 'Will you have another drink, D. W.?' " Once, thinking it would amuse him, Sterne brought Griffith a matchbook with Vera Hruba Ralston's picture on it. These were put out by her great and good friend Herbert Yates, then head of Republic Pictures, who was determined to make a major star out of his lover, whose main distinction in life was finishing second to Sonja Henie in the 1936 Olympic figure-skating championships. When one opened the matchbook a legend read, "The most beautiful Woman in the World," or some such. Griffith studied this for a moment and then said, "My God, I wasn't that silly about Miss Dempster."

His old press agent, Bennie Zeidman, saw him for the last time at the Brown Derby. He was alone and his air was isolate. He passed Zeidman's table but turned back when he was hailed. He sat down and, as was his wont, engaged in a rambling conversation in "a voice that had grown more throaty," about the old days. "I let him talk, reliving the past," Zeidman said. "I felt so bad about him. He had had so much. He had been the only one once."[59] Another time, in the same restaurant, Leatrice Gilbert, John Gilbert's daughter, then a young actress, was dining with Frances Goodrich and Albert Hackett: she was startled to hear herself addressed from an adjoining table in booming, theatrical tones. "That voice. That voice. It is the voice of the woman I love." It was Griffith, though who her voice reminded him of—Gish? Dempster? Evelyn?—no one can say. But he had his excuse to join their table for yet another meandering monologue.[60]

But many of his encounters were anything but benign. There was a fight in a bar about the service and Griffith was knocked down by a punch, perhaps thrown by an insulted barman. And Alva Johnson, the *New Yorker* writer, told Gerrit Lloyd that Griffith "gets crocked and insults women in the cocktail bars daily." He reported witnessing a scene in which Griffith made such unpleasant advances to a young woman that her escort threatened to beat him up if he did not desist. Around this time Griffith approached Johnson, whose most famous article was a hilarious profile of Samuel Goldwyn, a work that is the ultimate source for most of the producer's famous malapropisms, about doing a similar piece on him. The writer visited him in his hotel suite, where he found that "the Old Man was slobbering and poetic and rambling," a sure sign that he was "hitting the black bottle" as Lloyd phrased it.[61]

Even the faithful Sterne was not immune to this ugliness. He would remember one of his last meetings with him, when he had broken a date in order to have dinner with Griffith at the latter's insistence ("What's more important—a date or D. W. Griffith?"), only to find the older man at his most abusive. He made Sterne a drink—he favored orange blossoms, and kept the oranges for them on his window ledge—and then suddenly demanded, "What are you doing here?"

"You invited me, remember?"

"If you think you can cadge food off of me, you're crazy."

"I'll leave."

"It can't be soon enough for me."

A week later Griffith was back on the phone, reinviting Sterne, as if nothing had happened.

All of this formed the context of Goodman's famous final interview. By this time Griffith had, in effect, withdrawn his long-standing approval of an attempt to write a biography of him by the sober, reliable and industrious Barnet Bravermann, perhaps realizing from the extent and tone of Bravermann's interviewing that his approach, though respectful, was not going to be hagiographic. He agreed instead to favor the suit of his half-mad acolyte Seymour Stern, who would spend more than two fruitless decades on the project, before finally publishing some paranoid ramblings on the production of *Birth* in a film journal. It was a mistake typical of Griffith in these last years. When asked by Herb Sterne why he had given his backing to Seymour Stern, Griffith replied with bland amusement, "Herb, it meant so much to Seymour, and it didn't mean a thing to me." At any rate, it was this strange creature that Goodman contacted in hopes of meeting Griffith. Stern told him that Griffith had now gone entirely to ground, having his food and liquor sent in to him, but conceived a plan to breach the wall he had erected around him. It involved recruiting a girl Goodman knew to call Griffith from the hotel lobby and ask for an invitation to visit him in his room. Griffith agreed to let her in, but when he opened the door to her knock, Stern and Goodman, lurking behind her, forced it wide enough to gain access to his presence. He kept grabbing for the young woman (who had never heard of him) throughout the talk that followed.

It was odd, that talk. What Griffith said was less immediately sensational, less memorable-seeming than the vividly rendered circumstances surrounding it. It is true that he was rambling and somewhat incoherent. But it is also true that he seemed to sense that this might be his last chance for a summing up, and from somewhere he summoned up some last reserves of eloquence, even elegance. For once he spoke without excesses of bitterness, self-pity, self-hatred. What he managed was what any poet should be able to manage—something close to a graceful dying fall.

He spoke generously of those he thought were his inheritors, of Sturges and Capra, of William Wyler and Orson Welles. As usual he spoke enthusiastically of the latest technical innovation—the wide screen, which he thought would give film a stagelike illusion of depth and reality. He also visited his contempt on the House Un-American Activities Committee's investigation of communism in Hollywood. He offered the same opinion of California that he had offered Lillian Gish many years before. He spoke of "the dreadful sameness in the sunshine out here," adding that somehow Southern California attracted "the most brainless people in all the world."

But then he spoke of the old days, and his tone took on the warm hues of nostalgia. "I would love to be again at Forty-fourth and Broadway and love again to see George M. Cohan walking down the street. . . . But most of all I would love to see John and Lionel Barrymore crossing the street as they used to be, when they were . . . full of youth and vitality, going to a Broadway theater. They'd stop traffic, arm in arm, when they were young, in the blessed days when they were young."

But more than that, he missed a certain beauty he thought had disappeared from film, from the way people saw life—"the beauty of moving wind in the trees, the little movement in a beautiful blowing on the blossoms in the trees. That they have forgotten entirely. . . . We have lost beauty." On that note, Griffith fell silent. On that note, his intruders withdrew. On that note, if one were directing the scene, one would begin a slow pullback. Whatever had become of him, whatever had become (or would become) of the medium that he had been the first to conceive of as an art, that fragile essence of his sensibility at its best, and of one of cinema's potentials at its most generous, he had now fleetingly evoked one last time. For him, there was nothing left to say.

The problem was not merely that pictures now talked. Or that they had become big business. Or that a new age of anxiety was upon the movies as television (and the application of the antitrust laws, forcing the studios to divest themselves of their great profit-source, their theater chains) destroyed everyone's confidence. No, it was more than that. It was, really, that everyone had now arrived where Griffith had arrived perhaps two decades earlier—at a place where innocence was lost, and with it the capacity to wonder at the miracle of a medium that could, if it would, show us, in the flicker of a ten-frame cut, something of our "inward life," or, if you will, find in the trembling of a leaf, the symbol of an unknown yearning, an unspoken dream. In all the long years of wandering and confusion, in all the long years when his own peculiar demons drove him down strange paths, in all the long years when, being the product of his bustling times and this often vulgar place, he had lost touch with his best self, his best and simplest hopes for this thing he had made. But now, at the end, he remembered. It was the last of his last-minute rescues.

7
——————

Sometime in the morning of July 23, 1948, Griffith was seized by an agonizing pain. He staggered from his rooms to the lobby of his hotel, where he asked for help and then collapsed. He had suffered a cerebral hemorrhage. He was taken to the Temple Hospital in Hollywood, and his nearest kin, his nephew, Willard, and his niece, Ruth, were summoned to his bedside. He did not regain consciousness and he was pronounced dead at eight twenty-four the next morning.

Only a few people called at the funeral parlor where he lay in state, and the only famous one to do so was Cecil B. DeMille. The rest of the industry would wait for the formal services on the twenty-seventh. These were held at the Hollywood Masonic Temple. The friends were there, and many who owed the beginnings of their careers to him. Some, like Searle Dawley and Lionel Barrymore, Mack Sennett and Dell Henderson, went back to the Biograph and before with him; some, like Richard Barthelmess and Walter Huston, entered his chronicle later; some, like Raoul Walsh and von Stroheim, had been at his side when he was defining the nature of the director's art on the job, on the set. Some, like Walter Wanger and Jesse Lasky, might not have been entirely welcome on this occasion had Griffith had anything to say about it. Some, like Herb Sterne, avoided the company of such other honorary pallbearers as Louis B. Mayer and Sam Goldwyn because they could have given Griffith something to do with his final years and did not. But if any were needed, the proof that the history of his life was the history of the movies in America up to then was gathered here.

The floral tributes were heaped high around the casket. Members of the Robert Mitchell Boys Choir were observed by early comers to be giggling as they rehearsed their hymns. As the time for the service drew near, only about half the seats in the auditorium were filled, so the crowd that had gathered outside to watch the celebrities come and go—as if this were a premiere and not an ending—was invited in to fill the empty places. The occasion struck Gerrit Lloyd as cold, perhaps in part because one of the two eulogists, Charles Brackett, the screenwriter who was serving a term as president of the Motion Picture Academy, had never known Griffith. He found it difficult to achieve the right tone, veering from the emptily melodramatic (his last years were characterized as "a frenzied beating on the barred doors") to the banal ("Griffith gave the public what it wanted") to the self-congratulatory (for Griffith's honorary Academy Award). Overall, Jay Leyda, the film historian who was present, thought Brackett achieved, at best, "a polite note of regret."

Donald Crisp did better, daring at least to chastize the film people for their neglect of Griffith. "It was the tragedy of his later years that this active, brilliant mind was given no chance to participate in the advancement of the industry. Difficult as it might be for him to have played a subordinate role, I do not believe that the fault was entirely his own. I cannot help feeling that there should always have been a place for him and his talents in motion pictures. . . ."

And then, as Leyda was to recall it, someone sobbed loudly, inarticulately. But it sounded as if he or she had cried out, "Yes, yes—why not!" "This one note of genuine emotion overturned the passive insincerity of the occasion," he wrote. When Crisp tried to go on, his voice broke, and as he struggled to regain control and proceed, "the emotions of the speaker and the audience were loosed and real"—until "the efficiency of the memorial service took over again, and the boys' choir singing 'Abide with Me' drowned out the sobs."[62]

And then it was over. Griffith's remains were flown home to Kentucky, where he was buried in the graveyard beside the Mount Tabor Methodist Church, where his family had worshiped when he was a boy. A rail fence, said to have been created from wood taken from the Griffith farm, surrounds the gravesite, which has been marked, since 1950, by a stone contributed by the Directors Guild of America, and bearing its insignia. The fence is rough-hewn; the stone is sleek. The congruence of the nostalgic and the moderne is curious but somehow correct. They are like the elements in a simple montage, resonating to each other, suggesting by their juxtaposition fleeting metaphors, hints of meanings, greater than the sum of those elements. We have new ways of seeing and thinking and perhaps even being which literally did not exist until the man who lies buried here began his work. And began that chain of artistic invention which has enabled us to see the world through fresh eyes, in a new light.

Acknowledgments

Since the basic source for this book is the D. W. Griffith collection at the Museum of Modern Art in New York City, my largest debt—indeed, it is quite incalculable—is to Eileen Bowser, the museum's chief film archivist. She was an unfailingly helpful, knowledgeable, patient and kindly guide to what was for me a truly daunting morass, and I cannot thank her enough for the many hours she spent, so many years ago, in helping me take the first vital steps on a road that turned out to be much longer than either of us anticipated.

As with files, so with films. The museum is by far the largest repository of Griffith's motion pictures, and Ms. Bowser's wise conversations while I screened his work unknowingly helped me form and test some of the critical opinions expressed here—not that I wish to burden her with several with which I know she disagrees. James Card, former director of the film department of the George Eastman House in Rochester, was equally helpful in arranging screenings of the Griffith material held by that distinguished center of film scholarship, while his colleague, George Pratt, an enormously gifted scholar of the silent film, was more than generous in sharing his knowledge of this subject, pointing me to innumerable sources I would not otherwise have found. Paul Killiam, whose Killiam Shows, Inc., distributes many of Griffith's films commercially, was also very good about arranging screenings for me of yet more Griffith films. William K. Everson, another distinguished expert on the silent film, also helped greatly by permitting me to view his print of *Hearts of the World*. And Nelsa Gidney, then of WNET/13 in New York, helped me to get second screenings of a number of Griffith films at a moment when that service was vital to my work. Finally, Jay Leyda, then teaching at Yale, arranged for me to see some short films that were in that institution's archive. Thanks to all these people, I was able to form my own fresh critical impressions of all Griffith's longer films and of his most sig-

607

nificant Biograph productions. None of the opinions expressed outside quotation marks in this book are secondhand, and though I do not want or expect agreement with all my re-evaluations of Griffith's work, I do hope some of my judgments will cause re-evaluation of some of the received opinions that—depressingly—one can often trace down from the first newspaper reviews to some of the very latest film histories.

Another of my large debts is to Walt Lowe. In the late sixties and early seventies, when he was a director-cameraman for television station WAVE-TV in Louisville, he conceived the notion of doing a film biography of Griffith and invited me to collaborate with him on it as host and co-writer. In the course of that work he placed at my disposal the transcripts of a number of interviews he had conducted and helped me to get in touch with several people whose lives had crossed Griffith's. He was also a genial guide to the city and the state that formed Griffith and to which in bitter age he retreated. A little later, Kevin Brownlow, whose contributions to the history of the silent cinema, both on film and in print, are awesome, shared his wisdom and material with me and generously read a portion of the manuscript. My debt to him is also large. Another friend, Henry Romney of the Rockefeller Foundation, introduced me to the appropriate staff members of that institution and they aided me in applying for, and obtaining, a grant from the foundation which was crucial to financing some of the research and writing of this book. Two researchers, Mary De Marzo and Doreen Barth, helped me to comb newspapers and periodicals for references to Griffith and his work, and I thank them for their diligence and skill.

The kindness of friends is precious. The kindness of strangers is often astonishing. One of the most pleasant aspects of this project was the opportunity it gave me to interview people whose lives were in some way entwined with Griffith's. They were all patient, kindly and very often inspiring in their gallant old age. One of the saddest aspects of bringing this book to its belated conclusion is that the majority of them have passed on, before I could record this formal expression of my gratitude to them not just for their assistance but for the grace of their lives and—in many cases—their gifts to the screen. They are Roy E. Aitken, William Bantell, William Beaudine, Sr., Miriam Cooper, George Cukor, Allan Dwan, John Ford, Lillian Gish, Ruth Griffith, Neil Hamilton, Raymond Klune, Evelyn Baldwin Kunze, Mrs. Edward Larson (Carol Dempster), Anita Loos, Lewis Milestone, Jean Renoir, Richard Reynolds, Hal Roach, Philip Scheuer, Herb Sterne, Raoul Walsh, Bennie Zeidman, Adolph Zukor. In less formal conversations Frank Capra, Douglas Fairbanks, Jr., Leatrice Gilbert Fountain and George Stevens, Sr., gave me some brief insights that helped inform this work.

Two men gave unstintingly of their loyalty to book and author. One is my agent, Sterling Lord, whose work in its behalf has been well above and beyond the call of duty. The other is Michael Korda, my editor at Simon and Schuster, whose faithfulness, through more years than either of us would care to calculate, remains for me one of the mysteries and blessings of my life. In the later stages, his associate John Herman has been enormously helpful in seeing the book through the press.

Finally, it must be recorded that even with all this help there would have been no book if Carol Rubinstein had not entered my life and with her love, patience and understanding, transformed it. She made it possible for this book to grow, at last, to its completion.

Notes

D. W. Griffith's papers are for the most part filed chronologically at the Museum of Modern Art (MOMA). Therefore the dates and brief identifying notes supplied here are all that are required to direct the researcher to material he requires for further study. Griffith's own writings may be found by reference to their titles. The Bitzer and Bravermann material, and the Griffith scrapbooks, are filed separately, but the references herein should be all the student requires to find what he needs. In order not to burden these already lengthy notes, only the briefest citations of material from books and major periodical writings by and about Griffith are offered. These will guide the reader to the proper place in the bibliography, where full references are given. More ephemeral journalism is referred to by the name and date of the publication where it was found, but it is not bibliographied. Other manuscript and interview material is also cited only briefly. I should note, however, that since I used it the United Artists material has been transferred to the Wisconsin Center for Theatre Research, Madison, Wisconsin, where it has been indexed in a manner that is different from that employed when I used it. In these notes, I have indicated documents obtained from UA and from Paramount, in order to set them apart from the MOMA material.

Chapter One

1. Long, *David Wark Griffith*, p. 25.
2. DWG/Bravermann, May 22, 1943.
3. D.W. Griffith, "Autobiography," MS pp. 1–2. This material exists in two slightly variant versions. Both are the products of a collaboration between Griffith and a free-lance journalist, James Hart, in 1938–39. Hart published the second draft as *The Man Who Invented Hollywood: The Autobiography of D. W. Griffith* in 1972. Almost all the variations in this unfinished work, which is about 25,000 words long, and breaks off with the completion of *Intolerance*, consist of excisions from the first draft of material Griffith apparently thought too intimate or emotionally revealing. In these notes I have referred to material from the slightly freer (but no more reliable) first draft, which was titled "D.W. Griffith and the Wolf" (by which he meant the wolf

of poverty), as "Wolf." I have referred to the second draft, originally called "The Hollywood Gold Rush," as "Hollywood," partly because it shares that key word with the title of the book Hart eventually published. Page citations are to the more conveniently available published version.

4. Ruth Griffith, interview with author.

5. Bravermann MS, chap. I, p. 1.

6. The sources for the Griffith and Oglesby family histories are several. Griffith's short version of his genealogy is to be found in "Hollywood," p. 24. The MOMA file marked "1895–1900" contains copies of legal documents found by genealogists Griffith hired, as well as an extensive report, "The Oglesby Family in Virginia and Kentucky," by Florence E. Youngs (Apr. 4, 1927), which was commissioned by him. Still more information is to be found in Bravermann, chap. I, pp. 1–7.

7. "Wolf," p. 6.

8. W. W. White, quoted in Bravermann, pp. 1–12.

9. "Wolf," p. 6.

10. "Hollywood," p. 24.

11. Bravermann, I, 6.

12. Bravermann, I, 8. Griffith does not mention this incident, but Bravermann, trusting his interview sources, recounts it with no hesitation.

13. Kirwin (ed.), *Johnny Green*, p. 12.

14. "Wolf," p. 4.

15. Thompson, *History of the Orphan Brigade*, p. 906.

16. *War of the Rebellion*, vol. 4, p. 723 (see under "W" in Bibliography).

17. Kerr (ed.), *History of Kentucky*, vol. 5, p. 639. Griffith tells the story similarly, but places it at a different location in "Hollywood," p. 25. The inscription on Jacob's gravestone, prepared under Griffith's direction, however, follows Kerr. In his MS, Griffith states he heard the story for the first time from Sir John French, the sometime commander of the British Expeditionary Force (and a cavalryman) when he visited Britain during World War I.

18. There is no official record of these promotions, but that does not mean the claim to them was false. In the final agony of the Confederacy, record-keeping was not high among its priorities.

19. "Hollywood," p. 25.

20. Bravermann, I, 14.

21. Bravermann, I, 14. The material regarding Jake's poor adjustment to civilian life is from the same source, I, 13–23.

22. "Wolf," pp. 3–4.

23. Quoted in Bravermann, I, 18.

24. Jacob Griffith/Mattie Griffith, Jan. 4, 1887.

25. Bravermann, I, 18.

26. "Wolf," p. 11.

27. These reminiscences are drawn from "Wolf," pp. 4–11; "Hollywood," pp. 27–33.

28. Bravermann was able to discover this man's identity, I, 22.

29. "Hollywood," pp. 28–29.

30. Bravermann, I, 25.

31. "Wolf," p. 6.

32. All material on the family's financial condition is from Bravermann, II, 1–4.

33. Griffith's school memories are drawn from "Wolf," pp. 7–11, and "Hollywood," pp. 25–38.

34. "Wolf," p. 11.
35. "Wolf," p. 11; "Hollywood," pp. 37–38.
36. Griffith, "It Never Happened." ND.
37. "Hollywood," p. 37.
38. *Ibid.*, p. 33.
39. *Ibid.*, p. 39.
40. Hays, *Response to Industrialism*, p. 126.
41. "Hollywood," p. 39.

Chapter Two

1. Jackson, "To Be a Boy in Louisville."
2. Griffith sometimes encouraged the notion that he had once been a professional newsman, but Bravermann talked to several reporters who observed that he had never been a staffer for the *Courier-Journal*, and Griffith then admitted to his biographer that he had served as a stringer—that is, as a free-lancer paid space rates for accepted items—for only about three months.
3. McMeckin, *Louisville*, pp. 176–80.
4. Rucker, "The Great D. W."
5. "Wolf," p. 12.
6. DWG/Willard Griffith, Apr. 8, 1933.
7. "Wolf," p. 15.
8. Material drawn from *Last Night at Macauley's* (see under "L" in Bibliography).
9. Rucker, "The Great D.W."; see also Rucker, interview with Walt Lowe.
10. Griffith's musical interests are detailed in Bravermann, II, 6–13.
11. Long, *op. cit.*, p. 29.
12. Bravermann, II, 6.
13. *Ibid.*, II, 8.
14. "Hollywood," p. 43.
15. Rucker interview.
16. "Wolf," pp. 13–14.
17. "Hollywood," p. 47.
18. New York *Dramatic Mirror*, Dec. 12, 1896. This notice is quoted in Russell Merritt and George Pratt, "A Chronology of D. W. Griffith's Stage Career 1896–1907," unpublished. Unless otherwise noted, I have relied on this marvelous work of scholarship, based on a detailed examination of the theatrical trade press of the time, for my account of Griffith's career as an actor.
19. DWG/Mary Griffith, undated, 1897 (in Bravermann papers).
20. "Hollywood," pp. 48–50.
21. "Wolf," pp. 30–31.
22. Quoted in Bravermann, II, 20–21.
23. New York *Dramatic Mirror*, June 25, 1898. Quoted in Merritt and Pratt, *op. cit.*
24. Long, p. 36.
25. *Ibid.*, p. 41.

Chapter Three

1. "Wolf," p. 29.
2. "Wolf," pp. 67–68. See also Bravermann, III, 4.

3. "Hollywood," p. 56.
4. *Ibid.*
5. *Ibid.*, p. 58.
6. Merritt and Pratt, *op. cit.*
7. "Wolf," p. 73. The anecdote is repeated in "Hollywood," pp. 66–68, but with a more innocent, and jocular, twist.
8. Tyler, *Hollywood Hallucination*, p. 46.
9. *Ibid.*, p. 50.
10. Bravermann, IV, 5.
11. "Hollywood," pp. 54–55.
12. Long, pp. 37–38.
13. Griffith's odd jobs are discussed in "Hollywood," pp. 68–69.
14. Merritt and Pratt, *op. cit.*
15. *Ibid.* See also Long, p. 33.
16. Merritt and Pratt, *op. cit.*
17. Bravermann, III, 15.
18. "Hollywood," pp. 60–61.
19. Morris, *Curtain Time*, pp. 162–63.
20. Bravermann, IV, 10.
21. *Ibid.*
22. George Stevens, in conversation with the author.
23. Mrs. D. W. Griffith, *When the Movies Were Young*, p. 14.
24. *Ibid.*, p. 10. This and subsequent descriptions of DWG in San Francisco are taken from this source, pp. 8–21.
25. "Hollywood," p. 61. See also Bravermann, IV, 10.
26. Mrs. Griffith, p. 15.
27. Bravermann, IV, 12.
28. Merritt and Pratt.
29. Quoted in Bravermann, IV, 15.
30. Mrs. Griffith, p. 16. Here, as elsewhere in her account, she has muddled the chronology of Griffith's theatrical bookings.
31. Vardac, *From Stage to Screen*, p. 247.
32. Mrs. Griffith, p. 17.
33. Lloyd/Bravermann. ND.
34. Mrs. Griffith, p. 19.
35. "Notice of Intention to Marry," May 14, 1906.

Chapter Four

1. Mrs. Griffith, p. 19.
2. *Ibid.*, p. 20.
3. Griffith, *A Fool and a Girl*. MS.
4. Quoted in Cook, *Fire from the Flint*, p. 145.
5. Quoted in Bloomfield, "Dixon's The Leopard's Spots," in Wynes (ed.), *The Negro in the South*, p. 84.
6. *Ibid.*, p. 89.
7. Quoted in *ibid.*, p. 97.
8. Stampp, *The Era of Reconstruction*, p. 11.
9. Reviews quoted in Vardac, p. 85.
10. Quoted in Cook, p. 149.
11. Mrs. Griffith, p. 23.
12. Long, pp. 39–40.

13. Quoted in Mrs. Griffith, p. 25.

14. "Hollywood," p. 70.

15. Reviews from the publications named, Oct. 1, 1907.

16. *Washington Post*, Oct. 6, 1907.

17. *Washington Herald*, Oct. 1, 1907.

18. DWG/Editor, *Washington Herald*. MS. ND.

19. Griffith, *War*. MS.

20. Bravermann, III, 29.

21. Long, p. 43.

22. Barry, *D.W. Griffith: American Film Master*, p. 8.

23. Long, p. 41.

24. Grace Dawley/Bravermann, Mar. 12, 1949. All information about the production of *Rescued from the Eagle's Nest* is drawn from this source.

Chapter Five

1. Quoted in Ramsaye, *A Million and One Nights*, p. 425.

2. Quoted in Pratt, *Spellbound in Darkness*, p. 20.

3. Quoted in Hendricks, *Beginnings of the Biograph*, p. 40.

4. Quoted in *ibid*., p. 42.

5. Reprinted in Pratt, p. 42.

6. Ramsaye, p. 455.

7. *Ibid*., p. 469.

8. *Ibid*.

9. Mrs. Griffith, p. 31.

10. Bitzer "Notes." MOMA.

11. Mrs. Griffith, p. 32.

12. *Ibid*., p. 43.

13. Quoted in Henderson, *D.W. Griffith: The Years at Biograph*, p. 33.

14. Ramsaye, p. 457.

15. Mrs. Griffith, p. 49.

16. *Ibid*., p. 49.

17. "Hollywood," p. 75.

18. Mrs. Griffith, p. 49.

19. Bitzer, *His Story*, pp. 55–56. The quotation from Marvin appears in Bitzer's first-draft MS (which is cited herein as "Notes," but not in the published version of them, which is cited as *His Story*). As with Griffith's autobiographical work, there are many variations between MS and printed work. The published version is cited here wherever possible.

20. "Hollywood," p. 75.

21. Mrs. Griffith, p. 43.

22. Bitzer, *His Story*, p. 63.

23. Mrs. Griffith, p. 51.

24. Bitzer, *op. cit*. p. 67.

25. Mrs. Griffith, pp. 51–52.

26. *Ibid*., pp. 53–54.

27. *Ibid*.

28. *Ibid*., p. 66.

29. Quoted in Eisenstein, *Film Form*, p. 205.

30. For material on Dickens, I have drawn on Wilson, "Dickens: The Two Scrooges."

31. This and other material on early technical innovations is drawn from Bitzer's "Notes."

32. Wagenknecht, *The Movies in the Age of Innocence*, pp. 93–94.

33. Quoted in Ramsaye, p. 474.

34. Wagenknecht, p. 52.

35. Mrs. Griffith, p. 59.

36. "Wolf," p. 88.

37. Sennett and Shipp, *King of Comedy*, pp. 52–53.

38. *Ibid.*, p. 51.

39. William Beaudine, Sr., interview with author.

40. Bitzer, *His Story*, p. 67.

41. Lillian Gish, interview with author.

42. Quoted in Henderson, *Biograph*, p. 30.

43. Eisenstein, p. 198.

44. *Ibid.*

45. Baudelaire, *The Painter of Modern Life*, pp. 4–5.

Chapter Six

1. Pratt, p. 57.

2. Quoted in Henderson, p. 61.

3. Mrs. Griffith, p. 58.

4. Blanche Sweet, interview with author.

5. Bitzer "Notes," pp. 69–72.

6. Bitzer, pp. 72–75. See also Bitzer's "Notes."

7. Beaudine interview.

8. Pickford, *Sunshine and Shadow*, pp. 102–3.

9. "Wolf," p. 86.

10. Pickford, pp. 105–10.

11. Bitzer "Notes," p. 60. See also Bitzer, *His Story*, pp. 73–74.

12. *Ibid.*

13. Brownlow, *The Parade's Gone By*, p. 123.

14. *Ibid.*, p. 124.

15. Croy, *Starmaker*, chap. XII.

16. These reviews are reprinted in Pratt, pp. 57–58.

17. Quoted in Henderson, p. 80.

18. Mrs. Griffith, p. 119.

19. Beaudine interview.

20. *Ibid.*

21. Sennett and Shipp, p. 75.

22. "Hollywood," p. 82.

23. Bitzer "Notes," pp. 63–64.

24. Reprinted in Pratt, p. 64.

25. *Ibid.*

26. Bitzer "Notes," p. 65.

27. Wagenknecht, p. 89.

28. Reprinted in Pratt, pp. 67–68.

Chapter Seven

1. Mrs. Griffith, p. 142.

2. This account of the first Griffith company to work in Los Angeles follows Mrs. Griffith, pp. 143–72.

3. Beaudine interview.
4. Reprinted in Pratt, p. 84.
5. Mrs. Griffith, p. 164.
6. Reprinted in Pratt, pp. 84–85.
7. Bankbook and contract in MOMA, 1910 file.
8. Review reprinted in Pratt, pp. 86–87.
9. Pickford, p. 134.
10. Quoted in Card, "The Films of Mary Pickford."
11. Sweet interview.
12. *Ibid.*
13. Bitzer, p. 75.
14. Review reprinted in Pratt, p. 90.
15. Mrs. Griffith, p. 202.
16. Beaudine interview.
17. Raoul Walsh, interview with the author.
18. *New York Journal-American*, Mar. 27, 1937.
19. Christy Cabanne, interview with Bravermann, unpaginated notes.
20. Barrymore and Shipp, *We Barrymores*, pp. 140–41.
21. *Ibid.*, p. 146.
22. *Ibid.*, pp. 147–48.
23. *Ibid.*, p. 151.
24. Sweet interview.
25. *New York World-Telegram*, June 17, 1946.
26. Sennett and Shipp, p. 67.
27. Review reprinted in Pratt, p. 92.
28. Pickford, p. 139.
29. Cabanne, interview with Bravermann.
30. George Beranger, interview with Bravermann, unpaginated notes.
31. Kael, "The Current Cinema," *The New Yorker*, Feb. 24, 1968.
32. Quoted in Gish and Pinchot, *The Movies, Mr. Griffith and Me*, p. 94.
33. Rosenberg and Silverstein, *The Real Tinsel*, p. 211.
34. *Ibid.*, p. 210.
35. Pickford, pp. 144–47.
36. Records of these transactions are to be found in the MOMA files, 1911–13.
37. Gish and Pinchot, p. 34.
38. "Hollywood," pp. 82–83.
39. Gish and Pinchot, pp. 36–38.
40. Bitzer "Notes."
41. Gish and Pinchot, p. 76.
42. Cabanne, interview with Bravermann.
43. Pickford, pp. 149–50. See also Gish and Pinchot, p. 76.
44. Quoted in Brownlow, p. 126.
45. Gish and Pinchot, p. 77.
46. Agee, *Agee on Film*, pp. 315–16.
47. Lillian Gish, interview with author.

Chapter Eight

1. Pratt, p. 105.
2. Henderson, *Biograph*, p. 119.

3. Gish and Pinchot, pp. 95–96.
4. *New York Times*, Apr. 22, 1913.
5. Lindsay, *The Art of the Moving Picture*, pp. 86–93.
6. Wagenknecht, p. 95.
7. Gish and Pinchot, p. 107.
8. *Ibid.*
9. Loos, *A Girl Like I*, pp. 76–87.
10. Sweet interview.
11. *Ibid.*
12. Ramsaye, p. 609.
13. Adolph Zukor, interview with author.
14. Aitken and Nelson, *The Birth of a Nation Story*, p. 22.
15. Gish and Pinchot, p. 110.
16. Bitzer "Notes."
17. Billy Bitzer, interview with Beaumont Newhall. Updated, pp. 45–47. MOMA.
18. Sweet interview.
19. Blaisdell, "At the Sign of the Flaming Arcs."
20. Robert E. Welsh, "David W. Griffith Speaks."
21. Aitken and Nelson, pp. 20–36.
22. Gish and Pinchot, pp. 112–13.
23. Seldes, *The Seven Lively Arts*, p. 277.
24. Aitken/Griffith, Apr. 15, 1914. (wire)
25. Aitken/Griffith, Apr. 15, 1914. (letter)

CHAPTER NINE

1. "Wolf," pp. 52–53.
2. See Stampp, chap. I, for a vivid and exemplary study of the historiography that influenced Griffith. These quotations are drawn from that work, pp. 5–6.
3. "Hollywood," p. 91.
4. Quoted in Barry, p. 19.
5. Gish interview.
6. Raoul Walsh, interview with author.
7. Quoted in Seymour Stern, "Griffith I: The Birth of a Nation," p. 45.
8. Gish and Pinchot, p. 133.
9. Tyler, p. 77.
10. Cooper and Herndon, *Dark Lady of the Silents*, p. 59.
11. Anita Loos, interview with author.
12. Rosenberg and Silverstein, p. 213.
13. Cooper and Herndon, p. 60.
14. Karl Brown, *Adventures with D.W. Griffith*, p. 57.
15. This report is on file among the Griffith papers.
16. Brown, p. 75.
17. Walsh interview.
18. Brown, pp. 52–54.
19. *Ibid.*, p. 75.
20. Loos interview with author.
21. Brown, p. 79.
22. Stern, p. 55.
23. Bitzer, *His Story*, p. 109.

24. John Ford, interview with author.

25. Brown, pp. 66–70.

26. *Ibid.*, pp. 73–74.

27. Sarris, "Birth of a Nation or White Power Back When," in Silva (ed.), *Focus on The Birth of a Nation*, pp. 108–10.

28. *Ibid.*, p. 107.

29. Aitken and Nelson, p. 41.

30. St. Johns, *The Honeycomb*, p. 56.

31. Bitzer, *His Story*, p. 111.

32. Gish and Pinchot, p. 144.

33. *Ibid.*, p. 143.

34. For a detailed discussion of the score, see Stern, pp. 103–4. I have drawn on his extensive researches for this passage.

35. Gish, pp. 152–53.

36. Majestic Pictures Corp. Balance Sheet–1914.

37. Brown, p. 88.

38. *Ibid.*, p. 89.

39. *Ibid.*, p. 95.

Chapter Ten

1. Cook, p. 168.

2. *Ibid.*, pp. 169–70.

3. Quoted in Cripps, "The Reaction of the Negro to the Motion Picture The Birth of a Nation," in Silva (ed.), p. 115.

4. Cook, p. 170.

5. Cripps, *Slow Fade to Black*, p. 52. This quotation, perhaps the most famous words ever spoken about a film, is accepted by this distinguished scholar, as by many of his predecessors. I accept it, too. Yet no one has been able to fully authenticate it. In print, so far as I can determine, its provenance is based entirely on secondary sources.

6. Quoted in Cripps, *Slowfade*, p. 53.

7. Aitken and Nelson, p. 53.

8. *Ibid.*, p. 55.

9. Crowther, *Hollywood Rajah*, pp. 61–62.

10. Epoch Producing Corp. Minutes, Mar. 2, 1915.

11. *Moving Picture World*, Mar. 13, 1915.

12. *New York Times*, Mar. 4, 1915.

13. Reviews from the newspapers cited, Mar. 3–4, 1915.

14. *New York American*, Mar. 5, 1915.

15. *New York Journal*, Mar. 5, 1915.

16. *Variety*, Mar. 12, 1915.

17. Robert M. Henderson, *D. W. Griffith: His Life and Work*, p. 160.

18. Crowther, p. 160.

19. Epoch statement to Stockholders, Dec. 31, 1917.

20. "Fighting Race Calumny." *The Crisis.* 10 (May–June 1915). Reprinted in Silva (ed.), pp. 66–73. This unsigned article is a valuable record, in diary form, of the NAACP's campaign against *Birth*.

21. *New York Post*, Mar. 10, 1915.

22. Hackett, "Brotherly Love," *New Republic*, Mar. 20, 1915.

23. This account of the Mayor's hearing is drawn from contemporary press accounts, notably the *New York News-Courier*, Mar. 31, 1915.

24. Cripps, *Slow Fade*, p. 57.

25. Parkhurst, "The Birth of a Nation." Reprinted in Silva (ed.), pp. 102–3. It appears that this remarkable document was commissioned by the producers and offered free to newspapers as the film opened around the country.

26. This account of the meeting is drawn from a report in the *New York Age*, Apr. 10, 1915.

27. *New York Globe*, Apr. 6, 1915.

28. *New York Press*, Mar. 7, 1915.

29. *New York Mail*, Mar. 13, 1915.

30. *Christian Science Monitor*, Mar. 20, 1915.

31. *New York Globe*, Apr. 10, 1915.

32. *New York Post*, Apr. 15, 1915.

33. This account of the Boston meeting is based on Fox, *The Guardian of Boston*, p. 191, and Cripps, *Slowfade*, p. 59.

34. This account of the Boston riot and its aftermath follows Fox, pp. 192–97.

35. Cripps, *Slow Fade*, p. 60.

36. *Philadelphia North American*, Sept. 21, 1915.

37. Quoted in *Oakland Tribune*, May 26, 1915.

38. Quoted in Fox, p. 189.

39. *Olean* (N.Y.) *Times*, Apr. 30.

40. Quoted in Fox, p. 189.

41. Griffith, "The Motion Picture and Witch Burners." In Silva (ed.), pp. 96–99.

42. Griffith, "Movies As Yet Only in Swaddling Clothes," *St. Louis Post-Dispatch*, Apr. 11, 1915.

43. Griffith, "The Future of the Two-Dollar Movie."

44. Griffith, "Swaddling Clothes," *op. cit.*

CHAPTER ELEVEN

1. Griffith, *The Rise and Fall of Free Speech in America*. Unpaginated.

2. Gish and Pinchot, p. 166.

3. Roy E. Aitken, interview with the author.

4. Brown, p. 134.

5. Loos, p. 93.

6. Bernard Hanson, "D.W. Griffith: Some Sources."

7. Material on Griffith's San Francisco trip is from Brown, pp. 114–24.

8. Henabery's recollections of this work are in Brownlow, *The Parade's Gone By*, pp. 50–52.

9. Brown, p. 135.

10. *Ibid.*, pp. 150–54.

11. Bitzer, pp. 139–40.

12. Brown, p. 148.

13. *New York Morning Telegraph*, Mar. 11, 1917.

14. Loos, p. 94.

15. Bitzer, p. 134.

16. Brown, p. 161.

17. Besides Brown, Bitzer and Gish, I have drawn on Robert Cannom, *Van Dyke and the Mythical City, Hollywood* (pp. 57–60) and the unpub-

lished MS of Sidney Franklin's autobiography (pp. 72–73) in Kevin Brownlow's possession.

18. Jean Darnell, "The Personal Side of David W. Griffith."

19. Bitzer, *His Story*, pp. 144–45.

20. Bessie Love, *From Hollywood with Love*, pp. 26–29.

21. Peter Bogdanovich, *Allan Dwan: The Last Pioneer*, pp. 38–39.

22. Epoch Producing Corp. Treasurer's Report, Jan. 1, 1916.

23. Wark Producing Corp., Statement of Receipts and Disbursements. Undated (but reflecting transactions through Sept. 5, 1916). See also Stockholder's List, undated, and minutes and legal documents executed at the Dec. 1915 Wark board meeting.

24. Wark Producing Corp., Statement of Receipts and Disbursements.

25. Allan Dwan, interview with author.

26. Quoted in Brownlow, p. 52.

27. Loos, pp. 102–3.

28. Brownlow, pp. 62–63.

29. Quoted in *New York Times*, Sept. 2, 1916.

30. *Ibid.*

31. *New York Times*, Sept. 10, 1916.

32. Lindsay, "Photoplay Progress," *New Republic*, Feb. 17, 1916.

33. Johnson, "The Shadow Stage," *Photoplay*, Dec. 1916.

34. Eisenstein, *Film Form and Film Sense*. See especially pp. 235–44.

35. Gish and Pinchot, p. 180.

36. *Los Angeles Herald*, Oct. 5, 1916.

37. *Cumberland* (Ind.) *Times*, Oct. 9, 1916.

38. *Philadelphia North American*, Dec. 23, 1916.

39. DWG/Aitken, Oct. 16, 1916.

Chapter Twelve

1. Lady Cynthia Asquith, *Diaries 1915–1918*, p. 88.

2. Long, pp. 89–91.

3. Kevin Brownlow, *The War, the West and the Wilderness*, p. 145.

4. *Moving Picture Herald*, May 26, 1917.

5. *Dramatic Mirror*, Apr. 21, 1917.

6. Brownlow, *The War*, p. 144.

7. "Hollywood," p. 20. See also his collaborator's recollections of Griffith's wartime reminiscences in the same volume, pp. 122–23.

8. Brownlow, *The War*, p. 144.

9. Harry C. Carr, "Griffith, Maker of Battle Scenes, Sees Real War." See also draft radio script, Mar. 30, 1932 (MOMA) and *Chicago Tribune*, Oct. 31, 1917.

10. This account of Griffith and party in wartime London is based on Gish and Pinchot, pp. 185–203; Bitzer, *His Story*, pp. 180–91; and Albert Bigelow Paine, *Life and Lillian Gish*, pp. 127–36.

11. Noel Coward, *Present Indicative*, p. 61.

12. Thomas Quinn Curtiss, *Von Stroheim*, pp. 85–88.

13. William K. Everson, *American Silent Film*, p. 98.

14. Carr, "Griffith . . . Sees Real War," *op. cit.*

15. *Chicago Tribune*, Oct. 31, 1917.

16. Brown, pp. 196–98.

17. *Ibid.*, p. 198.

18. Quoted in Brownlow, *War*, p. 153.
19. *New York Times*, Apr. 5, 1918.
20. Gish and Pinchot, p. 201.

CHAPTER THIRTEEN

1. DWG/Albert Grey, Nov. 9, 1918.
2. *New York News*, June 8, 1918.
3. Gerrit J. Lloyd/Bravermann, June 27, 1949.
4. *New York Times*, Aug. 5, 1918.
5. Exhibitor's Trade Review, Jan. 4, 1919. Quoted in Wagenknecht and Slide, *The Films of D. W. Griffith*, p. 110.
6. DWG/Motion Picture Editor, *Washington Herald*, Jan. 6, 1919.
7. Quoted in Wagenknecht and Slide, p. 110.
8. Brown, pp. 203–4.
9. DWG/Banzhaf, Oct. 6, 1918.
10. Barthelmess "Reminiscences," dictated Mar. 30, 1945, MOMA.
11. Brown, pp. 203–4.
12. Gish, interview with author.
13. DWG/Morris Gest, Nov. 9, 1918.
14. E.C. Bidwell/J.C. Epping, Aug. 5, 1919.
15. Adela Rogers St. Johns, "Love, Laughter and Tears, The Hollywood Story," *American Weekly*, Oct. 8, 1950.
16. Barthelmess reminiscences.
17. *Ibid*.
18. Gish and Pinchot, p. 220.
19. Quoted in Slide, *The Griffith Actresses*, p. 95.
20. Gish and Pinchot, p. 220.
21. *Theatre*, Jan. 1918.
22. DWG/Marshall Neilan, Feb. 25, 1919.
23. DWG/Banzhaf, Oct. 10, 1918.
24. Albert Grey/DWG, Nov. 20, 1918.
25. J.C. Epping/Bravermann, June 10, 1944.
26. This account of the founding of UA is drawn primarily from Tino Balio, *United Artists: The Company Built by the Stars*, pp. 13–29; Charles Chaplin, *My Autobiography*, pp. 221–25; and Budd Schulberg, *Moving Pictures: Memoirs of a Hollywood Prince*, pp. 71–79 and 95–99.
27. DWG/First National Contract, Jan. 21, 1919.
28. Quoted in Balio, p. 13.
29. *Los Angeles Herald-Examiner*, Feb. 5, 1919.
30. DWG/UA, Memorandum of Agreement, Feb. 5, 1919.
31. *New York Times*, May 14, 1919.
32. Julian Johnson, "The Shadow Stage," *Photoplay*, Aug. 19, 1919.
33. Quoted in Pratt, p. 252.
34. *Variety*, May 16, 1919.
35. United Artists Minutes, Aug. 28, 1919 (UA).
36. United Artists Minutes, Jan. 20, 1920 (UA).
37. John Belton in Wagenknecht and Slide, pp. 119–20. Reprinted from *The Silent Picture*, Nov. 17, 1973.
38. S.E.V. Taylor/E.C. Bidwell, Dec. 22, 1919.
39. Barthelmess "Reminiscences."
40. Gish and Pinchot, p. 211.

41. Ralph Graves/Bravermann, May 3, 1944.

42. Adela Rogers St. Johns, *Love, Laughter and Tears: My Hollywood Story*, pp. 75–76. This book reworks and greatly expands material first presented in the *American Weekly* series cited above.

43. Graves/Bravermann, May 3, 1944.

44. Everson, p. 157.

Chapter Fourteen

1. Gish interview.

2. Lloyd/Bravermann, 1946, ND.

3. Lloyd/Bravermann, Aug. 1948, ND.

4. Lloyd/Bravermann, Dec. 14, 1948.

5. D.W. Griffith Inc./Prospectus, June 4, 1920 (advance proof).

6. Raymond Klune, interview with author.

7. DWG/H.O. Schwalbe, Sept. 5, 1919.

8. *New York Times*, Mar. 22, 1922.

9. *Ibid.*, Aug. 23, 1920.

10. Bitzer, *His Story*, p. 206.

11. Mrs. Ethel Bitzer, interview with Walt Lowe.

12. DWG/Josephus Daniels (undated draft). The rest of this account follows Bitzer, *His Story*, pp. 222–26. Barthelmess's experiences are in his "Reminiscences."

13. *Boston Evening Transcript*, June 1, 1920.

14. Gish and Pinchot, p. 229.

15. Stanley Kauffmann, "Griffith's 'Way Down East,' " *Horizon*, spring 1972.

16. Mrs. Bitzer interview with Lowe.

17. Leigh Smith/DWG, Apr. 3, 1920.

18. Clifton/DWG, Apr. 4, 1920.

19. V. I. Pudovkin, *Film Technique and Film Acting*, p. 129.

20. Kauffmann, *op. cit.*

21. Harry Carr, "Griffith: Maker of Motion Pictures," *Motion Picture*, August 1922.

22. DWG/ "To the Public . . . ," undated MS.

23. Bitzer, *His Story*, p. 236. See also Gish and Pinchot, pp. 235–36.

24. New York *Times*, Sept. 4, 1920.

25. Review reprinted in Pratt, p. 254.

26. Review reprinted in Kauffmann and Henstell (ed.); *American Film Criticism*, pp. 111–12.

27. Quoted in Paine, *Life and Lillian Gish*, pp. 162–63.

28. *Omaha World-Herald*, Feb. 9, 1921.

29. United Artists Minutes, Dec. 6, 1920 (UA).

30. Fairbanks/DWG, Jan. 12, 1921.

31. Banzhaf/Dennis O'Brien, Jan. 13, 1921.

32. DWG/Fairbanks, Jan. 17, 1921.

33. Pickford/DWG, Jan. 17, 1921.

34. DWG/Pickford, Jan. 18, 1921.

35. Pickford, Fairbanks, Chaplin/DWG, Jan. 20, 1921.

36. D.W. Griffith Inc./Projected Budget, Dec. 18, 1920.

37. D.W. Griffith Inc./Minutes, Jan. 7, 1921.

38. M.C. Praeger/J.C. Epping, May 24, 1921.

39. DWG/Grey, June 3, 1921.
40. *Newport (R.I.) News*, May 16, 1921.
41. *New York Telegram*, May 3, 1921.
42. *Cleveland Plain Dealer*, May 8, 1921.
43. *Minneapolis Journal*, July 31, 1921.
44. *New York Picture Play Magazine*, July 1921.
45. *Montreal Star*, May 14, 1921.
46. *Ibid.*
47. *Boston Evening Transcript*, Oct. 10, 1921.
48. DWG/"Enormity," Aug. 14, 1921.
49. Klune interview.
50. DWG/W.R. Hearst, Oct. 12, 1921.
51. *New York Times*, Jan. 4, 1922.
52. Review reprinted in Kauffmann and Henstell, p. 131.
53. *Chicago American*, Feb. 1, 1922.
54. *Philadelphia Evening Bulletin*, Feb. 28, 1922.
55. *Chicago Tribune*, Feb. 4, 1922.
56. *Omaha Daily News*, Feb. 19, 1922.
57. DWG/Class "A" Stockholders, Dec. 31, 1921.
58. Wagenknecht and Slide, pp. 183–84.

CHAPTER FIFTEEN

1. *Boston Post*, Dec. 26, 1921.
2. *Boston Evening Transcript*, Oct. 10, 1921.
3. *New York Call*, May 13, 1922.
4. Lloyd/Bravermann, June 27, 1949.
5. *New York American*, Nov. 5, 1922.
6. Lloyd/Bravermann, June 27, 1949.
7. *One Exciting Night* Program. ND.
8. *New York Tribune*, Nov. 12, 1922.
9. Reviews from the newspapers specified, Oct. 24, 1922.
10. *Boston Telegram*, Oct. 10, 1922.
11. Woods/DWG, Apr. 4, 1922.
12. DWG/Marsh, Apr. 27, 1921.
13. Marsh/DWG, Oct. 7, 1921.
14. Mrs. Edward Larson (Carol Dempster), interview with the author.
15. *The White Rose* Press Book. ND.
16. Unidentified clipping, Griffith Scrapbooks.
17. William Bantell and Hal Sinzenich, interview with Walt Lowe.
18. DWG/Weeks Hall, Sept. 11, 1923.
19. Epping/Banzhaf, Mar. 19, 1923, Mar. 21, 1923.
20. *The White Rose* Program. ND.
21. *New York Times*, May 21, 1923.
22. *New York Herald*, May 27, 1923.
23. *New York World*, May 23, 1923.
24. Jolson/DWG, June 23, 1923.
25. Banzhaf, "Memoranda [*sic*] Regarding Griffith–Al Jolson Matter." ND.
26. DWG Inc./Grey, July 26, 1923; Frey/Banzhaf, Aug. 7, 1923.
27. *New York Daily News; New York World*, Sept. 15, 1926.
28. Affidavit, Benjamin Popper, Nov. 12, 1926.

29. Capt. George F. Sherks, "The 1923 Battle of Bunker Hill," *America*
Souvenir Program. ND.

30. Neil Hamilton, interview with author.

31. DWG/Weeks Hall, Sept. 11, 1923.

32. Robert W. Chambers, "The Sacrifice," MS. ND, MOMA.

33. Chambers/Griffith, Jan. 23, 1924.

34. Powers/Bravermann, Aug. 10, 1944.

35. *New York American*, Feb. 22, 1924.

36. *New York World*, Feb. 23, 1924.

37. *New York Herald*, Feb. 22, 1924.

38. *New York Journal*, Feb. 22, 1924.

39. *New York Post*, Feb. 22, 1924.

40. *New York Daily News*, Mar. 5, 1924.

41. *New York Commercial*, June 23, 1924.

42. *New York World*, May 9, 1924.

43. Griffith, "The Movies 100 Years from Now."

44. Details of this complex economic passage are drawn from: Central
Union Trust/DWG Inc., June 25, 1924, and July 25, 1924; "Agreement,"
DWG Inc., DWG and Empire Trust Co., July 1, 1925; DWG Inc.; "Letter
to Class A Stockholders," Mar. 21, 1925. Balio has a good account of the UA
side of the matter, pp. 49–51, but misplaces, by three years, a Griffith letter
complaining about distribution practices.

45. Neil Hamilton, interview with author.

46. DWG/Banzhaf, July 24, 1924.

47. Banzhaf/DWG, July 26, 1924.

48. *The Film Daily*, Aug. 7, 1924.

49. *Ibid.*, Sept. 17, 1924.

50. DWG/Dawes, Sept. 25, 1924.

51. Dennis T. O'Brien/Banzhaf, Sept. 18, 1924.

52. Banzhaf/Grey, Nov. 13, 1924. See also Banzhaf/Griffith, Nov. 13,
1924.

53. DWG/Banzhaf, Nov. 14, 1924. See also Grey/Banzhaf, Nov. 13,
1924, and Schenck/DWG, Nov. 13, 1924.

54. *New York Times*, Dec. 1, 1924.

55. *New York Morning Telegraph*, Dec. 6, 1924.

56. *New York World*, Dec. 6, 1924.

57. *Exhibitor's Trade Review*, Dec. 13, 1924.

58. *Motion Picture News*, Dec. 13, 1924.

59. Deed of Sale, DWG Inc. and Edgewater Point Inc., Jan. 2, 1925;
Memorandum of Agreement, UA, DWG Inc., DWG, Jan. 10, 1925; Agreement, DWG Inc., DWG and Famous Players–Lasky, Jan. 20, 1925.

Chapter Sixteen

1. Sarris, *The American Cinema*, pp. 51–52.

2. *Boston Herald*, Oct. 4, 1925.

3. Fields/Dorothy Herzog. ND.

4. Reviews from the newspapers cited, Aug. 3, 1925.

5. Sherwood, "The Silent Drama," *Life*, Oct. 15, 1925.

6. Memorandum re Famous Players Contract, Aug. 11, 1926. The author of this memo, intended for circulation among DWG Inc. executives, is
unknown.

7. DWG/Zukor, Nov. 10, 1926.

8. *Toronto Star*, Dec. 26, 1925.

9. Grey/DWG, Oct. 15, 1925.

10. *The New Yorker*, Jan. 16, 1926.

11. Louis E. Swarts/Jesse Lasky, June 29, 1926 (Par.).

12. Graham/Henry L. Salisbury, Jan. 16, 1924 (Par.).

13. DWG/Gordon Hillman, Mar. 8, 1927.

14. Wanger/Swarts, June 29, 1926 (Par.).

15. Norman Bel Geddes in *Miracle in the Evening* (Kelly, ed.), pp. 319–20.

16. DWG/Zukor, Nov. 10, 1926.

17. Zukor/DWG, Nov. 24, 1926.

18. *New York Times*, Oct. 13, 1926.

19. *New York Sun*, Oct. 17, 1926.

20. DWG/Zukor, Nov. 29, 1926.

21. Bantell-Sintzenich, interview with Walt Lowe.

22. Bel Geddes, *op. cit.*, p. 321.

23. Gerrit J. Lloyd, "What Will Griffith Do Now?" *Picture Play*, Sept. 1925.

24. *New York World*, June 10, 1926.

25. Frederick James Smith, "He Might Be the Richest Man in the World," *Photoplay*, Dec. 1926.

Chapter Seventeen

1. DWG/Schenck, Oct. 26, 1926.

2. Famous Players–Lasky/DWG Inc., Release of Contract, Jan. 5, 1927.

3. Agreement: Art Cinema Corp./DWG Inc., DWG, Apr. 19, 1927.

4. Klune/Banzhaf, June 17, 1927.

5. Cripps, *Slow Fade to Black*, p. 163.

6. Klune/Banzhaf, June 17, 1927.

7. Klune/Conway, Oct. 30, 1928.

8. Quoted in Slide, *op. cit.*, pp. 162–63.

9. Evelyn Baldwin Kunze, interview with the author.

10. Sarah Baldwin/DWG, May 27, 1927.

11. Reviews from newspapers cited, Jan. 25, 1928.

12. Klune/Lindeman, July 2, 1928.

13. DWG/Banzhaf, July 11, 1928.

14. Goodman/DWG, Mar. 19, 1928.

15. Klune/Lindeman, July 2, 1928.

16. Lichtman/DWG, Aug. 3, 1928.

17. Quoted in Wagenknecht and Slide, p. 234.

18. *New York Herald Tribune*, Oct. 13, 1928.

19. *New York Telegram*, Oct. 13, 1928.

20. *Variety*, Oct. 17, 1928.

21. Klune/Lindeman, July 2, 1928.

22. *New York Herald Tribune*, Mar. 11, 1929.

23. *New York Telegram*, Mar. 11, 1929.

24. Picon/Bravermann, June 7, 1944, July 10, 1944.

25. Linda Griffith/DWG, Sept. 15, 1930.

26. Quoted in Alexander Walker, *The Shattered Silents*, p. 68.

27. *Exhibitors Herald-World*, Jan. 21, 1929.

28. *New York Sunday World*, Mar. 24, 1929.

29. "Talk to Be Broadcast over Radio and Television by Mr. Griffith on Sunday, February 3, 1929." MS.

30. *New York Times*, Feb. 4, 1929.

31. Balio, p. 86.

32. Banzhaf/DWG, May 31, 1929.

33. Baldwin/DWG, Aug. 26, 1929.

34. Baldwin/DWG, Sept. 29, 1929.

35. Baldwin/DWG, July 11, 1929.

36. Sandburg/DWG, Oct. 30, 1929.

37. Klune/Banzhaf, Nov. 26, 1929. See also Griffith/Schenck memo, Nov. 19, 1929; Banzhaf/DWG, Nov. 8, 1929; Epping/DWG, Nov. 8, 1929.

38. Charles Fenton, *Stephen Vincent Benet*, pp. 232–41.

39. Aaron Latham, *Crazy Sundays*, pp. 55–56.

40. DWG/Schenck. ND.

41. Considine/DWG, May 15, 1930.

42. Considine/DWG, July 27, 1930.

43. *New York Evening Journal*, Aug. 14, 1930.

44. Reviews from the newspapers cited, Aug. 26, 1930.

45. Schenck/DWG, Nov. 28, 1930.

46. DWG/Schenck. ND.

Chapter Eighteen

1. *New York Graphic*, Dec. 19, 1931.

2. *Time*, Dec. 21, 1931.

3. Reviews from newspapers specified, Dec. 11, 1931.

4. Anita Loos, interview with author.

5. Loos interview.

6. Kunze interview.

7. John Houseman, *Run-Through*, pp. 84–85.

8. See Wagenknecht and Slide, pp. 252, 258.

9. Linda Griffith/DWG, Dec. 10, 1931.

10. Hearst/Griffith, Dec. 10, 1931.

11. *New York Times*, Dec. 11, 1931.

12. DWG/UA Stockholders, July 8, 1932 (UA).

13. DWG/Ruth Griffith. ND.

14. Klune interview.

15. DWG Inc.; Minutes, Apr. 15, 1932. The salary claims are from Minutes, Feb. 7, 1933.

16. DWG/UA Stockholders, July 8, 1932 (UA).

17. Schenck/DWG, Nov. 25, 1932 (UA).

18. DWG/UA Stockholders, Nov. 26, 1932 (UA).

19. Oglesby/O'Brien, Dec. 2, 1932 (UA).

20. Quoted in Balio, p. 89.

21. Oglesby/Schenck, Jan. 14, 1933.

22. *Motion Picture Herald*, Feb. 13, 1933.

23. Balio, pp. 89–90.

24. Agreement; DWG/Oglesby, Sept. 20, 1933.

25. Gish and Pinchot, p. 313.

26. DWG/Ruth Griffith, Feb. 9, 1934.

27. Linda Griffith/DWG, Dec. 16, 1932.

28. Bitzer "Notes."

29. *New York Times,* Mar. 17, 1933.

30. Hepburn/Carl Hunt, Nov. 1, 1932.

31. Linda Griffith/DWG, June 9, 1932.

32. S.L. Smith/DWG, May 30, 1934.

33. DWG/Sheehan, May 26, 1934.

34. Ackland and Grant, *The Celluloid Mistress,* pp. 55–56.

35. *New York Times,* Nov. 17, 1935.

36. Ballard Clark, interview with Walt Lowe.

37. Evelyn Baldwin Kunze, interview with Walt Lowe.

38. Frank Capra, *The Name Above the Title,* pp. 208–9.

39. Boyd Martin, "D.W. Griffith: The Maker of the Movies." *Louisville Courier-Journal Magazine,* Aug. 1, 1948.

40. Richard Reynolds, interview with Walt Lowe.

41. Evelyn Kunze, interview with author. All subsequent quotations from her are from the same source.

42. Griffith, *The Treadmill.* MS.

43. Martin, *op. cit.*

44. Reynolds interview with Lowe.

45. Griffith, *The Musquito* [sic], MS.

46. Griffith, "An Old-Timer Advises Hollywood," *Liberty,* June 17, 1939.

47. Material on Griffith's attempt at autobiography is from James Hart's introductory memoir in *The Man Who Invented Hollywood,* pp. 3–8.

48. Hal Roach, interview with author. Subsequent quotations from Roach are drawn from the same source.

49. *Ibid.*

50. *New York Times,* Dec. 2, 1939.

51. Lewis Milestone, interview with author.

52. Quoted in Gish and Pinchot, p. 341.

53. Goodman, *The Fifty Year Decline and Fall of Hollywood,* pp. 1–15.

54. Jean Renoir, interview with author.

55. Jean Renoir, *My Life and My Films,* pp. 45–46.

56. Herb Sterne, interview with author. Subsequent quotations from Sterne are drawn from the same source.

57. George Cukor, interview with author.

58. Gish and Pinchot, p. 353.

59. Bennie Zeidman, interview with author.

60. Leatrice Gilbert Fountain, conversation with the author.

61. Lloyd/Bravermann. ND.

62. Jay Leyda, "The Art and Death of D.W. Griffith," *Sewanee Review,* fall, 1948.

Bibliography

THE principal manuscript source for this work is the Museum of Modern Art Film Library in New York City. It is the repository for Griffith's personal papers (including his unpublished writings, which consist of poems, plays, short stories, screen stories and his unfinished autobiography) as well as the voluminous records of his corporation. Besides this material, the Museum holds other important Griffith source material. This includes Richard Barthelmess's "Reminiscences," in which he recollects his years with Griffith, dictated March 30, 1945; Barnet Bravermann's "Biography," slightly more than three chapters of which appear to be nearly finished work, together with his notes of interviews with, and correspondence with, the many Griffith coworkers, friends and business associates who were still alive when Bravermann was working on his tragically unfinished book in the 1940s; G. W. Bitzer's manuscript autobiography, which was later published in an edition that left out some material, notably a short chapter regarding Griffith's life in New York in the 1930s, after the failure of *The Struggle*. Finally, the Museum possesses the Griffith Corporation scrapbooks, which are indispensable for determining press response to many of Griffith's most significant films as well as for following his public life when his celebrity was at its height.

Other primary material came from several sources. I was able to see pertinent portions of Sidney Franklin's unpublished autobiography and a section of an interview with David Butler in which he discussed his work for Griffith, thanks to Kevin Brownlow. An unpublished chronology of Griffith's career as an actor was given me by George Pratt, who compiled it with Russell Merritt. Transcripts of interviews with William Bantell, Ethel Bitzer, Ballard Clark, Evelyn Baldwin Kunze, Richard Reynolds, Edmund Rucker and Hal Sintzenich were supplied to me by Walt Lowe and were an invaluable supplement to my own interviews with some of them. As my acknowledgments indicate, I was able to speak, as well, to many other individuals whose lives were bound up with Griffith's, and their specific contributions to this book, having been footnoted, I have not thought necessary to cite again here. The same is true of papers obtained from Paramount and United Artists.

Finally, a word about printed sources. Perhaps the most important of them were the trade journals and that handful of early magazines that, before they turned into "fan" publications, attempted to write with reasonable seri-

629

ousness about the movies for the general public. For my purposes I found these to be the most valuable: *Exhibitor's Trade Review, Motion Picture, Moving Picture Classic, Moving Picture World, New York Dramatic Mirror, Photoplay, Variety.* Of the general circulation publications, of course, the *New York Times* is invaluable; but especially in the 1920s, many of the other New York dailies generally had more literate and knowledgeable movie reviewing, so I found the files of the *Tribune* (latterly the *Herald Tribune*), the *Sun* and the *World* to be particularly illuminating. Among the general magazines, *Life* (the humor magazine, not the picture magazine) was blessed first by Robert Bench- ley, then by Robert E. Sherwood, as the film critic; and the *New Republic* was, from its beginning, a home for serious reviewing. If my researches had been confined to this relative handful of publications, it might have been possible to bibliograph all of the journalism I consulted. But I made a determined effort to at least sample reviews from other major cities in the United States and, of course, Griffith's career was an extraordinarily wide-ranging one. To list all the relatively ephemeral sources that recorded his work and his passages would be to extend this bibliography to unconscionable lengths. The notes, citing merely those sources quoted in the text, will, I hope, suggest the range of my inquiries. But the list of printed sources which follows records only the major periodical sources and those books that are either directly quoted or that, in some mea- sure, shaped my view of D. W. Griffith's life and times. In the citations of books, the place of publication is New York unless otherwise indicated.

Rodney Ackland and Elspeth Grant, *The Celluloid Mistress, or The Custard Pie of Dr. Caligari.* London: Alan Wingate, 1954.

James Agee, *Agee on Film.* McDowell-Obolensky, 1958.

Roy E. Aitken, as told to Al P. Nelson, *The Birth of a Nation Story.* Mid- dleburg, Va.: Denlinger, 1965.

George Amberg (ed.), *The New York Times Film Reviews, 1913–1970.* Quadrangle Books, 1971.

The American Film Institute Catalogue of Motion Pictures Produced in the United States. Vol. F2; *Feature Films 1921–1930.* R. R. Bowker, 1971.

Lady Cynthia Asquith (E. M. Horsley, ed.), *Diaries 1917–1918.* Alfred A. Knopf, 1969.

Tino Balio, *United Artists: The Company Built by the Stars.* Madison, Wis.: University of Wisconsin Press, 1976.

Fred J. Balshofer and Arthur C. Miller, with the assistance of Bebe Berg- sten, *One Reel a Week.* Berkeley, Cal.: University of California Press, 1967.

Reyner Banham, *Los Angeles: The Architecture of Four Ecologies.* Harper & Row, 1971.

Iris Barry, *D.W. Griffith: American Film Master* (with an annotated list of films by Eileen Bowser). Museum of Modern Art, 1965.

Lionel Barrymore, as told to Cameron Shipp, *We Barrymores.* Appleton- Century-Crofts, 1951.

Charles Baudelaire (trans. and ed., Jonathan Mayne), *The Painter of Modern Life and Other Essays.* Phaidon, 1965.

Richard Berry, "Five Dollar Movies Prophesized." *The Editor,* Apr. 24, 1915.

G. W. Bitzer, *Billy Bitzer: His Story.* Farrar, Straus & Giroux, 1973.

George Blaisdell, "At the Sign of the Flaming Arcs." *Moving Picture World,* Jan. 23, 1914.

Peter Bogdanovitch, *Allan Dwan: The Last Pioneer*. Praeger, 1971.

Eileen Bowser (ed.), *Biograph Bulletins, 1908–1912*. Octagon Books, 1973.

——— (ed.), *Film Notes*. Museum of Modern Art, 1969.

Karl Brown (Kevin Brownlow, ed.), *Adventures with D.W. Griffith*. Farrar, Straus & Giroux, 1973.

Kevin Brownlow, *Hollywood: The Pioneers*. London: Collins, 1979.

———, *The Parade's Gone By*. Alfred A. Knopf, 1968.

———, *The War, the West and the Wilderness*. Alfred A. Knopf, 1979.

Edward D. C. Campbell, Jr., *The Celluloid South: Hollywood and the Southern Myth*. Knoxville, Tenn.: University of Tennessee Press, 1981.

Robert Cannom, *Van Dyke and the Mythical City, Hollywood*. Culver City, Cal.: Murray & Gee, 1948.

Frank Capra, *The Name Above the Title*. Bantam Books, 1972. (Reprint of 1971 edition.)

James Card, "The Films of Mary Pickford." *Image*, Dec. 1959.

Harry C. Carr, "Griffith, Maker of Battle Scenes, Sees Real War." *Photoplay*, Mar. 1918.

———, "Griffith, Maker of Pictures." *Motion Picture*, Aug. 1922.

———, "How Griffith Picks His Leading Women." *Photoplay*, Dec. 1918.

C. W. Ceram, *The Archaeology of the Cinema*. Harcourt, Brace & World, ND.

Charles Chaplin, *My Autobiography*. Simon & Schuster, 1964.

Raymond Allen Cook, *Fire from the Flint: The Amazing Careers of Thomas Dixon*. Winston-Salem, N.C.: John F. Blair, 1968.

Miriam Cooper with Bonnie Herndon, *Dark Lady of the Silents: My Life in Early Hollywood*. Indianapolis: Bobbs-Merrill, 1973.

Noel Coward, *Present Indicative*. Garden City, N.Y.: Doubleday, Doran, 1937.

Thomas Cripps, *Slow Fade to Black: The Negro in American Film 1900–1942*. Oxford University Press, 1977.

Bosley Crowther, *Hollywood Rajah: The Life and Times of Louis B. Mayer*. Dell, 1961. (Reprint of 1960 edition.)

———, *The Lion's Share: The Story of an Entertainment Empire*. E. P. Dutton, 1957.

Homer Croy, *Starmaker: The Story of D. W. Griffith*. Duell, Sloan & Pearce, 1959.

Thomas Quinn Curtiss, *Von Stroheim*. Farrar, Straus & Giroux, 1971.

Jean Darwell, "The Personal Side of David W. Griffith." *Motion Picture*, Jan. 1917.

Sergei Eisenstein (ed. and trans., Jay Leyda), *Film Form*. Harcourt, Brace & World, 1949.

William K. Everson, *American Silent Film*. Oxford University Press, 1978.

Charles Fenton, *Stephen Vincent Benet: The Life and Times of an American Man of Letters, 1898–1943*. New Haven, Conn.: Yale University Press, 1958.

Gene Fowler, *Father Goose: The Story of Mack Sennett*. Covici-Friede, 1934.

Stephen R. Fox, *The Guardian of Boston: William Monroe Trotter*. Atheneum, 1970.

Philip French, *The Movie Moguls: An Informal History of the Hollywood Tycoons.* London: Weidenfeld & Nicolson, 1969.

A. R. Fulton, *Motion Pictures: The Development of an Art from Silent Films to the Age of Television.* Norman, Okla.: University of Oklahoma Press, 1960.

Harry M. Geduld (ed.), *Focus on D. W. Griffith.* Englewood Cliffs, N.J.: Prentice-Hall, 1971.

Lillian Gish with Ann Pinchot, *The Movies, Mr. Griffith and Me.* Englewood Cliffs, N.J.: Prentice-Hall, 1969.

Eric Goldman, *Rendezvous with Destiny.* Vintage, 1978. (Reprint of 1952 edition.)

Ezra Goodman, *The Fifty-Year Decline and Fall of Hollywood.* Simon & Schuster, 1961.

Henry Stephen Gordon, "The Story of David Wark Griffith." *Photoplay*, June–Nov., 1916.

D. W. Griffith (James Hart, ed.), *The Man Who Invented Hollywood: The Autobiography of D. W. Griffith.* Louisville, Ky.: Touchstone Publishing, 1972.

D. W. Griffith, "An Old-Timer Advises Hollywood." *Liberty*, June 17, 1939.

———, "Are Motion Pictures Destructive of Good Taste?" *Arts and Decoration*, Sept. 1933.

———, "Don't Blame the Movies!" *Motion Picture*, July 1926.

———, "Five Dollar 'Movies' Prophesied." *The Editor*, Apr. 24, 1915.

———, "The Greatest Theatrical Force." *Moving Picture World*, Mar. 26, 1927.

———, as told to Myron M. Stearns, "How Do You Like the Show?" *Collier's*, Apr. 24, 1924.

———, "Life and the Photodrama." *Motion Picture Classic*, Dec. 1918.

———, "Motion Pictures: The Miracle of Modern Photography." *The Mentor*, July 1, 1921.

———, "The Motion Picture Today and Tomorrow." *Theatre*, Oct. 1927.

———, "The Movies 100 Years from Now." *Collier's*, May 3, 1924.

———, "Pace in the Movies." *Liberty*, Nov. 13, 1926.

———, "Pictures vs. One-Night Stands," *Independent*, Dec. 11, 1916.

———, "The Real Truth About Breaking into the Movies." *Woman's Home Companion*, Feb. 1924.

———, *The Rise and Fall of Free Speech in America.* Los Angeles: privately printed pamphlet, 1916.

———, "What I Demand of Movie Stars." *Moving Picture Classic*, Feb. 1917.

———, "What Is Beauty in Motion Pictures?" *Liberty*, Oct. 19, 1929.

———, "Youth, and the Spirit of the Movies." *Illustrated World*, Oct. 1921.

Mrs. D. W. Griffith (Linda Arvidson), *When the Movies Were Young.* Benjamin Blom, 1968. (Reprint of 1925 edition.)

Francis Hackett, "Brotherly Love." *New Republic*, Mar. 20, 1915.

Benjamin B. Hampton, *History of the American Film Industry: From Its Beginnings to 1931.* Dover Publications, 1970. (Reprint of 1931 edition.)

Ralph Hancock and Letitia Fairbanks, *Douglas Fairbanks: The Fourth Musketeer.* Henry Holt, 1953.

Bernard Hanson, "D. W. Griffith: Some Sources." *The Art Bulletin,* Dec. 1972.

Lewis Reeves Harrison, "David W. Griffith: The Art Director and His Work." *Moving Picture World,* Nov. 22, 1913.

William S. Hart, *My Life East and West.* Benjamin Blom, 1968. (Reprint of 1929 edition.)

Molly Haskell, *From Reverence to Rape: The Treatment of Women in the Movies.* Holt, Rinehart & Winston, 1974.

Charles Edward Hastings, "A Biography of David Wark Griffith and A Brief History of the Motion Picture in America." *Exhibitor's Trade Review,* 1920. (Offprint of article from publication cited.)

Samuel P. Hayes, *The Response to Industrialism.* Chicago: University of Chicago Press, 1957.

Robert M. Henderson, *D. W. Griffith: His Life and Work.* Oxford University Press, 1972.

———, *D. W. Griffith: The Years at Biograph.* Farrar, Straus & Giroux, 1970.

Gordon Hendricks, *Beginnings of the Biograph: The Story of the Invention of the Mutoscope and the Biograph and Their Supplying Camera.* The Beginnings of American Film, 1964.

Stanley Hochman, *From Quasimodo to Scarlett O'Hara: A National Board of Review Anthology.* Frederick J. Ungar, 1982.

Frederick J. Hoffman, *The Twenties: American Writing in the Postwar Decade.* Viking Press, 1955.

John Houseman, *Run-Through.* Simon & Schuster, 1972.

Theodore Huff, *"Intolerance," The Film By David Wark Griffith: Shot-by-Shot Analysis.* Museum of Modern Art, 1966.

———, *A Shot Analysis of D. W. Griffith's The Birth of a Nation.* Museum of Modern Art, 1961.

Will Irwin, *The House That Shadows Built.* Garden City, N.Y.: Doubleday, Doran, 1928.

Joseph Hays Jackson, "To Be a Boy in Louisville." *Louisville Courier-Journal Magazine,* Jan. 28, 1968.

Lewis Jacobs, *The Rise of the American Film: A Critical History.* Harcourt, Brace, 1939.

Pauline Kael, "The Current Cinema: A Great Folly, and a Small One." *The New Yorker,* Feb. 24, 1968.

Ephraim Katz, *The Film Encyclopedia.* Thomas Y. Crowell, 1979.

Alfred Kazin, *On Native Grounds.* Garden City, N.Y.: Doubleday (Anchor), 1956. (Abridged reprint of 1942 edition.)

Stanley Kauffmann with Bruce Henstell (eds.), *American Film Criticism: From the Beginnings to Citizen Kane.* Liveright, 1972.

———, "D. W. Griffith's 'Way Down East.' " *Horizon,* spring 1972.

William Kelly (ed.), *Miracle in the Evening.* Garden City, N.Y.: Doubleday, 1960.

Judge Charles Kerr (ed.), *History of Kentucky* (by William L. C. Connoly and E. M. Coulter). Chicago: American Historical Society, 1922.

Albert D. Kirwin (ed.), *Johnny Green of the Orphan Brigade.* Lexington, Ky.: University of Kentucky Press, 1956.

Arthur Knight, *The Liveliest Art: A Panoramic History of the Movies.* Macmillan, 1978.

Richard Koszarski (ed.), *The Rivals of D. W. Griffith: Alternate Auteurs, 1913–1918.* Minneapolis, Minn.: Walker Art Center, 1976.

Gavin Lambert, *On Cukor*. G. P. Putnam's Sons, 1972.

Jesse L. Lasky with Don Weldon, *I Blow My Own Horn*. Garden City, N.Y.: Doubleday, 1957.

Last Night at Macauley's: A Checklist, 1873–1925. Louisville, Ky.: The Printing Shop, University of Louisville, ND.

Aaron Latham, *Crazy Sundays: F. Scott Fitzgerald in Hollywood*. Viking Press, 1971.

Jay Leyda, "Film Chronicle: The Art and Death of D. W. Griffith." *Sewanee Review*, fall 1948.

Vachel Lindsay, *The Art of the Moving Picture*. Liveright, 1970. (Reprint of 1915 edition.)

———, "Photoplay Progress." *New Republic*, Feb. 17, 1917.

Gerrit J. Lloyd, "What Will Griffith Do Now?" *Picture Play*, Sept. 1925.

Robert Edgar Long, *David Wark Griffith: A Brief Sketch of His Career*. D. W. Griffith Service, 1920.

Anita Loos, *A Girl Like I*. Viking Press, 1966.

———, *The Talmadge Girls: A Memoir*. Viking Press, 1978.

Bessie Love, *From Hollywood with Love*. London: Elm Tree Books, 1977.

Dwight Macdonald, *On Movies*. Englewood Cliffs, N.J.: Prentice-Hall, 1969.

Kenneth Macgowan, *Behind the Screen: The History and Technique of the Motion Picture*. Delta, 1967. (Reprint of 1965 edition.)

Isabel McLennan McMeckin, *Louisville: The Gateway City*. Julian Messner, 1946.

Mae Marsh, *Screen Acting*. Los Angeles: Photo-Star Publishing, 1921.

Boyd Martin, "D. W. Griffith: The Maker of the Movies." *Louisville Courier-Journal Magazine*, Aug. 1, 1948.

Brian Masters, *Now Barabbas Was a Rotter: The Extraordinary Life of Marie Corelli*. London: Hamish Hamilton, 1978.

Lary May, *Screening Out the Past: The Birth of Mass Culture and the Motion Picture Industry*. Oxford University Press, 1980.

Colleen Moore, *Silent Star*. Garden City, N.Y.: Doubleday, 1968.

Lloyd Morris, *Curtain Time: The Story of the American Theatre*. Random House, 1952.

Mary B. Mullett, "Greatest Moving Picture Producer in the World." *American*, Apr. 1921.

Hugo Münsterberg, *The Film: A Psychological Study*. Dover Publications, 1970. (Reprint of 1916 edition.)

Peter Noble, "A Note on an Idol." *Sight and Sound*, autumn, 1946.

Paul O'Dell, *Griffith and the Rise of Hollywood*. A. S. Barnes, 1970.

Albert Bigelow Paine, *Life and Lillian Gish*. Macmillan, 1932.

Geoffrey Perrett, *America in the Twenties*. Simon & Schuster, 1982.

Mary Pickford, *Sunshine and Shadow*. London: William Heinemann, 1956.

Fletcher Pratt, *A Short History of the Civil War*. Bantam Books, 1968.

George Pratt, *Spellbound in Darkness: A History of the Silent Film*. Greenwich, Conn.: New York Graphic Society, 1973.

V. I. Pudovkin (trans. and ed., Ivor Montagu), *Film Technique and Film Acting*. Grove Press, 1970. (Reprint of 1958 edition.)

Frank Rahill, *The World of Melodrama*. University Park, Pa.: Penn State University Press, 1967.

Terry Ramsaye, *A Million and One Nights: A History of the Motion Picture through 1925*. Simon & Schuster, 1964. (Reprint of 1926 edition.)

Jean Renoir, *My Life and My Films*. Atheneum, 1974.

David Robinson, *Hollywood in the Twenties*. A. S. Barnes, 1968.

Selma Robinson, "Don't Blame the Movies, Blame Life!" *Motion Picture*, July 1926.

W. R. Robinson (ed., with assistance from George Garret), *Man and the Movies*. Baton Rouge, La.: Louisiana State University Press, 1967.

Bernard Rosenberg and Harry Silverstein, *The Real Tinsel*. Macmillan, 1970.

Paul Rotha, *The Film Till Now: A Survey of World Cinema*. Funk & Wagnalls, 1951. (Revised edition.)

Edmund Rucker, "The Great D.W." *Louisville Courier-Journal Magazine*, Feb. 17, 1957.

Adela Rogers St. Johns, *The Honeycomb*. Garden City, N.Y.: Doubleday, 1969.

―――, *Love, Laughter and Tears: My Hollywood Story*. Garden City, N.Y.: Doubleday, 1978.

―――, "Love, Laughter and Tears: The Hollywood Story." *American Weekly*, Oct. 8, 1950.

Andrew Sarris, *The American Cinema: Directors and Directions, 1929–1968*. E. P. Dutton, 1968.

Richard Schickel, *His Picture in the Papers*. Charterhouse, 1973.

Budd Schulberg, *Moving Pictures: Memories of a Hollywood Prince*. Stein & Day, 1981.

Gilbert Seldes, *The Seven Lively Arts*. A. S. Barnes, 1962. (Reprint of 1924 edition, revised 1957.)

Mack Sennett, with Cameron Shipp, *King of Comedy*. Garden City, N.Y.: Doubleday, 1954.

Fred Silva (ed.), *Focus on The Birth of a Nation*. Englewood Cliffs, N.J.: Prentice-Hall, 1971.

Anthony Slide, *The Griffith Actresses*. A. S. Barnes, 1973.

Frederick James Smith, "He Might Be the Richest Man in the World." *Photoplay*, Dec. 1926.

Kenneth M. Stampp, *The Era of Reconstruction, 1865–1877*. Vintage Books, 1967. (Reprint of 1965 edition.)

Seymour Stern, "An Index to the Creative Work of D. W. Griffith." Index Series—2, 4, 7, 8, 10. London: British Film Institute, 1944.

―――, "Griffith I: 'The Birth of a Nation.'" *Film Culture*, spring–summer, 1965.

Karl Struss: Man with a Camera. Bloomfield Hills, Mich.: Cranbrook Academy of Art, 1976.

Allene Talmey, *Doug and Mary and Others*. Macy-Masius, 1927.

Howard Taubman, *The Making of the American Theatre*, Coward-McCann, 1967.

Robert Lewis Taylor, *W. C. Fields: His Follies and Fortunes*. Garden City, N.Y.: Doubleday, 1949.

Ed Porter Thompson, *History of the Orphan Brigade*. Louisville, Ky.: Lewis N. Thompson, 1898.

Bruce T. Torrence, *Hollywood: The First 100 Years*. New York: Zoetrope, 1982.

Jim Tully, "David Wark Griffith," *Vanity Fair*, Dec. 1926.

Parker Tyler, *The Hollywood Hallucination*. Simon & Schuster, 1970. (Reprint of 1944 edition.)

A. Nicholas Vardac, *Stage to Screen: Theatrical Method from Garrick to Griffith*. Cambridge, Mass.: Harvard University Press, 1949.

Edward Wagenknecht, *The Movies in the Age of Innocence*. Norman, Okla.: University of Oklahoma Press, 1962.

Edward Wagenknecht and Anthony Slide, *The Films of D. W. Griffith*. Crown Publishing, 1975.

Alexander Walker, *Rudolph Valentino*. Stein & Day, 1976.

————, *The Shattered Silents: How the Talkies Came to Stay*. London: Elm Tree Books, 1978.

Raoul Walsh, *Each Man in His Time: The Life Story of a Director*. Farrar, Straus & Giroux, 1974.

War of the Rebellion: Official Records Atlas. Washington, D.C.: National Archives.

Robert E. Welsh, "David W. Griffith Speaks." *New York Dramatic Mirror*, Jan. 14, 1914.

Edmund Wilson, "Dickens: The Two Scrooges," in *Eight Essays*. Garden City, N.Y. Doubleday (Anchor), 1954.

————, *Patriotic Gore: Studies in the Literature of the American Civil War*. Oxford University Press, 1966. (Reprint of 1962 edition.)

Edward Mott Woolley, "Story of D. W. Griffith: The $100,000 Salary Man of the Movies." *McClure's*, Sept. 1914.

Charles E. Wynes (ed.), *The Negro in the South Since 1865*. Harper Colophon, 1968.

Larzer Ziff, *The American 1890s: Life and Times of a Lost Generation*. Viking Press, 1966.

Adolph Zukor with Dale Kramer, *The Public Is Never Wrong*. G. P. Putnam's Sons, 1953.

A Checklist of
D. W. Griffith's Films

FULL filmographies of Griffith's features are readily available in Iris Barry and Eileen Bowser's *D.W. Griffith: American Film Master* and in Edward Wagenknecht and Anthony Slide's *The Films of D.W. Griffith*. Both give fuller casts and credits than space permits here. The most complete listing of Griffith's Biograph work, including photographic credits, production and release dates as well as notes on casting and literary sources, is to be found in the appendices to Robert M. Henderson's *D.W. Griffith: The Years at Biograph*. I felt it would be convenient for readers and students to draw the most important information from these three sources together in one place, and for me to resolve, where possible, a few minor errors and discrepancies that came to my attention. I have marked with asterisks those Biograph features that seem to me the most interesting artistically or important historically; most of them are discussed more fully in the text. I have also added a few notes in the hope that they will help the reader to keep his bearings in the flood of film Griffith unloosed in the years 1908 to 1912. Biograph films are listed under the year of their production; the later, longer films are listed under the year of their release.

1908

The Adventures of Dollie*
The Redman and the Child*
The Tavern Keeper's Daughter
A Calamitous Elopement
   (Billy Bitzer's and Florence Lawrence's first film for Griffith)
The Greaser's Gauntlet
The Man and the Woman
For Love of Gold
   (unacknowledged adaptation of Jack London's story "Just Meat" and an often cited early example of Griffith's changing camera angle in the midst of a scene)

The Fatal Hour*
   (often cited as an effective early use of cross-cutting)
For a Wife's Honor
Balked at the Altar
   (Mack Sennett's first film for Griffith as an actor)
The Girl and the Outlaw
The Red Girl
Betrayed by a Hand Print
Monday Morning in a Coney Island Police Court
Behind the Scenes
The Heart of O'yama

637

Where the Breakers Roar
The Stolen Jewels
A Smoked Husband
The Zulu's Heart
The Vaquero's Vow
Father Gets in the Game
The Barbarian, Ingomar
(Wilfred Lucas's first film for Griffith)
The Planter's Wife
The Devil
The Romance of a Jewess
The Call of the Wild
(one-reel adaptation of the Jack London novel)
After Many Years
(the first of Griffith's explorations of the "Enoch Arden" theme)
Mr. Jones at the Ball
Concealing a Burglar
The Taming of the Shrew
The Ingrate
A Woman's Way
The Pirate's Gold
The Guerrilla
The Curtain Pole*
(Mack Sennett in a starring role)
The Song of the Shirt
The Clubman and the Tramp
Money Mad
Mrs. Jones Entertains
The Feud and the Turkey
The Test of Friendship
The Reckoning
One Touch of Nature
(Kate Bruce's first Griffith film)
An Awful Moment
The Helping Hand
The Maniac Cook
The Christmas Burglars
A Wreath in Time
The Honor of Thieves
(Owen Moore's first Griffith film)
The Criminal Hypnotist
The Sacrifice
The Welcome Burglar
A Rural Elopement
Mr. Jones Has a Card Party
The Hindoo Dagger
The Salvation Army Lass
Love Finds a Way
Tragic Love
The Girls and Daddy

1909

Those Boys
The Cord of Life
(Adolphe Lestina's first Griffith film)
Trying to Get Arrested
The Fascinating Mrs. Frances
Those Awful Hats
Jones and the Lady Book Agent
The Drive for Life
The Brahma Diamond
The Politician's Love Story
The Joneses Have Amateur Theatricals
Edgar Allan Poe*
The Roué's Heart
His Wife's Mother
The Golden Louis
His Ward's Love
At the Altar
The Prussian Spy
The Medicine Bottle
The Deception
The Lure of the Gown
Lady Helen's Escapade
A Fool's Revenge
(adaptation of Rigoletto) *
The Wooden Leg
I Did It, Mama
A Burglar's Mistake
The Voice of the Violin*
(Griffith on the subject of anarchy)
And a Little Child Shall Lead Them
The French Duel
Jones and His New Neighbors
A Drunkard's Reformation
The Winning Coat
A Rude Hostess
The Road to the Heart
(James Kirkwood's first Griffith film)
The Eavesdropper
Schneider's Anti-Noise Crusade
Twin Brothers
Confidence
The Note in the Shoe
Lucky Jim
A Sound Sleeper
A Troublesome Satchel
'Tis an Ill Wind That Blows No Good

The Suicide Club
*Resurrection**
  (adaptation of the Tolstoy novel)
One Busy Hour
A Baby's Shoe
Eloping with Auntie
The Cricket on the Hearth
  (adaptation of the Dickens story)
The Jilt
Eradicating Auntie
What Drink Did
Her First Biscuits
  (Mary Pickford's first Griffith
  film)
*The Violin Maker of Cremona**
Two Memories
*The Lonely Villa**
  (scenario credited to Mack Sen-
  nett)
The Peach Basket Hat
The Son's Return
His Duty
A New Trick
The Necklace
The Way of Man
The Faded Lilies
The Message
The Friend of the Family
Was Justice Served?
Mrs. Jones' Lover, or I Want My
  Hat!
The Mexican Sweethearts
*The Country Doctor**
Jealousy and the Man
The Renunciation
The Cardinal's Conspiracy
The Seventh Day
Tender Hearts
A Convict's Sacrifice
  (Henry Walthall's first Griffith
  film)
A Strange Meeting
Sweet and Twenty
The Slave
They Would Elope
Mr. Jones' Burglar
*The Mended Lute**
*The Indian Runner's Romance**
With Her Card
The Better Way
His Wife's Visitor
The Mills of the Gods
Pranks

Oh, Uncle
*The Sealed Room**
  (George Siegmann's first Griffith
  film)
1776, or The Hessian Renegades
The Little Darling
In Old Kentucky
  (some of the themes of *The Birth
  of a Nation* are prefigured here)
The Children's Friend
Comata, the Sioux
Getting Even
The Broken Locket
A Fair Exchange
  (adaptation of *Silas Marner*)
The Awakening
*Pippa Passes**
  (adaptation of the Browning
  poem; first film review in the *New
  York Times*)
Leather Stockings
Fools of Fate
Wanted, a Child
The Little Teacher
A Change of Heart
His Lost Love
*Lines of White on the Sullen Sea**
  (Dell Henderson's first film for
  Griffith as an actor)
The Gibson Goddess
In the Watches of the Night
The Expiation
What's Your Hurry
The Restoration
Nursing a Viper
Two Women and a Man
The Light That Came
A Midnight Adventure
The Open Gate
Sweet Revenge
  (Robert Harron's acting debut)
*The Mountaineer's Honor**
In the Window Recess
The Trick That Failed
The Death Disc
  (adaptation of the Mark Twain
  story)
Through the Breakers
In a Hempen Bag
*A Corner in Wheat**
  (unacknowledged adaptation of a
  Frank Norris short story, "A Deal
  in Wheat")

The Redman's View
(a particularly sympathetic portrayal of the American Indian)
The Test
A Trap for Santa Claus
In Little Italy
To Save Her Soul
Choosing a Husband
The Rocky Road
(Blanche Sweet's first major role for Griffith)
The Dancing Girl of Butte
Her Terrible Ordeal
The Call
The Honor of His Family
On the Reef
The Last Deal
One Night and Then—
The Cloister's Touch
The Woman from Mellon's
The Duke's Plan
(Miriam Cooper's first Griffith film)
The Englishman and the Girl

1910

The Final Settlement
His Last Burglary
Taming a Husband
The Newlyweds
(Griffith's first film in California)
The Thread of Destiny
In Old California
The Man
The Converts
Faithful
The Twisted Trail
Gold Is Not All
*As It Is in Life**
A Rich Revenge
A Romance of the Western Hills
Thou Shalt Not
The Way of the World
The Unchanging Sea
The Gold Seekers
Love Among the Roses
The Two Brothers
Unexpected Help
An Affair of Hearts
Ramona
(one-reel adaptation of the popular novel by Helen Hunt Jackson)
Over Silent Paths

The Implement
In the Season of Buds
A Child of the Ghetto
In the Border States
A Victim of Jealousy
The Face at the Window
The Marked Time-Table
(Frank Woods's first recorded original scenario)
A Child's Impulse
Muggsy's First Sweetheart
The Purgation
A Midnight Cupid
What the Daisy Said
A Child's Faith
The Call to Arms
Serious Sixteen
A Flash of Light
As the Bells Rang Out
An Arcadian Maid
The House with the Closed Shutters
Her Father's Pride
A Salutary Lesson
*The Usurer**
The Sorrows of the Unfaithful
In Life's Cycle
*Wilful Peggy**
A Summer Idyll
The Modern Prodigal
Rose O'Salem Town
Little Angels of Luck
A Mohawk's Way
The Oath and the Man
The Iconoclast
Examination Day at School
That Chink at Golden Gulch
The Broken Doll
The Banker's Daughters
The Message of the Violin
Two Little Waifs
Waiter No. 5
The Fugitive
Simple Charity
The Song of the Wildwood Flute
A Child's Stratagem
Sunshine Sue
A Plain Song
His Sister-in-Law
The Golden Supper
The Lesson
When a Man Loves
Winning Back His Love
*His Trust**

His Trust Fulfilled*
(with previous title, Griffith's first
two-reel subject)
A Wreath of Orange Blossoms
The Italian Barber
The Two Paths
(Donald Crisp's first Griffith film)
Conscience
Three Sisters
A Decree of Destiny
Fate's Turning
What Shall We Do with Our Old?*
The Diamond Star
The Lily of the Tenements
Heart Beats of Long Ago

1911

Fisher Folks
His Daughter
The Lonedale Operator*
(scenario credited to Mack Sen-
nett)
Was He a Coward?
Teaching Dad to Like Her
The Spanish Gypsy
The Broken Cross
The Chief's Daughter
A Knight of the Road*
Madame Rex
(scenario by Mary Pickford)
His Mother's Scarf
How She Triumphed
(scenario by Linda Arvidson)
In the Days of '49
The Two Sides
The New Dress
Enoch Arden, Part I*
Enoch Arden, Part II*
The White Rose of the Wilds
The Crooked Road
A Romany Tragedy
A Smile of a Child
The Primal Call
The Jealous Husband
The Indian Brothers
The Thief and the Girl
Her Sacrifice
The Blind Princess and the Poet
Fighting Blood*
(Lionel Barrymore's first Griffith
film)
The Last Drop of Water*
Robby the Coward

A Country Cupid
The Ruling Passion
The Rose of Kentucky
The Sorrowful Example
Swords and Hearts
The Stuff Heroes Are Made Of
The Old Confectioner's Mistake
The Unveiling
(Mabel Normand's first Griffith
film)
The Eternal Mother
Dan the Dandy
The Revenue Man and the Girl
The Squaw's Love
Italian Blood
The Making of a Man
Her Awakening
The Adventures of Billy
The Long Road
The Battle
Love in the Hills
The Trail of the Books
Through Darkened Vales*
Saved from Himself
A Woman Scorned
The Miser's Heart
The Failure
Sunshine Through the Dark
As in a Looking Glass
A Terrible Discovery
A Tale of the Wilderness
The Voice of the Child*
The Baby and the Stork
The Old Bookkeeper
A Sister's Love
For His Son
The Transformation of Mike
A Blot on the 'Scutcheon
(adaptation of the Browning
poem)
Billy's Stratagem
The Sunbeam
A String of Pearls
The Root of Evil

1912

The Mender of the Nets
Under Burning Skies
A Siren of Impulse
Iola's Promise
The Goddess of Sagebrush Gulch*
The Girl and Her Trust*
The Punishment

*Fate's Interception**
*The Female of the Species**
Just Like a Woman
One Is Business, the Other Crime
  (Mae Marsh's film debut)
The Lesser Evil
*The Old Actor**
A Lodging for the Night
His Lesson
When Kings Were the Law
*A Beast at Bay**
An Outcast Among Outcasts
Home Folks
A Temporary Truce
The Spirit Awakened
Lena and the Geese
  (scenario by Mary Pickford)
An Indian Summer
The Schoolteacher and the Waif
*Man's Lust for Gold**
*Man's Genesis**
Heaven Avenges
A Pueblo Legend
*The Sands of Dee**
  (Linda Arvidson's last film for
  Griffith)
Black Sheep
The Narrow Road
A Child's Remorse
The Inner Circle
A Change of Spirit
An Unseen Enemy
  (film debut of Lillian and Doro-
  thy Gish; Harry Carey's first Grif-
  fith film)
Two Daughters of Eve
Friends
So Near, Yet So Far
A Feud in the Kentucky Hills
In the Aisles of the Wild
The One She Loved
The Painted Lady
*The Musketeers of Pig Alley**
Heredity
Gold and Glitter
My Baby
The Informer
The Unwelcome Guest
Pirate Gold
*Brutality**
*The New York Hat**
  (Anita Loos's first scenario)
*The Massacre**

My Hero
Oil and Water
The Burglar's Dilemma
  (scenario by Lionel Barrymore)
A Cry for Help
The God Within
Three Friends
The Telephone Girl and the Lady
Fate
An Adventure in the Autumn Woods
A Chance Deception
The Tender-Hearted Boy
A Misappropriated Turkey
Brothers
Drink's Lure
Love in an Apartment Hotel

1913

Broken Ways
A Girl's Stratagem
Near to Earth
A Welcome Intruder
The Sheriff's Baby
The Hero of Little Italy
The Perfidy of Mary
A Misunderstood Boy
The Little Tease
The Lady and the Mouse
The Wanderer
The House of Darkness
Olaf—An Atom
Just Gold
His Mother's Son
The Yaqui Cur
  (2 reels)
The Ranchero's Revenge
A Timely Interception
Death's Marathon
The Sorrowful Shore
The Mistake
*The Mothering Heart**
  (2 reels)
Her Mother's Oath
During the Round-Up
The Coming of Angelo
The Indian's Loyalty
Two Men of the Desert
*The Reformers, or The Lost Art of
  Minding One's Business*
  (2 reels)
*The Battle at Elderbush Gulch**
  (2 reels)
Brute Force

(also known as *Wars of the Pri-*   *Judith of Bethulia**
mal Tribes; 2 reels)   (4 reels)

1914

The Battle of the Sexes. Scenario by Griffith, based on the novel by Daniel Carson Goodman. 5 reels. Produced by Reliance-Majestic, distributed by Mutual. Premiere and general release, Apr. 12, 1914. Leading players: Lillian Gish, Owen Moore, Mary Alden. Only a fragment of the film survives. Photography: G. W. Bitzer. Unless otherwise noted, he is the cinematographer of all subsequent Griffith films.

The Escape. Scenario by Griffith, based on the play of the same title by Paul Armstrong. 7 reels. Produced by Reliance-Majestic, distributed by Mutual. Premiere, Cort Theater, New York, June 1, 1914; general release date unknown. Leading players: Blanche Sweet, Mae Marsh, Robert Harron, Donald Crisp, Owen Moore. No prints are known to exist.

Home, Sweet Home. Scenario by Griffith. 6 reels. Produced by Reliance-Majestic, distributed by Mutual. Premiere, Clune's Auditorium, Los Angeles, May 4, 1914; general release date unknown. Leading players: Henry B. Walthall, Lillian Gish, Dorothy Gish, Mae Marsh, Spottiswoode Aitken, Robert Harron, Miriam Cooper, Mary Alden, Donald Crisp, James Kirkwood, Jack Pickford, Courtenay Foote, Blanche Sweet, Owen Moore, Edward Dillon.

The Avenging Conscience. Scenario by Griffith, suggested by Edgar Allan Poe's "The Telltale Heart" and other works by Poe. 6 reels. Produced by Reliance-Majestic, distributed by Mutual. Premiere, Strand Theater, New York, Aug. 2, 1914; general release on the same date. Leading players: Henry B. Walthall, Blanche Sweet, Spottiswoode Aitken, George Siegmann, Ralph Lewis, Mae Marsh.

1915

The Birth of a Nation. Scenario by Griffith and Frank Woods, based on the novel and the play *The Clansman*, by Thomas Dixon, with additional material from Dixon's *The Leopard's Spots*. 12 reels. Produced and distributed by Epoch Producing Corp. Premiere, as *The Clansman*, Clune's Auditorium, Los Angeles, Feb. 8, 1915; as *The Birth of a Nation*, Liberty Theater, New York, Mar. 3, 1915. Released thereafter as a road show attraction. Leading players: Lillian Gish, Mae Marsh, Henry B. Walthall, Miriam Cooper, Mary Alden, Ralph Lewis, George Siegmann, Walter Long, Robert Harron, Wallace Reid, Joseph Henabery, Elmer Clifton, Josephine Crowell, Spottiswoode Aitken, André Beringer, Maxfield Stanley, Donald Crisp, Howard Gaye, Raoul Walsh.

1916

Intolerance. Scenario by Griffith. 14 reels. Produced and distributed by Wark Producing Corp. Premiere, Liberty Theater, New York, Sept. 5, 1916. Leading players: Lillian Gish, Mae Marsh, Robert Harron, Fred Turner, Sam de Grasse, Vera Lewis, Miriam Cooper, Walter Long, Ralph Lewis, Howard Gaye, Margery Wilson, Eugene Pallette, Spottiswoode Aitken, Josephine Crowell, Constance Talmadge, Elmer Clifton, Alfred Paget, Seena Owen, Tully Marshall, George Siegmann, Elmo Lincoln.

1918

Hearts of the World. Scenario by Griffith, writing under two pseudonyms. 12 reels. Produced by Griffith, distributed by Paramount-Artcraft. Premiere, Clune's Auditorium, Los Angeles, Mar. 12, 1918; New York premiere, 44th St. Theater, Apr. 4, 1918. Leading players: Lillian Gish, Robert Harron, Dorothy Gish, Adolphe Lestina, Josephine Crowell, Jack Cosgrove, Kate Bruce, Ben Alexander, George Fawcett, George Siegmann.

The Great Love. Scenario by Griffith and Stanner E. V. Taylor, under a pseudonym. Exact footage unknown. Produced by Griffith, distributed by Paramount-Artcraft. Premiere, Strand Theater, New York, Aug. 11, 1918; general release, Aug. 12, 1918. Leading players: Lillian Gish, Henry B. Walthall, Robert Harron, Maxfield Stanley, Gloria Hope, George Fawcett, Rosemary Theby, George Siegmann. With appearances by Alexandra, the Queen Mother, Lady Diana Manners, Elizabeth Asquith, and the Princess of Monaco as themselves. No prints are known to exist.

The Greatest Thing in Life. Scenario by Griffith and Stanner E. V. Taylor, under a pseudonym. 7 reels. Produced by Griffith, distributed by Paramount-Artcraft. Premiere, Los Angeles, Dec. 16, 1918; New York premiere, Strand Theater, Dec. 22, 1918. Leading players: Lillian Gish, Robert Harron, Adolphe Lestina, David Butler, Elmo Lincoln, Edward Piel, Kate Bruce, Peaches Jackson. No prints are known to exist.

1919

A Romance of Happy Valley. Scenario by Griffith, under a pseudonym. 6 reels. Produced by Griffith, distributed by Paramount-Artcraft. Premiere, Strand Theater, New York, Jan. 26, 1919. General release on the same date. Leading players: Lillian Gish, Robert Harron, Kate Bruce, George Fawcett, George Nichols, Adolphe Lestina, Porter Strong.

The Girl Who Stayed at Home. Scenario by Stanner E. V. Taylor. 7 reels. Produced by Griffith, distributed by Paramount-Artcraft. Premiere, Strand Theater, New York, Mar. 23, 1919; general release on the same date. Leading players: Carol Dempster, Clarine Seymour, Richard Barthelmess, Robert Harron, Adolphe Lestina, George Fawcett, Kate Bruce.

Broken Blossoms. Scenario by Griffith, based on "The Chink and the Child," by Thomas Burke. 6 reels. Produced by Griffith, distributed by United Artists. Premiere, George M. Cohan Theater, New York, May 13, 1919; general release, Oct. 20, 1920. Leading players: Lillian Gish, Richard Barthelmess, Donald Crisp. Photography: Bitzer; "Special Effects," Henrik Sartov.

True Heart Susie. Scenario by Marion Fremont. 6 reels. Produced by Griffith, distributed by Paramount-Artcraft. Premiere, Strand Theater, New York, June 1, 1919; general release the same date. Leading players: Lillian Gish, Robert Harron, Wilbur Higby, Loyola O'Connor, George Fawcett, Clarine Seymour, Kate Bruce, Carol Dempster.

Scarlet Days. Scenario by Stanner E. V. Taylor. 7 reels. Produced by Griffith, distributed by Paramount-Artcraft. Premiere, Rivoli Theater, New York, Nov. 10, 1919; general release, Nov. 30, 1919. Leading players: Richard Barthelmess, Carol Dempster, Clarine Seymour, Ralph Graves, Eugenie Besserer, George Fawcett, Walter Long.

The Greatest Question. Scenario by Stanner E. V. Taylor, based on a story by William Hale. 6 reels. Produced by D.W. Griffith, Inc., distributed by First National. General release, Nov. 1, 1919. Leading players: Lillian Gish, Robert Harron, Ralph Graves, Eugenie Besserer, George Fawcett, Tom Wilson, Josephine Crowell, George Nichols.

1920

The Idol Dancer. Scenario by Stanner E. V. Taylor, based on the story "Blood of the Covenanters," by Gordon Ray Young. Produced by D.W. Griffith, Inc., distributed by First National. Premiere Strand Theater, New York, Mar. 21, 1920; general release, Mar. 22, 1920. Leading players: Richard Barthelmess, Clarine Seymour, Creighton Hale, George MacQuarrie, Kate Bruce, Porter Strong, Anders Randolf.

The Love Flower. Scenario by Griffith, based on the story "The Black Beach," by Ralph Stock. 7 reels. Produced by D.W. Griffith, Inc., distributed by United Artists. Premiere, Strand Theater, New York, Aug. 22, 1920; general release that month. Leading players: Carol Dempster, Richard Barthelmess, George MacQuarrie, Anders Randolf, Florence Short, Crawford Kent, Adolphe Lestina.

Way Down East. Scenario by Anthony Paul Kelly and Griffith, based on the play by Lottie Blair Parker, Joseph R. Grismer and William Brady. 13 reels. Produced by D.W. Griffith, Inc., distributed by United Artists. Premiere, 44th St. Theater, New York, Sept. 3, 1920; general release Aug. 21, 1921. Leading players: Lillian Gish, Richard Barthelmess, Lowell Sherman, Burr McIntosh, Kate Bruce, Mary Hay, Porter Strong, Creighton Hale, Mrs. Morgan Belmont, Emily Fitzroy, Vivia Ogden, Edgar Nelson, George Neville. Photography: Bitzer, Sartov.

1921

Dream Street. Scenario by Griffith, under a pseudonym, based on two stories, "Gina of the Chinatown" and "The Sign of the Lamp," by Thomas Burke. 10 reels. Produced by D.W. Griffith, Inc., distributed by United Artists. Premiere, Central Theater, New York, Apr. 21, 1921; general release May 16, 1921. Leading players: Carol Dempster, Ralph Graves, Charles Emmett Mack, Edward Peil, W.J. Ferguson, Porter Strong, Tyrone Power (Sr.), Morgan Wallace. Photography: Sartov.

Orphans of the Storm. Scenario by Griffith, under a pseudonym, based on the play *The Two Orphans,* by Adolphe d'Ennery and Eugene Cormon. 12 reels. Produced by D.W. Griffith, Inc., distributed by United Artists. Premiere, Tremont Theater, Boston, Dec. 28, 1921; general release Apr. 30, 1922. Leading players: Lillian Gish, Dorothy Gish, Joseph Schildkraut, Frank Losee, Catherine Emmett, Morgan Wallace, Lucille La Verne, Sheldon Lewis, Frank Puglia, Creighton Hale, Leslie King, Monte Blue, Sidney Herbert, Lee Kohlmar, Marcia Harris, Adolphe Lestina, Kate Bruce. Photography: Sartov, Paul Allen, Bitzer.

1922

One Exciting Night. Scenario by Griffith, based on his own pseudonymous story. 11 reels. Produced by D.W. Griffith, Inc., distributed by United Artists. Premiere, Apollo Theater, New York, Oct. 23, 1922; general release Dec. 24, 1922. Leading players: Carol Dempster, Henry Hull, Porter Strong, Morgan

Wallace, C.H. Crocker-King, Margaret Dale, Frank Sheridan, Frank Wunder-lee, Grace Griswold. Photography: Sartov.

1923

The White Rose. Scenario by Griffith under a pseudonym. 10 reels. Produced by D.W. Griffith, Inc., distributed by United Artists. Premiere, Lyric Theater, New York, May 21, 1923; general release, Aug. 19, 1923. Leading players: Mae Marsh, Ivor Novello, Carol Dempster, Neil Hamilton, Lucille La Verne, Porter Strong. Photography: Bitzer, Sartov, Hal Sintzenich.

1924

America. Scenario by Robert W. Chambers, based in part on his novel *The Reckoning.* 12 reels. Produced by D.W. Griffith, Inc., distributed by United Artists. Premiere, 44th St. Theater, New York, Feb. 21, 1924; general release Aug. 17, 1924. Leading players: Neil Hamilton, Carol Dempster, Erville Anderson, Charles Emmett Mack, Lionel Barrymore. Photography: Bitzer, Sartov, Marcel Le Picard, Sintzenich.

Isn't Life Wonderful. Scenario by Griffith, based on the short story by Maj. Geoffrey Moss. 9 reels. Produced by D.W. Griffith, Inc., distributed by United Artists. General release Nov. 23, 1924. Leading players: Carol Dempster, Neil Hamilton, Helen Lowell, Erville Anderson, Frank Puglia, Marcia Harris, Lupino Lane. Photography: Sartov, Sintzenich.

1925

Sally of the Sawdust. Scenario by Forrest Halsey, based on the musical play *Poppy,* by Dorothy Donnelly. 10 reels. Produced by Famous Players–Lasky, distributed by United Artists. Premiere, Strand Theater, New York, Aug. 2, 1925; general release same date. Leading players: Carol Dempster, W.C. Fields, Alfred Lunt, Erville Anderson, Effie Shannon, Charles Hammond. Photography: Harry Fischbeck, Sintzenich.

That Royle Girl. Scenario by Paul Schofield, based on the novel by Edwin Balmer. 11 reels. Produced by Famous Players–Lasky, distributed by Paramount. General release Dec. 7, 1925. Leading players: Carol Dempster, W.C. Fields, James Kirkwood, Harrison Ford, Marie Chambers, Paul Everton. Photography: Fischbeck, Sintzenich. No prints are known to exist.

1926

The Sorrows of Satan. Scenario by Forrest Halsey, adaptation by John Russell and George Hull, based on the novel by Marie Corelli. 9 reels. Produced by Famous Players–Lasky, distributed by Paramount. Premiere, George M. Cohan Theater, New York, Oct. 12, 1926; general release Feb. 5, 1927. Leading players: Carol Dempster, Ricardo Cortez, Adolphe Menjou, Lya De Putti, Ivan Lebedeff, Marcia Harris, Lawrence D'Orsay. Photography: Fischbeck.

1928

Drums of Love. Scenario by Gerrit J. Lloyd. 9 reels. Produced by Art Cinema Corp., distributed by United Artists. Premiere, Liberty Theater, New York, Jan. 24, 1928; general release Mar. 31, 1928. Leading players: Mary Philbin, Lionel Barrymore, Don Alvarado, Tully Marshall, Eugenie Besserer, Charles Hill Mailes. Photography: Karl Struss, Bitzer, Harry Jackson.

The Battle of the Sexes. Scenario by Gerrit J. Lloyd, based on the novel *The Single Standard*, by Daniel Carson Goodman. 10 reels. Produced by Art Cinema Corp., distributed by United Artists. Premiere, United Artists Theater, Los Angeles, Sept., 1928; general release Oct. 13, 1928. Leading players: Jean Hersholt, Phyllis Haver, Belle Bennett, Don Alvarado, Sally O'Neil. Photography: Struss, Bitzer.

1929

Lady of the Pavements. Scenario by Sam Taylor, based on a story by Karl Volmoeller. 10 reels. Produced by Art Cinema Corp., distributed by United Artists. Premiere, United Artists Theater, Los Angeles, Jan. 22, 1929; general release, Feb. 16, 1929. Leading players: Lupe Velez, William Boyd, Jetta Goudal, Albert Conti, George Fawcett, Henry Armetta, Franklin Pangborn. Photography: Struss, Bitzer.

1930

Abraham Lincoln. Screenplay by Stephen Vincent Benét and Gerrit J. Lloyd. 10 reels. Produced by Art Cinema Corp., distributed by United Artists. Premiere, Central Theater, New York, Oct. 25, 1930; general release Nov. 8, 1930. Leading players: Walter Huston, Una Merkel, Kay Hammond, E. Alyn Warren, Hobart Bosworth, Fred Warren, Henry B. Walthall, Frank Campeau, Francis Ford, Lucille La Verne, W.L. Thorne, Ian Keith, Oscar Apfel, Jason Robards, Sr., Cameron Prudhomme. Photography: Struss.

1931

The Struggle. Screenplay by Anita Loos and John Emerson. 9 reels. Produced by D.W. Griffith, Inc., distributed by United Artists. Premiere, Rivoli Theater, New York, Dec. 10, 1931; general release, Feb. 6, 1932. Leading players: Hal Skelly, Zita Johann, Charlotte Wynters, Jackson Halliday, Evelyn Baldwin. Photography: Joseph Ruttenberg.

Index

Titles of D. W. Griffith's films are followed by their dates in parentheses.